Colombian Constitutional Law

Praise for
Colombian Constitutional Law

"Prepared by two leading experts on Colombian constitutional law, this volume will become an absolutely essential research and teaching tool in the comparative constitutional canon. With fluid and readable translations, it affords insights into the background and jurisprudence of one of the most innovative constitutional courts in the world—excerpting case-law on social welfare rights, on 'unconstitutional states of affairs' (suffered by a massive internally displaced population), on victim's and indigenous rights, and on other rights of personal liberty (including freedom of expression), equality, and dignity. Other chapters illustrate the Court's effort to reinvigorate a weakened legislature and restrain an over-empowered executive. Constitutional theorists will find much to reflect on as well in the closing chapter on unconstitutional amendments. Highly recommended!"

Vicki C. Jackson, author of
Constitutional Engagement in a Transnational Era

"For the last several decades the Colombian Constitutional Court has created some of the most bold and humane constitutional jurisprudence on the planet. Sadly, the reach and influence of this remarkable body of work has been limited by the lack of readily available translations. It is a cause for rejoicing that *Colombian Constitutional Law* now remedies this unfortunate barrier."

Robert C. Post, Dean, and Sol & Lillian Goldman Professor of Law,
Yale University Law School

"This valuable collection of materials and commentary on the work of the Colombian Constitutional Court makes accessible to students of comparative constitutional law a wide range of the work of one of the world's most interesting and important courts. The work of everyone in the field of comparative constitutional law will be deepened by reflecting upon the cases and materials provided here."

Mark Tushnet, William Nelson Cromwell Professor of Law,
Harvard University Law School

Colombian Constitutional Law

Leading Cases

Manuel José Cepeda Espinosa

David Landau

OXFORD
UNIVERSITY PRESS

OXFORD
UNIVERSITY PRESS

Oxford University Press is a department of the University of Oxford. It furthers the University's objective of excellence in research, scholarship, and education by publishing worldwide. Oxford is a registered trademark of Oxford University Press in the UK and certain other countries.

Published in the United States of America by Oxford University Press
198 Madison Avenue, New York, NY 10016, United States of America.

Library of Congress Cataloging-in-Publication Data

Names: Cepeda Espinosa, Manuel José, author. | Landau, David E., author.
Title: Colombian constitutional law : leading cases / Manuel José Cepeda Espinosa, David Landau.
Description: First edition. | New York : Oxford University Press, 2017. | Includes bibliographical references and index.
Identifiers: LCCN 2016043880 | ISBN 9780190640361 (hardback)
Subjects: LCSH: Constitutional law—Colombia—Cases. | Colombia. Corte Constitucional.
Classification: LCC KHH2921 .C438 2017 | DDC 342.861—dc23 LC record available at https://lccn.loc.gov/2016043880

Note to Readers

This publication is designed to provide accurate and authoritative information in regard to the subject matter covered. It is based upon sources believed to be accurate and reliable and is intended to be current as of the time it was written. It is sold with the understanding that the publisher is not engaged in rendering legal, accounting, or other professional services. If legal advice or other expert assistance is required, the services of a competent professional person should be sought. Also, to confirm that the information has not been affected or changed by recent developments, traditional legal research techniques should be used, including checking primary sources where appropriate.

(Based on the Declaration of Principles jointly adopted by a Committee of the American Bar Association and a Committee of Publishers and Associations.)

Contents

Preface

This book aims to introduce readers to Colombian constitutional law through the case law of the Colombian Constitutional Court. Since its creation as part of the Colombian Constitution of 1991, the Court has become known for its work across a number of different domains covered in this volume, both on global topics such as same-sex marriage, abortion, and the defense of socioeconomic rights, and more particular issues such as the protection of indigenous cultural diversity and autonomy, the rights of victims of the country's brutal and long-running internal armed conflict, and the striking down of constitutional amendments on the grounds that they replace rather than truly amend core parts of the existing constitutional text. The Court's case law is a prime example of transformative constitutionalism aiming to overcome entrenched economic and social inequalities. And it has exercised a significant impact on the political order, perhaps most prominently in the decision striking down a proposed constitutional amendment that would have allowed the popular President Alvaro Uribe to exercise a third consecutive term in office.

Yet the Court's decisions have largely been unavailable to non-Spanish speakers because very few decisions have been translated. This volume aims to fill that gap by providing lucid and succinct translations of the Court's most significant decisions in these and other areas. As these decisions are often hundreds of pages long and contain many pages recounting procedural history, the positions of intervenors, and other issues, we have focused on providing those extracts that contain the core of the reasoning and will be most useful to comparative constitutional lawyers. We have not aimed to be fully comprehensive (an impossible task at any rate) but rather have focused on those issues likely to be of greatest interest to the field because they show the Court wrestling with common problems in particular ways, demonstrate noteworthy doctrinal innovation, or highlight judicial intervention on undertheorized but significant issues.

Alongside the cases themselves, we have provided materials intended to orient the reader. Chapter 1 contains no cases, but instead serves as a brief introduction to the history of the 1991 Constitution and the Constitutional Court, as well as providing essential concepts needed to understand the constitutional text and the organization, powers, role conception, and interpretive style of the Court. In all subsequent chapters, we have included introductory materials for each topic and notes following many of the cases. Our goals here are to give readers a sense of the historical, social, and political context within which these decisions were made, as well as to provide a comparative perspective on major decisions. In addition, the notes aim to give readers a sense of the ways in which the principal cases have been viewed in subsequent political debate and case law, and thus of how the Court's doctrinal interventions have evolved over time.

We expect this book to be of use to both students and scholars of comparative constitutional law who are interested for comparative purposes in learning about the case law of a significant but understudied constitutional system, as well as judges and other practitioners who may be interested in referencing comparative materials for their work. In addition, we hope this book will be useful to other scholarly communities. For example, constitutional theorists may be interested in the Court's doctrinal innovations on the control of constitutional change, structural remedies for socioeconomic rights, and other issues, and international lawyers might study the Court's thick engagement and incorporation of international law into the domestic constitutional order.

The genesis of this book were the discussions at Yale Law School's annual Global Constitutionalism Seminar, which brings together a group of high courts judges from around the world with Yale faculty, and at which one of the authors of this volume has participated for many years. Translations of some of these decisions were first produced for that seminar, and we therefore thank all or the judges and faculty who helped to raise issues essential to this volume. We are particularly grateful to Dean Robert Post, who encouraged and supported the publication of this book.

We are also grateful for the assistance of several organizations and people with some of the translations included in this volume. The Human Rights program of the United States Agency for International Development (USAID) helped to fund some translations, as did the PPODRE program in public policy, constitutional rights, and regulations at the school of law of the University of Los Andes in Bogotá, Colombia. We would also like to thank Guillermo Otalora for assisting with some of the translations included in this volume.

Finally, we have benefitted from conversations and support from numerous colleagues, which have helped to ensure this book reached print and to shape its final form. We would especially like to acknowledge the invaluable advice and assistance of Professor Vicki Jackson of Harvard University.

1

Introduction to the Colombian Constitution of 1991 and the Constitutional Court

Since the Colombian Constitutional Court was first created in 1991, few if any courts in the world have had such a profound impact on different spheres of society and public policy. The object of this volume is to give the reader a sense of the Court's functioning and its most important case law, within a comparative perspective. To give just a few examples: the Court has decriminalized drug possession and assisted suicide, holding that criminalization of either violates the right to free development of personality (see Chapter 3). It has given civil union status to same-sex couples, holding that the failure to do so is a violation of equality and human dignity (see Chapter 4). It has enacted massive structural remedies to protect the socioeconomic rights of internally displaced persons who have suffered because of Colombia's civil violence and to reform the country's troubled healthcare system (see Chapter 6). It has protected the core content of social rights and adopted systemic remedies aimed at the reform of the entire healthcare system in order to end inequality between poor Colombians and those who have capacity to pay for health insurance (see Chapter 6). It has protected the rights of indigenous groups to conduct their own autonomous justice systems and to have an influence over what happens in their traditional territories (see Chapter 8). It has placed limits on the executive's ability to use emergency powers to confront guerrilla groups (see Chapter 9). And in probably its most politically significant decision, the Court struck down a referendum aimed at amending the constitution to allow a politically popular president to run for a third term in office, holding that the amendment would constitute a substitution of the existing constitutional order rather than an amendment of it (see Chapter 11).

This introduction treats key elements needed to understand the Court's jurisprudence in a historical and comparative context. Colombia has a long history of judicial review, which before 1991 was carried out as one of the functions of the Supreme Court. During the

Colombian Constitutional Law: Leading Cases. Manuel José Cepeda Espinosa and David Landau.

Constituent Assembly of 1991, however, drafters created a specialized Constitutional Court and imbued it with the constitutional powers previously held by the Supreme Court, as well as new powers. This introduction briefly explores relevant political and constitutional history before and during the Constituent Assembly of 1991. It then examines the structure, powers, decision-making, and role of the Constitutional Court. Finally, this introduction lays out the methodology and plan of the rest of the book.

A. The Prelude to the 1991 Constitution: Institutional Decay and a Crisis of Public Order

During the twentieth century, the Colombian state enjoyed a relatively high degree of institutional stability. It maintained the same Constitution, the Constitution of 1886, for over 100 years, and it avoided any long periods of military dictatorship.[1] The same two traditional parties, the Liberal and Conservative parties, dominated political life throughout most of this period.

Furthermore, the 1886 Constitution and its amendments set up the framework for a relatively independent system of judicial review. The 1886 Constitution established a Supreme Court, divided into several chambers, which combined powers of constitutional judicial review and cassation or interpretation of ordinary law. Since 1910, the Constitution has allowed for a "public action" of unconstitutionality, where any citizen could challenge before the Supreme Court, on abstract review, any law for any constitutional reason.[2] Throughout the period under study, these constitutional claims were heard by the entire Supreme Court, which was mostly made up of specialists in other fields such as civil law and criminal law.[3]

The public action is an important mechanism in Colombian history and has been maintained up to the present day, although since 1991 the Constitutional Court (rather than the Supreme Court) has had jurisdiction over these claims. As recent scholarship has demonstrated, the Supreme Court used the public action to play a significant role in public law matters throughout most of the twentieth century. It carried out a number of different functions, including mediating disputes between the parties or their factions and

1. For basic background on the history of Colombia, see DAVID BUSHNELL, THE MAKING OF MODERN COLOMBIA: A NATION IN SPITE OF ITSELF (1993); MARCO PALACIOS, BETWEEN LEGITIMACY AND VIOLENCE: A HISTORY OF COLOMBIA, 1872–2002 (Richard Stoller trans., 2006); MALCOLM DEAS, INTERCAMBIOS VIOLENTOS: REFLEXIONES SOBRE LA VIOLENCIA POLÍTICA EN COLOMBIA (1999).

2. For background on the creation and early use of the public action, see JORGE GONZÁLEZ-JÁCOME, ENTRE LA LEY Y LA CONSTITUCIÓN: UNA INTRODUCCIÓN HISTÓRICA A LA FUNCIÓN INSTITUCIONAL DE LA CORTE SUPREMA DE JUSTICIA, 1886–1915 (2007). Abstract review is a system where a citizen challenges a law without reference to its application in any concrete dispute. *See* MAURO CAPPELLETTI, THE JUDICIAL PROCESS IN COMPARATIVE PERSPECTIVE (1989).

3. Although the Court gained a specialized Constitutional Chamber in 1968, this Chamber only had the power to do a preliminary study of public actions; decisions were made by the full Supreme Court and the members of all of its chambers.

legitimating important changes in the direction of law and politics.[4] Although its approach to constitutional interpretation tended to be formalistic and deferential to the political process concerning rights, the Supreme Court played a crucial role in the development of the rule of law in Colombia and consolidated a durable tradition of judicial review. Colombia's equivalent to *Marbury v. Madison* was decided in 1887.[5]

Despite these institutional advantages, Colombia was also plagued by violence throughout much of this period.[6] During the period following the assassination of the important Liberal political leader Jorge Eliécer Gaitán in 1948, Colombia was plunged into a 10-year period of intense civil strife called "La Violencia," in which affiliates of the country's two traditional parties (the Liberals and Conservatives) fought throughout the country.

After a brief military dictatorship under President Gustavo Rojas Pinilla from 1953 to 1957, the leaders of the two parties agreed to set up a political regime called the National Front.[7] This regime, which was written into the Constitution, basically divided up all major institutions, such as Congress, equally between the two parties, and guaranteed alternation in the presidency (so that a Liberal president would succeed a Conservative president and vice versa). The judiciary was also initially divided up between the two parties, but its independence was protected by a system called "cooptation"—members served for life, and existing members of the Court would pick their own replacements as seats opened up due to death or retirement.[8] The National Front formally ended in 1974, but it exercised a continuing influence on Colombian political culture. and some of its key provisions (such as the cooptation provisions governing appointment to the Supreme Court) were continued until the new constitution was written in 1991.

The National Front was initially effective at restoring order to the country. However, as time went on the regime developed certain notable problems. It gave the two traditional parties a near monopoly on political power, thus creating an exclusionary political system. The nation's most prominent guerrilla groups in the late twentieth century, such as the FARC and M-19, result from this period. Moreover, the ideological differences between the parties lost some meaning, and much political competition became intra-party, creating strong factions within both traditional parties. Finally, the regime caused a particular configuration of political institutions. As the executive branch had clear preeminence, and

4. For a detailed and careful look at the jurisprudence of the Supreme Court throughout the 20th century, see MARIO ALBERTO CAJAS SARRIA, LA HISTORIA DE LA CORTE SUPREMA DE JUSTICIA DE COLOMBIA, 1886–1991 (2015).

5. For a contrast of the approaches of the Supreme Court and the Constitutional Court, see MANUEL JOSÉ CEPEDA, POLEMICAS CONSTITUCIONALES (2007)

6. Between 1899 and 1902, the two traditional parties and their factions fought another significant civil war called the Thousand Days War. For background on the War and surrounding events, see CHARLES W. BERQUIST, COFFEE AND CONFLICT IN COLOMBIA, 1886–1910 (1986).

7. For details on the design and functioning of the National Front, see JONATHAN HARTLYN, THE POLITICS OF COALITION RULE IN COLOMBIA (1988).

8. For background on the National Front, see BUSHNELL, *supra* note 1, at 223–48.

as the public order situation in the country worsened, the president often governed alone, using emergency powers or broad delegations of legislative power from Congress. The president and not Congress thus became the main legislator.[9] Both the State of Siege (included in the Constitution of 1886) and the State of Economic and Social Emergency (which was added in a constitutional reform in 1968) became increasingly common instruments of governance. Colombia was governed under one of these states of exception a remarkable 82 percent of the time between 1970 and 1991.[10]

The Supreme Court during and after the National Front was criticized for not effectively limiting executive power, either by enforcing constitutional rights or by stopping the president from governing unilaterally via emergency powers. As an example, it developed doctrines holding that it could not review the necessity for declaring a State of Siege, which was essentially a political question entrusted to the president, but would only review whether the declaration had gone through the proper procedures (i.e., whether it had been signed by the president and his ministers). Although the Court did review decrees issued during such a declaration, it rarely struck them down, upholding even decrees that severely constrained fundamental rights or that were only very loosely connected to the stated reason for declaring the State of Siege. In the 1980s, as the Colombian crisis of public order deepened, the Court became somewhat more activist in reviewing these decrees, for example reversing its long-standing jurisprudence allowing civilians to be tried by military courts martial for political crimes.[11]

The Supreme Court was also criticized for blocking important efforts at constitutional change, particularly ones that would have dismantled institutional configurations dating from the National Front. In 1978, for example, the Court struck down a constitutional amendment passed by President Alfonso López Michelsen that would have called a "small Constituent Assembly" to work on key issues of constitutional reform.[12] In 1981, it struck down a set of reforms that has passed through Congress, among them changing the structure and powers of the Court.[13] Thus, the Supreme Court, along with other institutions like Congress, was critiqued for creating a "blocked society" that was incapable of necessary institutional reforms.[14]

The road to the 1991 Constitutional Assembly was paved by a combination of this perceived institutional stress with an increasingly visible and urgent crisis of violence

9. For an analysis of the institutional dynamics during and after the National Front period, see Ronald P. Archer & Matthew Soberg Shugart, *The Unrealized Potential of Presidential Dominance in Colombia*, *in* PRESIDENTIALISM AND DEMOCRACY IN LATIN AMERICA 110 (1997).

10. *See* Rodrigo Uprimny, *The Constitutional Court and Control of Presidential Extraordinary Powers in Colombia*, 10 DEMOCRATIZATION 46, 65 tbl.3 (2003).

11. *See id.* at 55.

12. *See* MARIO CAJAS SARRIA, EL CONTROL JUDICIAL A LA REFORMA CONSTITUCIONAL: COLOMBIA, 1910–2007, at 59–72 (2010); FERNANDO CEPEDA ULLOA, LA PEQUEÑA CONSTITUYENTE (1977)

13. *See* CAJAS SARRIA, *supra* note 12, at 76–83.

14. *See* Mario Latorre Rueda, *Colombia: ¿una Sociedad Bloqueada? Artículo 120: Espíritu Nacional Y Participación Adecuada Y Equitativa*, *in* HECHOS Y CRITICA POLITICA 121 (1986).

and public order. During the late 1980s, a worsening problem of guerrilla activity combined with high levels of violence connected to the drug trade. In 1985, for example, the Colombian Palace of Justice, which housed both the Supreme Court and the Council of State (the high administrative court) was stormed by the M-19 guerrilla group. Following a military raid to retake the Court, half of the Supreme Court's magistrates, and many more staff members, were killed.

In 1988, President Virgilio Barco announced that he would call for a referendum to amend the Constitution in order to create alternative means to reform the Constitution. In spite of wide popular support for this initiative, President Barco refused to act unilaterally and instead made a political pact with conservative opposition to call a referendum allowing amendment to the Constitution either by Congress, direct popular vote, or by the Constituent Assembly, but this pact was invalidated by the Council of State. After the assassination of a Liberal candidate for president, Luis Carlos Galan, in August 1989, an active student movement took to the streets to support Barco's original idea and then to demand the calling of a Constituent Assembly to draft a new Constitution. They called for a seventh ballot (*septima papeleta*) non-binding vote on whether to hold such an Assembly, which would be held contemporaneously with other congressional and local elections on March 11, 1990. Informally, such a vote was held, and indicated overwhelming support for the measure.

President Barco then issued a decree allowing for a formal counting of the votes on a specific ballot on whether to call a popularly elected Constituent Assembly, which was heard on the same date as the May 1990 presidential election. The Supreme Court, in a unanimous decision, upheld the decree. The yes votes received 5,236,863 of the 5,891,117 votes cast. The new president, the Liberal Cesar Gaviria, who was Minister of Government in 1988, had been an early supporter of the idea and pushed forward. Based on an accord with the other major political forces, he issued a decree calling for elections for a Constituent Assembly. Unlike in traditional congressional elections, almost all of the members of the Assembly would be elected using a purely proportional formula based on one nationwide electoral district. Both traditional parties and new political movements could launch candidates. Free access to television and public funds was granted to the parties and movements. The Supreme Court, in a closely divided decision, upheld Gaviria's calling of elections for a Constituent Assembly (despite the fact that it was not explicitly contemplated in the Constitution as a mechanism of reform), under the theory that the people retained the ultimate power to create a new constitutional order.[15]

B. The Making of the 1991 Constitution

Elections for the 72-member Assembly appeared to indicate a significant opening for groups that had historically been left outside of the National Front. Although the Liberals

15. The full text of this decision, as well as other institutional detail on the prologue to the Assembly and the Assembly itself, is reprinted in RAFAEL BALLEN M., CONSTITUYENTE Y CONSTITUCION DEL 91, at 156–232 (1991).

won a plurality of seats in the Assembly (25), the second largest group consisted of the now-demobilized guerrilla group that had stormed the Palace of Justice, the M-19 (19 seats), and the third largest group was an alliance of dissident conservatives called the Movement of National Salvation (11 seats). The traditional Conservatives won only five seats, while independent conservatives affiliated with them won another four. The few remaining seats were made up by a mix of ex-guerrilla groups (four seats), Protestants (two seats), and indigenous movements (two seats).[16] The resulting Assembly worked largely by consensus between the traditional parties and the newcomers; the then-president, Cesar Gaviria, and his ministers and advisers also took an overarching role in shaping the constitutional text.[17]

The Constituent Assembly had several major goals. Most important, it sought to create an environment that would bring about peace. The most important goal, in other words, was to construct a set of institutions and values that would end the high levels of violence in the country. Article 22, for example, defines peace as both a right and a duty.

The designers were very interested in ending the pervasive violations of human rights that had been carried out by guerrilla groups and paramilitaries, and also by the state itself. The document thus contains an extensive list of rights. Moreover, the Assembly sought to go well-beyond the liberal constitutionalism of the 1886 text—it enshrined a long list of socioeconomic rights, such as the right to housing, health, education, and social security, and it also included collective rights such as the right to protection of the environment. Colombia's indigenous organizations, which had historically been repressed, were represented at the Assembly and won important rights to autonomy over their land, institutions, and traditional cultural practices, which have since been important in Constitutional Court case law.

The normative vision of the Constitution was transformative. Aside from the emphasis on socioeconomic rights, which focused attention on the need to greatly reduce poverty in the country, the Constitution included a vision of equality that stressed the need for material as well as formal equality. For example, Article 13 explicitly contemplates affirmative action measures: "The state shall promote the conditions so that equality may be real and effective and shall adopt measures in favor of groups which are discriminated against or marginalized." As noted in Chapter 4, the Constitution has often made use of this material conception of equality to approve or require actions on behalf of traditionally disadvantaged groups such as women and the disabled.

16. Full electoral results can be found in John Dugas, *El Desarrollo de la Asamblea Nacional Constiuyente*, *in* LA CONSTITUCION DE 1991: UN PACTO POLITICO VIABLE? 45, 47 tbl. 1 (John Dugas ed., 1993). Two additional members of guerilla groups, representing Quintin Lame and the EPL, had a voice but no vote in the Assembly. For a description of coalition building and voting behavior on key issues within the Constituent Assembly, see MANUEL JOSE CEPEDA, LA CONSTITUYENTE POR DENTRO (1992).

17. *See* MANUEL JOSE CEPEDA, INTRODUCCION A LA CONSTITUCION DE 1991: HACIA UN NUEVO CONSTITUCIONALISMO 450 apx.2 (1992) (presenting a table showing the similarities between the government project and the final Constitution from the perspective of the then-presidential advisor both to Barco and Gaviria on how to call a constituent assembly); HUMBERTO DE LA CALLE, CONTRA TODAS LAS APUESTAS: HISTORIA INTIMA DE LA CONSTITUYENTE DE 1991 (2004) (giving an account of the Assembly from the perspective of the then-Minister of Government, who was a key interlocutor with the Assembly).

The drafters also put great emphasis on importing and using international human rights law in order to bolster and transform the domestic legal order. The most important provision is Article 93, which reads as follows:

> **Article 93.** International treaties and agreements ratified by Congress that recognize human rights and that prohibit their limitation in states of emergency have priority domestically.
>
> The rights and duties mentioned in this Charter shall be interpreted in accordance with international treaties on human rights ratified by Colombia.

Thus, the Constitution requires incorporation of international law in two distinct ways. First, provisions of international human rights treaties that cannot be limited during emergencies are directly incorporated as the highest norms of the Colombian legal order. Second, other provisions of international human rights treaties must be used as aids for interpreting domestic constitutional law. The Constitutional Court has used these concepts to elaborate on the French concept of a "constitutional block." Using Article 93, they have held that constitutional law includes not only the domestic text, but also relevant parts of international law (see Chapter 2).[18]

Perhaps the best way to get an overall sense of the Colombian constitutional framework is to consider its first article, which reads as follows:

> **Article 1.** Colombia is a social state of law organized in the form of a unitary republic, decentralized, with the autonomy of its territorial units, democratic, participatory and pluralistic, based on respect for human dignity, on the work and solidarity of the individuals who belong to it, and on the predominance of the general interest.

Article 1 thus lays out the aims of the Colombian state. The centrality of the focus on "human dignity," which was taken from postwar European constitutionalism, has been evident in much of the case law.[19] It has underlined the Court's jurisprudence on autonomy, equality, and social rights. But the core concept in Colombian constitutional law is the idea of a "social state of law" (*estado social de derecho*), which is a complex but critically important idea. It includes the notion of the rule of law, and particularly the idea that nobody should be subject to arbitrary action by either state or nonstate actors. But it also includes a social-democratic dimension: the shift from the *estado de derecho* or rule of law in the old constitutional order to the *estado social de derecho* in the new one suggests that the state

18. For the seminal French decision from 1971, see CC Decision 71-44 DC, July 16, 1971, Rec. 29. For a general discussion of the ways in which different constitutional orders incorporate international and comparative law into the domestic legal order, see VICKI C. JACKSON, CONSTITUTIONAL ENGAGEMENT IN A TRANSNATIONAL ERA (2010).

19. For an overview of the concept and its migration from German constitutional law, see CATHERINE DUPRÉ, THE AGE OF DIGNITY: HUMAN RIGHTS AND CONSTITUTIONALISM IN EUROPE (2015).

must provide a safety net to protect the poorest and to transform the socioeconomic structure, which it perceived as highly unequal and with distressing levels of extreme poverty. The Constitutional Court has made extensive use of this concept to create, for example, an implied right to a minimum level of subsistence (*minimo vital*), which has underpinned its jurisprudence on socioeconomic rights and has become another of its basic orienting principles. Both of these principles are explored in more depth in Chapter 6, but will recur throughout this book.

The structural part of the Colombian constitution was dominated by the need to reinvigorate institutions that had been ossified by the National Front and to rectify the imbalance caused by an excessively strong president and an excessively weak Congress. The Assembly sought to open up the political system to new parties and movements. For example, it changed the method for electing the Senate so that all 100 members are now elected via proportional representation from a single nationwide district.[20] It also aimed at limiting presidential power to legislate unilaterally. Most important, although the president retained certain emergency powers under the new constitution, these powers were subjected to new controls and regulations. As explained in detail in Chapter 9, the Constitutional Court has used these new limitations to aggressively police the use of emergency powers by the president and to greatly reduce the amount of time that the country has spent under a state of exception. Unlike in the period before 1991, the Court has reviewed declarations of states of exception (not just decrees issued during those states), and has often struck down those declarations when it has felt that they were unjustified by the gravity or nature of events on the ground. The country has managed both the guerrilla and drug-trafficking threat primarily with reference to ordinary legal instruments, rather than emergency decrees—a sharp change from the situation before 1991.[21]

The Assembly also created a number of new control institutions charged with ensuring that the rights included in the Constitution were actually protected. Thus, along lines argued by Bruce Ackerman, it supplemented traditional democratic institutions such as the legislature with a number of other bodies meant to reinforce and protect the democratic order and individual rights.[22] For example, the new Constitution created a *Defensoria del Pueblo* or Ombudsman, who is given the power to investigate and publicize rights violations. It also created a national prosecutor's office and shifted the criminal justice system away from an inquisitorial model and toward an adversarial one more like that found in the United States. The most important of these new institutions, of course, was the creation of a specialized Constitutional Court to carry out judicial review, as detailed below.

Finally, the Assembly created a complex but flexible system of constitutional change. The Constitution may be amended either by the vote of a majority of the members of Congress in two consecutive sessions (in the second round approval must be by an absolute

20. *See* Article 171.

21. *See* Uprimny, *supra* note 10, at 65 tbl.3 (showing that Colombia dropped from spending 82.1 percent of its time in a state of exception between 1970 and 1991, but only 17.5 percent between 1991 and 2002.

22. *See* Bruce Ackerman, *The New Separation of Powers*, 113 HARV. L. REV. 633 (2001).

majority), or by the people in a referendum after Congress has approved a law calling one to vote on the text of the new articles proposed by Congress.[23] The ordinary amendment threshold is therefore fairly low. Further, the Constitution also allows, if approved in a referendum, the calling of a popularly elected Constituent Assembly in order to reform the existing constitution or even to write an entirely new one.[24] Somewhat unusually, then, the Constitution contains a provision regulating its own replacement.

This multilayered system of constitutional change forms the basis for one of the Court's most important doctrines—the "substitution of the constitution" doctrine.[25] This doctrine holds that constitutional amendments can be substantively unconstitutional if they are in reality replacements for the existing constitution rather than amendments. Such replacements may only be done via Constituent Assembly, and not via amendment. The Court has used this doctrine several times (see Chapter 11), most famously in 2010 to strike down a referendum that would have amended the Constitution to allow President Alvaro Uribe to run for a third term.[26]

C. The Structure and Powers of the Colombian Constitutional Court

One of the most important decisions of the 1991 Constituent Assembly was to create a specialized Constitutional Court that would exercise the judicial review powers previously held by the Supreme Court, as well as hearing new constitutional mechanisms. In addition to creating the Constitutional Court, the Assembly also gave that body an impressive array of powers by adding an individual complaint mechanism (the *tutela*) to the traditional public action, allowing the Court to have a significant voice on public policy.

The debate and vote on the proposal made by the government to create a specialized Constitutional Court (thus divesting the Supreme Court of some of its key powers) was an unusually contentious one for the 1991 Assembly.[27] Furthermore, because the country already had a long history of judicial review via the Supreme Court's review of the public action, it focused not on general questions (as in Europe) about whether ordinary judges were unsuited for constitutional adjudication, but instead on more particular themes of Colombian history and jurisprudence. The Conservative delegates, as well as some of the

23. *See* Articles 375 & 378; *see also* Chapter 11 (discussing these methods in detail).

24. See Article 376.

25. This doctrine is similar to the Indian "basic structure" doctrine. *See* Rosalind Dixon & David Landau, *Transnational Constitutionalism and a Limited Doctrine of Unconstitutional Constitutional Amendment*, 13 Int'l J. Const. L. 606 (2015) (comparing the doctrine across those two contexts).

26. For references to the unconstitutional constitutional amendment doctrine with respect to the re-election case in light of theory of constituent power, see Mark Tushnet, *Peasants with Pitchforks, and Toilers with Twitter: Constitutional Revolutions and the Constituent Power*, 13 Int'l J. Const. L. 639 (2015).

27. For an overview of the debates through which the Colombian Constitutional Court was created, see David Landau, Beyond Judicial Independence: The Construction of Judicial Power in Colombia 105–18 (unpublished Ph.D. dissertation, Harvard University, 2015).

M-19 delegates, voted against the proposal. They argued that the old system had worked well, and moreover appealed to the tragic guerrilla attack on the Supreme Court in 1985 (a particularly poignant issue for the demobilized M-19, which had led that attack). Paradoxically, the government considered the creation of the Constitutional Court a priority in order to give a fresh start and a new guardian to the new Constitution, as well as to have an organ with the institutional capacity to handle all of the new claims that were expected to be filed. The majority was thus swayed by the need for a more focused and specialized body that would defend and amplify the rich catalogue of rights included in the new constitution. The criticisms of the Supreme Court noted above, in its perceived failure to develop rights protections and to check executive power, as well as its role in blocking constitutional change, also played a role in the decision. The Constituent Assembly, however, maintained the Supreme Court as a court of cassation on civil, criminal, and labor issues, and also maintained the Council of State as the nation's high administrative court. Thus, the Colombian system has multiple high courts, which has led (as described below) to some jurisdictional conflicts.

The designers of the Constitutional Court sought a selection mechanism that would ensure an adequate level of independence, while also trying to avoid the insularity of the cooptation system of the old Supreme Court, where justices served for life and picked their own successors. The nine magistrates of the Constitutional Court are selected to eight-year, nonrenewable terms, with the president, Supreme Court, and Council of State each sending lists of three names to the Senate, which makes the final selection from the names on each list.[28] Thus, a president has some influence over the composition of the Court, but no one actor or institution is able to play a decisive role in composing it.[29] This proved to be critically important in 2009, when most of the Court turned over shortly before the Court would hear its case on whether the popular president Alvaro Uribe could seek a third term (see Chapter 11 for the decision).[30] The president had some influence over the new court because he had drafted lists for the selection of three of its justices, but lost the case, seven to two. The dissenters defended the competence of the Court to strike down the amendment, and the president of the Court, Mauricio González Cuervo, announced the judgment of the Court to the public and explained its reasoning even though he was one of these dissenters. Moreover, in order to support the Court in this critical moment they did not immediately make their dissent public, but instead waited for the written decision to be drafted in order to do so.

The Court was given a strong set of powers by the Constituent Assembly. The Assembly maintained the traditional public action, but switched jurisdiction from the old Supreme Court to the new Constitutional Court. As has been true since its creation in 1910, the

28. *See* Article 239.

29. The selection mechanism is somewhat similar to that found in some European systems, where appointment power is also split between several political and judicial actors, but diminishes the risk of court-packing by political majorities. *See* ALEC STONE SWEET, GOVERNING WITH JUDGES: CONSTITUTIONAL POLITICS IN EUROPE 49 tbl.2.3 (2000).

30. This is Decision C-141 of 2010 (excerpted in Chapter 11).

public action allows any Colombian citizen to raise a challenge to any law or decree-law, in the abstract, at any time. Unlike in many other countries within and outside of Latin America, the power to initiate abstract review is not limited to certain defined groups of actors (such as political groupings or institutions), but extends to every citizen.[31] The lack of standing or other requirements makes it very easy for the Court to hear challenges to laws.[32] The Court must hear these actions if they have been properly filed, and the National Inspector General (*Procurador General de la Nación*) is required to intervene in them and give an opinion on the relevant constitutional issues. Any citizen, as well as public institutions, may also intervene in favor or against the constitutionality of the challenged norm. Amicus curiae are widely allowed.

These challenges are always heard by the full Court of nine justices, and are generally denoted with a "C" before the number of the decision and the year. These actions have *erga omnes* effect, meaning that if they prevail, the unconstitutional law or decree is erased from the legal order. The Court's power to hear public actions extends to all laws, decree-laws issued with the force of law, and even, for certain designated purposes, constitutional amendments.[33] Further, some types of legal instruments, such as international treaties, emergency decrees, and certain designated "statutory laws," are sent to the Court automatically for review.[34]

The Constituent Assembly also created a new action, the *tutela*, which has become an important symbol of the new constitutional order. The *tutela*, a kind of individual constitutional complaint or special writ for the protection of fundamental rights, was the linchpin of the strategy to make constitutional rights real rather than theoretical.[35] Article 86 describes the *tutela* as follows:

> Every person has the right to file a *tutela* before a judge, at any time or place, through a preferential and summary *proceeding*, for himself/herself or by whomever acts in his/her name for the immediate protection of his/her fundamental constitutional rights when that person fears the latter may be violated by the action or omission of any public authority.

31. *See* STONE SWEET, *supra* note 29, at 47 tbl.2.2; Julio Rios-Figueroa & Matthew M. Taylor, *Institutional Determinants of the Judicialisation of Policy in Brazil & Mexico*, 38 J. LAT. AM. STUDS. 739 (2006).

32. The Constitution does require that claims based on the procedure through which a given norm was passed be filed within one year of the publication of that norm. *See* art. 242, cl. 3.

33. Article 241, clause 1 of the Constitution gives the Court the power to review constitutional amendments "exclusively for errors of procedure in their makeup." But as noted in Chapter 11, the Court has built a doctrine of substitution of the constitution that is similar to the Indian basic structure doctrine, in addition to reviewing constitutional amendments for procedural errors.

34. *See* Article 241, cl. 7, 8, 10.

35. *See* MANUEL JOSÉ CEPEDA ESPINOSA, LA TUTELA: MATERIALES Y REFLEXIONES SOBRE SU SIGNIFICADO (1992) (summarizing and analyzing the debates that led to the creation of the instrument). The *tutela* is in the family of individual complaint mechanisms commonly found in Latin America and often referred to as an *amparo*. *See* ALLEN BREWER-CARIAS, CONSTITUTIONAL PROTECTION OF HUMAN RIGHTS IN LATIN AMERICA: A COMPARATIVE STUDY OF *AMPARO* PROCEEDINGS (2008).

> The protection will consist of an order issued by a judge enjoining others to act or refrain from acting. The order, which must be complied with immediately, may be challenged before a superior court judge, and in any case the latter may send it to the Constitutional Court for possible revision.
>
> This action will be available only when the affected party does not enjoy another means of judicial defense, except when it is used as a temporary device to avoid irreversible harm. In no case can more than 10 days elapse between filing the *tutela* and its resolution.
>
> The law will establish the cases in which the *tutela* may be filed against private individuals entrusted with providing a public service or whose conduct may affect seriously and directly the collective interest, or in respect of whom the applicant may find himself/herself in a state of subordination or defenselessness.

This article establishes several key points. First, the *tutela* is designed to be highly informal and fast. It can be filed by anyone at any time, and it must be decided within 10 days. The Constitutional Court has prevented the legal system from putting formalities or other requirements on the bringing of *tutelas*. Like the Indian Supreme Court, the Colombian Court has been interested in ensuring that constitutional justice remains accessible and free of technical barriers.[36] This informality and speed partially accounts for the popularity of the mechanism, especially as ordinary legal cases often take many years to decide.

Further, the *tutela* can be filed both against any "public authority" and against private individuals, mainly private organizations, in circumstances where they are "providing a public service" or against whom the applicant finds himself in a situation of "subordination or defenselessness." *Tutelas* are often taken against private schools, health insurance companies, and other similar actors, for example. There has been considerable debate about whether "public authority" includes judges, but the Constitutional Court has long held that *tutelas* may be taken against judicial decisions in some situations. The ordinary courts, especially the Supreme Court and the Council of State, have at times resisted this conclusion, engaging in very public fights with the Constitutional Court that the media has called "train crashes" (*choque de trenes*). These conflicts appear to be fairly common in comparative perspective in contexts such as the Colombian where there is more than one high court.[37] The ability to hear *tutelas* involving private action both directly (by suing private parties in some circumstances going beyond the so-called third-party effect doctrine) and indirectly (by challenging ordinary judicial decisions and thus shaping ordinary legal doctrines) has given the Constitutional Court considerable power to shape the legal system.[38]

36. *See* CHARLES R. EPP, THE RIGHTS REVOLUTION: LAWYERS, COURTS, AND ACTIVISTS IN COMPARATIVE PERSPECTIVE 71–89 (1998) (describing the Indian Supreme Court's aggressive attempts to lower barriers to access through Public Interest Litigation).

37. *See* Lech Garlicki, *Constitutional Courts versus Supreme Courts*, 5 INT'L J. CONST. L. 44 (2007).

38. For a comparative perspective on the impact of constitutionalism on private parties, see THE CONSTITUTION IN PRIVATE RELATIONS: EXPANDING CONSTITUTIONALISM (András Sajó & Renáta Uitz eds., 2005).

Further, *tutelas* can be taken only to protect "fundamental constitutional rights." The Constitution contains no clear definition of what is or is not a "fundamental constitutional right," although it does include Article 85, which lists those rights that are "applicable immediately." The list of rights that are "applicable immediately" excludes the socioeconomic and collective rights in the constitutional text. At any rate, the Constitutional Court has refused to engage in a strictly textual read of the issue of which rights are fundamental. It has instead engaged in a more complex consideration, focusing on the precise nature of the right and the context in which it is being applied, as is allowed in the decree-law regulating the *tutela*.[39] The Court has, from its inception, treated social rights as justiciable via *tutela*, initially because of their connection with other fundamental rights such as the right to life, and later sometimes as being fundamental on their own. For example, T-760 of 2008, excerpted in Chapter 6, established that the right to health could be a fundamental right on its own accord, some aspects of which could be enforced directly via *tutela*. T-418 of 2010, also excerpted in Chapter 6, has made the same step with respect to the right to water for human consumption.

Tutelas are heard in three stages: they first go to a judge within the ordinary judiciary, and can then be appealed to another, higher-ranking judge within that same judiciary. These second-instance decisions (and the first-instance ones if not appealed) are all sent to the Constitutional Court, which enjoys a certiorari-like discretionary power to select and revise only those decisions that it wishes to review. Thus, although the Court has little direct docket control over public actions, it has complete docket control over the flow of *tutelas*. *Tutela* decisions are screened and selected by a special selection panel of the Constitutional Court, consisting of two justices who are selected each month by lot.[40] Both justices must agree in order for a *tutela* to be selected. If selected, *tutelas* are normally heard in panels of three judges and denoted by a "T" before the number and year. However, *tutelas* can be sent to the full court in order to settle a problematic doctrinal point or a split between different chambers on the Court; these judgements are denoted with an "SU".

Tutelas are only directly binding on the parties to the action itself. However, the Constitutional Court has developed doctrines to broaden the effect of its decisions in this area, as discussed in detail in Chapter 2. First, it has held that equality norms in the Constitution require that like cases be decided alike, and thus that prior *tutelas* on the same topic must be given precedential weight within both the Constitutional Court and all other courts in the country. The construction of a system of precedent is a distinctive (albeit far from unprecedented) feature for a civil law court.[41] Second, it has developed remedies that have reached beyond the individual case. The most important example here is the "state of

39. *See* Decree 2591 of 1991, art. 2 ("Rights protected by the tutela. The tutela action guarantees fundamental constitutional rights. When a tutela decision refers to a right not expressly stated in the Constitution as fundamental but whose nature permits it to be protected in concrete cases, the Constitutional Court will give it priority in the revision of this decision.").

40. *See* Reglamento Interno de la Corte Constitucional, Acuerdo 05 de 1992 (with amendments), art. 49, at http://www.corteconstitucional.gov.co/lacorte/reglamento.php.

41. Mexico, for example, has long had a variant of the doctrine of precedent in *amparo* cases, through which five reiterated and consistent jurisprudential "theses" become binding. *See* STEPHEN ZAMORA ET AL., MEXICAN

unconstitutional conditions" doctrine, in which the Court declares that an entire area of public policy is rife with unconstitutional action, and thus requires a structural remedy.[42] This mechanism, similar to the United States doctrine of structural injunctions,[43] was used to protect about 3 million internally displaced persons in a case that began in 2004 and where supervision is ongoing (see Chapter 6).

D. The Constitutional Court's Decision-Making Process and Interpretive Style

The Court has had a significant workload since its inception. In 2014, according to statistics from the Court's administrative office, it rendered 194 decisions of abstract review (popular action and automatic review), and 789 *tutela* decisions.[44] As Table 1.1 shows,

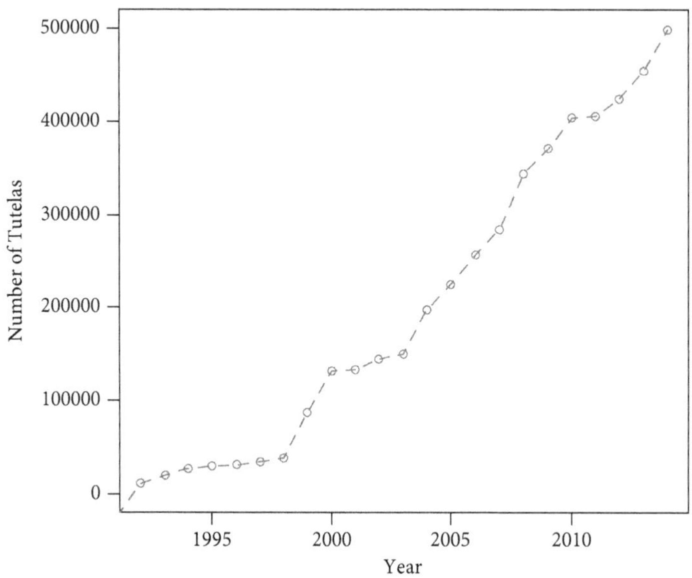

FIGURE 1.1 Total *Tutelas* Filed, 1992–2014. Defensoria del Pueblo, La *Tutela* y el Derecho a La Salud 2014, at 69 tbl. 1 (2015).

LAW 85 (2004); *see also* INTERPRETING PRECEDENTS: A COMPARATIVE STUDY (D. Neil MacCormick & Robert Summers eds., 1997).

42. *See* CÉSAR RODRÍGUEZ-GARAVITO & DIANA RODRÍGUEZ-FRANCO, RADICAL DEPRIVATION ON TRIAL: THE IMPACT OF JUDICIAL ACTIVISM ON SOCIOECONOMIC RIGHTS IN THE GLOBAL SOUTH (2015).

43. For an overview of the U.S. practice with structural injunctions, see OWEN R. FISS, THE CIVIL RIGHTS INJUNCTION (1978).

44. The Court also issued 406 ancillary orders following up on its structural decisions and various other orders. The historical statistics for the Court's workload, going back to 1992, can be found here: http://www.corteconstitucional.gov.co/relatoria/estadisticas.php (last visited September 20, 2016).

TABLE 1.1 **Constitutional Court Workload, 1992–2014 (Select Years)**

	1993	2000	2007	2013	2014
Abstract Review	204	396	204	198	194
Tutelas	394	1340	903	764	789

Source: http://www.corteconstitucional.gov.co/relatoria/estadisticas.php.

both numbers have in fact decreased somewhat in recent years, from their peak in 2000. Given that 498,240 *tutelas* were filed throughout the country in 2014, the Court in fact reviews only a very small percentage of these claims using its discretionary review power.[45] Furthermore, as Figure 1.1 demonstrates, the total number of *tutelas* filed nationwide has risen very sharply and consistently since the 1991 Constitution went into effect (20,181 were filed in 1993, 131,764 in 2000, and 344,468 in 2008).[46]

Cases heard by the Court are normally assigned to a single justice who acts as reporter or *ponente* for the decision. The *ponente* is listed at the beginning of the decision. The practice of the Colombian Constitutional Court also includes a tradition of justices writing both dissenting opinions (*salvamento de voto*) and concurring opinions (*aclaración de voto*). This tradition, which has deep roots in Colombian history and predates the creation of the Constitutional Court, means that the Colombian practice is more individualistic than the practice of many other civil law countries.[47]

Because the workload of the Court is so significant and its jurisprudence is so specialized, the justices rely heavily on their professional legal staffs. Each chambers has a number of law clerks or *magistrados auxiliares* (generally three per justice), as well as a larger number of lesser legal and non-legal staff members. These clerks are highly paid and generally very experienced; many of them are also professors at top universities in Bogotá. Clerks often stay at the Court for a number of years; moreover, it is fairly common for incoming justices to maintain the law clerks of their predecessors, or otherwise to draw on clerks who have had previous experience on the Court.

A word should also be said about the Court's interpretive methodology. The Court has not been particularly originalist or textual; it has focused more on carrying out the purpose or spirit of the 1991 text, as guided by its fundamental principles such as human dignity and the social state of law. The Court's interpretive methodology has been heavily influenced by the work of the German Constitutional Court. The Colombian Constitution is a long and very detailed text; the result is that constitutional provisions routinely conflict. The Court has utilized the technique of proportionality in order to weight these conflicting rights and

45. *See* DEFENSORIA DEL PUEBLO, LA TUTELA Y LOS DERECHOS A LA SALUD Y A LA SEGURIDAD SOCIAL 2014, at 69 tbl.1.

46. *See id.*

47. Across some courts in Europe, decisions are presented as unanimous and/or dissenting and concurring votes are not published or are very rare. *See* STONE SWEET, *supra* note 29, at 48; MITCHEL LASSER, JUDICIAL DELIBERATIONS: A COMPARATIVE ANALYSIS OF TRANSPARENCY AND LEGITIMACY (2006).

interests.[48] Under this technique, the Court asks whether the state's action that infringes on a constitutional right is aimed at protecting or furthering an important end; if it is, the Court will go on to ask whether the action impairs the affected right as little as possible, and whether the injury to the right is proportional to the aim achieved. Proportionality is of course an extremely widespread tool in the field of comparative constitutional law.[49]

The Court has also been heavily influenced by the way that European Constitutional Courts have modulated their decisions to fit a given circumstance.[50] Under the traditional model of abstract review, as developed by Hans Kelsen, the Court acted as a "negative legislator"—its decisions immediately removed the offending norm from the legal order but had no other effects.[51] But the Court has used a number of remedial tools to shape public policy in a more nuanced way. Like many European courts, the Colombian Constitutional Court has held that it has the power to issue conditional decisions.[52] Under a conditional decision, which is seen throughout this volume, the Court holds a given provision constitutional only if it is interpreted in a certain way, and this interpretation is supposed to be given binding effect by other authorities and courts in the system. The Court has also issued a variety of other decision types—for example issuing a decision with deferred effects, where a provision is held unconstitutional, but the Court delays removing it from the legal order until the legislature has time to write a new system. An example is given in the housing case found in Chapter 6. The Court has also, at times, issued integrative decisions, where it will essentially add to a statute to cover some previously excluded group or situation. For example, in a case in Chapter 4, the Court held that the legal concept of "marital union in fact" (essentially a type of common law marriage) had to be read to include same-sex couples. In short, the Court has developed a number of tools for strengthening its supervision over the constitutionality of public policy. Appendix 1 contains a lengthier explanation, along with examples, of the different types of orders issued by the Colombian Constitutional Court.

E. The Constitutional Court in the Post-1991 Political Context

Some of the hopes embodied in the 1991 Constitution were realized; others have proven much more elusive. The peace that the country sought did not immediately materialize: the 1990s proved to be a difficult situation from a security standpoint. Considerable progress

48. For more on the concept of proportionality, see, e.g., Lorraine E. Weinreb, *The Postwar Paradigm and American Exceptionalism*, in THE MIGRATION OF CONSTITUTIONAL IDEAS 84, 93–98 (Sujit Choudhry ed., 2006).

49. *See* AHARON BARAK, PROPORTIONALITY: CONSTITUTIONAL RIGHTS AND THEIR LIMITATIONS (2012); ROBERT ALEXY, A THEORY OF CONSTITUTIONAL RIGHTS (Julian Rivers trans., 2009); David Law, *Generic Constitutional Law*, 89 MINN. L. REV. 652 (2005). Carlos Bernal, EL PRINCIPIO DE PROPORCIONALIDAD Y LOS DERECHOS FUNDAMENTALES (2007) (assessing proportionality in the Colombian context).

50. For a recent summary of the use of these tools by the Italian Constitutional Court, see VITTORIA BARSOTTI ET AL., ITALIAN CONSTITUTIONAL JUSTICE IN GLOBAL CONTEXT 82 (2015).

51. *See* HANS KELSEN, GENERAL THEORY OF LAW AND STATE 269 (Anders Wedberg trans., 1945).

52. *See* STONE SWEET, *supra* note 29, at 51–53.

has been achieved since the administration of President Alvaro Uribe (2002–2010), when the state began enacting very tough anti-guerrilla measures under a program called "democratic security."[53] At the same time, these measures raised questions from the standpoint of Colombian constitutional law, international humanitarian law, and international human rights law, producing some of the Court's most important case law. These cases are treated throughout the book, but particularly in Chapters 7, 9, and 11. Subsequently in the administration of President Juan Manuel Santos (2010–present), the state has pursued a fruitful but long and difficult process of peace negotiations with the FARC. This process again has raised important questions, particularly from the standpoint of the rights of victims of armed conflict. These issues are explored in Chapter 7.

Furthermore, the institutional reconfiguration desired by the 1991 Constituent Assembly has not occurred in every sense. Although Congress was opened up to additional political forces, it did not immediately become a stronger or more functional body.[54] The two-party monopoly in Congress was replaced by a fluid group of parties and movements, many of short-lived duration and without a solid ideological platform. Moreover, Congress continued to be plagued by scandals—a very high number of congressmen were investigated and jailed for links with illegal groups. Political reform (especially in 2003) addressed some of these problems by strengthening and consolidating the party system, but other aspects such as high levels of clientelism and patronage have persisted.[55] The result of these factors is that Congress has not materialized into a powerful or cohesive influence on policymaking. The executive branch has remained the major locus of power, but now controlled by a powerful constitutional tribunal. The other branches of government have also not been major carriers of constitutional norms and values, leaving the Court as the main branch charged with ensuring enforcement of constitutional norms and developing a constitutional culture.[56]

In this environment, the Constitutional Court emerged in an unusually active role, as the major developer of constitutional values and as a significant check on the executive branch. The Court suggested this role in one of its first landmark decisions, T-406

53. President Uribe's "democratic security" policy is considered in Fernando Cepeda Ulloa, *Colombia: Democratic Security and Political Reform*, *in* CONSTRUCTING DEMOCRATIC GOVERNANCE IN LATIN AMERICA 209 (Jorge I. Dominguez & Michael Shifter eds., 3rd ed. 2008).

54. For a discussion of these continuing problems, see Eduardo Pizarro Leongomez, *Giants with Feet of Clay: Political Parties in Colombia*, *in* THE CRISIS OF DEMOCRATIC REPRESENTATION IN THE ANDES 78 (Scott Mainwaring et al. eds., 2006).

55. Indeed, the Court itself has not been entirely free of these influences. In 2015, it was hit with a major scandal when one of its justices was accused of demanding a bribe to issue a decision favorable to a corporate party. The plenary of the Court called for his resignation. He claimed to be innocent and refused to resign. The resulting impeachment process, initiated by another justice of the Court, is ongoing, with the House of Representatives approving the charges in late 2015 and sending the case to the Senate. *See* Jessica Walsh, A Double-Edged Sword: Judicial Independence and Accountability in Latin America 22 (International Bar Association Human Rights Institute Thematic Paper No 5, Apr. 2016).

56. *See, e.g.*, Robert J. Post & Reva B. Siegel, *Popular Constitutionalism, Departmentalism, and Judicial Supremacy*, 92 CAL. L. REV. 1027 (2004) (arguing that judicial supremacy and popular constitutionalism in the United States may work in tandem, rather than in opposition).

of 1992 (excerpted below in Chapter 2), where it wrote: "The difficulties derived from the unchecked growth of the executive power in the interventionist state and of the loss of political leadership of the legislative organ, must be compensated, in constitutional democracy, by the strengthening of the judicial power. . . . Only in this manner can a true equilibrium and collaboration between the powers be achieved; otherwise, the executive power will predominate."

Moreover, the first set of justices on the new court carried a new legal approach called *nuevo derecho* or "new law," which was also associated with then-president Cesar Gaviria's administration.[57] Colombian constitutional law had historically been formalistic and concerned mostly with structure rather than rights. The new framework instead emphasized the need to make rights real, and to privilege the material aspects of constitutional law over its formal aspects.[58] These themes are clear, again, from T-406, where the court refers to a "greater preoccupation for material justice and for solutions that respond to the specific facts at issue" and to its understanding that "the Constitution is conceived in such a way that the organic part of it only acquires significance and meaning as an application . . . of the principles and rights inscribed in the dogmatic part of the text." Finally, this new vision of law has tended to give international human rights law a prominent place in its discourse—the Court has thus been aggressive in incorporating international law and creating the Constitutional Block referred to above. This new vision of law has also been more up front about the fact (as T-406 states) that "legislation and the judicial decision are both processes of the creation of law." As we show below in Chapter 2, the Court has thus attempted to construct a system of precedent, based for example on the constitutional right to equality as well as on other constitutional provisions and principles.

More broadly, one can say that the political context within which the Court has operated—with an extremely powerful president; a perceivably weak, dysfunctional, and clientelistic Congress; and recurrent concerns about regulatory failures and bureaucratic capacity and performance—has been an important determinant of the Court's activism across areas.[59] The Court's social rights jurisprudence (treated in Chapter 6) is a good example. The Court's widespread *tutela* jurisprudence on issues such as the right to health has been driven in part by a public perception of institutional failure among both private and public entities operating in that area. Similarly, the Court's structural interventions (such as its cases treating the rights of internally displaced persons and the healthcare system)

57. Although an economist, President Gaviria openly advocated for "new law" and "new constitutionalism" as a necessary consequence of the characteristics of the 1991 Constitution. *See* MANUEL JOSÉ CEPEDA ESPINOSA, INTRODUCCION A LA CONSTITUCION DE 1991: HACIA UN NUEVO CONSTITUCIONALISMO (1992) (excerpting important speeches from President Gaviria on this topic).

58. *See* DIEGO EDUARDO LÓPEZ MEDINA, TEORIA IMPURA DEL DERECHO: LA TRANSFORMACIÓN DE LA CULTURA JURÍDICA LATINOAMERICANA (2004). The shifts within Colombia are to a degree paralleled elsewhere in Latin America, under the label "new constitutionalism." *See* Javier Couso, *The Transformation of Constitutional Discourse and the Judicialization of Politics in Latin America*, *in* CULTURES OF LEGALITY: JUDICALIZATION AND POLITICAL ACTIVISM IN LATIN AMERICA (Javier Couso et al. eds., 2010).

59. *See* David Landau, *Political Institutions and Judicial Role in Comparative Constitutional Law*, 51 HARV. INT'L L.J. 319 (2010).

have often been motivated by a sense of widespread bureaucratic failure and a lack of state capacity.[60] The role conception of the Court is thus one perhaps typical across some other countries of the "global south"—it is based on a skepticism, and at times distrust, of the capacity and will of political and bureaucratic actors to carry out the constitutional project.[61] The perceived need to further the resolution of deep conflicts and very divisive issues through institutional means in a violent context also helps to explain the sustainability of judicial activism in Colombia.[62]

Throughout its history, the Court has faced attacks on its powers and structure, either from political actors such as the president and members of Congress or from the other high courts. Generally speaking, these attempts have not succeeded.[63] The strongest such effort occurred in 2002, when the administration of the newly installed president Uribe sought a sweeping set of reforms that would have eliminated the Court's ability to review declarations of states of exception, required a supermajority for the Court to strike down laws or constitutional amendments, and eliminated the *tutela* against judicial decisions of the ordinary courts or to enforce socioeconomic rights. Despite the new president's popularity and control of a governing coalition in Congress, the proposal faced stiff political opposition and did not advance. The public popularity of the *tutela*, which had been made into a powerful symbol of the 1991 Constitution because of the Court's jurisprudence, appeared to be relevant in dissuading Congress from moving forward.[64]

F. Methodology and Plan of This Volume

The remainder of this volume takes a casebook form—it consists primarily of translated excerpts from decisions issued by the Colombian Constitutional Court since its inception in 1991. This book is thus intended to give readers a sense of the Court's major doctrinal contributions, rather than making an argument about the sources of the Court's power or its political effect. As most of the Court's decisions are quite long and rather technical (the decision on President Uribe's proposed second re-election, along with all concurrences and dissents, runs about 224,000 words!), the excerpts are edited to focus on the core of reasoning rather than being complete translations of the decisions. The excerpts focus on the majority decisions of the Court, although we have sometimes summarized or included

60. *See* RODRÍGUEZ-GARAVITO AND RODRÍGUEZ-FRANCO, *supra* note 42, at 38.

61. *See* DANIEL BONILLA, CONSTITUTIONALISM OF THE GLOBAL SOUTH: THE ACTIVIST TRIBUNALS OF INDIA, SOUTH AFRICA, AND COLOMBIA (2013).

62. *See* Manuel José Cepeda Espinosa, *Judicial Activism in a Violent Context: The Origin, Role, and Impact of the Colombian Constitutional Court*, 3 WASH. U. GLOBAL STUD. L. REV. 529 (2004).

63. As noted in Chapter 11 (Decision C-288 of 2012), in 2011 during Juan Manuel Santos's first term, Congress did pass an amendment enacting a principle of "fiscal sustainability" and creating a special action that allowed public officials to ask the high courts to consider the budgetary impact of their orders. This amendment was clearly a reaction to the jurisprudence of the Constitutional Court, but as Decision C-288 of 2012 points out, it was weakened in critical ways during its passage in Congress.

64. For a more complete recounting of the various attempts to curb the Court's powers, see Landau, *supra* note 27, at 292–315.

brief excerpts from important concurring and dissenting opinions. We have also included introductory notes to give readers a sense of the significance of each case in a Colombian and comparative perspective, and notes on subsequent developments where we make reference to later Constitutional Court decisions or developments that help to give the reader a sense of the impact of the Court's jurisprudence.

In our selection of cases, we have not aimed to be comprehensive, but instead have selected the topics and cases most likely to highlight the Constitutional Court's most distinctive contributions or those that are most likely to be of interest to the broader comparative constitutional law community. This book is organized around the different doctrinal problems the Court has faced. Some of these problems such as the balance between speech and reputation or the right to abortion are broadly familiar across countries, while others such as the rights to victims of armed conflict to justice or of citizens to a minimal level of subsistence are more distinctive to conflict-ridden and developing societies such as the Colombian one. All of these issues are strongly marked, however, by the context, particularly long-running civil conflict and high levels of poverty.

Part I (which includes Chapter 2) includes introductory materials on the role of the Constitutional Court itself. This chapter reproduces the seminal decisions through which the Court justified an assertive institutional role and a new conception of constitutional interpretation. It also contains case law on the Court's creation of a system of precedent in a civil law country, and its use of the "Constitutional Block" concept in order to lay out an expansive role for international law within the domestic constitutional order.

Part II (Chapters 3–8) deals with the rights jurisprudence of the Court on several topics. Chapters 3, 4, and 5 deal with a set of basic rights issues that will be familiar to many readers from other constitutional contexts—autonomy and dignity, equality, and the freedoms of speech and religion. Nonetheless, the way these concepts are used is innovative and distinctive to the Colombian context. The principle of human dignity and the right to free development of personality in the Constitution have been used to liberalize abortion laws by requiring exceptions in cases involving rape, incest, and threats to the life or health of the mother. These norms have also been used to legalize possession of small amounts of drugs and euthanasia, and to prevent a girl with an intersex condition from being operated on without her consent.

Equality is a particularly interesting issue in Colombia, because Colombian society has historically privileged some religious, ethnic, and gender groups and greatly disadvantaged others. The Court has thus undertaken a difficult and transformative project in this area. It has aimed not only to ensure formal equality, but also to encourage the state to take affirmative measures to ensure material equality, for example in its cases upholding quotas for women in politics and requiring mass transportation companies to create equal access for the handicapped.

The free speech context shows how the Court has balanced conflicting constitutional rights to speech and to other values, such as the rights to privacy and to a good name. The Court has, for example, enforced a right of rectification for politicians who were impugned of being linked to guerrillas after sloppy journalism. Finally, the freedom of religion context again shows how the Court has used its jurisprudence to change the historical ties between the state and Catholicism (as in a case striking down much of the Concordat treaty between Colombia and the Vatican), and to strengthen the rights of religious minorities.

Chapters 6, 7, and 8 treat a set of rights that are more distinctive to the Colombian context, and perhaps to other contexts of the "global south"—socioeconomic rights, the rights of victims of armed conflict to justice, and indigenous rights. Chapter 6, on social rights, covers one of the Colombian Constitutional Court's best-known contributions to comparative jurisprudence. The Court has wrestled with the problems associated with the enforcement of these rights as much as any court in the world, and the jurisprudence on this topic is on par with that of the Indian and South African courts. The Court has also experimented with a number of different remedial approaches. On the right to health, for example, it began by issuing largely individual remedies, but has since shifted to a more structural approach over concerns that the individual remedies were not fixing the system, that they clogged the courts, and that they benefitted mostly wealthier plaintiffs. And the large-scale and long-lasting case of internally displaced persons, where the Court issued another structural remedy and has ordered the state to construct a public policy to deal with these people, is one of the most interesting and difficult examples of the Court's remedial creativity.

Chapter 7 deals with the Court's novel construction of a jurisprudence that emphasizes the rights of victims to the country's long-standing armed conflict. The Court has used the constitutional block concept to ensure that victims receive not just the protection of domestic constitutional provisions, but also of international humanitarian law. As the chapter explains, this line of jurisprudence, and its incorporation of principles from international humanitarian law, has played an important role during the ongoing peace process by setting parameters for negotiations. Chapter 8 looks at the Court's jurisprudence aimed at protecting the rights of indigenous groups. It focuses on two major issues: the right of the indigenous group of meaningful consultation and input before outsiders undertake economic activities on their historical lands, and the balance between their autonomous powers of governance and the fundamental individual rights of their various members.

Part III (Chapters 9–10) focuses on structural constitutional law in the distinctive Colombian political context, which includes a somewhat unbalanced political context with a very strong executive and weak legislature. Chapters 9 and 10 focus on the executive and legislature respectively, with Chapter 9 looking at ways in which the Court has tried to rein in and control a historically very strong executive, and Chapter 10 looking at the Court's attempts to rationalize and strengthen a historically weak and non-deliberative Congress. The Court has been successful in some of these tasks (such as limiting the president's use of emergency powers) and less successful in others (such as improving the rationality of the legislature).

Finally, Part IV (Chapter 11) considers the mechanisms of constitutional change. Here the Court has faced the dilemma of policing a Constitution that is rather flexible and easy to change—amendments can be passed by majority approval in a referendum (so long as certain other conditions are met) or by an absolute majority of Congress in two consecutive sessions. The Court has responded by meticulously policing both the legislative process through which amendments have been approved and the wording and processes of referenda. And in one of its best-known doctrinal innovations, it has developed the "substitution of the constitution" doctrine, which allows it to strike down constitutional amendments if they alter fundamental elements of the existing constitutional order. The Court has held that "substitutions of the constitution" can only be carried out by Constituent Assembly, rather than by ordinary constitutional reform procedures. The doctrine was most famously used when President Alvaro Uribe sought to amend the constitutional text to allow him to run for a second and later a third term in office. The Court held that allowing a second term was not a substitution of the constitution, but allowing a third term was. However, as Chapter 11 shows, the Court has also deployed, or threatened to deploy, the doctrine in a number of other significant cases.

PART ONE

The Constitutional Court

2

The Role of the Constitutional Court

This chapter covers the Constitutional Court's core jurisprudence on its conception of judicial role. The concepts introduced in this chapter will recur throughout the rest of the book.

Decision T-406 of 1992 (Part A) was one of the Court's first decisions and contains perhaps its most striking pronouncements on judicial role. In this decision, a *tutela* involving socioeconomic rights issues, the Constitutional Court lays out a potentially activist space within Colombian politics and society. Subsequent decisions and events have often confirmed this conception of role.

In justifying this bold role conception, the Court relies in large part on its institutional context, and particularly the presence of both a very strong president (see Chapter 9) and at times a weak, dysfunctional, and clientelistic Congress (see Chapter 10). As the Indian Supreme Court has sometimes done, it thus relied in part on the failures of the political system as justification for activism.[1] The relationship between the Court and the political context is a complex topic that will recur throughout the book.[2] For example, the Court's creation of structural injunctions in socioeconomic rights cases (Chapter 6), and its construction of the "substitution of the constitution doctrine" that places substantive limits on the scope of constitutional amendment (Chapter 11), are both in part responses to this context.

In Decision T-406, the Court also emphasized a new conception of constitutional law that represented a sharp break from the constitutional jurisprudence of the Supreme Court before the Constitution of 1991. In its view, the 1991 Constitution replaced a formal conception of law and the separation of powers with a more material conception that emphasized the actual enjoyment of constitutional rights by Colombian citizens. This move away from a

1. *See* Nick Robinson, *Expanding Judiciaries: India and the Rise of the Good Governance Court*, 8 WASH. U. GLOB. STUDS. L. REV. 1, 16–17 (2009).

2. For more detail on the relationship between the Court and its political context, see Manuel José Cepeda-Espinosa, *Judicial Activism in a Violent Context: The Origin, Role, and Impact of the Colombian Constitutional Court*, 3 WASH. U. GLOB. STUDS. L. REV. 529 (2004); David Landau. *Political Institutions and Judicial Role in Comparative Constitutional Law*, 51 HARV. INT'L L.J. 419 (2010).

Colombian Constitutional Law: Leading Cases. Manuel José Cepeda Espinosa and David Landau.

rigid, formal understanding of the separation of powers, and toward a more flexible understanding that focused on the material effectiveness of constitutional rights, made the Court both an early participant and leader in the "new constitutionalist" movements that have been important throughout the region.[3]

The second part of this chapter covers a series of decisions in which the Court asserted the power to determine the reach of its own decisions. This line of jurisprudence has been important for two purposes. First, it has formed the basis of the Court's ability to modulate the effect of its own decisions, by for example holding that legislation is constitutional only if interpreted in certain ways (conditional decisions), or by deferring the effects of unconstitutionality for a period of time so that the legislature has a chance to write new legislation (deferred decisions). Appendix 1 contains examples of the many different ways in which the Court has modulated its decisions.

These principles have also been important in constructing a system of judicial precedent. Civil law countries are often thought to be hostile to systems of case law or precedent. This hostility has generally been evident in Latin America, although in fact some countries have used variants of systems of precedent.[4] In its text, the Colombian Constitution of 1991 appears to maintain the relatively minor role for judicial precedent that has obtained throughout most of the country's history. Article 230, for example, states that judges are "bound exclusively to the rule of law" and that "fairness, jurisprudence, and the general principles of law and doctrine are [merely] auxiliary criteria of judicial proceedings." Given the historical context, this provision was thought to have given case law a low status within the system of sources. Nonetheless, the Court has leveraged constitutional equality norms and other concepts in order to hold that its jurisprudence, whether in abstract review cases or in *tutela* cases, is entitled to significant weight. The Colombian system of constitutional precedent is relatively common-law like in its core features—it is judge-made and utilizes concepts such as the distinction between holding and dicta, as well as rules concerning distinguishing, following, and overruling past precedents.

The final part of the chapter treats the Court's construction of a "constitutional block" that includes many important instruments and principles from international law. Although the concept derives from French constitutional law, the Colombian Constitutional Court has used it to carve out a robust role for international law within the domestic constitutional order. In so doing, it has perhaps pushed Colombian constitutionalism beyond even what Vicki Jackson calls "engagement" and toward "convergence," at least with international law.[5] In constructing the constitutional block, the Constitutional Court placed great emphasis on Article 93 of the Constitution, which states first that international treaties ratified by Colombia that recognize human rights and prohibit their limitation during states

3. *See* Javier A. Couso, *The Transformation of Constitutional Discourse and the Judicialization of Politics in Latin America*, *in* CULTURES OF LEGALITY: JUDICIALIZATION AND POLITICAL ACTIVISM IN LATIN AMERICA (Javier A. Couso et al. eds, 2010).

4. For an overview of some of this variation, see Teresa M. Miguel-Sterns, *Judicial Power in Latin America: A Short Survey*, 15 LEG. INFO. MGMT. 100 (2015).

5. *See* VICKI S. JACKSON, TRANSNATIONAL ENGAGEMENT IN A TRANSNATIONAL ERA (2010).

of exception "have priority" over other norms in the Colombian Constitutional order, and second that the rights provisions of the Constitution must be "interpreted" in light of ratified treaties on human rights.

In the Court's jurisprudence, some provisions of international human rights law (those that cannot be limited during states of exception) literally become part of the domestic constitutional order, whereas many others become mandatory as a source of interpretation of the Colombian Constitution. The Court has also routinely given great weight to decisions of international tribunals (particularly those who are authorized interpreters of a given statutory scheme). And it has on occasion referred to sources of international "soft law" (for example in the internally displaced persons case found in Chapter 6). Uses of the constitutional block concept will be found throughout this book, most intensely in Chapter 7 on the rights of victims.

A. The Role Conception of the Constitutional Court

In the decision below, the Court examined a case regarding a neighborhood located in Cartagena where work to build a sewage system was begun but then suspended. This resulted in the neighbors having to put up with the overflow of waste water, nauseous smells, and environmental contamination. The Court protected the dwellers' rights to public health, human dignity, and life. It ordered the Public Service Company of Cartagena "to finish the construction of the sewage system in Vista Hermosa neighborhood. The conclusion of these works must be accomplished in a reasonable period of time which cannot exceed three months. While this is done, the company must immediately take adequate provisional measures aimed at putting an end to the trouble and damages to which inhabitants of the neighborhood are being subjected." Likewise, the Court held that in all other similar cases "when unfinished public works have an impact on public health, the constitutional doctrine established in the present decision will be mandatory for all authorities."

Decision T-406 of 1992 (per Justice Ciro Angarita Barón)

[The Court began by reflecting on the role of the judge in the new constitutional order. It noted that social and legal changes] had produced in law not only a quantitative transformation given the increase in the volume of statutes, but also a qualitative change, given the surge of a new manner of interpreting law, whose key conception can be summarized as follows: *the loss of the sacred importance of the legal text understood as an emanation of the popular will and a greater preoccupation for material justice and for solutions that respond to the specific facts at issue.* These characteristics acquire a special relevance in the field of constitutional law, given the generality of its texts and the consecration given there to the basic principles of political organization. Thus the enormous importance that the constitutional judge acquires in the social state of law.[6]

6. As noted in the Introduction, Article 1 of the Colombian Constitution defines the political order as a "social state of law."

The complexity of the system, both in terms of the facts that are being regulated and the regulations themselves, renders absurd the rationalist pretension that consists in laying out every possible social conflict so that it can later be given a corresponding legal solution. In the legal system of the social state of law, we are dramatically confronted with the problem of the necessity of adapting, correcting, and conditioning the application of law by means of judicial intervention. But this *intervention is not only manifest as a necessary mechanism to solve a dysfunction, but also, and above all, as an indispensable element to improve the conditions of communication between law and society*, in other words, to favor the achievement of justice (of the communication between law and reality). . . .

The increase in the factual and legal complexity of the contemporary state has brought as a consequence a decrease in the regulatory capacity of general and abstract norms. In these circumstances the legal text loses its traditional predominant position, and principles and judicial decisions, previously considered secondary sources within the normative system, acquire exceptional importance. This redistribution occurs, above all, for functional reasons: since the law can no longer determine all of the possible solutions through legal texts, one needs teleological criteria (principles) and instruments of a concrete solution (judges) to achieve better communication with society. But this shift also occurs for substantial reasons: the new role of the judge in the social state of law is the direct consequence of the energetic attempt to give validity and effectiveness to the substantive content of the Constitution, clearly signaled in its Article 228 ("The actions [of the administration of justice] will be public and permanent with the exceptions established by law, *and in these actions substantial justice will prevail.*").

But this is not the only reason explaining this change: the development of constitutional democracy renders it obvious that the legislative organ, the traditional repository of the popular will, must be accompanied by judicial review [by the courts], which across the history of modern constitutional law has been shown to be the most effective organ in defending the rights of citizens and democratic principles. The difficulties derived from the unchecked growth of the executive power in the interventionist state and of the loss of political leadership of the legislative organ, must be compensated, in constitutional democracy, by the strengthening of the judicial power. . . . Only in this manner can a true equilibrium and collaboration between the powers be achieved; otherwise, the executive power will predominate.

The dispersion of interests in the present capitalist society has reduced the importance of the public interest, thus affecting the legitimacy of the legislative organ and of the law itself. This deficiency of traditional legitimacy has been compensated by the strengthening of state capacity to create consensus and to find solutions that are a product not only of the law but of negotiation and of particularization to the specific circumstances of the conflict. In these conditions, the idea of judicial control appears as the functional key to avoid an imbalance of power and to achieve an adaptation of law to social reality. Since he is the repository of a wisdom that is remote from society and which thinks in terms of objective values, and also because of the advantages based on hearing, every day, the "living reality of the litigants," the judge is plainly capable, like no other organ in the political system, of playing this role. In synthesis, the control exercised by judges and tribunals in the contemporary constitutional state is the formula for the best relationship between legal security and justice.

Thus we derive the idea that the judge, in the social state of law, is also a carrier of the institutional vision of the public interest. The judge, upon putting the Constitution—its principles and its norms—in dialogue with the law and the facts, makes use of an interpretive discretion that necessarily defines the political meaning of constitutional texts. In this sense legislation and the judicial decision are both processes of the creation of law. . . .

The Colombian constitution is broadly based on the normative postulates of the social state of law. This is rooted not only in the list of principles and the Charter of Rights, but also in the organization of the state apparatus. Article 1 of the Constitution is the normative key that irradiates the entire constitutional text.

> **Article 1.** Colombia is a social state of law organized in the form of a unitary republic, decentralized, with the autonomy of its territorial units, democratic, participatory and pluralistic, based on respect for human dignity, on the work and solidarity of the individuals who belong to it, and on the predominance of the general interest.

The meaning . . . of Article 1 cannot be entirely determined by an interpretation reduced to an analysis of its text. Each one of the words of the article possesses an enormous semantic charge, which across the history of western constitutionalism, have been decanted into a series of basic notions that delimit their meaning and make them coherent and reasonable. An interpretation which ignores the national and international context in which the concepts of Article 1 have been formed could give way to contradictory and concocted solutions.

In synthesis, the Constitution is conceived in such a way that the organic part of it only acquires significance and meaning as an application . . . of the principles and rights inscribed in the dogmatic part of the text. The bill of rights, nationality, citizen's participation, the structure of the state, the functions of the powers, the mechanisms of control, elections, the territorial organization and the mechanisms of reform are understood and justified as an instrumental transmission of these principles and constitutional values. It is impossible, then, to interpret an institution or proceeding listed in the Constitution outside of the basic material contents of its principles and fundamental rights. [The Court classified constitutional provisions into three categories: specific norms, principles, and values. Values formed the "axiological catalogue across which is defined the purpose and ends of other constitutional provisions"—these included things such as work, peace, and liberty. The Court noted that values have "an enormous generality and thus an open interpretive texture," which made them better suited for legislative rather than judicial development. Principles, in contrast, "consecrate general legal prescriptions that have a recognized political and axiological meaning; thus, they restrict the space of interpretation [and] are norms of immediate application." The Court classified the social state of law and the prevalence of the general interest as principles. The holding that higher-level norms such as principles may be judicially enforced paved the way toward a more aggressive and systematic judicial interpretation of the Constitution.]

[Finally, the Court tackled the question involved in this particular case. The major issue was whether the rights claimed in this case, which were social and economic rights, were "fundamental" in nature. The question was important because only fundamental rights may be enforced via *tutela*.[7] The Court held that fundamental rights: "(i) must have a direct connection with constitutional principles; (ii) must be directly effective from the constitutional text, even without any additional statutes or regulations, and (iii) must have an essential content or basic core recognizable by the judge without having to resort to additional sources."]

[The Court held that the criteria to identify fundamental rights may be analytical, factual, or historical. The Court mentioned the following analytic criteria: (i) A clear textual enshrinement, as "regarding some rights, the Constituent Assembly clearly stated its will to establish them as fundamental. This is the case of the rights consecrated in the first section of the second chapter of the Constitution, as well as in Article 44 on the rights of children"; (ii) a clear reference to international law, as in the case where the Constituent Assembly refers a topic to international treaties and covenants; (iii) a direct link with other rights clearly enshrined as fundamental, as "some rights are not clearly established as fundamental [but] their link with other fundamental rights is of such nature that when the latter are not duly protected, they will virtually disappear or their effective protection will become impossible"; (iv) their nature as intrinsic rights of individuals: "the criteria which determine the fundamental nature of a right go beyond its enshrinement in the text and depend on the existence of a historical consensus and a collective will regarding its specific character and all of its implications with regard to essential content, its link with principles and its direct effectiveness."]

[The Court defined the factual criterion for identifying social rights as being about "the factual importance" of the right for the person at issue, within the context of a given case. On this matter, the Court held that the factual context would be critical in determining how a right would be protected. As a result, the process of protecting a given right would be "mainly inductive, as the interpretation given by judges to the relation between the text of the law and the facts will be the base to establish the scope of the rights." Finally, concerning the historical criterion, the Court pointed out that: "[T]his approach has two implications: a) Not all fundamental rights have

7. Article 86 of the Constitution only allows the *tutela* to be brought to protect "fundamental rights." However, the constitutional text contains no clear definition of which rights are fundamental, although Article 85 does list some rights as being "applicable immediately" (social and economic rights are not on that list). For more on the court's jurisprudence on the enforceability of social and economic rights via *tutela*, see *infra* Chapter 6.

been considered fundamental at all times, and some may have this nature only in a transitory way because of the evolution of civil society, and b) the fundamental essence of a right is linked to the collective representations of a topic at a given time [or], in other words, to the way in which society envisages the right."]

[T]he majority of the [social, economic, and cultural] rights in question entail the provision of some benefit by the state and, consequently, expenditures which usually depend on political will. Based on this argument, the Court holds that the constitutional clauses which embody these rights cannot be subject to judicial decisions until Congress has adopted the regulations required to apply them; otherwise, and according to the doctrine of the separation of powers, the judge would be invading spheres which are outside of his competence.

Judges must act with equal caution and firmness. In the first place, judicial intervention in the case of economic, social, or cultural rights is necessary when it is deemed indispensable to enforce a constitutional principle or fundamental right. In these circumstances, judges act under similar conditions to those present when they must deal with problems related to a gap or incoherence in the law. It is clear that in all these cases, judges decide upon matters that are, in principle, part of the legislator's jurisdiction. However, in this specific situation, the absence of a solution by the political branch that is entitled to act opens the possibility for another branch, in this case the judiciary, to decide with the sole objective of safeguarding the validity and effectiveness of the relevant constitutional provision. . . .

The Constitution is a legal norm valid in the present and it must be enforced and honored without delay. Hence, maintaining that social, economic and cultural rights are merely a link of political responsibility between citizens and the legislator is not only naïve with respect to the existence of such a bond, but also a flagrant distortion of the meaning and coherence which the Constitution must keep. If the responsibility for the effective realization of these rights were exclusively in the hands of the legislator, constitutional provisions would have no value and the validity of the will expressed by the constituent assembly would be subordinated to the legislator's volition.

[Finally, the Court analyzed the case in question by resorting to the opinions of several specialists who underlined the importance of public health and its relation with the right to life, as in poor sanitation conditions such as those described in the *tutela*, many diseases can be unleashed affecting all exposed populations.]

The right to have access to sewage services in those circumstances where it has an evident impact on fundamental constitutional rights and principles, such as those enshrined in Articles 1 (human dignity), 11 (life) and 13 (rights of vulnerable groups), must be considered as a right that can be protected through *tutela* actions. This being the case, and taking into account the concepts rendered by the experts. . . , on the one hand, and the fact that it has been clearly proven that there is a lack of vital services in Cartagena's Vista Hermosa neighborhood with foreseeable disastrous effects on its inhabitants, on the other, this Review Panel considers that in the present case there is a clear violation of a fundamental right. The unfinished sewage system has resulted in the overflow of waste water on neighborhood streets. It is also important to note that this is a poor neighborhood . . . where the economic resources of dwellers to face the problem are surely insufficient and, therefore, hygiene and sanitation conditions must be precarious.

The infringement of Vista Hermosa neighborhood dwellers' right to public health has special connotations given the fact that the construction work on the sewage system was started and then suspended. The decision to build the sewage system and the initiation of the corresponding public works was a positive answer to these people's complaints, while non-completion created an additional frustration for them.

Also, the fact that the construction of the sewage system was actually initiated [before being suspended] refutes the main objection to the effective realization of the right to access vital public services, the lack of financial resources. Indeed, the decision to build the sewage system had to be accompanied by the allotment of adequate public funds. The Public Service Company of Cartagena never expressed its stance during the *tutela* proceedings, although its representatives were summoned by the judge to explain the reasons which may have prevented the completion of the works. This shows a blatant neglect in their handling of the problem.

B. Precedent and the Effects of Constitutional Court Decisions

1. The Power of the Constitutional Court to Determine the Effects of Its Own Decisions

Decision C-113 of 1993 (per Justice Jorge Arango Mejía)

[In a unanimous decision, the Constitutional Court declared parts of Decree 2067 of 1991 unconstitutional. The decree laid out "the procedures to be followed . . . before the Constitutional Court." The contested legal provision was the second clause of Article 21 of Decree 2067 of 1991, which established that: "The rulings handed down by the Court will have effect only as of their date of enactment, except to safeguard the principle of favorability in criminal . . . and disciplinary matters." In other words, the provision at issue generally prevented rulings of the Constitutional Court from having retroactive effect.]

Besides the Constituent Assembly, what other authority has the jurisdiction to determine the effects of the rulings handed down by the Constitutional Court. . . ? Only the Constitutional Court is vested with this power, and it must obviously rest with the Court given the text and the essence of the Constitution.

Hence, only the Constitutional Court, in compliance with the Constitution, can determine the effects of one of its own decisions. This principle, which is true more generally, is especially true when it comes to decisions related to constitutional matters.

Consequently, the President of the Republic committed an error when he issued the norm in question, since he exercised functions ascribed by the Constitution to the

> Constitutional Court. Specifically, the president infringed Article 121, according to which "no authority of the state may exercise functions different from those assigned to it by the Constitution and statute." He also infringed the third clause of Article 113, which establishes that "the various organs of the state have separate functions. . . ."
>
> [I]t would be inadmissible to deprive the Constitutional Court of its faculty to determine the effects of its own decisions, always, we must insist, abiding strictly by the Constitution. . . . The competence of the Constitutional Court to determine the effects of its own decisions in accordance with the Constitution was established in Article 241, which entrusts the Court with safeguarding "the integrity and supremacy of the Constitution." To comply with this mandate, the first and most indispensable step is the interpretation developed in a decision, in order to describe its own effect. In short, not even a piece of paper may be placed between the Constitutional Court and the Constitution, whenever the former interprets the text of the latter.

Note on the Court's Control Over Its Decisions. The principles established in Decision C-113 of 1993 have proven fundamental for subsequent case law, particularly the construction of a system of precedent (as noted below). An important subsequent case was **Decision C-037 of 1996 (per Justice Vladimiro Naranjo Mesa)**.

In C-037, the Court held partially unconstitutional several provisions of the Statutory Law on the Administration of Justice. The key provision attempted to limit the precedential effects of Constitutional Court decisions. It stated that only the resolution of an abstract review decision would be binding for the future; the reasoning of abstract review decisions and all parts of *tutela* decisions (both the reasoning and the resolution) would be merely persuasive or auxiliary authority. Furthermore, the article stated that only Congress (and not the Court) could issue constitutional interpretations of a "general mandatory nature."

These provisions about the nature of precedent and the distribution of interpretive authority between Congress and the Court represented an important battle in a broader interpretive war between the two institutions. In general these provisions closely tracked the traditional view on precedent and interpretive authority in Colombia, and thus the Court's rejection of them marked a step toward the construction of a system of precedent, as well as an assertion of judicial power.

In its analysis, the Court reiterated the core principle of Decision C-113 of 1993: "[T]he legislator cannot limit the scope of or establish rules regarding decisions adopted by the Court in the exercise of its chief task as guardian of the Constitution." It also struck down the attempt to give only the Congress sole interpretive authority:

> Case law has clearly defined the duty of the Constitutional Court aimed at safeguarding the supremacy and integrity of the Constitution, which means that the Court is in charge of the authoritative interpretation and definition of the scope of constitutional precepts. In this line of discussion, it is overtly unconstitutional to claim, as is the case in the norm under study, that only the Congress of the

> Republic has the authority to interpret laws. . . . [A]s has been previously stated, the interpretation that the Constitutional Court carries out in the exercise of its authority has a general mandatory character.

Finally, the Court adopted rules for the adoption of precedent that differed in significant ways from those found in the law under study. In analyzing abstract review decisions, the Court held that binding, *erga omnes* effects extended not only to the resolution itself, but also to those parts of the reasoning that have a "close, direct and inseparable connection with the judgment, in other words, those elements of the reasoning which are deemed totally central, necessary and indispensable to back the resolutions adopted in the decisions and which have a direct incidence on them."

In analyzing *tutela* judgments, the Court held that although these decisions were formally binding only on parties to the judgment, constitutional principles of equality required that past decisions be given weight.

> [T]he constitutional doctrine concerning the contents and scope of constitutional rights established by the Constitutional Court in its exercise of reviewing *tutela* rulings goes beyond the specific situations involved in them and becomes the rule which unifies and guides the interpretation of the Constitution. The principle of judicial independence must be in agreement with the principle of equality in the enforcement of the law; otherwise, there is always the risk of falling into arbitrariness. The case law established by jurisdictional high courts through doctrinal unification seeks the realization of the principle of equality. . . . [I]f judges decide not to follow past decisions, they must give a sufficient and adequate justification for not doing so as to avoid infringing the principle of equality.

Justices Hernando Herrera Vergara and Vladimiro Naranjo Mesa concurred in the judgment, but wrote separately to lay out a more traditional view. "[T]he reasoning of the decisions handed down by the Constitutional Court generally include a series of concepts, arguments, appraisals and quotes from doctrinal experts which are deemed necessary by the Justice in charge of presenting the discussion to illustrate his arguments; if such arguments are accepted by the Plenary, they are included in the decisions. However, it is unthinkable to conceive of all these concepts, opinions or arguments as having the same status of final judgment that the judgment has. . . . [O]nly those specific sections which have a direct and precise relationship with the judgment have binding force."

The principles and analysis found in Decisions C-113 of 1993 and C-037 of 1996 are the basis for the system of precedent later constructed by the Court, as noted below. They are also the basis for a jurisprudence in which the Court has adopted a wide variety of different decisions to face different situations. In issuing abstract review decisions, the Court has been a frequent user of modulated decisions including: (1) conditional decisions, where the Court holds a norm constitutional only on the understanding that it be interpreted in a certain way; (2) deferred decisions, where the Court strikes down a norm but only after a lapse of time, so that the legislature has the ability to develop a new system; and

(3) integrative decisions, where the Court orders that new content be read into existing law, in order to cover new groups or situations.

The Court has also used its power over its own decisions to develop modulated orders in concrete *tutela* decisions. Perhaps most important, where it finds through the presentations of the parties or its own prior case law that problems underlying a *tutela* judgment are widespread, the Court has asserted the ability to issue structural orders to governmental authorities in many instances. This is true despite the fact that the *tutela* was designed as an individual remedy to address concrete problems. In extreme cases of widespread violations, the Court has declared a "state of unconstitutional conditions" and/or maintained jurisdiction over the case for long periods of time. Some of the Court's structural *tutela* judgments are found throughout the book, but especially in Chapter 6 on socioeconomic rights. Furthermore, there are examples and deeper explanations of all of these types of orders, both on concrete and abstract review, in Appendix 1.

Neither type of order is unique to the Colombian context. The modulation of decisions of course is found in the practice of many Constitutional Courts throughout the world, particularly in European contexts.[8] The issuance of structural orders out of individual cases has comparative parallels as well, especially in the United States practice with structural injunctions, but also in other contexts such as India.[9] Nonetheless, the Colombian experience has been distinctive in the way some of these orders have been used. For example, the sheer size of the Colombian structural cases, and the nature of the monitoring scheme established by the Court, has been seen as a model in comparative practice.[10]

2. The Construction of a System of Precedent

The Constitutional Court gradually introduced the concept of precedent into constitutional law. The first step was done in abstract review decisions; these decisions clearly have *erga omnes* effects in the sense that a legal norm found contrary to the Constitution is expelled from the legal order, cannot be applied by anyone, and cannot be adopted again by Congress or by any other authority. The innovation of the Court was linking this effect on the formal norm judged to the most important parts of the reasoning as well. In C-037 of 1996 (see Section 1 above), the Court held that the part of the reasoning that has a "close, direct and inseparable connection" with the court's order also has *erga omnes* effects.

8. *See, e.g.*, ALEC STONE-SWEET, GOVERNING WITH JUDGES: CONSTITUTIONAL POLITICS IN EUROPE 61–73 (2000).

9. MALCOLM M. FEELEY & EDWARD L. RUBIN, JUDICIAL POLICYMAKING AND THE MODERN STATE: HOW THE COURTS REFORMED AMERICA'S PRISONS (1998) (tracing structural injunctions in United States courts in the prisons area, and concluding that they had some successes and justifications); DONALD L. HOROWITZ, THE COURTS AND SOCIAL POLICY (1977) (offering a skeptical take on United States structural injunctions in schools, juvenile justice, and other areas); Michael C. Dorf & Charles F. Sabel, *A Constitution of Democratic Experimentalism*, 98 COLUM. L. REV. 267 (1998); Jessica Corsi, *Between Starvation and Globalization: Realizing the Right to Food in India*, 31 MICH. J. INT'L L. 691 (2010) (discussing a major structural case on the right to food from India).

10. CÉSAR RODRÍGUEZ-GARAVITO & DIANA RODRÍGUEZ-FRANCO, RADICAL DEPRIVATION ON TRIAL: THE IMPACT OF JUDICIAL ACTIVISM ON SOCIOECONOMIC RIGHTS IN THE GLOBAL SOUTH (2015).

The second step was made in *tutela* decisions, which officially have only *inter partes* effects, that is, they are binding only between the parties to that individual case. The Court nonetheless held that *tutela* decisions have considerable weight for future *tutelas* of a similar type. It based this holding, as noted in Decision C-037 of 1996, on constitutional principles such as equality, legitimate expectations, and due process.

Over time, the Court has deepened and extended the meaning of precedent, for example by holding that governmental and some private actors as well as courts have a duty to give weight to past Constitutional Court decisions. The current regime of precedent, with the difficult issue of its application to private parties, is explained below in Decision T-292 of 2006.

Decision T-292 of 2006 (per Justice Manuel José Cepeda Espinosa)

[In this decision, the Court protected the rights of a woman who filed a *tutela* against a shipping company known as CIFM.[11] The Court considered that the woman's rights to due process of law, to the free development of personality, and to equality had been infringed when the company "suspended the payment of her late husband's pension, to which she had been entitled since the year 2000, by arguing that her right had ceased when she remarried." The claimant argued that the company's decision was based on a regulation whose contents had long been declared unconstitutional by the Constitutional Court. In Decision C-309 of 1996, the Court had declared unconstitutional "all regulations in force before the 1991 Constitution which suspended pension payments due to surviving spouses as a consequence of their marrying or cohabitating with new partners." In earlier instances, lower courts acting as *tutela* judges nonetheless rejected her claim.]

The legal problem under discussion in the present case is whether [CIFM] . . . has *manifestly violated the Constitution* by suspending the pension payments due to Mrs. Gómez, arguing that she had married again, and given that, apparently, previously binding constitutional case law had established that those regulations suspending pension payments to surviving spouses due to their remarrying infringed the right to the free development of personality and to equality. In other words, does a private company engage in a *manifest violation of the Constitution* when its decision is based on the enforcement of a regulation whose normative contents, according to binding case law, are unconstitutional? That is to say, is CIFM obliged to apply the holding of the decision (*ratio decidendi*) contained in a constitutionality ruling which . . . declared unconstitutional the legal regulations establishing the suspension of the right to continue receiving late spouses' pensions due to the holder's new marriage, since they were held contrary to the 1991 Constitution?. . .

11. Article 86 of the Constitution allows the *tutela* to be filed against a private party, rather than the state, if that party is "entrusted with providing a public service or . . . may affect seriously and directly the collective interest or in respect of whom the applicant may find himself/herself in a state of subordination or vulnerability." The Court held that the test in Article 86 was met in this case.

Decision C-309 of 1996 (per Justice Eduardo Cifuentes Muñoz) has been cited in the present writ . . . as a constitutionality ruling which should have been observed for this specific case by CIFM. . . . However, are the reasons given in Decision C-309 binding in this case? Are they part of the holding of Decision C-309? If C-309 is a precedent for this case, (1) does precedent bind private parties as well as the state? And (2) what is the scope of *stare decisis*—which parts of the decision does it cover?. . .

The reliability of legal provisions within a normative system is founded on the respect given to constitutional norms which permeate the whole legal system, as well as to the unity and coherence among different levels of courts in relation to [the interpretation of] constitutional provisions. The Constitutional Court . . . has precise legal powers to ensure the effectiveness and predominance of constitutional mandates within our legal system. Since the Court is in charge of maintaining the integrity and predominance of the Constitution, its decisions are a source of law for authorities and private citizens when, in the exercise of its constitutional competence, it establishes a binding interpretation regarding provisions contained in the Constitution. Consequently, the main objective of the interpretation of the Constitution . . . is to guide the legal system in order to keep it in harmony with constitutional principles and values. . . .

It may be difficult . . . to determine which decisions or parts of decisions are legally binding and which ones are not.

To ensure that the case law on the binding character of constitutional precedents is sufficiently clear, we will review some of the Court's decisions which have helped to lay the foundations of this doctrine. This description will focus on relevant aspects deemed necessary to resolve the present *tutela,* which may be summarized as follows: (i) Is the reasoning of the decision in Constitutional Court rulings binding? What is the constitutional basis for its binding character?; (ii) Which specific elements in the reasoning of the decision in Constitutional Court rulings are binding?; (iii) How can these elements be identified?; (iv) Is there a difference among the different types of rulings issued by the Court in this respect?; and (v) What does "binding precedent" mean and what is the judicial obligation concerning precedent? These questions have been resolved by the Court in different stages of the development of its case law.

[Concerning the first question of whether the reasoning of a Constitutional Court decision was binding, the Court pointed out that during] its first few sessions, the discussion on the reach of its own rulings centered around determining if beyond the ruling itself, any of the statements contained in the reasoning expressed constitutional motives of a binding nature for all legal authorities involved.

At that time, the Court discussed the issue of the mandatory nature of the reasoning for the decision in constitutional rulings mainly from the point of view of their *legal effects*. . . .

Regarding the effects of rulings, one of the first decisions which touched upon the binding character of constitutional case law was decision C-113 of 1993 [see Section

B.1. above]. . . . [The Court held that] only the Court itself was entitled to determine the effects of its own decisions, without any restrictions set by other bodies or authorities. . . .

This appraisal . . . opened the possibility of advocating for the binding nature of specific elements contained in the reasoning for the decision in constitutional rulings, as it allowed for extending the *erga omnes* concept beyond Acts formally judged unconstitutional to include the subject matter addressed by the decision and thus to the material issue which was resolved. . . .

[D]ecision C-037 of 1996 [see Section B.1 above] on the Statutory Law on the Administration of Justice, included some key considerations regarding the scope of abstract review and *tutela* rulings. . . . [This] ruling confirmed that judicial interpretations of the Constitution have binding authority and, therefore, the expression which established that only the interpretations issued by the Congress could be considered as having a "general mandatory nature" was declared unconstitutional. The court's reasoning stated that "the authoritative interpretations made by the Constitutional Court have a general mandatory character. . . ."

The constitutional bases for the binding nature of the reasoning of abstract review decisions are the following: (i) respect for the *erga omnes* principle found in Article 243 of the Constitution [for abstract review decisions], which extends to certain elements of the reasoning; and (ii) the position and institutional mission of the Court, which imply that its interpretations have authority and general binding character. . . . Likewise, and especially regarding decisions on *tutela* actions, the Court has referred to other principles in support of the binding nature of the ratio decidendi, as follows: the principles of equality, legal security, due process of law, and legitimate expectations. . . .

[The Court next analyzed its prior case law on the parts of a decision for precedential purposes, and especially the distinction between the *decisum,* ratio decidendi, and obiter dicta. The Court defined the *decisum* as the concrete ruling in a case, whereas the ratio decidendi was "the general formulation of . . . the principles, regulations or reasons which lie at the base of specific rulings, in other words, the direct normative grounds of the ruling." Finally, obiter dictum or dicta referred to "considerations presented by the judge in the argumentative presentation of the ruling which are not strictly necessary for the decision, i.e., incidental opinions expressed by the judge along his line of argument."]

The *decisum* is usually binding only for the parties involved and it must be seen as *res judicata* only for the parties except in the case of abstract constitutional review, in which case rulings have *erga omnes* effects. . . . However, since the ratio decidendi is constituted by the "necessary grounds for the decision," judges are obliged to apply the ratio decidendi when ruling on similar cases. Finally, obiter dicta are non-binding, as their goal is essentially that of persuasion.

Generally the identification of the *decisum* is not difficult. This part clearly follows the term "Orders" or "Resolves" in Constitutional Court decisions. However, how can the ratio decidendi of a specific decision be identified?

In this respect, the Court has pointed out that it is necessary to take into account three main elements regarding abstract control decisions: (i) the norm subject to the examination of the Court; (ii) the constitutional norms which backed the ruling, and (iii) the decisive criterion of the ruling. . . .

On these grounds, we may say that the ratio of a decision has been properly identified when: (i) The ratio by itself constitutes a rule with sufficiently defined specificity so as to allow a clear response to the question of whether or not the norm under examination complies with the Constitution. Any other element outside of this immediate identification shall not be considered as part of the ratio of a ruling; (ii) The ratio is equivalent to a norm which implies an authorization, a prohibition or an order derived from the Constitution; and (iii) Generally the ratio resolves the legal problem under examination in a case and is formulated as a rule derived from case law, which sets the meaning of the constitutional provision invoked by the Court in its analysis of the legal problem in question. . . .

The ratio decidendi in [both] abstract review and *tutela* decisions is binding for all legal operators. . . . First, the ratio decidendi (i) reflects the qualified and authoritative interpretation of the Constitution by the Court according to its powers, as has already been stated. Therefore, the interpretation is generally binding since the ratio decidendi responds to the authoritative examination of the competent body in the terms established by Article 241 of the Constitution.

Additionally, the ratio decidendi is formally binding (ii) according to the Statutory Law on the Administration of Justice and to the conditions established in decision C-037 of 1996, which was previously discussed.

Lastly, the ratio decidendi is mandatory (iii) because:

(a) It ensures that legal rulings are based on a uniform and consistent interpretation of our legal system;
(b) it guarantees the coherence of the system (legal security), and
(c) it favors respect for the principles of legitimate expectations and equality under the law enshrined in the Constitution. . . .

An applicable *precedent* can be defined as a previous *relevant* ruling whose reasoning entails a decisive rule—prohibition, order or authorization—to resolve a case where similar facts or constitutional matters are involved. In constitutional law, the application of precedents by judges must have the following characteristics:

(i) If the precedent stems from a ruling declaring a provision unconstitutional [on abstract review], the acting judge must refrain from applying the norms which have been struck down, and will be obliged, to the extent of his/her capacity, to apply the ratio decidendi of the decision to those cases with similar provisions. . . .
(ii) If the decision declares a law constitutional, the binding ratio decidendi requires that the judge not adopt a different interpretation. In the event of decisions declaring a law constitutional only subject to conditions, the ratio decidendi establishes the *constitutional interpretation* of the law, i.e., the meaning that the provisions under examination must follow in order to

comply with the Constitution, which will be in the precise terms set forth by the Court. . . .

(iii) In *tutela* matters, judges must acknowledge and embrace precedents to ensure equal access to the administration of justice, unless they find well-founded reasons not to follow them by meeting a burden of argumentation, showing why the precedent is wholly or partially contrary to the Constitution.

In all instances, judges and courts must follow decisions adopted by their superior tribunals so as to standardize and harmonize case law.

When a judge openly disregards a constitutional precedent, his/her ruling will certainly constitute a *gross error* which will place it outside the Constitution. In such a case, the ruling could be subject to a *tutela* action against it, if it contradicts "the mandatory rules set by the Court as authorized interpreter of the Constitution."

Based on the considerations presented so far, we can conclude that constitutional precedents bind all legal and civil authorities, and even individual citizens. . . .

In any case, although respect for precedents is essential in our legal system, it should not entail a freezing of the law. In this sense, judges may diverge from horizontal and vertical precedents, but only if they can rigorously back their position and present convincing arguments to legitimate their stand. Their arguments should prove that the precedent is wholly or partially contrary to the Constitution. The Court has also established other prerequisites in order to set aside a precedent.

[Past case law] clearly admits the possibility of diverging from precedents in some specific situations: (i) eventual errors in the case law which demand correction; (ii) interpretations which may have been useful and adequate to solve certain matters in the past, but whose present application would bring unexpected and unacceptable consequences in similar cases; and (iii) historic changes which render unreasonable the application of traditional interpretations. . . .

CIFM . . . had an obligation to observe the ratio decidendi applicable in this case in compliance with the Constitution. Hence, the claimant's rights to equality and to the free development of personality were infringed. CIFM, being as it is a private institution with no administrative restrictions, can freely modify its own measures to adjust them to the Constitution. Therefore, the Court orders it to reverse the suspension of the claimant's pension payments, and to revoke the measures which disregard the relevant ratio decidendi.

Note on the Colombian System of Constitutional Precedent. In a comparative perspective, and particularly with reference to other legal systems in Latin America, the Colombian system of constitutional precedent has some striking features. In Mexico, for example, a kind of precedent exists: legal texts state that the *tesis* [a summarized, very brief holding] of the Court can bind, in *amparo* cases normally only if reiterated in five cases in a consistent way.[12] The Mexican approach appears to be a way of accommodating the advantages of a system of precedent to a civil-law context. The jurisprudential *tesis* is a very brief and abstract

12. *See* Stephen Zamora et al., Mexican Law 85 (2004).

pronouncement separate from the underlying judgment; these circulate in widely distributed texts and can be found on a searchable database on the Mexican Supreme Court's website.

In contrast, the Colombian system of precedent is much closer to a common-law system, and in some respects (such as requiring that private entities be bound by those rules) is an attempt to construct an even stronger set of norms surrounding precedent. The Colombian system is judge-made, relies directly on the reasoning of its decisions, and utilizes distinctions between holdings and dicta. The Court has had some success in creating a system of constitutional precedent in Colombia. Judges, lawyers, law students, and scholars have begun to accept and pay attention to this case-law based system, which is a significant shift from the country's traditional views about legal culture.[13]

However, the path has been very difficult, and the Court has encountered both some inherent problems and significant resistance from other key actors. Other courts, administrative agencies, and private actors have often been ignorant of court decisions. As a result the Court has often had to decide similar claims in several subsequent cases, and litigants have very often been forced to file *tutela* claims even though their issues had already been decided in earlier cases. Case law is not nearly as widely read, or as widely available, in Colombia as it is in most common-law systems.[14]

Also, at certain points the ordinary courts, and particularly the two other high courts—the Supreme Court and the Council of State—have denied the authority of the Constitutional Court to issue rulings that would bind them. There have been some high-profile fights between these courts, which the media has dubbed the "train crash" (*choque de trenes*).[15] The issue of precedent is closely related to the Constitutional Court's power to hear *tutelas* against the rulings of these tribunals that are alleged to violate the Colombian constitution. The Supreme Court and Council of State have at times denied that the Constitutional Court possesses the power to hear *tutelas* against their judicial decisions.[16] This conflict simmered throughout the 1990s but the high point was reached in 2002, when President Uribe proposed a constitutional amendment that would, among other things, have (1) denied the Constitutional Court the power to take *tutelas* against judicial decisions, (2) limited the ability of judges to hear *tutela* cases involving social and economic rights, and (3) restricted the power of the Constitutional Court to create precedent. This proposed constitutional amendment was not passed by Congress, and the controversy regarding the *choque de trenes* has since cooled.

The Court has dealt with important issues surrounding the effects of its decisions outside of the judiciary, particularly on administrative actors. This role of precedent is

13. For the contours of the jurisprudential shift, see DIEGO EDUARDO LOPEZ MEDINA, EL DERECHO DE LOS JUECES (2d ed. 2006), which has been widely used to train lawyers and judges in the country.

14. There have been some attempts to create searchable databases of case law similar to Westlaw and Lexis in the United States—for example, LexBase, which can be found at http://www.lexbase.co/.

15. In comparative terms, disputes between ordinary courts and constitutional courts are fairly common, and are often called "wars of the courts." These disputes, broadly speaking, seem to be about protection of jurisdiction and questions of institutional supremacy. *See* ALEXEI TROCHOV, JUDGING RUSSIA: THE ROLE OF THE CONSTITUTIONAL COURT IN RUSSIAN POLITICS, 1990–2006, at 265–82 (2008).

16. Article 86 of the Constitution allows for the taking of *tutelas* against "any public authority." The controversy is about whether judges are "public authorit[ies]" within the context of Article 86.

important in protecting equal access to constitutional rights, as many citizens are wrongly denied a right by administrative authorities but never go to the courts. Anecdotally, it appears that administrative officials in many contexts do not regularly follow or adhere to judicial precedents. In **Decision C-816 of 2011 (per Justice Mauricio González Cuervo)**, the Court heard a challenge to a provision of the new Code of Administrative Procedure, which stated that "[t]he authorities must extend the effects of a jurisprudential unification decision released by the Council of State, in which a right has been recognized, to those who demand it and who demonstrate the same factual and legal situation." The goal of this provision is to extend constitutional precedent established by the high administrative court to administrative agencies, in order to improve bureaucratic performance and create a more equal application of the law. But the challengers argued that the law was unconstitutional because it only gave this effect to administrative decisions issued by the Council of State, and not decisions issued by the Constitutional Court. The Court held the provision conditionally constitutional, under the understanding that administrative authorities must also follow decisions of the Constitutional Court on relevant issues.

Another important problem is the issue of compliance with the Constitutional Court's orders. The Court has sometimes had trouble gaining compliance, particularly with its more complex structural orders such as the ones outlined in Chapter 6 on social rights. In **Decision C-006 of 2012 (per Justice Maria Victoria Calle Correa)**, the Court heard a challenge to a provision of the national budget, which stated that the budget would incorporate funds for compliance with judicial decisions "in agreement with the availability of resources." The Court struck down the provision, holding as follows:

> The Court must state with the greatest emphasis that compliance with judicial decisions issued against state entities, including those given by constitutional judges, may not be subject to the existence of available resources, according to whatever the government calculates and Congress approves for each fiscal period. To submit compliance with judicial decisions against the state to such a condition would in practice deprive them of any binding force, given that there is always the possibility of arguing a lack of available resources in order to justify noncompliance with corresponding judicial orders.

C. The Constitutional Block: Incorporation of International Law

The Colombian Constitution, following a trend in comparative constitutional law,[17] gives international human rights law a high status within the domestic legal order. The Court's key doctrinal construction is the concept of the "constitutional block." Under the theory of the constitutional block, the Colombian constitution includes not only the constitutional

17. For example, see CONST. S.A., art. 39 ("When interpreting the Bill of Rights, a court, tribunal or forum (a) must promote the values that underlie an open and democratic society based on human dignity, equality and freedom; (b) must consider international law; and (c) may consider foreign law."); *see also* CONST. ARG.,

text, but also certain principles of international law.[18] The concept is pervasive in Colombian constitutional law—decisions on social rights (Chapter 6), victims' rights (Chapter 7), and indigenous rights (Chapter 8) have all been heavily influenced by international law.

The key textual provision is Article 93 of the Constitution, which establishes first that international treaties and agreements ratified by Congress that recognize human rights and that prohibit their limitation in states of exception will "have priority" in the domestic legal order. Some provisions of international human rights treaties (those in treaties ratified by Congress that recognize human rights and prohibit their limitation in states of exception) are therefore part of the constitutional block in a "strict sense": they are morphed into constitutional provisions that themselves directly prevail over the entire domestic legal order.

Article 93 also states that rights and duties found in the Constitution will be "interpreted in accordance with" international human rights treaties ratified by Colombia. Thus, all other norms in human rights treaties ratified by Colombia are part of the constitutional block in a "broad sense": they are not themselves constitutional provisions, but they must be used to interpret rights and duties already included in the constitutional text.

Article 93 lays out a vision of the relationship between international law and domestic constitutional law that is quite integrated in comparative terms. An interesting point of reference is the South African constitution, which directs that courts "must" consider international law and "may" consider foreign law when deciding cases requiring interpretation of fundamental rights.[19] The Colombian constitution goes further by requiring that domestic constitutional rights be interpreted in light of international human rights treaties ratified by Colombia, and by giving some norms (those that cannot be limited even during states of exception) direct constitutional status.

The concept of the constitutional block has had a major impact on the jurisprudence of the Court, particularly (but hardly exclusively) on issues intersecting international humanitarian law. Such issues are frequent because of Colombia's ongoing problem of civil violence. The constitutional block most obviously includes the text of the relevant human rights treaties themselves, but the Court has also relied heavily on other sources of international law. It has held that customary norms of international humanitarian law, as well as general principles of law, are also part of the block.[20]

art. 75, sec. 22 (listing prominent human rights treaties and stating that they "have constitutional hierarchy . . . and are to be understood as complementing the rights and guarantees recognized herein"); Const. Mex., art. 1 ("In the Unites States of Mexico, all persons shall enjoy the rights recognized by the Constitution and international treaties to which the Mexican State is party, as well as guarantees for their protection, the exercise of which may not be restricted or suspended, except in cases and under conditions established by this Constitution."). *See generally* Jackson, *supra* note 5.

18. The concept of the constitutional block is French; the French Constitutional Council used this concept to incorporate into the 1958 Constitution fundamental principles drawn from other texts, such as the Declaration of the Rights of Man and of the Citizen. *See* John Bell, French Constitutional Law 64–73 (1992).

19. *See* Const. S.A., art. 39.

20. *See* Decision C-291 of 2007 (per Justice Manuel José Cepeda Espinosa) (briefly described in the note below).

The position of treaty interpretations by authorized interpreters of a given treaty regime—such as the United Nations Committee on Economic, Social, and Cultural Rights for the International Covenant on Economic, Social and Cultural Rights, and the Inter-American Court and Commission on Human Rights for the American Convention on Human Rights—is more ambiguous. The leading position is that they are not "automatically" incorporated into the block, but generally are entitled to great weight in ascertaining the meaning of the treaties at issue.[21] These interpretations are routinely used in constitutional jurisprudence. Finally, the Court has often relied on forms of "soft law," such as United Nations resolutions and guidelines, as interpretative aids in difficult cases.[22] The result of all these practices has been a thick engagement between domestic constitutional law and international law.[23] The Court mainly aims at harmonization between the national constitution and international norms. Judicial review integrates both national and international standards at the same time. The Court has not separated "constitutional review" from "conventionality review,"[24] as has happened for example in France.

International human rights are invoked in several decisions of the Court included in other chapters of this book, such as those on the peace process with the FARC (Fuerzas Armadas Revolucionarias de Colombia) in Chapter 7, the structural decision on internally displaced persons in Chapter 6, and the decisions on states of exception in Chapter 9. The case below examines the development of the constitutional block concept through the particular context of the rules of international humanitarian law (IHL) applied to Colombia's internal armed conflict, which has been a major area where the Court has incorporated and enforced international norms.

Decision C-225 of 1995 (per Justice Alejandro Martínez Caballero)

[In this case, the Court reviewed Colombia's ratification of the Protocol II addition to the Geneva Conventions, relating to the protection of victims of internal armed conflicts. Both the treaty itself and its relevant implementing legislation were declared

21. *See, e.g.*, Decision T-616 of 2010 (per Justice Luis Ernesto Vargas Silva) ("As the Court stated in Decision C-355/06, the observations and recommendations offered by the organs authorized to interpret international human rights treaties ratified by Colombia are relevant for clarifying the normative content of their dispositions and the meaning of the fundamental rights consecrated in the Constitution. Even though these documents are not automatically incorporated into the constitutional block, they do constitute a relevant hermeneutic criterion and a limit for the legislator.")

22. An example is the displaced persons case, Decision T-025 of 2004, found in Chapter 6, where the Court relied heavily on the United Nations Guiding Principles on Internal Displacement.

23. Article 53 of the Constitution contains a special provision regarding the status of ratified treaties written under the auspices of the International Labour Organization (ILO): the article states that "duly ratified international labor conventions are part of the internal legal system." In Decision C-401 of 2005 (per Justice Manuel José Cepeda Espinosa), the Court held that this phrase meant that *all* ILO treaties were part of the domestic legal system. However, not all ILO treaties are part of the constitutional block—only those treaties meeting the requirements of Article 93 of the Constitution would be considered as part of the block.

24. *See* Manuel José Cepeda-Espinosa. *The Functions of International and Comparative Law in Constitutional Adjudication: The Colombian Case*, *in* KEY DEVELOPMENTS IN CONSTITUTIONALISM AND CONSTITUTIONAL LAW (Lidija Basta & Tanasije Marinkovic eds., 2014).

constitutional. The issue had been subject to heated controversy for the previous 20 years. Opponents of ratification of Protocol II warned that it might change the status of guerrilla groups and take them a step toward being recognized as belligerents under international law. Furthermore, they argued that ratifying Protocol II would open the door to the internationalization of the Colombian armed conflict. In contrast, advocates of ratification argued that Protocol II aimed exclusively at humanizing the armed conflict and protecting the civilian population from its effects, including attacks by guerrilla groups.]

[Protocol II was argued to be constitutional by several government representatives, among them the President of the Republic and the Ministers of Defense, Health and Foreign Relations, as well as by the Ombudsman. Additionally, various representatives of civil society such as the Colombian Red Cross, several nongovernmental organizations (NGOs), the Colombian Episcopal Conference, and Professor Ciro Angarita Barón, a former Constitutional Court justice, participated in this discussion. The National Committee of Guerrilla Victims pleaded before the Court to declare Protocol II unconstitutional, arguing that it would legitimate armed groups acting against the state.]

[The Court began by finding that "the majority of international humanitarian law (IHL) treaties should be understood simply as the codification of already existing [customary] obligations rather than as the creation of new principles and rules."[25] The Court thus concluded that irregular armed groups such as guerrillas were already bound by IHL: "regular or irregular armed groups are . . . compelled to observe these norms that protect all those basic human principles that cannot be disregarded even in the worst situations of an armed conflict." Additionally, the Court pointed out that a party to the conflict could not justify its noncompliance with IHL by adducing its opponents' noncompliance, because "one of the features of [IHL] law is that its norms are inalienable guarantees structured in a singular manner: obligations are imposed on armed groups not for their own benefit but for the benefit of others, for the noncombatant population and the victims of armed confrontation."]

[The Court subsequently focused on resolving the problem derived from the tension between Article 93, which establishes that certain human rights norms prevail in the legal order, and Article 4 of the Constitution, which states that the Constitution prevails over any other law.[26]]

International humanitarian law treaties prevail in the internal legal system. What is the scope of this principle? Some legal experts and other observers following

25. Some rules in international law are considered to have *jus cogens* status; this means that they cannot be derogated from under any circumstances. For example, prohibitions on torture, genocide, and unlawful use of force are generally thought to have *jus cogens* status. *See generally* Gennady M. Danilenko, *International* Jus Cogens: *Issues of Law-Making*, 2 Eur. J. Int'l L. 42 (1991).

26. Article 4 states: "The Constitution is the norm of norms. In all cases of incompatibility between the Constitution and the statute or other legal regulations, the constitutional provisions shall apply. It is the duty of citizens and of aliens in Colombia to obey the Constitution and the laws, and to respect and obey the authorities."

> this process have expressed their view that this principle places these treaties above the Constitution, since they are *jus cogens* norms. This may be valid from an international law perspective, because according to Article 27 of the Vienna Convention on the Law of Treaties, no Party shall invoke provisions of their internal legal system as justification for non-compliance with a treaty. Even more clearly, no state may invoke its internal laws to disregard *jus cogens* norms such as those enshrined by international humanitarian law. However, from the perspective of Colombian constitutional law, this interpretation must be tempered given that the Constitution is the norm of all norms. . . .
>
> The concept of a "constitutional block," whose origin is to be found in French law. . . , allows for the harmonization of principles and provisions apparently in contradiction in Articles 4 and 93 of our Constitution.
>
> The constitutional block includes those rules and principles that, although not formally enshrined in the constitutional text, are used as parameters for constitutional control because they have been integrated as norms in the Constitution through different routes and by its clear dictate. These principles and rules, therefore, have truly constitutional value, i.e., they are conceived as being at the same level as the Constitution. . . . Treaties on human rights and international humanitarian law . . . form together with the other constitutional provisions a "constitutional block" that prevails over other levels of law.
>
> [Furthermore, the Court reflected upon the implementation of Protocol II in the Colombian internal legal system, stating that even though Article 1 of Protocol II establishes a relatively demanding set of obligations on states, it should be applicable in Colombia even during low-intensity armed conflicts. The Court based this conclusion on Article 214, clause 2 of the Constitution, which regulated states of exception and states in part that "in all cases, the rules of international humanitarian law shall be observed." The Court considered then the various provisions included in Protocol II, and verified that each of them conformed to the principles enshrined in the Constitution, especially those regarding human dignity, the primacy of individuals' inalienable rights, the conducting of international relations according to international law, and the right to life. Thus, the Court decided to declare Protocol II and the law by which it was approved to be constitutional.]

Note on IHL and the Constitutional Block. Because Colombia is a country that has long been in the grips of civil conflict, the relationship between IHL and domestic constitutional law has been litigated in many subsequent cases. For example, in **Decision SU-256 of 1999 (per Justice José Gregorio Hernández Galindo),** a *tutela* action, the Court protected the rights of children attending a school located close to police headquarters in an area where guerrilla groups were present. The Court ordered authorities to adopt the necessary measures to relocate the school or, otherwise, to relocate the police headquarters. The aim was to protect the children's fundamental rights before the threat posed by an eventual attack of armed guerrilla groups. In this decision, the Court took into account Articles 4 and 13 of Protocol II of the Geneva Conventions.

In **Decision C-291 of 2007 (per Justice Manuel José Cepeda Espinosa),** the Court litigated issues surrounding the definition of certain crimes in existing legislation, and clarified several important issues surrounding the nature and scope of the constitutional block. The Court held that Congress had a "wide margin of configuration to design criminal policies and criminal law," but that "such legislative authority is subject to the limits set by the Constitution and by the norms enshrined in the constitutional block. . . ."

The Court noted that the constitutional block fulfills two purposes: "an *interpretative* purpose, because it serves as a guiding parameter in the interpretation of the contents of constitutional provisions and the identification of admissible restrictions to fundamental rights, and an *integrative* purpose by providing specific constitutional guidance in the absence of express constitutional provisions." In this case, the Court added, the issue referred to the *integrative* purpose of the constitutional block because "our Political Constitution . . . does not include specific provisions literally establishing the contents of [IHL] within the constitutional text."

In its decision, the Court clarified various aspects of IHL, including the relationship between the constitutional block and different sources of IHL. To eliminate confusion resulting from past cases, the Court noted that not all IHL norms were *jus cogens* in nature, but only some "essential principles," such as "(i) the principle of distinction between civilians and combatants, (ii) the principle of precaution, and (iii) the principle regarding humane treatment and respect for basic guarantees and safeguards to which civilians and persons uninvolved in the conflict are entitled." Nonetheless, the Court stated that "all International Humanitarian Law provisions—be they substantive or procedural, conventional or customary in their origin, or general principles—are *mandatory* for the Colombian state as part of the constitutional block," regardless of whether they have *jus cogens* status. Thus, the Court held that the constitutional block reached beyond ratified treaties to also include other binding sources of international law, such as customary international law and general principles of law.

The Court used these principles to conduct a close examination of the legislation under review. The Court based its analysis on a number of international sources, including case law by the International Criminal Tribunal for the former Yugoslavia and the Inter-American Commission on Human Rights, as well as on the Rome Statute of the International Criminal Court. For example, it held conditionally constitutional a provision that punished the murder of "combatants who have surrendered their arms," holding that the provision was only constitutional if it was read to include participants in armed conflicts such as irregular guerrilla groups. The Court also struck down a part of the definition of the crime of taking of hostages, which held that the taking only constituted a crime if demands were made to "the other party" in the conflict. This implied that if demands were made to some organization other than "the other party" in the conflict, the crime would not have occurred. The Court again held that the limitation unjustifiably contracted the scope of protection found in IHL.

Chapter 7 contains other relevant decisions on the relationship between IHL and the constitutional block, from the particular perspective of the rights of victims.

PART TWO

Rights

3

Dignity and Autonomy

This chapter considers the Court's case law in enforcing the principle of human dignity and the right to free development of personality. Article 1 of the Colombian Constitution establishes "human dignity" as one of the fundamental principles of the Colombian state, whereas Article 16 establishes that "[a]ll persons have the right to free development of personality without limitations other than those imposed for the rights of others and the legal order."

These provisions, of course, lack a clear meaning on their face—human dignity, in particular, is a notoriously contested concept that might accommodate a range of relationships between the individual and the state.[1] The historic Colombian social context is one deeply influenced by Catholic social thought and corporatist ideology; in that context, the individual is often called upon to sacrifice her particular interests for the good of the community. One might have expected the Court to subordinate individual autonomy interests to the general will of the community. After all, Article 1 also establishes that the Colombian state is founded on "the predominance of the general interest."

However, since the Court's early years, it has focused on individual autonomy as a major strain of its jurisprudence. In contrast, the Court's jurisprudence on equality (Chapter 4) and socioeconomic rights (Chapter 6) are more material or substantive in conception, and require the state to take steps in order to overcome real inequalities created by historic circumstances or economic deprivation. In the concrete circumstances of Colombian constitutionalism, what might hold these different strains of jurisprudence together is an emphasis on social transformation. Both lines of jurisprudence, in other words, can be interpreted as an attempt to fight against ingrained patterns in Colombian society, particularly inasmuch as they affect historically marginalized groups.

1. For discussion of the meaning of the concept of human dignity in different contexts, see, for example, CATHERINE DUPRE, THE AGE OF DIGNITY: HUMAN RIGHTS AND CONSTITUTIONALISM (2015); DONALD P. KOMMERS & RUSSELL A. MILLER, THE CONSTITUTIONAL JURISPRUDENCE OF THE FEDERAL REPUBLIC OF GERMANY 355–72 (3d ed. 2012); CATHERINE DUPRE, IMPORTING THE LAW IN POST-COMMUNIST TRANSITIONS: THE HUNGARIAN CONSTITUTIONAL COURT AND THE RIGHT TO HUMAN DIGNITY (2003); Michèle Finck, *The Role of Human Dignity in Gay Rights Adjudication and Legislation: A Comparative Perspective*, 14 INT'L J. CONST. L. 26 (2016).

Colombian Constitutional Law: Leading Cases. Manuel José Cepeda Espinosa and David Landau.

Carlos Gaviria, who since became a senator and national leader for the leftist party *Polo Democratico*, wrote two of the Court's most interesting early decisions. In C-221 of 1994, the Court decriminalized possession (but not trafficking) of drugs, and in C-239 of 1997, it legalized assisted suicide for terminally ill patients. The Court has followed these lines to a variety of other contexts: in SU-642 of 1998, it protected the right of a four-year-old girl to maintain the personal appearance desired by her rather than the appearance ordered by school authorities; in SU-337 of 1999, it protected the right of an older child with an intersex condition not to have a risky operation despite the wishes of her parents. Finally, in C-355 of 2006, the Court applied similar principles to liberalize restrictions on abortion in cases where the pregnancy was a result of rape or incest, or threatened the life or health of the mother. It is notable that several of these cases—especially the drug possession, euthanasia, and abortion ones—received hostile reactions from the Catholic Church and governmental authorities, and remain among the Court's most controversial decisions.

A. Decriminalization of Narcotics for Personal Use

In a five-to-four decision, the Constitutional Court decriminalized the possession or use of narcotics for personal use in Colombia. The challenged provision established that possession of drugs for personal use was a crime, although it defined lesser penalties for possession for personal use than for other acts.

The provisions under examination by the Court, Articles 2(j) and 51 of Law 30 of 1986 (the National Statute on Narcotics), established the following:

> **Article 2.** The following definitions will be adopted for the present law:
>
> j) Dose for personal use: [T]he amount of narcotics that a person possesses or keeps for self-consumption.
>
> A dose for personal use is an amount of cannabis not exceeding twenty (20) grams; an amount of hashish not exceeding five (5) grams; an amount of cocaine or other substance prepared from cocaine not exceeding one (1) gram, and an amount of methaqualone not exceeding two (2) grams.
>
> Regardless of their amount, narcotics possessed by a person with the purpose of distribution or sale shall not be considered a dose for personal use.
>
> **Article 51.** In agreement with provisions established in the present law, a person possessing or using cocaine, cannabis or any other type of addictive drug in the amount considered a dose for personal use shall receive the following penalties:
>
> a) For a first offense, detention up to thirty (30) days and a fine amounting to one-half (1/2) the minimum monthly salary under the law.
>
> b) For a second offense, detention for one (1) month to one (1) year and a fine amounting to one-half (1/2) to one (1) minimum monthly salary if the deed takes place within the twelve (12) months following the occurrence of the first crime.

c) A user or consumer who, according to a medical examiner, is under the effect of drugs, regardless of whether or not this is his first offense, shall be interned in a public or private psychiatric or similar institution for as long as necessary for his recovery. In that case, no fine or arrest will ensue.

The relevant authority may entrust the drug addict to the care of his family or refer him under his family's responsibility to a clinic, hospital, or health center for treatment; such treatment will be administered for as long as is necessary for his recovery, which will be certified by the physician in charge and by the corresponding Forensic Medicine Office. The drug addict's family shall be liable for compliance with these duties, under bail determined by the competent authority according to the family's financial capacity.

The physician in charge shall periodically report to relevant authorities on the drug addict's health and rehabilitation process. If the family fails to comply with their duties, bail will be forfeited and the drug addict's hospitalization will be enforced.

Decision C-221 of 1994 (per Justice Carlos Gaviria Díaz)

Beyond the academic disputes about the nature of law, one can affirm with certainty that what characterizes that specific form of control of human conduct is having as the object of regulation . . . the actions of a person to the extent that they interfere with the sphere of action of another person or persons. If this does not occur, moral norms are the proper way to evaluate the conduct of the actor. . . .

In other words: the legislator can prescribe the form in which I must behave with others, but not the form in which I must behave with myself, to the extent that my conduct does not interfere with the sphere of action of anyone else. . . . Prohibiting conduct that does not interfere with the lives of others may only be justified in one of three ways: 1) by expressing a wish with no normative consequence; 2) by taking on the role of absolute ruler of people's behavior even in those realms that have nothing to do with others' conduct; 3) by taking into account the situation of other people that may be affected by the actor's conduct. . . .

The Court will examine these three possible hermeneutics, beginning with the last one . . . .

If it is assumed that criminal conduct occurs in consideration of the people around the drug addict, who will be deprived of his presence, his affection and eventually his economic support . . . then we must conclude that having loved ones and family obligations is part of the punishable conduct and thus those who are not found within such a situation cannot be punished for the crime in question. But the norm ignores any such conditions and makes criminal anyone who carries out the acts at issue, independently of whether or not they have a family or links of obligation with anyone. . . .

[O]ne can [also] invoke as a motive for punishment, the potential of aggressive conduct caused by drug consumption. To this point, one could make various responses. The first refers to the openly discriminatory treatment that the law gives to consumers of drugs versus the consumers of other substances of similar effects, ie. alcohol. . . .

Is it not an empirically verifiable fact that the ingestion of alcohol, in an elevated number of people, causes the relaxing of inhibiting ties and the consequent appearance of repressed violent attitudes, which is a factor in the commission of a innumerable number of crimes? Why, then, the openly distinct, discriminatory treatment for the alcoholic (who can consume without any measure or limit) versus the drug addict? . . .

[A] person cannot be punished for what he will possibly do, but only for what he effectively has done. This is true unless being a drug addict were considered punishable in and of itself, even though this behavior is within the most intimate orbit of the consumer[. T]his without doubt would be abusive because it invades a sphere precisely left for ordering by the free determination and dignity of the person (autonomy to choose one's own destiny), the basic pillars of any legal superstructure. . . .

[As for the second option, the Court held that it is based on the idea that] the Colombian state is assumed owner and master of the life and destiny of each person subject to its jurisdiction, and thus may prescribe behaviors that from a less absolutist perspective would remain their own decision and not that of the state. But, this tentative exegesis must be cast aside, because the philosophy that informs the Constitution of 91 is libertarian and democratic and not authoritarian or much less totalitarian.

But if, moderating the perspective, we assume that we are not dealing with an omnipotent state, with a desire to interfere in the most intimate decisions of its subjects, but a paternalistic state that seeks to protect its subjects and knows better than they themselves what their interests are. . . ; by that benevolent route one arrives at the same inadmissible result: the negation of individual liberty. . . .

There remains, then, as the only plausible interpretation a third possibility: that the norm only treats the expression of a desire of the community, of merely symbolic efficacy, carrier of a message that the emitting subject judges desirable—it is *good* for people to care for their health—but which does not carry normative connotations in the general legal order, much less of a criminal character. . . .

[First, the Court considered Article 51, requiring treatment for drug addicts.] The question that [Article 51] poses is obvious: is it a punishment for a crime, or a humanitarian measure for a sick person? If the first, then the norm is unconstitutional based on the prior analysis. . . . There is no doubt for the Court, that also under [the second] possibility, the disposition is openly unconstitutional, because each person is free to decide whether or not to care for his own health. . . .

Under the treatment of certain conduct judged "deviant," as illnesses, one hides the most ferocious repressive power, more censurable the more it is presented as a paternal (almost loving) attitude towards the dissident. The reclusion in psychiatric or similar establishments has for a long time been a vital mechanism used by totalitarian regimes to "cure" the heterodox. And contemporary societies have insisted on treating drug addicts as heterodox, and indeed as sick individuals who must be made to see the world as the rulers see it. . . .

In the cited norm there is an implicit and inadmissible discrimination between the drug addict who has economic resources and the one who lacks it, because while the first can go to a private clinic and receive treatment from specialists chosen by him, the second is forced to go to an establishment not chosen by him, and with all the connotations of a prison.

[Finally, the Court considered the constitutionality of Article 2(j), criminalizing the personal dose.] In order to explain in their totality the constitutionality of the norms that make the consumption of drugs a crime, it is important to relate these to a basic norm that, for this purpose, is decisive. This is Article 16 of the Constitution, which consecrates the right to free development of personality. It does so in the following terms: "All persons have the right to free development of personality without limitations other than those imposed for the rights of others and the legal order."

The phrase "without limitations other than those imposed for the rights of others and the *legal order*" deserves reflection, especially for the [emphasized] phrase. Because if any limitation were valid simply by being included in the legal order, the right consecrated in Article 16 would be nullified. In other words: the legislator cannot establish limits other than those which are in harmony with the spirit of the Constitution. . . .

[This norm] is the recognition of persons as autonomous in their dignity, that is, as an end in themselves and not a means for an end, with the full capacity to decide on their own acts and above all, on their own destiny. The first consequence that one derives from autonomy is that it is the person himself (and not anyone on his behalf) that must give meaning to his existence and, in harmony with that, a direction. . . . That is to say: it is in function of the liberty of others only that my liberty may be restricted. . . .

When the state resolves to recognize the autonomy of the person, what it has decided to do is nothing less than to delimit the sphere which corresponds to that person as an ethical subject: it leaves for him to decide . . . on the good and the bad, on the sense of his existence. If the person resolves, for example, to dedicate his life to hedonistic gratification, the state does not interfere in that way of life during such time as, *in concrete*, not in the abstract, it does not translate into damage to another. We may not share that ideal of life . . . but that does not make it illegitimate. These are the consequences that follow from assuming liberty as a directive principle within a society that, by that road, proposes to achieve justice. . . .

If the right to free development of personality has any meaning inside our system, we must conclude that, for the reasons noted, the norms that make consumption of drugs a crime are clearly unconstitutional.

One might then ask: what can the state do if it finds the consumption of drugs undesirable and it thinks that consumption should be avoided, without violating the liberty of persons? The Court believes that the only adequate way that is compatible with the principles that the state itself has promised to respect and promote, consists in bringing to . . . the people, the possibilities of education. . . . Each person should

> choose his way of life responsibly, and to achieve that objective, the greatest barrier must be removed: ignorance. . . .
>
> In dealing with thinking beings . . . , the only dignified and effective route consists in showing in an honest and rigorous way the causal connection between distinct ways of life and their inevitable consequences, without manipulation. . . .
>
> A state that is respectful of human dignity, of personal autonomy, and of the free development of personality cannot ignore its undeniable obligation to educate by substituting repression as a means of controlling the consumption of substances that it judges noxious for a person individually considered and eventually, for the community with whom that person is necessarily integrated.

Note on the Political Impact of the Court's Personal Dose Decision: More than 20 years after this decision was issued, the Court's ruling concerning the personal dose is still a matter of great controversy in the government, Congress, and civil society. The decision raised significant and continuing opposition, especially from the government. Shortly after the ruling was issued, both the outgoing administration of President César Gaviria and the incoming administration of President Ernesto Samper promoted a referendum to amend the Constitution in order to recriminalize the possession of a personal dose. However, the organizers were unable to collect the number of signatures required. Almost 10 years later, in 2003, President Álvaro Uribe's administration called for a referendum that sought citizens' approval for a draft constitutional amendment that included changes to several constitutional provisions, among them the law regarding narcotics possession. The question asked citizens whether they agreed with the following provision:

> To Protect Colombian Society, Particularly its Children And Young People, Against The Use Of Cocaine, Heroin, Marijuana, Bazuco, Ecstasy, And All Other Hallucinogens, Do You Approve The Following Article?
>
> To promote and protect a real development of personality, the law will strictly punish the farming, production, distribution, possession or selling of narcotic or addictive substances such as cocaine, heroin, cannabis, ecstasy or similar substances by establishing penalties according to the circumstances in which the offense is committed. The state will undertake active prevention campaigns against drug addiction and in favor of rehabilitation, and will punish with penalties other than imprisonment the use of such products for personal purposes if deemed advisable to protect individual and collective rights, especially those of children and young people.

The Court examined the constitutionality of this referendum question in **Decision C-551 of 2003 (per Eduardo Montealegre Lynett)** and declared it null and void. The Court held that the introductory note to the question included emotional language aimed at influencing citizens to vote in a specific way and thus infringed on the freedom of voters. Likewise, the Court stated that "the use of expressions such as 'to protect . . . against the use of cocaine' . . . links a socially desirable situation like control against the abuse of certain narcotics to the approval of the draft law." The Court also found a problem with regard to the "relation of causality that could be established between the introductory paragraph and the approval of an article that includes punishments against possessing and using narcotic substances when there are so many critical analyses of such penalty-centric strategies that show how these type of measures, far from protecting, tend to worsen users' situation as a result of their social marginalization."

After several other attempts by the Uribe administration failed, President Uribe finally passed a constitutional amendment regarding the personal dose, Legislative Act 2 of 2009. This amendment bans the possession and use of psychoactive substances, but does not include any punishment for users. Instead, it restricts its scope to the establishment of educational, prophylactic, and rehabilitation measures. The amendment reads as follows:

> The possession and consumption of psychotropic and narcotic drugs is prohibited, except in the case of a medical prescription. For preventative and rehabilitative ends the law will establish administrative measures and treatments of a pedagogical, prophylactic, and therapeutic nature for people who consume these substances. Submission to those measures and treatments requires the informed consent of the addict.
>
> Likewise, the State will grant special assistance to drug addicts and their families to strengthen their values and principles . . . by conducting permanent prevention campaigns against the use of narcotic substances and in favor of the recovery of drug addicts.

The part of this constitutional amendment that prohibited possession of a personal dose was challenged in front of the Constitutional Court in **Decision C-574 of 2011 (per Justice Juan Carlos Henao)**. The petitioners argued that the prohibition acted as an unlawful "substitution of the constitution" because it changed the fundamental principle of autonomy in the constitutional text. The Court, however, ruled that it lacked power to reach the merits, because the petitioners had challenged the prohibition language without including other relevant language indicating that no criminal penalties would apply and that the consent of the addict was required for any measures to be taken.

In subsequent case law, the Court verified that Legislative Act 2 of 2009, although prohibiting possession of the personal dose, foreclosed the criminal law as a means of enforcing that prohibition. Thus, in **Decision C-491 of 2012 (per Justice Luis Ernesto Vargas Silva)**, the Court upheld changes to the criminal laws on drug trafficking only on the understanding that they "do not include the criminalization of the carrying or conservation of doses of [drugs] exclusively destined for personal consumption."[2]

Although the Constitutional Court decriminalized possession of small amounts of drugs, it has consistently held that prohibitions on drug production and trafficking are

2. Little work has focused on the on-the-ground impact of the Court's intervention. A recent paper by two Colombian scholars found, based on interviews with members of the police force, that socioeconomic status was an important marker of how police treated those found with a personal dose. Lower-income consumers were more likely, for example, to be sent to detention centers, even if no charges were ultimately brought. *See* Julieta Lemaitre & Mauricio Albarracín, *Patrullando la dosis personal: la represión cotidiana y los debates de políticas públicas sobre el consumo de drogas ilícitas en Colombia*, *in* Políticas antidroga en Colombia: éxitos, fracasos y extravíos (Daniel Mejía et al. eds., 2011).

constitutional. In **Decision C-420 of 2002 (per Justice Jaime Córdoba Triviño)**, the Constitutional Court upheld crimes related to the production, selling, and distribution of psychoactive substances. On that occasion, the claimant contested those articles in Law 30 of 1986 referring to the production, transportation, and selling of narcotics.

The claimant first stated that the state's prohibition on drug trafficking was inconsistent with the reasoning of the personal dose case. The Court rejected this argument by stating that it was possible to verify the existence of

> a wide range of rights affected by narcotics trafficking. The criminalization of trafficking was first linked to the need to protect a specific legal good, i.e., public health, a position that was compatible with the duty assigned by the Constitution to all citizens to give integral care to their own health and that of their community. . . . Later this field of protection was widened to the point that today it is not only aimed at protecting public health, but also public security and social and economic conditions. The former because the high profitability of narcotics traffic has turned it into a financing alternative for organized criminal and armed groups that distorts the basic assumption of the State's exclusive control of the use of force as a guarantee for coexistence in society. The latter because narcotics trafficking is driven more and more by an excessive profit motive toppling every obstacle on its way, circulating huge amounts of capital and producing incommensurate wealth, which alters in a dramatic way the economy of those countries it impacts.

The Court stated that this holding was compatible with Decision C-221 of 1994 regarding the personal dose, because that decision made a clear distinction between decriminalization of "possessing, keeping or using narcotic substances in doses considered for personal use and narcotics trafficking, which is seen as an illegal activity driven by profit motives."

Second, the claimant argued that the prohibition on trafficking was unconstitutional because the constitutional rights to life and health included within themselves the right of buyers to consent to their infringement. The Court rejected this second argument as well by holding that "even if fundamental rights were at stake in this case, this would not hinder holding as criminal the conduct [at issue] if the legislator deems that the point in question involves a fundamental legal good that calls for protection against socially unacceptable damage or peril." Likewise, the Court held that the consent by the holder of a right could extinguish criminal liability only in those cases involving an individual legal right. The Court emphasized that in this situation the aim was to protect collective legal goods such as public health, public security, and social and economic conditions.

Finally, the claimant argued that the right to equality had been violated by treating drugs differently from alcohol and tobacco. The Court held that the fact that

> the legislator has not punished tobacco and alcohol production and merchandizing . . . , and instead has ordered prevention campaigns against their consumption . . . shows that it did not consider it necessary to resort to the use of criminal law in connection with these events. This decision . . . is also compatible with the subsidiary nature attributed to criminal law for a long time now, because it is . . . imperative

> that, given the extreme levels of institutional violence it calls for, society should resort to such an expedient only when it is definitely essential for the safeguarding of legal goods that are basic for coexistence. . . . The legislator's obligation to assess all social behaviors in the same way and, even more, to place them under the same measures of social control, cannot be inferred from the Constitution.

Last, the Court added that the criminalization of narcotics trafficking (as opposed to consumption) emerged from the international commitment contracted by Colombia with the ratification of the 1988 United Nations Convention Against Illicit Traffic in Narcotic Drugs and Psychotropic Substances, which was declared constitutional by the Court through Decision C-176/94.[3]

B. Euthanasia and Dignified Death

In the case below, the Court made two rulings. First, it held that a criminal provision regarding therapeutic homicides for altruistic reasons, which gives these kinds of homicides a lesser punishment than ordinary murder, was constitutional. As by definition therapeutic homicides are based on altruistic motives (putting an end to extreme suffering) and thus inspired by the constitutional principle of solidarity, establishing therapeutic homicide as an autonomous type of crime to be punished with a lesser penalty than that for ordinary homicide is constitutional. Second, the Court held that the provision at issue was only conditionally constitutional: in circumstances involving terminally-ill patients who had freely manifested their consent to die, the Court held that euthanasia carried out by a doctor had to be legalized altogether. The provision at issue stated:

> **Therapeutic Homicide.** A person who kills another one for pity to put an end to extreme suffering resulting from bodily injuries or severe or incurable illness shall be punished with imprisonment of six months to three years.

Decision C-239 of 1997 (per Justice Carlos Gaviria Díaz)

A person who kills another for pity in order to put an end to his extreme suffering acts is guided by altruistic reasons, and this is precisely the motivation that has led legislators to create a different criminal type punished with a considerably lesser penalty than that for simple or aggravated murder. This decision does not disregard the fundamental right to life found in Article 11 of the Constitution as, notwithstanding the motivation, the conduct is still against the law, but rather in consideration of the

3. In Decision C-420 of 2002, the Court limited itself to ruling on the validity of the provisions in Law 30 of 1986 that had been contested, and refrained from examining the corresponding articles of the new Criminal Code (Law 599 of 2000), which had not been challenged in this lawsuit. These provisions modified the penalties established for the conduct in question while maintaining the same definitions of criminal conduct. This motivated the filing of a new action of unconstitutionality by the same claimant to contest the provisions relating to narcotics trafficking contained in Law 599 of 2000. The Court examined the claim in Decision C-689 of 2002 (per Justice Álvaro Tafur Galvis), and after quoting extensively from the reasoning of Decision C-420 of 2002, it upheld the constitutionality of those new articles.

subjective element lessens the punishment, which expresses respect for the culpability principle derived from criminal law. . . .

[T]here is no therapeutic homicide when a person kills another person who is not subject to [extreme] suffering, even if he invokes motives of pity. In this case, which corresponds to homicide as such or even aggravated murder, death results from the offender's selfish motives to obliterate someone's existence, judging it valueless. By behaving in this manner, a person kills because he does not acknowledge his victim's dignity, while in the case of a therapeutic homicide as established in the Penal Code, the actor does not kill because of his disregard towards another individual, but due precisely to the opposite motive. The actor sees the victim as a person having his same dignity and rights, but subject to such excruciating suffering that death may be deemed as an act of compassion and mercy. . . .

[I]n a social state of law, punishment must maintain a reasonable proportionality with the degree of culpability of the action, and not only regarding the material and objective severity of the harm inflicted on the victim. . . .

If there exists a consensus that life is the necessary prerequisite to all other rights, an inalienable good without which the exercise of the others would be unthinkable, its protection in western legal systems, and the response regarding the duty to live when an individual suffers from an incurable disease that causes intense suffering, can be seen from two positions: 1) that which assumes life as sacred, and 2) that which assumes it is a valuable good but not sacred, because the religious beliefs and metaphysical convictions that ground its sacredness are only one among diverse options. In the first view, independently of the conditions in which the individual is found, death should arrive by natural causes. In the second, on the contrary, it is admitted that in extreme circumstances, the individual can decide whether or not to continue living, when circumstances that impact his life do not make it desirable or dignified to keep living, ie. when intense physical suffering that the person experiences has no possibility of being alleviated, and when his conditions of existence are so precarious that death appears to be a preferable option to survival.

In Colombia, in light of the Constitution of 1991, this question must be resolved from a secular and pluralist perspective, which respects the moral autonomy of individuals and the liberties and rights that inspire our superior order. . . .

Article 1 of the Constitution, for example, establishes that the Colombian state is founded on respect for the dignity of the human person; this signifies that, as a supreme value, dignity irradiates the group of recognized fundamental rights, which find their maximum expression in the free development of personality. . . .

Additionally, the same Article 1 of the Constitution, together with Article 95,[4] consecrates solidarity as one of the basic principles of the Colombian state, a principle that involves the positive duty of all citizens to relieve those who are found in need with humanitarian measures. And it is not difficult to find altruistic and solidarity-driven motives in a person who acts in response to his desire to put an end to others'

4. Article 95 states that the enjoyment of rights implies corresponding duties, and states that "social solidarity" is a duty of all Colombian citizens.

suffering, after surely having to overcome his own inhibitions and aversion towards an action aimed at destroying someone's life.

In these terms, the Constitution draws on the concept of a person as a moral subject capable of assuming in a responsible and autonomous manner decisions on matters that are above all of his own concern, while the state is limited to enforcing duties that concern other moral subjects with whom he has to coexist[. T]herefore, if the way individuals see death reflects their own convictions, they cannot be forced to continue living under the inadmissible argument that the majority deems it a moral or religious obligation, when, given the extreme situation they are in, they do not consider it desirable or compatible with their own dignity. . . .

[T]he state cannot demand heroic behavior from its citizens, much less if its grounds are to be found in religious beliefs or moral attitudes that may only be viewed as optional in a pluralistic society. Nothing can be so cruel as to force someone to live subject to degrading suffering on behalf of others' beliefs, even if the majority of the population judges these beliefs to be intangible goods. . . .

In sum, from a pluralistic point of view, the absolute duty to live cannot be ascertained. . . . [A] person who conceives a conduct as mandatory based on his religious or moral beliefs cannot expect to make it forcibly mandatory for all; he may only claim to be allowed to live fully and without interference according to such moral commands.

Besides, if respect for human dignity irradiates all of our legal system, it is clear that life cannot be considered sacred to the point of disregarding individuals' specific situations and the conception they have of the value of their own life. As stated by this Court: the right to life cannot be reduced to mere subsistence, since it entails living in adequate and dignified conditions.

The Constitution not only protects life as a right, but also deems it a value within the legal system, which implies competence for the state to intervene and even duties for the state and for individuals. . . . [T]he Constitution is not neutral towards the value of life but clearly in favor of it, a political option with implications, since it implies a duty of the state to protect life. However . . . , the state cannot comply with this obligation by disregarding the autonomy and dignity of people themselves. Thus, this Court has consistently held that any therapy must have the informed consent of patients who, therefore, may refuse treatments that would objectively lengthen their biological existence, but that they consider incompatible with their innermost personal convictions. Only the holder of the right to life may decide the point at which life is no longer desirable and compatible with human dignity.

The duty of the State to protect life must therefore be compatible with respect for human dignity and the free development of personality. Therefore, as regards terminal patients subject to extreme suffering, the state's duty must yield to the patient's informed consent regarding his desire to die with dignity. In such a case, the state's duty weakens considerably because, after examining medical reports, it may be said that beyond all reasonable doubt death is unavoidable in a relatively short time. And the decision on how to face death has decisive importance for terminal patients who are aware there is no cure for their ailment and that, therefore, are not choosing between death and many years of fulfilling life, but between dying as they decide to or dying some time afterwards in painful circumstances that they consider devoid of dignity. The fundamental right to live with dignity entails then the right to die with dignity, because forcing a person to prolong for a short time his life when he does not want to and when he is subject to intense distress is equivalent not only to cruel and inhumane treatment, which is forbidden by the Constitution, but also to an annulment of his dignity and autonomy as a moral subject. The person would be reduced to an instrument aimed at preserving life as an abstract value.

For all of these reasons, the Court concludes that the state cannot oppose the decision made by an individual who does not want to go on living and who requests help to die when he suffers from a terminal disease resulting in unbearable pain incompatible with his own conception of dignity. Therefore, if a terminal patient living under the objective conditions contemplated in the Criminal Code considers that his life must come to an end because he deems it incompatible with his dignity, he may exercise his freedom and proceed, as the state has no jurisdiction to oppose his purpose or to prevent a third party from helping fulfill his will through prohibition or punishment. This does nothing to diminish the importance of the duty of the state to protect life, but merely acknowledges that such an obligation does not result in the preservation of life only as a biological fact. . . .

It must not be forgotten that consent by [the sufferer] must be freely and unambiguously manifested by a person capable of understanding the situation. In other words, consent implies that the person has sound and reliable information about his illness and its prognosis and about therapeutic options, and that he has enough intellectual capacity to make a decision. For this reason the active subject must be a physician, as he is the only professional who has the ability both to supply adequate information to the patient and to offer him appropriate conditions to die with dignity. Therefore, in the case of terminal patients, physicians that carry out the action described in the criminal code and who have the [sufferer's] consent cannot be punished and, consequently, judges must remove responsibility from those acting in this way.

As the state is not indifferent to human life but . . . has a duty to protect it, it is necessary to establish very strict legal regulations on consent and on assisted suicide so as to avoid situations where people who want to continue living or who are not suffering extreme pain as a result of terminal illnesses are killed. These regulations must be intended to ensure that consent is genuine and not the result of a momentary depression. For example, the state could require that the request be expressed on more than one occasion, and that a reasonable time period pass between each of them. They might also consider the possibility that all cases require judicial authorization, in order to ensure the authenticity of consent and guarantee that all of the intervenors are concerned only with the dignity of the patient. They might equally order that, before the final request, the person meet with a support team that fully explains the situation and all of the possible alternatives to death. This signifies that the state . . . should offer the terminally ill patient . . . all of the possibilities so that he might continuing living, in particular, palliative treatments for pain. In sum, essential elements of the regulation are without doubt:

1. Strict verification *by competent professionals* of the patient's real situation, and of his unequivocal will to die.
2. A clear indication of the persons (qualified subjects) who should take part in the process.
3. The circumstances under which consent by the person who requests death or an end to suffering should be valid; the manner of expressing that consent; the subjects before whom consent should be granted; the verification of sound judgment by competent professionals, etc.
4. Measures that may be used by qualified professionals to achieve the . . . outcome.
5. Education programs that include topics such as the value of life and its relation to social responsibility, freedom and personal autonomy, so that these provisions are understood as the last resort in a process that could converge on other outcomes. . . .

As these regulations can only be established by the legislature the Court considers that while the topic is being regulated, in principle, all therapeutic homicides of terminal patients must result in corresponding criminal investigations . . . with the goal of allowing judicial officials to establish whether the conduct of the doctor has been illegal or not, in the terms discussed in this decision.

On the other hand, and for the sake of legal security, the Court exhorts the Congress to regulate the topic of dignified death in the briefest time possible and in a way that conforms to constitutional principles and elemental considerations of humanity.

[The decision included three dissenting votes. Justice Vladimiro Naranjo Mesa's dissent emphasized the role of palliative medicine as responding to the constitutional duty of solidarity and as a procedure that respects patients' dignity without causing their death. He further argued that the right to life is the basis for the exercise of all other constitutional rights, and that the existence of a right to die is a contradiction to the right to life. Justice Naranjo Mesa expressed that the right to the free development of personality is not absolute, but is restricted by social principles and by a minimum ethical standard at the base of legal concepts that the Court did not follow. Justice Hernando Herrera Vergara argued that the procedure of euthanasia is often applied to terminal patients who could exercise only a "fragile and weak consent." In a concurrence, Justices Jorge Arango Mejía and Carlos Gaviria Díaz expressed their agreement with the Court's decision and deemed it a "significant constitutional development," but argued that the option of dying with dignity should not have been restricted to terminal patients, "as there are dramatic cases of 'non-terminal' patients, such as quadriplegics, who should have the possibility of dying with dignity if they judge their suffering to be overwhelming."]

Notes on the Political Reaction to the Euthanasia Decision. The decision allowing doctors to carry out euthanasia on behalf of terminally ill patients in some circumstances was strongly opposed by the Catholic Church, which requested through the Archbishop of Medellin and through the President of the Colombian Episcopal Conference that the proceedings on the decision be declared null and void. In their petition, the Church officials argued that there was disagreement between the text of the decision and the recordings of the Court's general meeting, as well as a serious contradiction between the motives and the resolution sections of the decision, which had the effect of vitiating the concept of a social state of law enshrined in the Constitution. Additionally, they argued that these inconsistencies were evident in the contradictory declarations of justices before the press, and that the print media had reported widely on these problems. However, the Court refused to declare the decision null and void, noting that "press reports are inadequate evidence of the events happening within proceedings." The Court also stated that alleged inconsistencies between the text of the decision and what was approved by the majority of justices did not exist.

For many years, the Congress avoided issuing any of the regulations requested by the Court. In **Decision T-970 of 2014 (per Luis Ernesto Vargas Silva)**, a woman suffering from incurable colon cancer filed a *tutela* against her health insurance provider, arguing that the provider had improperly denied her claim for euthanasia (She died during the pendency of the claim). The health insurer argued that she had not given informed consent, and moreover that it could not act because of the absence of any legal regulation on the issue. After carrying out a broad survey of the practices in other countries, the Court issued a decision again exhorting Congress to pass a law, but also requiring the Ministry of Health to issue directives to healthcare providers within 30 days for the conformation of interdisciplinary committees that would determine the circumstances under which euthanasia could be carried out. These regulations were written, despite opposition from the Catholic Church and some elements of the state (particularly the National Inspector General). The country's first act of euthanasia under these new regulations occurred in July 2015.[5] In July 2016, the press widely reported on a well-known entrepreneur and "free thinker" who opted for euthanasia.[6]

The Colombian Court's ruling is unusual in comparative terms, particularly within traditionally Catholic and conservative Latin America, where no similar case appears to exist. In the United States, the Supreme Court has suggested a constitutional right of patients to refuse life support and other measures, but rejected any claim to have active measures taken either by the patient assisted by a doctor or by the doctor.[7] In a very small number of countries, including Belgium and the Netherlands, euthanasia administered by a doctor was legalized through political means, and in a slightly larger number of countries,

5. *See Ovidio González se convierte en la primera persona sometida a eutanasia en Colombia*, BBC MUNDO, Jul. 3, 2015, at http://www.bbc.com/mundo/noticias/2015/07/150703_eutanasia_ovidio_gonzalez_colombia_cch.

6. *See Eutanasia, la última voluntad de Tito Livio Caldas, fundador de Legis y Ámbito Jurídico*, EL ESPECTADOR, Jul. 21, 2016, at http://www.elespectador.com/noticias/judicial/eutanasia-ultima-voluntad-de-tito-livio-caldas-fundador-articulo-644676.

7. *See* Washington v. Glucksberg, 521 U.S. 702 (1997). Some states have passed laws allowing assisted suicide by a patient with aid from a doctor.

assisted suicide carried out by a patient with the aid of medical personnel is legal.[8] A fairly close parallel to the Colombian example may be Canada, where the Supreme Court in 2015 legalized assisted suicide carried out by the patient with help from a doctor.[9] The Canadian parliament passed new legislation implementing the decision in 2016.

C. Personal Appearance

Decision SU-642 of 1998 (per Justice Eduardo Cifuentes Muñoz)

[In a seven-to-two decision, the full Court protected the right to the free development of personality of a four-year-old child, after a kindergarten director tried to force her to cut her hair in order to prevent contagion with lice and gnats, against her stated preference not to have her hair cut. The Court protected the right to the free development of the girl`s personality and ordered the kindergarten to reform the school's regulations ordering children to wear short hair.]

[I]t is possible to discover, in an abstract and generalized way, the principle variables that one must take into account in the determination of the scope that the free development of personality has for a minor.

In the opinion of the chamber, the first variable is constituted by the psychological maturity of the minor who takes a determined decision, susceptible of being protected by the free development of personality. On this point, the Court has pointed out that the protection given by this fundamental right is more intense when the faculties of self-determination of the minor are greater; which, it is supposed, are complete from the age when the law fixes one as an adult. This rule . . . has been formulated as a relationship of inverse proportionality between the minor's capacity for self-determination and the legitimacy of any interventions taken against the minor's will. Therefore, the greater the intellectual and volitional capacity of the minor, the lesser will be the legitimacy of any interventions taken against her will. . . .

[To resolve the problem set out in this case, the Court asked for a psychologist's opinion; the psychologist stated that a four-year-old girl would start to show some degree of independence in certain activities, such as choosing her own outfits.] For the Court, it does not seem absurd or unreasonable to deduce from this that, if a four year-old girl can make a decision regarding her outfit, she can also do so regarding other aspects of her personal appearance such as, for example, the length of her hair. If a four year-old child possesses sufficient intellectual and volitional capacities to make a decision, in an autonomous manner, regarding the length of her hair, it is possible to state that such a decision is protected by the fundamental right to the free development of personality.

[The Court then stated that the measure at issue must be subjected to a test of proportionality.]

8. *See* JOHN GRIFFITHS & HELEEN WEYERS, EUTHANASIA AND LAW IN EUROPE (2d ed. 2008).

9. Carter v. Canada, 2015 SCC 5, [2015] 1 S.C.R. 331.

I[n] this type of case, measures that impose restrictions on the personal appearance of learners are unconstitutional, as they violate the fundamental right to the free development of personality, except when it is possible to demonstrate that they aim at the protection or effectiveness of a compelling and urgent constitutional interest with greater weight than the fundamental right noted above, in which case the measures would be considered adjusted to the Constitution.

According to what has been established above regarding the autonomy of four year-old children to decide on matters dealing with their personal appearance, it is possible to affirm that the kind of decision that has been limited in this case is not part of the essential nucleus of the right to the free development of personality. The decisions taken by four year-old children as to the length of their hair, although related to the child's bodily identity, admit relatively wide interventions, as long as they are carried out within the framework of a frank and friendly dialogue. In this sense, the scope of decision allows for restrictions whose compatibility with the Constitution will be determined by means of a judgment of proportionality which, in this case, must be particularly intense. Certainly, even when the decisions taken by children regarding their bodily identity are not part of the essential nucleus of the fundamental right to the free development of personality, the kind of decision involved in this case is indeed quite close to it, taking into consideration the thoroughness with which the Constitution protects all the matters related to the body itself and personal identity.

In the judgment of the Chamber, the purpose of the measure . . . is founded in clear constitutional dispositions. Health is, at the same time, a right of persons and an objective value of the order that grants the public authorities powers of intervention aimed at promoting the necessary conditions to make that reality effective. Additionally, in the case of children, health is a fundamental right that prevails over the rights of others, whose full exercise must be guaranteed by the family, society, and the state. . . .[10]

[T]he chamber finds that the measure . . . is ineffective to achieve its purpose, since a mere haircut is useless to prevent or combat contagion with lice and gnats. In addition, medical testing demonstrates that the purpose of the measure under constitutional review can be reached through alternative means to the haircut (the use of pesticides in lotion or shampoo), which involve less intrusion into the individual autonomy of students. In the Court's judgment, the use of measures that do not compromise or modify an individual's physical appearance will always be more reasonable and compatible with the fundamental right to free development of personality, even if the changes in physical appearance are only temporary.

Once it has been demonstrated that the measure under study is ineffective at achieving its end, there is no need to proceed with the other steps of the proportionality test. . . .

10. The Court cites Article 44 of the Constitution, which gives children a number of rights, including the right to health, and states that "[t]he rights of children take precedence over the rights of others."

Justices José Gregorio Hernández Galindo and Hernando Herrera, dissenting
It seems to us that the Court, in this ruling as well as in some previous rulings (such as C-222, dated May 5, 1994—decriminalizing illegal drug consumption- and C-239, dated May 20, 1997—decriminalizing euthanasia), has completely disfigured, in ways not intended by the Constituent Assembly, the right to free development of personality; the right, we feel, does not have an absolute character. Its exercise is limited, as the constitutional norm emphasizes, by the rights of others and by the legal order—in this case the legal order regulating the educational community.... Should this path continue, as the reaches of the right to free development of the personality are exaggerated, we will end up eroding fully and in an incomprehensible manner, the authority of educators, and frustrating both parents' and society's expectations regarding the education of children.

D. Intersex Rights

Decision SU-337 of 1999 (per Justice Alejandro Martínez Caballero)

[In a *tutela* decision aimed at unifying existing case law on patients' informed consent for hormonal and surgical interventions, the Constitutional Court confirmed a lower court's judgment denying a *tutela* filed by the mother of a seven-year-old child diagnosed with male pseudohermaphroditism, but who had been stated to be a girl at birth and who had been raised as a girl by her mother The mother requested that the state authorize surgery to alter the child's genitalia, removing the male sex organs and shaping them into female sex organs. The Institute for Social Security (ISS) refused to authorize the intervention because of prior constitutional case law establishing that such a decision should be made by the minor and not by the mother. A lower-court *tutela* judge agreed with the ISS that judges had no competence to grant such authorization because constitutional case law had established that "only the person involved could decide" whether or not to go through the surgery.]

[In arguing in favor of surgery, the mother contended that her "daughter is a minor and she cannot make decisions on her own," and "if we wait until she has the capacity to decide, it will be too late, and her psychological, physiological and social development will not be the normal one." On these grounds, and in her capacity as sole parent, the mother claimed to be in a position to authorize the surgical procedure. According to the Court, "the mother believes that ... her daughter's rights to equality, to the free development of personality and to special protection for children are being infringed, as the child is entitled to define her sexuality soon so as to ensure her normal personal and social development." Therefore, the mother requests that the *tutela* judge grant her, in her capacity as mother and sole parent, the possibility to authorize "the surgical interventions ... needed to remodel her genitalia and the medical treatment subsequently required."]

["To collect relevant scientific information," the Court asked advice from the Colombian Society of Urology and from medical doctors and specialists in the field.] The majority of experts consulted by the Court agreed with the mother's view on the need and convenience of surgical intervention to ensure the girl's welfare, and therefore, they considered that parents, aided by an interdisciplinary team, were well suited to authorize the surgery since these interventions must be undertaken early on during childhood in order to be successful. . . .

The *tutela* judge's decision, as well as other views included in the proceedings, were opposed to the above mentioned opinions[; these actors instead believed] that medical treatments in cases like this one were unnecessary, invasive, irreversible, and potentially harmful. These surgical and hormonal interventions should be postponed until the person has the capacity to give truly informed and free consent. . . .

The Constitutional Court not only does not deny but explicitly recognizes the complexity of the issue that it must decide, since it is not easy to come to a satisfactory conclusion. On one hand, chemical and surgical interventions on minors with genital ambiguity for the purpose of assigning them a masculine or feminine identity implies a very strong tension between multiple constitutional principles, especially those regarding the welfare and autonomy principles implicit in any medical treatment. And on the other hand, based on the medical, scientific, and sociological literature that this court has carefully examined, . . . whichever decision is taken appears to have an important cost in terms of human suffering and in affecting some fundamental constitutional principle. We are thus in the presence of a case that is not only difficult, but also tragic, since judges are under the obligation to rule, but any decision seems inadequate, and the situation can only be solved by adopting the decision that is the least humanly painful and has the least negative impact on the constitutional principles at stake. . . .

[The Court proceeded to clarify some of the ethical and legal principles at issue.] [F]rom the times of the Hippocratic oath, physicians have based their practice on the welfare principle, in its double dimension: it is their duty to contribute to patients' welfare (principle of benevolence), or at least to refrain from causing them physical or psychic harm (non-maleficence principle or *primun non nocere*). On the other hand, [they must also be guided by] the development of new medical techniques through scientific testing and research, in favor of the population and new patients, since it is a duty for the medical profession to provide the best treatment possible to the most people (principle of usefulness). In the third place, medical services should be distributed in an equitable manner to all persons, in development of the mandate according to which all people should have equal access to the benefits of science and culture (principle of justice). Lastly, in societies founded on personal inviolability, dignity and autonomy, any intervention on a human body must be authorized by the person involved (principle of autonomy). . . .

The obvious question that surges from the prior analysis is the following: how does one resolve the tensions that can be presented between those principles that govern medical activity? There is no easy answer to this question, whose solution depends in general on the balancing of the specific weight that those principles acquire given the particularities of the concrete case. But that does not mean all of these principles have exactly the same normative force since, in a society founded on pluralism and human dignity, principles regarding consent and autonomy have a prima facie prevalence over other concurrent principles. It has been a consistent doctrine of the Court that any medical intervention must have the informed consent of patients, who may refuse even those medical treatments aimed at prolonging their lives, but which they consider incompatible with their most important projects and personal convictions.

This prima facie preference in favor of the principle of autonomy and its obvious consequence, i.e., patients' consent, are strongly founded on our Constitution and on human rights treaties, since it is an inevitable result of the pluralism of contemporary societies and of the recognition of the dignity and autonomy of human beings. Thus, if individuals are free and autonomous beings, it is obvious that they should decide on how to care for their own health and, therefore, on which medical treatments they will authorize. . . .

In addition, if individuals are inviolable, so too are their bodies, and they cannot be subjected to interventions without consent. . . . [T]he individual is an absolute holder of the right to decide about his own body, and therefore, any intervention carried out on him without consent is one of the most typical and primordial offenses. . . .

[T]he clear authorization of patients may be unnecessary in certain cases in which the principle of autonomy must cede before the exigency of other concurrent principles, given the particularities of the concrete case, such as medical emergencies or other similar events. Therefore, the principle of autonomy has a prima facie but not absolute prevalence over concurrent principles, especially over the principle of welfare. Consequently, physicians must always obtain authorization to conduct a treatment, except when the specific features of a case justify disregarding the obligation. This means that a medical team wanting to disregard their duty to obtain informed consent has to prove beyond doubt the need to do so. . . .

In this context, it is relevant to distinguish between regular or non-invasive therapies, which have low risk and do not have a strong impact on patients' daily lives, and those exceptional medical interventions which are notably invasive and disturbing for patients' autonomy. . . . [Regarding the latter,] the duty to disclose information is far more demanding and the authorization of patients must be especially clear. Therefore, the more invasive a treatment is, the clearer and more complete the information should be so as to enable patients' truly informed consent.

Parents and guardians may make certain decisions regarding their children's medical treatments, sometimes even against their will. However, this does not mean that parents can make, in the name of their child, any medical decision regarding the minor, because children are not the property of anyone but instead represent a form of liberty and autonomy in development, which enjoys constitutional protection. . . .

Hormonal and surgical interventions on hermaphrodites are especially invasive and, therefore, according to the above mentioned criteria, informed consent by the person involved must be clear, complete and founded on a full knowledge of treatment risks and of possible alternative therapies. It is obvious, of course, that such a consent requires special maturity and autonomy from patients, who must be perfectly clear on what they want and must understand the risks involved in invasive, irreversible and exacting interventions. In such cases, therefore, medical teams must not only provide clear information to patients, but also establish procedures to make sure that their consent is genuine.

[The Court rejected the argument that parental consent should substitute for the consent of the child because of the operation's urgent nature]. [T]his cannot be assumed in a simplistic manner: first, because the minor involved in this case is already several years old. . . . [A]ccording to the dominant view, the surgical intervention . . . should be undertaken before the minor is two years old, which is the critical period for sexual identity processes in children. At that age, a minor's self-determination is almost non-existent and this adds to the legitimacy of a parent's substitute consent. However, the girl in the case under examination is more than eight years old, which means that she has amply surpassed the threshold of that critical period and, therefore, the urgency for a medical intervention has decreased. Moreover, her situation challenges the need for an immediate operation since she seems to have developed a significant sexual identity and, according to her medical record, she has not had any problems with psychological or social adaptation. Finally, at the age [of eight] a minor has greater autonomy, which calls for stricter constitutional protection, because as mentioned before by the Court . . . it is well established that the greater the autonomy of minors, the greater the constitutional protection that their right to the free development of personality deserves. . . .

[The Court conducted a review of the conflicting medical and sociological literature related to the procedure at issue, some of which viewed these procedures as beneficial and others of which viewed it as risky or harmful with no corresponding benefits.] In the issue under consideration, no evidence has been found to justify the urgency and the need for this therapy. On the other hand, according to the evidence collected during the proceedings and the many scientific articles consulted, it is clear for the Court that these surgical and hormonal interventions can produce physical and psychological harm to the girl. Since there is no conclusive data on the issue, it cannot be clearly established how harmful such interventions may be. . . . It is possible that future research will show that damage occurs only in exceptional situations and that these interventions are necessary and beneficial; however, the evidence available at the moment shows that the girl's risk to suffer irreversible and severe damage is highly probable. . . .

A consideration of these treatments as invasive and risky procedures has transcendental legal consequences for the legitimacy of the substitute consent of the parents of the minor. . . . The necessity of informed consent is still more important in the event of invasive and risky medical procedures, since that authorization is the only way to protect the dignity of patients. This special exigency is perfectly in accord with the Constitution since, as this Court has said on numerous occasions, children are not property of their parents but rather have their own individuality and dignity, and possess a developing autonomy. The rights of parents over their children therefore have as their only basis the protection of the superior interests of the minor, with the goal that he develop into an autonomous person. Article 18 of the Convention on the Rights of the Child, approved and ratified by Colombia, states that "[p]arents or, as the case may be, legal guardians, have the primary responsibility for the upbringing and development of the child," but also clarifies that "[t]he best interests of the child will be their basic concern." [11] Parents cannot submit their children to risky surgeries and treatments from which they will not derive a direct health benefit, since such a decision affects the superior interest of the child. . . .

[Finally, the Court considered] a last objection against the constitutional prohibition of surgery . . .: by adopting this kind of decision, judges seriously interfere in the family's autonomy and privacy because the girl's medical treatment is defined through a judicial decision and not by her mother. The family is not only society's basic unit but also one of the essential spaces in which pluralism, a constitutional principle of particular relevance, is nurtured. . . .[12]

[F]amily privacy is not absolute, which is why the Constitution also establishes that the state has a duty to protect the rights of children, who are among the weakest subjects in the family unit. . . .[13]

[T]here is a prima facie protection of parents' right to make decisions concerning their children's health, which springs from two basic assumptions: (i) that parents have a better understanding of their children's interests and that they are best suited to protect such interests, and (ii) that within certain limits, families may take alternative approaches to health problems. However, there exists strong evidence that parents only rarely develop alternative options in this area, and most importantly that they have great difficulty understanding the true interests of their children with genital ambiguities. In effect, the theme of hermaphroditism has been left in silence in our societies, so that the birth by chance of an intersexual child is traumatic for the parents, who do not understand the situation adequately. In those circumstances, it is perfectly human that the decisions of the parents tend to be based more in their own fears and prejudices, rather than on the real needs of the child. In a certain way, the parents are part of the social majority who have a defined biological sex, and who see in hermaphrodites strange beings whom they hope can be "normalized" as quickly as possible. The children run the risk of being discriminated against by their own parents.

Based on the foregoing, in the case of hermaphroditism, there are objective difficulties with the claim that the mother really understands and defends her daughter's

11. Convention on the Rights of the Child, Nov. 20, 1989, 1577 U.N.T.S. 3.

12. The Court cites several articles of the Colombian Constitution in this part, including Article 68, which gives parents the power to select education for their children, and Article 42, stating that the family is the "basic nucleus of society."

13. Article 44 of the Constitution states that "the family, society, and the state have the obligation to assist and protect children in order to guarantee their harmonious and integral development and the full exercise of their rights."

> interests, who is a minor apparently of an age to have greater consciousness of her body and individuality; likewise, it does not seem easy for this family to develop different options from those offered by the present treatment proposal, not only because the medical team offered early surgical intervention as the only alternative, but also because this option helped to reduce the parent's fears since she believes that the surgical procedure will make her child normal. In light of this, the Court recalls that one of the essential functions of constitutional judges is to protect minority groups. Therefore, the Court must speak for the minor involved in this case by legitimately . . . intervening in family privacy to protect her best interests while she gains greater autonomy to decide upon her sexual identity. By means of this decision, early surgical interventions and hormonal treatments should be postponed until the person involved can grant informed consent, since parental decisions may not always be aimed at truly protecting the best interests of children. . . .
>
> [T]he Court concludes that since the minor's life will not be put at risk if the surgical intervention is postponed, it is impossible for the mother to authorize the operation and hormonal treatment of her daughter, who is now more than eight years old. Therefore, these interventions may only be undertaken with the girl's informed consent and, consequently, the *tutela* writ is denied. . . . Moreover, the constitutional judge must take all necessary measures to protect the child's fundamental rights. Hence, the Court will protect the claimant's rights to sexual identity, to the free development of personality and to equality, and will order relevant authorities to adopt the necessary measures so that the child and her mother receive proper psychological assistance and interdisciplinary counseling to help them fully understand the situation they are going through. Likewise, an interdisciplinary team will be set up with not only medical doctors, but also a psychotherapist and a social worker, to give support to the child and her mother throughout the process. This team will establish when the girl possesses sufficient autonomy to give informed consent authorizing surgical interventions and hormonal treatments, if that is her decision.

Note on the Colombian Intersex Rights Jurisprudence. The Court's extensive and detailed jurisprudence on intersex rights demonstrates an intervention in an area where, as SU-337 of 1999 suggests, the state of science, medicine, and psychology remain unsettled. It also represents an intervention into an emerging area of human rights, with a relatively undeveloped international and comparative normative structure and case law.[14] The Court's jurisprudence on intersex issues has been the subject of comparative exploration and criticism.[15]

14. *See, e.g.*, U.N. Office of the High Comm'r on Human Rights [OHCHR], Discrimination and violence against individuals based on their sexual orientation and gender identity, U.N. Doc. A/HRC/29/23 (May 4, 2009); International Commission of Jurists (ICJ), Yogyakarta Principles—Principles on the application of international human rights law in relation to sexual orientation and gender identity (Mar. 2007), *available at* http://www.refworld.org/docid/48244e602.html.

15. *See, e.g.*, TRANSGENDER RIGHTS (Paisley Currah et al. eds., 2006); Ryan L. White, *Note: Preferred Private Parts: Importing Intersex Autonomy for M.C. v. Aaronson*, 37 FORD. INT'L L.J. 777 (2014).

The scientific debates and jurisprudential principles articulated in SU-337 of 1999 have been further articulated in a series of subsequent cases, usually involving the parents of children suing their health insurers for coverage of relevant surgery or treatment. The Court has generally allowed substitute consent by parents on behalf of very young children under the age of five, but only if that consent meets the demanding standard of "qualified and persistent informed consent."[16] For older children, the Court has generally allowed the procedure only if both the child and his or her parents give informed consent, and then only after extensive consultation with the interdisciplinary medical team described in SU-337 of 1999.[17]

E. Abortion

By a five-to-three vote, the Court held that the criminalization of abortion in all cases was unconstitutional. The Court stated three situations in which abortion could not be a crime: (1) rape, other pregnancy without consent, or incest; (2) fetal malformations incompatible with life outside the womb; and (3) a pregnancy threatening the life or health of the mother. In those three situations, the Court held that abortion must be permitted.

Decision C-355 de 2006 (per Justices Jaime Araújo Rentería and Clara Inés Vargas Hernandez)

[Four citizens filed a public action of unconstitutionality against the articles of the Criminal Code that criminalized abortion. The plaintiffs asserted that the articles and paragraphs in question violated the following constitutional rights: the right to human dignity, the right to life, the right to bodily integrity, the right to equality, the right to free development of personality, the right to reproductive autonomy,[18] the right to health, and obligations under international human rights law incorporated into the constitutional block via Article 93.]

The Court will begin by making reference to "life" as a relevant constitutional value and to the difference between this value and the fundamental right to life. The Court will also refer to the international treaties which are part of the constitutional block and it will refer to the fundamental rights of women found in the 1991 Constitution and in international law, which, in this case, must also be given consideration in order to establish whether they collide with the right to life and the duty to protect life.[19] Then, the Court will address the limits of the legislature's discretion

16. *See* Decision T-551 of 1999 (per Justice Alejandro Martínez Caballero). In T-551, the Court held that the standard for "qualified and persistent" informed consent was not met, because doctors did not give parents pluralistic advice on other options, and instead presented surgery as the only option.

17. *See* Decision T-912 of 2008 (per Justice Jaime Córdoba Triviño); Decision T-622 of 2014 (per Justice Jorge Ignacio Pretelt Chaljub).

18. The plaintiffs referred in particular to Article 42 of the Colombian Constitution, which states in relevant part that every couple has the right to "freely and responsibly" decide on the number of their children.

19. The constitutional block is a doctrinal concept created by the Court out of Article 93 of the constitution. The block includes not only the text of the Constitution and jurisprudence of the Court, but also international human rights treaties ratified by Colombia and its interpretations by international tribunals and in international "soft law." For more detail, see Chapter 2.

over criminal matters, in particular over matters related to the fundamental rights to human dignity, the free development of the individual, and health, as well as the constitutional block, and issues of reasonableness and proportionality. Finally, the Court will determine the constitutionality of the articles in question by weighing the different rights at issue against the obligation to protect life.

It can be said that by virtue of the mentions of "life" in various constitutional articles, the Constitution of 1991 is inclined to a general protection of life. From this point of view, all of the state's actions must focus on protecting life. This protection shall not be understood as an anthropocentric protection only. The duty to protect life as a constitutional value extends from the axiological sphere to the normative sphere and becomes a constitutional mandate with real obligations. Among those obligations is that all state authorities, without exception and to the extent of their abilities, must act within their legal and constitutional discretion with the purpose of achieving appropriate conditions for the effective development of human life. Public authorities' duty to protect life is the necessary flip side of life as a constitutionally protected value, and as such it has given rise to multiple jurisprudential lines of argument from this Court.

Following this reasoning, "life" and "the right to life" are different phenomena. Human life passes through various stages and manifests in various forms, which are entitled to different levels of legal protection. Even though the legal system protects the fetus, it does not grant it the same level or degree of protection as it grants to a human person. These differences are notable in most legal systems where, for example, the criminal punishment for infanticide or for homicide is greater than the punishment for abortion. That is, the protected life is not identical in all cases and therefore the legal implications of the offence carry different degrees of reprisal and thus a proportional punishment. These considerations must be taken into account by the legislature if it finds it appropriate to enact public policies regarding abortion. . . .

It cannot be said that an absolute or unconditional duty to protect the life of the unborn fetus derives from the various international human rights treaties that form part of the constitutional block. Both a literal interpretation and a context-driven interpretation require weighing the unborn fetus' right to life against other rights, principles, and values recognized in the 1991 Constitution and in other international human rights law instruments, an approach that has been followed by the Inter-American Court of Human Rights.

This approach requires identifying and weighing the rights at issue in conjunction with the duty to protect life, while taking into account the constitutional importance of the bearer of the rights; in these cases, the pregnant woman.

The 1991 Constitution expressly sets out the goal of recognizing and enhancing the rights of women, as well as of reinforcing these rights by protecting them in an effective and decisive manner. Thus, women are now entitled to special constitutional protection and their rights must be recognized and protected by government authorities, including those within the legal system, without exception. . . . Women's sexual and reproductive rights have finally been recognized as international human rights. . . .

[But this does not mean that] a mandate to decriminalize abortion or a prohibition on the legislature's adoption of criminal abortion laws derives from international treaties or constitutional articles on the topic. Congress has a wide range of discretion to adopt public policies on abortion. However, this discretion is not unlimited. As this Court has held, even in criminal matters, the legislature must respect two constitutional limits. First, the legislature cannot disproportionately encroach upon constitutional rights. Second, the legislature must not leave certain constitutional values unprotected. At the same time, the legislature must recognize the principle that criminal law, due to its potential to restrict liberties, must always be a measure of last resort.

[First,] when the legislature enacts criminal laws, it cannot ignore that a woman is a human being entitled to dignity and that she must be treated as such, as opposed to being treated as a reproductive instrument for the human race. The legislature must not impose the role of procreator on a woman against her will.

[Second, the law must respect an] individual's private decisions, which result in a person's life plan or in an individual's ideal of personal achievement. . . . The right to be a mother, or in other words, the right to opt for motherhood as a "life choice," is a decision of the utmost private nature for each woman. Therefore, the Constitution does not permit the state, the family, the employer or educational institutions to introduce any regulation or policy that infringes upon the right of a woman to choose to be a mother or that interferes with the rightful exercise of motherhood. Any discriminatory or unfavorable treatment of a woman on the basis of special circumstances that she might be facing at the time of making the decision of whether to be a mother (for example, at an early age, within marriage or not, with a partner or without one, while working, etc.) is a flagrant violation of the constitutional right to the free development of the individual.

[Third,] international human rights treaties, which, according to constitutional jurisprudence, are part of the constitutional block, provide a clear limit on the legislature's discretion over criminal matters. Accordingly, various articles of the International Covenant on Civil and Political Rights, the Convention on the Elimination of All Forms of Discrimination against Women, and the International Covenant on Economic, Social and Cultural Rights . . . are relevant in the analysis of the constitutionality of the total ban on abortion.

[Fourth] . . . the legislature may choose from amongst the different available measures those that it considers the most adequate for the protection of legitimate ends, and it may adopt criminal laws penalizing conduct that threatens or infringes upon constitutionally protected values, rights or principles. However, the legislature's discretion is subject to various constitutional limits, including the principle of proportionality. . . . A criminal law cannot impose a disproportionate restriction on the fundamental right in question. . . . Nor can it require a complete sacrifice of any individual's fundamental right in order to serve the general interests of society or in order to give legal priority to other protected values.

[Next, the Court examined decisions from courts of the United States, Germany, and Spain and concluded that] when constitutional tribunals have examined the constitutionality of laws governing the termination of pregnancy, they have coincided in the need to balance the various interests at stake; on one hand, the life of the fetus, which is constitutionally relevant and therefore should be protected, and on the other hand, the rights of the pregnant woman. Even though the various tribunals have differed on which of those interests must prevail in particular cases, they have shared common ground in affirming that a total prohibition on abortion is unconstitutional because under certain circumstances it imposes an intolerable burden on the pregnant woman which infringes upon her constitutional rights.

It is not the role of the constitutional judge to determine the character or the nature of the measures that the legislature should adopt in order to protect a particular state interest. That is an eminently political decision reserved for the legislative branch, which has the legitimate democratic ability to adopt those measures. The intervention of the constitutional judge comes *a posteriori* and only in order to examine whether the legislature has exercised its powers within the limits of its discretion.

If the legislature decides to serve legitimate ends by adopting criminal measures, its margin of discretion is limited due to the severity of such measures and their potential to seriously impair human dignity and individual liberties. In the case of abortion, the decision is extremely complex because the crime impacts various rights, principles and values, all of which are constitutionally relevant. Accordingly, defining which should prevail and in what measure is a decision with profound social repercussions which may alter as society transforms and public policy changes. The legislature has the ability to modify its decisions in response to such changes, and it is the branch responsible for providing the state's response to competing constitutional rights, principles and values.

Even though the protection of the fetus through criminal law is not in itself disproportionate and penalizing abortion may be constitutional, the criminalization of abortion in all circumstances entails the complete preeminence of the life of the fetus and the absolute sacrifice of the pregnant woman's fundamental rights. This result is, without a doubt, unconstitutional.

In effect, one of the characteristics of constitutional regimes with a high degree of axiological content, such as the Colombian Constitution of 1991, is the coexistence of different values, rights and principles, none of which is absolute and none of which prevails over the rest. This is one of the fundamental pillars of proportionality that must be utilized as an instrument to resolve the tension amongst laws in a structured and principled manner.

Thus, a criminal law which prohibits abortion in all circumstances extinguishes the woman's fundamental rights, and thereby violates her dignity by reducing her to a mere receptacle for the fetus, without rights or interests of constitutional relevance worthy of protection.

Determining under which circumstances it is excessive to require a woman to continue a pregnancy because it results in an infringement of a woman's fundamental rights is an exercise within the legislature's sphere. Once the legislature has decided that criminal law is the most appropriate way to protect the life of the fetus, then the legislature must set out the circumstances under which it is not excessive to sacrifice the rights of the pregnant woman. Nonetheless, if the legislature does not establish those circumstances, then it is up to the constitutional judge to prevent a disproportionate infringement of the fundamental rights of the pregnant woman. This does not mean, however, that the legislature lacks discretion to deal with this matter within constitutional limits.

Even though the Criminal Code contains a general prohibition of abortion, the articles in question demonstrate that under certain circumstances the legislature did establish mitigating factors and even provided the judiciary with the discretion to not impose a penalty in a particular case [where pregnancy results] from rape, sexual abuse, or non-consensual artificial insemination or implantation of a fertilized ovary.

In these circumstances, the legislature decided that the penalty for abortion should be mitigated in light of the fundamental rights of the woman involved.... However, the legislature decided that even in those circumstances, where the woman's dignity and free development of personality were imperiled, she should be tried and sentenced as a criminal. A measure such as this is disproportionate because the conduct continues to be criminal, which seriously infringes on the constitutional rights of the pregnant woman.

This Court is of the view that under the enumerated circumstances, abortion does not constitute a crime. This is not only because that result was originally contemplated by the legislature, but also because the absolute prevalence of the fetus' rights in these circumstances implies a complete disregard for human dignity and the right to the free development of the pregnant woman, whose pregnancy is not the result of a free and conscious decision, but the result of arbitrary, criminal acts against her in violation of her autonomy; acts that are penalized in the criminal code.

Pregnancy resulting from incest should also be included within these exceptional circumstances because it represents another example of a pregnancy resulting from a punishable act, where, in most cases, the woman does not consent. Even when there is no physical violence involved, incest generally infringes on a woman's autonomy. It also affects the stability of the family (an institution protected by the Constitution) and results in a violation of the constitutional principle of solidarity, which is, as has been held previously by this Court, a fundamental guiding principle of the Constitution. The criminalization of abortion in this circumstance amounts to a disproportionate and unreasonable infringement on the liberty and dignity of women.

When the pregnancy is the result of rape, sexual abuse, non-consensual artificial insemination or implantation of a fertilized ovary, or incest, it is necessary that such criminal acts be reported accordingly to the competent authorities.

To this end, the legislature may enact regulations as long as the regulations do not preclude access to abortion and do not impose a disproportionate burden on the rights of women. For instance, the regulations cannot require forensic evidence of actual penetration after a report of rape or require evidence to establish lack of consent to the sexual relationship. Nor can they require that a judge or a police officer find that the rape actually occurred, or require that the woman obtain permission from, or be required to notify, her husband or her parents.

The circumstances above are not the only ones in which it is disproportionate to criminalize abortion. When there is a risk to the health and life of the pregnant woman, it is clearly excessive to criminalize abortion since it would require the sacrifice of the fully formed life of the woman in favor of the developing life of the fetus. If the criminal penalty for abortion rests on valuing the life of the developing fetus over other constitutional interests involved, then criminalization of abortion in these circumstances would mean that there is no equivalent recognition of the right to life and health of the mother.

This Court has held on several occasions that the state cannot oblige a person, in this case a pregnant woman, to perform heroic sacrifices and give up her own rights for the benefit of others, or for the benefit of society in general. Such an obligation is unenforceable, even if the pregnancy is the result of a consensual act, in light of Article 49 of the Constitution, which mandates that all persons take care of their own health.

These obligations do not pertain only where the woman's physical health is at risk, but also where her mental health is at risk. It must be noted that the right to health, under Article 12 of the International Covenant on Economic, Social and Cultural Rights,[20] includes the right to the highest achievable level of both physical and mental well-being. Pregnancy may at times cause severe anguish or even mental disorders, which may justify its termination if so certified by a doctor.

A final circumstance that must be addressed involves medically-certified malformations of the fetus. Although there are different types of malformations, those extreme malformations incompatible with life outside the womb pose a constitutional issue that must be resolved. Those circumstances are different from having identified an illness of the fetus that may be cured during pregnancy or after birth. Rather, those circumstances involve a fetus that is unlikely to survive due to a severe malformation, as certified by a doctor. In these cases, the duty of the state to protect the fetus loses weight, since the life is in fact not viable. Thus, the rights of the woman prevail and the legislature cannot require her, under the threat of a criminal penalty, to carry a pregnancy to term.

Furthermore, in a situation where the fetus is not viable, forcing the mother, under the threat of criminal charges, to carry the pregnancy to term amounts to cruel, inhumane and degrading treatment, which affects her moral well-being and her right to dignity.

20. International Covenant on Economic, Social and Cultural Rights, Dec. 16, 1966, S. Treaty Doc. No. 95-19, 6 I.L.M. 360 (1967), 993 U.N.T.S. 3, art, 12 ("1. The states Parties to the present Covenant recognize the right of everyone to the enjoyment of the highest attainable standard of physical and mental health. . . .")

In both cases described above, where the continuation of the pregnancy puts the life or health of the pregnant woman at risk or when there are serious malformations of the fetus incompatible with life outside the womb, there should be a medical certificate to validate the circumstances. . . . Such determinations are to be made by medical practitioners acting within the ethical standards of their profession.

It must be noted that conscientious objection is not a right that legal entities or the state can exercise. It is only possible for natural persons to exercise this right. Hospitals, clinics or other health centers cannot raise a conscientious objection to performing an abortion when all the requirements established by this decision are met. When it comes to natural persons, it must be underscored that a conscientious objection relates to a religious belief and the opinion of the doctor with regard to abortion which should not be questioned. However, women's fundamental rights cannot be disregarded; thus, if the doctor raises a conscientious objection, the doctor must immediately refer the pregnant woman to another medical practitioner who can perform the abortion. That referral is without prejudice to a determination that may be made afterwards, through mechanisms established by the medical profession, regarding whether the objection was legitimate.

[The Court also considered a provision of the Criminal Code that "penalizes abortion when it is performed without the consent of the woman or when it is performed on a woman of less than 14 years of age. The challenged article established a presumption that a woman of less than 14 years of age is legally incapable of consenting to an abortion and therefore her consent is irrelevant from the perspective of the criminal penalty."]

[C]onstitutional jurisprudence has recognized that minors possess the right to the free development of personality and may consent to medical treatments and interventions, even when they are of a highly invasive nature. Purely objective criteria such as age have been rejected as the only standard for determining whether minors can consent to medical treatments and interventions. With regard to abortion, the legislature, if it deems appropriate, may establish rules in the future regarding representation of minors or the assertion of minors' rights, which shall not invalidate the consent of a minor of less than 14 years of age.

From this perspective, any protective measure that nullifies the legal effect of a minor's consent, such as the challenged expression in Article 123 of the Criminal Code, is unconstitutional because it completely annuls the minor's rights to the free development of the individual, autonomy and dignity. . . .

[Finally, the Court held that] the legislature in its discretion may decide that abortion should not be penalized in additional circumstances. . . . The legislature may foresee other cases in which public policy calls for the decriminalization of abortion, taking into consideration the circumstances under which abortions are performed, as well as socio-economic situations and other public health policy objectives.[21]

21. Three justices (Marco Gerardo Monroy Cabra, Rodrigo Escobar Gil, and Álvaro Tafur Galvis) dissented, arguing that the Constitution protected life from the moment of conception.

Note on the Law and Politics of Abortion. By comparison for example with the United States, the intervention of the Constitutional Court in abortion could be seen as relatively modest. However, the holding opened the door for Congress to legalize abortion in additional circumstances, and the concept of health of the mother included psychological as well as physical health, as Justice Manuel José Cepeda Espinosa pointed out in a concurring opinion that was based on an extensive study of comparative law. Moreover, in comparison to most of the rest of Latin America and to a historically conservative Catholic context, the jurisprudence of the Court represented a significant departure. Many major countries in the region still prohibit abortion altogether, and others make only narrower exceptions such as for the life of the mother.[22] Although courts throughout the region have played a role in shaping public debate, they have often done so in quite restrictive contexts and with more modest interventions.[23]

This case was brought by a public interest organization, and in this sense it may illustrate the accessibility of the Colombian public action, even in the face of strong popular opposition to abortion.[24] On the other hand, on-the-ground changes in response to this decision have been very slow. For example, a study by the Guttmacher Institute found that there were 400,000 abortions in Colombia in 2008, but the vast majority (at least 99.9 percent) were done clandestinely, using misoprostol or other methods taken outside of a formal medical environment. The overall rate of abortions remained much the same as it had been in 1988, and most healthcare sites in the country had no facilities for abortion.[25]

The Court has recently issued a number of decisions aimed at clarifying and amplifying this judgment in concrete cases, particularly in situations where it has faced substantial resistance. For example, in **Decision T-388 of 2009 (per Justice Humberto Antonio Sierra Porto)**, the Court encountered a situation where a health insurer, despite the opinion of several doctors that an abortion should be performed because of a risk to the health of the mother, demanded a judicial order to realize the procedure. Further, the first instance judge had refused to hear the case, stating that he had a conscientious objection to allowing abortion.

The Court held that the insurer could not require a judicial order to carry out an abortion, but rather had to act once a medical certification had been obtained. Moreover, the Court held that although an individual healthcare provider possessed a right to conscientious objection in these cases (along with a duty to provide someone who would carry out the service), neither institutions as a whole nor administrative officials such as judges possessed these rights.

22. *See* Guttmacher Institute, Fact Sheet: Abortion in Latin America and the Caribbean (May 2016), at: https://www.guttmacher.org/sites/default/files/factsheet/ib_aww-latin-america.pdf.

23. *See* Paola Bergallo & Augustina Ramón Miguel, *Abortion*, *in* THE LATIN AMERICAN CASEBOOK: COURTS, CONSTITUTIONS, AND RIGHTS 36 (Juan F. Gonzalez-Bertomeu & Roberto Gargarella eds., 2016).

24. For information on the legal strategy behind this case, see ISABEL CRISTINA JARAMILLO SIERRA & TATIANA ALFONSO SIERRA, MUJERES, CORTES Y MEDIOS: LA REFORMA JUDICIAL DEL ABORTO (2008).

25. Elena Prada et al., Unintended Pregnancy and Induced Abortion in Colombia: Causes and Consequences (2011), *available at* http://www.guttmacher.org/pubs/Unintended-Pregnancy-Colombia.pdf.

Finally, the Court emphasized that the right to have an abortion in the circumstances decriminalized by the Court was a fundamental right, and that it creates a set of corresponding obligations in the healthcare system. Some of these were of a negative nature—the state and healthcare providers may not place additional obstacles in the path of the woman, or pressure her. Others are of a positive nature—these same actors must create sufficient infrastructure such that safe and high-quality abortion services are available in all regions of the country. The Court listed the corresponding rights of a woman as follows:

> (i) Women in a situation contained in decision C-355 of 2006 have the right to decide free of pressure, duress, urgency, manipulation, and in general any sort of inadmissible intervention. . . .
>
> (ii) All women must be able to count on sufficient, broad, and adequate information to be able to exercise their sexual and reproductive rights capably and freely. . . .
>
> (iii) Abortion services in the circumstances contemplated in Decision C-355 of 2006 must be available in the entire national territory . . .
>
> (iv) Healthcare professionals and staff who assist women on abortion-related matters must offer them a guarantee of confidentiality and must respect their rights to privacy and dignity. . . .
>
> (v) Neither women who opt to voluntarily interrupt their pregnancy . . . , nor those who assist them, can be victims of discrimination or practices that in any way limit or impede their access to workplaces or educational centers, or their affiliation to the general healthcare or insurance systems.
>
> (vi) The departments, districts and cities are required to ensure sufficient availability of services in the public network with the goal of guaranteeing to women effective access to high-quality, sanitary abortion services.
>
> (vii) No healthcare provider—public or private, religious or lay—can deny abortion services when a woman is experiencing one of the circumstances established in Decision C-355 of 2006, regardless of her affiliation to the social security system or her social or economic condition, age, payment capacity, or sexual or ethnic orientation.
>
> (viii) It is absolutely prohibited to place any obstacles, requirements, or barriers beyond those established in Decision C-355 for the practice of abortion in the circumstances stated. The following are among the inadmissible barriers:
>
> To create medical boards for appeal or approval which cause unjustified wait times . . .
>
> To prevent children under 14 years who have freely given their consent from having an abortion, when their parents or legal guardians do not agree to the abortion.
>
> To place additional obstacles such as: (a) reports of forensic medicine, (b) judicial orders, (c) health examinations that are not quickly provided, (d) authorization from relatives, legal advisors, or auditors. . . .

> To claim a collective conscientious objection that triggers institutional and unfounded objections.
>
> To make individual or collective agreements in order to refuse to practice abortion.
>
> To create [plans or working arrangements] which mean that hospitals do not have doctors disposed to offer abortion services, either because these professionals are discriminated against or because they are pressured to abstain from realizing abortions.
>
> To disqualify medical opinions offered by psychologists recognized as healthcare professionals [by law]. . . .
>
> To not offer abortion services within some public networks of healthcare providers at the municipal, district, or departmental levels.

The scope of the Court's reasoning in this case gives one a sense of the obstacles that it was confronting on ground-level compliance with its abortion decision.

In **Decision T-841 of 2011 (per Justice Humberto Antonio Sierra Porto)**, the Court heard the case of a very poor, twelve-year-old girl who had sought an abortion. Despite the fact that several doctors certified that the pregnancy was placing both her mental and physical health at risk, her health insurance company did not take any action on her request for an abortion, and doctors refused to provide one until the insurance company had provided approval. Further, the insurance company argued that the pregnancy was too advanced by the time she sought a *tutela* (around five months), and that an abortion could not be performed after eight weeks of pregnancy without placing the life of the mother at risk. The Court held that the insurer had violated her rights by not providing the abortion quickly and by placing additional obstacles in her path. Moreover, the Court emphasized that both the insurance company and the lower court had wrongly stated that an abortion could not be safely performed after eight weeks; in fact existing law did not create a temporal limit on when an abortion would be allowed. It held that even an abortion very close to birth (which was not the case with the petitioner here) could be appropriate in some circumstances, and that the risks of performing the procedure should be weighed, concretely, against the risks of not performing it in each concrete case.

4

Equality

Colombian society has historically been stratified and hierarchical, with certain groups enjoying significant privileges in public and private life while others were consigned to subordinate roles. Women, indigenous groups, Afro-Colombians, sexual minorities, and religious minorities faced substantial discrimination.

The Constituent Assembly attempted to inculcate a transformative conception of equality that would benefit many of these historically marginalized groups. It thus laid out a substantive conception of equality that, for example, contemplated measures of affirmative action. The key provision is Article 13, which reads as follows:

> All individuals are born free and equal before the law, shall receive equal protection and treatment from the authorities, and shall enjoy the same rights, freedoms, and opportunities without any discrimination on account of gender, race, national or family origin, language, religion, political opinion, or philosophy.
>
> The state shall promote the conditions so that equality may be real and effective and shall adopt measures in favor of groups which are discriminated against or marginalized.
>
> The state shall especially protect those individuals who on account of their economic, physical, or mental condition are in obviously vulnerable circumstances and shall sanction the abuses or ill treatment perpetrated against them.

Thus, the Colombian Constitution goes beyond laying out a non-discrimination norm on behalf of protected groups. Its latter two sentences, in particular, require the state to "adopt measures" on behalf of groups facing marginalization and discrimination, and to "especially protect" vulnerable groups. Both of these provisions require state action to overcome past or inherent injustices, rather than simply formal non-discrimination.

Each of the three sections in this chapter emphasizes a different part of Article 13's guarantee of equality. The first section focuses on the Constitutional Court's case law between 2007 and 2016 that began by giving rights to same-sex couples and eventually legalized same-sex marriage. These three cases blend the non-discrimination mandate found in the first phrase of Article 13 with the rights to human dignity and autonomy that were explored in Chapter 3. The second section excerpts the Court's decision on gender quotas for political posts, which emphasized the second phrase's mandate to "adopt measures" in favor of a group that was historically subject to discrimination in the public sphere. The Court upheld the quotas as a constitutionally-permissible form of "affirmative action." Finally, the third section focuses on the need for the state to adopt measures to "especially protect" the access of the handicapped to public transportation in order to ensure that they can fully participate in society. In that case, the Court ordered the mass transportation system of the City of Bogotá to develop a plan to make more of its system handicapped-accessible.

At a social and political level, what unifies these decisions is the use of political and judicial power to overcome the effects of social injustice and hierarchies, a difficult and gradual constitutional project.[1] The sequence of cases leading to same-sex marriage have been significant in a traditionally conservative and Catholic social context, in which sexual minorities have often been subject to severe repression. The gender quota law that the Court upheld in 2000 was an attempt to transform the political sphere by overcoming entrenched historical barriers to the participation of women in public life. Finally, the decision requiring that Bogotá's public transportation system be made handicapped-accessible aimed at aiding a group that has often been stigmatized or simply ignored by the majority.

The Court's doctrinal approach to equality has been influenced by several different traditions. As both the same-sex marriage and gender cases show, the Court has used the concept of "suspect classes" and stated that classifications involving those classes will be particularly heavily scrutinized. It has also stated that different levels of scrutiny will be used for different kinds of cases. Both concepts draw on the case law of the United States Supreme Court, even as the Colombian Constitutional Court's view of both the groups and tiers is more fluid and less categorical than the U.S. vision. (For example, it sometimes combines an assessment of the tiers of scrutiny with proportionality analysis, as in the gender quota case below).

The Court's approach also reflects more substantive visions of equality, drawing for example on the recent jurisprudence of the European Court of Human Rights.[2] The Colombian Constitutional Court has departed from the U.S. doctrinal tradition in holding that affirmative action measures aiding historically-disadvantaged groups should be

1. Similarly, Gary Jacobsohn has argued that India possesses an "ameliorative" conception of equality aimed at overcoming deeply-entrenched hierarchies based on caste, religion, gender, and other factors; there too, affirmative and special measures on behalf of historically-disadvantaged groups are explicitly contemplated. *See* GARY J. JACOBSOHN, THE WHEEL OF LAW: INDIA'S SECULARISM IN COMPARATIVE CONSTITUTIONAL CONTEXT (2003).

2. *See* Sandra Fredman, *Emerging from the Shadows: Substantive Equality and Article 14 of the European Convention on Human Rights*, 16 HUM. RTS. L. REV. 273 (2016).

treated as less suspect than measures discriminating against those groups.[3] More broadly, the Court has insisted that the state must take positive steps to overcome entrenched inequalities, rather than merely refraining from discriminatory classifications.

A. The Equality and Dignity Rights of Same-Sex Couples

This section presents the evolution of the Court's jurisprudence on same-sex couples by excerpting three cases from 2007, 2011, and 2016. Before 2007, the Court's case law had protected individuals from discrimination based on sexual orientation in a number of cases. But the Court had consistently refused to grant constitutional protection to same-sex couples. In reaching this conclusion, the Court had given political authorities a broad scope to define legally-recognized marital relationships. Moreover, the Court at times had relied on Article 42 of the Constitution, which states in part:

> The family is the basic nucleus of society. It is formed on the basis of natural or legal ties, through the free decision of *a man and woman* to contract matrimony or through the responsible resolve to comply with it (emphasis added).

Thus, the text of the 1991 Constitution was arguably hostile to the recognition of any right of same-sex marriage. Nonetheless, beginning in 2007 the Court began an expansion of rights that ended only in 2016. First, in Decision C-075 of 2007 and subsequent decisions, the Court recognized that same-sex couples had the right to the protections found in a regime called the marital union in fact, essentially a form of common-law marriage that had traditionally been used for heterosexual couples who were cohabitating and formed a permanent partnership but had not formally married. This decision received broad support from both progressive and conservative justices. In Decision C-577 of 2011, the Court held that there was still a "deficit of protection" in the law: although same-sex couples could now be recognized as a marital union in fact, they still could not enter into a formal marriage contract. However, the Court refused to order direct relief, instead "exhorting" Congress to legislate on the issue and giving it a defined period of time to do so. Finally, in Decision SU-214 of 2016, after Congress did not act and same-sex couples were left in legal limbo, the Court ordered same-sex marriage to be legalized throughout the country. The 2011 decision recognized same-sex couples as families, whereas the 2016 decision moved beyond the "deficit of protection" concept by recognizing that the core issue was one of discrimination.

These decisions reflect both change and stasis in the political and social environments. In Colombia, as in much of Latin America, the conservative Catholic culture has historically been hostile to homosexuals and same-sex couples, who have therefore faced

3. For an example of the United States' practice applying scrutiny to all race-based classifications, whether intended to undermine or promote historically-disadvantaged groups, see, e.g., Regents of the University of California v. Bakke, 438 U.S. 265, 290–91 (1978).

substantial discrimination and marginalization.[4] It is surprising, then, that the expansion of marital unions in fact to same-sex couples was unanimous, and indeed the decision was authored by a justice from the Court's religious conservative wing. In contrast, the granting of marital rights to same-sex couples has proven to be more controversial, and has faced resistance from conservative elements in civil society, politics, and the Court itself.

The Court's evolving jurisprudence on same-sex marriage demonstrates some parallels to other political contexts where courts seem concerned about backlash and about getting too far ahead of public opinion. In the United States, federal judicial interventions followed a long series of decisions, and backlash against those interventions, at the state level. Even then, the United States Supreme Court moved cautiously, in 2013 issuing a decision that recognized same-sex marriage, where allowed by state governments, at the federal level,[5] and only in 2015 legalizing same-sex marriage throughout the country.[6] In Mexico, the Supreme Court since 2013 has undertaken a fairly slow-motion legalization of same-sex marriage through the accumulation of individual complaint or *amparo* actions on a state-by-state basis.[7] Finally, in South Africa, as in Colombia, the Court in the 2005 *Fourie* case attempted to incentivize the legislature to regulate same-sex relationships rather than mandating same-sex marriage directly.[8] Unlike in Colombia, however, the South African parliament passed a law in 2006 extending marriage to same-sex couples.

Finally, it is worth noting the reasoning of the Colombian Constitutional Court in these three cases. All involve a mix of dignity, autonomy, and equality considerations. In focusing on dignity, the decisions emphasize the fundamental nature of the marital decision for individuals and families. In stressing autonomy, they highlight the constitutional relevance of individuals making their own decisions on such an important matter. In discussing equality, they stress the historically marginalized position of sexual minorities in Colombia and the absence of sufficient reasons for denying same-sex couples benefits extended to heterosexual ones. Although a comparative literature has analyzed the judicial choice among dignity, autonomy, and equality and has attempted to analyze the meaning of the right through different frames, the Colombian reasoning style may suggest that courts may be most comfortable and persuasive combining these different factors.[9]

4. *See, e.g.*, Germán Lodola & Margarita Corral, *Support for Same-Sex Marriage in Latin America*, *in* SAME-SEX MARRIAGE IN LATIN AMERICA: PROMISE AND RESISTANCE 41 (Jason Pierceson et al. eds., 2013).

5. United States v. Windsor, 133 S. Ct. 2675 (2013).

6. Obergefell v. Hodges, 135 S. Ct. 2584 (2015).

7. *See* Estefanía Vela Barba, *Same-Sex Unions in Mexico: Between Text and Doctrine*, *in* SAME SEX COUPLES—COMPARATIVE INSIGHTS ON MARRIAGE AND COHABITATION 49 (Macarena Sáez ed., 2015).

8. *See* Minister of Home Affairs v. Fourie, [2005] ZACC 19, 2006 (1) SA 524 (CC), 2006 (3) BCLR 355 (CC).

9. For some recent examples of this literature, see Kenji Yoshino, *Comment: A New Birth of Freedom:* Obergefell v. Hodges, 129 HARV. L. REV. 147 (2015); Michèle Finck, *The Role of Human Dignity in Gay Rights Adjudication*, 14 INT'L J. CONST. L. 26 (2016).

Decision C-075 of 2007 (per Justice Rodrigo Escobar Gil)

[Law 54 of 1990 established regulations regarding the "marital union in fact"—the association between a man and a woman who are "permanent companions," and that can result in the creation of a common property regime and other rights and duties even though the parties are not formally married. The law established a presumption that a joint property regime was formed whenever parties existed as a "permanent and singular community of life" for more than two years. It also stated that a couple in such a situation could declare its existence by, for example, mutually making a statement before a notary. However, the entire regime was limited to heterosexual couples. The claimants argued that this restriction left same-sex couples unprotected and placed them in a discriminatory position. In a ruling that was unanimous as to its core principle,[10] the Constitutional Court declared the common property regime in Law 54 of 1990 constitutional only under the condition that its benefits be extended to same-sex couples.]

[The Court first resolved a preliminary question. It noted that a previous decision, **Decision C-098 of 1996 (per Justice Eduardo Cifuentes Muñoz)**, had declared the provisions questioned in the case to be constitutional. Prior constitutional decisions have a res judicata effect on all actors, including the Constitutional Court, but this effect extends only to the holding of the case. The Court found that the previous analysis had been limited to a consideration of Law 54 of 1990 as a measure for family protection, and thus "left the door open for a new examination" of whether the provisions had a "negative impact on homosexuals." The Court therefore decided to examine whether Law 54 implied a "lack of protection" for same-sex couples and constituted "discriminatory treatment as compared with heterosexual couples." Furthermore, given the way the demand was drafted, the Court also restricted its examination to the property regime established by the Act, and did not consider collateral consequences in, for example, criminal and labor law.]

Constitutional jurisprudence in Colombia, in both *tutela* and constitutionality decisions, has signaled that homosexuals have been a group traditionally subject to discrimination, and thus in light of the [Constitution] all differences in treatment based on the sexual orientation of persons are presumed unconstitutional and are submitted to strict constitutional control.

In this context we have stated that "within the ambit of personal autonomy, sexual diversity is clearly protected by the Constitution, precisely because the Charter, without any doubt, aspires to be a framework in which 'the most diverse forms of humanity can coexist.'"[11]

Notwithstanding the foregoing and the weight of the many pronouncements in which the Court has acted to prevent and repair discriminatory events based on the

10. Justice Jaime Araujo Rentería dissented because he believed that the ruling should have been broader, and also analyzed other types of discrimination against same-sex couples aside from property rights.

11. The Court is quoting from Decision T-268 de 2000 (per Justice Alejandro Martínez Caballero) (involving a gay pride parade in the city of Neiva).

sexual orientation of persons, in the complaint and in various interventions it was expressed, with justification, that while the constitutional order creates a prohibition on discrimination based on sexual orientation that has been declared in existing case law, the effectiveness of this postulate, although increasing at the individual level, has not manifested in the sphere of same-sex couples, who lack legal recognition.

In other words, the legal order recognizes the rights that homosexual persons have as individuals, but at the same time it deprives them of instruments that would permit them to develop fully as a couple, an essential sphere for personal realization not only in its sexual aspects, but also in other dimensions of life.

In this respect one can observe that the prohibition on discrimination based on sexual orientation stems from international norms that form part of the constitutional block and that in a generic way proscribe all forms of discrimination.... [P]ronouncements of international institutions and tribunals of different states have advanced in the definition of the sphere of protection of homosexual persons and couples, and in the identification of factors that can be seen as discriminatory based on the sexual orientation of persons.

As expressed by one of the intervenors in this process "during the last 10 years, recognition of sexual orientation as an inadmissible reason for discrimination has become a habitual norm," and "courts and human rights institutions all over the world ... have sustained that the dispositions on equality of protection that prohibit discrimination based on sex intrinsically prohibit them as well based on sexual orientation."

Specifically, distinct pronouncements have been aimed at identifying the cases in which the difference in treatment between heterosexual and homosexual couples can be considered a form of discrimination based on sexual orientation. To that effect it seems pertinent to cite two pronouncements of the U.N. Human Rights Committee, the organ responsible for interpreting the International Covenant on Civil and Political Rights (ICCPR), in which it was stated that, in relation to Article 26 of the Covenant,[12] the prohibition on discrimination based on sex includes the category of "sexual orientation," which thus constitutes a suspect criteria of differentiation. Additionally, while according to the consistent jurisprudence of the Committee not every distinction constitutes illicit discrimination if based on reasonable and objective criteria, where there is no argument demonstrating that a distinction affecting same-sex couples is reasonable and objective...., nor any proof revealing the existence of factors justifying that distinction, it must be considered contrary to Article 26 of the Covenant.

In Colombia, constitutional jurisprudence on this topic has developed along the following lines: (i) in accordance with the Constitution, all forms of

12. Article 26 of the ICCPR reads: "All persons are equal before the law and are entitled without any discrimination to the equal protection of the law. In this respect, the law shall prohibit any discrimination and guarantee to all persons equal and effective protection against discrimination on any ground such as race, colour, sex, language, religion, political or other opinion, national or social origin, property, birth or other status."

discrimination based on sexual orientation are prohibited; (ii) there exist differences between heterosexual and homosexual couples, and thus there is no constitutional imperative for equal treatment between them; (iii) it corresponds to the legislator to define the measures necessary to attend to the requirements for protection of distinct social groups and to advance gradually in the protection of those found in a situation of marginalization, and (iv) all differences in treatment between people or groups ... are only constitutionally admissible if they obey a principle of sufficient reason....

[O]ne sees that this law, by regulating the marital union in fact, establishes a joint property regime for heterosexual couples, but it does not do the same for homosexual couples. In principle, one can say that the way in which property protection is given to those who have decided to become a couple as a permanent and singular plan of life is within the legislative sphere of configuration, because there is no single constitutional formula on that issue and the required protection may be obtained through distinct routes. However, that legislative sphere of configuration is limited by the Constitution and the fundamental rights of persons. To the Court, the absence of protection for the joint property of homosexual couples harms the dignity of the human person, is contrary to the right of free development of personality, and is a form of discrimination prohibited by the Constitution.

With respect to the dignity of persons and the free development of personality, the Court emphasizes the importance that the legal recognition of the economic relationships that by nature exist between those who opt to live as a couple has for ... the realization of a common plan of life in conditions of equality.

This Court has expressed that human dignity is a superior value and a foundational principle of the social state of law, according to which all people must be treated in accordance with their humanity....

In constitutional jurisprudence, human dignity has been treated as an expression of individual autonomy, as an expression of certain material conditions of existence, or as an expression of the intangibility of physical and moral integrity. In that context, the constitutional provision establishing that the state is based on respect for human dignity imposes on authorities the duty to adopt indispensable measures of protection to safeguard the legal goods that define man as a person, including liberty, autonomy, physical and moral integrity, the exclusion of degrading treatment, personal and family intimacy, and certain material conditions of existence.

In the topic currently being studied by the Court, the manifestations of dignity in the sphere of personal autonomy have particular relevance.... In accordance with the Constitution, personal autonomy is limited by the rights of others and by the legal order. By that the Court has understood that the right to free development of personality consecrates a general protection in the Constitution for self-determination under which people can follow their own rules and develop their own plans of life whenever they do not affect the rights of third-parties or the legal order....

As a general matter ... human dignity as a foundational principle of the state is the essential prerequisite to the consecration and effectiveness of the system of rights and guarantees contemplated in the constitution and therefore it has an absolute value that cannot be limited under any circumstance.

Thus, while it is true that the Constitution imposes as a limit to the free development of personality the rights of others and of the legal order, this limit cannot be carried to such an extreme that it makes the person into an instrument for the benefit of the general interest in ways that affect his dignity.

Finally, it is worth saying that . . . the principle of human dignity includes not only a constitutional mandate including the negative duty of non-interference, but also the positive duty of protection and maintenance of the conditions needed for a dignified life.

Within the scope of the problem that the Court must resolve, it is clear that the lack of legal recognition of the reality of homosexual couples is an affront to their dignity because it harms their autonomy and capacity for self-determination by preventing their decision to share a common plan of life from producing legal effects, which means that . . . they remain in an unprotected situation. . . . There is no reason justifying the submission of homosexual couples to a regime that is incompatible with a vital option which they have chosen in the exercise of their right to free development of personality. . . .

[T]he absence of a legal regime that, in the sphere of property rights, specifically applies to homosexual couples implies that those couples must be governed by ordinary civil law, which limits their autonomy to regulate the consequences of their decision to live as a couple . . . , with potentially harmful consequences in the event that they end their relationship. . . . Put another way, the legislative decision not to include same-sex couples in the property regime created for marital unions in fact is an unjustified restriction on the autonomy of the members of those couples and can have harmful effects, not only because it hinders the realization of their common project of life, but also because it does not offer an adequate response to the situations of conflict that can present themselves when for whatever reason the relationship ends. . . .

The same considerations establishing that there is a deficit of protection for the property regime of same-sex couples brings us to the conclusion that [the law], since it applies exclusively to heterosexual couples and excludes homosexual couples, is discriminatory. Notwithstanding the objective differences that exist between the two types of couples, and the specific considerations that led the legislator in 1990 to establish this regime of protection because of the need to protect women and families, it is no less certain that . . . same-sex couples present analogous needs for protection and there are no objective reasons justifying differential treatment. . . .

Based on the foregoing criteria and without ignoring the sphere of configuration of the legislator . . . , the Court finds that it is contrary to the Constitution to maintain a legal regime of protection exclusively for heterosexual couples and thus it will declare [the law] constitutional on the understanding that the regime of protection found there also applies to homosexual couples.

This is to say that same-sex couples complying with the conditions stated in the law for marital unions in fact, a community of life that is permanent and singular and which has been maintained for a period of at least two years, may accede to that regime of protection. . . .

Note on the Extension of C-075 and the Drive for Same-Sex Marriage: Over the next few years, the Court extended the protection due to same-sex couples constituting a "material union in fact" to many other spheres. In **Decision C-811 of 2007 (per Justice Marco Gerardo Monroy Cabra)**, the Court mandated health coverage for same-sex couples on the same terms as for heterosexual couples, and in **Decision C-336 of 2008 (per Justice Clara Inés Vargas Hernández)**, the Court did the same with respect to retirement pensions. In **Decision C-029 of 2009 (per Justice Rodrigo Escobar Gil)**, the Court granted same-sex couples the protection established by law regarding all of the following benefits given to heterosexual couples: (i) state protection in the case of heinous crimes, (ii) social security benefits for members of the police and armed forces, (iii) state subsidies for low-income families, (iv) housing subsidies, (v) access to property in rural areas, (vi) insurance compensation coverage in case of accidents, (vii) impediments in access to public positions, (viii) civil liability for alimony, (ix) migration regulations, and (x) criminal laws relating to spouses.

After these and other decisions had been issued, the economic and legal regime for same-sex couples forming a marital union in fact looked quite similar to the regime for opposite-sex couples. But same-sex couples still had no option to enter into a formal marriage contract. The legal issues dealing with same-sex marriage were both legally and politically more difficult than those dealing with unions in fact. Textually, Article 42 of the Constitution seemed to contemplate marriage as being limited to between "a man and a woman." Politically, the religious connotations of marriage in Colombia, a historically conservative Catholic country, made the issue very controversial.

In 2011, however, a group of citizens (some affiliated with progressive civil society groups) challenged the marriage regime found in the Civil Code and in other legal provisions. A Court that was unanimous on the core issue responded with a significant but limited ruling. It held that same-sex couples constituted a family under the Constitution and thus required protection of their relationship that went beyond the marital union in fact. The Court held in particular that same-sex couples had to be offered the option of a formal and contractual relationship more analogous to marriage. However, they upheld the Civil Code provision at issue and refused to order same-sex marriage directly. Instead, they gave Congress two years to pass legislation that would resolve this "deficit of protection."

Decision C-577 of 2011 (per Justice Gabriel Eduardo Mendoza Martelo)

[A series of individuals challenged a provision of the Civil Code that defined marriage as a contract between "a man and a woman, entered into with the purpose, among others, of living together, procreation, and rendering mutual assistance." They also challenged other provisions in two different laws that defined a "family" as being created through "the free choice of a man and a woman." This language closely tracks that of Article 42 of the Constitution, which states in part that a family is formed "through the free decision of a man and woman to contract matrimony or through the responsible resolve" to form one. The Court began by considering whether same-sex couples constituted a family under the Constitution.]

[W]e will proceed to determine whether or not there is a relationship between the existence of homosexual couples and the family, given the diversity of family ties and the evident difference between family and marriage. . . .

Up until this moment, constitutional jurisprudence relative to the concept of a family has been based, essentially, on a literal interpretation of Article 42 [thus conceptualizing a family as "heterosexual and monogamous"].

In order to examine the solidity of this interpretation it is indispensable to contrast it with the diverse forms of family . . . , with the objective of establishing if there is some common denominator to all of them. The Court notes that when speaking of families made up of single mothers and their children, which can be created through scientific assistance, the status of that relationship as a protected family is not based on the existence of a couple and thus, heterosexuality does not seem to be indispensable in the understanding of a family. . . . [The Court also mentioned other situations, such as aunts or uncles raising the children of their siblings, to support this point.]

Any argument to the contrary would imply a contradiction between Article 5 of the Constitution which, in general terms and without any distinctions, places the state in charge of protecting "the family as the basic institution of society," and Article 42 which, according to the dominant interpretation of the Court, introduces discrimination between different types of families by proclaiming that, despite their diverse forms, only the heterosexual one is the object of protection and recognition, as opposed to others which lack that special characteristic.

This contradiction between the texts, derived from the interpretation that has been the majority one in this Court, is without doubt also a contradiction with reality, because one cannot forget that the family is a sociological institution that exists prior to the state, and the state thus does not constitute it but merely recognizes its existence and evolution. . . .

Heterosexuality is not, then, a predictable characteristic of all families, and neither are blood relations . . . , therefore something else must be the common denominator of the family institution in its diverse manifestations. . . .

[T]he Court considers that there are no arguments legally worthy of consideration to sustain that between members of a homosexual couple one need not recognize the affection, respect, and solidarity that inspires their common, permanent plan of life, or that those personal conditions only deserve protection when they are professed between heterosexuals but not same-sex couples.

Thus, the protection of homosexual couples cannot remain limited to the property aspects of their permanent union, because there is an affective and emotional component that drives them to live together and that is translated into solidarity, manifestations of affection, and mutual aid and assistance; personal components that one also finds in heterosexual unions or any other union that, even though it is not characterized by heterosexuality, constitutes a family.

Ties of affection are present in the families integrated by aunts and uncles with the nephews under their care, grandparents responsible for their grandchildren, and the mother or father who is the head of a household with children who may or may not be his or hers biologically; therefore it is those bonds that constitute the common denominator of all types of families[. S]ince those bonds exist between members of homosexual couples that live together in a permanent manner, it must be concluded that [same-sex] couples also form a family that, like the others, is a basic institution and fundamental nucleus of society and deserves protection from society and the state. . . .

Cohabitation sustained by affection and emotional bonds generates a community of life that is manifested in a common search for means of subsistence, in mutual company or moral support, and also in the realization of a shared project for the benefit of each one of the members of the family and for the achievement of their happiness, all of which is experienced by the members of a same-sex union and which in any form constitutes a family, however it might be constituted. . . .

[W]e must change the interpretation [of Article 42] that has predominated in the Court [up until now] and clarify that, under Article 42 . . . , it is now improper to say that legal links are only constituted by marriage between heterosexuals, and natural links are only constituted by the marital union in fact of two people of distinct sex. . . .

[The Court then turned to the question of whether the Constitution required recognition of same-sex marriage entered into by contract, as distinct from marital unions in fact.]

[M]arriage is a form of constituting a heterosexual family where the couple, integrated by a man and a woman, manifest their consent and celebrate it, while the free and responsible will to form a family is the source of other type of families like the marital union in fact or that type composed by homosexual couples. . . .

This implies that, notwithstanding the variety of family forms, through a decision of the Constituent Assembly there exists an express recognition of the heterosexual family . . . based on the marital link. . . . [The Court cites Article 42 and other parts of the Constitution where marriage is mentioned in a heterosexual or religious context.]

Marriage as a way to constitute a family appears to be unequivocally linked to the heterosexual couple and this decision . . . corresponds to language that the Constituent Assembly included in the Constitution in such a clear and profuse way . . . that we can only say that in this case "the real and clear will of the Constituent Assembly is the text of the Constitution." . . .

Of course, in 1991 the question had not evolved in Colombia to the point that the need to expressly recognize the acceptance of homosexual movements . . . was so visible and urgent; . . . thus by giving express treatment to [heterosexual] marriage . . . , it expressed the predominant viewpoint of society at the time. . . .

[The existing jurisprudence of the Court on same-sex couples] has operated in the property-rights sphere, in which the Court has previously recognized a deficit of protection . . . and where above all, action was taken in the legal regime . . . of the marital union in fact in order to extend its provisions dealing with social benefits and duties so that they would also include [same-sex] couples. . . .

For some of the intervenors these protective measures . . . are sufficient to guarantee the recognition and protection of homosexual couples, who thus can aspire to nothing more. However, the consideration of these unions as a family . . . prohibits us from circumscribing constitutional protection to a few measures that, while important, have a clear economic content, and which far from exhaust the requirements of a stable and formalized union called a family, above all in the affective and emotional spheres which . . . are the common denominators of all families. . . .

[E]ven though the marital union in fact is the closest figure to marriage, it does not overcome the deficit of protection to which homosexual couples are submitted because it does not give rise to a legal bond, does not permit the elevation of moral commitments existing between the members of a couple to a legal imperative, and it does not offer the possibility of tying the non-compliance with those promises to the dissolution of the marriage or the maintenance of some obligations even after it has been terminated.

Beyond this, [the material union in fact] does not constitute a conjugal society from its initiation . . . , it does not create a civil status because the civil status of "permanent companion" does not exist, and it does not offer complete coverage, because the Court has not extended to permanent companions all of the aspects making up the framework for the protection of marriage. . . .

The marital union in fact, which same-sex couples can enter, is an available but insufficient alternative . . . , because its existence as the only way for those couples to create a family implies a deficit of protection . . . , and also ignores the right to free development of personality and thus of autonomy and self-determination.

In effect, heterosexual couples that want to start a family have at their disposal two routes: marriage and the marital union in fact, and they can make a free decision to opt for either route depending on whether they wish to submit themselves to the regulations of marriage or escape from them, while if we insist that the union in fact is the only alternative for homosexuals, same-sex couples will only be able to choose that option. . . .

This means that in order to guarantee that the free development of personality of homosexuals is respected and to overcome the deficit of protection to which they are subjected in the sphere of family law, the legal order must have a contractual institution, distinct from the union in fact, that permits them to choose between . . . a higher grade of formalization and protection and . . . the union in fact that is already recognized. . . .

It is also important to note that the existence of a contractual mechanism to formalize the commitment makes it possible to publicize the link that unites a same-sex couple, which gives the relationship legitimacy in society . . . and advances the dignity of homosexual persons, who are no longer forced to hide their relationship or the affection that led them to form a family. . . .

[T]he decision about the option taken to guarantee the possibility of choice in the case of homosexual couples who decide to form a family and its concrete development does not belong to the Constitutional Court, but to the Congress of the Republic, among other reasons, because aside from being the democratic forum par excellence . . . , the social transcendence [of the family] demands its protection through measures adopted by the representative organ, limited by rights that are inherent to the family or its individual members. . . .

The legislator will have the power, then, to determine the way in which same-sex couples may formalize and solemnize their legal bond, and the Court understands that the representative organ has the freedom to assign the label it wishes to that bond, as well as defining its scope, under the understanding that, more than the name, what is important are the specific ways in which the rights and obligations of the relationship are identified and the manner in which it can be formalized and perfected.

In a panorama in which homosexuality has become more visible and more accepted, arguments should be heard not only before the Constitutional Court, but additionally and above all before the Congress of the Republic, where, according to the dynamics of politics, minorities can ally themselves with other parties and movements to configure . . . a majority coalition capable of advancing projects in which they have an interest. . . .

As the Magistrates Eduardo Cifuentes Muñoz and Vladimiro Naranjo Mesa said in a concurrence to Decision C-098 of 1996, "we have opened a space for controversy and arguments about justice, which can be transmitted in the public forum of democracy" without waiting "for the simple expedient of a analogical interpretation to substitute what should be the fruit of a determined and courageous political fight." . . .

Given that . . . same-sex couples should have the possibility of acceding to the celebration of a contract that permits them to legally formalize and solemnize their link as a means to constitute a family with greater commitments than those stemming from a union in fact, and given that the regulation of this topic corresponds to the legislator, . . . this Court considers it pertinent to exhort the Congress to take up the analysis of this question and to produce a law that regulates that contractual institution . . . in a systematic and organized way.

The Chamber notes that, as always, this exhortation is formulated with total respect for the powers corresponding to the Congress; however, in order to promote collaboration between the Court and the representative body . . . and to guarantee attention to the rights of those involved where the deficit of protection affecting same-sex couples is evident and demands an urgent institutional response, the Court considers it indispensable to fix a time limit within which the Congress should issue the regulation that is respectfully requested.

> The duration of time for which one should wait for the representative body . . . depends on the importance of the material, and in this case the Court observes that the absence of any provision has the undesirable effect of prolonging an unprotected state; but the Court also acknowledges that the Congress requires a sufficient lapse of time to debate a controversial topic and to give it the shape that it considers pertinent; therefore the weighing of the two variables permits us to conclude that two legislative sessions constitutes adequate time to discuss and resolve the issue. . . .
>
> [I]f on June 20, 2013 the corresponding legislation has not been issued, same-sex couples may go before a competent notary or judge to formalize and solemnize the contractual link that will permit them to constitute a family. . . .
>
> [The Court thus declared the reference to "a man and a woman" in the Civil Code to be constitutional, held that it could not reach the challenges to the other laws defining a family because they merely reproduced the language of Article 42, and "exhorted the Congress to legislate, before June 20, 2013 and in a systematic and organized way, on the rights of same-sex couples with the goal of eliminating the deficit of protection that . . . affects those couples." If Congress had not acted by that date, same-sex couples would be able to go before a notary or judge to "formalize and solemnize their contractual bond."]
>
> [Four justices wrote a concurring opinion agreeing with the Court's ruling but writing separately to emphasize that its analysis was reductionist in referring exclusively to "homosexual" and "heterosexual" couples without taking into account other individuals and situations such as intersexuals and transsexuals. One justice, María Victoria Calle Correa, issued a partial dissent and argued that the Court should have gone further in defining and explaining the legal rules that would be applied by judges and notaries in the event that Congress did not act within the two years given by the Court.]

Note on the Political and Legal Impact of the "Dialogical Remedy" in C-577: The Court's order was a form of dialogical order—the Court identified a legal problem and asked Congress to resolve it with a constitutionally-acceptable solution.[13] However, Congress did not act on the invitation within the time period set by the Court. In response to C-577, several pieces of legislation were introduced in Congress. However, by June 20, 2013, it had not passed a law legalizing same-sex marriage. Nor had it passed a law creating any other type of formal union for same-sex couples. The political environment in which this legislation was debated was difficult, as there was significant opposition from conservative and religious forces, and same-sex marriage remained unpopular from the standpoint of public opinion.

Because Congress did not legislate within the Court's stated two-year time frame, on June 20, 2013, the provision of C-577 allowing parties to go directly to judges and notaries to "formalize and solemnize their contractual bond" went into effect. But the resulting

13. *See, e.g.*, Anne Meuwese & Marnix Snel, *Constitutional Dialogue: An Overview*, 9 UTRECHT L. REV. 123 (2013). For another example of a similar remedy from South Africa, see *Fourie*, *supra* note 8.

regime had a significant degree of uncertainty built into it. Some judges and notaries granted civil marriage licenses to same-sex couples. Other judges and notaries refused and attempted to grant other types of contractual relationships that were not labeled as a marriage. Furthermore, some institutions of state, especially the National Inspector General's office, opposed same-sex marriage and took action to block local judges and notaries from granting it.

In response to this legal uncertainty, a number of *tutelas* percolated through the legal system. In 2016, the Court sought to develop a unified jurisprudence by accumulating several claims and adjudicating them in plenary session. That decision is reproduced here. In a six-to-three decision, the Court held that courts and notaries had an obligation to act even in the absence of a specific legislative framework, in light of Decision C-577 of 2011. It further held that same-sex couples had a fundamental right to receive a civil marriage license. Finally, the Court extended the effects of its decision to all similarly-situated couples. Thus, the Constitutional Court legalized same-sex marriage throughout Colombia.

Decision SU-214 of 2016 (per Justice Alberto Rojas Ríos)

[This case involved the accumulation of several claims: Same-sex couples from around the country sought marriage licenses from notaries and judges. In some of the accumulated cases, the notaries and judges declined to provide these licenses; in others, officials from the National Inspector General's Office (which opposed same-sex marriage) sought to nullify licenses that had been provided. In one of the claims, a couple from Cali sought a marriage license from that city's Fourth Notary's Office on June 20, 2013, the very day on which the period for Congress to act set out in Decision C-577 of 2011 expired. The notary declined to issue the license, arguing that it lacked the power to grant it because Congress has not legislated. The Office also argued that the Constitutional Court in Decision C-577 had spoken of a "contractual bond between partners of the same sex," not a marriage contract as such. After surveying the history of its own jurisprudence on sexual orientation rights and comparative practice from a number of jurisdictions, the Court began by describing the relevant constitutional principles related to the case.]

From the principle of human dignity one derives the full autonomy of the individual to choose the person with whom he or she wants to sustain a permanent marital bond, whether natural or solemn, for the purposes of mutual company, support, and intimate association.... This free and autonomous election forms part of the dignity of each person individually considered and is intrinsic to the most intimate and relevant aspects of the ethos of self-determination in three concrete spheres recognized by constitutional jurisprudence: "live as you choose," "live well," and "live without humiliation."

In that sense, the state cannot tolerate the existence of two legal classes of solemn unions for the heterosexual and homosexual communities, since that would signify differential treatment based on sexual orientation that would undermine the dignity of the human person. For this Court, where there is a will to join together in a permanent manner to form a family, there exists a bond that deserves equality of rights and the protection of the state.

Liberty does not consist in being submitted to rules, but in setting one's own bases of action, which we commit to in our lives in order to be truly free.

The constitutional liberty to unite oneself to someone else, whether through a natural legal link or solemnly through the celebration of marriage, is a right that is based on the reasoning of man, whose nature . . . includes the need to relate him- or herself to another person in order to share existence and develop a common plan of life. The permanent bond of this freely-chosen option is based on the most vital and elemental ties and sentiments of the human condition. This is true to such an extent that in many cases its effects transcend life itself, because even after death, people continue to be characterized and determined based on the bond called "marriage" by diverse cultures.

The autonomy that a human being possesses to contract marriage, without distinctions based on social class, ethnicity, race, or sexual orientation, is a predicate of human dignity. Thus, constitutionally the only admissible limitations are those related to consanguinity, age, absence of free consent, or the existence of another marital bond. . . .

In comparative law, for example, the Supreme Court of the United States, in *Loving* v. *Virginia* (1967),[14] invalidated prohibitions on interracial relationships, stating that the celebration of marriage is "one of the vital personal rights essential to the orderly pursuit of happiness by free men." And more recently, in a Decision of June 26, 2015, in the case *Obergefell* v. *Hodges* (2015), the Supreme Court considered that "the right to personal choice regarding marriage is inherent in the concept of individual autonomy."[15] In addition: "Choices about marriage shape an individual's destiny."

The right of both heterosexual and same-sex couples to celebrate a formal marital union, whose principle expression is constituted by civil marriage, is also a manifestation of the fundamental right to equality of treatment. . . .

Constitutional jurisprudence has designed a specific methodology to address cases related to the supposed infraction of the principle and fundamental right to equality: the integrated test of equality. . . . This test starts with an examination of the legal regime and the subjects in comparison, with the object of determining if there is reason to suggest a problem of differential treatment for subjects that have common elements which, in principle, would require equal treatment on the part of the legislator. Next the Court establishes whether in the factual and legal planes there is unequal treatment between equals or equal treatment between unequals. Finally, the Court determines the intensity of the test of equality given the nature of the affected constitutional rights, in order to realize a proportionality test with its distinct stages—adequacy, suitability, and proportionality in a strict sense. . . .

14. 388 U.S. 1 (1967).

15. 135 S. Ct. 2071 (2015).

Because of the diverse realms in which state action can occur, it has been useful to include in the study of equality by the constitutional judge, hermeneutic tools that make it possible to carry out scrutiny with different levels of intensity.

As a general rule, this Court applies a *weak or flexible* control, in which the test is limited to determining whether the measure adopted by the legislator is potentially adequate or suitable to achieve an end that is not prohibited by the Constitution. Intermediate scrutiny is applied in situations in which the state has adopted measures of positive differentiation (affirmative action). In this analysis, the examination consists in determining whether the sacrifice by part of the population is proportional to the expected benefit from the measure for the group that it intends to promote. Finally, *strict scrutiny* is carried out when the legislator bases discriminatory treatment on suspect classes, like race, sexual orientation, or political affiliation. In that case, the legislator must pursue an overriding goal, and the measure must be the only adequate means to achieve it.

In the concrete case, establishing differential treatment between heterosexual and same-sex couples, in the sense that the first can form a family through a marital union in fact or civil marriage, while the second can do so only through [a marital union in fact], affects a suspect class (based on sexual orientation), and the state cannot overcome strict scrutiny with its measure since it does not pursue any constitutionally admissible goal. . . .

There exists no constitutionally admissible reason for the state to deny this right to some people based on their sexual orientation, because that would work against the guarantees of human dignity, liberty, and equality that irradiate the legal order. . . . To affirm the contrary would be to negate the structural changes that occurred with the entry into force of the Constitution of 1991.

In light of this conception, the Constitution of Colombia, in view of the principles of human dignity, liberty, and equality, is blind to race, color, ethnic origin, religion, sexual orientation, social status or any other quality that could give rise to discrimination or differential treatment between people.

Therefore, the principles of human dignity, individual liberty, and equality mean that all human beings may contract civil marriage in accordance with their sexual orientation.

Article 42 of the Constitution expressly states that marriage stems from the bond between a man and a woman. While this text gives a right to heterosexual persons, it does not follow that there is any prohibition on others exercising that right under equal conditions. To insist that men and women may marry each other does not mean that the Constitution excludes the possibility that this bond might be celebrated between women or between men as well. . . . In light of this, this [Court] finds that the Constitution does not exclude the possibility of same-sex marriage in any of its parts. . . .

[T]o interpret the constitution so that same-sex partners could carry out a solemn contract distinct from civil marriage would lead, among other things, to the following results: (i) they would not formally constitute a family, (ii) there would be no duties of support and mutual assistance, (iii) the contracting parties would not modify their civil status, (iv) a conjugal society would not be created, (v) the contracting parties would not enter into their respective regime of succession, (vi) it would be impossible to sign prenuptial agreements, (vii) there would be no clarity about the causes of termination of the bond between the contracting parties, (viii) upon arriving to establish their residence in other countries, the respective authorities would not give them the legal protection that married parties enjoy . . . and (ix) in the area of taxation they could not invoke certain benefits for having a spouse or permanent companion. In conclusion, no unnamed or atypical solemn contract, celebrated between same-sex partners, could produce the same effects on persons and property as civil marriage. . . .

[Last, the Court considered the question of the scope of the order to be given in this case involving several accumulated *tutelas*, and decided that the effects of judgment should be extended to all similarly-situated same-sex couples throughout the country rather than only protecting those who had brought suit.]

The effects of *tutela* judgments are *inter partes* [among the parties], as a general rule. However, in some cases, given the existence of an objective universe of people found in the same situation as the petitioners, the Court has modulated its decision with the goal of ensuring the exercise of the right to equality.

There exist very special circumstances in which a *tutela* claim is not limited to being a subsidiary judicial action aimed at avoiding the harm or threat of harm to fundamental rights of parties to the process. . . . [T]he *tutela* judge can issue a judgment . . . with *inter pares* [among equals] effects with the goal of protecting . . . the fundamental rights of those who have not come directly before the Court but require equal protection. . . .

Based on Decision C-577 of 2011 and the persistent deficit of constitutional protection in the exercise of fundamental rights by same-sex couples, there have been diverse interpretations of the ideal contractual bond to formalize and solemnize the relationships of same-sex couples. This lack of legal definition in the constitution of the family has meant that some same-sex couples have been unable to formalize and solemnize their contractual bond. . . .

With the goal of (i) overcoming the deficit of protection recognized in Decision C-577 of 2011 in relation to same-sex couples in Colombia; (ii) guaranteeing the full validity of the Constitution, and more concretely the fundamental right to form a marital bond . . . ; and (iii) protecting the principle of legal security in relation to the civil status of persons, the Court will extend the effects of the present unification decision to all similar cases, in other words, to all same-sex couples that, since June 20, 2013, (i) have gone before judges or notaries in the country and have had their request for marriage denied because of their sexual orientation; (ii) have celebrated a contract to formalize and solemnize their bond, without the title or legal effects of civil marriage; (iii) have celebrated a civil marriage, but the National Marriage Registry had refused to inscribe it and (iv) from this point forward, will seek to formalize and solemnize their bond through civil marriage. . . .

Note on Other Cases Related to Sexual Orientation and Identity: Same-sex marriage has been the most prominent issue in this area for the past several years. However, it has not been the only controversial issue. Adoption by same-sex couples has also been a politically-salient recent topic. Existing law appeared not to contemplate adoption by same-sex couples, but only other categories such as individuals, heterosexual spouses, and heterosexual unions in fact. In 2015, the Court issued two decisions on this topic. The first, **Decision C-071 of 2015 (per Justice Jorge Iván Palacio Palacio)** was relatively narrow in scope—it held the relevant norms conditionally constitutional on the understanding that adoption by both members of a same-sex couple would be allowed if the adoptee was the biological child of one member of the couple. In the second, **Decision C-683 of 2015 (per Justice Jorge Iván Palacio Palacio)**, the Court issued a broader decision and held these same norms conditionally constitutional only "with the understanding that, by virtue of the superior interest of the minor, same-sex couples forming a family should also be included within their sphere of application." In this latter decision, the Court called for more educational measures so that society would be accepting of same-sex couples with adopted children, and declined to issue a decision like the one in C-577 of 2011 where it would give Congress time to fill a "deficit of protection."[16] Instead, it ordered direct relief.

Finally, it is worth noting that the Court has issued a number of decisions dealing with other aspects of sexual identity. One example is the Court's jurisprudence on intersex minors, included in Section D of the last chapter. Additionally, the Court has issued several decisions protecting the rights of transsexuals. These include decisions giving transsexuals the right to have their sex, name, and other information changed in official registries and documents;[17] requiring health insurers to cover sex-change procedures;[18] and holding that transsexual individuals should be treated in accordance with their stated gender identity. In **Decision T-099 of 2015 (per Justice Gloria Stella Ortiz Delgado)**, for example, the Court held that state authorities could not demand that transgender women either undertake military service or pay a fine, because those norms, applicable to men, could not be applied to a transgender woman.

B. Equality, Affirmative Action, and Gender Quotas

Decision C-371 of 2000 (per Justice Carlos Gaviria Díaz)

[In a decision that was unanimous on its key points, the Constitutional Court upheld most of the so-called "gender quota law." The draft statutory law under examination by the Court established measures to increase women's participation in public sector

16. The Court also presented statistical evidence suggesting a significant mismatch between the number of children in need of adoption and the existing supply of individuals and couples willing to adopt.

17. *See, e.g.*, Decision T-063 of 2015 (per Justice María Victoria Calle Correa) (right to change of sex in civil registry and documents such as identity card and passport); Decision T-086 of 2014 (per Jorge Ignacio Pretelt Chaljub) (right to name change).

18. *See, e.g.*, Decision T-552 of 2013 (per Justice María Victoria Calle Correa).

decision-making. Its key article established that prospectively, at least 30 percent of officials in "maximum" and "other decision-making levels" in the public sector should be made up of women.]

[The Court first noted that the law aimed at] achieving greater women's representation in the state's highest decision-making levels, as well as greater participation in the private sector and other arenas of civil society.

It is evident that there is something implicit in the goal set by the legislators for the draft law, i.e. women are not duly represented in the above mentioned sectors.

Is this the real situation? If so, are there cultural, economic, social or academic factors that may justify such a situation? Can the state grant preferential treatment to women in order to remedy it? . . .

[T]he mechanisms established in the statutory law under study constitute, in general terms, affirmative action. This term refers to policies or measures aimed at favoring specific people or groups, whether to eliminate or reduce social, cultural, or economic inequalities affecting them or to achieve greater inclusion for members of underprivileged groups, usually those subject to discrimination.

[These actions] differ from [others] in two ways: 1) Because they take into account aspects such as sex or race that are usually deemed to be suspicious or potentially forbidden criteria . . . , and 2) because inverse discrimination occurs in situations where there is a scarcity of desirable goods, as is usually the case with access to jobs or universities, which can lead people to the conclusion that benefits granted to certain people result in damage to others. . . .

[The Court posed the question] of whether in light of our constitutional system it is possible to adopt inverse discrimination measures. Or . . . whether the legislator may grant preferential treatment as regards the distribution of goods, rights or obligations based on the criterion of the recipients' sex. The answer, undoubtedly, must be drawn from Article 13 of the Constitution.

The first clause of this constitutional article enshrines the general principle that "all persons are born free and equal before the law and are entitled to equal protection and treatment by the authorities, and to enjoy the same rights, freedoms, and opportunities without discrimination on the basis of gender, race, national or family origin, language, religion, political opinion, or philosophy."

These criteria enshrined in the Constitution . . . allude to categories deemed suspicious, as their use has been historically associated with behaviors tending to undervalue and disadvantage certain people or groups such as women, blacks, homosexuals, and indigenous peoples, among others.

Ultimately, suspicious criteria are categories that "(i) are based on people's permanent features that they cannot change through their own will without risking their identity; (ii) have been traditionally subjected to patterns of cultural appraisal that tend to belittle them, and (iii) do not comprise, per se, criteria enabling a rational and fair distribution of goods, rights or social obligations."

[W]hen such characteristics or factors are invoked in order to establish differences regarding treatment, an infringement on the right to equality is assumed.

However, this does not mean that a discriminatory action always occurs when one of these criteria has been utilized, as clause 2 of Article 13 establishes that "the state shall promote the conditions so that equality may be real and effective and shall adopt measures in favor of groups which are discriminated against or marginalized."

Affirmative action is, therefore, clearly authorized by the Constitution and, consequently, authorities may invoke race, sex or any other suspicious category not to exclude certain people or groups or to perpetuate inequalities, but rather to reduce the harmful effects of social behaviors that have placed this same people or groups in unfavorable conditions.

In synthesis, not all utilization of forbidden criteria is discriminatory, because as this Court has affirmed, "the State cannot effectively try to improve the situation of a marginalized group without supplying regulations that mention the factor that provoked that segregation. Thus, if the law seeks to improve the situation of women . . . , or indigenous groups . . . , it is obvious that it must resort to ethnic or sex-based classifications."

But in the end, *inverse discrimination* does not utilize the same criterion that serves as a basis for *unjust discrimination*. To illustrate this affirmation with an example, while in the discrimination that the Constitution prohibits, X is given a distinct treatment by the simple fact of being a woman or being black; in the cases of inverse discrimination, preferential treatment is given based on the fact that X is a person who has been (unjustly) discriminated against for being a woman or for being black. . . .

Now, having accepted that the constitution authorizes measures of inverse discrimination, it must be clarified that: 1) "the validity of these measures depends on the real presence of discrimination. [The subjective opinion of] a woman, for example, is not enough to establish the constitutionality of measures allegedly in favor of women; [actual] conduct or practices must [demonstrate discrimination]." 2) Not all inverse discrimination measures are constitutional, as one of the claimants appears to suggest. Each case should be examined to see if the discriminatory treatment established is reasonable and fair. 3) Affirmative action should be temporary; once "real and effective equality" had been achieved, it would no longer be necessary.

A frequent argument against affirmative action . . . is that in an equalitarian world, only the conditions at the starting point should be equalized. In other words, if the state adopts positive measures in favor of certain groups in order to guarantee them a *real and effective* equality of opportunity, these must target the starting point rather than the ending point.

It could thus be argued . . . that if the legislator aspires for women to occupy posts at the highest levels, the important and in principle only permissible mechanism is to develop policies stimulating access of women to superior education and removing obstacles clashing with that objective. And once substantial equality has been achieved at the starting point, the particular merit of each person will determine the quantitative composition at the end point. This is somewhat similar to the Darwinian thesis of the survival of the fittest or the free play of the laws of the market in the economic sphere, which cannot and should not—from those perspectives—be corrected through artificial means at risk of gravely distorting the natural or social spheres.

Apart from whatever might be said about the ethical and political consequences of Darwinism or economic liberalism, that argument overlooks an unavoidable factor, which can be verified by empirical observation and statistically corroborated: the percentage of the population trained to carry out high political charges is . . . equally distributed between men and women, and indeed the balance is tipping over time more in favor of the latter.

If despite the existence today of equality at the point of departure, the situation at the point of arrival continues to be inequitable, this is because merit is not determining (at least not completely) who will receive these high posts.

Conscious of that situation, the Constituent Assembly of 1991 established in the last subsection of Article 40 that "the authorities shall guarantee the adequate and effective participation of women in the decision-making ranks of the public administration," in evident harmony with subsection 2 of Article 13, which upon [calling for affirmative action measures] does not prejudge the stage at which those actions will be appropriate and thus legitimates and even obligates action by public authorities aimed at correcting any inequality derived from discriminatory factors expressly proscribed in that article.

Thus, if the goal is to guarantee a real and effective equality of opportunity, it is necessary to remove obstacles at the point of departure as well as at the point of arrival.

[The Court then examined the current state of gender equality in the Colombian public administration, finding that there was equality between women and men in entry level jobs, but not at the highest decision-making levels. In particular, the Court made the following findings:]

(a) That although there is a clear balance between women and men qualified to occupy posts at the highest decision-making levels, that balance is not reflected in the actual representation [of women] at those levels.
(b) That the scarce representation of women results from discrimination rather than from alleged natural inferiority or from cultural and academic training, is proved beyond any doubt by the fact that women occupying posts supposedly provided through merit throughout the [entire] administration outnumber men.
(c) That it is necessary to remove the obstacles preventing women's participation through measures aimed at two goals: an immediate goal of reducing the lack of participation, and a long-term goal of changing attitudes that are incompatible with the purposes established by an egalitarian and democratic Constitution like ours.

[The Court the analyzed the key provision providing a 30 percent quota for women in "maximum decision-making levels" and "other decision-making levels" within the state. For this purpose, it used the proportionality test:]

[T]he constitutional judge should determine (1) whether the measure pursues a valid end in light of the constitution, (2) whether the differential treatment is adequate to achieve that end, (3) whether the measure is "necessary" in the sense that there is no less onerous way, in terms of the sacrifice of other constitutional principles, to achieve the end, and (4) whether the differential treatment is "proportional in the strict sense," that is to say, whether it does not sacrifice values, principles, and rights (including equality) that have a greater weight than those which it is trying to achieve through the measure.

It is clear to this Court that the first goal of the analyzed measure is to increase, within a short time, the participation of women in directive and decision-making posts within the state, in such a way that little by little they achieve equitable representation. In addition, the quota tries to habituate officials to select women for these posts, or in other words . . . to correct a selection system that continues to work in detriment to the female population. These objectives, without doubt, are constitutional. . . .

In terms of the relationship between the means and proposed end, the Court has no doubt that setting quotas is an efficient measure because it ensures that at least 30 percent of women will be performing posts at the "maximum decision-making level" and at "other decision-making levels," thus increasing significantly their participation. The quota ensures, then, that the purpose of the law will be fulfilled. . . .

[An] argument against the efficacy of the quota could be expressed as follows: it aims exclusively at eliminating or reducing the underrepresentation of women, but does not attack the causes that provoke that low participation.

While the main objective of the legislator is precisely to reduce a lack of balance in representation and in this sense . . . the measure is effective, the Court considers that the measure under discussion will also counteract some of the underlying causes of the imbalance.

One of these causes is the long patriarchal tradition according to which the role of women principally corresponds to the private sphere. That tradition has meant that trained women, disposed to participate in public life, remain "invisible."

[S]etting a quota for women's participation in decision-making levels within the state not only forces appointing authorities to search for qualified women—who undoubtedly exist, and in large numbers—but also enables women to become "visible." Thus, the habit or custom of taking women into account and acknowledging them as fully proficient to occupy the highest ranks of public administration will gradually gain ground. . . .

In addition to this symbolic purpose, women's entrance into decision-making positions . . . points the way towards the proposal and design of other policies in favor of women as a whole. Hence, the measure benefits not only those women who are in high positions, but also others who, given their economic, social and educational situation, have no access to those spheres of power.

For all of these reasons, setting a quota is really effective at achieving the goal at issue. . . .

[Next, the Court considered whether other measures might have achieved the same goal in a less burdensome way, focusing on the possibility of measures aimed at education and training.]

[T]hat a man and a woman have the same qualifications because they have a similar education means that they have similar starting conditions, but that does not necessarily mean that they have the same opportunities to reach certain posts. For the Court it is a fact that women, even when they have a superior education to that of a man, must confront greater obstacles to be promoted, which are at their peak if one mentions the highest posts in the political hierarchy.

In synthesis, this Court understands that the stimulus of education for women ... is without doubt essential, but it alone does not guarantee ... that women, in a short period of time, will really reach the directive posts at the top of the public sector hierarchy, which is the objective sought by the legislator.

An illustration to this respect is that the percentage of women graduating from institutions of superior education is higher than that of men. However, in the workplace, and specifically in the posts at issue, their representation is significantly less. . . .

It is clear that in the analysis as to whether less onerous alternatives exist, one must inquire about alternatives that will be equally effective at achieving the proposed end, and it is worth insisting that the promotion of education, or simple measures to promote the "equality" of women, are important but not sufficient. . . .

There is no other measure that both complies with the Constitution and is as efficient as establishing quotas. . . .

Having shown that the measure is adequate and necessary, it must now be established whether unequal treatment harms rights and principles that may have a greater weight than those protected through that treatment. In following the line of discussion developed up to now, this Court considers that the best way to examine this issue is to go through the objections that are usually adduced with regard to quotas and that have been voiced by some of the parties interested in the matter.

First argument: The measure establishes an unreasonable difference in opportunities to access posts at the "highest decision-making level" and "other decision-making levels," which infringes men's right to equal treatment and work.

Upon examining this objection ... the Court poses the following question: does the diminishing of a privilege that one group has enjoyed thanks to the marginalization of another group imply a significant disadvantage for those who have held the privilege? To answer affirmatively would no doubt be a big concession against egalitarian reasoning. Just as the abolition of slavery cannot be conceived as a disservice for slave "owners", alleviating women's marginalization cannot be seen as a significant disadvantage for men. . . .

Second argument: Setting quotas ultimately results in discrimination against women. The quotas suggest that women are inferior or disabled because they cannot access posts at the highest levels through their own merit.

The Court does not share this objection, as it considers that measures based on affirmative action such as the one under study are adopted precisely because it is understood that women have the same capacity as men to carry out senior state positions. However, the Court acknowledges that state intervention is required to remove the obstacles that women have had to face throughout history. In other words, this mechanism aims at rectifying social behaviors that give rise to unequal conditions, and it is not a measure based on state paternalism that treats women as if they were "under age." . . .

Third argument: Establishing quotas goes against the principle of free appointment and dismissal from [certain] public posts. . . .

[Although] it is true that the measure imposes restrictions on the power to freely appoint and dismiss from a post, this limitation is reasonable and does not affect the essential core of the power. First of all, because the appointing authority has a wide range of choice, i.e., 51 percent of the population, and secondly, because the restriction has the constitutional purpose . . . to ensure women's equal participation in the exercise of power within a democratic state. . . .

Fourth argument: Setting quotas harms administrative effectiveness and efficiency because it imposes selection rules that disregard merit. Gender is placed above quality.

What has already been said rebuts this argument. Establishing a selection rule such as the one under study does not mean that the people selected need not comply with requirements established by the Constitution and the law to perform public functions or, in other words, that appointing authorities have to choose any woman just because she is one. On the contrary, the provision implies that when making appointments for positions at the "maximum decision-making level" and "other decision-making levels," the women selected must meet all the necessary requirements and merits to occupy the said positions; these requirements are of course also applicable to men.

[Based on this proportionality analysis, the Court upheld the quota system at issue. However, it did strike down a separate provision creating a 30 percent quota for women in the executive boards and candidate lists of political parties or movements. The Court held that upholding this provision "would imply state intervention in the internal organization of parties, which is forbidden by the Constitution." Thus, political parties were exempted from the quota requirement. In addition, the Court reduced the effectiveness of the quota system for some very high public positions that are selected by Congress from a list created by another political actor with three or more nominees on it. The Court held that the law could require that at least one woman be included in the three member lists or an equal number of men and women in larger lists, but that it could not place a legally binding duty on Congress or other selection body to choose an equal number of women and men for these positions.[19]]

Note on the Law of Gender Quotas in Colombia and Elsewhere: In comparative terms, gender quota laws exist across most of Latin America, including in the major countries of Argentina,

19. For example, Constitutional Court magistrates are selected by the Senate from a list of three names established by one of three institutions—the Council of State, Supreme Court, and the president. At least one of the nominees on each list must be female, but the law does not require the Congress to choose any particular percentage of women for the Court itself. In its history, the Court has had only three female justices.

Brazil, Mexico, and Peru, as well as in parts of Europe, Africa, and Asia. Research has generally found that these measures do help to increase the statistical representation of women in the public sphere.[20] However, this research has also highlighted a number of potential trouble spots, including the social perception of women, who are assumed to have been selected or elected due to a quota, and the relationship between gender quotas and informal norms such as clientelism and nepotism, which may ultimately blunt their transformative effect.[21]

The quota law has resulted in some improvement in the distribution of higher-ranking jobs in the public sector.[22] At the same time, given the Court's exclusion of political parties from the law's scope, analysts continued to find significant problems with gender equity in elected political posts. For example, a report found that in 2010, women made up only about 8 percent of members of the lower house of Congress and only about 10 percent of the Senate, with similar levels of representation in city and departmental assemblies.[23] In 2009, Congress passed a set of constitutional reforms addressing the political party system. Among other measures, these reforms established that parties must be founded on the principle of "gender equity." In reliance on the change, in 2011 Congress passed a new quota law requiring that the candidates on many electoral lists be at least 30 percent female.

C. Discrimination against the Disabled and the Positive Dimension of Equality

Decision T-595 of 2002 (per Justice Manuel José Cepeda Espinosa)

[A petitioner filed a *tutela* writ against "Transmilenio S.A.," Bogotá's urban mass transport company. He argued that "the company was infringing his rights to the freedom of movement (Article 24[24]), to equality and to accessibility because it disregarded the special protection that the state was required to grant to people with disabilities (Article 47[25]) by not making the buses that run on secondary routes of the system accessible to people using wheel chairs." Because of this, the petitioner was forced to go 15 blocks to a bigger Transmilenio station that did accommodate his disability. The

20. *See, e.g.*, Mark P. Jones, *Gender Quotas, Electoral Laws, and the Election of Women: Evidence from the Latin American Vanguard*, 42 COMP. POL. STUDS. 56, 68 (2009).

21. *See* Susan Franceschet et al., *Themes and Implications for Future Research on Gender Quotas*, *in* THE IMPACT OF GENDER QUOTAS 229 (Susan Franceschet et al. eds., 2012).

22. *See* United Nations Development Programme, Gender Equality and Women's Empowerment in Public Administration: Colombia Case Study 17-18 (2012), *available at* http://www.undp.org/content/dam/undp/library/Democratic%20Governance/Women-s%20Empowerment/ColombiaFinal%20-%20HiRes.pdf.

23. *See id.* at 8.

24. Article 24 states: "Any Colombian citizen, except for the limitations established by statute, has the right to move about freely across the national territory, to enter and exit the country, and to remain and reside in Colombia."

25. Article 47 states: "The state shall promote a policy of planning, rehabilitation, and social integration for those who are physically, emotionally, or psychologically handicapped and who shall receive the specialized attention that they need."

claimant requested that the *tutela* judge protect his rights by ordering Bogotá's city government to make the necessary Transmilenio secondary bus routes accessible to the handicapped.]

[Transmilenio representatives responded that "it is not possible to adapt the buses on secondary routes so they are accessible to people with disabilities using wheel chairs, as the corresponding costs would negatively affect the present economic and financial planning of the Company and . . . users' fares would have to be increased. Besides, buses for people with disabilities (wheelchair lift-equipped buses) require special lanes and public space conditions which do not exist in the city areas where secondary bus routes usually operate."]

[The lower court denied the *tutela*. However, the Constitutional Court revoked the ruling under review, and instead protected the claimant's rights. It ordered Transmilenio to prepare, within a two-year period, a plan aimed at guaranteeing full accessibility to the city's transport system for people using wheelchairs.]

The 1991 Constitution contemplates special protection for all of those marginalized and disadvantaged groups in society who, because of their situation, are limited in the exercise and effective enjoyment of their fundamental rights. This mandate is expressly consecrated in the first and second sections of Article 13 (right to equality) and Article 47 of the Constitution. The first of those indicates that it is the duty of the state to promote the conditions required for *real and effective* equality and to adopt measures in favor of vulnerable groups or those subject to discrimination, as well as to grant special protection to those people who given their economic, physical or intellectual condition are in a situation of manifest disadvantage and to sanction any abuse or ill treatment against them. In turn, Article 47 orders the state to implement policies of care, rehabilitation and social inclusion for people with physical or intellectual disabilities who are entitled to the required specialized assistance. . . .

In light of these constitutional provisions, international treaties on the topic, other pertinent legal dispositions, and constitutional caselaw, our conclusion is that the scope of protection of the freedom of movement of a person with disabilities includes the possibility to access the city's transport system in equal conditions, i.e., without having to face restrictions resulting in an excessive burden. Handicapped groups have the right to demand the removal of disproportionate burdens preventing them from fully participating in society. . . .

The freedom of movement is usually seen as a right of a negative or defensive nature because it is understood that its goal is to limit the power of the state in defense of individual freedoms. The view that its effective realization exclusively involves restrictions on state action . . . has resulted in an assumption that liberties are guarantees which do not require public investment. The Court does not share this view. In cases such as the one presently under review, it is evident that fundamental rights considered as freedoms, such as the freedom of movement, can have a positive, service-provision aspect. As has already been stated, in modern cities the freedom of movement greatly depends on public transportation. Without that transportation, it would be difficult to move around a large city, even for people without a physical disability.

The belief that the [first generation] rights to freedom do not involve investments while social, economic and cultural rights do, has led to the safeguarding of the immediate protection of the former, but not the latter. The Court has already noted this distortion in its caselaw, in the following terms:

> Constitutional rights involving the provision of services have a broad relationship with the social, economic and cultural rights mentioned in Chapter 2, Title II of the Constitution, but are not the same. The rights of liberty—fundamental civil and political rights—can also have a dimension of service provision. In general terms, this dimension of service provision requires the possibility of demanding from public authorities, and sometimes from private institutions, things that must be done or delivered in order to enjoy the right as established in the Constitution.[26]

The service-providing aspect of liberties stems from their positive dimension. Traditionally doctrine identified basic liberties with negative rights. . . . The state was only obliged not to impede the enjoyment and exercise of the rights of the person, without it being conceivable to speak of a service-providing dimension involving liberties. At present, however, it is generally acknowledged that the realization of even the most basic liberties, such as the freedom of movement and expression, requires material conditions. In modern societies where the enjoyment of individual freedom depends on public actions and service delivery—public transport, telecommunications, health, etc.—and personal safety must be paid for, it is impossible to insist on the thesis of the negative nature of basic freedoms. On the contrary, the infrastructure required to enable the exercise of fundamental liberties, the right to a lawyer and to due process, or political rights, demands considerable funds, as well as the state's permanent and coordinated intervention. Police forces, the administration of justice, and electoral systems, although seemingly obvious in a democratic state, represent the dimension of fundamental liberties that involves the provision of services.

We must point out, however, that the positive nature of rights and liberties does not always imply that they have a [merely] progressive character. The gradual nature of the positive realization of a right does not deny the possibility of claiming it [immediately] through legal action when non-compliance with the minimum correlative obligations causes the holder of the right imminent and unjustified harm. . . . The *urgency* of the rights holder's situation creates the possibility of legally demanding protection for the right in question through provision of those services which would prevent irreparable damages. . . .

Without question, the budget required to change the present infrastructure so to make it accessible to people with severe physical disabilities is considerable, since a good part of it was built without considering those requirements. The right at issue

26. The court is quoting Decision T-427 of 1992 (per Justice Eduardo Cifuentes Muñoz).

involves undertaking a democratic decision-making process on public investment and adjusting facilities that have been built over hundreds of years, which cannot be done in an instant. In this respect the Court has noted:

> It is not out of place for the Court to point out that the process of design and reconstruction of the physical infrastructure of cities with the goal of covering the necessities of people with physical and mental limitations, merits numerous investments that should be gradually carried out. While the planning and implementation of "humane" architectural projects becomes a reality, public authorities must contribute to the removal of those legal and cultural barriers which reinforce discrimination against people with disabilities. Indeed, usually people with disabilities are subject to discrimination by default when general regulations are enforced. . . . Given this social situation, and in compliance with clear constitutional principles (Article 13), the State must intervene by adopting measures in favor of groups subject to segregation or discrimination.[27]

Thus, the fact that time is required to plan and design, as well as the necessity of appropriating and directing resources to adapt existing conditions, is evidence that one is discussing a programmatic benefit whose full realization cannot be demanded instantaneously. The diverse policies that ensure the full inclusion of the handicapped into society will be implemented gradually. . . .

The programmatic nature of a benefit protected by a fundamental right does not imply that it may not be demanded or that its satisfaction may be postponed indefinitely. The freedom of movement, in its positive aspect, is a constitutional right which must be respected, developed and protected just like any other right, especially if it aims to remove obstacles that hinder the access of a person with disabilities to the city's public transport system with the goal of achieving the full and effective realization of equality.

That is how progressivity acquires its full constitutional nature. Taking rights seriously means taking progressivity seriously as well, as competent international institutions have stated.[28] First, progressivity is a part of the effective enjoyment of a right and, therefore, social groups cannot be excluded from its realization. Since certain social groups, given their physical, cultural, or socioeconomic conditions, can fully enjoy benefits protected by a right only if the state adopts policies backed by public funds and administrative measures, the state cannot be completely indifferent to the needs of those groups if that indifference would perpetuate a situation of marginalization that is incompatible with the fundamental principles of a participatory democracy. Second, the progressive nature of certain benefits requires that the state

27. The Court is quoting Decision T-288 of 1995 (per Justice Eduardo Cifuentes Muñoz).

28. The Court referred specifically to the General Observations of the United Nations Committee on Economic, Social and Cultural Rights, which interpreted the International Covenant on these issues, and to the 1993 Annual Report of the Inter-American Commission on Human Rights.

include in its policies, programs, and plans the funds and measures to ensure the gradual fulfillment of those goals so that all citizens effectively enjoy all the rights they are entitled to. Third, through its relevant institutions, the state can define the magnitude of the commitments that it will make to its citizens to achieve its objectives and can also determine the pace at which it will advance in their implementation. However, these publicly-adopted decisions must be serious, in other words they must be backed by a *rational* decision-making process that structures public policies which can be implemented, in such a way that the democratically-acquired commitments do not become empty promises. Thus, when those commitments have been enshrined in laws and reflect indispensable measures to ensure the effective enjoyment of fundamental rights, citizens are entitled to appeal to the courts to demand compliance with the corresponding benefits.

The following question thus emerges: Is there any aspect of the benefits included in the constitutional rights involved in the present case that can be enforced by *tutela*? Can the petitioner claim any of the special protection that the state should offer him? For this Court, the answer is yes.

While it is true that Transmilenio cannot guarantee the immediate access of [the petitioner] to the public transportation system without undertaking excessive costs, it must at least protect the programmatic benefit stemming from the positive dimension that the freedom of movement possesses in a social state of law and a participatory democracy, which implies adopting a program or plan aimed at ensuring the effective realization of his rights and those of all others with physical disabilities.

It is understandable that the benefit implied by the right in question cannot be granted immediately for the reasons already mentioned, but the lack of an adequate plan aimed at effectively guaranteeing its enjoyment is inadmissible from a constitutional perspective. The progressive nature of a benefit cannot be invoked in order to justify a continuous lack of action on the part of the state. Precisely because these are guarantees which involve designing and implementing public policies, the fact that no plan has been drawn up constitutes a violation of the Constitution. . . . This is the logical consequence of the constitutional case law on programmatic benefits, which establishes that their full realization will be gradual. This case law has established that the scope of demands will increase with the passage of time, as administrative capacity improves, as budgetary resources are enhanced, and . . . as the democratic decisions adopted by the Congress and enshrined in laws fix goals and determine the scope of commitments aimed at achieving the effective enjoyment of those benefits. . . .

First, there must be a public policy generally outlined in a plan. This is the minimum that those who have the obligation to guarantee the benefit at issue must do. The positive dimension of a fundamental right and its programmatic implications are disregarded *when not even a plan has been drawn up* that aims to gradually but seriously and sustainably guarantee and protect them.

Second, the plan should aim at guaranteeing the effective enjoyment of a right; Article 2 of the Constitution fixes this duty with complete clarity. The defense of rights cannot be formal. The mission of the state is not restricted to issuing laws and regulations which merely acknowledge the entitlement to rights on paper. The minimum rationality of the state demands that those norms be followed by real actions. These actions must be designed to aid people in enjoying and fully exercising the rights that were recognized in the Constitution.

It is constitutionally unacceptable to lack policies in these matters, but so is the maintenance of a plan or program which (i) *only exists on paper* and whose implementation has not begun, or (ii) one which, albeit in the process of implementation, is evidently *pointless* either because it does not answer the real problems and needs of rights holders, or because its implementation has been indefinitely or unreasonably postponed.

Third, the plan must be sensitive to the participation of citizens when demanded by the Constitution or the law. This mandate stems from various constitutional provisions, including Article 2, which states that it is an essential goal of the state to "facilitate the participation of everyone in the decisions that affect them and in the economic, political, administrative, and cultural life of the nation. . . ."

[A]lthough [the petitioner] does not have the right to the immediate and personalized enjoyment of the benefits he claims, he does have the right to demand at least the existence of a plan. The lack of a plan aimed at gradually guaranteeing his *access* to Bogotá's public transport system infringes both his freedom of movement and his right to equality, besides threatening the different rights whose effective realization depend on the possibility of movement, such as the right to work, to education, to health, and to the free development of personality. Therefore, the ruling issued by the first-instance *tutela* judge will be revoked and Transmilenio will be ordered . . . to develop a plan that will guarantee the programmatic character of the fundamental rights invoked by the petitioner.

[The Court thus ordered Transmilenio, "within a maximum term of two years . . . , to design a plan oriented towards guaranteeing the access of the petitioner to the basic public transportation system of Bogotá . . . and, once the plan is designed, to immediately begin the process of executing that plan in conformity with the timeline included in it." It also ordered Transmilenio to "report to the petitioner every three months, in his capacity as a member of the board of directors of the Colombian Association for the Development of People with Disabilities, on the progress of the plan so that he and the Association can participate in the phases of design, execution, and evaluation."]

Note on Positive Equality and the Disabled: The Court has fleshed out the constitutional rights of the disabled in many other cases and contexts. For example, in **Decision T-030 of 2010 (per Justice Luis Ernesto Vargas Silva)**, the Court required government buildings in the city of Popoyan to build ramps and take other measures to provide access to disabled citizens. Similarly, in **Decision T-553 of 2011 (per Justice Jorge Ignacio Pretelt)**, the Court held that judicial facilities around the country must be made accessible to the disabled, and issued a structural order to the Superior Council of the Judiciary (in its capacity as administrator of the judicial branch) to develop a plan to make judicial buildings accessible within five years.

The Court returned to the question of the access of disabled citizens to Bogotá's public transportation system in **Decision T-192 of 2014 (per Justice Gabriel Eduardo Mendoza Martelo)**. That case involved a complaint that many public buses providing transport around the city were inaccessible to the handicapped, and the petitioner stated that this harmed her constitutional rights. The Court ordered the city to develop a plan to make the entire urban transportation system handicapped-accessible within six months and to execute that plan within two years. It also ordered the state to file a report to the first-instance *tutela* judge every three months in order to gauge progress on those orders.

The positive aspects of equality cases of course implicate concerns that are similar to those found in socioeconomic rights cases. In both types of cases, courts must push state authorities to spend bureaucratic effort and resources on particular spending priorities identified by the judiciary. These kinds of orders often take time, and success may depend on the remedy and monitoring of compliance carried out by a court or by another actor. In short, the issues seen here will recur in Chapter 6.

5

Freedom of Speech and Freedom of Religion

This chapter considers the interlinked rights to freedom of religion and speech. The constitutional provisions and basic contours of the Court's case law may seem somewhat familiar to readers who have expertise in other constitutional systems, but the context is quite distinctive. Article 20 of the Colombian Constitution guarantees every person "the freedom to express and diffuse his/her thoughts and opinions, to transmit and receive information that is true and impartial, and to establish mass communications media"; it also states that "there shall be no censorship." Further, Article 73 guarantees the "freedom and professional independence" of journalism.

At the same time, these rights must often be balanced against others' rights and interests with which they might conflict. Article 15, for example, gives all citizens a right to "personal and family privacy" as well as to a "good reputation," and Article 20 gives citizens a "right to rectification in equitable conditions" for speech that injures these or other personal interests. Other constitutional provisions give the president and other political institutions the power to maintain public order, including if necessary by declaring one of several types of states of exception.

The Court has responded by adopting a position that offers strong protection to free speech, but is less categorical than the United States' approach and often has more similarities to European jurisprudence.[1] What is perhaps most notable about these cases is the context in which they have arisen, particularly the country's civil conflict and resultant problems of public order.

Section A deals with the conflict among speech, public order, and morality. Public order has been a particularly significant concern in the Colombian context, with its long-lasting and severe problems of civil violence. In Decision C-045 of 1996, the Court upheld

1. For comparative experiences from Europe, see, e.g., Donald P. Kommers & Russell Miller, The Constitutional Jurisprudence of the Federal Republic of Germany 441–537 (3d ed. 2012); John Bell, French Constitutional Law 327–38 (1992).

Colombian Constitutional Law: Leading Cases. Manuel José Cepeda Espinosa and David Landau.

an emergency decree preventing the publication of communiques and other texts of armed groups, holding that this publication of those instruments helped to empower guerrilla movements and thus weaken public order. But it has been unwilling to uphold restrictions in other contexts where the state interests in order or morality have been vaguer.

Section B treats the conflict between freedom of speech and interests in reputation and privacy. Here, the Court has given protection to media outlets only where they can demonstrate that they have taken steps to ensure that their reporting is truthful and impartial. The Court has not given defendants the same level of insulation enjoyed by United States' defendants under *New York Times* v. *Sullivan*[2] and other cases, even when the defendants are reporting on public figures or matters of the public interest. It should be underlined, however, that the *tutela* remedy is constitutional, not criminal nor civil. In T-066 of 1998, the Court protected the rights of mayors who were accused of being tied to illegal armed groups, based on leaked but unverified government documents. The Court held that the newspaper that published the information should have taken additional steps to inquire into its truthfulness, particularly given the threat to the life and family of the mayors stemming from this publication, and ordered that an adequate rectification be published.

Section C briefly considers the issue of speech and finance during political campaigns. Here too, the Court has largely followed the European model (and eschewed the U.S. model) in treating political campaigns as a separate realm that can be regulated by the state through caps on donations and total spending caps.[3] The Court's main concern instead has been in maintaining equality among competing candidates and political movements.

Finally, the last two sections treat a series of issues related to the freedom of religion. The 1991 Colombian Constitution contains several provisions on religious equality and freedom. Article 19 guarantees the freedom of religion, gives all individuals the right to freely profess and practice their religion, and states that all religions and churches are "equally free before the law." Article 18 guarantees "freedom of conscience," and states that no citizen may face retaliation on account of her beliefs or be forced to act against them. More broadly, the 1991 Constitution reflected a much more secular vision of the relationship between Church and state than the previous 1886 constitution. For example, Article 42 of the new Constitution contemplated divorce (which had previously been proscribed) and placed the control of family law in civil courts rather than with Church authorities.

The extent of the clash between the secular constitutional provisions and Colombia's deeply-grounded Catholic history became clear in the 1992 Concordat case, which is reproduced in Section D and was one of the Court's first major decisions. The treaty between Colombia and the Vatican reflected Catholicism's privileged status in many different ways in the spheres of education, politics, and law, but much of that treaty was declared unconstitutional in that decision.

2. 376 U.S. 254 (1964) (requiring that plaintiffs who are public figures prove that media defendants acted with "actual malice" in publishing allegedly libelous stories about them).

3. *See, e.g.*, KOMMERS & MILLER, *supra* note 1, at 269–85; Rick Hasen, *Regulation of Campaign Finance, in* GLOBAL PERSPECTIVES IN CONSTITUTIONAL LAW 198 (Vikram Amar & Mark Tushnet eds., 2009).

Finally, Section E treats the issue of accommodation for religious beliefs, which has become an important issue in Colombian politics and constitutional law. At times, this has reflected increasing pluralization in religious beliefs within a country that was historically dominated by Catholicism, and thus the accommodation of minority beliefs. At times, it has also reflected resistance by the Catholic majority against some secularizing measures, such as in the area of abortion. In Decision C-728 of 2009, the Court examined Colombia's tradition of obligatory military service, which makes no exception based on religious belief. The Court held, based on analogies to other areas where it has allowed conscientious objection, that the right had to be allowed on an individualized basis, and that in the absence of legislative regulation, the courts would recognize such a right via *tutela*. The chapter concerning the rights of indigenous peoples also includes decisions with religious connotations, although the Court often speaks of "worldviews" or "traditional beliefs."

A. Limitations on Speech for Security and Decency

In 1985, the media carried live broadcasts of an operation carried out by the armed forces to recapture the Palace of Justice in Bogotá, after the M-19 guerrilla group held hostage many justices from the Supreme Court of Justice and the Council of State (the country's highest administrative court). The operation ended with a very high loss of life. This live broadcast ignited heated controversy on the role of mass media in encouraging or publicizing terrorist acts, and led to legal regulations and judicial decision on the issue.

In **Decision C-425 of 1994 (per Justice José Gregorio Hernández Galindo)**, the Constitutional Court struck down an ordinary law that placed limitations on the media's ability to publish communiqués released by illegal armed groups. However, in **Decision C-179 of 1994 (per Justice Carlos Gaviria Díaz)**, the Court upheld parts of a statutory law that contemplated similar restrictions on mass media during states of exception. In 1995, in the context of attacks waged by the FARC guerrilla group to take over some cities and towns, and after the assassination of the conservative leader Álvaro Gómez Hurtado, the president declared a state of internal commotion (a type of state of exception aimed at curbing civil unrest or violence).[4] During this state of internal commotion, the president issued a decree that limited the media's ability to publish statements issued by illegal armed groups. Like all decrees issued during a state of internal commotion, this one expired when the state of exception itself expired; it was a temporary rather than a permanent measure. The decision reviewing that decree is excerpted below.

Decision C-045 of 1996 (per Justice Vladimiro Naranjo Mesa)

[By a vote of six-to-three, the Court upheld an emergency decree that, in relevant part, prevented the media from publishing "communiqués or any other kind of statements released by guerrilla groups [or] criminal organizations linked to subversive or

4. *See* Article 213 (giving the president the power to declare a state of internal commotion in the event of a "serious disruption of the public order imminently threatening the institutional stability and security of the state or the peaceful coexistence of the citizenry," and where ordinary police powers are inadequate).

terrorist activities" and "the dissemination . . . of interviews with members of guerrilla groups or criminal organizations linked to subversive or terrorist activities."]

As the Court has stated repeatedly, there are no absolute rights or freedoms. This stems from the necessary limitations on rights and liberties in conditions of peaceful coexistence; if the rights of any one person were absolute, these could predominate over the rights of others, and thus pluralism, coexistence, and equality would cease to operate. . . .

Thus, it is worth making a distinction based on the legal reality: It is one thing to say that fundamental rights are inviolable, and another very distinct thing to say that they are absolute. They are inviolable, because human dignity is inviolable: in effect, the essential nucleus of the humanity of the subject of a right, his rationality, is unalterable. . . . In other words, one can say that [fundamental] rights, within their limits, cannot be altered; their essential nucleus is untouchable. That is why the Constitution states that human rights may not be "suspended" even in states of exception and that, in any case, those states of exception must always be in conformity with the principles of international humanitarian law. One can deduce that when the essential nucleus of a fundamental right is affected, the right has been either violated or suspended.

The vision of public order as a restriction on rights, is a vision that we have already overcome. Public order, in the first place, is a guarantee of the rights and liberties that it contains. . . . Thus, the public has a right to public order, because this works in favor of the general interest, which should prevail.

For the Court it is clear the public order does not only consist in the maintenance of peace but also, and above all, in the harmony of the rights, liberties, and powers within the state. The real vision of public order, then, is nothing else than to be the guarantor of public liberties. It consists . . . in the peaceful coexistence between power and liberty. There is no liberty without order, and no order without liberty. . . . All situations of insecurity nullify liberty, because a person who is submitted to psychological pressure, who is in fear of being attacked by others constantly and for no reason, is not truly free. Public order, then, implies the liberation of man, because it ensures the effectiveness of his rights, by ensuring that others cannot abuse them. . . .

Reasonable limitations occasionally adopted under the law as to the exercise of the right to information do not constitute censorship, which is clearly forbidden by our Constitution (Article 20). Censorship implies that the state selects, based on ideological and doctrinaire criteria, the information and opinions to be disclosed, thus acting openly against political or intellectual pluralism, something totally inadmissible in a state ruled by democratic laws.

But we are in a very different situation where the liberty of expression and the right to information are used as an apology for crime and violence. In a state such as ours, where the Constitution deems the aim of ensuring peace as an essential asset, and where peace is enshrined as both "a right and a duty," promoting violence and crime through the media is nothing less than a contradiction. Freedom of expression and information is one thing, but it is something else to use those freedoms to foster illegal activities, especially criminal behavior and violence . . . by spreading communiqués or statements directly or indirectly released by members of such groups. The utilization of the mass media for those ends, in a society like ours, creates a greater climate of chaos and magnifies the actions of criminals in the eyes of civil society.

We reiterate that "limiting" is not the same as "suspending". . . . In effect, while limiting is the act of defining the sphere of action of something, suspending . . . denotes the temporary exhaustion of its force. Since fundamental rights are inherent to all persons because of their human dignity, they cannot be suspended, but they can be limited. . . .

The presidential decree does not prohibit information about a criminal fact, but tries to prevent criminals and subversives, protagonists of organized crime, from making an apology for violence through communications and public declarations. Democracy cannot harbor the seeds of its own destruction because within the framework of a social state of law, democracy is not a means but rather an end. . . .

The decree under examination does not establish censorship, but merely establishes reasonable measures to prevent the means of communication from being manipulated by organized crime, thus altering public order. It is evident that terrorism depends in large part, for the achievement of its final objectives, on the impact that the media gives to its aims and violent actions, which produces public disorder . . . and allows those groups to take advantage of a state of social panic. The media must cooperate to consolidate peace rather than being an instrument of terrorism and organized crime, by abusing the freedom of the press to convince the public that the actions of these groups are normal, thus creating a situation that partly legitimates their violent ways.

Note on Free Speech, Public Order, and Public Morals: In upholding this emergency decree, the Court emphasized the political and social context: the existence of an ongoing state of internal commotion, a crisis of public order, the temporary nature of the decree, and the scope of the threat of violence. This case might thus be seen within the broad framework of "militant democracy"—the set of ideas, originating in Germany, which require the state to take active steps (such as the banning of anti-democratic political parties and certain forms of speech) to weaken and eliminate anti-democratic elements that might otherwise threaten its existence.[5] In this sense, the recent political context may demonstrate a weakening of this threat. The relevance of states of exception to Colombian public life has dropped significantly since the 1990s; indeed no state of internal commotion has been successfully declared since 2002, and other states of exception are now mostly used to deal with natural disasters and similar events.[6]

5. *See* Samuel Issacharoff, *Fragile Democracies*, 120 Harv. L. Rev. 1405, 1409 (2007).

6. *See* Rodrigo Uprimny, *The Constitutional Court and Control of Presidential Extraordinary Powers in Colombia*, 10 Democratization 46, 57 tbl.1, 65 tbl.2 (2003).

At other times, the Colombian state has also invoked grounds of morality or public decency to limit the freedom of expression. A leading case is **Decision T-391 of 2007 (per Justice Manuel José Cepeda Espinosa)**, where the Court protected the rights to due process of law and freedom of speech of the firm RCN, broadcaster of the radio program *El Mañanero de La Mega*. In this case the Court also synthesized core doctrinal concepts involving the freedom of speech.

The program's target audience was mainly young people, and it frequently resorted to sexually explicit language, which prompted lawsuits from parental associations. In ruling on a collective legal action brought against the program, the Council of State (the country's high administrative court) ordered the government to restrict the broadcasting of the program and ordered RCN to alter its content.[7] The Council of State also set up a committee to monitor compliance with the decision. RCN filed a *tutela* against the decision, arguing that its right to freedom of speech had been violated.

The Court emphasized the "practically universal consensus" surrounding freedom of expression, and found that the right had a "special legal status:" "This privileged position . . . is principally justified with five types of arguments: (1) philosophical considerations regarding the search for truth, (2) reasons derived from the development of democracies, (3) motives related to individuals' dignity and self-fulfillment, (4) considerations regarding the preservation and enhancement of society's cultural and scientific heritage, and (5) historical and practical motives concerning states' inability to intervene adequately in this field. . . ."

The Court noted several constitutional presumptions protecting the right to freedom of expression: a presumption that any expression is protected by the Constitution unless there is a "convincing" demonstration to the contrary, a presumption that freedom of expression will prevail over other rights in the event of a conflict, a presumption that restrictions on the right are unconstitutional and thus subject to a "strict test" of control, and an irrefutable presumption against censorship, based on the constitutional text. The Court also noted that in seeking to restrict the freedom of expression, the state bore the burden of specifically explaining the legal and factual basis for any restriction, rather than simply stating in the abstract that it is based on "public morals."

Next, the Court defined some relevant features of the freedom of speech: "(1) its entitlement is universal . . . and it can involve public or collective interests, as well as the private interests of the speaker; (2) notwithstanding the presumptive constitutional protection of any form of expression. . . ., there are certain specific types of expression that are not protected according to virtually universal agreements enshrined in international treaties which are binding in Colombia; (3) there are different degrees of constitutional protection for the freedom of speech [and] some types of discourse enjoy greater protection than others, . . . [and (4)] the freedom of speech covers socially accepted expressions, as well as

7. Article 88 of the Constitution establishes the right to bring collective legal actions in order to seek "protection for collective rights and interests." Through these collective actions, any citizen is entitled to request before the courts protection for collective rights regarding issues such as the environment or public morals. These actions may result in orders addressed to authorities and individuals, as well as the establishment of monitoring committees.

unusual or alternative ones including offensive, shocking, indecent, outrageous and eccentric expressions . . . because the constitutional freedom protects both the content of the speech and the way it is said. . . . "

The Court noted several types of expression that are altogether excluded from constitutional protection, based on a study of relevant international human rights treaties. These include (1) propaganda in favor of war, (2) "appeals to racial, religious, or other types of hatred which may foster discrimination, hostility or violence against persons or groups (this type of expression includes categories commonly known as hate speech, discriminatory speech, and incitements to crime and violence)", (3) child pornography, and (4) direct public incitement to genocide.

However, the Court held that sexually-explicit speech was not such a category of unprotected expression. The Court noted debates and legislation found elsewhere, especially in the United States and the United Kingdom. However, it held that those debates were not particularly relevant in Colombia, as Colombian "legislation does not punish obscenity or pornography. . . . " The Court also pointed out that "Colombian society, constitutionally defined as a pluralistic structure based on respect for diversity, has not established a unique stance or attitude regarding expressions with sexually explicit content. . . . " Consequently, the Court held that "in principle, sexually explicit language is assumed by the Constitution to be protected by freedom of speech, by the suspicion of unconstitutionality to which any type of state restriction in this sense is subject to, and by the preference which that freedom is granted over other rights with which it may be in conflict."

The Court went on to resolve the specific case in question, concluding that the expressions broadcast in the radio program *El Mañanero de la Mega* were protected by freedom of speech, and thus that the restrictions enacted by the Council of State were unconstitutional. It pointed out that there were no clear and precise regulations allowing for restrictions on the freedom of speech for the benefit of children's rights. It noted Article 47 of the Code of Children and Adolescents, which required members of the media to "refrain from broadcasting or publishing information that is against the moral, psychic or physical integrity of minors, fosters violence, incites crime, or contains depraved or pornographic descriptions," but held that the law was too vague to be invoked as a ground for restricting the freedom of speech. Further, the Court held that the various restrictions adopted by the Council of State and by other authorities were not well justified and thus were unable to overcome the presumption of constitutional protection enjoyed by expression. The Court held that the radio station was required to take measures in order to protect underage audiences, but noted that these regulations should be adopted exclusively by RCN without any intervention from the state.

B. Limitations on Speech for Privacy and Reputation

Article 15 of the 1991 Constitution explicitly protects rights to privacy and reputation. Moreover, Article 20 creates a "right to rectification in equitable conditions" of anyone who has been slandered or libeled, or who has been victimized by the publication of false information. The Constitutional Court has protected this right via *tutela* in cases involving the publication of "false, mistaken, or inaccurate information harming the reputation and good name of a person." This instrument has been described by the Court as "a means of defense characterized by its efficiency—since rectification is published close in time to the harm—and which is less intimidating than criminal punishment."[8] The Court has routinely allowed *tutelas* to be brought by those seeking rectification against private mass media outlets.[9] If ordered by a Court, as the decision below makes clear, the rectification must be "under equitable conditions"—in other words, as prominent as the original article that is being corrected.

The Colombian "right of rectification" is in fact somewhat less generous than the "right of reply" found in some contexts. A right of reply, which is found in some Latin American and European countries, including Germany, France, and Brazil, extends beyond a right of rectification by requiring that a news outlet use its own space to print or broadcast replies by a party affected by negative information about that person, rather than merely issuing prominent corrections (which can be drafted by the news organization itself) of inaccurate information. Article 14 of the American Convention on Human Rights, of which most Latin American countries are signatories, requires all countries to have some provision for either "reply" or "correction."[10] In contrast, the United States Supreme Court held that a Florida law giving political candidates the right to reply to any attacks on their candidacy or record was unconstitutional because it violated the freedom of the press and chilled speech by effectively penalizing content critical of those candidates.[11]

Under the Colombian criminal code, libel and slander can also be punished with imprisonment and fines as crimes against "moral integrity."[12] Through **Decision C-489 of 2002 (per Justice Rodrigo Escobar Gil)**, the Constitutional Court acknowledged the constitutionality of criminalizing libel and slander, but only as a last resort. Thus, it upheld a provision establishing that retraction absolved authors of criminal responsibility for libel and slander if the retraction occurred before a judicial decision was issued, despite the non-consent of the offended person.

Decision T-066 of 1998 (per Justice Eduardo Cifuentes Muñoz)

[In a unanimous decision, the Court protected the fundamental rights to life, to personal integrity, to reputation and good name, to privacy, and to due process of law

8. Decision T-1198 of 2004 (per Justice Rodrigo Escobar Gil).

9. As noted in the Introduction, the Colombian constitution allows the *tutela* to be taken against private actors when those actors are providing a public service or when the petitioner is in a state of subordination or defenselessness before them. *See* Article 86.

10. American Convention on Human Rights, Nov. 21, 1969, 1144 U.N.T.S. 143, art. 14.

11. *See* Miami Herald Pub. Co. v. Tornillo, 418 U.S. 241 (1974).

12. The penalty for criminal libel, included in Article 220 of the criminal code, is imprisonment of one-to-three years and a fine of between 10 and 1,000 minimum monthly salaries. The penalty for criminal slander, included in Article 221 of the same code, is imprisonment of one-to-four years and a fine of between 10 and 1,000 minimum monthly salaries.

of a municipal mayor who had been mentioned in an article as having links with illegal armed groups. The article, published by *Semana* magazine under the title "The Guerrilla Mayors," disclosed an intelligence report from the National Army, which included the names of several mayors alleged to be allies of rebel groups. The Court held that there were several legal issues to be tackled successively:]

Whether, in the first instance, the armed forces are authorized to collect information of this type for the elaboration of their article. After that, we will need to establish whether the media can publish information contained in documents with a classified character. If the answer is yes, we must then determine whether that authorization extends to situations in which the classified information permits one to deduce a series of incriminating facts against distinct individuals, even when there is no proof against any of them.

If the response to that last question is also yes, we will then need to define which conditions the media must meet in order to publish that material and what consequences they will face if they do not meet those requirements.

At the outset it is important to clarify . . . as a general framework that the country is going through difficult times regarding law and order which affect citizens and their activities. . . . The interpretation of constitutional principles should always take into consideration the specific and changing conditions of society. . . . Therefore, constitutional judges must always take heed of the actual situation in which constitutional provisions will be applied. . . .

[The Court noted that the military has the obligation to collect information of this type, because it "can and must have all necessary information for the normal, adequate, efficient, legitimate, and democratic exercise of their functions."]

But this power is not unlimited. . . . It has been established that in the process of collecting information human rights and due process must be respected. Also, . . . it has been established that state security organs must maintain any information obtained in the strictest confidence. . . .

Further, it must be noted that the information which has been collected must be strictly necessary, in such a way that it does not affect the right to privacy of those involved. In order to carry out an investigation about certain people, there must be reasons to presume, in a reasonable manner, that those people have committed a crime. If this condition were not met, we would be opening the door to a police state, to the detriment of individual liberty. . . .

In the situation under study, the military collected a series of information about the possible links between mayors in the country with guerrilla groups. This is obviously a topic that interests the military, given its obligation to guarantee the constitutional order and preserve the peace. From this point of view, there is no reason to reproach the military.

The copy of the intelligence report did not include any proof about the allegations made within it. . . . [T]he allegations made about people should always be formulated in a conditional and questioning manner, in order to make it clear that there is no proof of those allegations. This condition, which appears to be merely formal . . . , demonstrates its importance precisely in facts like those involved in this *tutela*, when the confidential documents are sent in an irregular way to media outlets.

Moreover, the military violated the fundamental condition on its investigative activities: maintaining the confidentiality of any information gathered.

If one takes into account the violent situation facing the country and the physical vulnerability of its mayors, one can only conclude that the published allegations may have generated situations of risk to the life and personal integrity of the mayors mentioned in the publication. Furthermore, the allegations contained in the article threatened the honor and good name of the mayors, since they accused them of links with illegal organizations. Thus, the *tutela* against the military should be granted.

[Next, the Court examined the conduct of the magazine that published the article.]

As this Court has repeatedly stated, the liberty of the press is an essential prerequisite for the existence of democracy. In effect, a free press contributes to informing and shaping citizens; it serves as a vehicle for the realization of debates on topics of social controversy; it helps to form public opinion; it acts to check public and private powers, etc. In addition, the freedom of the press is fundamental for the full exercise of the right to free development of personality, because in order for a person to be able to define and follow in an appropriate manner the direction that they wish to give to their life, they must have the possibility of understanding distinct forms of conceiving of life and communicating their own vital choice.

The importance of the freedom of the press for the proper functioning of the political system and for the free development of personality of all people explains the broad protection that this guarantee receives in modern constitutionalism. However, this liberty also generates legal difficulties since it frequently collides with other fundamental rights or purposes of the state.

In effect, the mass media has become an important center of power in society . . . that can affect the rights of individuals, which is even more significant because those individuals may have very few ways to defend themselves against those actions. . . .

This explains why in diverse modern constitutions and international human rights treaties, limits are placed on the freedom of the press, even while censorship is prohibited. The Constitution of 1991 exists within this tendency. . . .

The document that served as the basis for the article . . . had a classified character. . . .

But, does the classified nature of the information also bind the media? In other words, in the event the media has access to a secret document, is it obliged to keep it confidential or can it divulge it? . . . [I]n principle, the mandate of confidentiality does not bind journalists or media outlets.

This is explained by the role of the press within a democratic system. As has been expressed, the media plays a role in checking public power. This task cannot be fully carried out if the media can only publicize documents given to it. Indeed, the checking function played by the media demands that they not rely solely on official communications and data given by interested parties, but that they go further in search of the truth. . . .

In its jurisprudence, this Court has stated that when there are conflicts between the right to information and the rights to honor, good name, and intimacy, in the case of people and facts of public importance, *prima facie* the first right prevails. In these events, the right to information should be preferred, in principle, because of the checking function that the media has been assigned. . . . If there were strong restrictions on the press in these areas it would prejudice in a notable way their capacity and vigilance regarding the correct functioning of these powers. . . .

Article 20 of the Constitution draws a distinction that is accepted in the jurisprudence and doctrine of other countries. . . . On the one hand, the article establishes the freedom to express and diffuse one's own thoughts and opinions, while on the other it creates a freedom to inform others and receive information that is truthful and impartial. The first freedom refers to the right of all people to communicate their conceptions and ideas, while the second applies to the right to inform and be informed about everyday facts and events.

The two freedoms receive distinct treatment: while the freedom of expression has no *prima facie* limits, the freedom to inform is constitutionally tied to two conditions: truth and impartiality. The explanation of the unequal treatment of these two liberties stems from the following: in a democratic and liberal society one cannot stop each person from having their own opinions, but it is something different to state facts that do not correspond to reality or to give a partial version of them, thus tricking the audience. . . .

[I]n accordance with this principle, the journalist must maintain a certain distance with respect to the sources and not accept in a unreflective way all of the allegations and incriminating statements that are made. On the contrary, this information must be compared with distinct versions of the same facts. . . .

The magazine *Semana* argues that the responsibility for the allegations made in the article . . . rests solely with the national army. . . . It recognizes that the allegations made in the document have no evidentiary value, but it argues that the obligation of the magazine is limited to establishing whether the document itself exists, without verifying the allegations made within it.

The Court does not share this position. . . . The statements made in the intelligence report . . . would be serious in any country, because they suggest that local officials are involved in crimes. But in the Colombian case, they carry an immense gravity given the degree of violence in the country, which has particularly affected its mayors. . . .

[T]hrough the publication of this type of article, the media plays a role in checking public power. The constitutional judge cannot hold the magazine accountable

> for publishing this report. . . . [W]hat is required is that when a publication contains incriminating information like that found in [the article at issue,] it makes an attempt to establish the truth. It should, at a minimum, give the accused a chance to make a statement about the allegations; and if this should prove impossible, it should obtain the opinions of knowledgeable people that would permit the appreciation of those statements from a different perspective. . . . Non-compliance with this procedure constitutes . . . grave negligence that, in this case, harmed the right of citizens to receive truthful and impartial information, affected the honor and good name of the mayors, and put their life and personal integrity at risk.
>
> As this Court has repeatedly noted, people who consider themselves affected by the publication of information that they believe to be false have the right to demand that these be corrected. The right of rectification has been defined by the Court as "a right of the same fundamental nature as the speaker's right to inform and of the rights to honor and to a good name."
>
> [The Court thus granted the *tutela*. The military was ordered to adopt policies to prevent the release of information of this type and to make its investigative policies consistent with the Constitution. *Semana* was ordered to provide a note vindicating the mayor's right to rectification. This correction must "clarify that the magazine had no evidence whatsoever regarding the affirmations in the article; acknowledge the mistakes that had been made in the handling of the news, and publish the rectification in the same section [where the original article was published] highlighting it in the same way."]

Note on the Colombian Law of Defamation: The Court has wrestled with the balancing of the rights to reputation and to a good name against the right to freedom of expression in many other cases. In **Decision SU-1723 of 2000 (per Justice Alejandro Martínez Caballero)**, for example, the Court unanimously denied the protection requested by a famous singer who claimed that his rights to privacy, reputation, and good name had been infringed by the broadcast of a television program. The program dramatized the facts that led to the death of a friend of the singer while at a drug-fueled party at the singer's house in Bogotá. According to the Court, the program showed in a "neutral" but dramatized way the woman's death and how her body had later been dumped, events in which the plaintiff was allegedly involved. The singer claimed that in the television series "intimate facets of his private life, his sexual behavior and his health had been shown and specific names, designations and circumstances had been disclosed without his authorization." A criminal investigation against the singer was underway and had not concluded at the time that the television series aired.

The Court first defined the concept of "good name" by stating that it "corresponds to one's expectation of having a good reputation resulting from his virtues and merits and as a consequence of his actions." The right thus includes the "power to prevent the actions of others that may unfairly discredit a person's reputation." Nevertheless, the Court emphasized that the right to a good name is not infringed when the harm to a person's reputation originates in his own behavior.

The Court also defined the right to privacy as "related to the most intimate sphere of an individual and his family, that is to say, to the events, situations, behaviors and information that are usually deemed as private or family affairs in which others cannot interfere." However, the Court noted that such events ceased to be covered by privacy protection when they had been disclosed to others by the right holders themselves or when they were already public knowledge.

Concerning cases of conflict between the freedom of information and other fundamental rights such as the right to a good name or to privacy, the Court noted that it may be necessary to balance those rights. However, in order to be entitled to the freedom of information, mass media should comply with three principles: "a) *public relevance, b) truthfulness*, and c) *impartiality*."

According to the Court, "the principle of *public relevance* refers to the requirement that the information meet tests of general interest concerning the issue in question. In this sense, two aspects are of importance: a person's status and the informational content involved." People who "have become public figures are unavoidably forced to accept the risk of being subject to comment, opinions or adverse revelations as a good deal of public attention focuses on their ethical and moral behavior. In such a case, the right to inform becomes broader. . . ."

Thus, the Court pointed out that "public relevance is a relative concept that may vary according to the public or private status of the individual referred to in the news or to the public attention regularly drawn to the person". Furthermore, quoting the Spanish Constitutional Tribunal (Decision STC-171/1990), the Court stated that "public figures or people who have given their professional project a public face must accept the cost this implies . . . , which may result in the possibility of intrusion in their private lives and exposure to comments, opinions and unfavorable revelations."

The Court then stated that the informational content of the report had to respond to "a real and legitimate general interest in keeping with its importance and social impact." In the Court's view, this "legitimate interest" differs from "simple general curiosity" (recalling on this issue the Paris Court of Appeals case *Soc. de Presse Marcel Dassault v. Brigitte Bardot*) and must also be "current" (citing cases from the Spanish (STC-231/1988) and German (*Lebach* case from 1973) Constitutional Tribunals).

Concerning the principle of *truthfulness*, the Court held that "it is not necessary that the information be strictly true, but only that it has gone through a reasonable process of verification, even though its absolute accuracy may remain a matter of controversy." Finally, the Court explained that the principle of *impartiality* "implies that the media will avoid making value judgments that may affect the audience's perception of facts."

Regarding the issue under examination, the Court observed that "the aforementioned principle of relevance had been doubly met" because the case involved both a public figure and content worthy of public debate. The Court also noted that "the company undertook a process to collect and select the information that served as the basis for the television series." According to the Court, this effort showed "respect not only for the principle of truthfulness, but also for the principle of impartiality, since the program dramatizes the versions that each of the parties defended during interviews, adopting a neutral position, while presenting some reasonable conjectures."

Thus, the Court denied the *tutela* at issue. In 2002, the petitioner in the case was sentenced to manslaughter for his role in the death publicized on the television program.

Nevertheless, in other cases the Court has granted requests for rectification even in those involving public figures. For example, in **Decision T-626 of 2007 (per Justice Jaime Córdoba Triviño)**, the Court ordered a news program to provide a correction of information broadcast regarding a public official involved in a corruption scandal. The Court considered that the news program had violated the principles of truthfulness and impartiality by (i) merging facts and subjective appraisal in the same report; (ii) adhering in the report to only one party's version of a lawsuit currently underway; (iii) disseminating incorrect data regarding the claimant's family ties that would have led to a conflict of interest, and (iv) omitting an important fact when presenting the story.

C. The Freedom of Expression and Political Campaigns

The Constitutional Court has dealt with a number of cases involving the regulation of political parties and campaigns. Many of these cases have involved the rules governing the financing of these organizations. The Court's approach in this realm has generally been to allow and even to require state regulation of campaign finance so long as it is carried out in a way that comports with the constitutional mandate of equality. In this sense, the Colombian approach is far closer to the approach across most European countries, where state financing of parties and campaigns is common and even-handed campaign finance regulations are generally upheld, then it is to the approach of the United States, where attempts to regulate campaign finance are subject to high levels of scrutiny as violations of freedom of speech.[13] Two of those cases are excerpted in Section 1 below. Section 2 excerpts one of the Court's early cases dealing with access to the televised debates. The Court's approach in that case, which privileged the freedom of the press over claims made by lesser presidential candidates, stands as something of a contrast to its financing cases.

1. Financing Political Parties and Campaigns

Decision C-089 of 1994 (per Justice Eduardo Cifuentes Muñoz): the Constitutional Court reviewed the "Basic Statute of Political Parties and Movements." By an eight-to-one vote, it upheld the majority of its provisions regarding the financing of political parties and movements, although a few articles were declared either unconstitutional or only conditionally constitutional.

The Court began by considering the overall constitutional scheme governing political parties: "Granting constitutional status to parties aims to . . . establish clear rules of the game in order to improve the conditions for the pluralistic political confrontation which is the foundation of any democratic system, and hence, it reveals and controls an activity which is essential to political power and its public role."

13. *See* Hasen, *supra* note 3.

Articles 12 to 17 of the law referred to the regulations applicable to state and private financing of political parties and movements. According to Article 12, the state must finance political parties and movements through a fund to be managed by the National Election Commission. That provision of the law also established a formula for distributing the money in that fund: 10 percent would be distributed equally among parties and movements, 50 percent would be distributed to them depending on the number of seats they obtained in elected bodies, 30 percent was reserved for certain particular kinds of expenses of parties and movements, and 10 percent was given to organizations dedicated to women, young people, indigenous group, Afro-Colombian groups, the disabled, and unions.

The Court considered that "[t]he creation of a fund financed with public funds and designed to contribute to the election campaigns of legally registered political parties and movements is fully supported by Article 109 of our Constitution. . . .[14] The purpose of this financial support—which is partial . . . , since it cannot and should not cover all costs of political activity, is to neutralize the dependence and subjection of political organizations on private interest groups whose support may be used to influence political decisions and demand favors, thus deteriorating collective morals and undermining the faith of citizens in the performance of their representatives, which should only respond to the general interest."

Regarding the specific formula for determining funding, the Court found that "the equality principle demands that funding based on the levels at which movements are [actually] represented supplement funding which gives money to all parties equally. . . . The criteria established by the law enable a reasonable system of financial allotment and take into account the differences among the various parties and movements."[15]

Finally, the Court upheld Articles 14 through 16 of the law, which established limits on private financing of campaigns.[16] Article 14 directed the National Electoral Council to set limits on the total amount of private money that a candidate could spend on his campaign, Article 15 established that private funds for campaigns had to be given directly to the candidate or his organization, and Article 16 stated that donations by legal persons such

14. The current text of Article 109 states in relevant part: "The State shall contribute to the financing of political parties and movements with legal personality, in accordance with the relevant statute. The election campaigns conducted by candidates put forward by parties and movements with legal personality and by relevant citizen groups which put candidates on the ballot shall partly be funded with state resources. An Act shall determine the percentage of votes necessary to qualify for the right to such funding. The expenses which parties, movements, relevant citizen groups or candidates may incur in election campaigns, as well as the maximum amount of private contributions may also be limited in accordance with the applicable statute. A percentage of this funding shall be directed to parties and movements with effective legal personality and relevant citizen groups which put forward candidates prior to the election or ballot in accordance with the conditions and guarantees determined by statute and with the authorization of the National Election Commission." The article was amended in 2003, but its original text was similar on relevant points.

15. The Court did however strike down a provision stating that 30 percent of funding could only be used for certain specific expenses such as publishing magazines and journals, organizing events, or attending international seminars. The Court held that this provision violated the autonomy that parties enjoyed over their internal affairs.

16. The initial penalty for violating these provisions was loss of public funding. However, following the adoption of Legislative Act 1 of 2003, which modified Articles 108 and 109 of the Constitution, the punishment is dismissal from public office.

as corporations had to be approved by their governing bodies. The Court considered that these provisions sought to "base political confrontation on equality as much as possible, and have candidates' intellectual and moral competence and ideological platforms play the main role in elections."[17]

More recently, the Court reviewed campaign finance regulations issued after the passage of Legislative Act 2 of 2004, a constitutional amendment that established, for the first time in modern Colombian history, the possibility of presidential election. As noted elsewhere in this volume, the Legislative Act was issued in contemplation of the end of the first term of then-president Alvaro Uribe, who sought these constitutional changes and in 2006 won presidential re-election. As Chapter 11, Section C notes, in Decision C-1040 of 2005, Legislative Act 2 of 2004 was upheld by the Constitutional Court against charges that it was passed by an improper procedure and that it constituted a "substitution of the constitution." The Legislative Act required Congress to issue a statutory law to preserve "electoral equality among candidates running for President of the Republic" and to counterbalance the advantage that the incumbent president might otherwise have during an electoral campaign.

Decision C-1153 of 2005 (per Justice Marco Gerardo Monroy Cabra): The Court reviewed the Law of Electoral Guarantees issued by Congress for the purpose of regulating the presidential re-election contemplated in Legislative Act 2 of 2004. By a seven-to-two vote, the Court upheld most provisions regulating the financing of presidential campaigns. In particular, it upheld provisions establishing systems of public financing and setting limits on the private and total financing of campaigns. However, it did strike down some important articles, most important those allowing *any* campaign contributions by corporations and other legal rather than natural persons.

The Court began by explaining why the basic scheme of the law was constitutional as a way to limit the incumbency advantage that had been created by allowing presidential re-election. "Given that the duty of the Congress is to guarantee that the presidential election is defined by ideas and not by the weight of power, it must adopt measures to minimize the effect of the incumbent president's advantages. . . . [P]ublic financing of political campaigns seeks to ensure financial balance among candidates running for president, since it guarantees equal conditions for the confrontation of ideas in a setting where candidates should be more concerned with expressing their views than with finding resources for their campaigns." The Court next stated:

> Public funding for political campaigns aims at preventing corrupt practices in democratic processes. As campaigns have become increasingly sophisticated and now involve experts, general campaign staff, publicists, consultants, etc., their costs have also increased. In this sense, the demand for contributions and donations from citizens has endangered the moral integrity of campaigns. . . . Regulation of these matters is indispensable in a re-election process, given that the incumbent president

17. In a subsequent decision, the Court upheld similar limits on private citizens for citizens' initiative campaigns, which allowed individuals to place proposed legislation before the voters. *See* Decision C-180 of 1994 (per Justice Hernando Herrera Vergara).

> has access to public funds and that private interests may see him as the main target for funding because of his privileged position....

The court also examined the problem of money in political campaigns more generally, explaining why tight regulations were constitutional in the electoral realm. "The growing role played by the huge amounts of money being spent in election campaigns involves serious risks for democracy. Such risks result from the economic interests of private groups that support candidates and act as powerful pressure groups whose regulation is essential to prevent distortions in voters' will.... The distortion resulting from the financial needs of parties affects not only their campaigns, but also the exercise of the posts for which their candidates run. The Court held as follows:

> Although it is difficult to measure the actual influence of financial capital in campaigns, it is clear that the advantages derived from greater resources have an impact on candidates' public image by increasing their publicity. That is why the term "equal opportunities in electoral campaigning" (taken from the English concept of "leveling the playing field" or the German term *Chancengleichheit*, contemplated in Article 21 of the German Basic Law)... became a founding element of regulations related to democratic fairness for political campaigning in almost all western democracies after World War II.

Article 11 of the law laid out the public financing to be given to each presidential candidate. In accordance with Legislative Act 2, it required that the state finance the "preponderance" of the expenses in presidential campaigns, which the Court understood to mean that "the state must finance more than fifty percent of the expenses of presidential campaigns waged by those political and social parties or movements which comply with the legal requirements." Article 11 also established that only a certain percentage of the public funds could be destined for political advertising, while the remaining funds must be used for other expenses. The Court upheld this limitation.

Article 12 established an upper limit for presidential campaign expenses: no campaign could spend more than a certain amount from combined public and private sources. The Court found that "setting a limit for political campaigns expenses is a measure which has several objectives in democratic systems. One is decreasing resource inequalities among parties, movements or groups and thus favoring electoral equality. Another is controlling private contributions and, therefore, limiting possible corruption. Article 109 of our Constitution contemplates these limits."[18] The Court held that the campaign spending limits were conditionally constitutional.[19]

18. *See supra* note 14 (giving the text of Article 109).

19. The condition stemmed from the following: The Court noted that the cap on total spending for the 2006 presidential election was less than the cap for the 2002 presidential election. It held that this was particularly unfair to any non-incumbent presidential candidates "since the aim [of the law] is to compensate for the advantages involved in his being in office for almost four years." It therefore held that for any non-incumbent presidential candidate (not currently president or vice president), the decrease would not apply and the relevant cap on campaign spending would be the one from the 2002 election.

Article 14 established that only 20 percent of the maximum amount allowed to campaigns in Article 12 could come from private donations. Additionally, no single private individual's contribution could exceed 2 percent of the limit, whereas the limit for a single legal person's donations was 4 percent, and a single holding company's limit was 5 percent. The Court held that the 2 percent limit to contributions by natural persons "abides by the constitutional provision which establishes that campaign financing should be done mainly through public funds; [the] restriction seeks to prevent corruption from invading political practices given that elected candidates and parties may be involved in serious conflicts of interest when they owe a high percentage of their campaign's resources to only one natural person. This mechanism, then, seeks to protect a very important constitutional principle: ensuring transparency in public administration by preventing conflicts of interest." The Court thus upheld the limits on campaign donations by individuals.

However, it struck down the provisions allowing campaign contributions by non-natural persons such as corporations and holding companies, finding that these entities must not be permitted to make any contributions. "[I]t is unconstitutional to allow legal persons it contribute to presidential campaigns.... This possibility disregards the constitutional principle of electoral equality which should guide presidential campaigns because it enables wealthy natural persons to contribute amounts which exceed the limit set for them by working through legal persons. Furthermore, in a democratic system, only natural persons are entitled to political rights such as political participation.... Finally, granting legal persons the ability to contribute funds to the incumbent president distorts the balance sought by the legislature, whose aim is to promote equality in a scenario where re-election is now possible, when it established the rules of the game."

2. Access to Televised Debates

Decision T-484 of 1994 (per Justice Jorge Arango Mejía)

[In a unanimous decision, a panel of the Constitutional Court denied a *tutela* filed by two presidential candidates who were excluded by two influential television networks from participating in a televised debate for the 1994 presidential election. The debate organizers invited only the candidates who received more than 10 percent of the vote in national opinion polls. One of the excluded candidates, Antonio Navarro Wolff, was a national figure and leader of a party created after a successful peace process with the M-19 guerrilla group in 1990.]

In Colombia the freedom of the press exists, not as the fruit of a conquest in recent times, but as the result of a century-long tradition....

[The Court reviewed constitutional history and quoted parts of Article 20 (freedom of speech) and Article 73, which reads as follows:]

> "Journalistic activity is protected to guarantee its freedom and professional independence...."

The freedom of the press, then, is protected by the Constitution. Of that there is no doubt. And there is ... a prohibition on censorship at any time....

The freedom of information is guaranteed by the Constitution from various points of view.

If one considers the situation of the recipient of the information, he has a right to receive truthful and impartial information.

He who participates in the facts that are the topic of the information, has a right not to have his honor harmed, and also has a right to ensure that the information is truthful.

He who broadcasts the information not only has a right to do so, but a duty to be truthful and impartial. But that duty to be truthful and impartial is related exclusively to the facts, and not to the opinions of journalists. *Their judgment or appraisal of the facts implicates the freedom of opinion and the freedom to express such opinions on their own accord.*

That freedom of opinion must necessarily be related to a core principle of the Constitution: the absolute prohibition on censorship contained in Article 20. . . .

But, one may ask: Is forcing a journalist to emit certain opinions or information, another form of censorship or a violation of the freedom of expression? Put another way: is the freedom of the press compatible with imposing on journalists the obligation to publish certain information . . . or the opinions of certain people? The answer, without doubt, is that *the prohibition of censorship, and freedom of the press, is violated when a journalist is forced to publish certain information or opinions, in the same way as when its publication is blocked*. . . . It is [the journalist] who must decide what, when, and how to publish. . . .

The foregoing allows us to analyze the relationship that exists between the journalist and those who seek public office. In concrete terms, to establish whether there is a fundamental constitutional right of all candidates to receive exactly the same treatment from journalists, and an obligation from them to dedicate the same time and attention to all of them. In this case, and limiting ourselves to the 1994 presidential election, one must take into account that in the first round there are 18 candidates.

When various candidates aspire to the same charge of public election, public opinion will favor them to varying degrees. There will be a logical interest on the part of the greater number of people to know the opinions of those who have the most public support.

Based on the foregoing, it is absolutely understandable that television debate organizers would limit participation to candidates having at least ten percent support in the polls. This offers the public precisely what they want, rather than imposing something contrary to their preferences.

Forcing people to watch . . . something they are not interested in is not only antidemocratic, but doomed to failure, since in the end, viewers decide what to watch. And if things reach the point where all channels are broadcasting things they do not like, they can always choose to turn off their television sets. . . .

Applying all of the foregoing to this case, it is clear that none of the fundamental rights of the candidates were violated. No candidate has the right to place the news channels or spaces of public opinion . . . at his whim, or to force the media to work according to certain obligations.

D. Religious Establishment

Colombia is a Catholic country, and the 1886 Constitution adopted a confessional state. A 1936 amendment weakened the establishment of Catholicism in the state, but stated that the Catholic religion was the religion of the nation and allowed the state to agree on a Concordat with the Holy Sea. In 1974 the Concordat was reformed but still regulated many matters such as marriage, religious education, the presence of the Catholic Church in regions of Colombia, and the influence of the Church in important institutions such as the military. The power of the Catholic Church has been an issue in Colombia since independence and a source of conflict among the two historic parties up to the 1960s: the Conservative party was allied with the Church, and the Liberal party was generally at favor of pluralism and at times anticlerical.

In the 1991 Constitution, all major political forces agreed to promote religious pluralism. Thus, for example, Article 19 guarantees freedom of religion, gives all people a right to freely profess individually or in groups, and states that all religions are equal before the law. Article 13 also prohibits discrimination against people based on religion. However, the members of the Constituent Assembly still clashed on specific issues, reflecting the historic Liberal-Conservative party split. For example, most conservatives opposed a constitutional provision (Article 42) allowing for divorce, an initiative of the Liberal president of the republic that was adopted despite their opposition. The Constituent Assembly did not say anything about the Concordat. However, many of its provisions, and particularly Article 19, seemed to fit uncomfortably with the treaty's privileged treatment of the Catholic religion. The Court dealt with this problem in one of the most controversial decisions of its first several years.

Decision C-027 of 1993 (per Justice Simón Rodríguez Rodríguez): In this decision the Court studied the constitutionality of Act 20 of 1974, which implemented the Concordat and Final Protocol between the Republic of Colombia and the Vatican. In an eight-to-one decision, the Court declared some articles of the Concordat constitutional and others unconstitutional.

The Court first dealt with the crucial preliminary issue of whether it even had jurisdiction to hear the challenge to the Concordat. The Constitution of 1991 established a special procedure for judicial review of treaties—they are automatically reviewed before they go into effect.[20] The Court held that this a priori review procedure was not exclusive—the treaty could also be challenged via a normal public action after it has gone into effect. Justice José Gregorio Hernández Galindo dissented on this point, arguing that the a priori review procedure for treaties should be considered exclusive in nature and thus that the case should not have been heard.

In a very long decision, the Court analyzed each article of the Concordat individually. This section excerpts some of the key articles that were declared unconstitutional.[21] Most of these violated the principle in Article 19 of equality of religion; however, some

20. *See* Article 241, cl. 10.

21. The Court also struck down, for example, Article XIII, which gave the Church privileged access to marginalized economic zones; Articles XIV and XV, which gave the president of the Republic a say in the

violated other constitutional rules, such as the new divorce regime found in Article 42 or the principle of autonomy for indigenous communities found throughout the constitution and explored in detail in Chapter 8.

a. ***Article XI.*** *In order to support the right of families to freely choose the places of education for their children, the state will equitably contribute, with funds from the domestic budget, in order to sustain Catholic schools.*

The Court held that this article of the Concordat violated the principle of equality of religions. "Article XI creates a preferential treatment for the children of Catholic families, and thus ignores the constitutional principle of equality for all religions. . . . , even though we acknowledge that the Catholic Church is the creed of the vast majority of the Colombian people."

b. ***Article XII.*** *To realize the right of Catholic families to have their children receive religious education according to their faith, education in government schools at the primary and secondary levels will include religious teaching and education according to the Church's teachings. . . . [T]he competent ecclesiastic authority must provide the curricula, approve religious textbooks, and oversee how this teaching is done. . . .*

The Court stated that this disposition was contrary to Articles 19 and 68[22] of the Constitution, as "students in a government school, whether or not they are Catholic, will receive the teachings of the Catholic Church, because educational plans must include such teachings. In addition, [this provision] discriminates against other religions."

"By declaring this article unconstitutional, this Court is not stating that the children of Catholic families may not receive religious education. . . . [W]hat is being struck down under the new Constitution is the fact that the teaching is mandatory and is the only form of religious instruction given in the state's schools, without providing for instructions in other religions or for the possibility of a student abstaining from religious education. . . . [T]he Catholic Church must be given the same religious access in the state's educational institutions that is given to other faiths. Students who do not want to receive any religious education must be free to do so; in this manner the principle of equality for all religious creeds would be respected since the academic program would fulfill the students' religious interest according to their own beliefs, and no one would be obliged to take religious classes."

c. ***Article XVII.*** *The spiritual and pastoral attention given to the members of the Armed Forces will be carried out by the Military Vicar, according to norms and regulations issued for such a purpose by the Holy See in agreement with the government.*

appointment of Church authorities in Colombia; and Article XXII, which defined the illegitimate exercise of church functions as a crime called usurpation of public functions. Article XVIII, which exempted priests from military service, was held constitutional under the condition that the same exemption be given to other faiths.

22. Article 68 states: "In state institutions, no person may be required to receive religious instruction. . . ."

"This Corporation considers that this article limits the fundamental right to the freedom of religion held by active-duty military members, at the same time, it discriminates against the other beliefs and churches that exist in Colombia."

"There is an obvious contradiction between this article of the Concordat and Article 68 of the Constitution in its fourth paragraph: the latter expresses that 'in state institutions, no person may be required to receive religious education' while the former establishes that the armed forces must receive spiritual assistance from the Catholic Church."

"This does not prevent the Catholic Church on its own . . . from providing its religious and pastoral services to members of the military who voluntarily wish to receive them, under the same rules as apply to any other religion."

> **d.** ***Article XIX.*** *Civil actions involving clerics and religious personnel . . . as well as criminal actions against them for crimes outside the ecclesiastic ministry. . . , must be taken to the courts of the state. . . . There is an exception, however, for criminal processes against bishops. . . . , which are the sole competence of the Apostolic Headquarters.*

"[T]here is no constitutional foundation to grant this sort of immunity in favor of bishops . . . on criminal issues, thus creating an exclusive competence that high members of other churches existing in the country do not enjoy. In addition, these ecclesiastic persons would be placed outside the jurisdiction of the state, whereas all the country's other residents would be subjected to this jurisdiction."[23]

> **e.** ***Article XXIV.*** *Ecclesiastical properties can be taxed in the same manner as the properties of common citizens. However, considering their distinct purpose, sites destined for worship, curial dioceses, Episcopalian houses, parishes, and seminars are exempted. . . .*

The Court declared this article conditionally constitutional, by extending the tax benefit to all religions operating in the country.

> **f.** ***Article VIII.*** *The causes for the nullification or dissolution of canonical marriages, including sacramental and unconsummated marriages, are the exclusive competence of ecclesiastical courts and congregations of the Apostolic Headquarters.*
>
> *The decisions of [the Headquarters], when they are firm and executable according to canonic law, will be transmitted to the [civil] court of the territorially competent judicial district, which will decree its execution . . . and will order its recording in the civil registration book.*

23. The Court similarly struck down Article XX, which set up special procedures for criminal cases involving priests.

The Court declared this article unconstitutional as applied to divorce. It emphasized Article 42 of the 1991 constitution, which granted the civil law the power to regulate marriage and divorce.[24] "As of the issuance of the new Constitution and especially its Article 42, the civil effects of Catholic marriage have ceased and divorce is now decreed according to civil norms. . . ."

> **g. *Article IX*.** *The high contracting parties agree that the causes of separation of a marriage will be dealt with by state judges, in the first instance before the corresponding higher court, and in the second instance before the Supreme Court of Justice.*
>
> *Upon request from either spouse, the case will be suspended in the first instance and for one time only, for thirty days, to allow for the Church's conciliating and pastoral actions. . . .*

The Court likewise held this norm unconstitutional, and particularly its last paragraph, as "the separation of marriages is under the state's jurisdiction[, and t]he competence to hear these cases lies with civil law judges."

> **h. *Article VI.*** *The Church and state will collaborate on the rapid and effective promotion of human and social conditions for the indigenous population. . . .*
>
> *A permanent commission composed of officers designated by the national government and priests elected by the Episcopalian Conference, with regulations reached through common agreement, will . . . supervise the proposed development of the plans adopted. The functions of the permanent commission will be carried out regardless of the state's own planning authority and without the Church performing activities that are foreign to its nature and mission.*

"[T]he 1991 Constitution offers a new socio-political conception of Colombian ethnic groups, . . . lifting indigenous groups out of the legal and constitutional marginalization in which they had found themselves, in order to recognize their ethnic, political, social, cultural, and religious identity."

"Thus, the Constitution recognizes the evolution and signs of improvement that marginalized zones of the country have had . . . which opens the possibility of them assuming consciousness of their own identity and thus they are expressly given rights of self-determination and self-government. The new Constitution contemplates the formation of indigenous territorial entities. . . ."

"For their part the indigenous territories will be governed by councils composed and regulated according to the uses and customs of their communities, to which various functions will be attributed. . . ."

24. Article 42, section 9 states that "[t]he form of marriage, age and legal capacity needed to enter into it, duties and rights of spouses, and separation and dissolution of marriage ties will be determined by civil law." Further, section 11 reads as follows: "The civil effects of any marriage will cease by divorce as established by civil law."

"Article VI is not in conformity with these provisions of the new Constitution in favor of indigenous autonomy, and in addition, when it creates a special canonical regime, it cannot be reconciled with the right of freedom of religion, which allows any person to fully practice their faith, and makes all religious beliefs free before the law."[25]

Note on the Establishment of Religion in Colombia: Negotiations between Colombia and the Vatican to adopt a new Concordat or separate agreement ended in deadlock. Thus the Concordat as modified by the Court's decision still regulates relations between the Catholic Church and the state. Subsequently, Congress passed a statutory law regulating freedom of religion, which created a process for the registration of churches and religions and established protections and rights for religions and their practitioners on equal terms. For example, the new law established provisions for religious education in schools (see Article XII above), but allowed students to get instruction in the religion of their choice or to refuse this education altogether. It also allowed all religions to minister to adherents within the military on equal terms (see Article XVII above). Most of the provisions in this law were upheld by the Court in **Decision C-088 of 1994 (per Justice Fabio Moron Diaz)**.

The Constitution of 1991, through its interpretation by the Court and in the statutory law governing freedom of religion, has moved Colombia somewhat away from a setting where Catholicism was an endorsed or preferred religion by the state and toward a setting where the state has cooperated with or accommodated religions in a pluralist setting.[26] Thus, the new regime grants tax exemptions to all religions and other formal benefits (such as educational access) to all religions equally. Practice, of course, remains more complex. Statistically, Colombia remains a very Catholic country—80 percent of citizens identified as Catholics in a 2014 poll, whereas most of the rest identified with a Protestant denomination.[27] This has had a marked impact, for example, on attitudes towards social issues including same-sex marriage and abortion.

E. The Accommodation of Religion and Conscientious Objection

Colombia provides for mandatory military service for its male citizens, although this legislation has historically included various exemptions and exceptions. Current law does not allow for any right of conscientious objection. However, Article 18 of the Constitution recognizes freedom of conscience and states that no person will be "obliged to act against

25. Articles XVI and XXVI of the Concordat, which further regulated Catholic missions in indigenous areas, were also declared unconstitutional for the same reasons.

26. For this framework, see W. Cole Durham, *Perspectives on Religious Liberty: A Comparative Framework*, *in* RELIGIOUS HUMAN RIGHTS IN GLOBAL PERSPECTIVE (Johan D. van der Vyver & John Witte, Jr., eds., 1996).

27. Pew Research Center, Religion in Latin America: Widespread Change in a Historically Catholic Region 14 (Nov. 13, 2014), *available at* http://www.pewforum.org/2014/11/13/new-pew-research-center-report-explores-changing-religious-landscape-in-latin-america/.

his conscience." In the case that follows, the Court recognized a right of conscientious objection from military service and held that it could be vindicated through a *tutela* in the absence of legislative regulation. In deciding the case, the Court relied on its jurisprudence establishing the right to religious exemptions in other contexts such as working schedules, educational policy, and abortion.

Decision C-728 of 2009 (per Justice Gabriel Eduardo Mendoza Martelo)

[Two citizens proffered a demand against Article 27 of Law 48 of 1993, which regulated obligatory male military service in Colombia. The article exempted several categories of people from having to serve at any time or to pay any compensation, including indigenous groups and those with physical or sensory handicaps. Article 28 created various other exemptions, after payment of compensation and only during times of peace, for orphans, only children, priests, and certain other groups of people. However, the articles included no provision for conscientious objection based on religious or other beliefs.]

[The petitioners argued that the legislature incurred a "relative legislative omission" by failing to include conscientious objectors alongside the various exemptions that were included. Under established constitutional doctrine, the Constitutional Court has the power to correct such "relative legislative omissions" by adding the omitted group. However, the Court cannot fix "absolute legislative omissions," where the legislature completely fails to regulate a given issue. "Relative legislative omissions" can, among other devices, be corrected via what the Court has called an "integrative decision," where the Court requires the provision to be read as though it included an exemption for the excluded group.[28] The Court began its analysis by laying out the right to conscientious objection under the Constitution:]

In accordance with Article 18 of the Constitution, "freedom of conscience is guaranteed" and "no one shall be importuned on account of his/her convictions or beliefs or compelled to reveal them or obliged to act against his/her conscience."

In general, the Constitutional Court has signaled that conscientious objection exists when compliance with existing law demands that persons behave in a way that their conscience prohibits. In other words, the Court has said that conscientious objection requires the presence of a discrepancy between the law and a moral code. The Court has defined conscientious objection as resistance to a legal imperative through the invocation of a dictate of conscience that prevents someone from subjecting him- or herself to the prescribed norm.

Constitutional jurisprudence has noted a clear link between conscientious objection and freedom of thought, freedom of religion, and freedom of conscience, to the point where one can affirm that conscientious objection is one of the necessary corollaries of those liberties. From that perspective, there is a sphere of human

28. The concept of an integrative decision is examined in more detail in Appendix I, which details the different kinds of orders issued by the Constitutional Court.

realization inside which state interference is either inadmissible or demands a higher burden of justification. Thus, those who object for reasons of conscience enjoy a *prima facie* presumption of moral correctness. The state must therefore make arguments that would justify an intervention in a sphere that is in principle immune from any interference.

In this context, this Corporation has pronounced on various opportunities about conscientious objection, on subjects like education, the obligation to provide an oath, workplace obligations, and health care.

The jurisprudence that has defined the right to conscientious objection has established that it is not an unlimited right, but instead that it can be submitted to restrictions. . . .

The basis for conscientious objection is the existence of legal duties that may consist of mandates expressly consecrated in the Constitution, or in legal norms, or as the result of a legal relationship that enables a person to demand from the other certain conduct. . . . In all of these cases, the objector states that compliance with that legal duty is contrary to his conscience.

The Court has stated that constitutional duties are complementary to the rights consecrated in the Constitution, such that the human person, center of the constitutional order, is not only the bearer of fundamental rights but is also subject to duties and obligations which are essential for social life.

For the Court, inside the social state of law founded on solidarity, dignity, work and the prevalence of the general interest, the reasoning that affirms, on the one hand, the immediate effectiveness of fundamental rights also recognizes, on the other hand, that the duties consecrated in the Constitution are imperatives that directly link individuals and whose compliance is a condition of peaceful coexistence.

In this context, constitutional duties, the Court has said, are those conducts and behaviors of public character, demanded by the law . . . , which impose physical or economic burdens and which affect, as a consequence, the sphere of personal liberty. These are behaviors imposed on individuals in consideration of the general interest of the community and which respond to criteria under which all people are required to contribute to the maintenance of the conditions permitting harmonious coexistence. These duties find their roots in the principle of solidarity and are the basis of order and of the very existence of society and of law. . . . [T]heir obligatory nature is based on the consideration that if each person could, according to the dictates of his own conscience, decide which laws to obey and which not to, order would be broken and organized community would be rendered impossible.

The Court has specified that, in general, the obligatory nature of constitutional duties requires legislative development and, in that sense, the duties consecrated in the Constitution give the legislature an opportunity to develop and concretize the sanction for noncompliance with the basic parameters of social conduct fixed by the Constituent Assembly. However, this does not prevent . . . the *tutela* judge from taking constitutional duties directly into account when weighing constitutional values, since they constitute an indispensable hermeneutic criteria for delimitating fundamental rights. The complementary relationship between rights and duties demands that the constitutional interpreter read them together. . . . The Court has stated that in exceptional cases, constitutional duties are directly justiciable and that this [may] occur when one person's noncompliance with a duty threatens the fundamental rights of another person, which demands the opportune intervention of constitutional judges to prevent irreparable harm.

[Next, the Court dealt specifically with the question of conscientious objection to military service, questioning whether it should change its existing jurisprudential criteria and recognize a right of conscientious objection to military service.]

[Historically,] conscientious objection was only allowed when it was expressly stated in law. That has been the position of the Constitutional Court in Colombia in relation to conscientious objection to obligatory military service, an aspect that will be analyzed specifically in the remaining parts of this decision.

In the 1991 Constitution, however, the topic has been treated in a broader way, such that under Article 18 of the Constitution, the right to be protected from acting against one's conscience is not subordinated to the law. Thus, in scenarios distinct from that of military service, we have not demanded a law developing the right in order to make it effective.[29]

We must define the criteria through which we can make the immediate application of the right effective, keeping in mind that not every conscience-based reservation can prevail over legal duties, nor, in the other extreme, can all legal duties be considered absolute over the conscience of individuals.

The Court must undertake a balancing that takes into account the nature of the conscientious objection, the seriousness with which it is assumed, the effect that its overriding would produce on the subject, against, on the other side, the importance of the legal duty . . . and the circumstances in which it has been developed, examining for instance the possibility of requiring the objector to fulfill the duty in another way, or substituting another duty of a similar nature that does not create a conflict of conscience. In this last case, the Constitutional Court has written about the possibility of reconciling compliance with the duty with tasks that do make it incompatible with considerations of conscience.

One criterion for establishing the seriousness and significance of the conscientious objection proposed by the objector is its link with religious liberty. Thus, if religious considerations exist, "it would be incongruous for the legal order, on the one hand to guarantee religious liberty, and on the other hand to refuse to protect its most valuable manifestations of spiritual experience, such as those dealing with aspirations

29. The Court cited several examples here, including Decision T-547 of 1993 (per Justice Alejandro Martínez Caballero) (refusal to take oath in criminal process), Decision T-588 of 1998 (per Justice Eduardo Cifuentes Muñoz) (refusal to participate in certain school activities), and Decision T-982 of 2001 (per Justice Manuel José Cepeda Espinosa) (refusal to work on the sabbath).

towards coherence between what one practices and what one believes. This element, which can pertain to the essential nucleus of religious liberty, also defines an aspect that is central to freedom of conscience. . . ."

While the constitutional guarantee under which it is possible to lodge conscientious objections to distinct duties needs legislative development, the absence of that development does not imply the ineffectiveness of the right, which in its essential nucleus can be made directly effective under the Constitution.

In this way, the possibility of presenting a conscientious objection is subjected to a weighing performed in each concrete case between the elements that create the objection and the nature of the duty that gives rise to it. If in light of this analysis it is concluded that the conscientious objection is well-founded, lack of legislative development cannot be taken as an obstacle to the effectiveness of the right, which may be exercised directly under the Constitution. In this sense the Court declines to follow the interpretation under which, in the past, we have arrived at the conclusion that the National Constituent Assembly, after rejecting a proposal to include conscientious objection to military service expressly in the text of the Constitution, had excluded the possibility of such an objection from the constitutional order. . . .

In addition, given that conscientious objection to military service is often linked to religious considerations, the refusal to recognize it would also affect the freedom of religion, which has as its object ensuring that people may follow religious beliefs of their choosing, as well as allowing them to adjust their behaviors and external actions to the dictates of their internal beliefs. For the Court it is unreasonable to require a person to offer military service when the overarching ends sought by that measure, such as repaying the state for benefits received, contributing to the protection of the nation and the state, and achieving social cohesion, may be sought by other means. It is unnecessary to seek these ends through the provision of military service which, in the case of conscientious objectors, creates a profound conflict between the constitutional duty and professed convictions or beliefs.

The above interpretation is in harmony not just with jurisprudence of the Court that has recognized explicitly the possibility of conscientious objection from workplace, educational, and professional duties, but with normative references in the constitutional block . . . [I]n General Comment 22 of 1993, about the right to freedom of thought, the [United Nations Human Rights] Committee observed that "[t]he Covenant does not explicitly refer to a right to conscientious objection, but the Committee believes that such a right can be derived from Article 18, inasmuch as the obligation to use lethal force may seriously conflict with the freedom of conscience and the right to manifest one's religion or belief."[30] The Committee expressly invited the State Parties to "report on the conditions under which persons can be exempted from military service on the basis of their rights under Article 18 and on the nature

30. UN Human Rights Committee, *CCPR General Comment No. 22: Article 18 (Freedom of Thought, Conscience or Religion)*, CCPR/C/21/Rev.1/Add.4 (July 30, 1993), § 11.

and length of alternative national service." Recently, as various interventions have mentioned, in the Final Observations of the Human Rights Committee: Colombia (2004), the Committee stated "with concern" that Colombian legislation "does not allow conscientious objection to military service." As a consequence, it observed that the state "should guarantee that conscientious objectors are able to opt for alternative service whose duration would not have punitive effects."[31] . . .

The Court holds that the convictions or beliefs that give rise to the refusal to offer military service must be profound, fixed and sincere, so that the freedom of conscience and religion is really threatened.

In the first place, the convictions or beliefs that are the object of constitutional protection must define and condition the behavior of people. In other words, [it must affect] their *external* behavior. These cannot be convictions or beliefs that only live in the *internal* sphere of a person, and which do not affect actions. . . . In that sense, all conscientious objectors have the minimum obligation to demonstrate the external manifestation of their convictions and beliefs. It is their duty to prove that their conscience has conditioned and determined their behavior in such a way that offering obligatory military service would act against it.

Now, the convictions or beliefs invoked, in addition to being external manifestations that can be proven, must be profound, fixed, and sincere.

Profound means that they are not a superficial conviction or personal belief, but instead that they affect the life of the person and his manner of living in an integral way, as well as the totality of his decisions and appreciations. These must be convictions or beliefs that form part of his way of life and that condition his actions in an integral manner.

Fixed implies that they are not changeable, and that one is not dealing with convictions or beliefs that can be modified easily or rapidly. . . .

Finally, *sincere* implies that they are honest, rather than false, accommodating, or strategic. . . .

Also, the Court clarifies that the convictions or beliefs . . . can be of a religious, ethical, moral, or philosophical character. Constitutional and international norms, as was noted, are not limited to religious beliefs, but contemplate human convictions of other types, which structure the autonomy and personality of all people.

Finally, it is enough to point out that until a special procedure is created, regulated by the legislator, objections of conscience that are presented by youths must be heard in an impartial and neutral manner, in accordance with the rules of due process and, in every case, the constitutional right to conscientious objection may be the object of protection by judges via the *tutela*.

[Finally, the Court considered the proper remedy. The Court held, contrary to the demand, that the provision's failure to include an exemption for conscientious objectors did not constitute a "relative legislation omission" that could be corrected

31. UN Human Rights Committee, *Concluding Observations: Colombia*, CCPR/CO/80/COL (May 26, 2004), § 17.

by the Court. The Court held that the provision at issue provided categorical exemptions for easily-identified groups of people, whereas conscientious objection was a subjective right that needed to be evaluated on an individual basis. Thus, the provision did not omit an exemption for a class of people similar to those to which it gave an exemption. The Court instead held that the legislature had incurred in an "absolute legislative omission" that could not be corrected by the Court.]

In this case, the real problem is that the legislator has not issued a law to regulate conscientious objection in the sphere of military service, which is an absolute legislative omission.... [A]s we have noted on other occasions, while a legislative omission having an absolute character cannot be corrected by an integrative decision of the Court sitting on abstract review, this does not mean that the right to conscientious objection . . . cannot be exercised, but merely that it must be applied by directly applying the Constitution . . . via *tutela* action....

Given that the legislative omission attacked by the petitioners is not derived from Article 27 of Law 48 of 1993, we will declare that provision constitutional. However, for the Court it is clear that the recognition of the right to conscientious objection, without a legal framework defining the conditions and procedures for its exercise, generates certain doubts and gaps in the legal system, and that the definition of those rules and conditions corresponds to the legislator as the paradigmatic agent of representative democracy. For this reason, we exhort Congress to regulate the topic by defining, in light of the Constitution, the conditions under which the right will prosper, as well as the alternatives that can be offered to objectors so that they will be able to comply with their constitutional duty without having to set aside their convictions or religious beliefs.

[The Court thus held the provision at issue to be constitutional, while encouraging the legislature to pass a law on the matter. Meanwhile, conscientious objectors to military service can bring *tutelas* to effectuate their rights. Four justices—Maria Victoria Calle Correa, Juan Carlos Henao Perez, Jorge Ivan Palacio Palacio, and Luis Ernesto Vargas Silva—dissented. They agreed with the analysis holding conscientious objection to military service to be a fundamental right, but would have held that the legislature did incur in a "relative legislative omission" in failing to include an exemption for conscientious objectors in the relevant law. Further, they criticized the majority's decision for creating uncertainty about when the right to conscientious objection should succeed.]

Note on Conscientious Objection in Colombian Law: If the Court had held that the failure to include a right of conscientious objection from military service was a "relative" rather than "absolute" omission in the existing law regulating mandatory military service, it could have issued an integrative decision and read that exemption into existing law. But such a decision would have left procedural gaps, for example in how conscientious objectors could petition for an exemption, who would decide whether they were entitled to one, and what standard would be used. The Court instead chose to leave the omission in place but to allow conscientious objectors to seek relief via the judiciary, by filing a *tutela*. This, of course, required that potential objectors understand their judicially-created rights and be able to access the courts.

Despite the exhortation of the Court, Congress has not yet passed a law regulating conscientious objection from military service. In **Decision T-018 of 2012 (per Justice Luis Ernesto Vargas Silva)** and once again in **Decision T-455 of 2014 (per Justice Luis Ernesto Vargas Silva),** the Court found in the course of adjudicating *tutelas* that the military generally refused to consider petitions for conscientious objection to military service, and took the view that it could not consider these claims to exemption until they had been regulated by Congress. In the second case, the Court ordered the relevant military authorities to establish and implement procedures to respond to these petitions. In 2015, the military finally created a set of regulations to regulate conscientious objection, even though Congress still has not acted.

A second area where religious accommodation has played a significant recent role is in abortion policy. As noted above in Chapter 3, Section E, the Supreme Court in Decision C-355 of 2006 legalized abortion in certain designated circumstances where the life or health of the mother is at risk, where the pregnancy is a result of rape or incest, or where the fetus suffers from a severe illness that is incompatible with life outside the womb. In such a Catholic context, this decision provoked substantial controversy.[32] In its jurisprudence developing that decision, the Court has held that individual doctors do have a right to conscientiously object to the carrying out of abortion procedures where contemplated by law. However, it has emphasized that the objection must be specific, that it must be individual rather than collective on behalf of an entire institution, and that the doctor carrying it out has a duty to immediately refer the patient to another physician who will perform the procedure.

For example, in **Decision T-209 of 2008 (per Justice Clara Inés Vargas Hernández)**, the Court examined the case of a 13-year-old girl who had been impregnated as the result of rape. Despite due notification to a special unit of the prosecutor's office (which stated that an abortion should be carried out) and to the health insurer, the abortion was not performed. A first hospital stated that all of its gynecologists and other relevant medical staff had a conscientious objection and sent the family to a second hospital, which gave the same response. The Court reiterated its jurisprudence that objections be individualized rather than collective, founded on specific objections, and that the objector take immediate steps to ensure the abortion is carried out. It found these steps flagrantly disregarded in the case at issue—and it has found similar problems in other cases. The problem of conscientious objection to abortion thus demonstrates some of the complexities that can arise when this right is exercised by a majority population rather than a small minority.

32. *See* Pew Research Center, *supra* note 27, at 73 (finding that 23 percent of Colombians favored legal abortion in 2014 and 73 percent opposed it).

6

Social Rights

From the inception of the Constitutional Court, the enforcement of social rights has been a priority. Statistically, Colombia remains a developing country with significant problems of poverty. Roughly 50 percent of the population lived below the national poverty line as recently as 2002; by 2015, that number had dropped but remained at 28 percent. As of 2013, 14 percent of the population continues to live on less than US$3.10 per day.[1] Although the state has developed a number of programs to respond to poverty and inequality, deficiencies in state capacity and clientelistic models for the provision of benefits have compounded problems in some areas.

The materials in this chapter treat three broad themes needed to give the reader a sense of the variety of approaches that the Colombian Constitutional Court has taken on socioeconomic rights issues. The first considers the Court's interpretation of these rights. As noted in the Introduction, the Colombian Constitution includes a long list of social rights, including health, housing, social security, and education, and the Court's case law has ranged broadly across different issues. However, two concepts have proven central for the interpretation of all of these rights—the vital minimum and the social state of law principle.[2]

The vital minimum was synthesized in one of the Court's first decisions (T-426 of 1992, excerpted in Section A) from the various social rights found in the constitutional text. It gives individuals a right to receive at least the minimum level of subsistence and enjoyment of rights needed to survive under dignified conditions. In subsequent case law, the vital minimum has become more than a subjective right: it is a principle that tells the Court and the Colombian state that it must prioritize the immediate needs of the poorest and most marginalized members of society. The principle of a social state of law, which is

1. These statistics are from the World Bank website, at http://povertydata.worldbank.org/poverty/country/COL (last visited Aug. 1, 2016).

2. For more detail on these two concepts, see David Landau, *The Promise of a Minimum Core Approach: The Colombian Model for Judicial Review of Austerity Measures*, *in* Economic and Social Rights after the Global Financial Crisis 267 (Aoife Nolan ed., 2014)

Colombian Constitutional Law: Leading Cases. Manuel José Cepeda Espinosa and David Landau.

expressly stated in Article 1 of the Colombian Constitution, has been described in Decision T-772 of 2003 (excerpted in Section E) as "a cardinal principle" of the constitutional order, and as requiring that the Colombian state take action for "the promotion of conditions of dignified life for all people and the resolution of the real inequalities present in society." In other words, the social state principle requires that the state design and implement programs to reduce poverty and to achieve substantive equality.

These two concepts map loosely onto approaches found in international and comparative doctrine. The vital minimum doctrine has some correspondence with the minimum core approach in international law.[3] Using this doctrine, the Court has demanded that programs give urgent priority to the desperate needs of the poorest and most marginalized Colombians. In some cases, including the internally displaced persons' case excerpted in Section D, the Court has also defined a minimum entitlement of socioeconomic rights for affected individuals. The social state principle, in turn, has some similarity to concepts of progressiveness found in international law.[4] The state is required by the Court to undertake affirmative steps over time to alleviate poverty and ensure substantive equality, and backward steps (retrogression) will be viewed with suspicion. The Court has therefore used a number of interpretive approaches to enforcement of social rights, depending on the circumstances.

The second broad theme of this chapter is the question of remedies, where the Court has also used a number of different approaches depending on the circumstances.[5] Social rights cases raise complex questions as to how a court can best remedy deficient provision of social programs without exceeding its legitimacy or capacity. The Court's first forays into the enforcement of social rights involved the *tutela*, and gave individual relief for an individual claim, for example ordering the provision of a pension or medical treatment for a given petitioner. These cases remain statistically important, at times in the last decade constituting about half of all *tutelas* filed in the country.

But since the late 1990s, the Court has also utilized various forms of structural relief in certain cases, using its power (outlined in Chapter 2) to define the effects of its own decisions. Therefore, where necessary the Court has asserted the power to issue broad orders reaching beyond the individual petitioners even in *tutela* cases. The two most prominent structural cases are T-760 of 2008, involving the healthcare system and excerpted in Section

3. *See* Committee on Economic, Social, and Cultural Rights (CESCR), General Comment 3: The Nature of States' Parties Obligations, U.N. Doc. E/1991/23, ¶ 10 (1991) ("The Committee is of the view that a minimum core obligation to ensure the satisfaction of, at the very least, minimum essential levels of each of the rights is incumbent upon every state party."). For discussions of the minimum core, see, e.g., DAVID BILCHITZ, POVERTY AND FUNDAMENTAL RIGHTS: THE JUSTIFICATION AND ENFORCEMENT OF SOCIO-ECONOMIC RIGHTS (2008) (defending the concept); Katharine G. Young, *The Minimum Core of Economic and Social Rights: A Concept in Search of Content*, 33 YALE J. INT'L L. 113 (2008) (arguing that the concept lacks definition).

4. *See* General Comment 3, *supra* note 3, ¶ 9.

5. For theoretical contributions to the debate about designing remedies for social rights violations, see, e.g., BRIAN RAY, ENGAGING WITH SOCIAL RIGHTS: PROCEDURE, PARTICIPATION, AND DEMOCRACY IN SOUTH AFRICA'S SECOND WAVE (2016); KATHARINE G. YOUNG, CONSTITUTING ECONOMIC AND SOCIAL RIGHTS (2012); MARK TUSHNET, WEAK COURTS, STRONG RIGHTS (2008).

C, and T-025 of 2004, involving internally displaced persons and excerpted in Section D. In each of these cases, the Court has created a robust system of monitoring in order to ensure compliance, and has issued numerous follow-up orders. As this chapter shows, the Court has also issued structural orders in a number of other cases.

A third theme has involved the beneficiaries of the Court's interventions.[6] Both the social state of law principle and the concept of the vital minimum suggest that the state must take steps to prioritize the needs of the poorest members of society. But the Court's jurisprudence has not always been as successful as one would like at reaching these groups. As Sections B and C show, for example, critics of the Court have raised concerns that some of its individual and large-scale interventions benefitted relatively affluent groups such as middle-class civil servants rather than the most marginalized. In other cases, such as those involving internally displaced persons (Section D) and street vendors working in the informal sector (Section E), the Court's decisions have clearly been targeted at impoverished and extremely marginalized groups.

The materials included in this chapter are designed to explore these themes while taking a loosely historical perspective, thus allowing the reader to gain a sense of the evolution in the Court's approach over time. Immediately after the creation of the Constitution of 1991, a major question was about whether the new social rights were judicially enforceable at all. The Court's creation of the vital minimum doctrine as related in Section A allowed it to answer this question in the affirmative, and the Court began issuing a small but increasing number of *tutelas* protecting these social rights.

The next major test for the Court (see Section B) occurred during a very deep economic crisis in the late 1990s, which caused an explosion of *tutelas* and other claims involving socioeconomic rights from a broad cross-section of society (including middle-class groups). These claims resulted in the Court intervening on behalf of claimants both collectively, for example in housing and public sector-salaries, and individually, by issuing an increasingly high number of *tutelas* protecting healthcare, pensions, and other social rights.

Following the crisis and turnover in the Court's personnel, as Sections C (health) and D (internally displaced persons) show, the Court began issuing structural remedies in certain areas where it found systematic deficiencies in state capacity affecting vulnerable groups. These remedies were undertaken to fix large-scale bureaucratic problems and to overcome the inequity and congestion caused by issuing a large number of individual *tutela* remedies, but they raised new challenges regarding capacity and compliance.

Finally, Sections E and F focus on two areas that the Court has most recently emphasized. Section E considers the problem of informal and marginalized workers such as street vendors, informal recyclers, and sex workers, who often face discrimination and are left

6. *See* David Landau, *The Reality of Social Rights Enforcement*, 53 Harv. Int'l L.J. 190 (2012) (arguing that some enforcement of social rights, both in Colombia and elsewhere, has not focused on the very poor). For a comparative perspective on this problem in relation to Brazil, see Octavio Luiz Motta Ferraz, *Harming the Poor through Social Rights Litigation: Lessons from Brazil*, 89 Tex. L. Rev. 1643 (2011).

outside of social safety nets entirely. Section F treats the right to water, which is a major problem across parts of Colombia and has become a significant theme in recent case law.

A. Foundations of Justiciability: The Right to a Minimum Level of Subsistence

In this early decision dealing with social rights, the Court deduced a right to a minimum level of subsistence (*derecho al mínimo vital*) from several clauses of the Constitution. The Constitution does not explicitly state such a right, but the Court found that it existed, based on specific social rights found in the Constitution (health, social security, housing, etc.), and based on broader clauses setting out constitutional principles (the principles of dignity and social state of law, for example).

The invention of the right to a minimum level of subsistence has played two major functions in the Court's case law. First, from a procedural perspective it allowed for the enforcement of various social rights via the *tutela*, which was initially left ambiguous by the constitutional text. Article 86 of the Constitution states that *tutelas* can only be used to protect "fundamental" rights, but the Constitution contains no definitive list of which rights are fundamental and which are not. Article 85, however, lists certain rights as being of "immediate application," but the social rights are generally excluded from this list.

The vital minimum allowed the Court to overcome this ambiguity and enforce social rights via *tutela* in some cases. The Court held that even if social rights are not fundamental in and of themselves, they become fundamental if they impact the vital minimum of the petitioner, because in that case they also affect other rights such as the right to life and human dignity. The right to a minimum level of subsistence therefore acted as the genesis for the Court's "connectivity" doctrine, which in the Court's early jurisprudence explained the circumstances under which social rights could be directly enforced by individuals. More recently, and as explained below with respect to both health (Section C) and water (Section F), the Court has held that some aspects of social rights can be deemed fundamental in their own right, thus rendering the connectivity doctrine unnecessary.

Second, from a substantive perspective, the right to a minimum level of subsistence has played a prioritization function for social rights in Colombian constitutional law. Like the international law concept of the "minimum core" with which it shares some similarities, the right to a minimum level of subsistence suggests that the state must prioritize the basic needs of the poorest members of society. Although the Court and the Colombian state have not always succeeded in adhering to this principle, it acts as a basic guiding ideal for the enforcement of social rights by the Court.

Decision T-426 of 1992 (per Justice Eduardo Cifuentes Muñoz)

[In a unanimous decision, the Court protected the right to the minimum level of subsistence of the petitioner, a senior citizen who requested that he be given the proceeds of a pension that had previously been earned by his late wife. Even though the petitioner clearly had this right under existing law as a surviving spouse, the authorities took no action on it. The petitioner defined himself in his complaint as an "elderly person without resources" and stated that the failure to recognize his right to a pension "forced him to live under the protection of his daughter, imposing an additional burden on her, and without being able to satisfy certain elemental necessities because of a lack of resources, including a surgical intervention required by his precarious state of health." After one year of receiving no response, the petitioner filed a *tutela*. The first-instance *tutela* judge found that the authorities had violated his constitutional right to petition[7] by giving him no response, and ordered the authorities to make such a response within one month. However, it also found that the petitioner's socioeconomic rights had not been violated. Finally, 16 months after the request had been filed, the relevant authorities granted his request and began paying him his late wife's pension.]

The condition of abandonment and social marginalization of thousands of elderly people is unacceptable. . . .

Long lines of the elderly waiting to be paid pensions needed to survive, a lack of government services to assist senior citizens as well as physically or mentally handicapped persons, unlike in other societies, and which are needed to guarantee the satisfaction of their basic needs and, in general, the absence of an adequate system of protection and assistance, are objective factors that place this social group in circumstances of manifest marginalization and weakness.

The Colombian constituent power wanted to respond to this injustice. . . . Thus, clause 2 of Article 46 of the Constitution establishes: "The state shall guarantee to [the elderly] services of integral social security and food subsidies in cases of indigence."

Within this social and cultural context . . . we must evaluate the *tutela* action brought by [the petitioner] in his condition as an elderly man. Social reality nourishes constitutional law. In the application of constitutional norms to concrete cases we must take into account that one of the essential ends of the state is the progressive realization of the aspirations of the constituent power aimed at transforming reality when that reality generates unfairness, injustice, and inequality. . . .

Even though the Constitution does not consecrate a right to subsistence, it can be deduced from the rights to life, to health, to work and to assistance, and to social security. People require a minimum of material elements to survive. The acknowledgement of fundamental rights in the Constitution aims to guarantee the economic and spiritual conditions necessary for the dignity of the person and the free development of his personality. . . .

The social state of law has a relationship to the form of political organization that has as one of its objectives combatting economic and social poverty and the disadvantages of diverse sectors, groups, or persons of the population, by lending them assistance and protection.

From the principle of the social state of law one deduces various constitutional mandates and obligations: first, the Congress has the task of adopting the legislative

7. Article 23 of the Colombian Constitution guarantees to all individuals "the right to present respectful petitions to the authorities . . . and to secure prompt resolution of same."

measures that are necessary to construct a just political, economic, and social order. In addition, the state and society together, in conformity with the principles of human dignity and solidarity, must guarantee to all persons the vital minimum needed for a dignified existence.

The social state of law demands the construction of the indispensable conditions needed to ensure all inhabitants of the country a dignified life within achievable economic conditions. The goal of empowering human capacity requires that the authorities act effectively to maintain or improve living standards, including food, housing, social security, and those scarce monetary resources needed to get along in society.

Everyone has the right to a minimum of conditions for his material security. The right to a vital minimum—the right to subsistence as the petitioner calls it—is a direct consequence of the principles of human dignity and of the social state of law, which define the just political, social and economic organization chosen as a goal by the Colombian people in their Constitution. . . .

The right to a vital minimum not only includes the power to neutralize situations violating human dignity, or to demand assistance and protection by victims of discrimination or marginalization or by those under circumstances of manifest weakness, but also, above all, aims to guarantee equality of opportunities and social leveling in a society that has historically been unjust and unequal, with cultural and economic factors that have had a serious incidence on this "social deficit."

The right to a vital minimum does not grant a subjective right for an individual to demand, directly and without considering the special circumstances of the case, an economic guarantee from the state. Even though the social duties of the state may eventually generate such a guarantee, as long as it remains infeasible, the state has the obligation to promote real and effective equality before the inequitable distribution of economic resources and scarcity of opportunities. . . .

The right to social security is not expressly acknowledged in the Constitutions as a fundamental right. Nonetheless, this right, established in a generic manner in Article 48 of the Constitution,[8] and in a specific manner regarding elderly persons (Article 46, clause 2), acquires the character of fundamental when, according to the circumstances of the case, not acknowledging it raises the possibility of endangering other fundamental rights and principles such as life, human dignity, physical and moral integrity or the free development of personality of the elderly.

The concrete situation of a great number of elderly people makes the right to assistance and social security fundamental given their circumstances. According to [the records of] the Constituent Assembly, "in Colombia it is estimated that in 1990 there were 2,016,334 people over sixty years of age, out of which 592,402, more than

8. Article 48 states in part: "Social Security is a mandatory public service which shall be delivered under the administration, coordination, and control of the state, subject to the principles of efficiency, universality, and solidarity within the limits established by statute. . . . All inhabitants are guaranteed the irrevocable right to Social Security."

one fourth, lack the resources necessary for subsistence. Further, it is known that most individuals who are senior citizens suffer from some type of social abandonment and very few have access to social security. That figure does not reach even 1 percent across the entire national territory." That is why the Constitution guarantees senior citizens the rights to integral social security and to a food subsidy if they are indigent. . . .

Even though the interventionist thesis has been accepted in the past to ameliorate the effects of the capitalist system and with the objective of promoting social justice, what is debated today is whether persons and groups who are gravely in need enjoy a constitutional right to assistance and social security. The restrictive character of the exercise of individual rights before the state is opposed to the recognition of constitutional rights aimed at the immediate satisfaction of basic needs and the consequent obligation of the state to guarantee them.

In certain political spheres a conception persists that the private sector is the primary and ultimate guarantor of the satisfaction of basic needs, not the public sector. The vision that underlines this thesis is that human welfare is best guaranteed by the "free market," which offers infinite economic opportunities to achieve prosperity, and not by the assumption of social obligations by the state.

However, the myth of economic equality of opportunity has been contradicted by global demographic realities.

In the international sphere this has given rise to the establishment of mechanisms for compliance with human rights. The International Covenants on Civil and Political Rights and Economic, Social and Cultural Rights . . . ratified by Colombia through Law 74 of 1968, develop and concretize the rights stated in the Universal Declaration of Human Rights. . . .

Especially, Article 9 of the International Covenant on Economic, Social, and Cultural Rights establishes: "The States Parties to the present Covenant recognize the right of everyone to social security, including social insurance."

The principle of interpretation of rights and duties in conformity with international human rights treaties ratified by Colombian (Article 93), demands that we affirm the fundamental character of the right to social security for those persons with basic unsatisfied needs and who are found in conditions of manifest weakness because of their economic, physical, or mental condition. . . .

Finally, it is important to note that the protection of and the assistance to elderly persons is not an obligatory function of the state, society, or family standing alone. The three institutions must cooperate to fulfill this social function, without it being possible for any of them to abstain from this legal obligation under the pretext that the others must do it. When the burden of protection or assistance to senior citizens is for their families of such a magnitude, given their economic conditions, that it becomes a grave inconvenience for them . . . , then the state or society must step in to guarantee the fulfillment of this obligation. Because of this, the argument given by the judge in this case that the state should not be obliged to provide protection and assistance to the petitioner, because this is an obligation of his family, is unacceptable.

The failure to resolve the pension issue in this case violated the concurrent obligation of the state to protect and assist the elderly.

[The Court confirmed that the state must recognize the petitioner's pension, and required that it pay damages in favor of the petitioner for the excessive delay (beyond the four to five months that is standard in these cases) in recognizing it. Furthermore, it warned the state not to take the same actions regarding other petitioners.]

B. The Court and Economic Crisis

Some of the Court's most aggressive interventions on social rights occurred in the late 1990s, during a very deep recession that originated in the financial sector. Economic growth expanded only 0.6 percent in 1998 before contracting 4.2 percent in 1999. Unemployment also spiked to nearly 20 percent in 2000.

As one observer has noted in detail, this economic crisis had an impact on the docket and case law of the Court.[9] The total number of *tutelas* filed increased sharply, and many of these involved the socioeconomic rights of those who had their healthcare, pensions, housing, or other goods threatened by the crisis. The Court's jurisprudence on the vital minimum shifted in this period: by the late 1990s it was protecting socioeconomic rights en masse, without undertaking the individualized assessment carried out in T-426 of 1992 as to whether the exact petitioner at issue lived in marginal conditions. Many of those seeking relief during the economic crisis of the late 1990s were struggling members of the middle class, rather than extremely poor.

Section C covers some of the individual *tutela* jurisprudence from this period and afterward, through a study of the right to health.

This section instead discusses two of the Court's larger-scale interventions from this economic crisis, on housing and public sector salaries, respectively. These decisions are of interest first because they give an example of a court wrestling with socioeconomic rights during economic crisis and in reaction to austerity measures. Moreover, they demonstrate an area where the Court faced strong criticisms both from the government and the economic establishment for its initial decisions, and those decisions evolved somewhat through time within the basic framework of the social state of law.

1. The Housing Finance Crisis

One byproduct of the financial crisis was to threaten about 100,000 mostly middle-class homeowners with foreclosure. The system for financing housing purchases called UPAC (units of constant acquisitive power) was created by the national government in 1972. The aim was to create a stable system that would finance mortgages for middle-class borrowers. Initially the system worked very well: long-term mortgage loans were linked to UPAC units, which in turn were closely tied to inflation. But beginning in the early 1990s, UPAC units

9. *See* Pablo Rueda, *Legal Language and Social Change during Colombia's Economic Crisis*, *in* CULTURES OF LEGALITY: JUDICIALIZATION AND POLITICAL ACTIVISM IN LATIN AMERICA 25 (2010).

were also tied to the prevailing interest rates in the broader economy. Thus, as Colombia faced a financial crisis in the late 1990s and interest rates spiked, increases in UPAC rates began to greatly outpace the rate of inflation. This was compounded by a rapidly increasing unemployment rate. The combination of these two factors left many homeowners unable to pay their debts.

The Board of Directors of the Central Bank, an autonomous entity created by the Constitution, failed to take any action to ameliorate the increase in UPAC rates. Neither Congress nor the executive intervened. Embattled debtors organized themselves into civil society groups and turned to the Constitutional Court by filing a series of lawsuits in front of it, and the Court thus issued several different decisions in 1999 and 2000. Some of those decisions are summarized here:

First, in **Decision C-308 of 1999 (per Justice Alfredo Beltrán Sierra)**, a seven-to-two judgment, the Court struck down a law according to which the value of UPAC units was determined by the Board of the Central Bank "so that the units would reflect the fluctuations of interest rates in the [broader] economy." The Court considered two issues: whether the law violated the principle of central bank autonomy found in the Constitution, and whether it violated the right to acquire and keep a dignified home established by Article 51, which also establishes that the state must create an "appropriate" financing system for this purpose.[10]

On the first issue, the Court highlighted discussions that took place during the Constituent Assembly and that suggested that the Bank was intended to exercise a high degree of "functional and technical autonomy" so that it would be free from political interference. It held that the Congress had the power to assign functions to the Central Bank, but that the Bank had to be given autonomy in determining how these functions would be carried out. In other words, Congress could give the Bank the power to set UPAC rates, but it interfered with the Bank's exclusive competence when it went further and ordered these rates to be established so that they reflected the fluctuations in interest rates in the broader economy.

On the second issue, the Court pointed out that the Constitution establishes "the right to dignified housing" as a social and economic right which, due to its inherent characteristics, cannot be immediately materialized, but can only be carried out in a progressive way.

> [T]he Constitution orders the State to "determine the conditions necessary to give effect to this right," as well as to promote "plans for public housing" and "appropriate systems of long-term financing." That is, according to the Constitution, the purchase and preservation of housing by Colombian families cannot be considered as a matter foreign to the state's concerns but, on the contrary, . . . authorities have . . . a specific mandate to assist [citizens] in purchasing housing and in facilitating payment under adequate long-term conditions, including by setting up specific plans for the less

10. Article 51 states: "All Colombian citizens are entitled to live in dignity. The state shall determine the conditions necessary to give effect to this right and shall promote plans for public housing, appropriate systems of long-term financing, and community plans for the execution of these housing programs."

> wealthy sectors of the population, an issue that the Constitution itself defines as of "social interest."
>
> "For the Court it is clear that for reasons of equity, the purchasing power of money must be preserved; for this reason monetary obligations can be adjusted according to [the rate of inflation]. [But] including as a factor for adjustment . . . the fluctuation of the interest rates in the economy causes an excessive increase in the initial obligation, since the obligation is increased not only to preserve purchasing power, but with one additional factor which destroys the balance between what was initially owed and what is in the end paid; it is precisely for this reason that this practice seems contrary to equity and justice as supreme goals of law; that is, in opposition to the 'enforcement of a just order' as stated in Article 2 of the Constitution."
>
> "Likewise, the determination of the value in pesos of the UPAC according to the fluctuation of the economy's interest rates is in direct contradiction with the 'equitable generalization of credit' ordered by Article 335 of the Constitution,[11] which is one of the basic postulates in the conception of a social state of law since . . . [such a state] is reached when . . . credit is not granted only to those who have money and goods, but is available to a greater number of the country's inhabitants. . . . [T]his requires the provision of effective possibilities for personal and familial development in egalitarian conditions, every day."
>
> "[W]e hold that including the variations in economy-wide interest rates in order to determine the value in pesos of the UPACs completely distorts the just preservation of the amount of the debt, in such a manner that it generates as a consequence a benefit for the lending entity and a direct and proportional negative effect on the debtor. . . ."

Justices Vladimiro Naranjo Mesa and Eduardo Cifuentes Muñoz dissented, arguing that the congressional power to define the functions of the Central Bank includes the possibility of determining criteria for their fulfillment, and that the Constitution sets no specific methodology for financing housing. Further, they argued that the Court was overstepping its role in important ways, taking on functions that should properly be exercised by more democratic branches.

> Respect for the rule of law and democracy requires the Court to abstain from extending its jurisdiction to social problems that require political instruments wielded by other organs of the state. The Court in this decision mistakenly defines as a constitutional problem what is in reality a complex topic involving only issues of convenience and of the design of policies by institutions charged with economic management. The lack of leadership in a country that fails to confront its great conflicts momentarily hides the impropriety of the Court's actions and allows the public to look with indulgence on those actions. But the enormous costs of these

11. Article 335 states: "The financial, stock exchange, insurance, and any other activities related to the handling, exploitation, and investment of . . . resources . . . are of public interest and may only be exercised following the prior authorization of the state, in accordance with the applicable statute, which shall regulate the government's form of intervention in these areas and promote the equitable generalization of credit."

kinds of interventions, even if they may be for the moment very popular, will eventually reflect negatively on this Court.

Next, in **Decision C-700 of 1999 (per Justice José Gregorio Hernández Galindo),** the Court in a six-to-three decision declared the law regulating the entire UPAC system to be unconstitutional. In the course of hearing this case, the Court held a one-day public hearing at which representatives of the different civil society groups representing debtors, economists and other experts, representatives of various state authorities, and other politicians presented to the Court evidence on the extent and nature of the housing crisis. Nonetheless, the grounds for striking down the UPAC system were ostensibly technical. According to the Court, the law was issued as a presidential decree when it should have been issued as a "framework statute" by Congress. The Court ordered that the effects of the decision be deferred for a time so as to avoid chaos in the housing sector, while allowing Congress to design a new system, and it ordered any new law to be consistent with its earlier and later decisions on the right to housing.

The Court noted that the 1991 Constitution created a new system for regulating certain issues. In areas such as financial regulation, Congress was given the power to adopt the general parameters of policy via a framework statute, and the president was then empowered to construct the details of policy within that broad framework. The Court found that the current UPAC system had been promulgated by a 1993 presidential decree, but that it should have been established by a framework law passed by Congress instead.

However, the Court deferred the effects of its decision in order to give Congress time to construct a new system: "For the Court it is clear that, in order to carry out an adequate transition between the two systems, without generating trauma in the economy, the law held unconstitutional must temporarily remain in force while Congress, using its powers, can write the framework statute which has been omitted, and the Executive, through administrative decrees, can develop that statute concretely." The Court thus allowed the current system to remain in force until the end of the then-current legislative period—June 20, 2000.

Justices Vladimiro Naranjo Mesa and Eduardo Cifuentes Muñoz again dissented. They considered that the constitutionality of the provisions at issue had already been decided in earlier cases, and that under stare decisis principles, the earlier decisions had to stand. Further, they pointed out that the 1993 decree was merely a reordering (with no changes other than the numbering of articles) of an earlier legal decree that predated the 1991 Constitution and its new distribution of powers. In sum, they argued that the Court had used a formal argument as a pretext to make a decision that was really about the wisdom of public policy, and that should have been discussed in a more democratic forum. "To insist on assuming judicial definition of more or less popular causes, outside the framework of constitutional parameters, will condemn the country to the impoverishment of politics and citizen's participation. The constitutional judge cannot anesthetize with its decision the real existence of democratic principles. On the contrary, its mission is to defend and stimulate the existence of an open democratic process. The artificial constitutionalization of all social problems will give the Constitutional Court a power than can be totalitarian and which will act as an obstacle to the deepening of a true constitutional culture."

In **Decision C-747 of 1999 (per Justice Alfredo Beltrán Sierra),** the Court in a six-to-three decision struck down a provision of the UPAC law that allowed long-term mortgage financing to be structured so that unpaid interest would capitalize onto existing loan balances. In other words, loans could be structured in such a way that the debtor's payments in some periods do not even cover the accruing of interest in those periods, and the unpaid interest is added on to the principal of the loan. Future interest then accrues on this new principal, with the unpaid interest added in.

The Court examined whether the right to dignified housing under Article 51 of the Constitution was being violated by the law, because "the capitalization of interest on loans granted to obtain long-term housing cannot be part of an 'appropriate system' for [obtaining dignified housing]; and, likewise, because [capitalization] prevented the debtor from obtaining true and impartial information on the real amount of her or his credit obligations . . . ."

"[T]his Corporation finds that the 'capitalization of interest' on medium and long-term loans does not violate the Constitution per se, so it cannot be declared unconstitutional in a general and definite manner for any type of credit. However, when dealing with credit to acquire housing, it is evident that the 'capitalization of interest' does violate Article 51 of the Constitution. . . ." The Court also emphasized that Congress, in its pending creation of a new framework statute to regulate the system of housing finance, must comply with its holding in this case.

Justices Naranjo and Cifuentes again dissented, in this case citing empirical research by the Central Bank and other economists to question whether the Court's decision would actually help to realize the right to housing laid out in Article 51. They argued that the Court's decision might hurt, rather than help, the poorest homeowners, because "contrary to the Court's intuition, the capitalization of interest is conceived with the purpose of permitting lower-income households to access the housing finance system, in cases in which the mechanism of fixed quotas without capitalization of interest would overrun their actual payment capacity and thus they would be unable to acquire the housing they desire. . . . ."

To comply with these decisions—and particularly Decision C-700 of 1999, which struck down the entire housing finance system but deferred the effects of that ruling until the end of the 2000 congressional session—the government introduced and Congress adopted a framework statute that created a new system to finance housing, called the Real Value Unit (UVR by its Spanish acronym). The new law responded to the weaknesses in the existing system by fixing the real interest rate over the life of the loan. It also provided funds to bail out existing homeowners in the old system and ending foreclosure proceedings against those homeowners. The law finally incorporated the prior jurisprudence of the Constitutional Court by, for exampling, prohibiting the capitalization of interest.

The constitutionality of this new system was examined in **Decision C-955 of 2000 (per Justice José Gregorio Hernández Galindo)**. The Court declared most of the new law constitutional, but struck down some sections and held major provisions of the law to be only conditionally constitutional. For example, the Court allowed real interest rates to be charged on housing loans in accordance with the law, but required that they must be "always below the lowest real interest rate being charged" in other sectors, as certified by the

Superintendent of Banking, because of Article 51's mandate to promote housing. The Court also struck down some provisions that limited the availability of relief to some categories of existing homeowners.

The new law, along with economic improvement, ameliorated the housing crisis. But the Court has continued to hear a number of *tutelas* involving the system. In the years after the new law was issued, a number of these cases involved the conditions under which existing debtors could refinance under the new system. Even more than 15 years later, the Court has also continued to hear a number of *tutelas* involving the conditions under which debtors should have been entitled to refinancing and a termination of foreclosure actions against them.

2. The Budgetary Crisis and Public Sector Salaries

The same economic crisis sharply increased public sector deficits. At the end of 1999, the Colombian government received a three-year financial support package from the IMF totaling $2.7 billion, and pledged to introduce various structural reform measures to reduce the deficit and achieve other goals. The 2000 budget therefore contemplated freezes in nominal salaries for higher-income public sector servants, with nominal increases roughly offsetting the rate of inflation for poorer workers making less than two minimum salaries. Given that inflation was running around 10 percent in this period, most public sector workers would see a significant decline in their real, inflation-adjusted wage.

In **Decision C-1433 of 2000 (per Justice Antonio Barrera Carbonell)**, the Court held that all public sector workers, regardless of socioeconomic status, must receive salary increases at least equal to the rate of inflation. The Court considered that employees had a right to preserve the purchasing power of their salaries; therefore, the salary provision of the budget was held unconstitutional and the Court ordered the state to pass a new provision in which all salaries in the public sector would be increased at least in accordance with the inflation rate of the prior year. The core of the Court's reasoning was as follows:

> From the provisions of the Constitution surges the constitutional duty of the state to conserve not only the acquisitive power of the salary, but to ensure its increase, taking into account the need to ensure that workers receive incomes according with the nature and value of their work and which allows them to ensure a vital minimum according to the requirements of a standard of living adjusted to dignity and justice. In effect, this duty is derived (i) from the necessity of ensuring a just social and economic order; (ii) from the philosophy that inspires the social state of law, founded in the principles of human dignity, solidarity, and the consecration of work as a value, a subjective right, and a social duty; (iii) from the purpose attributed to the state of promoting and guaranteeing prosperity and general welfare, the improvement of the quality of life of persons, and the effectiveness of the principles, rights, and duties consecrated in the constitution; (iv) from the principle of equality in the formulation and application of law; (v) from the necessity of ensuring equality of opportunities for all persons and a minimum essential and flexible remuneration;

> (vi) from the recognition of equal treatment in salaries for active workers and pensioners; (vii) from the duty of the state to intervene in a special manner to ensure that all people, especially those with lower incomes, have effective access to basic goods and services, and (viii) from the prohibition on the government weakening the social rights of workers, naturally including a salary, during an economic state of emergency, which indicates that in times of normality it is even clearer that these rights cannot be reduced. . . .
>
> It is convenient to recall that the budgetary law for 2000 was conceived within the context of a series of macroeconomic criteria, among which a determining weight was given to the need to restrict salary increases. The law at issue recognizes two groups of public servants in relation to the increase or adjustment in salary: those making up to two minimum monthly salaries, who will receive an increase, and the others who are excluded from that right.
>
> This signifies, without doubt, a discriminatory treatment to the prejudice of a vast sector of public servants, under the criterion that the majority of workers should make a sacrifice as a contribution to the health of public finances. This treatment violates the principle of equality because all workers are equally affected by the economic situation and especially, by inflation. And if the state must preserve the real value of salaries, as we have seen, there is no reasonable basis for this only to happen in relation to certain workers and not others. . . ."
>
> The fiscal situation of the country is an insufficient argument for ignoring the adjustment of salary for public servants, because it requires management that is adjusted to the constitutional order and from that order surges, with meridian clarity, the constitutional duty of the government to conserve the real value of salary. . . .

Decision C-1433 of 2000, along with the UPAC decisions summarized above, was the subject of extensive criticism, particularly from state officials and economists. These critiques focused on several major points. First, they noted the very substantial cost of both the housing and salary decisions for the state, as they required the state to appropriate bailout funds for the housing sector and to raise salaries for all public sector workers. Second, the critics argued that the Court issued these decisions without having a sufficient understanding of the overall macroeconomic context, and without understanding why the decisions were sound. Third, they questioned the legitimacy of the Court to enter into matters involving the formulation of public policy. Finally, some commentary questioned the distributive impact of the Court's decisions, suggesting that both the housing decisions (which mainly aided formal-sector workers with a decent income) and the budgetary decision (by requiring that the state raise salaries for higher-income workers) benefitted the middle class more than the very poor.

Allies of the Court in civil society, academia, and the press defended the Court, noting for example that it was often the only institution defending constitutional values and social groups ignored by other actors. In the case of UPAC, for example, debtors turned to the Court in part because other political institutions were not responsive to their pleas for relief from a problematic system. The defenders of the Court also argued that it had played a useful role in protecting that system, which otherwise would have collapsed from political inattention. 2000 and 2001 were years in which most justices from the first full court ended their eight-year terms; thus these decisions, and their underlying debates, became issues in the election of Constitutional Court justices. They were raised, for example, in the congressional hearings from which the Senate elected the new justices, and discussed in the press.

After turnover in the Court's personnel, it modified its jurisprudence. In a five-to-four decision reproduced below, the Court declared the budget for 2001 to be conditionally constitutional. Given the ongoing fiscal crisis, the Court allowed for a budget that would make full adjustments for inflation only for lower-income public sector workers making less than the average salary; more affluent workers could receive lesser adjustments in order to allow the state to fulfill its constitutional duties to fund social programs.

Decision C-1064 of 2001 (per Justices Manuel José Cepeda Espinosa and Jaime Córdoba Triviño)

[The annual budget was challenged on the ground that all public salaries were not increased in a percentage equal to the previous year's inflation and therefore the principle of a "minimum essential and flexible remuneration" of work, as well as the right to preserve the real acquisitive power of salaries, had been violated]

Among the concrete manifestations of the fundamental principle of the social state of law we can find, for example, general mandates to promote real and effective equality through the adoption of measures favoring marginalized or discriminated groups; to especially protect people who, because of their economic, physical or mental standing, are found to be under manifest weakness; to protect pregnant women, the female head of a family, children, adolescents, elderly, disabled, retired, and ill persons; to provide support for the unemployed; to foster full employment as well as improvements in quality of life for persons with lower incomes; and, in general, to give priority—over any other allocation—to social expenses in order to resolve the unsatisfied health, education, environmental and potable water needs of the nation and territorial entities' plans and budgets.

To appeal to the reinforced solidarity of a social state of law cannot, however, reach the extreme point of eliminating individual and social freedom by means of the materialization of a state which, under the pretext of exercising its functions of directing the economy, transforms itself into a totalitarian one. The social state of law aims at "creating the implicit social conditions of the same liberty for everybody"; that is, suppressing social inequity. In this sense, the principle inherent in the social state of law is a mandate to the legislator, which obliges him or her to provide justice and equity when making decisions in agreement with the constitutional framework, but which grants an ample margin of respect for the options of public policies as exercised by the elected authorities. The social state of law does not impose any social or economic model, but neither is it indifferent to the realization of values such as a fair social order or human dignity. Such an interpretation provides power for the Congress to design legislative programs, and for the executive to design government programs; it aims to reconcile these powers with the material contents that the Constitution itself requires, and which bind all public authorities.

[Next, the Court provides a historical review regarding the right to work in the Colombian Constitution, and concludes that] work has, thus, multiple means of expression within the constitutional order in force, since it is not only a right by which the individual obtains resources that allow him or her to cover his or her basic needs, but is also a social obligation that translates itself into a mechanism to imbed the person into the community as an individual who dignifies herself or himself by means of the contribution he or she makes to a community's development, as well as a duty that every worker has to contribute . . . to the construction of a society that is more participatory both in political and economic terms and—in this manner—is more democratic and pluralistic.

Section 1 of Article 53 of the Constitution sets out, within the fundamental principles that must be developed by the Labor Statute, the right to "minimum essential and flexible remuneration.". . . [The] Constitutional Court considers that a systemic interpretation of the Constitution requires that the means to construct a just social order must utilize the fundamental principles of a social state of law. [These principles include] human dignity, solidarity, and work, and the state's social duties—among these the ones that promote and guarantee prosperity and general wellbeing; the improvement of quality of life; and the effectiveness of principles, rights and duties set out in the Constitution in order to take measures so that equality is made real and effective, especially to protect work in all forms; to guarantee the means so that pensions maintain their constant acquisitive power; to ensure equality of opportunities for all persons;—as well as the state's mandate to intervene in a special manner to ensure that all persons, especially those with lower incomes, have effective access to basic goods and services. [Based on these principles,] it is possible to establish the foundations for a constitutional right held by workers to preserve the real purchasing power of their salary.

We reach a similar conclusion from constitutional interpretation in light of international treaties and agreements regarding the protection of salaries.

[T]he Court believes that the requirement of "minimum essential and flexible remuneration" does not lead to a single rule for altering salaries, in particular because a salary increase depends on multiple factors that cannot be reduced to a single criterion.

[Likewise the] constitutional right to preserve the real acquisitive power of a salary is not an absolute right, since no right in a social and democratic state is absolute. . . . However, rights cannot be ignored through the mere invocation of the principle of general interest. . . .

As has already been noted, this case necessarily sets up a confrontation of several constitutional rights, ends and principles, since the effectiveness of the social state of law depends on the realization of a series of acts that require economic resources. This circumstance reveals the close relationship between the concretization of the ends required of the state in social matters and the need to have a macroeconomic structure that permits not only the fulfillment of those objectives but also the normal functioning of the state. Because of this, we must carry out a balancing exercise, which takes into account (i) the relevant legal antecedents for the issue being analyzed, and (ii) the public rights and ends at play in order to establish the reasonableness of the measures being questioned in the real context in which the norm being contested was created and applied.

[The Court] confirms the main premises of C-1433 of 2000[, which required that all public salaries be increased at least by the rate of inflation]. However, it differs from the conclusions derived within it about the right to preserve the acquisitive power of salaries. . . . [T]he order from the Court [in that case] did not constitute an accurate interpretation of the constitutional regime regarding the legal nature and issuance of the budget.

[The Court held in C-1433 that] equality prevented the salaries of some public servants from being raised while others were not, even though all salaries were equally affected by inflation. [Yet] this interpretation of the principle of equality ignores a line of precedents upheld by this Court that has interpreted [it] to mean that equal people must be treated equally and unequal ones, unequally. And public servants who earn the equivalent to 1 or 2 minimum wages are not equally affected [by a decrease in real salary] as compared to those who earn between 10 and 20 minimum wages, just to mention one example.

[Finally,] a decision such as the one in C-1433 of 2000, which starts out by asserting the absolute right of workers to a salary readjustment according to a fixed criterion—the inflation rate—, and which considers that such a right, formulated under the terms of an inflexible rule, cannot be limited due to justifiable constitutional reasons, falls afoul of the uniformly-followed practice of interpretation and application of constitutional rights according to which the latter are susceptible of being balanced against other constitutional rights, ends and principles.

[T]he Court certifies that even though there does not exist a line of precedents on the constitutional relevance of macroeconomic policy or on the constitutional value of economic progress within a just order as part of the general interest, in C-1433 of 2000 the weight of the real situation of the country or the greater or lesser importance of the ends being pursued by macroeconomic policy were not considered. . . .

[Regarding] the right to preserve the acquisitive power of the real salary of public servants whose salary is lower than the . . . average one, the Court points out that the right is untouchable because of the reinforced protection provided by the Constitution. That is, it is a right that although non-absolute, has a special resistance, constitutionally acknowledged, before possible limitations resulting from actions by public authorities. It is a right that, in spite of the fact that the country is in the midst of an economic [crisis], cannot be touched. . . . Four arguments of constitutional character support this statement.

First, as the Political Constitution itself points out in Article 334, one of the ends the state must aim to fulfill when it intervenes in the economy is to "ascertain that all individuals, especially those with a low income, may have effective access to all basic goods and services."

Second, when the Constitution enacts the right to equality in Article 13, it states that "the state shall promote the conditions so that equality may be real and effective and shall adopt measures in favor of groups which are discriminated against or marginalized." The Constitutional Court, as an organ of the state, is called upon to fulfill this mandate and may not ignore it. The preservation of the real purchasing power of the salary of lower-income public servants, even under extraordinary circumstances, calls into play this mandate since it aims at closing the breach between those who earn less and those who earn more.

Third, failing to preserve the acquisitive power of the salary of public servants with lower incomes can significantly affect their rights and the rights of the persons who economically depend on them to live a dignified life, since the state is dealing with people who are more vulnerable and in critical economic situations.

The fourth reason has to do with the state's economic ends. Considering the arguments set forth in this case, the justification for limiting the right in question of those who are in the higher salary scale is the mandate on the state to give priority in the allocation of resources to servicing the basic desires of those most in need. The group of public servants with lower incomes, together with their relatives, are part, precisely, of that group of people who constitutionally deserve special protection in a social state of law, particularly in economic situations like the one taking place over the last three years. . . .

In the case of public servants who earn the highest salaries, the situation is different. On the one hand, the factual context studied by the Court shows that their situation is not as grave as the one that the majority of the population is facing; on the other hand, the legal context indicates that they are not subjects [who] should receive reinforced constitutional protection. . . .

The Court then asks itself what, in the midst of a critical socio-economic situation like the one of the last few years, could justify limiting the right of the higher-earning public servant to receive a salary that at least preserves its real purchasing power. . . .

[The proportionality test] presupposes three steps. The first consists in analyzing the end looked for through the decision made by the Government; the second, of analyzing the means to reach such an end; and the third, of studying the relationship between means and end. . . . The Court warns that in this case strict scrutiny must be applied because the norm being challenged may affect constitutional rights such as the person's salary, their minimum vital means of subsistence, and their dignity.

[The Court highlighted the following as a valid goal of the legislation: "to ensure that social investment not be reduced as a consequence of allocating scarce resources under a fiscal deficit to paying rather onerous salary increases." The Court found that this goal arose directly from Article 366 of the Constitution.[12] Once the Court had concluded that the measure sought to fulfill an end of constitutional status

12. Article 366 states: "The general well-being and improvement of the population's quality of life are social purposes of the state. A basic objective of their activity shall be to address the unsatisfied public health, educational, environmental, and drinking water needs of those affected. For such an outcome, in the plans and budgets of the nation and of the territorial entities, public social expenditures shall have priority over any other allocation."

which could justify a limitation, it continued to the second and third stages of the proportionality test:]

[The means used] are not only permitted but also foreseen in the Constitution itself. In fact, Article 366 . . . points out that in order for the state to reach the social ends mandated by the Constitution, "in the plans and budgets of the nation . . . , public social expenditures shall have priority over any other allocation." . . .

The real context that gives life to the meaning of the Constitution indicates that it is necessary for the state to decline to allocate resources for certain expenditures, in order to have the necessary funds for public social spending. It is, then, necessary to limit certain allocations in order to benefit impoverished persons so that the mandates for the intervention of the state in the economy are fulfilled, everybody is able to have access to goods and services, and the unsatisfied needs for health, education, environment, and potable water are taken care of.

[Regarding] budgetary issues, means are considered necessary when their weight is of such a magnitude that it becomes a necessary condition to obtain a determinate end, even if it is not at the same time a sufficient condition; that is, even if the attainment of the end requires the concurrence of other means.

In the case being studied, considering on the one hand the critical economic situation and the great demands of the social expenditures demanded by the Constitution; and, on the other hand, that expenditures on salaries are one of the items that weigh most heavily in the state's operating expenses, the Court considers that the means selected by the Congress are necessary ones. . . .

[Thus,] it is not disproportionate to limit public servants with better salaries . . . in order to liberate and allocate resources to cover needs related to public social spending.

Thus, the following question arises . . . : Under what exact conditions would the limitation be disproportionate? The Court considers that it is not within its competence to determine the exact nature of such a limitation. This decision must be made in political forums. Nevertheless, the Constitution does enunciate certain criteria to determine how far it is possible to limit the right at issue, criteria the Court will now discuss:

First, authorities must decide that they are carrying out a limitation and not a restriction or annulment of the right. The right to preserve the purchasing power of the salary of public servants with high salaries can be limited but not ignored, [and thus even employees with higher salaries must receive] some kind of salary increase, in nominal terms. . . .

The answer . . . cannot be an exact figure . . . ; it must consist instead of indications of constitutional criteria that must be observed. . . . The first two criteria are equity and progressiveness. . . . The other criterion . . . is proportionality. . . .

[The] degree of any salary increase for workers with higher incomes cannot be equal to or higher than the increases for those with lower incomes. Otherwise, the principles of equity and progressiveness would be ignored. In addition, the differences between the percentage of salary increase of two workers found at slightly different salary grades should not be too large, in order to avoid disproportionate differences. Within these general criteria, it is the task of the competent authorities to determine the percentage increase for each salary grade. It is beyond the Court's competence to give specific percentages. That rests in the discretion of the competent authorities.

The Court emphasizes that it is the fulfillment of the State's fundamental and overriding social goals that justifies the limitation of the right and no other goal; thus the fiscal savings must be effectively aimed at public social spending. . . . Therefore, in order to comply with this decision, measures must be adopted ensuring that the fiscal savings obtained as a result of the adjustment of the salaries of public servants leads to an effective increase in public social spending. . . .

The considerations [outlined in this decision] offer a reasonable margin of configuration for the competent authorities to define public salary policy. The Court does not ignore the fact that under extraordinary circumstances the criteria enunciated might become a barrier to macroeconomic policies of a greater social benefit for all the country's workers, both the employed and the unemployed, as well as for those Colombians with lower income, especially those living below the poverty line. The Constitution does not prevent such criteria from being weighed, giving special consideration to such extraordinary circumstances. Nonetheless, the justification and defense of a public salary policy that includes the weighing of extraordinary macroeconomic circumstances, of their constitutional relevance, and of their imperative character is within the competence of the authorities who adopt it. The Court certifies that in this case such a burden was not met by the authorities upon whom it fell. . . .

[Justices Clara Inés Vargas Hernández, Jaime Araujo Rentería, Alfredo Beltrán Sierra, and Rodrigo Escobar Gil dissented, arguing that the issue had already been decided in C-1433 of 2000 (which involved the prior year's budget) and therefore could not be re-litigated. They thus believed that the budget should have been held unconstitutional because it did not preserve the real purchasing power of all public sector salaries.]

Note on the Court's Austerity Jurisprudence: In response to the Court's 2001 decision, the government complied by maintaining nominal increases at roughly the rate of inflation (9 percent) for those making less than two minimum salaries, and then issuing progressively smaller increases for higher-income workers, with all workers receiving at least an increase of 2.5 percent. In 2002, the government maintained increases equal to the rate of inflation (7.65 percent) but only for those workers making equal to or less than one minimum salary; all other workers received smaller nominal increases. During this period, economic growth improved markedly, although the deficit remained large by historical standards and the debt increased.

In **Decision C-1017 of 2003 (per Justices Manuel José Cepeda Espinosa and Rodrigo Escobar Gil)**, the Court studied the budget for 2003, which had once again failed to provide for salary increases sufficient to preserve the real value of all public sector salaries. The Court noted that the intervening budget of 2002 had not complied with the Court's reiterated jurisprudence on this issue, because the executive and Congress had not justified a continued deterioration in salary policy even for low-income workers making more than one minimum salary. In addition, it emphasized that many public sector workers had now experienced several years of real salary decreases due to austerity, without noted improvement in the budgetary situation. Finally, it pointed out that the president and Congress had called a referendum to reform the Constitution and effectively reverse the Court's salary jurisprudence. The referendum received a majority of all votes cast, but failed because less than the constitutionally-required minimum of 25 percent of all registered voters participated.

The Court thus issued a more direct set of instructions to the political branches. It required that the real purchasing power of all public sector workers making less than two minimum salaries be preserved, and it held that all workers should receive increases at least equal to 50 percent of inflation, in order to preserve the "essential nucleus" of the right. It also stated that the government must develop a plan to give all public sector workers salary increases at least equal to the rate of inflation within a short period of time, it required that any deviations from such an increase be justified by increasingly weighty reasons, and it held that any savings should be used only on public social spending. The Court finally issued a stronger remedy in this decision: it held the 2003 budget conditionally constitutional in the terms stated by the Court, and it ordered the president and Congress to effectuate "the corresponding budgetary additions and transfers" to ensure that any necessary increases in appropriated funds would actually occur.

The Court's decisions in this section, and particularly those involving public sector salaries, are worth considering in a broader comparative perspective. They are part of a broader family of decisions protecting socioeconomic rights during economic crisis, and in particular responding to austerity measures taken as a step to overcome that crisis. Several courts around the world have struck down parts or all of government measures designed to cut salaries or benefits in response to economic or fiscal crises.[13] Courts undertaking these interventions have at times been criticized for being overly rigid, or for protecting affluent civil servants and formal-sector workers rather than the very poor. The Colombian Court's jurisprudence in C-1064 of 2001 might be viewed as an attempt to provide protection for constitutional rights during crisis, prioritizing the rights of the very poor while giving the state flexibility to make cuts upon sufficient justification.

C. The Right to Health: From Individual to Structural Remedies

The 1991 Constitution refers to the right to health in several articles. Article 49 states that "public health and environmental protection are public services for which the state is responsible" and guarantees to all individuals "access to services that promote, protect and restore health." The same article gives the state the leading role in the design and operation

13. *See generally* Economic and Social Rights after the Global Financial Crisis, *supra* note 2.

of the system, which should follow principles of "efficiency, universality and solidarity." Furthermore, Article 44,[14] which gives the rights of children "precedence" over the rights of others, mentions health as a basic right of children.

In 1993, Congress issued Law 100, through which the General Social Security System was created.[15] The Congress chose to create a complicated healthcare system that mixed private and public elements. The law established two main types of health plans: contributory plans and subsidized plans. Contributory plans cover those who have the financial capacity to pay into the system (workers or independent contractors), whereas subsidized plans cover those who cannot afford to pay and are therefore subsidized by the state. According to the law, the inclusion of poorer people who require subsidies into the healthcare system would be a gradual process that prioritized those most in need based on a survey of socioeconomic status. Meanwhile, those not included in either of the two systems would have access to public healthcare centers when they were sick, but were not entitled to a specific healthcare service package and were forced to pay a percentage of their healthcare costs in certain cases.

Those covered by either a contributory or subsidized plan would have the right to a government-mandated package of services known as the Mandatory Healthcare Plan (POS). The subsidized POS, though, was initially much smaller than the contributory POS. One goal of Law 100 of 1993 was to gradually equalize the quality of the two plans over time. Thus, the basic package of healthcare services is defined by regulation rather than being left to individualized healthcare contracts as in the United States.

The system is not government-operated. A set of private institutions called Health Promotion Entities (EPSs) are charged with ensuring that individuals receive healthcare services included in the POS, and they contract with individual healthcare providers for that end. Users are free to choose their EPS, and can switch EPSs over time. In exchange for delivery of all services included in the POS, EPSs receive a fixed fee from the government for each consumer affiliated with their organization. This per-capita fixed fee is paid from a public fund whose budget is collected mainly from fees paid by those who are affiliated to the contributory system. The entire system was supervised and regulated by a fragmented system of state entities.

Law 100 of 1993 was highly successful along some dimensions. For example, it allowed for a substantial expansion in health insurance coverage. However, from the very start, the law has had significant problems. Some important or lifesaving treatments that were very costly (such as those for chronic diseases) were not included in the POS. This was a problem in both systems, but was particularly problematic within the subsidized POS, which remained much smaller than the contributory POS. Other treatments were

14. Article 44 states: "The following are basic rights of children: . . . health and social security. . . ."

15. For general overviews of the contours and jurisprudence on the right to health in Colombia, see Katharine G, Young & Julieta Lemaitre, *The Comparative Fortunes of the Right to Health: Two Tales of Justiciability in Colombia and South Africa*, 26 HARV. HUM. RTS. J. 179 (2013); Alicia Ely Yamin, Oscar Parra-Vera & Camila Gianella, *Colombia: Judicial Protection of the Right to Health: An Elusive Promise?*, *in* LITIGATING HEALTH RIGHTS: CAN COURTS BRING MORE JUSTICE TO HEALTH? 103 (Alicia Ely Yamin & Siri Gloppen eds., 2011).

included in the POS, but were improperly denied by the EPSs, which were not effectively supervised by state entities. Finally, in many cases it was unclear whether a given treatment was included or excluded from the POS, and there was no efficient mechanism to resolve those disputes.

1. Individualized Enforcement

Following the Court's creation of the vital minimum in Decision T-426 of 1992, it became possible for petitioners to bring *tutelas* to protect the right to health. As noted in the Introduction, Article 86 only allows the *tutela* to be taken to protect "fundamental" rights. Although the Court did not in this period hold that the right to health was fundamental in-and-of-itself, *tutelas* could be taken to protect the right whenever a failure to do so would affect the vital minimum of the petitioner. In other words, the right to health could be protected whenever its enforcement was connected to rights that were clearly fundamental, such as the rights to life and human dignity. This was referred to in the Court's jurisprudence as the "connectivity" doctrine, and it was the main way social rights could be enforced by *tutela* in the Court's early years.

The first cases of the Court were idiosyncratic and turned heavily on the individual circumstances of the petitioner and a showing that the denial of rights at issue impacted that person's vital minimum. In **Decision T-534 of 1992 (per Justice Ciro Angarita Barón),** the Court ruled on the case of a young man who was recruited by the national army for compulsory military service. From the beginning of his training, he declared that he had health problems, but his commanders paid no attention to his complaints. Before taking the oath of enlistment and while on a temporary leave, he visited a private doctor and was diagnosed with lung cancer. When he reported this to his superiors in the army, they refused to authorize the healthcare he required because the formal oath of enlistment ceremony had not taken place. Instead, he was declared unsuitable for service and dismissed. The soldier then filed a *tutela* requesting access to the healthcare he required. The Court ordered his transfer to the healthcare center suggested by his physician.

According to the Court, the fact that the right to life is enshrined in Article 11 of the Constitution implies that the state has the "duty" to "protect citizens' lives by adopting all those measures that would allow them to live in dignified conditions." And therefore, "since the soldier is a Colombian citizen, his dignity entitled him to receive from the state efficient and timely care for his health and life from the moment he was recruited and put under the authority of his immediate commanders. The lack of a symbolic ceremony cannot be pleaded as an excuse, even less so when the soldier was serving the country to the best of his ability."

Soon, however, the Court began to be called upon to interpret the rules regulating the system in light of constitutional principles. In **Decision SU-043 of 1995 (per Justice Fabio Morón Díaz),** for example, the Court examined the case of a 14-year-old girl who had tuberous sclerosis, which caused significant symptoms and was incurable but controllable with medical treatment. The girl was registered as a beneficiary of her parents' affiliation to the healthcare system, and she had received medical treatment all her life. One day, however, the girl's mother was informed that it was impossible to continue delivering the service because the disease was classified as "non-curable" and therefore not covered under an exclusion from the POS. The girl's mother, a low-wage worker, filed a *tutela* claiming that the girl's fundamental rights to life, health, and social security had been infringed. In a unanimous decision, the full Court ordered the health insurance company to deliver the healthcare services she required. Reiterating prior case law, the Court noted that the right to health of children was especially protected in the Constitution. It found that the healthcare provider had interpreted the POS too narrowly; properly interpreted in light of the Constitution, it covered the services required because it also covered treatments that were aimed at "support, maintenance, and for the relief of pain."

Subsequently, the Court began to require EPSs to cover even treatments located outside of the POS if they were fundamental to a citizen's rights to life or human dignity. In **Decision SU-480 of 1997 (per Justice Alejandro Martínez Caballero)**, for example, the Court protected the rights of several people living with HIV/AIDS who had filed *tutelas* requesting the delivery of medication required for their treatment (such as antiretroviral drugs). These drugs were not included in the POS. In a unanimous decision, the Court ordered that the drugs be provided. However, the Court also gave the EPSs the ability to seek reimbursement from the state for the cost of medications that were not included in the POS. The Court stated that "since we are dealing with a contractual relationship, the EPS only has an obligation to provide the specified services . . . ; if they go beyond what is in the regulations, it is fair that medicines given to save lives be defrayed . . . by the state."

By the early 2000s, a confluence of factors created a very rapid expansion in the number of *tutelas* filed on the right to health. First, the basic weaknesses of the design of the system became exacerbated through time. The POS was vaguely designed and updated only in an ad hoc way; it was often difficult to determine whether a given treatment was inside or outside of the POS. Furthermore, as regulatory oversight was fragmented and insufficient, the EPSs had an incentive to deny even treatments within the POS, forcing individuals to seek relief via *tutela*. The Court's jurisprudence also played a role in the expansion—it required coverage for non-POS treatments and allowed the EPS to seek reimbursement from the state, but the government did not establish a sufficient formal system for seeking such reimbursement. This gave the EPSs a further incentive to deny treatments, in the hope that a court would order it to be outside the POS, allowing the EPS to perform these often expensive treatments while getting paid by the state.

At any rate, as Figure 6.1 shows, from 1999 through 2008, health claims represented an increasingly high percentage of all *tutelas* even as the total number of *tutelas* increased sharply.[16] In 1999, there were 21,301 *tutelas* on the right to health in Colombia, which represented 25 percent of all *tutelas* filed. By 2008, there were 142,957 health *tutelas*, 42 percent of all *tutelas* filed in the country. Half or more of these claims were for treatments or medicines that were included in the POS and thus should not have been denied by the EPS. Statistics also demonstrate that the petitioners won the vast majority of these cases. Claims for cosmetic or fully elective procedures were denied, but petitioners would ordinarily

16. For a statistical overview, see Defensoría del Pueblo, *La tutela y los derechos a la salud y la seguridad social 2014*, at http://www.defensoria.gov.co/public/pdf/LatutelaylosderechosalaSalud.pdf.

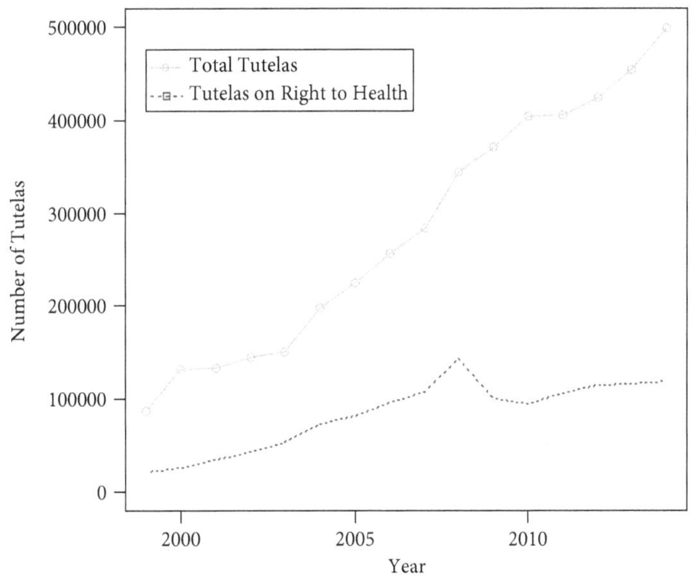

FIGURE 6.1 Total *Tutelas* and Health *Tutelas*, 1999–2014. Defensoria del Pueblo, La *Tutela* y el Derecho a La Salud 2014, at 86 tbl. 7 (2015).

win whenever they could show that a given treatment affected their life or human dignity, regardless of whether the treatment was included in the POS. The Court's jurisprudence thus shifted over time. Rather than undertaking an individualized assessment of whether a given situation impacted the vital minimum of a petitioner, it began indicating that relief should be issued in a more categorical manner.

By the 2000s, the judiciary was playing a substantial role in the governance of the healthcare system. This helped ameliorate some problems: Colombians denied services because of the vagueness of the POS and inadequate oversight of the EPSs could seek rapid relief from the courts. Moreover, the Court's role was fundamental in establishing health as a right rather than a mere public service, and thus requiring treatment even for expensive treatments left outside of the standard plans when necessary to protect the life and dignity of the petitioner.

At the same time, citizens were often forced to resort to the courts to seek meaningful relief, as the quality of the healthcare providers did not markedly improve, the POS continued to be ambiguous and outdated in many respects, and regulatory oversight of the system continued to be deficient. This in turn had a worrisome equity effect—in many cases, only those who sued reaped the benefits of the system. And empirical data suggested that those accessing the courts tended to be relatively affluent in comparison with those who did not. Most claims, for example, originated from the contributory regime for formal sector workers with a stable income, even though more workers were attached to the subsidized regime for informal workers and the unemployed. Finally, the sheer volume of *tutela* claims on health clogged the dockets of the Constitutional Court and the judiciary as a whole.

2. Structural Enforcement

It was in this context that the Court issued **Decision T-760 of 2008 (per Justice Manuel José Cepeda Espinosa)**. The decision sought to shift away from the individualized remedy model and toward a structural model that would fix major problems within the entire healthcare system. To this end, the Court aggregated various *tutela* writs requesting access to medical treatments and procedures prescribed by physicians in charge, but denied by EPSs. Some of these services were included within the POS, whereas others were not. The Court also reviewed *tutela* writs that had been filed by EPSs requesting reimbursement from the state for services already delivered and not included in the mandatory health plan. In the course of making its determination, the Court collected information from EPSs and other healthcare providers, civil society organizations, government regulatory agencies, and institutions charged with overseeing and controlling the state. After examining all of the evidence collected in the proceedings, the Court found that there were pervasive regulatory failures that had led people to resort to a flood of *tutela* actions.

The Court first held that "the right to health is a fundamental constitutional right" in and of itself, which can be protected by *tutela* in certain circumstances. Thus, the Court completed a shift in the foundations of the justiciability of the right. It moved away from its traditional "connectivity" doctrine, where the right to health was protectable by *tutela* only if it was linked to other fundamental rights such as life and human dignity, and toward a model where the right to health could be directly protected by *tutela* because of its fundamental nature.

> [Taking into consideration] that fundamental rights are "(i) those considered as such by general consensus and (ii) those subjective rights aimed at ensuring human dignity," the Court has pointed out that the right to health is fundamental in an "autonomous manner" when it can be operationalized in subjective guarantees derived from the norms which govern its fulfillment. Some of these guarantees, the Court has found, are to be found in the Constitution itself, others in the constitutional block, and the majority in the laws and rules established to govern the National Health System and define specific services to which people are entitled. . . .
>
> Following this same line of discussion, the full Constitutional Court has underlined that health is a fundamental right to which all individuals are entitled. If it is not protected, an inadmissible constitutional breach ensues. . . .
>
> Constitutional case law has rightly pointed out that acknowledging the fundamental nature of a right does not entail that all of its aspects are susceptible to protection via *tutela*. First because constitutional rights are not absolute; in other words, they may be restricted according to rational and proportional criteria established through constitutional case law. Second because the possibility of demanding the enforcement of obligations derived from fundamental rights in general and the adequacy of doing so by resorting to a *tutela* action are two clearly different things.
>
> The progressive nature [of social rights] explains the impossibility of demanding by legal process, in concrete individual cases, immediate fulfillment of all the obligations derived from the field of protection of a constitutional right, but this in

no way means that the state is licensed to refrain from adopting adequate measures to comply with such obligations as they gradually come into being. . . .

The Court then presented examples of medical care services that it had refused to protect via *tutela*, such as dental care and fertility treatments. It considered that these exclusions from the POS were legitimate because the Constitution does not establish that these plans are or should be unlimited. Further, the Court discussed the contours of the right to health in the General Comments of the Committee on Economic, Social, and Cultural Rights, in its interpretations of the International Covenant on Economic, Social, and Cultural Rights.

Based on these foundations, the Court proceeded to establish "the scope and contents of the right to access health care services in the light of constitutional case law, focusing on judicial standards applicable to the cases under consideration in the present process." The Court referred to the following judicial standards:

1. Operation of a health system capable of ensuring access to health care services.
2. Affiliation with the system and guarantees for health care service delivery.
3. Adequate and necessary information to freely and easily access health care services.
4. The right to demand from institutions access to high-quality, efficient and timely health care services.[17]
5. Special protection for individuals under special constitutional protection, such as children.

Based on these standards, the Constitutional Court posed the question of whether "the problems under discussion in specific cases . . . went beyond particular situations, reflecting, instead, structural failures in the health and social security system arising from regulatory issues and other factors." The Court noted a sharp increase in litigation related to the right to health: "[T]he number of *tutela* writs [requesting protection for the right to health] quadrupled between 1999 and 2005." The Court also examined some factors that may have caused this increase. First, the Constitutional Court found that the POS had not been comprehensively updated since shortly after the passage of Law 100 of

17. The Court issued a more detailed explanation of the components of this principle, as follows:

[1.] The right to access "necessary" health care services.
[2.] The expert opinion of the physician in charge being the main, but not the exclusive criterion in establishing whether a health care service is really required.
[3.] Access to health care services, whether or not included in the [POS].
[4.] Regulations on how to resolve conflicts between the physician in charge and scientific committees [charged with arbitrating claims of medical necessity].
[5.] Reasonable fees in all cases, which cannot become barriers to access to health care for those who do not have the economic capacity to pay. . . .
[6.] [EPSs] may not inhibit access to health care as a way to demand payment.
[7.] Health care institutions must deliver timely, efficient and good-quality service. . . .
[8.] There is a duty to ensure access to health care services without subjecting users to unnecessary and cumbersome administrative procedures.
[9.] The principle of continuity: Access to health care services must not be subject to sudden interruptions.

1993. It ordered that such an update occur with the input of both users of the plans and medical organizations. It pointed out that

> although specific changes introduced in the POS have helped to improve coverage and service delivery, they do not constitute an actual update as established in the law. A proper update implies more than just specific changes, but rather a systematic revision of the POS according to (i) demographic changes; (ii) the country's epidemiological profile; (iii) the technology available in the country, and (iv) the financial conditions of the system. Taking into account that the present POS was adopted in 1994, when the [Law] had just started to operate, i.e., fourteen years ago, it is reasonable to suppose that it is time to modify it and adapt it to the country's new conditions. . . . [B]esides problems related to medical services not included in benefit plans, many *tutelas* respond to the doubts of consumers regarding which services are or are not included in the POS, and to the lack of institutional mechanisms within the system to resolve those doubts.

The Constitutional Court also noted that *tutela* writs filed by citizens to request protection for their right to health frequently sought access to healthcare services actually included in the POS. It pointed out that "according to a study undertaken by the National Ombudsman's Office . . . most *tutela* writs had been filed to demand access to health services that were actually included in the mandatory health plan. In effect, around 56.4 percent of *tutela* actions filed during the period under study were filed to demand a service to which users were legally entitled and which, therefore, should have been delivered without resorting to a lawsuit."

> [T]he state is not protecting people's right to health if it allows violations that clearly disregard this right by hindering people's access to services already included and paid for in mandatory health plans. This situation of constant and unjustifiable infringement of the right to health has come about because many of the relevant actors have incentives and disincentives that do not promote its effective enjoyment, and because surveillance and control mechanisms have not been duly applied.

In order to fix these regulatory failures, the Court ordered the Ministry of Social Protection and the National Health Supervision Committee to adopt measures aimed at identifying those EPSs and health providers that most frequently refuse to deliver services included in the POS, and to report on the measures adopted to penalize them.

Further, the Court found that competent authorities had failed to equalize the POS in the contributory regime with the POS in the subsidized regime (which included many fewer treatments and medicines), despite the fact that this was clearly required to be completed by the year 2000, according to Law 100 of 1993. The Court pointed out that the orders it had issued would be "insufficient as long as the difference between benefit plans for contributory and subsidized affiliates persist."

> [The Court has been able to verify that] to date no program has been designed to set specific goals regarding the progressive equalization of benefit plans backed by a schedule with precise deadlines for each goal. . . .

> The need to unify benefit plans is even more necessary in the case of children. . . , as the Constitution grants them special protection, giving priority to their fundamental right to health.

To amend this regulatory failure, the Court ordered the government to design a plan and a schedule to gradually advance toward the standardization of a single POS in both types of plans. Additionally, it ordered the government to strive to eliminate differences regarding children within several months, warning that if the definition of a new POS for children was not fulfilled by the deadline, the Court would itself order that subsidized affiliates enjoy the same plan as contributory affiliates without any further delay.[18]

Last, the Court found that "the country's health system is not operating in accordance with the principle of universal coverage, which is one of the founding principles of social security in our Constitution. . . . "

> The importance of ensuring universal health care coverage was underlined from the very first stages of discussion around Law 100 of 1993. [The Law] later established that the general social security system had to have universal coverage. In the first clause of Article 162, the legislator set a deadline to fulfill this goal [before 2001]. . . . Despite the aforementioned, the deadline set by Law 100 of 1993 to achieve universal coverage has not been fulfilled.
>
> In 2006, the Congress of the Republic discussed an amendment to Law 100 of 1993, which emphasized once more the need to achieve universal health care coverage. . . . The amendment was enshrined in Law 1122 of 2007. . . . Article 9 of that law established a new deadline [of 10 years] to achieve universal health care coverage. . . .

The Court emphasized "the need to comply with the new deadline set by the legislator. Thus, the present decision will order the Ministry of Social Protection to adopt the necessary measures to ensure sustainable universal coverage of the [system] before the deadline set by the legislator, and to report every six months to the Constitutional Court and to the National Ombudsman's Office on partial progress achieved toward fulfillment of this goal. If the goal proves not to be attainable by the deadline established in the law, noncompliance must be explained and justified and a new deadline set."

Finally, the Court discussed the general state of the healthcare system and explained the reasoning behind its structural intervention:

> For more than a decade, people have had to resort to *tutela* actions requesting legal intervention to solve controversies that could have been settled by competent

18. The Court recognized that this equalization could cause a perverse effect: it could incentivize some people who could afford to be affiliated with a contributory plan to instead affiliate with a subsidized plan, as they would be of the same quality and yet the subsidized plan would be free. The Court thus exhorted the state to come up with regulatory measures that would restrict subsidized plans only to those "who truly lack economic capacity."

> regulatory bodies. This fact clearly points to regulatory failures in the health system, which in turn explains the general orders herein issued to correct them. Consequently, the decision to be adopted by regulatory bodies aimed at complying with the present decision must result in improved access to health care services and, eventually, in a reduction in the amount of *tutela*s filed for this purpose.
>
> For this reason, and without prejudice to the power of health sector authorities to design and implement the indicators which they consider adequate, the Court will order the Ministry of Social Protection to report before this panel . . . on the number of *tutelas* filed to request protection of the right to health, particularly in regard to the legal issues described in the present decision. If the measures to be adopted by the regulatory bodies are suitable, people will gradually stop resorting to *tutela* actions and their number will consequently be reduced. . . .

The Court thus issued two sets of orders in Decision T-760 of 2008: orders designed to resolve the individual cases aggregated by the Court, and structural orders aimed at the system as a whole. The latter orders were numerous and complex. Among the most important were for the authorities to (1) develop a plan aimed at equalizing the contributory and subsidized POS within a reasonable period of time (and for children, within a very short period of time), (2) carry out a comprehensive update and clarification of the POS, (3) implement measures to identify and sanction EPSs and other actors that have abused the system by denying treatments that should have been covered, and (4) take action to improve the regulation of treatments that are necessary for the life or dignity of the patient but excluded from the POS, by creating internal systems within EPSs for the approval of these treatments and by improving the flow of resources for reimbursement by the state of the EPS once they have been carried out. The Court also held that the structural orders concerning the reform of the health plan should be carried out by the relevant state regulatory authorities through a process that: (i) gave participation opportunities to associations of patients and physicians, (ii) fixed priorities based on serious studies concerning the health needs of all Colombians in a transparent way, and (iii) preserved the financial sustainability of the healthcare system.

T-760 was the second Constitutional Court decision in which the Court established an extensive monitoring system for compliance with the judgment. The first was T-025 of 2004 on internally displaced persons, which is included in Part D immediately below. In enforcing T-760, like T-025, the original *tutela* panel has maintained jurisdiction over the case and has issued numerous follow-up orders called *autos*. Second, the Court in key periods had law clerks and other high-ranking staff members working only on compliance with this case. Third, the Court has required regular reports on the state of compliance from governmental agencies, as well as from control institutions such as the National Ombudsman's Office and the National Inspector General. The Court has also invited reports from civil society institutions, especially civil society commissions that the Court has authorized in its *autos* to follow different aspects of compliance with the judgment. Finally, the Court has held periodic public hearings (sometimes televised) at which it has asked state authorities to explain and justify their actions in response to its orders, and it which it has also asked control institutions and civil society groups to make comments.

The implementation of the Court's structural orders has proven difficult, although significant progress has been made after some years of stalemate. The number of *tutelas* filed on the right to health dropped immediately after the decision was filed but has since been on an upward trajectory, reflecting the continued structural problems in the healthcare system. About one year after the Court issued Decision T-760 of 2008, the administration of President Alvaro Uribe declared a state of social and economic emergency in 2009 aimed at overcoming a financial crisis in the system. The decrees, for example, established new taxes on cigarettes, alcohol, and games of chance, which were aimed at easing resource limitations with the healthcare system, and also took certain measures aimed at improving the flow of resources within the system. However, some also clashed with the Court's jurisprudence on the right to health. For example, one of the decrees renamed treatments found outside of the POS as "exceptional healthcare benefits," contemplated that individuals should exhaust all of their personal resources (including pensions) before seeking state assistance, and noted that these treatments would only be covered by the state until the state special fund established by that purpose was exhausted. Another contemplated sanctions against doctors who ordered treatments that they judged as medically-necessary but which were excluded from the POS and had not been ordered by special scientific committees as "exceptional healthcare benefits."

In short, President Uribe's emergency envisioned healthcare less as a fundamental individual right, and more as a service in which individual needs must cede to collective concerns and resource limitations.[19] In **Decision C-252 of 2010 (per Justice Jorge Ivan Palacio Palacio)**, the Court struck down the entire economic and social emergency. As explained in more detail in Chapter 9 (which treats presidential power), it applied its long-standing jurisprudence that the emergency could not stand because the facts that motivated it were chronic and structural rather than truly new and unexpected. However, in an unusual move, the Court maintained the new taxes that had been created during the emergency in place for an indefinite period of time. The Court held that these taxes were necessary to help ameliorate a "grave" financial crisis in the system, and therefore held that it would "modulate" its decision by refusing to immediately strike down the new taxes. The emergency had sparked protests by organizations of patients and medical professionals, and the Court's decision was greeted by a cheering crowd in the Plaza Bolivar, the central square of Bogotá.

During the administration of Juan Manuel Santos, who took office in 2010, the Court has had more success in making progress on its orders. In sum, the main results of the implementation of Decision T-760 have been (1) the initial expansion of the health plan applied to poor children, followed by (2) the equalization of the two health plans, thus ending the differences in coverage that excluded the poor from almost half of the services

19. For a lucid analysis of why the human rights approach to health not only challenges power relations but also constitutes a change of paradigm, see ALICIA ELY YAMIN, POWER, SUFFERING, AND THE STRUGGLE FOR DIGNITY: HUMAN RIGHTS FRAMEWORKS FOR HEALTH AND WHY THEY MATTER (2016).

provided to those with ability to pay, (3) the revision and actualization of the new health plan to include important drugs and treatments, (4) advances toward universal coverage, (5) a significant increase in the budget for health services, and (6) a deep reform of the administrative regulatory structure of the system.

Moreover, the interventions of the Court prompted a wide debate concerning not only the content, scope, and limits of the right to health, but mainly about the architecture of the healthcare system itself. In 2015, the Congress passed a new Statutory Law governing health. In general, this new law establishes an approach that is consistent with the Court's jurisprudence. Article 1, for example, defines health as a "fundamental right," and the remaining articles lay out principles to protect the rights of patients and the autonomy of doctors. The law helps to define the scope and limits of the right. According to the law, the right to health requires the fulfillment of positive obligations to provide all drugs, diagnosis, and treatments that have not been expressly excluded by the regulator through a transparent, participatory, and evidence-based procedure. The law also requires the regulator to strike a balance between the financial sustainability of the system and the effective enjoyment of the right. Finally, it contemplates measures to control the prices of drugs and prohibits any requirement of preauthorization for the provisions of urgent healthcare services. The Constitutional Court upheld the law with some conditions in **Decision C-313 of 2014 (per Justice Gabriel Eduardo Mendoza Martelo).**

D. A Structural Remedy for Internal Forced Displacement

Because of Colombia's long-running civil conflict, Colombia has long had a very large number of internally displaced persons (IDPs), mostly caused by guerrilla and paramilitary groups. IDPs are individuals who have been forced from their homes due to conflict and violence, but who have not crossed international borders and instead remained in Colombia. According to the United Nations High Commissioner on Refugees, Colombia had the highest number of internally displaced persons in the world at the end of 2015—6.9 million people, or about 14 percent of the national population.[20]

From the perspective of law and public policy, IDPs pose a number of complex issues. Many IDPs have been forced to relocate to the poorest neighborhoods of big cities such as Bogotá, Medellin, and Cartagena. Many were poor even before being forced to leave their homes; their displacement has often greatly increased their marginalization. IDPs potentially need to be identified by the state so that they can receive socioeconomic assistance along a number of dimensions, including emergency economic aid, housing, healthcare, education, and job training and employment opportunities. In addition, IDPs are victims of the Colombian armed conflict, and as such should be entitled to learn the truth about what was done to them, and receive justice against the perpetrators, reparations for the

20. *See* United Nations High Commissioner on Refugees (UNHCR), *Global Trends: Forced Displacement in 2015*, June 20, 2016, at http://www.unhcr.org/576408cd7.

resulting harm, and restitution of the land that was taken from them.[21] Finally, the state as a whole has a potential obligation to prevent future incidents of internal displacement.

Law 387 of 1997 laid out many of these rights and established the outlines of a public policy for displaced persons. Nonetheless, the network of state agencies that was supposed to attend to the problem was extremely fragmented, and in practice little was done. By 2004, the Court had been receiving an increasingly high number of *tutelas* from IDPs (often aided by civil society groups) who complained of a lack of state aid or even recognition of their status. The Court protected the rights of these individual complaints, but individual relief did not ameliorate a massive social problem affecting millions of people. Thus, in 2004 the Court aggregated a large number of individual *tutelas* and issued a structural remedy.

In the unanimous decision below, a chamber of the Court protected the fundamental rights of persons displaced due to Colombia's ongoing armed conflict. The Court aggregated 108 *tutelas* filed by displaced families against different state institutions such as the Social Solidarity Network, the Presidential Administrative Department, the Ministry of Public Finance, the former Ministries of Health, Labor and Social Security (the present Ministry of Social Protection), the Ministry of Agriculture, and the Ministry of Education. The claimants were men, women, and children demanding access to assistance programs for the displaced population, especially those regarding housing, employment opportunities, healthcare, and education.

Through this decision, the Court protected not only the individual claimants and their families, but also all other IDPs. It did so by declaring a state of unconstitutional affairs, a doctrine used since 1997 on nine occasions to respond to massive and repeated violations of rights due to structural causes affecting specific groups of population, such as prisoners, elderly public servants deprived of their pension rights in poor territorial entities, and public notaries exposed to political patronage. For example, the first declaration of a state of unconstitutional affairs was used to protect the rights of prisoners held in jails in overcrowded and unhealthy conditions (**Decision T-153 of 1998 (per Justice Eduardo Cifuentes Muñoz)**). On the basis of this declaration, the Court issued structural orders regarding public policy in the area, and maintained jurisdiction over the case in order to monitor compliance and issue follow-up orders.

Decision T-025 of 2004 (per Justice Manuel José Cepeda Espinosa)

[First, the Court summarized the applicable law, relying heavily on relevant international principles. For example, the Court emphasized the Guiding Principles on Internal Displacement adopted by the United Nations High Commissioner on Refugees "as a tool that contributes to the interpretation of this population's rights." Based on these international principles and on relevant domestic law, the Court found a plethora of basic rights to which IDPs were entitled but were often not enjoying: for example, the right to a dignified life, the right for especially vulnerable groups such

21. In the context of the ongoing Colombian peace process, many of these rights are examined in Chapter 7.

as the elderly and children to be specially protected, the right to choose their home, the rights to healthcare and education, the right to family, and the right to work. The Court next compiled statistics suggesting non-compliance with these rights. For example, it found that only between 15 and 30 percent of IDPs were receiving government assistance, 80 percent of the population lived in conditions of severe poverty, and 92 percent had some basic need that was not being met.]

The public policies on assistance for IDPs have failed to counteract the serious deterioration of their already vulnerable condition, to ensure the effective realization of their constitutional rights, or to overcome the circumstances resulting in the violation of those rights. . . .

It is true that the unfortunate situation faced by IDPs is not caused by the state, but by the internal armed conflict, especially the actions carried out by illegal armed groups. However, by virtue of Article 2 of our Constitution,[22] the state has a duty to protect the population subject to this situation, and therefore, the obligation to respond to it.

[The Court then carefully analyzed each of the public policies aimed at assisting IDPs, based on documents gathered from government institutions, human rights organizations, and international agencies, and on the answers to a survey prepared by the Court. Based on this data, the Court concluded that there were two main problems: "(i) Limited institutional capacity to implement policies and (ii) insufficient funds." Regarding the first problem, the Court reasoned that difficulties were related to three aspects: "(i) the design and regulatory development of public policies on forced displacement; (ii) their implementation, and (iii) their monitoring and evaluation." Concerning the second problem, the Court stated that:]

From a constitutional point of view, it is imperative to allot the required budget to ensure that displaced people's fundamental rights are fully realized. The state's constitutional obligation to guarantee adequate protection to citizens that are facing shameful life conditions due to internal forced displacement cannot be postponed indefinitely. As established by Article 350 of the Constitution,[23] public social spending should be prioritized over any other allocation. Law 387 of 1997 acknowledged that assistance to displaced people is urgent and has priority. Through case law the Court has repeatedly insisted on prioritizing funds to deliver assistance to this population and thus to resolve the social and humanitarian crisis that their situation implies. . . .

22. Article 2 states in part: "The essential goals of the state are to . . . guarantee the effectiveness of the principles, rights, and duties stipulated by the Constitution . . . and to ensure peaceful coexistence and the enforcement of a just order. The authorities of the Republic are established in order to protect all individuals residing in Colombia, in their life, honor, property, beliefs, and other rights and freedoms, and in order to ensure the fulfillment of the social duties of the state and individuals."

23. Article 350 states in part: "Except in case of foreign war or for reasons of national security, public social expenditure shall have priority over any other allocation."

However, this was not done here and in this way the Constitution, the laws passed by Congress, and even the plans of the executive branch have been ignored.

With the purpose of correcting this situation, it is necessary for the distinct national and territorial entities charged with attending to the displaced population to fully comply with their constitutional and legal duties and adopt, within a reasonable period and within their respective spheres, the corrective actions needed to ensure a sufficient budgetary appropriation. By ordering this type of measure, the Court is not ignoring the separation of powers established by our constitution, nor displacing other authorities in the execution of their duties.

The Court is not suggesting that the *tutela* may be used to order non-budgeted expenses or to modify budget planning as established by the legislature. It is not defining new priorities or modifying policies designed by the legislature and developed by the executive. On the contrary, the Court, taking into account the legal instruments [already] established to develop policies of assistance for displaced persons, as well as the design and engagements taken on by different state entities, is invoking the constitutional principle of harmonic collaboration among the branches of government in order to ensure compliance with the obligation to offer effective protection to the rights to which all residents in our national territory are entitled. This falls within the province of constitutional judges in a social state of law whenever rights that have a clear welfare dimension are being violated.

The Court concludes that the state response has not resulted in the effective enjoyment of constitutional rights by all displaced persons. We will give some examples:

Emergency humanitarian aid, which seeks the satisfaction of the basic needs of the displaced population, covers only 43 percent of the registered population. In this way, the rights to life, the vital minimum, equality, and health of those persons who do not receive that aid are ignored, in other words more than half of the registered population. The measures designed to execute policies regarding the generation of income by the same IDPs has a coverage of 19.5 percent of the registered population. The impossibility of generating income prevents IDPs from autonomously satisfying their basic needs for food, housing, health, and education in the case of minors. This aggravates the vulnerable situation of these persons. Further, that the IDP population sometimes returns [to their homes] without minimal conditions of security and without ensuring their socio-economic stabilization in their place of return, clearly exposes them to threats against their rights to a dignified life, to personal integrity, to a vital minimum, to equality, and to work. In addition, the help with housing ordered in the law has only reached 3.7 percent of the potential demand. In the same way, the policies of protection of the possessions or property abandoned because of displacement, as well as the properties designed to adjudicate and restore land to IDPs, have not been implemented. Finally, the state has not developed systematic instruments to evaluate results, which would identify problems in the design and implementation of policy and suggest mechanisms for resolving them.

Because of the magnitude of the problem of displacement and its grave impact on the protection of the rights of IDPs, including the petitioners in this case, the

Court will ask whether it should proceed to declare a state of unconstitutional affairs.

When treating the repeated and constant infringement of fundamental rights, which affect many people, and whose solution requires the intervention of distinct entities to attend to structural problems, this Court has declared the existence of a state of unconstitutional affairs and has ordered remedies that reach not only those who have filed a *tutela* to protect their rights, but also others found in the same situation but who have not filed a *tutela*.

In its most recent decisions treating the phenomenon, this Court has stated that a state of unconstitutional affairs exists when (1) there is a repeated violation of the fundamental rights of many people, who therefore resort to *tutelas* claiming protection for their rights and overcrowding judicial courts—and (2) the origin of such an infringement is not exclusively ascribable to the authorities accused, but also to structural factors.

Among the factors evaluated by the Court in order to determine whether a state of unconstitutional affairs exists, it is worth mentioning the following: (i) the massive and generalized violation of various constitutional rights affecting a significant number of people; the prolonged omission of the authorities in compliance with their obligations to guarantee rights; (ii) the adoption of unconstitutional practices, like the incorporation of the *tutela* as part of the procedure to guarantee the right at issue; (iii) the failure to issue legislative, administrative, or budgetary measures needed to avoid the infringement of rights; (iv) the existence of a social problem whose solution requires the intervention of various entities, requires the adoption of a complex and coordinated set of actions and demands a level of resources that demands an important additional budgetary effort; (v) if all of the people affected by the same problem were to utilize the *tutela* to protect their rights, greater judicial congestion would be produced....

[O]nce a state of unconstitutional affairs has been declared, the Court has extended the effects of the *tutela* in order to order remedies that have a material and temporal relationship to the magnitude of the violation and to protect, based on the principle of equality, the rights of those found in a similar situation to the petitioner, but who have not filed *tutelas*. Thus, taking into account the duty of the authorities to "protect all individuals residing in Colombia, in their life, honor, property, beliefs, and other rights and freedoms, and in order to ensure the fulfillment of the social duties of the state and individuals" (Article 2) as well as the duty that the branches of government have to "cooperate harmoniously for the realization of their goals" (Article 113), the Court has declared the existence of a state of affairs contrary to the Constitution so that authorities may adopt, within their respective spheres of competence, the corrective measures that will permit them to overcome that situation.

In consequence we have ordered, among other things and according to the case, that (i) the policies, plans, and programs that will adequately guarantee the fundamental rights ... be designed and put into effect; (ii) that the necessary resources to guarantee those rights be appropriated; (iii) that the practices and organizational and procedural failures that violate the Constitution be modified; (iv) that the legal framework whose failures have contributed to the state of unconstitutional affairs be reformed; and (v) that the administrative, budgetary, and contractual measures indispensable to overcome the infringement of rights be carried out. . . .

Various elements confirm the existence of a state of unconstitutional affairs concerning IDPs . . . .

First, the seriousness of the violation of rights faced by displaced people was overtly acknowledged by the legislature by addressing displaced people's conditions and highlighting massive violations of multiple rights. . . .

Second, another element that confirms the existence of a state of unconstitutional affairs regarding forced displacement is the considerable and growing amount of *tutelas* filed by IDPs to access aid, as well as the fact mentioned by some of the documents analyzing these policies that the *tutela* has been incorporated as a necessary step in the administrative procedure in order to obtain assistance.

In addition, even though there has been some development regarding the issue, it is also true that several of the problems tackled by the Court are not new and, nonetheless, authorities have still not found the necessary solutions.

Among these, emphasis should be placed on the lack of resources actually destined at delivering assistance to the various policy components, as well as on problems regarding institutional capacity that affect state policy development, implementation, and monitoring. . . .

Third, the cases accumulated in the present *tutela* confirm this state of unconstitutional affairs by revealing that infringements affect the majority of IDPs around the country and that authorities have not taken steps to adopt the necessary corrective measures. . . . [T]he different institutions in charge of assistance for displaced persons have already detected several omissions and shortcomings in policies and programs. Likewise, human rights organizations have identified problems regarding coordination, lack of resources, administrative obstacles, unnecessary paper work and procedures, deficient design of some policy instruments, as well as prolonged omission by authorities to adopt necessary corrective measures. [This] situation has worsened the vulnerable condition of the displaced population and the massive violation of their rights.

Fourth, the continued violation of the rights of IDPs is not the responsibility of a single institution. As mentioned earlier, several state institutions, by act or omission, have tolerated this continued violation of displaced persons' fundamental rights, especially national and local institutions in charge of ensuring adequate budget allocation so that the different policy components offer real and equal benefits to all displaced persons. . . .

Fifth, the violation of the rights of displaced persons springs from structural factors . . . , among which one may highlight the lack of balance between what the law establishes and the means to comply with its provisions; an aspect that acquires significant relevance *vis á vis* insufficient funding levels and the lack of institutional capacity to respond in a timely and efficient manner, as compared with the scope and growing impact of the displacement problem.

In conclusion, the Court will formally declare the existence of a state of unconstitutional affairs relative to the conditions of life of the internally displaced population, and will adopt the corresponding judicial remedies while respecting the sphere of competence and expertise of the authorities responsible for implementing the corresponding policies and executing the pertinent laws. For this purpose, the national authorities as well as the territorial ones must adopt the corrective actions within their spheres of competence to overcome the state of unconstitutional affairs. . . .

[The Court next discussed the kinds of obligations that existed on the Colombian state, distinguishing "progressive" rights that could be realized over time and "minimal" rights that should be realized immediately. In making this distinction, the Court relied heavily on the doctrine of the Committee on Economic, Social, and Cultural Rights charged with interpreting the International Covenant on Economic, Social, and Cultural Rights.]

When the state declines without a constitutionally acceptable justification to take measures before the marginalization suffered by some members of society, and that refusal violates a fundamental constitutional right, the function of the judge "is not to replace the organs of public power, but to order them to comply with their duties."

In the case of the displaced population, in order to ensure the effective enjoyment of their fundamental rights, the response of the state must include positive actions highlighting the welfare dimension that, together with the dimension of defense against arbitrariness, is possessed by all the rights whose violation convinced the court to declare the state of unconstitutional affairs. . . .

In the present case, because of an insufficient budgetary appropriation and the lack of correction of the principle weaknesses in institutional capacity . . . the progressive advance in the satisfaction of the rights of the displaced population has not only slowed, but has also deteriorated with the passage of time in some respects. . . .

This retrogression is prima facie contrary to the constitutional mandate to guarantee the effective enjoyment of the rights of all IDPs. The first duty of the competent authorities is to avoid that retrogression in the level of protection of the rights of all IDPs where it has presented itself, even if it is a result of the evolution of the problem and of factors beyond the will of the responsible officials. The gravity, magnitude, and general complexity of a problem, by itself, does not justify a grade of protection of rights which does not correspond to constitutional mandates. . . . Neither is it constitutionally admissible for the achievement of that protection to diminish in practice, without . . . adopting corrective measures in a timely and adequate manner. . . .

[T]he welfare dimension of certain rights and the progressive nature of their realization, demands rationality in order to attain a transparent, serious, and coherent design and articulation of public policies related to such rights. . . . Transparency requires clear information on the benefits that will be granted, as well as on the institutions responsible for ensuring compliance with what has been legally established. Seriousness implies that policies enshrined in legal instruments, such as laws or decrees, must be observed as enforceable regulations, not as political or rhetorical statements. . . . Coherence points to the harmony that should exist between, on the one hand, what the state "promises" and, on the other, the financial resources and the institutional capacity to fulfill those promises, especially if those promises have become legal regulations. Coherence implies that if the state has created a specific welfare right through a law, it should plan on the resources required to ensure its effective realization and the institutional capacity needed to respond to demands generated by the creation of that specific right. . . .

[G]iven the present extent of displacement in Colombia, as well as resource limitations for the achievement of goals, it is essential that when designing and implementing public policies aimed at protecting displaced people, relevant authorities should weigh all factors and set priorities where timely and efficient assistance must be delivered. Therefore, it may be impossible to satisfy simultaneously and up to the maximum possible level the welfare dimension of all constitutional rights . . . given present material limitations and the actual extent of displacement in the country.

However, the Court emphasizes that there are certain minimum rights to which displaced people are entitled, and which must be satisfied in all circumstances since they involve the dignified survival of individuals in these situations. What, then, are those minimum rights that must be always satisfied?

In order to define the minimum level of satisfaction of the constitutional rights of IDPs, a distinction must be made between (a) respect for the essential nucleus of their fundamental rights, and (b) compliance by authorities with certain duties of a benefit-providing character derived from rights internationally and constitutionally recognized to IDPs.

[I]t is clear that authorities' actions may not in any circumstance result in disregarding, damaging or threatening the essential nucleus of the fundamental rights of displaced persons—just as they cannot act in any way that may affect the essential nucleus of the rights of any person settled in Colombian territory. In this sense, displaced people cannot be subject to actions carried out by authorities that may work, for example, against their physical integrity or their freedom of expression.

[T]he Court notes that the majority of rights recognized to IDPs according to international law and our Constitution impose on authorities clear welfare obligations that evidently require public expenditure—which does not inhibit classifying some of them as fundamental rights because, according to case law established by this Court, both fundamental and economic, social and cultural rights have a welfare dimension that the state has a responsibility to address. According to the Court, those welfare rights that are part of the minimum that should always be guaranteed to IDPs are those closely related to the preservation of life in dignified conditions proper for autonomous human beings. It is precisely on this point, i.e. the preservation of basic conditions required to lead a dignified existence, where a clear line should be established between state obligations of a mandatory and urgent nature concerning the IDP population, and those that obviously should be satisfied, but do not have the same priority. [Of course,] the state should use all possible institutional resources to ensure the full realization of all displaced people's rights.

[The Court listed those rights possessed by IDPs that formed part of this minimum and thus should always be satisfied by the state. These included, for example, the right to a minimum level of subsistence and the consequent right to receive emergency humanitarian aid for at least three months, extendable by another three months if necessary. However, certain vulnerable groups such as children, elderly, or female heads of household must be given aid for indefinite periods of time because they were unable to generate income.]

Note on the Monitoring of Decision T-025 of 2004: In its decision the Court not only issued orders aimed at remedying the specific complaints of the petitioners in this case, but also complex orders designed to remedy the underlying structural issues. These orders, for example, required the government to measure the number of IDPs and their unsatisfied needs, as well as developing a plan to redefine public priorities and to attain the necessary budgetary resources, within time frames established by the decision.

The Court also ordered that decisions on measures to be adopted by the executive to comply with the Court's orders must involve the participation of displaced people's organizations, and required the authorities to distribute a charter of basic rights for IDPs created by the Court in its decision. This charter includes nine rights: (1) the right to be registered as an IDP; (2) the right to special protection as an IDP, along with the rights protected of all other citizens; (3) the right to receive emergency humanitarian aid for at least three months, extendable for another three months; (4) the right to be enrolled in a healthcare plan; (5) the nonobligatory right to a secure return to their place of origin if they so choose; (6) the right to aid in finding work, if applicable; (7) to right to education if under 15 years old; (8) the right to immediate access to all of these rights without needing to file a *tutela*; and (9) the right as a victim to truth, justice, and reparations.

Within the Colombian context, a novel feature of this decision is that the three-justice panel issuing the initial decision maintained jurisdiction over the case.[24] It has received frequent reports from state officials, control institutions, and civil society groups and has issued frequent follow-up orders or *autos*. Indeed, the Court has spent a considerable amount of time and resources monitoring compliance with this decision. Several staff members have worked full time on this case, and a Monitoring Commission composed of ex-magistrates and leaders of various civil society groups has been involved in reporting on compliance and generating policy ideas subsequently adopted by the Court or by the state.

The Court has carried out several public hearings attended by representatives of the national government and of the displaced population, as well as by the monitoring

24. For a comprehensive study of the monitoring process for Decision T-025 of 2004, see CÉSAR RODRÍGUEZ GARAVITO & DIANA RODRÍGUEZ-FRANCO, RADICAL DEPRIVATION ON TRIAL: THE IMPACT OF JUDICIAL ACTIVISM ON SOCIOECONOMIC RIGHTS (2015).

commission and by other NGOs. The Office of the United Nations High Commissioner for Refugees (UNHCR) also became actively involved by participating in public hearings and by presenting reports on relevant issues.

Based on this monitoring process and the resulting dialogue, the Court has issued numerous follow-up orders giving greater specificity and content to its initial orders. The following are some of the most significant orders that have been issued:

Measurement of results: From 2005 to 2007, the Court was flooded with long government reports, some of which were returned to the government because of their vagueness or irrelevance. The Court found that it was very difficult to measure whether or not public policy was improving and was achieving results. The Court thus demanded that the government propose a set of statistical indicators aimed at measuring progress.

In a subsequent order, the Court ruled on a set of proposed indicators presented by relevant government agencies. On their own accord, the Monitoring Commission, some NGOs, and the UNHCR also presented proposals. Many of these indicators measured the actual enjoyment of rights by IDPs, whereas others aimed to measure the reach of state programs. The Court required the government to redesign some key indicators, and in many cases adopted indicators proposed by the Monitoring Commission or other actors instead of those proposed by the state.

Responsible national entities presented a preliminary report on all indicators at the end of 2008 based on data collected from relevant agencies. The Monitoring Commission used well-known experts to prepare an independent report based on a field survey. Both reports were presented simultaneously in a public hearing before the Court with the participation of IDP organizations. Subsequent reports are being presented regularly to the Court to show progress on effective realization of rights, until the Court determines that the state of unconstitutional affairs has been overcome. In 2008, Congress passed a statute demanding that these same indicators be applied by territorial entities (departments and municipalities) and that periodic reports be presented before each congressional chamber.

Differential focus. A number of subsequent orders have aimed at protecting the fundamental rights of the most vulnerable and heavily affected segments of the displaced population—namely women, children and adolescents, indigenous peoples, Afro-Colombian communities, and persons with disabilities. Throughout 2007 and 2008, by means of a complex process of hearings, the Court gathered a large amount of specialized information relating to each one of these groups. Thereafter, it issued orders that described the relevant situation and the special risks and needs of each group, assessed the impact of displacement on their effective enjoyment of fundamental rights, and issued corresponding orders to state authorities.

Auto 092 of 2008, for example, focused on the special needs and vulnerabilities of female IDPs. The Court "identified eighteen sex-related issues in forced displacement, i.e., aspects of displacement that impact women in a particular, specific, and heightened way in the context of the Colombian armed conflict." After assessing from a constitutional point of view each of these sex-related issues, and explaining their effect on the realization of the fundamental rights of the women involved, the Court ordered the creation of 12 specific programs by the national government aimed at resolving the most serious problems within a short period of time.

The Court also gave instructions to the national prosecutor aimed at resolving continued impunity concerning crimes against women, and ordered the prosecutor to report to the Court on the results of criminal investigations regarding violent crimes against women. The Court became aware of these crimes while reviewing reports presented by organizations of female IDPs. Likewise, the Court defined constitutional presumptions protecting displaced women, most important creating a "constitutional presumption of the automatic extension of emergency humanitarian aid for displaced women until their dignified self-sufficiency has been verified" by governmental authorities.

The orders regarding children and adolescents and people with disabilities follow the same basic lines. The orders regarding indigenous peoples and Afro-Colombian communities, on the other hand, include an important additional dimension: they demand the adoption of specific plans to prevent the ethnic extinction of specific communities that have been placed in grave danger because of the armed conflict. For example, Auto 004 of 2009 instructed the government to create a Program to Protect the Rights of Indigenous Peoples Affected by Displacement. Furthermore, after consulting with authorities from each endangered group, the Court ordered the government to adopt plans to protect each of the 16 indigenous peoples at risk of extinction or disintegration.

The persistence of the state of unconstitutional affairs. Before six new justices came into office in early 2009, the Court issued Auto 008 of 2009. The provision established that the state of unconstitutional affairs declared in decision T-025 of 2004 persisted. The Court arrived at this conclusion after determining that the government had not implemented adequate solutions in several basic areas. The Court emphasized, for example, that the state had not yet ensured that its policies were promoting the effective enjoyment of constitutional rights by the population, that it had not yet set up a regime to give special protection to the especially-vulnerable groups mentioned above, and that it had not taken adequate steps to ensure that IDPs could participate in decisions of the state regarding policies affecting them.

In 2014, on the 10-year anniversary of the declaration of a state of unconstitutional affairs, the Court issued another document assessing progress with the implementation of the decision. Looking backward, the Court noted that the decision itself had given a greater visibility to the problem of displacement both within the bureaucracy and the public, and had resulted in massive increases in the amount of the budget for IDP issues. The Court also emphasized the results of the monitoring process in establishing indicators to measure the extent of effective enjoyment of rights by the population, and in establishing programs and measures to give special protection to vulnerable groups. It also noted the passage of a Victim's Law in 2011, which codified many of the rights for IDPs that had been established in the Court's jurisprudence. However, the Court noted continuing difficulties in many areas, especially the prevention of displacement, the right of return, the generation of income by displaced individuals, and the real protection of vulnerable populations, and stated that in these areas, the state of unconstitutional affairs has not been overcome. The Court thus continues to issue follow-up orders and hold hearings, more than 12 years after the decision was first issued. A special chamber elected in 2009, presided over by Justice Luis Ernesto Vargas Silva, has issued *autos* focusing on the most vulnerable IDPs. Moreover, Decision SU-254 of 2013 (discussed in Chapter 7) is part of the efforts of the Court to protect the right of IDPs to reparation, with wider implications concerning the rights of victims of the armed conflict.

Note on Structural Remedies in the Colombian Context: In comparative terms, issuing structural remedies for violations of socioeconomic rights is unusual but not unique. The Indian Supreme Court, for example, has issued sweeping structural orders and has supervised compliance with those orders over long periods of time, most notably in litigation involving the right to food.[25] In contrast, other courts both inside and outside of Latin America seem to be more comfortable issuing individual remedies than they are in issuing structural relief. Still, the state of unconstitutional affairs doctrine developed in the IDP case has had some transnational influence: in 2015, the Brazilian Supreme Federal Tribunal adopted that label for a case involving prison conditions in that country.[26]

Decision T-025 of 2004, along with the healthcare Decision T-760 of 2008 discussed in the previous section, are the two decisions where the Constitutional Court has developed its most elaborate structure to monitor compliance. In both decisions, a panel of the Court has maintained jurisdiction over the case, staffed high-ranking personnel solely on the case at issue, issued numerous follow-up orders, required periodic reports from state agencies and control institutions, held public hearings, and created civil society commissions to aid in the monitoring process. Both decisions have resulted in some long-term impact on bureaucratic structure and policy; both have also been resource-intensive for a relatively small institution such as the Court.

However, the Court has issued structural relief in other cases. An unusual example occurred in 2013, when the governmental agency charged with administering pensions in Colombia (now called *Colpensiones*) approached the Court and asked that it declare a state of unconstitutional affairs against itself. The agency stated that it lacked the bureaucratic capacity to respond to requests for pensions or adjustments to pensions made against it, and moreover that it was facing a very large number of *tutelas* with which it lacked the capacity to comply and from which it feared contempt sanctions for continued noncompliance. The agency stated that the structural problems creating this backlog were long-standing but had become exacerbated in recent years.

Beginning in **Auto 110 of 2013 (per Justice Luis Ernesto Vargas Silva)**, the Court issued a series of structural orders binding all other *tutelas* against the same agency on this issue. The Court's orders established a plan for prioritization of claims against the agency, gave it time to respond to these requests without fear of contempt sanctions, ordered the agency to obtain sufficient budgetary resources and personnel to clear its backlog and

25. *See* Lauren Birchfield & Jessica Corsi, *Between Starvation and Globalization: Realizing the Right to Food in India*, 31 Mich. J. Int'l L. 691 (2010).

26. *See* Vanice Regina Lirio do Valle, *An Unconstitutional State of Affairs in the Brazilian Prison System*, Int'l J. Const. L. Blog, Sept. 25, 2015, at http://www.iconnectblog.com/2015/09/an-unconstitutional-state-of-affairs-in-the-brazilian-prison-system/.

respond to future requests in a timely manner, and required the head of the agency to report regularly to the Court on adherence to the plan. The Court monitored compliance through reports and public hearings, and updated and expanded this plan in subsequent cases. In 2015, the Court held that most although not all of these orders had achieved a high degree of compliance, and denied the agency's request for further relief from contempt sanctions because it was now unnecessary.

Finally, it is worth noting that the Court often makes structural orders in *tutela* cases without declaring a state of unconstitutional affairs—indeed, no such declaration was made in Decision T-760 of 2008. Regardless of the formal label used by the Court, it has held that it maintains the power to determine the effects of its decisions and issue structural orders whenever necessary to ensure compliance with the Constitution, as noted in Chapter 2. For example, in the street vendors case (Decision T-772 of 2003), the informal recyclers case (Decision T-291 of 2009), and the water case (Decision T-418 of 2010) below, the Court issued complex or structural orders designed to resolve the broader problem as well as simple orders designed to resolve the situation of the individual petitioners. Of course, the extent of the monitoring and follow-up undertaken in response to these structural orders has varied from case to case.

E. Informal and Marginalized Work

Both historically and up to the present day, many Colombians have been unable to find work in the formal sector. One recent study from the International Labour Organization found that around half of all Colombian workers were in the informal sector, based on analyses of contributions to the healthcare and pensions systems.[27] The causes of this phenomenon are multifaceted, but linked for example to weaknesses in educational and economic opportunities within a developing context, as well as issues connected to Colombia's long-running internal civil conflict and forced displacement (examined above in Section D).

In Colombia and throughout Latin America, working in the informal sector has often meant that employees are excluded from the protections of labor regulations and the provisions of the welfare system. These rights have historically been a privilege enjoyed by formal-sector workers, rather than a universal entitlement. Although Colombia has made some strides in this respect, for example by extending healthcare coverage and benefits to workers left outside the formal "contributory" system (see Section B above), very significant differences in labor and welfare rights persist.

As the cases in this section show, those earning money in the informal sector are also often marginalized from a social perspective. Street vendors, informal recyclers, and sex workers are all groups that continue to be subject to high levels of discrimination. These deep inequalities, in terms of both labor and welfare rights and social marginalization, implicate concerns emphasized by the transformative Colombian constitution, particularly

27. *See* Ximena Peña, *The Formal and Informal Sectors in Colombia: Country Case Study on Labour Market Segmentation* (Employment Working Paper No. 146, 2013), http://www.ilo.org/wcmsp5/groups/public/---ed_emp/---ifp_skills/documents/publication/wcms_232495.pdf.

human dignity, the vital minimum principle, the social state of law principle, and Article 13's requirement that the state ensure that "equality may be real and effective" and "adopt measures in favor of groups which are discriminated against or marginalized."

1. Street Vendors

Decision T-772 of 2003 (per Justice Manuel José Cepeda Espinosa)

[In a unanimous decision, the Court protected the fundamental rights to human dignity, to a minimum level of subsistence, and to due process of a Bogotá street vendor who sold food and relied on his business as his sole means of subsistence. The police arrested the vendor and seized his goods, under the argument that he was illegally occupying public space. Consequently, the Court issued a series of specific orders to protect the petitioner, and issued a set of more general orders to protect street vendors.]

Were the fundamental rights of the petitioner, as an informal vendor, violated through the police measures to recover public space by virtue of which his goods were seized and he was prevented from exercising the activity through which he earns his personal and family livelihood?

Was the petitioner's dignity violated by the treatment he was subjected to by the police officers who participated in the operation described in the writ to recover the public space?

Was the right to due process violated by detaining the claimant for a 24-hour period because of his activity as a street vendor? . . .

By mandate of Article 1 of the Constitution, Colombia is a social state of law. This is . . . the political formula of the Colombian state since 1991; . . . it is a *cardinal principle* of our constitutional order, which gives it a meaning, a character, and specific objectives . . . that are binding on the authorities, who must guide their actions towards the achievement of the goals of the system: the promotion of conditions of dignified life for all people, and the resolution of the real inequalities present in society, with an eye towards establishing a just order. . . .

From the foregoing one derives two classes of distinguishable duties for the state: (i) on the one hand, it must adopt and implement positive policies, programs or measures geared to reaching a real equality of conditions and opportunities among its members, thus fulfilling its international and constitutional obligations to fight poverty and to provide progressive realization of the population's basic economic, social and cultural rights—applying what constitutional jurisprudence has called a "clause to eradicate present injustices"—and, (ii) on the other hand, it must abstain from carrying out, promoting or executing ostensibly regressive policies, programs or measures in economic, social and cultural matters, which clearly and directly lead to more poverty than what the country presently suffers, and that worsen the exclusion and marginalization of certain sectors of society, especially those that live under poor economic conditions, even more so if, as a result of such policies, programs, and measures, the general material situation of those who are already living in extreme conditions is made worse. . . .

In this sense, state policies, programs or measures that become a source of poverty for affected individuals, and which do not foresee complementary mechanisms to counteract in a proportionate and efficient way those negative effects, are unjustified in light of the country's international obligations regarding the fostering of economic, social and cultural rights as well as in light of the constitutional principle of a social state of law and its various manifestations throughout the Constitution. For the same reason, the design and execution of those policies, programs and measures constitutes *prima facie* an act of ignorance of the state's duty to eradicate present injustices and to improve the population's living conditions due to their intrinsically regressive character, which has no support whatsoever within the framework of the constitutional order implemented in Colombia as of 1991.

Because of this, public policies, programs and measures designed and executed by the authorities in a social state of law must begin from a reasonable and careful evaluation of reality, and they must be formulated in such a way that they serve the factual outcome derived from such an evaluation . . . so that the effective enjoyment of the fundamental rights of persons is not affected. In other words, at the moment of their formulation and execution, all dimensions of reality that will be affected by the policy, program or measure must have been studied as technically as possible, including the effect on people who will see their rights severely harmed; they must be, consequently, placed in such a situation that they are not obliged to bear a disproportionate public burden, even more so if those who are affected by the pertinent policies, programs or measures are under a special condition of vulnerability and weakness due to their poverty or economic deprivation. Measures necessary to mitigate any damage to these persons or groups must be executed simultaneously with the policies in such a way that the essential nucleus of their right to the vital minimum and to subsistence under dignified conditions is respected.

Only then has the requirement of *proportionality* that must accompany any limitation of the effective enjoyment of the fundamental rights in a social state of law been fulfilled: in addition to (i) being aimed at fulfilling a legitimate and imperative right, and (ii) being developed through means fully adjusted to legality, which guarantee respect for due process and the dignity of persons; . . . (iii) they must be proportional within the context of the Constitution, that is, they cannot excessively sacrifice other interests that are constitutionally protected in order to foster a specific constitutional end. . . .

The facts submitted to this court during this litigation refer to the status of an informal vendor . . . who states that he has been doing that work for several years. . . . [T]he petitioner's concrete problem—which needs an urgent solution—derives from the deprivation by the authorities of the only means of personal and family subsistence that he has available in the context of a very high unemployment rate, a massive displacement of people towards the capital city, and high rates of poverty.

In other words, the Court not only asks in this case if the authorities have adopted abrupt eviction measures, in opposition to their previous course of action and in contradiction to the good faith of an informal vendor who was led to believe that he was legitimately carrying out his activity due to its tolerance for several years; it also asks, based on the facts stated in the file, if in agreement with the Constitution, persons who are forced to occupy public space to exercise their informal activities—since this is the only legal alternative for subsistence which they have at their disposal in the general context of the country's social and economic difficulties—can be deprived of their means of livelihood without receiving a viable alternative from the authorities. . . .

[After noting the high figures on poverty and unemployment in the country, the Court stated:] From this perspective, the recovery of public space by the authorities through the eviction of those who occupy it to exercise an informal trade, acquires a new connotation: more than the diligent fulfillment of a state duty geared to promote the collective welfare, it is equivalent to depriving those who are forced to exercise informal business (as an alternative to subsistence) of the legal means they have selected to earn their living through work, in the midst of the highest unemployment levels in the city's recent history, and without consulting the social reality upon which their decisions and acts would have an effect. We need to evaluate whether this is an excessive limitation of the effective enjoyment of fundamental constitutional rights.

It is obvious that, in a context of such grave poverty like that being suffered in [Bogotá], there are thousands of people who must make the decision to work in order to survive and, in the absence of opportunities in the formal sector, they use the public byways, squares and parks to sell varied kinds of articles, in order to satisfy, in this way, their families' and their own basic needs. . . . [T]he Court has already pointed out that the informal vendor evicted by the authorities from the public space, and who does not have within his or her reach economic alternatives, is thrown by these authorities into total unemployment. "[U]nder this scheme, it is contradictory to increase unemployment without providing alternatives to mitigate it and, therefore, justice cannot allow the use of force to worsen the crisis."

To carry out, under conditions like these, policies and programs to recover public space is hardly compatible with a social state of law based, among other things, on the rights to work and solidarity of the persons who constitute it, and it signifies the application of measures that are inadequate to the present dimensions of social and economic reality, . . . which presently is one of poverty and marginalization of enormous masses of people in the capital, a fact that cannot be hidden.

To deprive people who want to escape from poverty of their only available means in order to clean up urban public space, without offering them a dignified alternative, is equivalent to sacrificing the individual in a disproportionate manner in the face of a general interest formulated in abstract terms and ideals. . . . Even though the general interest in preserving the public space is placed above, in principle, the specific interest of the informal street vendors who occupy it to work, the authorities cannot adopt disproportionate measures to foster the public interest; they must look for conciliatory ways that harmonize the conflicting interests and satisfy in full the principles of the Constitution. Thus, as the Court has indicated, "eviction from public space is constitutionally permitted as long as there is a judicial or police process authorizing it, the rules of due process are fulfilled, and measures are taken in order to guarantee that its occupants will not be abandoned, because Colombia lives under a social state of law." Should these measures not be taken . . . , we would be witnessing . . . the sacrifice of individuals, families and whole communities to whom the state has not offered a viable economic alternative, who want to work in a legal way no matter how, and who must not become the forced martyrs to some general benefit.

To conclude: the authorities do have the constitutional duty and the power to carry out policies, programs and measures geared to recover and preserve public space, but such policies, programs and measures (i) have to be carried out according to due process and by giving the affected parties dignified treatment; (ii) they must respect the legitimate trust of the affected parties; (iii) they must be preceded by a careful evaluation of the reality upon which they will have effects, with necessary monitoring and updating in order to ensure their effectiveness and correspondence with reality, and to ensure the effective enjoyment of fundamental constitutional rights; and (iv) they cannot be carried out in such a way that the vital minimum rights of the most vulnerable and impoverished sectors of the population are disproportionately damaged, or so that those who do not have economic opportunities in the formal sector of society are deprived of their only legal and available means of subsistence.

Therefore, to apply the principle of the social state of law, and in the context of the present social and economic conditions of the capital city, competent district authorities have the constitutional duty to incorporate as an integral part of their policies, programs or measures to recover public space, a mandatory component that provides economic alternatives for those who depend on informal work activities for their vital subsistence[.] [T]hese alternatives must be formulated based on previous and detailed evaluation and monitoring of [Bogotá's] real and changing social and economic conditions, in order to ensure the effective enjoyment of the fundamental rights involved . . . [and] in such a way that there is correspondence between those policies, programs and measures, and the dimensions and characteristics of the social problem to be solved. In the absence of such a component, which must be offered to all persons affected before their eviction, the corresponding policy, program or measure will, on its face, be deemed damaging to constitutional mandates—that is, it will be inadmissible because of its disproportionate character.

[The Court also referred to the due process that must guide all acts of recovery of public space, and it concluded that in this case "the mentioned seizure" imposed on the petitioner was an arbitrary deprivation of his property, since it was not carried out according to the applicable substantial and procedural norms. Thus, it was held to violate Article 58 of the Constitution, which states in part: "Private property and the other rights acquired in accordance with civil laws are guaranteed and may neither be disregarded nor infringed by subsequent laws." Further, the Court held that there are certain parameters and limits that must be observed by those who are members of the police force or who exercise police power:]

- In as much as they are functions exercised within the framework of the rule of law, police power, functions and activity are immediately subjected—and in a strict way since they affect the rights and liberties of the persons—to the constitutional principle of legality. . . .
- Any police measure must be geared towards guaranteeing and preserving public order, which is conceived not as an objective in itself, but as a means to permit the exercise of the liberties and rights of the citizens; therefore, such a measure cannot become a simple repression of liberties, and it cannot be applied in order to limit the legitimate exercise of the rights of persons—but only to fight the disturbances to collective security, tranquility and health that threaten to prevent the full exercise of those rights. . . .
- The measures adopted by the police can only be those that are strictly necessary to preserve and reestablish public order in an effective way. . . .
- Police measures must be proportional, in agreement to the end being sought and the gravity of the circumstances within which they are applied; and any excess is forbidden. . . .
- When applying police measures, the constitutional principle of equality must be preserved. . . .

[The Court therefore issued an order requiring state authorities to offer the petitioner an alternative means of subsistence within one month, and returning his seized goods within 48 hours. It also issued structural orders to the Bogotá police department requiring that it comply with the rules governing eviction from public space laid out in the decision.]

2. Informal Recyclers

Decision T-291 of 2009 (per interim Justice Clara Elena Reales Gutiérrez)

[In this decision the Court protected the fundamental rights of informal recyclers who worked at the Navarro waste dump in the city of Cali, picking through trash that they would then use or resell in order to survive. They were left without a livelihood when the dump was closed. City authorities gave environmental reasons for closing the dump, and they initially promised jobs for the recyclers and other benefits so as to avoid the negative impact on their social and economic conditions. However, these promises were not kept and the informal recyclers were seriously harmed when they found themselves with no other income option. CIVISOL Foundation helped them file a *tutela* and described the conditions of poverty and vulnerability they were facing at the time.]

[The Foundation pointed out that: "In the context of urban poverty, the informal recyclers are the poorest among the poor. For many generations, Colombian elderly, men, women and children [have worked at the waste dump], including many great-grandchildren of the population displaced by the violence of the mid-twentieth century, who arrived at the cities as refugees from the violence that had sent them away from the countryside. For them, as for their great-grandchildren, the waste dumps have represented their only chance at a livelihood in the cities. Among the piles of waste created by the rest of society, these marginalized people have learned over the past decades to dig and select the materials that could be recovered for their own use or could be sold."]

Is the right to equality violated when a measure, program, or policy adopted by the administration causes severe impact on a marginalized group and no mechanisms are adopted in order to mitigate that impact?

Is the right to equality violated (i) when measures, at first impersonal, general and abstract, are adopted, generating the exclusion from the development of a productive activity of a group which historically had been developing such an activity and (ii) when such a group is in a special condition of vulnerability?

Is the informal recyclers' legitimate trust violated when, before the closure of the waste dump where they once obtained their livelihood, the authorities had agreed to grant them new employment, capacity-building programs, education and health; . . . commitments which were not met based on the argument that they are not formal contractors and that given the city's environmental obligations, they do not have any social obligations towards the informal recyclers?

The informal recyclers are a social group with a self-identity, about which . . . one can talk without having to refer to each one of its members. Furthermore, it is doubtlessly true that, considering the long existence of the Navarro waste dump and the presence, throughout the decades, of people who picked through the waste to find their source of income, a group with self-identity was formed, whose members understand that their life conditions depend on the conditions they can create as a collectivity. . . .

[T]he petitioners are part of a social group traditionally marginalized and discriminated against. A great part of the Colombian informal recyclers—both the ones who work in waste dumps and the so-called street recyclers—live in conditions of extreme poverty, affected by high levels of discrimination and exclusion. That population has used informal waste picking due to the impossibility of finding other means of subsistence. As one of the interveners in the present case indicates, it should come as no surprise that if people "only find opportunities among the waste of others, it is because they do not have other options for work and subsistence at their disposal."

It is not difficult to understand that the informal recyclers survive in a physically and socially hostile environment. They must face the multiple social stigmas generated by the simple association of an activity with elements discarded by society. . . . [T]he fact that the informal recyclers live and survive among the discarded items that are useless . . . [to] others generates a problem in terms of the construction of social imagination. Society rejects the waste and extends this rejection to those who work with it. That is why a series of stereotypes ultimately place the informal recyclers in the lowest level of society and generate a perspective that they are unpleasant, smell bad, commit crimes, jam traffic and get the city dirty. Prejudices against informal recyclers are so deep that they have culminated in "social cleansing" campaigns to "discard" them. . . .

[F]or the Court there is no doubt that the decision to close Navarro waste dump obeyed an imperative constitutional end, which is assuring appropriate environmental conditions and public sanitation. . . .

In the same way that the threat to the people from Cali and the environment represented by the Navarro waste dump is a proven fact, it is also an unquestionable fact that the decision to close the waste dump has caused a social impact of great proportions for the people whose vital minimum conditions depended on it. As previously indicated, the petitioners and other informal recyclers sold recyclable material obtained in Navarro in order to receive their only source of income. Therefore the closure jeopardized their basic needs, such as food, housing, and clothing. In other words, it is a decision that, although obeying considerations of the general interest, generated an adverse and disproportionate impact on a marginalized and discriminated group, which is why it should have been followed by complementary measures to mitigate its effects. As noted [in prior decisions], when a measure, program, or policy from the administration affects groups in a situation of special vulnerability, for example due to their conditions of poverty or economic precariousness, "necessary measures to minimize the damage, in such a way that the essential nucleus of their rights to a vital minimum and to subsistence in conditions of equality are respected" must be implemented in parallel with the execution of that measure, program, or policy.

Furthermore, as previously expressed in this Corporation's jurisprudence . . . , the intervention of the authorities must not be limited to compensation for any damage that has been caused, but also must be followed by measures designed to improve the living conditions of the marginalized group. . . .

Although the closure of Navarro was unavoidable and obeyed an imperative end regarding the general interest, the defendant authorities (i) neglected to design an appropriate response to the social consequences generated by the closure of Navarro; (ii) evaded their duty to provide special protection to a marginalized group especially affected by the decision; and (iii) did not comply with the promises made to the population, ignoring the trust legitimately placed in them by the informal recyclers. . . . [A]s proven by evidence provided to the Court, the informal recyclers have lived in extreme poverty since the closure of the Navarro dump.

[Additionally, the Court found several regulations regarding waste collection to be discriminatory and to have generated a negative and disproportionate impact on the informal recyclers. Some of these regulations, for example, forbade opening or picking through the contents of garbage bags in public places. This situation affected informal recyclers, because their activity demanded that they open the bags to separate and classify the waste. Some provisions also forbade transporting waste on improvised vehicles, which also had a negative impact on them as they tended to use vehicles moved by animals rather than motorized cars.]

Although the Court does not ignore the need for waste collection to be carried out in efficient and environmentally friendly conditions, it is certain that the administration, which bears the burden of proof, has not demonstrated in this action why the informal recyclers should be excluded from these activities . . . because of the goals of rendering an efficient service with optimal environmental standards, or why the informal recyclers should not be allowed to keep carrying out their economic activity in conformity with the protection of the environment, considering that they used to do so. Also, as highlighted by one of the intervening parties, it is surprising that when the recycling activity was not regarded as a profitable economic activity, the informal recyclers were allowed to develop it—and their function was in fact applauded—however, nowadays when it is clear that recycling is a highly profitable activity, the people who carried it out for years are excluded from all possibilities of participation in it.

However, even supposing that the exclusion furthers the goals of efficiency and environmental protection in the rendering of a public service, it is unjustifiable to say that the informal recyclers' participation in the management and use of solid waste, in a context such as the Colombian one, jeopardizes efficiency and the protection of the environment. On the contrary, what the Court observes is that in countries where the culture of separating waste at its source does not exist, such as in Colombia, the informal recyclers have a lot to contribute. . . .

[The Court issued two types of orders: specific orders to solve the issue under discussion and protect the fundamental rights of the *tutela* claimants[28] and other more complex orders "designed to solve the problems highlighted concerning the Navarro informal recyclers, as well as the informal recyclers from the city of Cali in general." The Court stated that the complex orders had two goals:]

First, compensating for the precarious material conditions in which the informal recyclers have been left due to the Cali's administration's noncompliance. Second, adopting measures to curb the disproportionate impact generated on the Navarro informal recyclers by the laws adopted in terms of the final disposal of waste and the new configuration of the processes of collection and disposal of waste.

[The Court ordered the suspension of the bidding process that was underway to award a contract for waste collection to a private company, and ordered the convening of a new bidding process for this public contract where informal recyclers could participate in an effective and real way. Additionally, the Court ordered local

28. The Court ordered local authorities to adopt "the necessary measures to uphold the effective enjoyment of their constitutional rights to health, education, and food, verifying in each concrete case the affiliation to the social security system related to health, access to education for the underage, and inclusion in the municipality's social programs in terms of food, housing, recreation, construction of labor capacity, and sports." Likewise, it ordered authorities to offer the claimants employment and alternative means of making a living, as was initially agreed by the government.

authorities to design, adopt, and implement "an effective policy for the inclusion of Cali's informal recyclers in the programs of collection, use and commercialization of waste, which strengthens their quality as entrepreneurs and their forms of collective organization." In this same sense, the Court ordered the creation of a committee that would work for the inclusion of informal recyclers in the formal market of waste collection in the City of Cali. It also ordered the city to "design and take a census of Cali's informal recyclers, in such a way that the information collected allows for progress in the process of inclusion of that population in the waste collection economy," as well as "civic and solidarity campaigns aimed at the citizens of Cali, with the objective of encouraging the city's population to (a) start separating waste at its source and (b) to hand over to the organized informal recyclers their recyclable waste. . . ." Finally, the Court ordered the city not to enforce each of the regulations having a disproportionate impact on informal recyclers "until the above mentioned measures had been totally and satisfactorily adopted," and it required state authorities and control institutions to issue periodic reports on compliance with its orders.]

Note on the Enforcement of T-291 of 2009: In 2014, the Court received reports of continued noncompliance from informal recyclers and civil society groups representing them. In response, it issued a follow-up order, **Auto 118 of 2014 (per Justice María Victoria Calle Correa)**, in which it found some effort to promote the rights of the informal recyclers by enrolling them in state programs and by giving them subsidies and other forms of state aid. However, it found many difficulties remaining, for example, with the access of recyclers to alternative work opportunities and with opportunities to participate in the bidding process for jobs related to trash collection. It thus issued a fresh set of more specific orders designed to comply with the goals of T-291.

3. Sex Workers

Decision T-629 of 2010 (per Justice Juan Carlos Henao Perez)

[A woman who worked as a prostitute at a bar brought a *tutela* against the bar, arguing that she had been illegally fired from the position when she became pregnant without receiving any social benefits or severance pay. She had begun work in the bar in February 2008, via what she called an "undefined and indefinite verbal contract" that required her to work between 3 pm and 3 am, seven days a week, with a free Sunday once every two weeks. She alleged that in January 2009, she informed the owner of the bar that she had a high-risk pregnancy, and shortly thereafter her employer denied her access to the bar in order to work, which left her unemployed. The owner of the bar responded that the petitioner "did not carry out in the bar . . . any function as an employee but rather exercised the actions of a sex worker, offering her services in an independent and irregular manner and without receiving on my part any type of salary even though she occasionally visited the establishment."]

Does a person dedicated to prostitution, in particular when she becomes pregnant, have the same constitutional protection that other types of workers enjoy, in terms of working stability, the right to social security and most importantly, the right to her own vital minimum and that of her unborn child?

Or looked at another way, is the argument laid out by the lower court judges correct, according to which . . . the petition based on labor law derived from offering sexual services is neither admissible nor may be guaranteed . . . because of its illicit purpose, as well as the fact that it is contrary to public order and good morals?. . .

As the Constitutional Court has said repeatedly, equality is one of the pillars upon which the Colombian state is founded.

On the one hand, it is a fundamental principal of political order on which is projected the abstract and general character of the laws, an essential element of the rule of law; and in public duties it calls for the satisfaction of constitutional rights through the guarantee of a minimum of material conditions which facilitates their exercise by all people. . . . On the other hand, it possesses an inextricable link with human dignity, source and purpose of all fundamental rights, as an attribute of all human beings and from which one derives their right to the full enjoyment of human rights. . . .

In effect, one of the expressions of equality is the protection of groups which have been traditionally discriminated against or marginalized, a condition that in the social state of law determines at the same time a mandate of abstention or prohibition on discriminatory treatment and a mandate of intervention, which recognizes demands on the state to take actions tending to overcome the conditions of material inequality faced by these groups.

[The Court next undertook a study of the legal status of prostitution under both Colombian and international law. The Court concluded as follows:] From the study of international law, as well as criminal, local, and urban law [in Colombia] which specifically and explicitly regulates prostitution in Colombia and in [Bogotá], the following keys to the legal order of prostitution are found: (i) the inducement of someone into prostitution for the purposes of economic gain or another economic benefit, is punished with a criminal sanction; (ii) this is because prostitution is related to the trade in human persons for the purpose of exploitation . . . ; (iv) however, the . . . protection of sexually exploited people is a duty of the state; (v) the "mere exercise of prostitution" is not punishable; (vi) nor is the existence and functioning of commercial establishments in which prostitution is exercised.

That is to say, the law prohibits someone from inducing another to prostitute herself for profit, regardless of whether that person is capable, conscious, and voluntarily accepts the transaction. . . . But the "mere exercise" of prostitution is not prohibited. . . .

Likewise, the law does not prohibit the existence of zones in which prostitution is exercised . . . ; the law protects those who exercise prostitution with public health measures, but at the same time imposes on the state the duty to promote its eradication and the rehabilitation of those working as sex workers.

[This is a system] that reflects the diverse tendencies of the legal tradition in dealing with prostitution. . . . Prohibitionist, abolitionist and regulatory measures operate at the same time and are not always in dialogue. . . . In any case, a regime is created . . . in service of dignity and liberty and for the elimination of any form of human exploitation against women. Thus the permanent tension between the tendency to eradicate the activity through prohibition . . . and the . . . recognition of rights for the people who exercise it. . . .

[T]he lower court accepted as an argument to not protect the rights invoked by the actor, the illicit purpose of the alleged contract. . . .

Given the supreme character of the Constitution, as the norm from which one derives the legitimacy of the laws and other measures . . . , it must be understood as a parameter to determine the reach of private autonomy. There are two constitutional elements that are of essential value for resolving the question about the licit or illicit nature of the contract at issue: liberty and human dignity. . . .

In terms of the general principle of liberty . . . , individuals are only responsible before the authorities for infringing the Constitution or the laws; what is not prohibited in them, prima facie is understood to be permitted. This is contemplated in the right to free development of personality . . . , in the fact that one can freely choose his profession or office, and in the fact that only a juridical order based on legal formalities can impose limits on the liberty of people in themselves, in their homes, or in their families. . . .

Together with liberty, in the sources determining the lawfulness of acts of private autonomy, one finds human dignity. This provision possesses an immense significance in the Colombian constitutional order as a founding principle, as a constitutional principle and as an autonomous fundamental right. It is recognized, on par with its axiological value as an ethical pillar or essential basis for the consecration and effectiveness of the entire system of rights and guarantees in the Constitution, as a right. . . . In this sense, it guarantees "(i) the autonomy or possibility of designing a life plan and to live according to its terms (to live as one wants), (ii) certain concrete material conditions of existence (to live well), (iii) the inviolability of . . . physical and moral integrity (to live without humiliation). . . ."

This is to say that, like the general principle of liberty, human dignity assures a sphere of autonomy and respect for individuality, and of material and immaterial conditions for its exercise, which must be respected by the public powers, by individuals, and by the holder of the right himself.

[The Court then referred to the concept of an illicit contract in the Colombian legal order, noting that contracts against "public order" and "good morals" were considered invalid under the Civil Code.]

[I]n light of the Constitution, this Chamber holds that the concept of "good morals" cannot be recognized except inside the law and not as a parallel figure to compete with it. In that sense, its development and recognition must respect the legal rules and the rights to liberty and dignity. . . . [T]he notion of good morals as an element to define the lawfulness of a service, obligation, or act, must operate in a spirit of tolerance as a way to respect the principles of liberty and also of difference without colliding with the rule of law and the principle *pro libertate*. . . .

[Based on] the ideals of a democratic society and respectful of fundamental rights, which seek to dignify in the highest level possible the life and personal development of individuals in society, it must be stated again that, within the limits imposed by law, prostitution is a lawful activity.

[The Court therefore refused to hold the contract unenforceable on the ground that it was "illicit." Next, the Court reviewed its constitutional law governing labor contracts, and in particular its principles governing the firing of pregnant women:]

For the case of women, who are the subjects of special protection in this matter, discrimination has generally been based on patriarchal conceptions of social organization and also in prejudices under which . . . law itself has viewed women as inferior and thus subordinated subjects. Thus, one of the fundamental purposes of the constitutional, social, and pluralist state has been precisely the recognition [of the] the many existing and intolerable inequalities [affecting] women, with the goal of overcoming them through politics of inclusion, recognition of specific rights, and special legal guarantees. For these reasons a series of affirmative actions have been created for the achievement of the equality of women in society. . . .

[The Court particularly emphasized special protections for two categories of women: (1) pregnant or nursing workers, and (2) those workers who are both single mothers and heads of households.]

In terms of the first category, a right to reinforced labor stability for pregnant or lactating mothers has been recognized by the Court as fundamental. . . . Through its exercise the dignity, equality, and free development of the woman is protected, guaranteeing her the choice to be a mother free of the imposition of adverse conditions in her working and social situation. . . .

This is, as well, a subjective protection expressly included in Article 53 of the Constitution, where the special protection of women and maternity is included as a principle that must govern the labor statute.[29] This protection in labor law is what has been called the maternity privilege, which includes "those specific mechanisms that law necessarily should give in favor of pregnant women, such as the right to paid leave before and after the birth, provision of medical and hospital services, paid breaks for nursing the recently born and reinforced labor stability. . . .

[T]here is a presumption that a firing is due to pregnancy when it occurs during the pregnancy or three months after birth and the employer had not sought authorization for the dismissal from the competent authority. In this case, with the objective of overcoming the presumption, the employer is required to show just legal cause for the termination of the working relationship.

Additionally, a working woman is also protected when she is a single head of household. This subject of special protection, contemplated in Article 43 of the Constitution,[30] is a figure that as was stated in the debates of the National Constituent Assembly, is a product of "diverse motives, such as violence—which has left a large

29. Article 53 states in part: "The Congress shall issue a labor statute. The appropriate law shall take into account at least the following minimal fundamental principles: . . . special protection of women, mothers, and under-age workers."

30. Article 43 states in part: "The state shall support the female head of household in a special way."

number of women as widows—the abandonment of the home by the man and his indifference to his child," facts that "have obligated women to incorporate themselves into the workplace and take responsibility for the economic survival of her home, without having been able to separate herself from the cultural norms that confine her to the domestic sphere and the care of her children. . . ."

The declaration and protection of specific rights for a female head of household, this body has stated, has the objectives of: (i) promoting real and effective equality between the sexes, (ii) recognizing the heavy burden that rests on a female head of household, (iii) creating a state duty to support her in all of the spheres of her life and in her personal development in order to compensate, alleviate, and make less burdensome the task of caring for her family, and (iv) to protect her family as the nucleus of society.

Thus . . . , in reiterated jurisprudence we have recognized the right to reinforced labor stability for female heads of household and have accepted that the possible violation of that right can be protected via *tutela*. This is a material and procedural legal position given to female heads of household, "not only due to the special conditions of discrimination faced by this group, but also because safeguarding the rights of female heads of household guarantees the effective rights for all of those who depend on her for their sustenance." Stated another way, to protect the right of labor stability for the female head of household creates "a direct link with the protection of underage or incapacitated children, where it is reasonable to suppose that the help offered will redound to the benefit of the entire family and not just to any one of its members in particular." . . .

[Finally, the Court held that these labor rights were applicable to a female sex worker when she works "at the service of a commercial establishment" and when there "existed subordination [to the employer] due to the character of the services offered, continuity, and payment of a previously defined wage."]

The alleged legitimate purpose in denying the lawfulness and enforceability of the labor contract between a prostituted person and the owner of a brothel . . . , is based on criteria that in and of themselves make it impossible to effectuate an equitable distribution of rights, obligations, and responsibilities, because to ignore [these contracts] only favors the interests of the owner of these establishments, with excessively grave consequences for those who actually offer sexual services.

Ignoring the labor rights of sex workers is also contrary to constitutional equality, because it restricts fundamental rights (to dignified treatment, to free development of personality and above all to earn a living, to work, and to receive a just and equitable wage) and it affects in an unfavorable manner a minority or social group traditionally discriminated against and which is found in conditions of manifest weakness.

Thus there is a constitutional imperative to recognize their minimum guarantees, to permit them to be linked not only to a system of protection in healthcare and self-defense, but also to a universal system of social security, to be able to receive social benefits such as retirement savings and unemployment insurance. It is important to begin to increase the visibility of their legal rights, not only from a liberal and individual perspective, but also from an economic and social perspective, since this concretizes legal rights to a just wage for their work.

[In light of these principles, the Court found that the petitioner had established that an employer-employee relationship existed along with a labor contract. After reviewing the evidence in the case, the Court concluded that some of the women worked only sporadic and irregular hours at the bar, but others such as the petitioner worked a "defined and regular" schedule and were fined when they did not comply with that schedule. The Court found that the petitioner had been fired during her period of pregnancy and that the employer had failed to overcome the presumption that she had been illegally fired because of that pregnancy. In light of existing labor law principles, the Court ordered the petitioner to be paid 60 days of salary and 12 weeks of paid leave in return for her unjust dismissal, estimating her salary by using the legal minimum wage then in force. It refused, however, to order her reinstated to her position, arguing that "because of the specific nature of the services offered by the petitioner and the fact that this activity is in tension with the liberal and rational ideas of human dignity in constitutionalism and in particular with the duties imposed by international law on states, this chamber will exclude such a remedy from the labor law guarantees of those who work in prostitution."]

F. The Right to Water

The right to water is not expressly stated in the Colombian Constitution. However, the Constitution does contain some relevant provisions. For example, Article 366 states that "[t]he general well-being and improvement of the population's quality of life are social purposes of the state. A basic objective of their activity shall be to address the unsatisfied public health, educational, environmental, and *drinking water* needs of those affected."

Nonetheless, the Court has issued many cases protecting an individual or group's access to water. In some of these cases, it held that the right to water could be protected via *tutela* because of its connection to other fundamental rights, particularly the right to life. In other cases, the Court protected the rights of access to water of indigenous groups, who as shown in Chapter 8 below are protected by their own set of constitutional norms. A recent example of the latter type of analysis is **Decision T-143 of 2010 (per Justice Maria Victoria Calle Correa)**, where two indigenous communities lost their access to water after a well failed in one and a pump broke in the other. Local authorities provided water via mobile tanks for 45 days, but took no other steps. The Court held that the inaction of the authorities violated the rights to water and to cultural survival of the indigenous groups, and ordered authorities both to extend the temporary provision of water and to form specific plans aimed at a long-term solution.

Recently, the Court has recognized the right to water as an autonomous fundamental right that can be protected via *tutela* in its own right, rather than merely through its connection to other fundamental rights. The decision below is an example.

Decision T-418 of 2010 (per Justice Maria Victoria Calle Correa)

[A group of people filed a *tutela* against the municipality of Arbalaez, alleging that the town had violated their rights to water, health, life, and equality. The petitioners lived in a rural area, and alleged that they had repeatedly asked the town to hook them up to the town's system of running water, but that their requests had been refused. The town stated that it lacked the technical capacity to expand the service outside of urban areas because of a lack of water pressure and inadequate pipes, and further that it lacked the money to upgrade its facilities. The town government also argued that the petitioners already had access to water from an aqueduct, but the petitioners claimed—and the Court found based on testing it ordered—that this water was unfit for human consumption and dangerous to public health. The town had promised long-run measures to improve the water quality of the aqueduct, but had not offered specifics about when or how these improvements would take place.]

From the beginning of its case law, the Constitutional Court has considered the right of all people to water to be a fundamental right, which can be the object of protection via a *tutela* action in many of its dimensions. . . .

"Water constitutes the source of life." This is a reality. The fundamental character of the right to water is the decision to recognize reality, not to create it. When Colombia adopted as its constitutional model a social state of law, founded on the defense of dignity of all people and on the respect, protection, and guarantee of their fundamental rights, especially their right to a dignified life, Colombia committed at the same time to protecting the fundamental right to water of all persons. It makes no sense to try and ensure life, either human or of any other species, without ensuring the right to water, in its basic dimensions, as fundamental. The essential nature of water for life has not merely been recognized from a scientific perspective. Many of the indigenous and Afro-Colombian cultures of the nation continue to believe in their ancestral knowledge in this respect, which insists on the importance of water to our vital essence; they carry ideas that anticipated much of the modern ecological debate.

The right to water acquires an irreplaceable value in the social state of law, in the current context, since it demands from the institutions and authorities charged with ensuring the effective enjoyment of the right, clear, decisive and efficient action in order to confront the challenges that are faced. All societies on planet earth confront great challenges to respect, protect, and guarantee this basic human right.

Currently, water is one of the rights that is most often denied. The Committee on Economic, Social, and Cultural Rights [CESCR] has found that this occurs "in developing as well as developed countries."[31] In the year 2002, it warned that '[o]ver one billion persons lack access to a basic water supply, while several billion do not have access to adequate sanitation, which is the primary cause of water contamination

31. Committee on Economic, Social, and Cultural Rights, General Comment 15: The Right to Water, U.N. Doc. E/C.12/2002/11, ¶ 1 (2002).

and diseases linked to water. The continuing contamination, depletion and unequal distribution of water is exacerbating existing poverty." According to the Committee, states "have to adopt effective measures to realize, without discrimination, the right to water."

In General Comment 15 (2002) of the [CESCR], the right to water is understood as the "right [of] everyone to sufficient, safe, acceptable, physically accessible and affordable water for personal and domestic uses."[32] The legal basis of this right, in addition to being found in various texts of international human rights treaties, stems from the necessary place that water has in protecting several human rights that are consecrated as basic guarantees of human dignity. . . .

The United Nations Report on Millennium Development Goals of 2010 finds that there have been advances in access to water in rural areas, but not in matters of quality, which continues being a problem. . . . The United Nations is currently close to declaring expressly and emphatically that access to potable water is a basic human right. . . .[33]

Even though this is not a right expressly stated by the Constitution, it must be understood to be included, taking into account the constitutional text approved by the Constituent Assembly in 1991, and especially its subsequent reforms.

[The Court then reviewed various relevant provisions included in the Constitution, including the preamble, the social state of law provision included in Article 1, and rights to life, dignity, and health. It concluded:]

The right to water is a complex constitutional right that has developed in recent years, especially based on the importance that it has as a prerequisite for other fundamental rights and their development. The right to water is . . . interdependent with other fundamental rights. In fact, the complexity of the right to water includes dimensions of a collective nature. . . .

The right to water contemplated in the Constitution . . . contemplates the right that every person has to have the state respect, protect, and fulfill his or her access to quality water.

Like any fundamental right, the right to water has positive aspects as well as negative ones. The right presupposes that necessary measures will be adopted to construct an adequate infrastructure of aqueducts and pipes such that the dignity and life of people will not be put at risk; but at the same time, it requires that measures not be taken that would, for example, contaminate water destined for human consumption.

The effective enjoyment of water requires, at least, three factors; (i) that water be available; (ii) that it be high-quality and (iii) the right to access it. In terms of availability, the [CESCR] has indicated that "[t]he water supply for each person must be sufficient and continuous for personal and domestic uses. . . . Some individuals and

32. *Id.* ¶ 2.

33. Shortly after this decision was issued, the United Nations General Assembly passed a resolution recognizing "the right to safe and clean drinking water and sanitation as a human right that is essential for the full enjoyment of life and all human rights." *See* G.A. Res. 64/292, U.N. Doc. A/RES/64/292 (Aug. 3, 2010).

groups may also require additional water due to health, climate, and work conditions."[34] With respect to (ii) quality, it warns that "[t]he water required for each personal or domestic use must be safe, therefore free from micro-organisms, chemical substances and radiological hazards that constitute a threat to a person's health." It signals that it must have a color, smell, and taste that are acceptable for personal and domestic use. Finally, on (iii) accessibility, it sustains that "[w]ater and water facilities and services have to be accessible to *everyone* without discrimination, within the jurisdiction of the State party." It establishes that four types of accessibility of water and its facilities exist: physical (. . . to all sectors of the population); economic (cost . . . may not be an obstacle); non-discriminatory . . . ; and informational (. . . the right to solicit, receive, and distribute information on questions dealing with water).

In accordance with the Constitution . . . , the right to water is a right of each and every person, but in the case of some subjects of special protection, it gives rise to special and specific obligations of respect, protection, and fulfillment. Thus, the [CESCR] observed that the state should "give special attention to those individuals and groups who have traditionally faced difficulties in exercising this right, including women, children, minority groups, indigenous peoples, refugees, asylum seekers, internally displaced persons, migrant workers, prisoners and detainees."[35] It warns that the measures adopted by the state must aim, among other purposes, to ensure that "[r]ural and deprived urban areas have access to properly maintained water facilities." Categorically, it establishes that "no household should be denied the right to water on the grounds of their housing or land status."

The obligations derived from a fundamental right suppose at least the obligations to respect, protect, and fulfill. In the case of water, the CESCR observed that the obligations to respect imply abstaining from directly or indirectly interfering in the exercise of the right to water; the obligations to protect involve preventing third parties from in any way lessening the enjoyment of the right to water; and the obligations to fulfill are divided in diverse ways, many of them positive and complex, oriented especially to ensuring the rights of those who cannot protect the right for themselves. . . .

As has been indicated, the obligations derived from the fundamental right to water can involve positive aspects, which demand complex measures by the state, like the realization of public works, or negative aspects, which require abstention from the state. This has been recognized in existing constitutional jurisprudence.

As an example of the protection of a positive aspect of the right, we can cite to the recent Decision T-974 of 2009 (per Justice Mauricio González Cuervo), in which the Constitutional Court protected the rights to life and to health of a community that was affected by the constant flooding of the *La Vieja* river. The petitioners alleged that the failure to construct a collector that would intercept runoff

34. General Comment 15, *supra* note 31, ¶ 12.

35. *Id.* ¶ 16.

before it arrived at the river and the lack of maintenance of some protective dykes were the cause of the floods that endangered the mentioned constitutional rights. The Constitutional Court decided to concede the *tutela* action, considering that (i) for more than three decades—from the middle of the 1970s—the administration has known about the problem . . . ; (ii) that the legal constitutional, regulatory, territorial, and treaty-based norms imposed a duty on the state to take measures; and (iii) that the rights of the petitioners were at risk.

Negative aspects of the right to water have also been protected. The Court considered that the right to access water has been violated . . . when by positive acts of the administration, even if justified, access to water . . . has been affected. This occurred, for example, in Decision T-381 of 2009 (per Justice Jorge Ignacio Pretelt Chaljub), in which, after recognizing the impact that a public works project had on the access to water on the land of the petitioners, the Court decided to order the adoption of adequate and necessary measures to ensure that the problem would find a definitive solution.

[Next, the Court proceeded to analyze the case at issue in light of these principles:]

The municipal administration in Arbalaez . . . violated the fundamental rights to life, health, and water of the petitioners and those of their families, by offering them a water service that was not drinkable . . . , by refusing to offer running water via a response that did not respond to their request, [and by declining] to create a plan that would assure, progressively, the effective enjoyment of their rights. In addition, since we are dealing with people that inhabit the rural sector of the town and who have limited economic resources, the omission of the municipal administration also ignores their right to be specially protected in access to potable water, guaranteeing them that they will not be "last in line."

The mayor of Arbelaez also violated the right to water of the petitioners by employing proceedings and processes before the administration as obstacles to the effective enjoyment of their rights. . . .

The constitutional judge does not have the option of "abstaining" from compliance with his constitutional obligation of protecting the effective enjoyment of fundamental rights, when he has discovered that those rights have been violated or threatened. The complexities that are involved in the actions of the public administration, for example regarding the design, elaboration, implementation, evaluation, and control of public policies, do not justify the *tutela* judge in abstaining from giving orders, within his competence, that will ensure the effective enjoyment of rights at least to the extent possible. . . .

When a *tutela* judge is obligated to adopt or impart complex orders with the goal of untangling what has been metaphorically called institutional paralysis, the judge must take into account, at least (i) that her measures be really effective . . . , which might require either direct or [indirect] supervision; (ii) that her measures respect the social state of law, and do not ignore the particular democratic and administrative competencies established by the constitution; (iii) that . . . she promotes, to the extent possible, the participation of . . . affected persons, as well as those who understand the situation through experience or study. . . .

The *tutela* judge must be conscious that when she imparts a complex order that her work with relation to the case does not end with the decision, but merely begins at that moment. The work that the *tutela* judge must carry out, in terms of supervision and control of compliance with these types of orders, can exceed, over time, the elaboration of the decision itself. . . .

Many of the [complex] orders imparted by a *tutela* judge . . . do not establish which specific measures of the administration or the individual should be taken in a concrete case, but are oriented to push the authorities or persons to adopt measures, in the proper conditions of a participatory democracy, and through a process of design, implementation, evaluation, and control. . . .

The Court will make reference to some of the measures that constitutional jurisprudence has considered relevant to adopt in order to . . . guarantee[] the effective enjoyment of the right to water, while respecting the technical and democratic competencies of the existing constitutional order. The Court has imparted, among others, the following orders: . . .

Realization of studies. In those situations where the required information to make a decision about the specific response to a violation or threat to a fundamental right does not exist, one measure is to order that adequate and necessary measures be taken to ensure that necessary "studies are realized" in order to obtain the required information. . . .

Construction or completion of construction of public works. The Constitutional Court has ordered that planned public works for a sewer system, which were never completed, be completed where that state of affairs constituted a violation of the rights of the persons who brought the *tutela*. . . .

Suspension of administrative proceedings. When the realization of a determined administrative proceeding puts fundamental rights at risk, the *tutela* judge can consider the possibility that that proceeding be postponed or suspended.

Establishment of working groups. The Constitutional Court has also tried employing other methods, like ordering the creation of a working group . . . [which] will be the body to determine the measures that should be adopted. . . .

Opening of spaces for participation. From the beginning of its jurisprudence, the Constitutional Court has valued the participation of people as an indispensable motor for the guarantee of the effective enjoyment of fundamental rights. . . .

Adoption of regulations. The Constitutional Court has ordered that regulations be adopted when they are required to ensure the right to water of persons, and when their absence constitutes an obstacle to the effective enjoyment of the right. . . .

Verification of compliance of an act of the administration. The Court has ordered that adequate and necessary measures be taken to ensure the effective compliance with an administration act, when the effective enjoyment of the right to water depends on it. . . .

> *Adoption of temporary measures.* When the Constitutional Court has recognized the need to carry out a series of actions to respect, protect, and fulfill the right to water, during the lapse of time while the decision is being complied with, the fundamental rights of persons can be gravely affected, perhaps irreparably. Thus, since the beginning of its jurisprudence, the Constitutional Court has indicated that in those cases where the orders are complex and their execution or implementation may take considerable time, it is proper to adopt temporary measures that prevent the sacrifice of fundamental rights while the primary order is receiving full compliance. . . .

Finally, the Chamber must raise two points for cases involving complex orders. The first is that the *tutela* judge must be open to dialogue with the administration so that, with the object of ensuring compliance with the *tutela* decision, changes can be introduced when indispensable and necessary. The second is that participation requires, at least, an adequate framework for governability. . . .

First, we will order the mayor of Arbelaez to adopt the adequate and necessary measures to design a specific plan for the rural community to which the petitioners pertain, in order to ensure that they will not be last in line to receive water. . . . The specific plan adopted for the community must have precise dates and timeframes that allow the community to follow the development of the plan. It must include mechanisms of control and evaluation that permit evaluation of grades of compliance with the plan. Also, it must have as its object ensuring the right to access and utilize water with regularity and continuity. . . .

The plan . . . must include effective and real spaces of participation for the persons affected and linked to the process of compliance with the present judicial decision, during the design, elaboration, implementation, evaluation, and control of the adopted plan. In particular, participation must be sought to determine the needs and specific problems of the community, and in order to control and supervise compliance with the actions undertaken.

The Chamber will order the mayor's office to realize a bi-monthly report, which will indicate, in a detailed and specific way—with dates, times, and concrete data—the actions that have been undertaken during that lapse of time in order to comply with what has been stated in the present decision. . . .

While the specific plan adopted is being implemented, the mayor's office in Arbelaez is ordered to adopt adequate and necessary measures to ensure access to a minimum of potable water to the people in the sector. By employing the measures that are considered adequate to that end and realizing the alliances and agreements that are apt, the mayor's office of Arbelaez must take temporary measures while the effective enjoyment of the right is being assured through the plan adopted for that end. As was indicated, it is understandable that the actions taken will take time to take effect, since they are complex orders; thus, while they are being effectively implemented, it is proper for the municipality to adopt temporary measures so that the constitutional rights affected are not left completely unprotected. These measures may only be suspended at the moment in which water service has been regularized and is being adequately offered.

Taking into account that some of the people in the area carry out agricultural work on their properties, the Chamber holds that the municipal administration must adopt adequate and necessary measures to ensure that none of the people in this sector are left without water for human consumption because it is being destined first to other ends like agriculture. . . . [T]he right to access water of one or various people is violated when positive actions are taken that limit the availability or access to it and when the authorities do not adopt the adequate and necessary measures to prevent that situation from continuing. . . .

[Justice Mauricio González Cuervo concurred in the decision. He agreed with the result of the case but would have held that the right to water was not fundamental in and of itself, but only when connected with other fundamental rights such as the right to life, health, or human dignity: "[T]he right to water cannot be understood as an autonomous fundamental right, but rather it is its connection with fundamental rights that determines its special protection by the *tutela* judge."]

Note on the Right to Water and the Minimum Core: Another common context where the right to water has arisen both in Colombia and in other countries is where the petitioner has access to water but is unable to pay for it because of extreme poverty. This situation raises a problem in stark form: Is it possible to define a minimum core entitlement to water, to which petitioners should be entitled regardless of ability to pay? In **Decision T-740 of 2011 (per Justice Humberto Antonio Sierra Porto)**, the Court held that it was possible to establish such a minimum core entitlement to water, which it set at least for purposes of that case at 50 liters per person per day.

The case dealt with the case of a 54-year-old, impoverished single mother head of household whose water service had been cut off because she was unable to pay the bill. The woman was instead forced to walk 20 minutes to access substandard water. In determining how to set a minimum quantity of water, the Court canvassed the statements of several international organizations on the issue. It particularly emphasized that "[t]he World Health Organization in its report on *Domestic Water Quantity, Service Level, and Health* stated that the minimum quantity of water that a person needs for the satisfaction of basic needs is 50 liters of water per day."[36]

The Court thus held that the utility company at issue had to re-establish the flow of water into the petitioner's home and was required to provide her with at least 50 liters of water per person per day. It could continue to try and collect the unpaid debt, but had to work with the petitioner to come up with a payment plan that would allow her to pay over time. Finally, the state was required to reimburse the utility for 50 percent of the cost of this minimum allotment of water granted to the petitioner.

36. Guy Howard & Jamie Bartram, *Domestic Water Quantity, Service Level and Health*, WHO/SDE/WSH/03.02 (2003). The report noted different ranges of water usage that were consistent with different levels of hygiene and personal consumption.

In its decision, the Court mentioned the jurisprudence of the South African Constitutional Court, particularly the 2009 judgment *Mazibuko v. City of Johannesburg.*[37] That decision overruled two lower court decisions setting a minimum entitlement to 25 liters and 42 liters of water per person per day respectively. The *Mazibuko* Court stated that it was beyond the competence of the Court to set a minimum core entitlement to water, and instead that it could only review whether the city's policies were reasonable, which it certified as being the case for the policy at issue. The South African Constitutional Court has consistently declined to set a minimum core entitlement to socioeconomic rights, holding that it lacks the legitimacy and capacity to do so. In contrast, the Colombian Court has been somewhat more willing to define a minimum core, as both this case and the internally displaced persons case found in Section D demonstrate. Nonetheless, it has used that technique as only one of several for interpreting the content of socioeconomic rights.

37. *Mazibuko and Others* v *City of Johannesburg and Others* (CCT 39/09) [2009] ZACC 28; 2010 (3) BCLR 239 (CC); 2010 (4) SA 1 (CC).

7

The Rights of Victims and Transitional Justice

The long-lasting and tragic civil conflict in Colombia has produced much suffering and many victims. As noted in the case on internally displaced persons excerpted in the previous chapter, millions of Colombians were forced from their homes because of the conflict. Furthermore, a large number of Colombians have suffered a range of other human rights abuses—such as murder, rape, destruction of property, and forced recruitment of minors to bear arms—related to the internal armed conflict. Historically, the state has not always been effective in protecting the rights of victims and in repairing violations of those rights; indeed, it has also committed violations in its actions related to the conflict.

Since its inception, the Court has held that victims have a range of rights, including the right to know the truth about what happened to them, to seek justice for the acts taken against them, and to have the perpetrator or the state make reparations for those acts. As Section A shows, these principles have been developed in the ordinary criminal context, where the Court has insisted that victims have the right to participate and seek reparations against criminals who have wronged them. But in the Colombian context, their most significant manifestation has been related to the internal armed conflict.

A particularly challenging context where these questions have arisen is in efforts to demobilize and make peace with the actors involved in the conflict. Sections B and C each consider legal efforts along these lines, first with paramilitary groups since 2005 and second with guerrilla groups since 2012. Peace is stated in Article 22 of the Constitution as both "a right and a duty," and was perhaps the overriding goal of the Constituent Assembly of 1991. Thus, efforts to end the conflict by demobilizing armed actors are consistent with the constitutional vision. But the Court has insisted that these efforts must be considered in light of the rights of victims to learn the truth of what has happened to them, seek justice for those events, and receive reparations for their losses. Thus, while maintaining a flexible

Colombian Constitutional Law: Leading Cases. Manuel José Cepeda Espinosa and David Landau.

vision consistent with a transitional justice regime, the Court has insisted on limits on the kinds of concessions that the state can make in return for peace.[1]

This area has been marked by the engagement between domestic and international law, particularly through the constitutional block doctrine explored in Section C of Chapter 2. Under this doctrine, codified in Article 93 of the Constitution, international treaties related to human rights either form part of the constitutional order directly or are used as criteria of interpretation for Colombian constitutional law. Colombia is party to a large number of international instruments that are relevant to the rights of victims, including the Geneva Conventions and Additional Protocols, the Inter-American Convention on Human Rights, and the Rome Statute of the International Criminal Court. The Court has thus frequently relied on these texts and on the bodies charged with interpreting them such as the Inter-American Court of Human Rights, which have had a significant influence on the law in this area. Key limits imposed by the Court, such as a prohibition on amnesty for the most serious crimes found in humanitarian law and human rights law, are based on international norms.[2]

That said, the relationship between the Constitutional Court and international law is more complex than one of simple incorporation or absorption. In the process of implementing international norms, the Court has translated and adapted them in light of the particularities of the Colombian context. In effect, the involvement of the Colombian Court in the peace process has contributed to a dialogue about how international norms and values must be interpreted in light of the pressing needs of Colombian society. The Court's vision has been fairly flexible in allowing special measures in pursuit of peace, but it has insisted on core protections for victims and prevention of regimes that would allow impunity for the most serious crimes.

In a broader sense, the Court's jurisprudence contributed to changes in political and public discourse. The traditional marginalization of victims has given way to an environment in which their rights have been recognized, if not always realized, by the state. The most tangible realizations of these changes are the Law of Victims and the Restitution of Land (passed in 2011 and excerpted in Section B) and the norms implementing the peace process with guerilla groups since 2012 (examined in Section C).

A. The Rights of Victims during Criminal Processes

Decision C-228 of 2002 (per Justices Manuel José Cepeda Espinosa and Eduardo Montealegre Lynett)

[In a unanimous decision, the Court protected victims' rights to truth, justice, and reparations by striking down some of the articles of the Code of Criminal Procedure. The relevant provisions limited the rights of a victim within a criminal proceeding to requesting only an economic indemnity for damages caused, and in addition limited

1. The seminal work on the concept is RUTI G. TEITEL, TRANSITIONAL JUSTICE (2000).

2. For an analysis of the emerging international norms governing peace-making processes, see CHRISTINE BELL, ON THE LAW OF PEACE (2008).

the access of the victim to the criminal proceedings in multiple ways. For example, the provisions required that victims participate only through counsel, and only once a formal criminal investigation of a defendant had been opened.[3] The Court decided that the rights of the victim, in addition to the right to reparations for any damages caused, also encompassed rights to truth and to justice. In addition, it ordered certain measures that would make it easier for the victim to participate in the criminal proceedings: it allowed victims to participate along with their lawyers, and allowed them to participate before a formal investigation has been opened.]

The right of victims to participate in the criminal process is related to respect for human dignity. Considering Article 1 of the Constitution, which states that "Colombia is a social state of law founded on respect for human dignity," victims and those wronged by a punishable act can demand from others treatment in accordance with their human condition. The victims' . . . dignity would be greatly violated by punishable acts if the only protection offered to them were the possibility of obtaining purely economic reparations. The principle of human dignity does not allow either the human being or the rights and legal goods protected by criminal law to be reduced to an economic analysis of their value. The acknowledgement of an [economic] indemnity for damage caused by a crime is one of the solutions that the lawmaker has chosen because of the difficulty of achieving a complete recovery of the rights and legal goods affected by a crime. But this is not the only alternative, nor is it the only one that fully protects each person's intrinsic value. On the contrary, the principle of dignity does not allow the protection of the victims of a crime to be exclusively of an economic nature. . . . It demands from the authorities that legal instruments be developed by the lawmaker to achieve the effective enjoyment of each victim's rights, and that these be geared towards their integral reestablishment. That is only possible if the victims of a crime are given, at a minimum, guarantees regarding their rights to know the truth, to obtain justice, and to receive full reparations for any damage that has been suffered.

[The Court also referred to victims' rights in international law. It underlined the growing tendency toward the acknowledgment and expansion of those rights, and it concluded that the victims have three relevant rights under international human rights law:]

1. The right to truth; that is, the possibility to know what happened. . . . This right is particularly important in the face of grave violations of human rights.
2. The right to have justice applied in the concrete case; that is, the right not to have impunity.
3. The right to reparations for the damage caused, which can be achieved by means of economic compensation, the traditional way in which the victim of a crime has been indemnified.

3. In Latin American and other civil law contexts, a long and quasi-formal process of interaction among prosecutors, judges, and police often precedes the decision on whether to open a formal investigation of criminal defendants.

> There must be real damage, concrete and specific ... that legitimizes the participation of the victim ... in the criminal process..., and this must be analyzed by judicial authorities in each particular case. Once the status of a person as a victim has been demonstrated ... that person may become the civil party, and may assert his claim exclusively in order to obtain justice and search for the truth, putting aside any economic objective, if the victim so desires. Moreover, even once economically indemnified, if victims have an interest in truth and justice, they can continue within the process in their condition as a civil party.... [V]ictims cannot be required to file a suit to obtain economic reparations.
>
> [The Court next stated that the requirement that the victim intervene in the criminal process only through legal counsel did not restrict or violate the victim's rights; on the contrary, it was aimed at ensuring the effective enjoyment of the rights to truth, justice, and reparation. Nonetheless, the Court clarified:] [T]his does not mean that the existence of technical arguments can prevent the exercise of a material defense directly by the victim, nor can the requirement of being represented by counsel become an obstacle to guaranteeing the victim's rights.... [B]oth the victims and their counsel may ask that evidence be submitted; both have the right to be informed of every procedural act adopted by the competent authority during the criminal process, as well as to contest all those procedural acts that may affect their rights to truth, justice and reparation.
>
> The victim and their counsel constitute a sole party: the civil party. Their intervention in the process must be subjected to the principle of equality. Consequently, the victim can directly file [motions] and can ask that evidence be submitted.
>
> [On the other hand, the Court declared unconstitutional a requirement that victims only participate in the criminal process after the authorities had adopted a resolution to formally open an investigation of a criminal defendant:] [T]he rights to truth, justice and economic reparation depend on the possibility that, before this stage, the civil party be permitted to actively intervene, submitting evidence, cooperating with judicial authorities, and knowing and questioning the decisions made before the formal opening of the investigation, especially the decision through which it is formally decided not to open an investigation.

Note on the Rights of Crime Victims: The Court's doctrine on the rights of victims within the criminal process has been further developed in several subsequent decisions. For example, in **Decision C-004 of 2003 (per Justice Eduardo Montealegre Lynett)**, the Court examined an article of the old Code of Criminal Procedure that allowed for the revision of criminal sentences on the following grounds: "after the sentence is issued, new facts or evidence arise, not known at the time of the decision, that establish the innocence of the condemned...." The Court declared this provision conditionally constitutional, under the understanding that it also cover some cases, involving international human rights law or international humanitarian law, in which new evidence would show that a previously acquitted or lightly-sentenced defendant actually had a higher degree of guilt. "[R]evision is also permitted in cases when the investigation has been precluded, procedures have ceased, or a decision has absolved the accused, as long as the crime has to do with violations of human rights or grave infractions of international humanitarian law, or as long as there was a decision from an international instance of supervision and control of human rights, formally accepted by our country, recognizing the existence of a new fact or evidence, not known before the criminal decision was adopted. Likewise, . . . revision . . . is allowed . . . in processes for the violation of human rights or grave infractions of international humanitarian law, even if there are no new facts . . . if an international judicial decision, or a decision from an international body [charged with] supervision and control of human rights . . . finds an evident non-fulfillment of the obligation of the Colombian state to seriously and impartially investigate the aforementioned violations." Thus, the Court allowed for investigations to be reopened and defendants retried in circumstances involving violations of international human rights law or grave breaches of international humanitarian law, in order to protect the rights of victims of these crimes.

In **Decision C-979 of 2005 (per Justice Jaime Córdoba Triviño)** the Court examined an article of the new Code of Criminal Procedure that explicitly allowed revised sentences in cases involving violations of international human rights law or grave breaches of international humanitarian law, but only in case of judicial decisions returning a verdict of innocence. The Court declared the limitation of revision only to verdicts of innocence to be unconstitutional. Thus, it allowed for revision in other circumstances as well, such as where light sentences are given for very serious crimes.

The Court has limited the rights of crime victims in some circumstances, particularly in order to preserve essential characteristics of the new adversarial justice system that was created by the 1991 Constitution.[4] The 1991 Constitution moved Colombia away from the inquisitorial criminal system that it has traditionally possessed (and where the judge plays the leading role in the criminal process), and toward an adversarial system more like the American system, where lawyers for each side act as the protagonists. In **Decision C-209 of 2007 (per Justice Manuel José Cepeda Espinosa)**, the Court held that at the trial stage only the prosecutor could be allowed to introduce the theory of the case and to exercise other faculties, such as examination and cross-examination of witnesses, in order to preserve equality between the defendant and the state.

B. The Rights of Victims during Internal Armed Conflict

In Colombia, the rights of victims are particularly salient with respect to the country's long-running and deeply violent internal civil conflict. Peace in this conflict has been achieved in a series of stages, beginning with negotiation with right-wing paramilitary groups. During the administration of President Alvaro Uribe (2002–2010), right-wing paramilitary groups

4. Many Latin American jurisdictions have switched from an inquisitorial to an adversarial system of criminal justice since the 1990s. *See* Máximo Langer, *Revolution in Latin American Criminal Procedure: Diffusion of Legal Ideas from the Periphery*, 55 Am. J. Comp. L. 617 (2007).

entered into a negotiation and demobilization process with the government by handing in their weapons. This demobilization process occurred in a context where the military, during the administration of President Alvaro Uribe, was perceived as successful in fighting left-wing guerrilla groups within the framework of a presidential policy called "democratic security."

When the conditions for demobilization had already been agreed in the midst of great national controversy, Congress (at the initiative of the government), adopted Act 975 of 2005, the Peace and Justice Act, which laid out special criminal provisions for the demobilized paramilitary groups, and eventually for some members of guerrilla groups as well. The law granted members of illegal armed organizations benefits under the criminal law in exchange for their demobilization and collaboration with the criminal system, but it did not demand their full confession for crimes committed, nor did it set any conditions requiring full reparations for these crimes. The main benefit was the establishment of a low punishment of between five and eight years for all crimes committed, including massacres and other atrocities, to any member of an illegal armed group who adhered to and was judged for any crime under the Peace and Justice Act.

Many citizens challenged this controversial law in front of the Court, and various NGOs, civil society organizations, and government agencies participated in the judicial process. These actors generally argued that the treatment given to paramilitaries violated both the Colombian constitution and international human rights law and international humanitarian law incorporated into the constitutional block.

The Court upheld the basic concept of the law, which provided a sharp reduction in sentences for demobilized paramilitaries, even if they had committed serious atrocities. The Court held that this system advanced the cause of peace in Colombia, which was a core value and impetus behind the 1991 Constitution. However, it also carefully examined the specific provisions of the Act in light of the right of victims to truth, justice, and reparations, and struck down significant parts of the law as a result.

Decision C-370 of 2006 (per Justices Manuel José Cepeda Espinosa, Jaime Córdoba Triviño, Rodrigo Escobar Gil, Marco Gerardo Monroy Cabra, Álvaro Tafur Galvis, and Clara Inés Vargas Hernández)

[The Court started with a general analysis of the scope of the right to peace as well as the right of victims to truth, justice, and reparation, based on international law and on the previous decisions of the Constitutional Court. The Court established that these rights and values were both important under the Colombian Constitution, and thus that they needed to be balanced against one another. Thus, the Court analyzed the concept of transitional justice in international law; it referred to binding treaties for Colombia and their relevance regarding the rights to peace, truth, justice, and reparation; it summarized the Inter-American Court's decisions regarding the standards on justice, non-repetition of crimes, truth, and reparation for the victims of grave violations of international human rights law and international humanitarian law; it discussed the United Nation's Updated Set of principles for the Protection and

Promotion of Human Rights through Action to Combat Impunity;[5] it summarized reports from the Inter-American Commission on Human Rights; and it summarized its own decisions on the rights of victims.]

[In the Court's judgment, the above concepts and decisions] emphasize the constitutional and international importance of peace, justice, and the rights of victims.] [They highlight] that the tension between these rights is manifest in a distinct way depending on diverse factors, among which, in this case, are the adoption of legislative and judicial instruments to foster the transition towards peace within a democratic context. . . .

Above all, it is worthwhile to pinpoint that the legislator has the competence to identify the dimensions within which that tension is expressed and to define the formulas to overcome it, exercising the attributions clearly granted by the Constitution. . . . It is the constitutional justice's competence to identify the limits on this power and to have them respected, without sacrificing any of the constitutional elements that are in tension, and without substituting for the legislature, which is exercising its own powers.

The Congress approved [the law] as an instrument to bring peace to the country; that is, as a means to overcome the internal armed conflict that has been affecting Colombia for several decades. . . . The value of peace has several manifestations in the 1991 Constitution, as was pointed out earlier. [I]it is worthwhile to highlight that peace is a right at the same time that it is a duty. To achieve the constitutional value of peace, Congress enacted in the Law diverse formulas which, in general terms, imply a reform to criminal procedures affecting the principle of justice—understood both as an objective value and also as one of the rights of the victims of violations of human rights. Thus, certain benefits under criminal law, and a special procedure before certain specific authorities, are established so that illegal armed groups will demobilize and reintegrate into civil life. . . .

The method of balancing (or proportionality) is appropriate to resolve the problems in this case, as it is not possible to materialize fully and simultaneously all of the different rights at play, that is, justice, peace, and victims' rights. The achievement of a stable and lasting peace that pulls the country out of the conflict through the demobilization of illegal armed groups can permit certain restrictions on the objective value of justice and the correlative right of the victims to justice . . . ; the historical experience of different countries that have overcome internal armed conflict has shown this. . . .

But peace does not justify everything. The value of peace cannot be granted an absolute reach, since it is also necessary to guarantee the materialization of the essential contents of the principle of justice and of the rights of the victims to justice . . . in spite of the legitimate limitations imposed on these rights in order to end the armed conflict. . . .

5. Commission on Human Rights, *Updated Set of Principles for the Protection and Promotion of Human Rights through Action to Combat Impunity*, E/CN.4/2005/102/Add.1 (Feb. 8, 2005).

[I]t was the legislator himself who, by opting to limit the value and right to justice to achieve peace, set the essential terms of the scale in which the balancing must be carried out. . . . Balancing must be carried out, consequently, taking into account the different ways in which the norms of the Act being contested affect justice and the other constitutional values and rights in need of protection, that is, peace, the right to truth, the right to reparation, and the right to non-repetition of crimes violating human rights. It is worthwhile to mention that the novel problem proposed by Law 975/05 is how much weight should be given to the value of peace. This is a complex issue, not only because of its novelty, but also because of the enormous transcendence that peace was given by the 1991 Constitution.

It is pertinent to highlight that justice (like peace) has great constitutional importance. . . . This does not imply that justice can, in its turn, be raised up to the category of an absolute right to such an extent that peace is sacrificed, or its materialization is prevented.

[By] examining the means designed by the legislator to reach the legitimate ends that he pretends to achieve, the Court will analyze whether they are the adequate means to reach those ends, and whether those means constitute a limitation on rights that is disproportionate. . . .

The fundamental charge against [the law] is that it constitutes a system of impunity, whose main effect is to grant a benefit under the criminal law so that those who have committed grave crimes, within the framework of the internal armed conflict, can be exonerated from a meaningful part of the punishment that would ordinarily be imposed on them for committing such crimes, without meeting the conditions set by international humanitarian law and human rights law for such measures to be valid. . . .

To issue a basic opinion on this charge, it is necessary to refer to the concept of the "alternative punishment." In essence, this is a benefit that consists of the suspension of the ordinary applicable punishment established by the general rules of the Criminal Code, so that instead of the regular punishment the condemned person receives a lesser alternative punishment, which is a minimum of five years and a maximum of eight years.

After a verdict of guilty, first, the regular punishment is set; and, second, that punishment is replaced . . . by an alternative punishment of five to eight years in prison. . . . Under the theory . . . adopted in [the Act], the regular punishment does not disappear—it is imposed by the verdict. But the convicted person who meets the requirements set by the Act benefits from a lower alternative punishment which must also be imposed in the verdict. This alternative punishment is the one that the convicted person must effectively fulfill in prison.

This configuration of the alternative punishment, as a measure geared towards the achievement of peace, is in agreement with the Constitution. [I]t does not imply a disproportionate burden on the value of justice, which is preserved by imposing the original regular punishment within the limits set in the Criminal Code, in proportion to the crime for which the person has been condemned, and which must be carried out if the sentenced person does not meet the commitments under which he or she was granted the benefit of suspension of the regular punishment. . . .

However, the Court considers that some [articles] of the Act deserve special consideration since they contain measures that, although aimed at the achievement of peace, could place a disproportionate burden on [the rights of victims to truth, justice, and reparations].

Article 3 conditions the suspension of the execution of the regular penalty . . . on the "collaboration with justice" [of the accused]. This demand is formulated in such generic terms, stripped of specific content, that it does not satisfy the right of the victims to the full enjoyment of their rights to truth, justice, reparation and non-repetition. . . . Consequently, the Court will declare that Article 3 is constitutional only on the condition that it be read under the understanding that "collaboration with justice" must be conducive towards the effective achievement of the rights of the victims to truth, reparation and non-repetition.

[The Court specified these requirements elsewhere in its decision—for example, it required that there be a "full and complete confession" in court by the accused. In another part of the decision, the Court examined provisions of the Act in light of the right of victims to truth.]

[We must ask] whether the norms questioned, aimed at the reintegration to civilian life of persons who have committed grave crimes, are the adequate procedural mechanisms to satisfy the right of victims of violations of human rights . . . so that (1) the crime is acknowledged by the state and is investigated within a reasonable period of time; (2) the responsible parties are known; and (3) the causes and the circumstances . . . of the crime are fully established. In addition, the Court asks whether such legal mechanisms will adequately serve in the reconstruction of macro-criminal phenomena [involving paramilitary organizations] and in the investigation of such crimes, including those that mankind as a whole has viewed as having the gravest characteristics.

For the Court, the Act being questioned does not clearly establish necessary and sufficient judicial mechanisms so that the macro-criminal phenomenon being studied can be resolved. Nor does it set judicial mechanisms that ensure that the truth will be known regarding the crimes committed by the members of specific groups that are demobilizing.

In the first place, the mechanisms designed by the Act do not in effect promote the full revelation of the truth. These mechanisms do not assign a consequence to lies or to the concealment of grave facts that the state has been unable to clarify, nor do they foster the complete and certain revelation of the truth regarding the crimes committed by members of such specific groups. . . .

As to any new crimes [by a defendant] that may be revealed by the state's investigations rather than from collaboration of the accused, the benefits of the law will still be applied [to him] so long as it is demonstrated that its omission from the confession was unintentional. . . . [Further,] it is the state's duty to provide evidence showing that the omission was intentional. If it is not possible to provide such evidence, and the person accepts the new charges, he or she will have the right, once again, to the benefits granted in [the Act]. So, the person responsible for crimes committed . . . as a member of such groups before demobilization who, at that time, did not confess, will probably still benefit from the alternative punishment according to the Act.

Taking into consideration the concept of accumulation of alternative punishments set by the Act, the new verdict—for crimes that could be massacres, forced displacement, or massive kidnappings—would not comprise an effective prison penalty. In fact, since the law establishes that . . . the total penalty [for all crimes] cannot exceed the eight-year maximum penalty stated by the Act under any circumstances, it might well happen that the person has already fulfilled this maximum penalty [before being sentenced for newly discovered crimes]. Therefore, in spite of the fact that the person can be the subject of a new alternative penalty, he would not be obliged to go to jail for even a single day, since the effective penalty cannot go beyond eight years.

This description clearly shows that the Act does not design a system of effective incentives that fosters the full and complete revelation of the truth. . . . However, the full and complete collaboration of the perpetrators is an indispensable measure to satisfy the right of the victims to truth, and to society's interest in the reconstruction of historical memory.

In the face of the type of crimes the questioned Act refers to, only the complete identification of the chain of crimes committed by each one of these specific armed groups allows us to know the true dimension of what occurred, to identify the victims, to give them redress, and to adopt serious and sustainable measures for non-repetition. . . .

[The Court thus held that the benefits provided to the criminal by the law should be repealed whenever a judge finds that the criminal has hidden additional crimes linked to paramilitary activities that were excluded from the initial confession.[6] The Court also dealt with several challenges based on the victims' right to justice. For example, it studied a provision of the law that allowed for the "possibility of counting as part of the punishment imposed the time that the sentenced person spent in the so-called demobilized zone," rather than in jail. Demobilized zones were areas set up by the state where paramilitaries could go in order to discuss demobilizing with representatives of the state. Petitioners argued that this provision violated the victims' right to justice by allowing criminals to count as part of their sentence time that was not actually spent in jail.]

[I]n order to facilitate talks, negotiations, and agreements within the framework of the demobilization processes of illegal organized armed groups, the National Government has created, after an agreement with spokespersons for such groups, the

6. The Court also heard another challenge to a provision of the law based on the right to truth. A provision conditioned the benefits of the law on the criminal's helping authorities to free any persons whom they have kidnapped. However, the law did not require paramilitaries to reveal the location of individuals who were victims of "forced disappearances" (and who presumably had been killed). The Court held that this exclusion was unconstitutional; actors would need to give information about these disappearances as well in order to receive the lighter sentences given under the law.

so-called temporary location or demobilized zones in specific spaces of the national territory. It is important to highlight that to enter these zones is a voluntary act by the members of the illegal armed groups. In some cases this has immediate legal effects, i.e. the suspension of arrest warrants against some representatives of those groups, in order to facilitate negotiations.

The Court notes that the questioned article . . . assimilates serving a sentence for a punishment imposed to the circumstance of [the criminal's] being located in a demobilized zone, in spite of the fact that there has not been any requirement from the state that these persons go to such a place. In this sense, staying in a demobilized zone for a long time is not a penalty, as it is not a coercive imposition on the demobilized paramilitary carrying with it the restriction of fundamental rights.

[The Court thus struck down the article of the law allowing time spent in those zones to count as part of the criminal penalty. It also held a related article, possibly allowing demilitarized paramilitaries to serve their sentences in "special places of reclusion" outside of the normal rules and regulations of the prison system, conditionally constitutional only on the grounds that the normal regulations of prisons apply to those places. The Court held that this condition was necessary to protect the "dignity" of victims and to ensure that the paramilitaries were not treated with "impunity." Finally, the Court considered challenges based on the victims' rights to reparations.]

The complainants consider that [the sections at issue] violate the right to reparations of victims since they state that only properties acquired illegally can constitute the source for the payment of indemnities.

The Court wonders whether the right to integral reparation guarantees that, even in transitional justice processes, those individuals responsible for crimes must redress with their own property the damage caused by their criminal activities.

[A] series of constitutional weaknesses are identified [in the law], which the Court cannot pass up or fail to identify. First, . . . there does not seem to be a constitutional reason that allows us to make an exception to the general principle that whoever causes illegal damage is obliged to redress it. . . . Second, even if it were accepted that the state can carry out such a transfer of responsibility, the truth is that it is not authorized to forgive—either in a criminal or a civil manner—those who have committed atrocious crimes of massive or systemic violence. To completely exempt from civil responsibility the person who caused damage is equivalent to an integral amnesty from due responsibility. Finally, it appears constitutionally disproportionate to renounce claims against the property of those responsible for the damage, at least in those cases where it can be proven that the responsible individuals have great fortunes while those who have suffered damage are facing painful conditions of poverty and homelessness. . . .

Further, the Court must define whether . . . the regulations that establish that demobilized individuals must hand in their property "if they have them," "when they have them available," or "if feasible," facilitate fraud because the demobilized individuals can exclude themselves from any obligation to make reparations by stating that they do not have properties or that they cannot dispose of properties that they do not own, in detriment to the rights of the victims to reparation.

In the same way that victims and society are required to accept a path towards legality of those who have committed extremely grave crimes and cruelty, it is only to be expected that the beneficiaries of this law act in good faith to return the properties to those who were dispossessed of them, and to economically compensate them for the damage caused due to their illegal actions. . . .

The clauses specifically questioned can be interpreted in such a way that the demobilized individual is not required to make any effort at all to uncover the businesses that have allowed him to hide his property or to locate illegal properties that are clearly identified, but are not presently in his possession. . . .

[The Court thus declared the relevant provisions unconstitutional. Finally, an important part of the decision of the Court dealt with charges in relation to budgetary limitations applicable to the Fund for the Reparation of Victims. Most paramilitary members are poor individuals recruited by chiefs that were or became very rich. The Act established that public money, put into the Fund, would be a major source of reparations. But the Act fixed limitations on the sources to establish the Fund. Complainants particularly attacked a provision establishing that the Fund would pay out judicially-ordered indemnities "within the limits authorized by the national budget."]

The complainants consider that the limitation of the . . . payment of the indemnities to the budgetary limit set in the national general budget is a violation of the rights of the victims to reparations, since it is equivalent to subjecting the state's obligation to pay such reparations on the availability of sufficient resources to do so.

In the Court's view, this limitation is disproportionate and becomes an excessive burden on the rights of victims to reparations. Once it has been ordered, as the result of a judicial process carried out according to the law's formalities, that a person who has been the victim of the violation of her or his human rights has the right to receive a determinate sum of money as an indemnity, this right in his or her favor cannot be subject to later modifications, much less when derived from the availability of resources in the national general budget. . . .

Additionally, the duty to pay reparations rests with the individual responsible for the crime that caused the damage, so the national general budget is not the only source of funds to finance payment of indemnities that have been judicially decreed. . . . The expression "within the limits authorized by the National Budget" . . . will be declared unconstitutional.

[As to the responsibility of the paramilitary group to provide an indemnity], the Court is quite clear that if the benefits set by the act are for a specific group or for its members as the result of their belonging to the group, the latter must have correlative responsibilities to pay indemnification, even aside from the determination of criminal responsibilities. This responsibility of any member of the group exists as long as the damage to the victim has been proven and the relationship of causation of the damage with the specific group's activities is established. . . .

[Three justices dissented. Justices Jaime Araujo Renteria and Humberto Sierra Porto argued that the law should be entirely struck down because it was passed through improper legislative procedures. Justice Alfredo Beltrán Sierra dissented on substantive grounds, arguing that the entire system of "alternative punishments" should have been declared unconstitutional as a disproportionate limitation on the rights of victims.]

Note on the Creation of a Discourse on Victims of Internal Armed Conflicts: The Law of Peace and Justice incentivized a large number of paramilitary actors to lay down their arms. However, it has been criticized for the slow pace in which investigations have been carried out and the low number of judicial decisions issued. Prosecutions are reliant on ordinary mechanisms of justice that are arguably insufficient for such large-scale crimes. Moreover, critics have claimed that some paramilitary groups only partially demobilized, and have not stopped carrying out illegal activities.[7]

In many of its decisions, including the ones on the Law of Peace and Justice and on internally displaced persons (included in the last chapter), the Constitutional Court has prioritized victims of the internal armed conflict and insisted that they were entitled to respect for certain rights, such as human dignity, truth, justice, and reparations. One effect of these decisions, over time, was to change the public and political discourse. In effect, the Court played a key role in framing those affected by the conflict as victims entitled to respect for a series of fundamental rights under domestic and international law.

In 2011, at the urging of the new president Juan Manuel Santos, Congress passed the "Law of Victims and the Restitution of Land," reflecting this changed national discourse. The law defines the concept of a victim of the armed conflict, and lays out a set of rights for those who have been harmed, displaced, or otherwise seriously affected by it. It makes extensive use of international human rights law, international humanitarian law, and the jurisprudence of the Constitutional Court in defining those rights. Article 4, for example, includes the following language as the basic principle behind the law:

> The fundamental basis of the rights to truth, justice, and reparations is respect for the integrity and honor of victims. Victims will be treated with consideration and respect, they will participate in the decisions that affect them so that they can obtain necessary information and assistance, and they will obtain effective protection for their rights. . . .
>
> The State commits to advance, with priority, actions aimed at strengthening the autonomy of victims so that the measures of attention, assistance, and reparations included in the present law will contribute to restoring them as citizens in full exercise of their rights and duties.

7. *See, e.g.*, *La ley de Justicia y Paz al banquillo*, Semana, Apr. 3, 2014, *available at* http://www.semana.com/nacion/articulo/justicia-paz-balance-de-ocho-anos/379367-3.

The law includes an extensive set of provisions giving the victims of armed conflict rights to safely participate in judicial proceedings, to humanitarian aid and other assistance with a range of benefits including health and education, to non-repetition of rights violations, and to reparations. It also contains principles protecting internally displaced persons and creating detailed special administrative and legal procedures for the restitution of land. Many of these provisions codified the existing jurisprudence of the Constitutional Court.

Many challenges to the law have involved its limitations on scope. For example, in **Decision C-250 of 2012 (per Justice Humberto Antonio Sierra Porto)**, the Court upheld a scheme of temporal limitations whereby only those people affected by the armed conflict since 1985 would be considered "victims" for purposes of the law, and only those affected since 1991 could request legal restitution of lands that they might have lost in the conflict. The Court was deferential to the limits placed in the law by the legislature: "We cannot forget that laws of transitional justice have temporal limits precisely because they make reference to the transition from one historical period to another; these limits therefore are an intrinsic characteristic of these laws, which always require exercises of legislative judgment."

In **Decision C-253A of 2012 (per Justice Gabriel Eduardo Mendoza Martelo)**, the Court upheld various other provisions of the law, including one that stated that members of illegal armed groups could not be considered victims under the law, and another that excluded victims of "common crime" from its ambit. And finally in **Decision C-781 of 2012 (per Justice María Victoria Calle Correa)**, the Court upheld a provision limiting the benefits in the law to victims of violations of international humanitarian law or grave breaches of international human rights law "that occurred by reason of the internal armed conflict." The Court held however that this phrase had to be understood "in a broad sense."

In designing policies for victims, a particularly problematic issue has been reparations. In **Decision SU-254 of 2013 (per Justice Luis Ernesto Vargas Silva)**, the Court developed a basic framework for the rights of victims of the armed conflict to reparations, especially internally displaced persons, based on the Constitution and the Law of Victims and its implementing regulations. In this decision, the Court established, for example, that the *tutela* could be used to protect this right because of the conditions of extreme vulnerability in which IDPs who were victims of the internal armed conflict found themselves. It also found that claimants inscribed in the national registry of IDPs were entitled to a presumption of truthfulness. Unless the state were able to overcome this presumption, the Court ordered it to pay the amount of restitution set in the relevant implementing regulations, and held that this amount must be independent of other economic support, such as housing subsidies or economic aid, that had previously been paid by the state. The Court thus clarified the law in an area where internally displaced persons had previously been denied a right to reparations by courts and administrative agencies based on a number of different grounds.

C. The Peace Process with Guerrilla Groups

In 2011, President Juan Manuel Santos announced that he would seek peace talks to end Colombia's long-running civil conflict by making peace with the country's guerrilla groups. This approach was a sharp departure from his predecessor, President Alvaro Uribe Vélez, who had pursued a "democratic security" approach and instead took a military-centered one against guerrilla groups such as the FARC.

One of the first steps in the peace process was the construction of a Legal Framework for Peace, a legal approach based on a transitional justice framework. Given constitutional constraints (including those stemming from the Court's own incorporation of international law), the Santos administration pursued a set of constitutional amendments. The constitutional amendments added new "temporary" provisions to the Constitution, including the following key article:

> **Temporary Article 66.** Instruments of transitional justice . . . will have as their overriding purpose facilitating the end of the internal armed conflict and the achievement of a stable and lasting peace, with guarantees of non-repetition and of security for all Colombians; and they will guarantee to the highest level possible the rights of victims to truth, justice, and reparations. A statutory law may authorize, through the framework of a peace agreement, differential treatment which will be given to the distinct illegal armed groups that have been part of the internal armed conflict and also to state agents. . . .
>
> A statutory law will establish instruments of transitional justice of a judicial and non-judicial character that will seek to guarantee the state's duties of investigation and sanction. In any case, mechanisms of an extrajudicial character will be applied for the purpose of clarifying the truth. . . .
>
> A law must create a Truth and Reconciliation Commission and define its objectives, composition, attributions, and functions. The mandate of the Commission can include the formulation of recommendations for the instruments of transitional justice, including the application of selection criteria.
>
> Prioritization and selection criteria are inherent in instruments of transitional justice. The General Prosecutor of the Nation will determine prioritization criteria for the exercise of criminal action. Without prejudice to the general duty of the state to investigate and sanction grave violations of human rights and international humanitarian law, . . . the Congress of the Republic . . . may through a statutory law: determine selection criteria that will permit the concentration of resources of criminal investigation on the top-level actors responsible for all the crimes constituting crimes against humanity, genocide, or war crimes committed in a systematic manner; establish the cases, requisites, and conditions in which punishments may be suspended, establish the cases in which extrajudicial sanctions, alternative punishments, or special modes of executing or complying with punishments may be applied; and authorize the conditional renunciation of criminal justice in all of the non-selected cases. . . .
>
> In all cases, special criminal treatment through the application of constitutional instruments . . . will be subject to compliance with conditions like the surrender of arms, recognition of responsibility, contribution to the clarification of truth and integral reparations for victims, the liberation of the kidnapped, and the disassociation of children illegally recruited and under the power of illegal armed groups.

The Legal Framework for Peace dealing with guerrilla groups makes an interesting comparison with the 2005 Law of Peace and Justice dealing mostly with paramilitaries. Both regimes allow reduced punishments for demobilized actors who comply with certain conditions. The Legal Framework envisions a fuller set of responsibilities for truth and reconciliation by these actors, along the lines suggested by the Constitutional Court's decision on the Law of Peace and Justice. However, the Legal Framework also implies that for many members of these groups who are not "top-level" actors who committed certain grave crimes under international law, the total renunciation of criminal punishment, and not just reduced sentences, may be appropriate. This selective approach was justified by Congress and the administration based on resource constraints stemming from the massive size of the conflict, on trade-offs with other goals such as the pursuit of truth, and on the need for incentives to end the conflict. In this sense, the drafters may have reacted in part to the slow pace and inadequate resources that have hindered enforcement of the Law of Peace and Justice.

In many countries, the incorporation of the Legal Framework for Peace in a constitutional amendment would effectively immunize that Framework from judicial review, at least of a non-procedural type. In Colombia, however, the substitution of the constitution doctrine (discussed in detail in Chapter 11, Section C below) allowed petitioners to challenge the constitutional amendment on the grounds that it conflicted so significantly with core principles of the existing text as to constitute a substitution, rather than an amendment. The case below was the most significant such challenge to the Legal Framework for Peace. As it sometimes does with cases of significance, the Court held a public audience at which a number of governmental and nongovernmental parties discussed the constitutionality of the reforms. In an unusual move, President Santos attended the hearing and personally argued in favor of the constitutionality of the law. He told the Court that "we are confronting a real possibility, in my opinion the best in our history, to put an end to the internal armed conflict."

Decision C-579 of 2013 (per Justice Jorge Ignacio Pretelt Chaljub)

[In this case, the petitioners challenged some of the language in temporary constitutional Article 66. In particular, they challenged the italicized language in the provision giving Congress the power to "determine selection criteria that will permit the concentration of resources of criminal investigation on the *top-level actors* responsible for all the crimes having the connotation of crimes against humanity, genocide, or war crimes committed in a systematic manner; . . . and authorize the conditional renunciation of criminal justice in *all* of the non-selected cases."[8] They argued that these pieces of the amendment disregarded the constraints of international humanitarian law and international human rights law, which are incorporated into the constitution through the constitutional block. Furthermore, they argued

8. The petitioners also challenged the phrase "in a systematic manner" in the language above. The Court held that this language only modified "war crimes" and did not substitute the constitution because under international humanitarian law, war crimes could only be committed in a systematic and not an isolated manner. In other words, according to the Court the phrase at issue should be read as confirming, and not modifying, the international definition of a war crime.

that these provisions disregarded those provisions to such a degree as to constitute a "substitution of the constitution," rather than an amendment of it. In effect, the petitioners argued that those parts of temporary constitutional Article 66 constituted an unconstitutional constitutional amendment. In a seven-to-two decision, the Court disagreed and held temporary constitutional Article 66 to be constitutional.]

[The Court first reiterated its long-standing doctrine on the substitution of the constitution doctrine. These tests are explored in detail in Chapter 10, Section C, and thus they will not be reproduced here. The Court then explored the concept of transitional justice and its meaning in international law:]

Transitional justice is constituted by a group of processes of profound social and political transformations in which it is necessary to utilize a great variety of mechanisms to resolve the problems derived from past abuses on a grand scale, with the purpose of having responsible parties account for their acts, thus serving justice and reconciliation. Those mechanisms may be judicial or non-judicial [and] they have distinct levels of international participation. . . .

[T]he Constitutional Court has defined transitional justice as "a legal institution . . . applied to societies to confront the consequences of massive violations and generalized or systematic abuses of human rights suffered in a conflict, through a constructive period of peace, respect, reconciliation and consolidation of democracy, which creates a situation of exception from the normal application of criminal institutions."[9]

Transitional justice looks to resolve the strong tensions that are presented between justice and peace, including the legal imperatives of the satisfaction of the rights of victims and the necessity of achieving an end to hostilities. For this reason it is necessary to follow a delicate balance between ending hostilities and preventing the return of violence (negative peace) and consolidating peace through structural reforms and inclusive politics (positive peace). For this purpose it is necessary to develop some special objectives:

Recognition of victims, who are not only affected by these crimes, but also by the lack of effectiveness of their rights. In this sense, victims must achieve through the process the reestablishment of their rights to truth, justice, and reparations. . . .

Reestablishment of public confidence through the reaffirmation of the relevance of the norms that the perpetrators violated. . . .

Reconciliation, which implies the overcoming of violent social divisions, referring both to the successful achievement of the rule of law as well as to the creation and recovery of a level of social trust, of solidarity fomenting a democratic political culture that permits people to overcome their horrendous experiences of loss, violence, injustice, pain, and hatred, so that they feel newly capable of coexisting with each other. In this sense, processes of transitional justice must look both forward and backward with the goal of realizing an adjustment of accounts about the past but also of permitting reconciliation with the future. . . .

9. The Court was quoting Decision C-771 of 2011 (per Justice Nilson Pinilla Pinilla).

The strengthening of democracy through the promotion of the participation of everyone, restoring a democratic political culture and a basic level of solidarity and social trust to convince citizens to participate in political institutions for reasons distinct from personal gain. . . .

Transitional justice implies the articulation of a series of measures, judicial or non-judicial, and can involve the trial of persons, compensation, the search for truth, institutional reform, the investigation of facts, removal from one's post or combinations of all of these, as the Security Council of the United Nations has recognized. . . .

While it is true that the understanding of justice by a part of the population is commonly linked with punishment, the complexity of processes of transitional justice and the necessity of responding to massive violations means that one cannot concentrate exclusively on criminal measures. Thus, criminal justice is only one of the mechanisms of transitional justice that should be applied together with measures of truth, reparations, and non-repetition in order to satisfy the rights of victims.

In any case, we must recognize that criminal processes suffer from multiple obstacles: (i) in politics, the central problem is the resistance of leaders to be questioned criminally; (ii) legally, in some cases solid evidence and material witnesses . . . are missing; (iii) materially, the requirements of cost and immense effort needed to open criminal processes in the number demanded by the massive atrocities committed in the war. . . .

Based on the foregoing, the application of criminal law in processes of transitional justice has special characteristics that can imply a more benign punitive treatment than the ordinary one, whether through the imposition of comparatively low penalties, the adoption of measures that—without extinguishing criminal responsibility—make conditional liberty possible, or at least a more rapid reduction in the imposed penalty. . . .

In this sense, the Court has signaled that the duty to judge and condemn those responsible for crimes to adequate and proportional sentences can only be subject to exception during processes of transitional justice, in which violations of human rights are fully investigated, the minimum rights of victims to truth and integral reparations are reestablished, and measures are taken to avoid repetition. . . .

[The Court then undertook a lengthy review of the characteristics of transitional justice projects found around the world, as well as the history of emergency powers in Colombia dating back to the nineteenth century, before turning to the question of whether the transitional justice regime is a substitution of the Constitution.]

The [provision at issue] consecrates a criminal justice system of transitional justice, but before studying it concretely we will analyze whether transitional justice per se constitutes a substitution of the Constitution.

Transitional justice seeks to resolve the strong tensions that are presented between justice and peace, between the legal imperatives of satisfaction of the rights of victims and the needs of achieving a cessation in hostilities[. I]t thus looks to comply with three criteria, the importance of which are recognized within our constitution: reconciliation, recognition of the rights of victims and the strengthening of the social state of law and democracy. Far from substituting the fundamental pillar of the guarantee of human rights, transitional justice develops it in situations of massive violations of human rights, in which the utilization of ordinary mechanisms can be an obstacle to their safeguarding. . . .

[After conducting a review of the state of international law on the rights of victims, the Court concluded that] in all of the pronouncements of international bodies, we can affirm that non-judicial and administrative mechanisms implemented by states in contexts of transitional justice are legitimate measures that can be adopted without triggering the international responsibility of the state. However, it is clear that these alternative mechanisms, like truth commissions, are complementary instruments to the judicial system and must function under many of the conditions essential for the judicialization of violations of human rights, such as independence, impartiality, effectiveness, reasonable time, and transparency. Additionally, the function of these alternative mechanisms must be aimed at clarifying the truth of the facts that produced violations of human rights and giving adequate reparations to victims; therefore, the active participation of those victims, and of society in general, is necessary. . . .

[The Court then turned to the specific question of whether the constitutional amendment at issue substituted what it called the "fundamental pillar" of the Constitution—"the promise of the Social and Democratic State to respect, protect, and guarantee the rights of society and of victims, from which is derived: (i) the obligation to investigate, judge, and in turn sanction (ii) grave violations of human rights and (iii) international humanitarian law."]

(i) The obligation to investigate, judge, and in turn sanction, implies the realization of all possible efforts to investigate, judge, and sanction grave violations of human rights and of international humanitarian law. In this sense, the investigation must be serious, impartial, effective, occur in a reasonable time, include the participation of victims, and punishment must be proportional and effective.

(ii) The grave violations of human rights recognized by the international community especially include the following: (a) extrajudicial executions, (b) forced disappearances, (c) torture, (d) genocide, (e) the establishment or maintenance of people in a state of slavery, servitude or forced work, (f) arbitrary and prolonged detention, (g) forced displacement, (h) sexual violence against women, and (i) forced recruitment of minors.

(iii) The crimes that constitute . . . grave violations of international humanitarian law at the international level are: crimes against humanity, war crimes, and genocide. . . .

[The Court conducted a detailed review of domestic and international legal sources from which it derived these definitions.]

[C]onstitutional jurisprudence has developed balancing as a resolution mechanism for conflicts that involve a collision between constitutional rights, principles, and values. . . . Balancing as a resolution mechanism for the collision of constitutional rights involves the unavoidable necessity of guaranteeing the unity of the constitutional text. . . .

The case under study involves a conflict between those constitutional values that oblige the state to persecute and sanction conduct that has generated violations of human rights, and the necessity of guaranteeing the effective enjoyment of peace as an optimization mandate. . . .

[T]he employment of mechanisms of transitional justice can create tensions from the point of view of the realization of [constitutional ends.] Some of those tensions are: (i) the anticipation of the justice of tomorrow can be an obstacle to the peace of today because retribution may contribute to the prolongation of the conflict; (ii) the justice of today can be an obstacle to the peace of tomorrow, since the imposition of severe penalties can limit the possibilities of negotiated exits and the construction of the truth; (iii) the search for the truth can be an obstacle to justice if the names of the perpetrators are published without due process; (iv) the truth can be an obstacle to justice if the symbolic measures of rehabilitation and excuse serve as a substitute for reparations; (v) the truth can be an obstacle to peace if the search for the identity of the perpetrators is not accompanied by sanctions; (vi) transitional justice will be an obstacle to distributive justice if the triumph requires conditions of extreme scarcity.

Thus, mechanisms of transitional justice generate constant collisions between the obligations of the state, including those derived from the duty of guaranteeing rights.

Those collisions require balancing. The duty of states is to design transitional models that do not ignore the minimum content of each duty and that contain a just balance of the principles in conflict. . . .

[I]t is possible to carry out balancing between the investigation, judgment, and sanction for grave violations of human rights and international humanitarian law and the other consequences of the obligations at issue:

The establishment of mechanisms that permit rapid judicial protection in case of a threat sometimes requires a special strategy of investigation and judgment, since the case by case investigation of violations of human rights can end in a generalized situation of impunity. . . . [T]he possibility of centering the investigation on a series of crimes committed by the most responsible and applying special measures to the less responsible stems from the factual impossibility of having a strategy of investigation that will proceed judicially against all suspects during a transitional justice process. . . .

The effectiveness of the rights of victims to obtain adequate reparations may imply a procedural strategy outside of a criminal process, through administrative mechanisms that will be more effective.

Assurance of the full and free exercise of human rights may mean that in order to guarantee rights like the right to the truth, special forms of investigation and criminal benefits will be applied in return for the revelation of facts. Additionally, in order to assure that there is no unjustified discrimination, one can establish legal mechanisms of prioritization, because if this does not occur the determination of which cases will be heard first will depend in practice on the discretion of the legal authorities.

Mechanisms of transitional justice require a precise balancing between these ends, through which limitations may be authorized in some cases. . . .

[The constitutional reform at issue] is not designed to treat some acts with impunity, but instead to replace the strategy of investigating violations "case by case," which makes it very difficult to guarantee the right to justice of victims of massive violations of human rights, with the construction of macroprocesses in which there is a massive participation of all the victims and which is not structured by chance, but by investigations based on context and on an analysis of the structures of organized crime. . . .

[T]his strategy consists in the construction of macro-processes that respond to a series of common elements determined by factors related to the gravity and representativeness of the crime such as the place, time, manner of commission, the victims or social groups affected, the perpetrators, the scale of commission, or available evidence, which should be determined by a statutory law.

Focusing effort on the criminal investigation of international crimes like crimes against humanity, war crimes, and genocide does not substitute the constitution, because it complies with the standards of the constitutional block for events that terminate armed conflict.

[The recognized constitutional norms] imply a duty to investigate, judge, and sanction grave violations of human rights and international humanitarian law. However, in cases of internal armed conflict one must take into account Article 6.5 of Additional Protocol II of the Geneva Conventions, which permits the application of generalized amnesties. . . .[10]

This norm changes the context of the obligation to investigate and in turn sanction grave violations of human rights and international humanitarian law, since it concentrates on a series of specific crimes. In this sense . . . there is an untouchable limit to [this duty], since crimes against humanity, genocide, and war crimes must be investigated. . . .

[The Court considered the phrase focusing judicial resources on "top-level" actors.] [I]f [the state] focuses only on the top-level actors and not on other authors of these crimes, the fundamental pillar [to investigate, judge, and punish grave violations of human rights and international humanitarian law] is limited but not substituted, for the following reasons:

First, the concentration of responsibility on top-level actors does not imply that some crimes against humanity, genocide, and war crimes will not be investigated, but rather that with respect to all of these only the top actors will be punished.

Second, in [the reform under study] the inclusion of the expression "top-level actors" has an additional legitimate end, directly related to the necessity of clarifying the structures of macro-criminality that lie behind each crime, by dedicating effort and resources to attend to present crime, dissuade future crime, and strengthen the social state of law. . . .

10. Article 6.5 of Optional Protocol II reads as follows: "At the end of hostilities, the authorities in power shall endeavour to grant the broadest possible amnesty to persons who have participated in the armed conflict, or those deprived of their liberty for reasons related to the armed conflict, whether they are interned or detained."

In this sense, the possibility of limiting (but not substituting) the fundamental pillar by investigating only top-level actors is based on a balancing with another consequence, . . . which is the obligation to prevent conduct that might put human rights at risk in the future. . . . [T]he potential for revealing structures of macro-criminality by trying top-level actors may aid in breaking up criminal organizations and revealing the chief violators of human rights. . . .

[The Court also studied the phrase allowing conditional renunciation of criminal liability in a range of cases.] While some cases involving conditional renunciation of criminal liability may limit the fundamental pillar, this limitation does not substitute the constitution for the following reasons:

First, the text itself . . . establishes some strict limits, including the impossibility of renouncing criminal prosecution for crimes against humanity, genocide, or war crimes committed in a systematic manner, as regards high-level actors. . . .

On the other hand, we must point out that the expression "conditional renunciation" has a very important consequence—if the actor does not comply with the requisites set out in the statutory law, which at a minimum should include . . . surrender of arms, recognition of responsibility, contribution to the clarification of truth and the integral reparation of victims, liberation of the kidnapped, and the freeing of [child soldiers], renunciation of prosecution can be immediately revoked and the state will recover all of its power to investigate, judge, and sanction those responsible for all crimes committed using the framework of ordinary justice. . . .

Finally, the limitation of the fundamental pillar is justified as a balancing between the obligation to investigate, judge, and sanction grave violations of rights and the duty to prevent the violation of rights. . . . This treatment fully guarantees the purposes of criminal law, which as the Court has noted are focused on prevention and not on retribution. . . .

[The reform] also authorizes conditional suspended sentences, non-judicial sanctions, alternative punishments, or special methods for the execution of punishment. . . .

[E]ach one of these consequences is applied to distinct events: a totally suspended sentence is applied to non-selected cases; therefore, if the conditional suspension is not total, it can be applied to selected cases; non-judicial sanctions will be applied as a consequence of non-judicial mechanisms, alternative punishments are punishments that will replace those that would ordinarily be applied and special methods for the execution of punishment can be applied if a sentence is imposed either in selected or non-selected cases.

In this sense, a totally suspended sentence cannot be used for selected cases; in other words, for those condemned as top-level actors for crimes against humanity, genocide, or war crimes committed in a systematic manner, but to other responsible parties. . . .

[A]lternative punishments and special mechanisms for carrying out punishments, as either ordinary mechanisms or as part of transitional justice, are fully accepted by the international community and have also been studied by this Court;

they do not violate any constitutional norm, and thus less still can they be considered a substitution of the constitution. These mechanisms are founded in the need to make justice compatible with reconciliation and the non-repetition of conduct in a system that is focused on the preventative goals of punishment more than on retribution. . . .

Although a correct reading of the [reform] permits us to conclude that it does not substitute the Constitution, this Court considers it necessary to fix a series of parameters in its interpretation to avoid it becoming an instrument for impunity or for ignoring the rights of victims.

The state must demand the termination of the armed conflict with respect to each demobilized group in the case of collective demobilization and the surrender of arms and non-commission of new crimes in that of individual demobilization, as a condition for the application of the Legal Framework for Peace. . . .

[I]f the armed conflict continues, measures of transitional justice and the balancing carried out lose all their meaning. . . .

[T]he termination of the armed conflict does not arrive with the simple surrender of arms, because it is also necessary to completely dismantle the organization and especially its forms of illegal financing, such as: drug trafficking, kidnapping, and extortion. Thus, among the guarantees of non-repetition, armed groups must eliminate all illegal activities supporting the conflict. . . .

[A]ll victims must receive at minimum the following guarantees: (i) transparency in the process of selection and prioritization, (ii) an investigation that is serious, impartial, effective, and carried out in a reasonable time and with their participation, (iii) the existence of a recourse to challenge decisions on selection and prioritization, (iv) specialized assistance, (v) the right to truth, which in the event of a case not being prioritized should be guaranteed through non-criminal judicial means and non-judicial means, (vi) the right to reparations, and (vii) the right to know where to find the rest of their family members.

As has already been explained, [the constitutional reform] is justified as a balancing between reconciliation and justice, and therefore it is necessary for armed groups not only to commit to ending the conflict, but also to contribute to the satisfaction of the rights of victims. . . .

Thus, for the criteria of selection and prioritization to proceed, the state must demand that the illegal armed group make a real and effective contribution to the clarification of the truth and reparation of victims, the liberation of all kidnapped and the disassociation of all children found in their power. . . .

The actors in the armed conflict should guarantee that they will clarify the truth about the violations of human rights that have occurred in this context, since this will contribute to personal and historical memory. The state should guarantee, for its part, effective resources to initiate investigations that are aimed at establishing the truth about the facts and based on those, take reparation measures responding to the gravity of the harm. . . .

[The Court thus declared the amendment at issue conditionally constitutional in the terms laid out in the decision. There were three concurring opinions, joined by five of the justices constituting the majority. These justices, although sharing the general approach of the majority opinion, argued that new questions would be raised when Congress passed its statutory law implementing the amendment, and that the majority opinion treated questions that it did not need to resolve and that were not raised in the complaint.]

[Justice Mauricio González Cuervo wrote a dissenting opinion. In his view, the provisions surpassed the acceptable limits of political discretion because they infringed on the "minimum obligation" of states, under international law, to investigate and punish "grave violations of human rights, crimes against humanity, genocide, and war crimes." As he stated: "Respect for this international imperative leaves open a broad margin for the flourishing of transitional justice solutions, but without sacrificing that minimum obligation, in such a manner that ... it is proper to declare the constitutionality of mechanisms for the prioritization of the exercise of criminal action, the prosecution of 'top-level actors,' suspended sentences, and the renunciation of criminal responsibility for non-selected cases, but only for conduct distinct from grave violations of human rights, crimes against humanity, genocide, and war crimes. The boundary drawn by the constitutional block, the imperative international order, the jurisprudence of the Inter-American Court of Human Rights and especially, the jurisprudence of this Constitutional Court establishes ... that transitional justice measures will only be legitimate, valid, and constitutional when they comply with the following conditions: (i) that they do not authorize the renunciation of investigation, judgment, and criminal sanction to those responsible under any rank for grave violations of human rights and international humanitarian law ... and, (ii) that they will not permit the application of a completely and unconditionally suspended sentence, for those cases of grave violations of human rights and international humanitarian law."]

Note on the Judicialization of the Peace Process in Colombia: Decision C-579 of 2013 was far from the end of the Court's involvement in the peace process. Indeed, the entire Colombian peace process has been marked by its interaction between political negotiation and legal and constitutional institutions.

In **Decision C-577 of 2014 (per Justice Martha Victoria Sáchica)**, the Court heard additional challenges to the Legal Framework for Peace, again on the grounds that the relevant constitutional amendments constituted a substitution of the constitution. In this decision, the Court heard a challenge to a different part of the Framework that regulated the potential political participation of demobilized guerrillas. In particular, the amendment allowed Congress to define which crimes were "connected to political crime";[11] those seen as "connected to political crime" would allow the convicted to participate in politics

11. The constitutional text at several points disallows convicted criminals from serving in elected or appointed posts. Article 179 for example disallows anyone sentenced to prison from serving in Congress, with the exception of those convicted of political crimes; Article 232 does the same with respect to justices on the high courts. Further, Article 35 prohibits extradition for political crimes.

(i.e., vote or be elected to office) once any punishment had been served because normal restrictions on the participation of convicted criminals would not apply. The Framework gave Congress broad discretion in this respect, subject only to the restriction that those convicted of "crimes against humanity and genocide committed in a systematic manner . . . will not be able to participate in politics or be elected." The petitioner argued that this limitation on congressional discretion to allow members of illegal armed groups to participate in politics was too narrow to be consistent with international law and the limitations on political participation found in the existing constitutional text.

The Court rejected this demand. Although the petitioner argued that the Constitution contained a fundamental principle requiring that political participation be exercised within a context of respect for human dignity and the protection of human rights, the Court held that this was not the proper framing of the fundamental principle at issue in light of a historical and holistic reading of the text. Instead, it stated that the fundamental principle at issue was "the democratic participatory framework": "political participation as a basic . . . principle of the Colombian constitutional regime is essential to the conformation, exercise, and control of power in a democratic state. . . . Its limits cannot be based on punishments imposed for the commission of political crimes or those connected to political crimes." In other words, the fundamental constitutional principle was political participation, not its limitation.

In proceeding to examine whether the amendment at issue substituted that principle, the Court emphasized that political participation was a separate issue from the political process, and any rights of political participation would only "begin from the point at which the criminal component ends." Further, rights of political participation would be contingent with full cooperation with all aspects of the peace process in the terms laid out in Decision C-579 of 2013. Understood this way, the Court held that the provision at issue in fact developed the fundamental principle at issue rather than substituting it, because it sought to prevent those convicted of political crimes from being excluded from politics. The Court also held that Congress had a broad "margin of appreciation" in defining political crimes, "which permits it to adapt its regulation to the specific necessities that may arise in processes that in pursuit of objectives like peace, require the adoption of frameworks of transitional justice, in which reconciliation always plays a central role."

The Court made a sharp distinction between criminal processes and political participation, holding that the latter was much less regulated in Colombian and international law: "participation in politics—or its prohibition—by convicted criminals . . . is not an aspect of criminal justice through which one looks to guarantee the rights of victims to truth, justice, or reparations. . . . [T]he duty to offer protection to victims of armed conflict does not oblige the constitutional reformer to exclude from spaces of political participation those responsible for war crimes, transnational crimes, acts of terrorism, or drug trafficking. . . . [F]or this Court, participation in politics by those who have been selected and condemned . . . does not per se affect any of the rights that must be guaranteed to victims of the armed conflict. Thus, the duty to investigate, judge, and sanction grave violations of fundamental rights does not impose on the constitutional reformer the obligation to restrict participation of those who are authors of those violations."

Beginning in 2012, the Santos administration undertook peace talks in Havana with by far the largest guerrilla group active in the country, the FARC. These talks took several years and were quite difficult. However, on June 23, 2016, the FARC and the government announced the definitive end of hostilities and that they were finalizing a peace agreement. Although this does not end all internal civil conflict in the country, because the FARC is not the only active guerrilla groups, it represents a historic step toward its termination as FARC has been active as a guerrilla group for almost 60 years.

The agreement contained provisions on a number of different issues, including the regulation of the demobilization process, the suppression of the successors to paramilitary groups, and reparations for victims, and on access to rural land and development for rural areas. The peace agreement contemplated the FARC entering politics as a party: it required temporary measures to give members of the FARC representation in Congress and created special electoral districts for areas especially affected by the conflict.

Most important for our discussion here, it contained provisions governing transitional justice. These provisions shared the basic approach of the Legal Framework for Peace, even though they differ in some respects. Transitional justice measures would be taken through the establishment of a special court system charged, among other tasks, with the punishment of grave human rights violations and grave infractions to international humanitarian law related to the conflict. A list of these conducts include crimes under the jurisdiction of the International Criminal Court. The National Tribunal for Peace that heads this jurisdiction would be composed of domestic justices, but a minority of foreign ad hoc justices may participate in special circumstances. Crimes linked to the crime of rebellion would be subject to amnesty through full participation in the peace process. However, members of guerrilla groups and the military who have committed crimes against humanity, grave war crimes, genocide, and grave violations of human rights including torture, extrajudicial execution, disappearances, forced displacement, sexual violence, the taking of hostages, and recruitment of minors would not be eligible for amnesty. The special jurisdiction for peace instead should try these crimes and may impose sanctions of up to 20 years in prison. However, if those responsible admit their responsibility early on, tell the whole truth about those events, and otherwise fulfill the conditions established in the peace agreement, they would receive punishments of between five and eight years involving "effective restrictions on liberty"[12] plus the obligation to do works and activities aimed at making reparations.

A 2015 statutory law allows for the holding of a plebiscite to approve or disapprove the peace agreement. The Constitutional Court upheld the law in **Decision C-379 of 2016 (per Justice Luis Ernesto Vargas Silva)**, which was issued in July 2016, but placed some conditions on it. The plebiscite would be considered approved if the yes votes exceed 13 percent

12. For some of the complex legal issues raised by the design of this transitional justice scheme, see Nicolás Carrillo-Santarelli, *An Assessment of the Colombian-FARC "Peace Jurisdiction" Agreement*, EJIL-Talk!, Sept. 25, 2015, *available at* http://www.ejiltalk.org/an-assessment-of-the-colombian-farc-peace-jurisdiction-agreement/; Claret Vargas, *The Peace Agreement in Colombia Matters, and It Could Set an Example for Entrenched Conflicts Elsewhere*, Feb. 9, 2016, *available at* https://dejusticiablog.com/2016/02/09/the-peace-agreement-in-colombia-matters-and-it-could-set-an-example-for-entrenched-conflicts-elsewhere/.

of registered voters and the yes votes exceed the no votes. The law also requires that the peace agreement be made widely available through a number of means at least 30 days before the vote, but the Court considered this too undetermined and required that the final peace agreement be published at the time the president submits to Congress a request to call a plebiscite. Further, the law states that the plebiscite would be "binding for constitutional and legal development" and on all institutions of state, but the Court held that the plebiscite could only bind the president. The Court also included a condition holding that if the plebiscite approved the agreement, it would not be automatically incorporated into the Constitution or legal order. As this book was going to press, the plebiscite was held on October 2, 2016, and narrowly failed to approve the peace agreement. However, the ceasefire held and a new agreement was reached in November 2016.

In 2016, Congress also approved a set of temporary constitutional amendments intended to provide legal certainty and political stability to the peace agreements with the FARC. These temporary amendments establish special legislative procedures for rapid congressional approval of the peace agreement itself, as well as during a six-month period for laws and constitutional amendments needed to implement and develop it. They also give the president broad authority to issue decrees with the force of law on topics designed to implement the agreement, also for a six-month period. Finally, the amendments state that the peace agreement constitutes a "special agreement" under Common Article 3 of the Geneva Conventions[13], and that after being approved by Congress through the special fast track procedure and reviewed by the Constitutional Court, it will immediately become "part of the constitutional block in a strict sense, in order to be taken into account during its period of implementation as a parameter of interpretation and reference for development and validity of the norms and laws of implementation and development of the final agreement." The amendment thus aims to give the peace agreement constitutional status. Of course, the Constitutional Court may soon need to interpret and apply these provisions, in considering challenges both to these temporary constitutional amendments and to any relevant implementing legislation or decrees. Surprisingly, the guerrillas that had rebelled against the established regime for half a century accepted that legal certainty could only be attained after the Constitutional Court exercised its powers of judicial review over the final peace agreement, previously incorporated in a statute approved by Congress after the will of the people was expressed in the plebiscite.

In comparative terms, the Colombian peace process has been strikingly judicialized at the domestic level: the Constitutional Court has played a pivotal role during its framing and negotiations. In contrast, in some other processes around the world, these issues have been left to the political process and/or been monitored by international actors,

13. Common Article 3, found in all four Geneva conventions, endeavors to set out minimal rules for all conflicts "not of an international character" where the full conventions do not automatically apply. These minimal guarantees include prohibitions, against "[p]ersons taking no active part in the hostilities," on violence, hostage-taking, outrages upon personal dignity, and the passing of sentences without prior judicial proceedings, as well as guarantees of care for the "wounded and sick." The provision also states in relevant part that: "The Parties to the conflict should further endeavour to bring into force, by means of special agreements, all or part of the other provisions of the present Convention."

institutions, and tribunals.[14] The heavy involvement of the domestic judiciary in a delicate political process raises potential risks both for the success of the process and for the Court's broader project aimed at incorporating international norms into domestic law. However, it has also given the Court an opportunity to emphasize the rights of victims and to remind negotiators that the process is shaped by both international and domestic legal constraints that are designed to protect their rights. At the same time, it has potentially contributed to a dialogue between various domestic and international actors as to how flexible the relevant international standards are and how those standards can best be adapted to the Colombian context.

14. In Africa, for example, international organizations and tribunals such as the International Criminal Court have been more directly involved. *See, e.g.*, ADAM BRANCH, DISPLACING HUMAN RIGHTS: WAR AND INTERVENTION IN NORTHERN UGANDA (2011) (critiquing the role of the ICC and other international actors during the Ugandan peace process).

8

The Rights of Indigenous Peoples

Colombia has a relatively small indigenous population by Latin American and particularly Andean standards, constituting perhaps 2 percent of the total population of the country, although indigenous territories constitute about one-third of all land in the country.[1] It is a population that has historically been subject to policies of assimilation, repression, and neglect. In part because this population is largely found in remote regions of the country, it has also been disproportionately impacted by Colombia's internal civil conflict.

The Constituent Assembly included two members of indigenous political movements, who pushed for increased recognition and autonomy of their cultures.[2] In the pluralistic environment of the 1991 Constituent Assembly, these goals were shared by a number of delegates from across the political spectrum. Thus, the final 1991 constitutional text marked a striking change in the direction of state policy toward indigenous communities. The text explicitly creates a multicultural framework that recognizes diversity rather than ignoring distinct cultures or seeking their assimilation.[3] Article 7 emphasizes that "[t]he state recognizes and protects the ethnic and cultural diversity of the Colombian nation."

Colombia's multicultural constitution of 1991 was at the start of a wave of changes throughout Latin America to adopt broadly similar models. Mexico, for example, adopted constitutional changes in 2001 recognizing the state as "pluricultural," and offers some forms of autonomy in electoral, legislative, and judicial functions, although it leaves many of these issues for definition at the state level.[4] The new Andean constitutions adopted in

1. *See* Donna Lee Van Cott, *Latin America's Indigenous Peoples*, 18 J. Democ. 127, 128 (2007) (noting that the indigenous population constitutes 71 percent of the population of Bolivia, 47 percent of the population of Peru, and 43 percent of the population of Ecuador).

2. For a summary of the debates on indigenous issues at the Constituent Assembly, see Beatriz Eugenia Sanchez, *El reto de culticulturalismo juridico: La justicia de la sociedad mayor y la justicia indigena*, *in* 2 El caleidoscopio de las justicias en Colombia: Análisis socio-jurídico 5, 68–69 (Boaventura de Sousa Santos & Mauricio García Villegas eds., 2001).

3. *See* Daniel Bonilla Maldonado, La Constitucion multicultural (2006).

4. *See* Const. Mex., art. 2 (1917, as amended in 2001).

Colombian Constitutional Law: Leading Cases. Manuel José Cepeda Espinosa and David Landau.

Ecuador (2008) and Bolivia (2009), which both have very large indigenous populations, also express the multicultural nature of those countries, but go further in defining the particular rights of indigenous communities to self-determination, to cultural identity, to ownership of land, and to legal autonomy.[5]

The Colombian Constitution contains several different provisions that are designed to protect the autonomy of indigenous groups within their own territories. The text establishes indigenous communities as "territorial entities" along with departments, districts, and municipalities and gives them considerable powers of self-governance.[6] For example, Article 330 establishes that councils formed to represent indigenous communities can collect and distribute resources, regulate uses of land and resources, design plans for economic and social development, promote public investment, and take action to preserve natural resources, among other functions. Article 246 also gives indigenous peoples the right to administer legal systems within their territories in "accordance with their own laws and procedures," so long as they are "not contrary to the Constitution and laws of the Republic."

The set of cases in Section A balance the rights of indigenous peoples to autonomy against the individual rights of their own members. The Court has given indigenous groups considerable autonomy to set their own procedures and punishments within their own legal systems, while at the same time seeking to maintain basic principles of constitutional law (such as human dignity) as an outer limit. The diverse cases in that section test the range of this autonomy on a diverse group of issues, including criminal punishment, tolerance for competing religion, and the treatment of individuals considered outcasts by cultural tradition.

Furthermore, the Constitution provides for special political rights for indigenous groups at the national level in order to ensure their representation. For example, Article 171 creates a senate in which 100 members are elected from one nationwide electoral district, and requires that two additional senators be elected from a "special national constituency for indigenous communities." Section B discusses the application of these rights to political participation. In Decision T-778 of 2005, the Court held that standard rules such as age requirements for participating in municipal, departmental, and national political bodies may need to give way in the case of indigenous representatives when those requirements clash with the ones accepted in their communities.

Finally, Article 330 gives indigenous groups special rights with respect to economic exploitation projects undertaken on their lands. The Article establishes that these projects must be carried out "without impairing the[ir] cultural, social, and economic integrity," and it states that in making these decisions, the government must "encourage the participation" of leaders from those communities. As Section C shows, Article 330 has been read together with international law provisions that form part of the constitutional block to create a right of "prior consultation" for indigenous groups before potentially disruptive economic projects are undertaken on their lands. The Court has used this right to strike down a

5. *See, e.g.*, Richard Lalander, *Rights of Nature and the Indigenous Peoples in Bolivia and Ecuador: A Straightjacket for Progressive Development Policies?*, 3 IBEROAMERICAN J. DEV. STUDS. 148 (2014).

6. Article 286 states in part as follows: "Departments, districts, municipalities, and indigenous (Indian) territories are territorial entities." Article 330 lays out the various functions of indigenous communities.

number of important economic projects and laws, and has strengthened its procedural contours through time. Given the resource-intensive nature of the Colombian economy and the fact that indigenous territories constitute such a high percentage of national territory where resources are located, the application of this doctrine has become a significant point of tension between indigenous and economic interests, and at times between indigenous peoples and the government.

A. Conflicts between the Rights of Indigenous Communities and Their Members

As noted above, the Colombian constitution contains numerous articles giving indigenous communities autonomy in the maintenance of their own affairs. The autonomy enjoyed by indigenous communities is far stronger than that enjoyed by other local governments, encompassing for example the power to set up separate legal systems and courts. This is in deference to the multicultural nature of the 1991 Constitution and its values of respect for indigenous economic, social, and cultural ways of life.

The text of the 1991 Colombian Constitution left unclear the limits to indigenous autonomy. Article 246, for example, gives indigenous communities the power to create their own legal systems, but also requires that these be in accordance with the "the Constitution and laws" of Colombia. As shown by the decisions below, the Court has given indigenous autonomy a broad read in light of the overriding purposes of the constitutional text. Rather than being restricted by all provisions of the constitutional and legal order, indigenous communities are free to deviate from these provisions so long as they adhere to certain basic principles that are a product of intercultural consensus—the prohibition on torture, for example, and fundamental conceptions of a fair criminal process.

The cases below demonstrate the application of these principles in several different contexts. The first considers and upholds forms of whipping and banishment as criminal punishments, even though neither is contemplated by the Colombian constitutional order. The second allows indigenous communities to prevent the entrance of representatives from other religions, in deference to the group's right to self-identity and despite competing principles of individual religious freedom. The third considers the process through which an indigenous community might dialogue with the broader Colombian society regarding a traditional practice (the abandonment to the elements of twin babies) that has been recognized by both sides as violating the minimum standards of the intercultural consensus.

1. Non-traditional Criminal Punishment

Decision T-523 of 1997 (per Justice Carlos Gaviria Diaz)

[In a unanimous decision, the Court denied a *tutela* filed by a member of the Páez indigenous community organized in the Jambaló reservation. The petitioner was investigated by the special indigenous jurisdiction for his alleged participation in the premeditated murder of the mayor of Jambaló. The Páez People's Assembly decided that the defendant was guilty and sentenced him to receive 60 lashes in front of the community and to be banished from the reservation. Among other issues, the petitioner challenged the constitutionality of the punishment he had received.]

The constitutional recognition of ethnic and cultural diversity responds to a new vision of the state, in which the human being is no longer conceived simply as an abstract individual, but as a subject with particular characteristics. . . . Values like tolerance and respect for difference are converted into imperatives in a society that is strengthened by diversity and in the recognition that each individual is a unique subject with the right to carry out his own life plan.

In this new model, the State has the special mission of guaranteeing that all ways of viewing the world can peacefully coexist, a difficult task since these conceptions are often antagonistic and even incompatible with the requisites that the state itself has chosen to guarantee coexistence. Especially, the tension between the recognition of cultural groups with diverse traditions, practices, and legal orders and the consecration of fundamental rights with supposed universal validity is clear. While the majority considers them to be untouchable principles, necessary for mutual understanding, others are opposed to the existence of super-cultural principles as a way of affirming their difference and in accordance with their worldviews. . . .

A first solution to this type of conflict has been suggested as an intercultural dialogue that is capable of drawing minimum standards of tolerance that cover different value systems. In other words, to achieve a consensus on the minimum necessary for coexistence between distinct cultures, without renouncing the essential postulates marking the identity of each. . . .

[T]he minimum limits based on human rights that indigenous authorities should apply in the exercise of their jurisdictional functions responds, in the opinion of the Court, to an intercultural consensus on acts that "are truly intolerable because they work against the most precious human values," in other words, the right to life, the prohibition on slavery, the prohibition on torture and the legality of the process, in criminal matters. . . . These measures are justified because they are "necessary to protect interests of a superior nature and are the least restrictive imaginable in light of the constitutional text."

These are the criteria that will be applied by the Court to decide this case. . . .

Does the punishment imposed on the claimant by the native General Assembly exceed established limits in the exercise of jurisdictional faculties by indigenous authorities? . . . .

[The Court used reports given by anthropologists in order to explain the Páez worldview and the process they follow when their members commit a crime.]

The punishment . . . is the only thing that can restore [a] broken equilibrium. Its public application plays a preventative and exemplary role, which seeks to dissuade other members of the community from committing these acts in the future and the accused from reoffending.

The most common punishments among the Páez people are: whipping, forced labor in communitarian enterprises, indemnification of the persons or families of the affected, and expulsion from the territory. Whipping and expulsion, the punishments used in this case, are common in Jambaló. The first, which consists in flagellation of the body with a "rope used to strike cattle" . . . is thought by the Páez as a mediator between light and darkness; in other words, as a purifying element. The second is the most serious punishment and is administered only to those who relapse in criminal behaviors or those who refuse to accept the council's authority. . . .

The punishment of whipping . . . clearly shows a tension between two types of thought: that of majoritarian society and that of the Páez indigenous community. In the first conception, one punishes *because* a crime has been committed; in the second, one punishes *to* reestablish the natural order and *to* dissuade the community from committing bad acts in the future. The first rejects corporal punishment as working against the dignity of man; the second considers them to be a purifying element, necessary so that the wrongdoer can feel liberated.

Confronted with these different conceptions, is it reasonable to privilege that of the majority? The Court has already answered this question: No, because in a society that defines itself as pluralistic, no single worldview should prevail or try to impose itself on others; and regarding the specific case of the worldviews of indigenous groups, our constitutional precepts demand the utmost respect. The sole acceptable restrictions would be, as already stated by this Chamber, the right to life, the proscription of slavery, and the prohibition of torture. This last possibility will be examined regarding the punishment by whipping, since in this case, according to the lower *tutela* judges, [whipping constitutes torture]. . . .

After reviewing international materials and particularly the Convention against Torture, the Court concluded as follows:]

The whipping consists in striking the body with a "rope used to strike cattle," which in this case is carried out in the lower part of the leg. . . . Although it certainly produces pain, its purpose is not to cause excessive suffering, but to represent the element that will serve to purify the individual. . . . It is a symbolic figure or in other words a ritual that uses the community to punish the individual and restore harmony.

In this case . . . , the Court concludes that the suffering that this punishment may cause the actor does not rise to the levels of seriousness needed to consider it as torture, since it produces minimal bodily damage. Neither can it be considered a degrading punishment . . . because it is a normal practice for the Páez and whose end is not to expose the individual to public "scorn," but to help him restore his place in the community. . . .

[Regarding the banishment, the Court concluded:]

Article 34 of the Constitution[7] proscribes the criminal punishment of banishment, since this would isolate the individual from his social world and condemn him to be ostracized. . . . Since indigenous communities can only exercise justice within their jurisdiction, the banishment is only from the reservation and not the entire

7. Article 34 states: "Punishments of exile, life imprisonment, and confiscation are prohibited."

national territory; thus, Article 34 has not been violated. In addition, the fact that the community decided to remove a member from its territory does not supersede the limits on the exercise of indigenous jurisdiction. . . .

Based on what has already been said, it is incompatible with the principle of ethnic and cultural diversity to impose on indigenous communities the sanctions and punishments contemplated by western tradition. . . . A contrary interpretation would promote the following contradictory reasoning: "The Constitution promotes the recovery of [indigenous] culture, but only in those practices that are compatible with the worldview of the majoritarian society." It is clear that reasoning of this type would respond to a cultural hegemony that is incompatible with the axiological pillar of pluralism which, among other things, permits indigenous communities to practice their culture whenever they do not violate the hard nucleus by engaging in acts that are truly intolerable because they work against the most precious human values. In addition, they would violate the constitutional principles that by recognizing the jurisdictional autonomy of the indigenous peoples, will make it possible to recover and reinterpret their own symbols and cultural traditions.

2. Religious Conflict and Diversity

Decision SU-510 of 1998 (per Justice Eduardo Cifuentes Muñoz)

[In a six-to-three decision, the Court denied a writ of *tutela* filed by the Colombian United Pentecostal Church (CUPCh) against several indigenous authorities belonging to the Ika community of the Arhuaco people. The claimant asserted that for the last 39 years, the CUPCh had been settled in the area and several Arhuaco natives had become members of the Church. The claimant further stated that these natives had been subjected to arbitrary acts and abuses by the Arhuaco authorities during the last 15 years. Such abuses, the claimant said, included a prohibition on carrying out worship services under threats of arrest, removal of biblical texts and personal objects, detention and imprisonment of Church members who were then forced to kneel down on stones, and the closure of the CUPCh's church building. Besides attracting public attention, the case divided the indigenous community. However, the parties involved stopped all activities related to the dispute in order to wait for the Court's decision.]

[T]he Court must resolve whether, in light of our Constitution, traditional indigenous authorities have the capacity to restrict the religious freedom of members of their communities in order to safeguard their cultural diversity and integrity. If the answer to this question is no, it would be unnecessary to examine each eventual restriction since all of them would infringe the right enshrined in Article 19 of the Constitution [protecting freedom of religion].[8] However, if it is accepted that . . .

8. Article 19 states: "Freedom of religion is guaranteed. Every individual has the right to freely profess his/her religion and to disseminate it individually or collectively. All religious faiths and churches are equally free before the law."

traditional authorities are authorized to restrict the enjoyment of this fundamental right, then it would be indispensable to examine each individual restriction—the closing of the Church, the prohibition on religious proselytism, etc.—to specifically determine its conformity with the Constitution.

Lastly, the Court must examine whether . . . traditional indigenous authorities can restrict access to the reservation of religious congregations that are alien to their culture or if by doing so, they are violating the right to religious freedom of those congregations, which includes the freedom to preach . . . everywhere in the country. . . .

In the context of the Ika community, the behaviors claimed to be infringing fundamental rights strictly correspond to their own cultural logic, whose aim is to maintain balance in the universe. According to this worldview, traditional authorities believe that the behavior of members of the community can produce a particular effect on the natural order that they seek to correct through their own means, namely, the authority of *mamos* [tribal priests] and purification rituals. It is not the role of the Colombian state to determine that it is unacceptable to pursue such balance in nature. . . . To impose a different interpretation or to modify the set of rules that guide indigenous authorities would signify cultural disrespect, something expressly forbidden by Article 7 of our Constitution.

Acknowledging the cultural significance of the contested behavior does not mean that it is in accord with the Constitution. It simply means that the Constitutional Court cannot judge indigenous authorities' actions or forbearance with the same strictness applied in other cases. This does not imply that the Court should adopt a lenient attitude. It simply underlines the fact that constitutional judges should proceed with caution and deference. On the one hand, the cultural violence implied in ignoring the categories through which indigenous communities understand the world around them, and which guides their behavior, should be avoided. On the other hand, the margin of indeterminacy in constitutional norms should allow the adoption of those interpretations that best capture the circumstances and cultural stance of indigenous communities and their members.

From an external point of view, the behaviors under examination could be deemed as infringing religious freedom. From the internal point of view of the indigenous community, they have a perfectly understandable cultural meaning as actions aimed at compensating for the imbalance introduced in the world, which should be remedied in a specific manner.

Taking into consideration this internal approach prevents a mechanical enforcement of constitutional regulations. By associating particular actions with cultural practices, it is possible to acknowledge their meaning and significance, and to determine if they are linked to the cultural diversity protected by the Constitution or if, on the contrary, they go beyond that protection, especially because they work against the minimum demands of dignity due to human beings. In other words, if constitutional judges ignore this internal point of view, they will be depriving the community and its members of their right to enjoy the protection granted to ethnic and cultural diversity.

In the present case, the actions of indigenous authorities are directly related to the core of those beliefs that constitute the Arhuaco worldview and through which they access and reproduce their identity as a distinct people. To expect a different behavior from indigenous authorities would entail forcing them to relinquish their most deeply-rooted beliefs, those on which they base their identity and, consequently, their distinctive ethnic and cultural identity. . . .

Membership in or proselytism of other religions within Arhuaco territory, regardless if it is done by community members or by outsiders, is a type of conduct that may be severely restricted by indigenous authorities because it works against the community's core beliefs. Indigenous communities, protected by the respect due to cultural diversity, may control their openness to external forces. If *tutela* judges were to allow a third party's proselytizing activities within Arhuaco territory, thus ignoring the community's legitimate claim to defense of its own cultural identity, they would be rapidly and efficiently paving the way for the destruction of this centuries-old culture. [Given] the recognition given to cultural diversity by the Constitution, the decision on when and to what extent cross-cultural contact should be allowed—contact that may have considerable impact on the community—is not . . . an issue assigned to national state authorities, but a constituent aspect of the functions left to the indigenous people themselves.

These severe restrictions on the religious freedom of a dissenting member of the indigenous community, concerning his ability both to express and practice his new faith, are incidental to his belonging to a community that revolves around religious factors. . . . However, no indigenous community may subject its dissenting members to treatments that disrespect their human dignity. Thus, non-believers, or those who practice a religion different from the official one, cannot . . . be subject to punishment or any kind of persecution. . . . [T]he collective exercise of religious activities can be forbidden within a community's territory, but it would be absolutely arbitrary to prevent believers in other religions from traveling to other places in order to share their creed with other members of their church.

Based on these considerations, the feasibility of building and opening an evangelical temple within Arhuaco territory must be freely and independently decided upon by indigenous authorities. . . . Respect for indigenous identity, which emerges from a direct ruling principle of the Constitution, would be completely undermined if [the state] forced Arhuaco community members, against their will and beliefs, to tolerate a foreign god demanding recognition within a territory dedicated to their own deity. . . .

As sole and absolute owners of their territory, the Ika community is entitled to autonomously decide who may gain entrance to it, and even more clearly to prohibit the construction of facilities by groups that are foreign to their culture. . . . For the Ika, the presence of strangers in their territory has a different significance than it may have for people who attach no deep religious and cultural significance to their land. From the point of view of the Arhuaco people, their territory on the mountain is sacred, as it is part of the all-encompassing body of their Mother, incarnated in the Sierra Nevada de Santa Marta. This is the dwelling place of their ancestors, where tradition is re-created and passed down from generation to generation. . . .

[I]n the case in dispute there is no higher constitutional concern than the fundamental rights of the Arhuaco people to ethnic and cultural integrity and to hold collective property over their reservation. In effect, even though the prohibition imposed by traditional authorities over CUPCh ministers and members not to enter their reservation or to build temples or carry out religious proselytism within its boundaries entails a restriction on the fundamental right to their religious freedom, that restriction is not unreasonable. Certainly, the restriction under examination is not based on arbitrary motives, as its sole foundation is to protect the cultural integrity of an indigenous group and to forestall influences from the majority society that may be harmful, an effort that, as evidenced in the present case, finds full constitutional justification in the provisions established in Article 7 of our Constitution.

Justices Jose Gregorio Hernández Galindo, Vladimiro Naranjo and Hernando Herrera, dissenting:

Indigenous people's traditional practices are not protected by preventing them from learning about new options regarding issues that may be of interest for the shaping of their own individual consciousness and for the spontaneous choice and pursuit of their personal religious ideas, as this entails a paternalistic approach that finds no justification in our Constitution, which besides the freedom of conscience and religion, proclaims the free development of personality and the right to receive information from the outside world, privileges from which the Constitution does not exclude members of indigenous communities. . . .

An infringement of fundamental human rights occurs when it is established that individuals born into a certain Amerindian culture, in this case the Arhuaco culture, cannot exercise their freedom of conscience and their freedom of religion without having to either abandon their culture or face discrimination. Referring to the Arhuaco people . . . , the [majority] opinion literally states that "when an individual gives up his religion, he also gives up the existential order that his cultural identity grants him." In other words, either he totally and unconditionally tolerates the indigenous priest's absolute and uncontestable religious and political authority . . . or he will be forced to live with his family and his community under permanent discrimination, as a person who is not granted the same rights to land and who may be punished for the behavior he has adopted as a result of his beliefs.

3. Cultural Practices and the Rights of Children

Decision T-030 of 2000 (per Justice Fabio Morón Diaz)

[In a unanimous *tutela* decision, the Court dealt with an issue that pitted the rights to health, life, and family of a pair of twins born in the U'wa indigenous community against the rights to self-determination and ethnic and religious diversity of the U'wa community. The Court examined the case of a couple belonging to the U'wa community who had twins; the twins were willingly handed over to the Cubará municipal healthcare center by their parents, who declared that it was impossible to take them back to their community. The U'wa people repudiate multiple births because they consider that those births contaminate the community. Traditionally, these children have been left outside to die. However, the U'wa community stated that taking into consideration constitutional provisions and international law, their members had decided to leave the twins temporarily (for at least seven months) under the custody of the Colombian Institute for Family Welfare (CIFW). During this time the U'wa would undertake an internal consultation process to arrive at a final decision.]

[The CIFW later sent the twins to a facility outside the indigenous community's municipality of origin in order to start a process of adoption. The president of the U'wa general indigenous council sent a letter to the CIFW expressing the U'wa people's opposition to the adoption process and requesting that the twins be sent back to the CIFW office in the municipality where the indigenous community was settled. The director of the facility then filed a *tutela* requesting that procedures to send the twins back to the U'wa community be stopped and that the adoption process be initiated. The lower court judges in charge of ruling on the *tutela* ordered the CIFW to proceed with an investigation "and if applicable, to declare the children to be abandoned" so that the adoption process could proceed. To comply with the provisions ordered by the *tutela* judges, the municipality's Ombudsman for Family Issues declared the twins to have been abandoned and ordered a start to the adoption process. However, the regional CIFW Director revoked the decision and instead ordered the return of the minors to their community and family.]

From an analysis of the content of the different declarations made during the administrative process [and the *tutela* suit], it is easy to conclude that the decision of the parents of the minors originated in a fear that they had that the tradition [of leaving twins outside to die] would be carried out. . . .

[O]nce the administrative process had begun, the indigenous community's internal governing bodies and authorities learned about the issue and proceeded, not by denying the existence of their belief, but by expressing their willingness to rethink it based on two specific reasons: one of an anthropological nature, implying that the community's contact with other communities and with "civilization" in general had taught them that it is not true that twins "contaminate" the community or are "carriers of bad luck"; and another of legal and political implications, forcing them to reconsider those traditions and habits because they infringe constitutional principles and . . . contravene the minimum standards established to safeguard harmonic coexistence in a context of respect for diversity and difference.

[A]lthough there is no doubt about the tradition that the U'wa community used to practice concerning children born from multiple births, and about the fact that within the framework of our legal system such a tradition is unacceptable because the right to life takes precedence over an indigenous community's right to self-determination, . . . it is also true that the community [in this case] did not intend to enforce it. This explains why . . . they decided to undertake a consultation and reflection process apparently motivated, among many other reasons, by the experience they have had through their intensive exchange with other cultures, which has led them to conclude that there is no risk in accepting in their community children resulting from multiple births since they are no different from other minors, and, therefore, to demand their return to the community and contest their adoption. . . .

[I]t is absolutely impossible to accept as legitimate the tradition practiced for centuries by the U'wa community regarding children born from multiple births . . . ., since that tradition patently contravenes the basic ethical principles underlying the existence of a social state of law, . . . and given that the protection due to these children's lives and integrity would naturally take precedence.

However . . . , how the community redefined, in a new context, this cultural notion and the fate of the children corresponded to [the special indigenous] jurisdiction; they had to make a decision, taking into account that any measures they adopted could not ignore or infringe our national legal order. In other words, the request presented by U'wa traditional authorities before the state, asking to keep the twins in custody (for seven months) while they undertook an internal consultation and reflection process to reach a final decision, was fully compatible with regulations and with the law; their decision, obviously, could not be to carry out the tradition, but instead it could reasonably leave the minors under the custody of people or families outside the community and keep in touch with them, authorize their adoption, or, as occurred in this case, demand their return to the community.

To claim that the time requested for the internal consultation was excessive, and consequently to declare the twins to have been abandoned, not only ignores the specific worldview of the community, their concept of time and space and the importance given to decisions resulting from internal consensus, i.e., constitutional principles recognizing and protecting ethnic diversity (Article 7) and indigenous peoples' right to self-determination, but also violates legal safeguards regarding the implementation of a measure that is characterized by its severity and irreversibility.

In effect, the Ombudsman for Family Issues . . . declared the U´wa twins to have been abandoned and gave instructions to start the adoption process without complying with the procedural requirements established in . . . the [law]. . . . [This was done while] the [community] was deciding on the way to handle a situation they could not and did not want to resolve by following the ancestral tradition . . . , but rather by rethinking it in a new context based on their acknowledgement that twins are the same as other children and do not carry contamination or bad luck. . . . [T]his behavior cannot be interpreted as abandonment, even less so when the community and the children's parents have clearly and persistently asked for their return and have expressed their opposition to adoption. . . .

[F]rom a legal point of view, the decision taken by the CIFW Regional Director . . . to revoke both the declaration of abandonment concerning the twins . . . and the instruction to start the adoption process, and to instead order their return to their family and community as requested . . . was correct. . . .

[The Court's decision allowed for the possibility of the return of the twins to the U'wa community, but also ordered the establishment of a "group of specialists (doctors, psychologists, anthropologists, and nutritionists) that under the coordination of the [Regional Director] would find the opportune moment to return the minors," and that was ordered to monitor the process for at least a year and issue follow-up reports. In 2002, personnel affiliated with the facility that was still holding the twins filed a second *tutela*, presenting evidence that the U'wa community had not changed its cultural practices and thus that the twins' lives would still be in danger if they were returned. Although lower courts issued relief, in **Decision T-444 of 2002 (per Justice Jaime Araujo Renteria)**, the Constitutional Court rejected the *tutela*. Instead, it left the issue in the hands of the Committee established by the previous decision, holding that the evidence presented in the action should be "taken into account" by it when deciding how to act, seeking above all respect and protection of the right to life of the children.]

B. Diversity and Political Representation

As noted in the introduction to this chapter, Article 171 of the Constitution provides special rights of representation for indigenous peoples in the national senate. Two indigenous senators are elected from special districts and must meet special criteria: they "must have exercised a position of traditional authority in their respective community or have been leaders of an indigenous organization." Article 176 contemplates the creation of special electoral districts in the House of Representatives for "ethnic groups and political minorities." As the case below suggests, members of indigenous communities may also compete for all other electoral posts found in the country. That case finds that in these cases, the general electoral requirements may need to be altered for indigenous candidates in light of the principles of pluralism and multiculturalism found in the Constitution.

Decision T-778 of 2005 (per Justice Manuel José Cepeda Espinosa)

[The claimant, an indigenous woman living in Bogotá but belonging to the Arhuaco community located far away, was elected to Bogotá's city council by the *Polo Democrático Independiente*, a left-wing political movement. Her election was contested before the administrative courts as not complying with the minimum age necessary to be a council member. The petitioner was only 23 years old, whereas the minimum age set by decree to be on the Council was 25. The first-instance administrative court therefore adjudged the petitioner's election to be void. The petitioner then brought a *tutela* seeking emergency relief from this measure, and the Constitutional Court unanimously suspended the administrative court's ruling while the highest administrative court in the country, the Council of State, considered the matter.[9]]

9. Article 86 of the Constitution notes that the *tutela* writ may be sought not only for permanent relief, but also as a "temporary device to avoid irreparable harm." This use of the *tutela* in this sense is much like a temporary injunction or provisional measure found in other legal systems. In this case, the petitioner justified her request for temporary relief by noting that given standard caseloads, the final decision by the Council of State may not occur until after the term for which she was elected had ended.

Does demanding compliance with age requirements not expressly included in the Constitution from an indigenous woman in order to access a popularly elected post, when such requirements differ from those observed in her community in order to exercise political rights, infringe her fundamental right to cultural identity . . . ?

In Colombian constitutionalism, multiculturalism is a pillar of nationality; therefore the state has the obligation to recognize and protect ethnic and cultural diversity and in addition to promote that diversity, on which harmonious coexistence within a participatory democracy depends. . . .

The right to cultural identity, as a right derived from the principle of ethnic and cultural diversity established in Article 7 of the Constitution, has been conceived as a fundamental right of indigenous communities and thus a right of a collective nature. The mentioned right materializes for example in the requirement that communities that do not share the majority's cultural and social values can exercise their fundamental rights in accord with their own way of viewing the world. This also implies that individuals pertaining to an indigenous community can express themselves and enjoy self-determination in accordance with their cultural worldview both inside and outside of their territories.

Thus, the right to cultural identity has two dimensions, one collective and the other individual. The first treats the constitutional protection given to the community as a subject of rights and the second the protection given to the individual in order to be able to preserve the rights of that collectivity. This suggests two types of protection for cultural identity: a direct route that protects the community as a subject of rights and an indirect one that protects the individual in order to protect the identity of the community. The protection of the cultural identity of the community as a subject of rights does not mean that the individual manifestation of that identity is left unprotected, since the protection of the individual can be necessary to realize the collective right of the indigenous community to which she pertains. . . .

The right to cultural identity of indigenous communities is a right that projects beyond the place where the respective community is located. This is because the principle of ethnic and cultural diversity is based in the peaceful and harmonious coexistence and respect for pluralism anywhere in the national territory, since it is a defining principle of the social and democratic state of law. This is a principle that is oriented towards inclusion within the recognition of difference, not exclusion on the pretext of respecting differences. To conclude that cultural identity can only be expressed in a determined place would be equivalent to establishing policies of segregation and separation. . . .

[The Court noted that the claimant did not run for office on a specifically indigenous electoral list, but held that this was not a prerequisite to asserting a right to ethnic cultural identity.]

Being a member of a political party or movement means sharing certain political views. . . . But this does not mean that the only thing a person may represent is that political party or movement. There are many personal features, for example a person's sex, that respond to social or cultural identities and have an additional effect on representation.

The failure to run for office on a specifically indigenous electoral list does not mean that a person no longer represents her people, since cultural identity does not depend on belonging to a particular organization or political party; it is a real and material phenomenon from a constitutional perspective.... [C]ultural identity is the consciousness that one has of sharing certain creations, institutions, and collective behaviors with the group to which one belongs, with its distinctive and specific worldview....

The exercise of political representation can also be a manifestation of cultural identity which overruns territorial boundaries, since the elected official is projecting a collective vision that feels identified with the personal qualities of a candidate as well as with her political ideology.

In this context, indigenous community representation does not disappear by virtue of one's belonging to another political group or movement, since the criterion to establish the scope of the right to cultural identity depends on whether or not a person is a part of an indigenous community, in other words, on the person's qualities and her link to the particular community.

[The Court confirmed that the claimant belonged to the Arhuaco indigenous people. Likewise, it sought the advice of expert anthropologists to establish when, under the petitioner's cultural norms, she would be entitled to exercise political rights.]

In accordance with the traditions and customs of the Arhuaco people, a woman acquires the power of voice and social and political responsibilities once she has passed through the rituals corresponding to baptism and menstruation. It is from that moment in which a woman ... begins to develop herself with full capabilities. For the Arhuaco people age is not a criterion for establishing whether or not a person has the capacity to exercise political rights....

[The petitioner] passed through the ritual of baptism three months after her birth and through the menstruation ritual in 1993; therefore in accordance with the customs of her people, she has the capacity and power to act publicly, that is, to exercise political rights....

[The Court also found that the petitioner "is a female member of the Arhuaco people who has been considered a leader among her indigenous community" and that she has become a leader in the political movement the Indigenous Social Alliance, which in turn established a coalition with the movement *Polo Democrático Independiente* that decided to include her on its electoral list.]

In this case we have found that the effective realization of the political rights of a woman who was elected by her community to represent them in Bogotá's city council has been hindered by the enforcement of a legal requirement concerning age that is not enshrined in the Constitution but in a decree. Although the exercise of the right to political participation is subject to parameters regulated by the law, in this particular case this legal requirement goes against the effective enjoyment of the right to cultural identity of an indigenous woman from the Arhuaco people, and, therefore, against her community's customs which establish that the claimant is fully capable and has all the qualities required for exercising political rights. If—as verified in the present ruling—the right to cultural identity in the exercise of representation rights is not restricted to a particular territory and can be exercised in any sphere, and if the representation of an indigenous worldview cannot be nullified by belonging to a non-indigenous political movement, then allowing for the exercise of the right to representation endorsed through popular voting and in agreement with the customs of the Arhuaco community is required under the constitutional mandate to promote the nation's distinct cultural values and to protect ethnic and cultural diversity. In accordance with these principles we must establish whether to directly apply the constitution and therefore to set aside the age requirement found in [the Decree] establishing requirements to be elected a member of the city council in Bogotá.

As the case law states, it is necessary to carry out cultural exceptions to general rules when those exceptions respond to the application of a constitutional mandate and that application does not violate any individual right or constitutional value that holds greater weight. . . . [Previously] we have established that those are respect for life, prohibition on torture, individual responsibility for one's acts, and proportionality of punishment to the seriousness of the wrong, all from the perspective of the worldview of each indigenous people.

Setting aside the age limit established in [the decree] does not touch any of these limits. However, [the age limit] does gravely affect the exercise of those rights distinguishing a multicultural democracy . . . and it fails to recognize or protect ethnic and cultural diversity. . . .

[The Court therefore suspended the administrative decision at issue and allowed the woman to assume her post on the city council.]

C. The Right to Prior Consultation

Several articles of the Colombian Constitution suggest that indigenous communities have special rights to participate in certain kinds of state decisions that have a particular economic or cultural effect on them. Article 330 of the Colombian Constitution states that any exploitation of natural resources in indigenous territories "shall be done without impairing the cultural, social, and economic integrity of" those communities and "must be carried out with the participation of" their representatives. Article 329 gives a similar right of participation in decisions delimiting the boundaries of indigenous territorial entities.

International law bolsters these rights. Convention 169 of the International Labour Organization (ILO) on indigenous and tribal peoples sets out a broad panoply of rights for indigenous groups, within the framework of multicultural respect and protection for their environment and way of life.[10] This Convention has been ratified by 22 states: most of these

10. Convention (No.169) concerning Indigenous and Tribal Peoples in Independent Countries, International Labour Organization, June 27, 1989.

are found in Latin America (including Argentina, Bolivia, Brazil, Chile, Costa Rica, Ecuador, Guatemala, Honduras, Mexico, Nicaragua, Paraguay, Peru, and Venezuela) and the remainder are scattered around the rest of the world. Colombia ratified the Convention in 1991.

The Convention, in particular, gives indigenous peoples a right to participate in development projects and other measures with particular impact on their culture or economy. Thus, Article 6 sets forth that states must "consult the peoples concerned, through appropriate procedures and in particular through their representative institutions, whenever consideration is being given to legislative or administrative measures which may affect them directly." It also establishes that consultations must be carried out "in good faith and in a form appropriate to the circumstances, with the objective of achieving agreement or consent to the proposed measures." Other provisions in the Convention further flesh out these rights.[11] The Convention envisions a consultation process that is flexible but substantial and robust rather than merely formal.

As the cases below show, the Constitutional Court used the constitutional block doctrine described in Chapter 2 to incorporate ILO Convention 169 into the constitutional order, thus creating a set of participation rights drawn both from the treaty and relevant constitutional provisions. This right of prior consultation extends beyond projects involving natural resources and also implicates any other measure having a direct impact on indigenous communities. The three principal cases excerpted here, along with the notes following the case, should give the reader a sense of the evolution of the Court's jurisprudence on this topic. In its early case law, the Court interpreted a right to participation on programs and projects having a direct effect on indigenous groups based on both international and domestic constitutional law, and held that the failure to carry out an adequate consultation violated fundamental rights that could be protected by *tutela*. Subsequently, the Court has broadened the scope of consultation, requiring it for example even for general laws that have direct effects on indigenous groups, as the General Forestry Law case below shows. Finally, over time the Court has given greater definition to the issue of what constitutes an adequate procedure for consultation. The answer depends on the context, but it is clear that indigenous communities must have ample opportunities for input and interchange, rather than simply being informed, and that the objective of a good faith negotiation should be consensus.

The procedural requirements of the right also appear to have deepened over time. As the scope of the right has broadened, and given the frequency with which resource exploitation and other economic projects target indigenous peoples holding one-third of all national land, opportunities for conflict between governmental and private economic interests, on the one hand, and indigenous peoples and their allies on the other, have increased.

11. *See id.* art. 7 ("1. The peoples concerned shall have the right to decide their own priorities for the process of development as it affects their lives, beliefs, institutions and spiritual well-being and the lands they occupy or otherwise use, and to exercise control, to the extent possible, over their own economic, social and cultural development. In addition, they shall participate in the formulation, implementation and evaluation of plans and programmes for national and regional development which may affect them directly. . . . 3. Governments shall ensure that, whenever appropriate, studies are carried out, in co-operation with the peoples concerned, to assess the social, spiritual, cultural and environmental impact on them of planned development activities. The results of these studies shall be considered as fundamental criteria for the implementation of these activities.").

1. Consultation on Projects Exploiting Natural Resources

Decision SU-039 of 1997 (per Justice Antonio Barrera Carbonell)

[In a five-to-four decision, the Court halted oil exploration projects planned on U'wa land until comprehensive prior consultation with the indigenous community could be carried out. The company Occidental Society of Colombia Inc. requested that the state grant it a license to undertake seismic explorations aimed at verifying the existence of oil wells or fields in a large area in the departments of Arauca and Norte de Santander, within which U'wa reservations are located. The Ministry of the Environment granted the license. It argued that any requirements of prior consultation with indigenous communities had been met through a meeting that was held with some members of the indigenous community on January 10 and 11, 1995, in the city of Arauca, and that included representatives from three state ministries, the Colombian state oil company (Ecopetrol), and the Occidental Society of Colombia Inc. The meeting mostly consisted of presentations by these officials regarding aspects of the project, followed by a brief question and answer period. Shortly afterward, the U'wa community held meetings where members expressed strong opposition to the project, but in February 1995, the license was granted after no further communication with the indigenous group.]

[The Court must determine,] within the framework of the Constitution, the conflict between the exploitation of natural resources in indigenous territories and the special protection which the state must grant indigenous communities so as to ensure the conservation of their identity and their ethnic, cultural, social and economic integrity. . . .

The exploitation of natural resources in indigenous territories makes it necessary to harmonize two contrasting interests: the need to plan natural resource management and use in those territories and ensure their sustainable development, conservation, renovation or substitution (Article 80[12]), and the need to guarantee protection for the ethnic, cultural, social and economic integrity of indigenous communities settled within those territories, in other words, the basic elements required for their cohesion as a social group. . . . This means that balance should be sought between the country's economic development, which demands the exploitation of resources, and the preservation of the integrity of indigenous groups, which is a condition for their survival as a human group. . . .

In order to guarantee that survival, the law has established that in the event of undertakings involving the exploitation of natural resources in indigenous territories, these communities have the right to participate in the decisions authorizing exploitation. The community's fundamental right to preserve its integrity is guaranteed and realized by exercising another fundamental right found in Article 40, clause

12. Article 80 states in part: "The state shall plan the handling and use of natural resources in order to guarantee their sustainable development, conservation, restoration, or replacement. Additionally, it shall caution and control the factors of environmental deterioration, impose legal sanctions, and demand the repair of any damage caused."

2 of the Constitution,[13] which instantiates a right to the participation of the community in the making of these decisions.

In the opinion of the Court, the participation of indigenous communities in decisions that may affect them related to the exploitation of natural resources . . . acquires the connotation of a fundamental right because it a basic instrument to preserve the ethnic, social, economic, and cultural integrity of indigenous groups. . . .

The indigenous right to participation as a fundamental right is reinforced by ILO Convention 169 . . . which is aimed at ensuring the rights of indigenous peoples to their territory and to the protection of their cultural, social, and economic values, as a way to ensure their survival as a human group. In this way, the cited Convention . . . forms part of [a] constitutional block intended to make the right to participation effective.

Based on . . . the Constitution and norms of Convention 169 cited above, the Court estimates that the institution of indigenous consultation . . . demands the adoption of a relationship of communication and understanding, underpinned by mutual respect and good faith between the communities and state authorities, with the purpose of:

a) Ensuring that the community will have full knowledge of projects whose purpose is to explore or exploit natural resources within its territory, as well as of all mechanisms, procedures and activities planned for the project's implementation.
b) Informing and enlightening the community on the ways the implementation of those projects may have an effect or a negative impact upon the elements at the root of their social, cultural, economic and political cohesion and which, therefore, constitute the basis of their survival as a human group with distinctive features.
c) Giving members of the group opportunities to freely and without outside interference convene their members or representatives to knowingly assess a project's advantages and disadvantages for the community and its members, to be heard regarding concerns and expectations about the defense of their interests, and to voice their opinion on the feasibility of the project. The objective is to ensure active and effective participation by the community in the decision-making process undertaken by authorities which should be, as far as possible, mutually agreed upon.

When agreement or consensus is impossible, the decision of the authority must be free of arbitrariness or authoritarianism; in consequence it must be objective, reasonable, and proportional to the constitutional end demanded by the state for the protection of the social, cultural, and economic identity of the indigenous community.

In all cases the mechanisms necessary to mitigate, correct, or restore the effects that the state measures may produce to the detriment of the community or its members . . . should be discussed.

13. Article 40 states in part: "Any citizen has the right to participate in the establishment, exercise, and control of political power. To make this decree effective the citizen may: 2. Participate in elections, plebiscites, referendums, popular consultations, and other forms of democratic participation."

Accordingly, consultation is not deemed to have occurred when the indigenous community simply receives information ... regarding natural resource exploration or exploitation projects. It is also necessary to comply with the above mentioned guidelines by presenting mechanisms to the community by which that they can express, through their authorized representatives, their approval or disapproval of those projects and their implications for their ethnic, cultural, social and economic identity....

It is clear that in the meeting held [over two days in 1995], the consultation required to grant the environmental license did not happen.... That consultation must also occur before the project is authorized, and therefore any actions taken afterwards, and which were designed to correct their inadequacies, lack any value or significance.

Nor can the many meetings that, according to the Occidental Society of Colombia Inc. company's representative, the company held with members of the U'wa community be deemed as complying with the consultation required, since this is an obligation that corresponds exclusively to state authorities with sufficient power of representation and decision over both indigenous communities and the country's interests concerning the need to exploit natural resources....

In conclusion, the Court estimates that the procedure for the issuance of the environmental license was carried out in an irregular way and violated the fundamental right of the U'wa community to prior consultation, which had to be carried out formally and substantively. Consequently, not only was the right to participation violated ... but also the right to due process.

[The Court thus granted the *tutela* and ordered that the consultation with the U'wa community be undertaken within 30 days. Justices Hernando Herrera Vergara, Vladimiro Naranjo Mesa, Fabio Morón Diaz, and Jaime Vidal Perdomo dissented. Although agreeing that the state had an obligation to consult with indigenous groups before undertaking projects on their land, the dissenting justices called for a congressional law to regulate the matter and expressed concerns that the majority may be pushing the right to prior consultation too far: "[T]he law does not establish that [the results of] consultation are binding on the government, or that it may be used as a veto, but that it should be an instrument to facilitate conciliation between purposes that ... may develop in parallel." The dissenters also argued that the *tutela* was not the proper mechanism to protect rights in this case, which instead should have proceeded before the administrative courts.]

2. Consultation on Government Programs

Decision SU-383 of 2003 (per Justice Alvaro Tafur Galvis)

[The Colombian state had carried out ongoing fumigation operations in the Amazon region of the country, aimed at eradicating illegal crops (such as the coca plant) across that part of Colombia. But the representatives of the indigenous groups in the region stated that fumigation was destroying crops that they needed for their livelihood, in addition to damaging their health and the environment, and had been undertaken without consulting with them. In a six-to-three decision, the Court ordered the state to "undertake effective and efficient consultations with indigenous peoples and tribes settled in the Colombian Amazon region regarding activities carried out by the Illegal Crop Eradication Program in their territories."]

[First, the Court examined whether the *tutela* mechanism was the appropriate one to use in this case—the government claimed that the consultation right was not a "fundamental right" and thus could not be protected by the *tutela*. The petitioners also argued that the consultation right was a "collective right" that should instead be protected through legal mechanisms found in administrative courts. The Court rejected these arguments:]

This Court has repeatedly sustained, given the special significance for the survival of indigenous peoples and tribes of their participation in decisions that can affect them through the mechanism of prior consultation, that this is a fundamental right. . . .

There is no mechanism distinct from the *tutela* through which indigenous peoples and tribes can demand the immediate protection of their right to be consulted, in order to ensure their right to cultural survival, and therefore the *tutela* judge has the power to issue orders ensuring this survival. . . .

Because of the need to achieve the material equality of indigenous tribes on the national territory given the real oppression, exploitation, and marginalization to which they have been submitted, this Court has said that the constitutional protection of the right to diversity and cultural integrity need not be individualized, because the right to survival of the members of indigenous and tribal communities . . . can only be understand as part of the group to which they pertain. . . .

[Next, the Court considered the international framework, focusing on the significance of ILO Convention 169:]

Colombia is among the countries which have ratified ILO Convention 169. . . . This convention protects the rights of indigenous peoples to land, and to participation, education, culture and development in the context of global efforts to protect their identities so they can enjoy their fundamental rights as fully as the rest of the population of member states, and acknowledges their special contributions to cultural diversity, to the social and ecological harmony of humankind, and to international cooperation and understanding. . . .

Therefore, Colombia, together with all other member states, is obliged to adopt all required measures so that indigenous and tribal peoples settled in their national territory may exercise control over their institutions, way of life, and economic development, by providing them with adequate tools to foster their identity, language and religion and to safeguard their members, assets, culture and territories. . . .

Within Convention 169 the right of these peoples to be consulted on decisions that affect them has a special significance. . . .

Convention 169 "assumes that these peoples can speak for themselves, that they have the right to participate in decision-making processes where the decisions affect them, and that their contribution shall be considered beneficial for the country where they are living," and thus Articles 6 and 7, which establish the right to prior consultation and the form in which this mechanism should be carried out, are considered . . . to be primordial.

ILO Convention 169, specifically regarding the right of indigenous and tribal peoples to prior consultation, forms together with our constitutional regulations a constitutional block . . . not only because it is contained in an ILO instrument which establishes the labor rights of these peoples, but also (i) because the right to participation of indigenous peoples in decisions regarding the exploitation of natural resources within their territories established in Article 330 of the Constitution cannot be interpreted as restricting a right to prior consultation regarding other issues related to their survival as differentiated communities; (ii) because the Convention is the most important international instrument governing discrimination against indigenous and tribal peoples; (iii) because the right to prior consultation by indigenous groups on administrative and legal measures that may have direct effects on those populations is the positive action favored and recommended by the international community to fight against the origin, forms, and contemporary manifestations of racial discrimination, xenophobia and related acts of intolerance towards indigenous and tribal peoples . . . and (iv) because Article 27 of the International Covenant on Civil and Political Rights establishes that ethnic minorities may not be denied their right to identity . . . .[14]

Article 34 of ILO Convention 169 establishes that the measures taken to give the Convention effect "shall be determined in a flexible manner, having regard to the conditions characteristic of each country," and this provision has been understood in our constitutional case law as requiring in-depth study of the cultural characteristics of peoples who are affected by decisions in order to determine their level of autonomy and, therefore, to maximize or minimize the nature and scope of both the consultation and the measures taken.

Consequently, it is necessary to determine whether the indigenous communities settled in the Amazon region have the social, economic and cultural conditions which would grant them the right to be considered as "peoples." Those conditions include: (i) their differentiation from other population groups in the country and their total or partial observance of their own customs and traditions or (ii) their condition as descendants of the groups who inhabited the national territory at the time of the conquest and colonization who have preserved their own social, economic, cultural and political institutions, or at least part of them. . . .

[T]he studies to which the chamber has made reference allow us to conclude that the indigenous and tribal communities settled in the Amazon region generally

14. *See* International Covenant on Civil and Political Rights (1966) ("In those States in which ethnic, religious or linguistic minorities exist, persons belonging to such minorities shall not be denied the right, in community with the other members of their group, to enjoy their own culture, to profess and practise their own religion, or to use their own language.").

comply with the conditions required in . . . ILO Convention 169 for its enforcement because they have inherited social, cultural and economic features that differentiate them from other groups of the country, they fully or partially follow their own customs and traditions, and they have occupied their territories from the time of the conquest and colonization of Colombia's present borders.

The definition of Colombia as a social state of law based on a participatory and pluralistic democracy, which acknowledges the ethnic and cultural diversity of its citizens, implies that indigenous participation and identity are foundations of our state and they are undeniable conditions to build a single nation truly founded on a viable diversity. . . .

Consequently, provisions regarding prior consultation and the right of indigenous people to participation are binding on the Colombian state according to the text of ILO Convention 169, its implementation guidelines and other ILO recommendations, and the relevant articles of our Constitution:

- Because Article 6 of Convention 169, adopted by the country through Law 21 of 1991, establishes that indigenous and tribal peoples have the right to be consulted without restriction before legal provisions or administrative measures directly affecting them are adopted.
- Because none of the provisions included in the Convention allow for indigenous and tribal peoples to be absorbed by the majority culture.
- Because the rights and duties enshrined in our Constitution are interpreted according to international human rights treaties ratified by Colombia.
- Because ILO Convention 169 is the most relevant and important international law instrument of protection of ethnic minorities' rights. . . .

Without prior consultation it is not possible to: (i) maximize the autonomy required by indigenous peoples settled in this region to preserve their ethnic and cultural integrity; (ii) determine which indigenous and tribal peoples consider coca plants as sacred given the implications they have in their culture; (iii) determine which peoples' survival depend on coca plantations as they offer shade to other essential crops in certain regions and periods of the year, and (iv) determine how significant the use of coca leaves is in their healing and ritual practices.

Only through consultations based on good faith and properly conducted with the peoples involved will it be possible to determine the implications that the Illegal Crop Eradication Program can have on their lives, beliefs, institutions, spiritual welfare and use of the land, and thus to define the nature and scope of measures to be adopted with the flexibility contemplated in Article 34 of the Convention. . . .

Although the eradication of illegal crops is a mechanism included in the state's criminal policy in response to its obligations towards the international community in order to confront the problems derived from narco-trafficking, and is generally compatible with our Constitution . . . , this does not mean that the duty of prior consultation with indigenous peoples can be disregarded, since the international community also requires the implementation without restrictions of the mechanism of prior consultation as a means of fighting against discrimination, and have further requested that illegal crop eradication not disregard human rights and interests in traditional uses for these crops. . . .

The defendants . . . must consult in an effective and efficient manner with indigenous and tribal peoples of the Colombian amazon about the decisions pertaining to the [eradication program] "with the objective of achieving agreement or consent to the proposed measures."[15]

This procedure must be initiated and completed in the three months following notification of this decision.

Within the first thirty days, the authorities of the indigenous peoples and the organizations representing them must be consulted, preferably (i) on the procedure and terms with which consultation will be carried out, (ii) with respect to its territorial scope, and (iii) on the determination of adequate measures to advance . . . on the eradication of illegal crops, either through aerial spraying or through an alternative method, so long as the chosen method guarantees real and effective enjoyment of the fundamental rights protected by this decision. . . .

Following the lines of Convention 169 of the ILO . . . , the consultations that are ordered cannot be reduced to a mere formality, given that their execution in good faith implies that the indigenous peoples of the Colombian amazon must be informed of the content of the program that will be carried out in their territories, with the goal of gaining their consent, about the impact of the measures in their habitat, cognitive and spiritual structures.

They must also be informed of the measures that are actually being carried out, with all their implications, with an eye towards having the peoples' consent to the . . . continuation of the program, and possess the capacity to discuss different proposals pertinent to the same goal and to formulate alternatives.

We must clarify that the right to prior consultation created in Convention 169 does not imply the right of indigenous peoples and tribes to veto legislative and administrative measures that affect them, but rather is an opportunity for the state parties to consider and value the positions that the representatives of national ethnic minorities have towards their decisions, in order to move towards an understanding and if possible, an agreement. . . .

[Justices Alfredo Beltrán and Clara Inés Vargas partially dissented. In their opinion the Court should also have protected indigenous peoples' rights to life and health by suspending all spraying immediately. "It is surprising that given the clear intention of the constitutional provisions invoked, the present decision has not ordered the immediate suspension of aerial crop eradication in the Colombian Amazon region, which disregards the regulations in force and the international covenants signed by Colombia on this issue. . . . [There is] abundant evidence mentioned and analyzed in the decision itself which fails to prove that glyphosate [the drug used in the spraying] is harmless for humans, animals, plants and water resources; on the

15. Convention (No. 169) concerning Indigenous and Tribal Peoples in Independent Countries, art. 6.

contrary, there is evidence that suggests that it does damage the health of adults and children. In light of all these considerations, the only possible decision should have been to order the immediate suspension of aerial fumigation with glyphosate."]

[Along similar lines, Justice Jaime Araujo's dissent stated: "International treaties on environmental protection, the Colombian Constitution, and the law have established the precautionary principle to ensure that if there is doubt as to whether a product affects the environment, its use should be suspended until there is absolute certainty that it is not harmful. The logic behind this principle is: in *dubio pro natura*, because if after 50 years of using a product certainty is established as to its polluting effect, it will have already affected several generations of living beings (men, animals, plants, etc.) and the damage will be irreversible. The scientific evidence gathered in this case showed that fumigations with glyphosate affect fundamental rights to life and personal integrity, and, therefore, the spraying should have been suspended. For the sake of argument, even if there were any doubts regarding its harmful effects, the precautionary principle should have been applied and the use of the product should have been suspended anyway."]

3. Consultation on Congressional Laws

Decision C-030 of 2008 (per Justice Rodrigo Escobar Gil)

[In a unanimous decision, the Court declared Law 1021 of 2006, the General Forestry Law, unconstitutional in its entirety because it violated the requirement of prior consultation with indigenous peoples. The Forestry Law aimed at regulating in a broad range of activities related to forests. The law was proposed by the government as a body of regulations that would allow the economic exploitation of timber through Colombia. The project that resulted in the issuing of the Forestry Law was criticized for focusing almost exclusively on economic exploitation while disregarding environmental issues and the economic and cultural relationships between indigenous and Afro-Colombian communities and forests. It was also challenged for a lack of prior consultation with indigenous communities before its passage.]

As this Court has noted and is clear from the text itself, Convention 169 of the ILO was adopted based on a new approximation of the situation of indigenous and tribal peoples in all regions of the world, according to which it was essential to eliminate the orientation aimed at assimilation . . . and replace it with a principle according to which the structures and ways of life of the indigenous and tribal peoples are permanent and everlasting, and the international community has an interest in safeguarding the intrinsic value of their vultures.

[W]hen measures are adopted in application of the Convention, one must distinguish two levels of effects on indigenous and tribal peoples: those concerning politics and programs that concern them in some manner, in which case a general right to participation should be made effective, and those concerning administrative or legislative measures that are susceptible of affecting them directly, in which case the duty of consultation must be carried out.

In terms of the general right of consultation, it is worth noting that the Convention is aimed at giving interested [indigenous] peoples opportunities to participate that are, at least, equivalent to those enjoyed by other sectors of the population in the adoption of decisions in elective institutions and administrative organisms. . . .

In a specific manner that general right of participation is manifested, within the sphere of legislative measures concerning indigenous and tribal peoples, (1) in the possibility that its members have of participating, in equal conditions with all Colombians, in the election of representatives in popularly-elected bodies; (2) in the fact that, in development of the public character of the legislative process, they can learn about initiatives that have been promoted, promote discussions, give opinions, solicit meetings, and (3) in the constitutional provisions on special indigenous electoral districts, because . . . these representatives are spokespeople, in a broad sense, of their particular worldview and can constitute effective channels of communication between legislative chambers and the authorities representing indigenous and tribal communities. . . .

In relation to the duty of consultation regarding measures that are susceptible of directly affecting indigenous and tribal peoples, the Court has said that it is a direct consequence of the right that these native communities have to determine their own priorities in the process of development and preservation of their culture and that this duty of consultation [constitutes] a fundamental right that may be protected by *tutela*, given its political importance and significance for the defense of identity and cultural integrity and its condition as a mechanism of participation. . . .

[T]he court finds it necessary to establish certain rules regarding the content of the duty of prior consultation . . . , particularly as it relates to the duty of consultation for legislative measures that directly affect indigenous communities. . . . In this matter it is important to consider three questions: (1) When is prior consultation necessary . . . for a legislative measure?, (2) Under what conditions of time, place, and manner should they be carried out?, and (3) What are the legal consequences of failing to carry them out?

First . . . , it is clear that the duty of consultation is not created with respect to all legislative measures that may affect indigenous communities, but only those that are susceptible of having a *direct* effect. . . .

It is also clear that what must be an object of consultation are those measures that may specifically affect indigenous communities as such, and not those laws that apply uniformly to all Colombians. . . .

In this sense, for example, in the case of a law that determines how the exploitation of petroleum will be carried out for reserves located on indigenous territory, consultation with the indigenous peoples susceptible to being affected must be carried out. . . .

But when one instead treats the adoption of a general framework for the petroleum policy of the state, there is no direct effect on indigenous or tribal communities . . . because the law is not oriented towards regulating the situation of those peoples specifically. . . .

Regarding the conditions of time, place, and manner in which the consultation should be carried out, . . . one must note the flexibility stated in [Convention 169] and the fact that . . . the process must be carried out under the principle of good faith, meaning that the state must define the conditions in which the consultation will be carried out and . . . must realize it in a manner that is conducive and effective. . . . The purpose is to create spaces of participation, which will permit useful interventions with sufficiently representative voices. . . .

[Next, the Court discussed the legal consequences of failing to carry out prior consultation for legislative measures.]

[S]ince . . . the norms governing prior consultation under Convention 169 of the ILO are integrated into the Constitution and since, more specifically, the duty of prior consultation has been seen as an expression of a fundamental right of participation which is linked to the fundamental right of cultural, social, and economic integrity, the omission of the consultation process in those cases where it is imperative in light of the Convention has immediate consequences in the internal legal order. . . .

[I]t would be possible, in some circumstances, to find that the law as such is unconstitutional, but it might also be possible in a general law concerning indigenous and tribal peoples, and which affects those peoples directly, to resolve the omission of consultation with a decision that excludes those communities from the sphere of application of the law; or a Court can declare . . . that what has been established is a legislative omission, and therefore that the law as such remains in the legal order, but that necessary measures must be undertaken to correct the legislative omission derived from the lack of measures specifically oriented towards indigenous and tribal peoples. . . . In that case, if the general law was called upon to be applied to indigenous groups, a court would decree a legislative omission because of the absence of specific, previously-consulted norms.

[The Court underlined that although there was a broad general debate regarding the law inside and outside of Congress, no specific process of consultation was undertaken with indigenous groups. The Court also stressed the economic and cultural importance of forests to indigenous and Afro-Colombian communities and established that most forests belong to indigenous or Afro-Colombian peoples: "Out of the total area covered by natural forests on the Pacific Coast and the Amazon region, 41.6 percent belongs to indigenous and Afro-Colombian communities. In fact, 72 percent of indigenous reservation areas, i.e., 22.5 million hectares, are covered by forests; in addition, 69.4 percent of the lands where Afro-Colombian communities are settled, i.e., around 2.6 million hectares, are covered by forests."]

It is undoubtable that a law regulating in an integral way the management of forests in the country has a direct and specific effect on indigenous peoples and tribes that live in zones with a high incidence of forests, not only for the interest that those communities have in participating in the definition of the elements of a national forest regime, but also because of the conflicts that distinct perspectives on the topic can cause, such as in this case when the legislative initiative emphasizes the promotion of wood as a strategic element for economic development. That emphasis can contradict the conception that the communities have regarding their land, which clearly suggests the necessity of a consultation oriented towards achieving a conciliation of interests. . . .

[N]otwithstanding the general character of the law—which is not directed at the special regulation . . . of the situation of indigenous and tribal communities—from its material content one derives the possibility of its specific impact on those communities, since its provisions regulate an object—the forest—that has particular relevance for them and has an intimate and binding relationship with their way of life. . . .

From the legislative history of the law one can conclude without great difficulty that . . . [it] did not go through the consultation with indigenous and tribal peoples that is required by Convention 169 of the ILO. There was, yes, a broad process of socialization that does not satisfy the criteria of the Constitutional Court because it was not specific, there is no evidence that the communities had been duly informed or given opportunities to present the impact that the project might have for them, nor were spaces for negotiation created.

Even if it is true that . . . there is a margin of flexibility surrounding the way in which consultation must be carried out . . . , it is no less certain that in a project with the size, complexity, and implications of one attempting to regulate forests in an integral way, the government, prior to the debate in Congress, should have carried out a specific exercise of consultation with indigenous and tribal communities. . . . That process would have permitted the identification of difficulties, established differences in perspective, searched for alternatives, and in any case enriched the debate in Congress. . . .

In order to have complied with the consultation, it would have been necessary for the government to have explained the project of law through sufficiently representative actors to the communities; illustrated its scope and how it might affect those communities; and given them effective opportunities to debate the project. That process was not carried out, and thus the Court concludes, given that the law treats a matter that is profoundly related to the worldview of those communities and their relationship to the land and that it is susceptible . . . to affecting them directly and specifically, that there is no alternative but to declare the law to be unconstitutional.

Note on the Evolution of the Right to Prior Consultation in Colombia: After this decision was adopted, the Constitutional Court ruled on the constitutionality of several other broad general statutes, such as the National Development Plan—**Decision C-461 of 2008 (per Justice Manuel José Cepeda Espinosa)** and the Rural Development Statute—**Decision C-175 of 2009 (per Justice Luis Ernesto Vargas Silva)**. Both cases referred to the duty of prior consultation for legislative measures. The solution adopted in each case differed given the type of law under examination, the objective of each, and its main contents.

Regarding the National Development Plan, the Court ruled Law 1151 of 2007 to be conditionally constitutional. According to the Constitution, a law embodying a national development plan must be issued every four years after presidential and congressional elections in order to adopt a national plan reflecting the new priorities of elected officials. The law includes a list of specific investments to be carried out, and listed several projects prone to affecting ethnic groups. Thus, the Court decided that projects, programs, or budgets "that may eventually have a direct and specific incidence on indigenous peoples or Afro-Colombian ethnic communities" would have to wait until the prior consultation demanded by ILO Agreement 169 had been carried out. The Court also ruled that prior consultation, being a mechanism of participatory democracy, could not be replaced by the presence of indigenous communities' representatives on the committee in charge of advising the government on the drafting of the National Development Plan.

In the Rural Development Statute case, the Constitutional Court, in a five-to-four decision, declared unconstitutional a law that aimed at globally regulating the use of rural land in Colombia. The Court considered that this law required compliance with the duty to consult because it issued general regulations regarding the relationship between individuals and land, and included specific provisions related to indigenous reservations and territories collectively owned by Afro-Colombian communities. Additionally, the Court determined that in accordance with the principle of good faith, that consultation had to be undertaken before sending the project to be debated in Congress, not during those debates. Thus, taking into account—as was the case with the Forestry Law—that the Rural Development Statute was a "general, integrated and systematic set of regulations," the Court declared it unconstitutional in its entirety.

The prior consultation doctrine has also been extended to the ratification of treaties. In **Decision T-615 of 2009 (per Justice Humberto Sierra Porto),** the Court struck down the congressional act that approved a treaty between Venezuela and Colombia concerning the Wayuu tribe because it was not subject to previous consultation with the affected indigenous communities living on the border between the two countries.

In **Decision T-129 of 2011 (per Justice Jorge Ivan Palacio Palacio)**, the Court dealt with a series of major projects that an indigenous community—the Embero-Katio community—alleged to be a violation of their constitutional rights. These included the construction of a highway, the building of electric lines that would link Colombia and Panama, and a gold mining project. The Court held, inter alia, that the right to prior consultation had been violated before these projects were carried out. The Court also clarified the question of whether, in some circumstances, prior consultation should be analogized to a veto right by the affected indigenous communities. The Court noted that consultation should be carried out with the goal of obtaining the "free and informed consent" of the affected community:

> Does free and informed consent constitute a veto power for ethnic communities facing investment projects? . . .
>
> The response to [this] question in accordance with the current jurisprudential and normative development is not easy, since one is dealing with a problem with two difficult extremes: on one side is previous consultation as a veto (which would be within the terms of [ILO] Convention [169] but would generate all types of resistance) and previous consultation as mere information (which would not conform to the Convention and frequently is employed to avoid compliance with

this instrument). Based on these considerations, for the Court the criterion that allows us to reconcile these extremes depends on the grade of affectation of the community [and] specific events in which consultation and consent can allow for the determination of the least harmful measure. . . .

[A]ny process must be judged in accordance with the distinctive characteristics of each concrete case, since what is in play is not only the expectation of receiving certain economic benefits through an economic project, but the present and future of a people, of a group of human beings who have rights of self-determination on which depend their physical and cultural existence, however "absurd or exotic" those customs or ways of life might seem to some.

On this point, the Court notes that it is necessary that the discussion not be planted in terms of whom gets to veto whom, since all [consultation] is a space for discourse between equals . . . , allowing time for state organs and concession holders to explain in a concrete and transparent way the goals of the project and giving the community a chance to explain its needs and points of view.

However, the distinct cases that have been revised by the Court on this topic allow us to conclude that prior consultation has not been carried with the rigor it deserves; . . . defendants have constantly seen the process of consultation as merely one of informal meetings without articulation or consideration for the rights that are in play. It is thus necessary, according to this Court, that the process not be limited to the stage prior to the intervention in ethnic territories. . . .

Based on these considerations, the Court finds it clear that the affected communities can make use of the possibility of revising and articulating their points of view about the intervention, not only beforehand but during and after the implementation of the work or plan of development. For this, in conformity to the specific features and demands of each case, at the moment of the initial consultation, times for revision in the short, medium, and long term must be fixed.

On the other hand, it is implausible to determine a single time for the materialization of the prior consultation and the search for consensus, because to homogenize this type of process would disrespect the differences and circumstances of the distinct ethnic groups. Thus, the process must be carried out from the stage where planning and feasibility studies are being created, and not at the . . . moment just before execution, since this type of practice ignores the interests and calendars of the ethnic community, situating the process of consultation and the search for consent as an obstacle and not as an opportunity to develop a dialogue between equals in which one side respects the thought of the other, including that of the businesspeople. . . .

[A]n ethnic community cannot be forced to renounce its way of life and its culture for the mere arrival of an infrastructure project or an exploitation project, and vice versa. Because of this, in exceptional or limiting cases the organisms of the state and in a residual form the constitutional judge, if the evidence indicates the necessity of the consent of the communities in order to determine the least harmful option, may order that course of action.

> This is a manifestation of the special protection that the Constitution gives ethnic minorities in those projects whose magnitude has the potential to warp or destroy their ways of life, which is why the Court finds it necessary that prior consultation and informed consent of ethnic communities in general seek to determine the least harmful alternative in those events that: (i) involve the moving or displacement of the communities due to the work or project; (ii) are related to the storage or release of toxic substances on ethnic lands, and/or (iii) represent a high social, cultural, and environmental impact on the ethnic community, which puts at risk its existence. . . .
>
> Now, in the event that the least harmful alternative is explored with the participation of ethnic communities . . . and in that process it is proven that . . . the intervention would carry with it the annihilation or disappearance of the group, the protection of the rights of ethnic communities must prevail, under the *pro homine* principal of interpretation.
>
> On this point, the *pro homine* principle of interpretation imposes the application of the legal norms that are most favorable to the human being and his rights; in other words, the imposition of that interpretation that is based on respect for human dignity and consequently on the protection, guarantee, and promotion of human rights and fundamental constitutional rights contemplated in the Constitution. This principle is contemplated in Articles 1 and 2 of the Constitution, which consecrate respect for human dignity as a basis of the democratic and social state of law. At the same time, the guaranteeing of the principles, rights, and duties consecrated in the Constitution is an essential end of the state, on the part of all authorities of the Republic in the protection of all persons in their life, honor, goods, and other rights and liberties.

A final point worth noting is the comparative dimension of the right to prior consultation. As noted above, most major Latin American states have ratified ILO Convention 169. High courts in other jurisdictions in the region are thus also beginning to issue decisions defining the scope of prior consultation. The Mexican Supreme Court, for example, has issued several decisions in recent years defending this right. In 2015 the Court reversed an administrative decision granting a license for Monsanto to undertake large-scale plantings of genetically-modified soy on the Yucatan peninsula and other areas of the country, holding that the required prior consultation had not been carried out.[16]

16. *See* Supreme Court of Mexico, Press Release N. 195/15, Nov. 4, 2015, at http://www.internet2.scjn.gob.mx/red2/comunicados/noticia.asp?id=3198.

PART THREE

The Separation of Powers

9

The President

Problems of Executive Overreach

Colombia has long possessed an exceptionally powerful chief executive. As noted in the Introduction, during the National Front period between the 1950s and the 1970s, the president become the main legislator in the system, using a combination of states of exception and delegated emergency powers to bypass Congress. This tendency worsened as the security situation in the country deteriorated and presidents relied increasingly heavily on states of exception, called at the time the "state of siege." Statistically, the country existed under a state of exception most of the time in the 1970s and 1980s. The heavy reliance on emergency powers raised concerns involving the quality of deliberative democracy (decisions were made in a technocratic fashion, bypassing the legislature), the abuse of constitutional rights (presidents used emergencies to carry out measures, such as the use of military tribunals to try civilians, that were unacceptable in times of normality), and the basic legitimacy and effectiveness of the state (even emergency measures were seen as increasingly incapable of responding to rising violence and disorder).[1]

One key goal of the Constituent Assembly in 1991 was to restore a more balanced separation of powers by taking measures to submit the president to stronger forms of control while strengthening and rationalizing Congress. The executive branch is considered in this chapter, whereas the legislative branch is treated in Chapter 10. The Assembly did not want to create a weak president, but it did seek to subject the executive branch to greater legal constraints while limiting the amount of time that the country would spend in abnormal legal states. For example, the Assembly maintained three different kinds of state of exception, but placed new limitations on the conditions for their use, duration, and scope. It also limited Congress's ability to delegate emergency lawmaking power to the president, and gave Congress new powers, such as voting motions of non-confidence on members

1. *See* Antonio Barreto Rozo, La generacion del estado de sitio: el juicio a la abnormalidad institucional en la Asamblea Nacional Constituyente de 1991 (2013) (analyzing the influence of the history of states of exception on the 1991 Constituent Assembly).

Colombian Constitutional Law: Leading Cases. Manuel José Cepeda Espinosa and David Landau.

of the Cabinet appointed by the president. Furthermore, the new Constitution included a range of institutions that were intended to check executive power as well as the actions of other political actors. These included the National Ombudsman and the Constitutional Court itself. Some powers were transferred to autonomous institutions, such as the Central Bank and other regulatory agencies. The National Inspector General and the Comptroller General, already existing organs, were granted more autonomy and powers. A new, independent National Prosecutor was created as an organ of the judicial branch, rather than the executive.

Since its inception, the Colombian Constitutional Court, like many other courts around the world, has wrestled with the problem of how to place effective limits on executive power. This is a topic, indeed, that is touched on in many other chapters of this book, for example on presidential restrictions on freedom of speech and of the press (see Chapter 5), presidential interference in the legislative process (see Chapter 10), and executive use of the constitutional amendment process to extend presidential term limits (see Chapter 11).

Even during times of institutional normality, the president before 1991 dominated the political order. The Court has tried to limit this power by subjecting executive powers to limits derived from the law and from the constitution itself, as noted in Section A below. Further, following the outlines of the constitution itself, the Court has developed a vision of the separation of powers that is flexible rather than formalistic—it invites harmonious collaboration among the branches in the pursuit of constitutional goals.[2] In this conception, the separation of powers is linked to the underlying substantive values of the 1991 Constitution: its purposes are to carry out the fundamental purposes of the text, such as the safeguarding of human dignity and the attainment of a social state of law. As Section B shows, the Court has limited executive concentrations of power when those concentrations threatened the achievement of these fundamental rights and principles, even when those concentrations purported to serve core state goals such as the maintenance of national security.

Finally, Section C considers the significant changes in the regime governing states of exception since the enactment of the Constitution of 1991. As it shows, the Court's doctrines since 1991 have exercised tighter control over declarations of states of exception themselves, as well as decrees issued during those states. Thus, although the states of exception found in the Constitution have not been rendered useless or impossible to deploy, the Court's doctrines have tended to reserve them for unexpected and severe crises. The result of the Court's doctrines and other institutional changes has been a sharp reduction in the percentage of time Colombia has spent in a state of institutional abnormality, from over 80 percent in the decades before 1991 to only about 18 percent in the 1990s.[3]

2. Article 113 states: "The branches of government are the legislative, the executive, and the judiciary. In addition to the organs which constitute them, there are others, autonomous and independent, for the execution of other functions of the state. The various organs of the state have separate functions but cooperate harmoniously for the realization of their goals."

3. *See* Rodrigo Uprimny, *The Constitutional Court and Control of Presidential Extraordinary Measures in Colombia*, 10 DEMOCRATIZATION 46, 65 tbl.3 (2003).

A. Limiting Executive Discretion

A basic goal of the 1991 Constitution was to restrict the arbitrary action by both state and nonstate authorities that had historically plagued citizens of Colombia. The *tutela* was designed, for example, as an instrument allowing citizens to get rapid redress against state (and in some cases private) actions that threatened their fundamental rights. At the same time, in a modern administrative state, discretion is inevitable. In the decision below, the Court distinguished "discretion" from "arbitrary action" in a sensitive context involving pervasive security or health crises in prisons. Discretionary administrative action, the Court maintained, was subject to strict restraints found in both the law and the Constitution.

Moreover, in this decision the Court distinguished situations of legal abnormality during specifically-defined states of exception (examined in Section C below) from situations of legal normality. During states of exception the president may temporarily combine his normal executive functions with some legislative functions, and may also suspend compliance with some existing legal requirements. But during normal periods, the executive branch must act in strict subjection to all existing legal and constitutional principles. Given the characteristics of Colombian history, and particularly the very powerful president that existed prior to 1991, these principles have proven significant for subjecting the president to the legal order and to the Constitution itself.

Decision C-318 of 1995 (per Justice Alejandro Martinez Caballero)

[In this decision, the Court analyzed the constitutionality of Article 168 of Law 65 of 1993,[4] which allowed the director of the prison system to call a "state of prison emergency" in some or all of the country's prisons in cases of grave threat due to disorder

4. Article 168 of the law states in part: "State of Prison Emergency. The General Director of INPEC (the National Prison Institute), with the consent of the Minister of Law and Justice, can decree a state of prison emergency in some or all penitentiaries . . . under the following circumstances:

a) When acts that gravely or imminently disturb or threaten prison order and security take place;
b) When grave problems of sanitation occur, which expose the prison center staff and inmates to contagion, or when hygienic conditions do not permit coexistence in that institution. . . .

In the cases dealt with in paragraph a) the General Director of INPEC has the power to take the necessary measures to overcome the situation presented, such as transfers, inmate isolation, rational use of extraordinary coercive measures and calls for support from the police. . . .

If staff members are involved in the events that alter the public order and security of the imprisonment center or centers, the Director of INPEC can suspend or replace them. . . .

In the cases dealt with in paragraph b) the Director of INPEC will call on the health or emergency authorities, both national and departmental and municipal, to obtain their assistance, which those entities are obliged to provide immediately in coordination with the affected prison centers.

The Director of INPEC can order the transfer of inmates to indicated places. Likewise, penitentiaries may be closed down. . . . Also, budgetary transfers and direct contracting of works necessary to overcome the emergency can be carried out, after due approval from the Institute's Directorate. The Director will also report the detainees' new locations to prison authorities. . . .

After the danger has been overcome and order has been reestablished, the Director shall report to the Directorate on the reasons for declaring the state of emergency and the justification for the measures implemented."

and violence or public health. Once such an emergency has been called, it allows the director to carry out various measures to overcome it, including the construction of new buildings and the transfer and isolation of inmates. In a unanimous decision, the Court upheld the law in question, while specifying limits on the exercise of discretionary administrative power in this and other contexts.]

The petitioner questions the attributions given to the administration in the prison emergency because it considers them ... because of their breadth ... to violate the rights of inmates. In addition some intervenors question the legitimacy of these states of emergency because they argue that the regime creates a state of exception that is not contemplated by the Constitution, and therefore the instrument is unconstitutional....

This Court does not share the opinion of those intervenors who assimilate the accused norm to the states of exception regulated by Articles 212 to 215 of the Constitution, because the state of prison emergency has a totally different legal meaning. The constitutional states of exception have, as one of their essential characteristics, the temporary assumption by the executive of legislative powers with the goal of overcoming a crisis....

During those states of exception, the president combines both administrative and legislative functions, with different intensities and limitations depending on the exceptional situation being confronted. In development of the foregoing, during a constitutional state of exception, the executive has the ability to restrict constitutional rights, but like the legislature cannot ignore their essential nucleus....

In contrast, the state of prison emergency does not imply that the executive assumes legislative functions because, in activating this instrument he is only carrying out the restrictions on the suspension of the right to physical liberty already determined by the legislature upon regulating the prison regime and fixing limits to the state of emergency at issue. Thus, the state of prison emergency is an administrative instrument, which simply ... allows the authorities to abbreviate certain procedures ... because of the crisis of security or health that they are confronting....

For all of the foregoing reasons, the Court holds it to be perfectly legitimate for the law ... to permit the Director of INPEC to decree a state of prison emergency. The hypotheses contemplated by the law are perfectly reasonable given situations of urgency, like those that gravely and imminently threaten or disturb order and prison security, or grave situations of a public health nature that expose people at the prison to contagion, or hygienic conditions that do not permit one to live there, or when there are serious threats of public calamity....

The Court believes that the essential element of the analysis ... is the administrative nature of the powers of INPEC.... This means that the accused norm cannot be interpreted in an isolated way without taking into consideration the norms and principles that govern the exercise of powers of the administration, especially when these have a discretionary content....

This point is essential because the actor ... insists that the attributions of INPEC are indeterminate, since its second clause allows the director "to take the necessary measures to overcome the situation presented." From this he infers that the law confers discretionary functions that are unconstitutional because they are outside of any control, they might legitimate arbitrary conduct by INPEC, and they ignore the submission of the administration to the principle of legality.

The Court does not share this argument because one cannot confuse discretion with arbitrariness. . . .

This difference between discretion and arbitrariness has a clear constitutional foundation in Colombia, since the Constitution allows administrative discretion but excludes arbitrariness in the exercise of public functions. Therefore, discretionary power is a necessary and essential legal tool in certain cases for good public administration, as it provides the public administrator with the possibility of making decisions, and using good judgment, without the rigidity of a detailed regulation that does not correspond to the situation that is being dealt with. Arbitrariness, however, is excluded from the Colombian legal order. In fact, even though the Colombian Constitution does not expressly include "a prohibition on arbitrariness by public authorities," as stated in Article 9-3 of the Spanish Constitution, this principle can be derived from specific norms of our Constitution. Thus, Article 1 defines Colombia as a social state of law founded on the prevalence of the general interest, which excludes the possibility that officers may exert their functions in a whimsical manner. In addition, Article 2[5] sets limits on the purposes of the state and the objectives of public authorities, and states that attributions exercised by authorities must be aimed at carrying out constitutional values and not at satisfying the officer's whim. This is complemented in Article 123,[6] which expressly states that public servants must serve the state and the community, and that they must carry out their functions in the manner foreseen by the Constitution, the law and regulations. Finally, Article 209[7] defines the principles that guide administrative agencies, and it pinpoints that these agencies are intended to serve general interests and that they must exercise power in an egalitarian and impartial manner.

In agreement with this, administrative power, and especially discretionary power, is subject to the principle of reasonableness, which states that under no circumstance may power become indefinite or limitless. In fact, it is subject to constitutional parameters because "in the social state of law, competences are regulated, and

5. Article 2 states: "The essential goals of the state are to serve the community, promote the general prosperity, and guarantee the effectiveness of the principles, rights, and duties stipulated by the Constitution; to facilitate the participation of everyone in the decisions that affect them and in the economic, political, administrative, and cultural life of the nation; to defend national independence, maintain territorial integrity, and ensure peaceful coexistence and the enforcement of a just order. The authorities of the Republic are established in order to protect all individuals residing in Colombia, in their life, honor, property, beliefs, and other rights and freedoms, and in order to ensure the fulfillment of the social duties of the state and individuals."

6. Article 123 states in part: "Civil servants are at the service of the state and of the community; they shall perform their function in the form prescribed by the Constitution, statutes, and regulations."

7. Article 209 states in part: "The administrative function is at the service of the general interest and is developed on the basis of the principles of equality, morality, efficiency, economy, speed, impartiality, and publicity through the decentralization, delegation, and deconcentration of functions."

the margin of discretion for public officers must be exercised within the philosophy of material values and principles of the new Constitution. . . . " [T]he power mentioned above is also limited by the definition of its field of action, by the determination of the purposes to be achieved, and by the determination of the means by which the action must be implemented. This means that power must always be understood as limited by the execution of specific means that have been assigned by the legal order. Thus, administrative power is only legitimate so long as it is exercised in accordance with the circumstances . . . established by the law that grants the power. That is why . . . the Administrative Code, under whose definitions the Court considers that INPEC's faculties must be interpreted during the state of prison emergency, clearly pinpoints that "as long as the content of a general or specific decision is discretionary, it must be adapted to the purposes of the law authorizing it, and it must be proportional to the facts that originated it."

Thus, discretionary action does not elude judicial control: it is possible to request annulment by the administrative courts of a discretionary act, either because the motives invoked to justify the act are false or because the act does not aim at achieving a legitimate public interest. . . .

In the case under examination, the state of prison emergency grants administrative power of a discretionary nature to the INPEC Director . . . , which provides him or her with flexibility as to the appropriate circumstances in which to adopt a specific action. In fact, the officer making the decision has a set of options among which he must decide according to criteria of opportunity and convenience and which are restricted, of course, by the law that granted the discretionary power.

This discretion seems reasonable because the unforeseen and complex nature of the security and sanitation crisis in the prisons justifies the law in granting authorities broader freedom to make, within the law's framework, the most convenient decision to face the crisis, since the law cannot determine in advance, in an abstract way, all the measures that are legally susceptible to be adopted. But . . . the liberty to make decisions under the boundaries of the law set cannot be confused with arbitrary action, which is action outside of the legal framework. . . .

[T]he Director of INPEC, both at a general level and when exercising discretionary powers derived from the state of emergency, is obligated to respect the constitutional rights of inmates. This limitation works, according to this Court, in a double sense. On the one hand, the prison authority cannot, under any circumstance, carry out any conduct that violates the constitutional rights that imprisoned persons retain. . . . On the other hand, when it is necessary to limit a right, the prison or penitentiary authority has a duty to take measures that are proportional. . . .

In particular, the Court finds that the measures adopted during the prison emergency cannot have the character of punishment against inmates, since they should be aimed exclusively at "overcoming the situation presented" as stated expressly . . . in the article. If those powers could give a power of punishment to the Director of INPEC, . . . then the article would be unconstitutional because it would violate the rules of due process and the principle of legality . . . in administrative sanctions. . . .

In the Colombian legal order, a transfer is not a punishment, but rather a managerial decision given available physical resources. . . .

In turn, isolation has two dimensions: it is both a sanction and a preventive action. Considering the nature of the state of prison emergency, the Court holds that the isolation of inmates contemplated in [the law] is of a preventive nature, as its sole purpose is to prevent the extension or continuation of the critical situation[. Thus,] the use of emergency powers to impose isolation to penalize inmates rather than to overcome the emergency would be an abuse of power. Once the security and sanitation problems have been overcome, the isolation must cease, given its preventive nature.

Additionally . . . , the adoption of these two specific measures must be appropriate, reasonable, and proportional and must respect the constitutional rights of inmates. For example, isolation that constitutes cruel or degrading treatment or which violates the dignity of inmates are not allowed, because these measures not only violate the Constitution but also clear norms of international human rights. Additionally, because of the principle of proportionality, the prison authority can only impose isolation when it is impossible to adopt appropriate measures for the overcoming of the crisis that are less harmful to the constitutional rights of the inmates.

Thus, the [law] does not confer on the Director of INPEC any arbitrary or unlimited power but a discretionary power that is subject to judicial and disciplinary controls . . . according to which the powers derived from a state of prison emergency should be interpreted in light of general and constitutional principles governing the validity of administrative acts. Under that understanding, the Court finds no constitutional flaw in the [law]. . . .

B. The Separation of Powers and National Security

For many years, Colombia has been in the midst of an internal civil conflict of varying degrees of intensity. The law examined here was passed during a difficult period in which security concerns were pressing. In response, Congress passed Law 684 of 2001, the so-called National Security Law. The law was broad and ambiguous in its core provision; however, it gave the president sweeping powers to safeguard national security. First, it created a new institution of government called the National Power, which was defined as the "capacity of the Colombian state to offer all of its potential in order to respond to situations that endanger the exercise of rights and liberties, and to maintain independence, integrity, autonomy, and national sovereignty. . . ." The National Power was directed by the president and his National Security Council, and charged with planning and implementing programs related to security, economic prosperity, and democracy. The law also authorized the president to call for a general national mobilization during states of exception.[8] Finally,

8. Article 62 of the law states: "[Mobilization] is [defined as] a permanent process of integration that consists in applying in all times and places the grouping of norms, precepts, strategies and actions that will permit the National Power to be adapted to . . . the public and private spheres in order to attend to and overcome any

the law contemplated the creation of "theaters of military operations"[9] in conflict-prone areas. These theaters would be governed by special rules: they would be under the power of military authorities commanded directly by the president, and their population would be required to register their name, address, and occupation with these authorities.

In the seven-to-two decision below, the Court struck the law down in its entirety. As the excerpt shows, the Court focused on two general problems with the law. The first was a violation of basic principles of the separation of powers, as according to the Court, in the name of public security it potentially allowed the president to consolidate too much power that properly belonged to other institutions of government.

The Court's vision of the separation of powers laid out in this decision is flexible—it emphasizes the statement in Article 113 that institutions of state have "separate functions" but should "cooperate harmoniously" in order to achieve fundamental constitutional goals including the safeguarding of human dignity and other basic rights and the social transformation of the state through the achievement of a social state of law. At the same time, the Constitutional Court's conception of the separation of powers is closely tied to the underlying substantive values of the Colombian Constitution. In effect, the Court emphasizes the role of restrictions on executive power in defending fundamental constitutional and human rights. Along these lines, one basic principle commonly found both in Colombian and comparative law is the "legal reserve" principle—restrictions on constitutional rights should ordinarily be established through democratic debate in Congress, and not through the unilateral action of the executive.[10] In the Court's view, the concentration of power in this law threatened these underlying constitutional principles.

A second problem identified by the Court was a blurring of abnormality and normality, or in other words the bleeding of standards temporarily applicable during states of exception into permanent ordinary law. The Constitution might tolerate some concentration of executive power and limitations on individual rights as a temporary measure during

emergency provoked by a public calamity or natural disaster. During states of exception, the president may, by decree, call a National Mobilization."

9. Article 54 of the law states: "Theater of Operations. A theater of operations is understood as a geographic area where it has been proven that possible threats to our constitutional order, or to the sovereignty, independence, and integrity of our territory exist. . . . [T]he President of the Republic will be empowered to . . . activate these Theaters of Military Operations, establish their scope, appoint commanders, set the extent of their authority and establish special control and protective measures for civilians and for resources and facilities in the given area according to international humanitarian law. Once the Theater of Operations is established, the president will have immediate command and operational control over all police forces and state security bodies deployed in the area. Upon establishing the Theater of Operations, the president will notify the Public Prosecutor's Office, the Inspector General's Office, and the Ombudsman's Office. In these Theaters of Operations, the president may confer on the commander . . . in the area the authority to carry out his instructions. Consequently, the instructions given by the president will be implemented immediately and will take priority over those issued by local governors and mayors. . . . The commander . . . will coordinate with the local civil authority on the registration of persons [in terms of their] identity, profession or trade, and address. Citizens who either change their address within the Theater of Operations or arrive there will have to appear before the corresponding civil authority for registration."

10. *See, e.g.*, ALLEN BREWER-CARIAS, CONSTITUTIONAL PROTECTION OF HUMAN RIGHTS IN LATIN AMERICA: A COMPARATIVE STUDY OF AMPARO PROCEEDINGS 26 (2009).

properly declared states of exception in response to true public crises (see Section C below), but it does not tolerate these measures as a permanent state of affairs.

Decision C-251 of 2002 (per Justices Eduardo Montealegre Lynett and Clara Inés Vargas Hernández)

Are the principles and basic institutional mechanisms of the national security and defense system included in [the law] in agreement with the principles and the model of the state established in our Constitution . . . .

One of the main goals of the Colombian authorities is the defense of national integrity and the preservation of public order and peaceful coexistence. . . .

Accordingly, our Constitution authorizes the Congress to adopt a defense and security system through which authorities in general, and especially the president, can establish policies and specific plans. . . . However, to be legitimate, any law on security and defense must fully respect the Constitution and the international commitments made by Colombia in the fields of international human rights and international humanitarian law. The law must abide by the Constitution, which is the highest set of norms, and it should also be adjusted to the democratic and social state of law established by our Constitution, which is founded on certain principles and institutional structures that cannot be disregarded by authorities. . . .

The principle according to which the Colombian state is founded on human dignity, on the prevalence of the rights of man, and on service to the community, has normative consequences that are very precise, both at the general level and particularly in the design of strategies of security and defense.

That constitutional formula proscribes any trace of authoritarianism. In effect, as is known, totalitarian states, like Nazism and fascism, which developed in Europe between the two world wars had some distinctive features: they were not only regimes of terror but also nations in which there were no limits between state and society, in fact society was absorbed by the state. Also, in these types of societies people were at the service of the state, which was considered an end in itself. In radical opposition to that type of philosophy, the Constitution of 1991 . . . makes dignity and the rights of the person the basis of the state. . . . Thus, it is clear that our constitutional order proscribes policies that would permit an absorption of society by the state, or the instrumentalization of persons for the aggrandizement or glorification of the state.

These characteristic features of the Colombian State have evident implications for security and defense policy. If our state is founded on human dignity and rights, then the preservation of public order is not an end in itself, but, as established by the Court, it is "subordinated to the respect for human dignity," and, therefore "preserving public order by overturning people's freedom is incompatible with democracy." Furthermore, if the state serves the community and the people, then obviously its authorities should protect and safeguard the security of persons instead of involving people in the protection of state security.

It is clear that adducing the general interest or the need to secure peaceful coexistence and public order cannot justify per se limitations or restrictions on constitutional rights, since there is no point in sacrificing these rights to allegedly ensure the conditions required to enjoy them. . . .

[I]t is the duty of the state to safeguard basic public peace and the conditions for peaceful coexistence, as without them people would be unable to fully enjoy their rights. This duty is so important that international instruments grant power to authorities when faced with especially serious situations to decree states of exception and to restrict the enjoyment of certain human rights. However, the obligation of states to ensure peace and order does not mean that authorities may forget their duty to respect and protect human rights. Therefore, security policies must always respect the limits imposed by human rights. . . .

The Court notes that the foregoing legal demands, derived from the basic constitutional formula that defines the Colombian state, continue operating in situations of armed conflict like the one that this country has experienced for many years. In effect, not only are the constitutional limits applicable to those situations but also, the Constitution establishes expressly that in "all cases" the rules of international humanitarian law must be respected.[11] International humanitarian law places minimum limits on the protection of human rights during armed conflict. This signifies that the basic principles of international humanitarian law, explained in detail by this Court in prior decisions, establish limits for security and defense policies.

[The Court next emphasized the importance of the principle of the separation of powers for security policy.]

[T]he separation of powers is . . . an essential mechanism for avoiding arbitrariness, maintaining the exercise of authority within permissible limits, and ensuring liberty and security. The logic of this disposition . . . is essential: the division of the public function between different branches allows power never to rest in the hands of one person or entity, so that the various organs can control each other reciprocally. . . .

The constitutional need to submit state action to law, and the principles of the separation of powers and popular sovereignty, have the following direct consequence: the law plays a transcendental role in the regulation and restriction of constitutional rights. In effect, in general the law establishes . . . a legal reserve for the regulation of constitutional rights. . . .

This legal reserve in the limitation and configuration of constitutional rights serves two purposes: it is a mechanism to avoid arbitrariness, because not only does it ensure that individuals know their rights but also stops the government from unjustifiably restricting them. The principle of legality is therefore a development of the rule of law. But it is also a development of the democratic state, because it allows restrictions on rights associated with certain security policies to be broadly debated in the paradigmatic democratic institution, which is the Congress. . . .

The definition of Colombia as a social state of law, the separation of powers, and the principle of legality, have obvious consequences regarding policies of security and defense. On the one hand, although the president has the responsibility to

11. With respect to states of exception, Article 214 of the Constitution states in part: "Neither human rights nor fundamental freedoms may be suspended. In all cases, the rules of international humanitarian law shall be observed."

ensure public peace and there is a duty of collaboration among state institutions in this field (Article 113[12]), security policies cannot infringe the principle of the separation of powers. It would be illegitimate then in the field of security and defense for all state bodies to be subjected to the government.... Also, given our legal framework, restrictions on constitutional rights must be established through a law, and if they refer to basic aspects of fundamental rights, they must be incorporated in a statutory law. Finally, the law must define in detail the specific obligations derived from the duties of citizens regarding public peace.

A systematic read of the law shows that its core is the so-called "National Power...."

According to Article 3 of the law, the National Power is the "capacity of the Colombian state to offer all of its potential in order to respond to situations that endanger the exercise of rights and liberties, and to maintain independence, integrity, autonomy, and national sovereignty.... "

[A] careful read of the [law] allows us to conclude that the National Power is not simply a reference to already existing state bodies and institutions, [but rather] the law seeks to create a new institutional reality—this National Power—with specific functions, duties and bodies....

[T]he law at issue would create a power-above-powers, the so-called National Power, which would have preeminence over the other branches of government in everything concerning national goals to be freely defined by the president himself with the support of the high commanders of the armed and police forces.... [T]he National Power will cover the entire state, including the Congress and judiciary, and it is directed by the president and the National Security Council, which is composed of governmental agents and high military and police officials. In turn, the distinct components of that National Power, which includes the other branches of government, must adjust themselves to the policies established by the government, since the law establishes that national defense is "the integration and coordinated action of the National Power." Finally the objectives to be achieved by that National Power are not only defined by the president with the direct assistance of military and police officials, but also have enormous breadth because they relate to almost all aspects of life[. T]he law states that they include the provision of means and mechanisms to make Colombia safer and more prosperous "especially in three spheres: achieving security with effective diplomacy and military forces ready to fight and win, increasing the prosperity of the economy, and promoting democracy." This signifies that under the law, the National Power is not only occupied with the classic functions of security, defense, and conservation of public order, but projects over almost all spheres of life for Colombians, and thus the National Power could become involved not only in models of development but ... also in the general political dynamic....

12. Article 113 states: "The branches of government are the legislative, the executive, and the judiciary. In addition to the organs which constitute them, there are others, autonomous and independent, for the execution of other functions of the state. The various organs of the state have separate functions but cooperate harmoniously for the realization of their goals."

No further analysis is needed to conclude that the National Power, as it has been regulated by this law, clashes directly with at least four basic constitutional principles: The separation of powers, the democratic principle, the preeminence of civil over military authority, and the president's command over the armed forces.

On the one hand, the law under examination ruptures the separation of powers because it subordinates the other branches of government to a National Power controlled by the president. In fact, this provision not only disregards the institutional framework established by our Constitution, which enshrines the independence of the three branches, but it also results in an excessive concentration of powers in the president, which is contrary to the rule of law, as reciprocal control among state bodies would disappear and all the branches would become part of this supreme national power in the hands of the president. This means that the law orders a fusion of the branches which the Constitution has separated in order to carry out what the president wishes, which not only threatens the separation of powers but also the rights of persons.

On the other hand, and which is equally serious, the National Power violates the democratic principle at least for the following two reasons: first, national goals are set exclusively by the government with no participation by the Congress, the main forum for democratic debate; . . . while it is true that the president is charged with conserving and reestablishing public order, that task should be exercised not only within the guidelines established by the legislature, but also subject to political control exercised by Congress.

[Second], the definition of the main elements included in security and defense strategies would be totally beyond the supervision and control of citizens and elected bodies. [Under the law,] the distinct primary and secondary documents are written by the Ministry of Defense and in part evaluated by the National Security Council to later be approved by the president, which signifies that neither the Congress nor the citizenry can be directly involved with their design. And if that were not enough, all those documents and deliberations are secret, since [the law] establishes that the primary and secondary documents, as well as the deliberations and acts of the councils, have a classified character for an indefinite period of time. One notes that those documents and deliberations do not refer exclusively to public order but also to economic, social, and political themes, as has already been explained, which shows the gravity of the effect on the principle of publicity. . . .

Lastly, the institutional design of the National Power undermines the principle requiring the subordination of military authority to civil authority because it undermines the principle that the police force should not deliberate on national policy (Article 219[13]). The reason is simple: the development of this National Power rests on a so-called planning activity, which implies the drafting of documents containing the goals of the security and defense system, as well as the different plans and programs

13. Article 219 states: "The public force is not deliberative: It shall not be able to assemble except by order of the legitimate authority nor direct petitions except on matters connected with the service and morale of the respective corps and in accordance with an Act."

required to achieve these goals.... The law orders the high command of the police force to discuss Colombia's challenges regarding political, economic and social issues and to design permanent strategies and plans to face such challenges.

The foregoing considerations are sufficient to declare the law creating the national power to be unconstitutional. But the situation may be even more serious, because that figure could affect other principles and constitutional values as well, since it may involve citizens in the National Power....

[T]he National Power and the security and defense system go beyond the sphere of the state because they imply the eventual permanent mobilization of the entire population to accomplish very broad "national goals" whose design corresponds to the Ministry of the Defense and to the high command of the police force, and which would be approved by the president. This institutional framework is totally inadmissible from the point of view of our constitutional principles because it not only infringes several provisions of the Constitution, but it also creates a type of state which is clearly incompatible with the fundamental constitutional regulations defining the nature of the Colombian state. In fact, besides violating the above mentioned constitutional principles (the democratic principle, the separation of powers, and the subordination of military authority to civil authority), the law also opens the way to the establishment of a totalitarian state by incorporating private sectors and individuals in the National Power, thus disregarding the autonomy of civil society and seriously affecting pluralism.

[T]he Court's analysis shows that the contested law would blend society and the state within one single National Power headed by the president, who would set national goals that all Colombians would need to support, and this is clearly contrary to the constitutional definition of the Colombian state. As has been explained in detail in the present decision, our Constitution recognizes the autonomy of civil society, as well as the political and ideological freedom of individuals, and it opposes any totalitarian effort aimed at the absorption of society by the state....

The foregoing violations of the autonomy of society and pluralism are supplemented by the manner in which this law imposes open-ended obligations on citizens in matters of public order, by incorporating them into the National Power and the system of security and defense.

The duties placed on individuals should be governed by the legal reserve principle ..., the obligations of people must be determined by the legislature, which should determine not only their scope but also the sanctions that can be imposed for disregarding them.

This law opens the door to the imposition of duties outside the law, since it incorporates individuals into the National Power and submits them to the direction of the government in order to achieve broad objects defined by the president. In other words, it permits duties to have a source other than the Constitution or law. Individuals not only must come to the mobilizations decreed by the government but must also be subject to duties not specified by the law and outside of democratic processes....

[The Court went on to consider some of the problems with specific provisions of the law. In particular, it examined the provisions creating theaters of war governed by military commanders rather than civilian authority and in which all citizens would need to register their name, profession, and address.]

[T]he norm says that the governors and mayors will be subject to the commanders of their theaters of operations, which violates the democratic principle of the primacy of civil power above military power. That situation casts aside the purpose of having limits between state and society, because as the Court has said: "The basis of the separation between the civil and the military is not a functional distribution of state tasks, but an essential principle in the organization of relationships between the state apparatus and the governed, which can be expressed as follows: the exercise of the public forces must be the minimum necessary to maintain the conditions of liberty permitting the exercise of fundamental rights. The enormous destructive capacity of the military power and its invasive and defense connotation makes it an improper entity to manage the everyday security of citizens."

[T]he Court has accepted that when a state of exception has been declared, limits on the freedom of movement can be established in such a way that circulation is temporarily restricted. However, we have also concluded that those restrictions cannot go to the extreme of provoking the uprooting of persons. . . .

[The law] designs a mechanism for registration of the population and demands that people send information when they change their residence. . . . It is broader [than measures considered in the past during states of emergency] because it includes a duty to reveal one's profession or office, which threatens other fundamental rights. Think for example of the situation of an activist belonging to a contested political group or a priest for a minority religion. The limitation on the freedom of movement and other rights through this mechanism does not help to protect liberty, but on the contrary facilitates the total control of the state over its subjects. . . .

[The Court finally discussed an argument made by some intervenors, according to which the "theater of operations" concept should be held constitutional because the Court had previously upheld "public order zones" during a state of internal commotion declared in 1996:]

As one can easily appreciate, the proposed analogy actually demonstrates the unconstitutionality of the measure. A careful analysis of the nature of the special zones of public order shows that they only make sense within a state of exception. . . . And it is within that context that the jurisprudence should be interpreted.

In accordance with Article 27 of the American Convention on Human Rights . . . , the suspension of rights can only be carried out during states of exception and during periods of time that are strictly limited by the demands of the situation. Thus, in order for the theater of operations to be able to limit the rights of persons, it would have needed to be conditioned by the prior declaration of a state of exception. That did not occur here, since as the law states, theaters of operations may be established [by the president] during situations of normality. . . .

The Court clarifies that the foregoing argument does not mean that the design of the law at issue on theaters of operation can be adopted during a state of exception, since the stated design—including the registration and control of the population and the loss of the supremacy of civil power to military officials—are materially unconstitutional, including during states of exception. We simply point out that the present regulation ignores the distinction between normality and abnormality defined in the Constitution and in human rights treaties. . . .

We cannot sustain that there are mechanisms for restricting rights that are more serious during states of normality than during states of exception. The state as a whole requires a system of security that protects the legal order. . . . However, that objective cannot be carried out through any means, which would end up instrumentalizing people in the service of the state and forgetting that the true relationship should be the opposite. The existence and function of the state can only be justified by service to society. In consequence the Court concludes that the figure of the theater of operations created by [the law] is also unconstitutional.

[The Court thus struck down the entire law. Justices Marco Gerardo Monroy Cabra and Rodrigo Escobar Gil dissented and argued that the majority had misinterpreted the meaning of the law. They stated in part that: "The three most important concepts in the law [the National Power, the theater of operations, and national mobilization] could have been interpreted to be in agreement with the Constitution; such a [conditional] interpretation should have been accepted out of respect for democracy . . .; The majority of the arguments adduced to declare [the law] unconstitutional come from things not explicit in it but which instead were inferred by the Court, which has led the Court to irrelevant conclusions. . . .]

C. States of Exception

Colombia has suffered public order problems of varied intensity, origin, and impact for two centuries, often deriving from violence and armed conflict. The 1886 Constitution allowed the president to declare a state of siege in case of grave perturbations of internal public order or of external war. After making such a declaration, the president could issue decrees with the force of law, signed by all the cabinet ministers. During a state of siege the president could restrict basic rights and suspend congressional statutes incompatible with the presidential decrees. No time limits existed. Legislative decrees were geared not only to solve public order problems but also to facilitate the exercise of governance by bypassing Congress and allowing the president to legislate directly. Thus, states of emergency became highly routinized within the Colombian system.

The Supreme Court of Justice, prior to the creation of the 1991 Constitution, held that it lacked the jurisdiction to substantively review the declaration of a state of siege because the issue was wholly within the competence of the president. It did review the legislative decrees issued during a state of siege, but it rarely struck them down. As the public order crisis deepened, the country was governed under a stage of exception with great frequency—82 percent of the time between 1970 and 1991.[14]

14. Uprimny, *supra* note 3.

This excessive use of emergency powers caused several problems. First, it worsened the sense of human rights abuses in the country, as it contributed to a regime in which the government as well as guerrilla and paramilitary groups were routinely violating basic human rights. Second, it contributed to an institutional dynamic where the president was too strong and the other branches of government, particularly Congress, were too weak. Finally, the emergency regime itself lost efficacy as it came to be seen as a chronic and routine event, which could do little to overcome Colombia's long-running civil conflict.

The 1991 Constituent Assembly saw the reform of the emergency powers regime as a major goal of the Assembly. After an intense debate, the Assembly decided to abolish the state of siege mechanism and replace it with a more nuanced regime consisting of three distinct instruments, each designed to deal with a distinct threat. First, the Constitution allows the president to declare a "state of exterior war" in the event of major international conflicts; this instrument has never been used. Second, it contemplates a "state of economic, social, and ecological emergency" for events threatening a "grave calamity" of an economic, social, or environmental nature—this instrument is examined in more detail in a note following the cases below. Finally, and most important, the Constitution created a "state of internal commotion" for internal civil conflict and disorder. This instrument is much more heavily regulated than the old state of siege.

The "state of internal commotion" is regulated by Article 213 of the 1991 Constitution, whereas Article 214 enunciates additional limitations that must be respected during any state of exception. The state of internal commotion may be declared by the president (with the signature of his entire cabinet) if there is a "grave disruption of the public order imminently threatening institutional stability, the security of the state, or the peaceful coexistence of the citizenry, and which cannot be met by the use of the ordinary powers of the police authorities."

It is worth highlighting several key points limiting this state of exception. First, the state of internal commotion is limited in duration—it can be called for only 90 days, and this period can be extended only twice, with the second extension requiring the prior approval of the Senate. Further, the measures taken are not permanent, but rather expire at the end of the state of internal commotion. Second, there is a duty not to suspend "human rights [or] fundamental freedoms," and "the rules of international humanitarian law shall be observed" in all cases. Third, any measures taken must be "strictly essential" to deal with the causes of the disruption. Finally, Congress was given the duty to adopt a statutory law further regulating these states of exception. Congress exercised this power by passing the Statutory Law of States of Exception (Law 137 of 1994); most of this law was upheld by the Constitutional Court in **Decision C-179 of 1994 (per Justice Carlos Gaviria Diaz)**.

The general approach of the 1991 Constituent Assembly was to maintain the Constitution's traditional distinction between normal and abnormal periods, rather than (as for example in the United States) trying to incorporate the management of true crises through a model of "business as usual."[15] At the same time, the new constitution attempted to

15. *See* Oren Gross, *Chaos and Rules: Should Responses to Violent Crises Always Be Constitutional?*, 112 Yale L.J. 1011, 1043 (2003).

place a number of different kinds of limits on these emergencies—textual restrictions on the calling of emergencies and the measures that may be used therein, limits based on international law, temporal restrictions on the length of emergencies, political control by Congress, and judicial control by the Court. In utilizing so many different kinds of limitations, the Constituent Assembly may have reacted to the difficulty of effectively controlling power in these moments, and uncertainty about which approach would ultimately prove effective.[16]

The constitutional text explicitly gives the Constitutional Court the power to review presidential decrees issued during states of exception. These decrees must immediately and automatically be sent to the Court for its review. However, the text is more ambiguous on declarations of states of exception themselves. Nonetheless, and in sharp contrast to the Supreme Court prior to 1991, the Constitutional Court quickly established that it had the power to review declarations of states of exception and could nullify the entire emergency if the facts were of insufficient gravity or nature to justify its declaration.

The Constitutional Court has since played a significant role in limiting declarations of states of emergency; indeed, this role has been called "one of the most important and original interventions of the Constitutional Court."[17] Presidents have attempted to declare a state of internal commotion seven times since 1991. Of these attempts, three have been declared totally unconstitutional (Decisions C-300 of 1994, C-466 of 1995, and C-070 of 2009), two have been partially upheld and partially struck down (Decisions C-027 of 1996 and C-802 of 2002), and two have been upheld (Decisions C-556 of 1992 and C-031 of 1993). Between 1991 and 2002, the country spent only 17.5 percent of the time under some kind of state of exception, down from over 80 percent in immediately prior decades.[18] Since 2002, there have been no successfully declared states of internal commotion, despite the fact that between 2004 and 2010 the harshest and most successful crackdown on guerrilla groups occurred during the presidency of Alvaro Uribe. From 2010 to 2012 President Juan Manuel Santos continued the military offensive, and then initiated a peace process with the guerrillas without calling a ceasefire. Thus, the most effective policies concerning the armed conflict have been designed and executed without declaring states of exception.

1. Review of the Declaration of a State of Internal Commotion

The president elected in 2002, Alvaro Uribe, took office in a difficult and violent environment in the country. He based his political campaign on the recovery of security in Colombia by means of a tough, confrontational policy called "democratic security." He announced amendments to the Constitution, arguing that the legal framework in force, according to the interpretations by the Constitutional Court, prevented the re-establishment of order. The same day he took office, homemade rockets fired by the FARC guerrillas hit the presidential palace, just several meters away from the capitol building where the ceremony was taking place.

16. *See* Bruce Ackerman, *The Emergency Constitution*, 113 YALE L.J. 1029, 1031 (2004).

17. *See* Uprimny, *supra* note 3, at 47.

18. *See id.* at 65 tbl.3.

The new president quickly declared a state of internal commotion in order to enact measures to combat the guerrilla groups. The declaration rested on several key facts, among others: (1) killings and other attacks against defenseless civilians, as well as crimes against humanity carried out by organized armed groups with significant financial power due to their participation in illegal activities; (2) acts of terrorism in recent weeks against the civil population and state infrastructure (including the attack on the president's official residence); and (3) threats to state officials from drug trafficking, extortion, and kidnapping.

The Court has reviewed declarations of states of exception since its inception in 1992. Nonetheless, President Uribe's minister of the interior stated that the Constitutional Court lacked the power to control the constitutionality of the declaration of a state of internal commotion, as it was a political and not a legal act. He thus said that the declaration was being sent to the Court as a mere "gesture of courtesy." Further, Article 3 of the declaration itself stated that "legislative decrees issued under and as a consequence of this declaration will be submitted to the Constitutional Court," thus implying that the declaration itself would not be susceptible to the Court's control. However, in the decision below, the Court examined the substantive constitutionality of the declaration using its accepted standards of review. Although it upheld most of it in a decision that was eight-to-one on its core argument, the Court also established limits on the scope of the state of internal commotion, effectively reducing it to a focus on truly exceptional events and on protecting potential victims.

Decision C-802 of 2002 (per Justice Jaime Córdoba Triviño)

[The Court began by recounting the context within which the 1991 Constitution dealt with states of exception, briefly examining the state of siege regime that existed before 1991.]

The abuses in the state of siege regime made it necessary for the Constituent Assembly of 1991 to construct a constitutional regime on states of exception that would be adjusted to the conditions of the democratic and social state of law. From the first debates of the National Constituent Assembly, serious questions were raised against the then-current regime of states of exception: the abuse of its nature as an exceptional mechanism for the reestablishment of public order and its transformation into a permanent mechanism for the executive to exercise exceptional powers; the erosion of the legislative power of Congress before the proliferation of norms of exception that ended up regulating all spaces of social life, with a consequent fracturing of the democratic principle and permanent restrictions on public liberties. Also, there was no distinction between the norms applicable to external war and for internal commotion, phenomena that have a distinct nature, and the powers conferred based on Article 121 of the Constitution were so broad that, in the words of the members of the Constituent Assembly themselves, in all cases the president was left with the attributions necessary to assume a total war.

For all of these reasons, it was necessary that the new regulation on states of exception consecrate greater powers for external war and fewer for events of internal commotion and, in relation to this, it was pertinent to establish limits tending to avoid excesses. . . . It is not difficult to conclude, then, that the reason for so many different provisions fixing limits on the power of the executive during states of exception was to prevent the excesses that had occurred with the state of siege. . . .

Article 214 of the Constitution, as a limit on legislative decrees issued by the executive under states of internal commotion, prohibits the suspension of human rights and fundamental liberties.

By making reference to "human rights and fundamental liberties," the Constitution refers to the rights and liberties recognized and guaranteed by what constitutional doctrine has called the constitutional block, that is, those legal norms that, even though they are not expressly consecrated in internal law, are fully applied in it. . . .

In the case of the constitutional law of exception, the constitutional block is composed of the Constitution, the instruments of international humanitarian law, the treaties consecrating human rights and rights that may not be suspended during states of exception and the statutory law [of states of exception].

[The Court then considered the contents of the constitutional block, focusing on relevant provisions in the International Covenant on Civil and Political Rights (ICCPR) and the American Convention on Human Rights.]

(1) Principle of intangibility of rights

The instruments exclude many rights from the scope of the extraordinary powers that are given to the executive during states of exception. In other words, one of the first limits imposed by the cited international norms is the impossibility of restricting, through exceptional measures, the essential nucleus of certain rights.

The American Convention considers as intangible the rights to legal personality, to life, to personal integrity, the prohibition of slavery and servitude, the principle against ex post facto laws, liberty of conscience and religion, the rights of the family, the right to a name, the rights of the child, the right to nationality, and political rights. The only intangible right in the [ICCPR] different from the ones already mentioned, is the prohibition against being incarcerated for the mere fact of owing a debt. . . .

(2) Principles of necessity and proportionality

The proclamation of a state of exception is only understood to be legitimate when it is motivated by a situation of grave danger to the life of the nation, or in the terms of the American Convention, a threat to the independence or security of the state. This [also] demands that the measures taken under the state of exception be strictly limited to those suitable to confronting the threat to the state, in other words, those which are necessary and proportional.

On this issue the European doctrine is relevant, which establishes that measures are legitimate only if (i) it is not feasible to use less serious measures, (ii) they are apt to contribute to the resolution of . . . the threat, (iii) the disruption cannot be ended through ordinary means, and (iv) there is no other measure of exception that will generate less impact on the protection of rights and guarantees.

(3) Principle of temporality

The specific characteristic of the application of measures of exception are their limited duration in time; in this sense, the international instruments studied oblige the states to apply such measures only for a strictly necessary period of time to overcome the facts that are threatening the nation's life. The principle of temporality also includes the need for the effects of the exceptional measures to have a defined duration and that, as a consequence of this criterion, the damage done to individuals affected by them must be repaired. . . .

(4) Principle of legality

The state of exception does not imply ignoring the basic postulates of the rule of law. International instruments demand that the state of exception be, above all, a system of powers subjected to the rule of law, with defined limits on state action, minimum requirements for measures adopted, and a list of applicable prohibitions.

From the principle of legality one derives that of judicial protection, on the understanding that it is precisely in the states of exception where we must reinforce mechanisms of control. . . .

(5) Requirements of form. Proclamation and notice

In addition to the principles that govern the utilization of states of exception and the restriction of guarantees, supranational norms set two procedural requirements whose purpose is to facilitate control by the other states in multilateral organizations. The first is the proclamation or declaration. . . . Notification, on the other hand, consists of the duty on the state to notify, through the Secretary General, the respective multilateral organization [of the declaration] and . . . the provisions it intends to restrict, the reason for those restrictions, and the date when those limitations should end. . . .

[After making these observations, the Court analyzed its own competence to decide on the constitutionality of the declaration of a state of exception.]

[C]onstitutional norms affirm the power of the Court to determine the constitutionality of the declaration of a state of internal commotion. A systematic read of the text allows us to infer the following:

(a) States of exception are special regimes conceived for situations of abnormality, but they are regimes conceived within the law, and not outside of it. That is to say, every state of exception is a regime of law . . . .
(b) The Constitution has placed the declaration of a state of internal commotion under various formal and material protections. Since the Court has been entrusted with the protection of the Constitution (Article 241[19]), the control that it exercises also extends to the norms dictated based on the constitutional dispositions that regulate the declaration of such a state of exception. . . .
(c) The Constitution is the norm of norms, the supreme norm. And in order for that superior legal nature not to be ignored by the powers of state, the Court has been entrusted with ensuring its supremacy. Within that framework, state entities may exercise the powers conferred upon them, but they must do so without ignoring the Constitution's supreme normative character. In the present constitutional regime

19. Article 241 states in part: "The safeguarding of the integrity and supremacy of the Constitution is entrusted to the Constitutional Court in the strict and precise terms of this Article."

there are no powers to issue legal acts without limits. . . . And since the imposition of those limits makes no sense if an instance of control is not set up, we can conclude that it is also true that there are no legal acts without an instance of legal control. . . .

(d) The constituent assembly has subordinated the declaration of the state of internal commotion to the existence of certain factual states of affairs and to a judgment about the sufficiency of ordinary police measures. It is fundamental that these requirements be met. . . .

It must thus be inferred that the Court does control these [declarations], and that this control must be adequate to defend the integrity and supremacy of the Constitution. And it is clear that this can only be achieved if the control is both formal and material.

[The Court thus declared Article 3 of the decree unconstitutional, as it suggested that the Court lacked competence to control the constitutionality of the declaration of a state of internal commotion and could only control decrees issued during the state of exception. The Court then proceeded to define the nature of its control of these declarations, emphasizing that there are three separate requirements from the text of the relevant articles—a factual finding that there is a "disruption of order," a value judgment that the disruption is "grave" and "imminently threatens institutional stability, the security of the State, or the coexistence of the citizenry," and finally a judgment that ordinary police measures are insufficient to overcome the problem.]

(a) Factual Finding

The Constitution imposes this requirement when it states: "*In case of . . . a disruption of the public order. . . .*"

[The president must verify] the occurrence of concrete facts, perceptible and consequently verifiable, that objectively generate an alteration of the conditions of security and tranquility demanded to exercise rights.

As an event of the phenomenological world, the factual presupposition under constitutional control is susceptible to an objective judgment. That is, the Constitutional Court must determine whether or not the disturbance of public order has occurred. . . .

(b) Value Judgment

The Constitution considers this requirement when it [allows a state of internal commotion] "in the case of a *grave* disruption of the public order *imminently threatening institutional stability, the security of the state, or the peaceful coexistence of the citizenry. . . .*"

As one can see, the prerequisite does not involve a fact as such . . . , but rather involves a value judgment based on the factual finding. It is an evaluation related to the intensity of the disruption and its consequences, an evaluation that corresponds to the president as the authority in charge of preserving public order.

In accordance with this prerequisite, on the one hand, it is not just any disruption of public order that will satisfy constitutional requirements but only a grave one. However, that value judgment is not a subjective decision of the president because it depends on an objective perception of the intensity of the disturbance.

On the other hand, according to the Constitution, the alteration of public order, in addition to being grave, must imminently threaten institutional stability, the security of the state, or the coexistence of the citizenry. That is, the alteration of public order, as a verifiable factual presupposition, in addition to being grave, must have the possibility of threatening, of placing in severe danger [or] of generating a risk for those areas of protection. And that grave danger must be imminent, that is; it cannot be a danger that is proposed as a distant or remote possibility for the institutions, the state or the citizens, but an effective risk that may materialize at any moment. . . .

[The Court's role here] is to determine whether the evaluation carried out by the President of the Republic as to the alteration of the public order is arbitrary, and whether or not that evaluation made a manifest error of appreciation. . . .

[T]hat is, once it has been established that the president's evaluation is neither arbitrary nor the result of manifest error, there is no place for the Constitutional Court to interfere. . . . [All other issues] must be judgments of opportunity or convenience, judgments that, as is known, are completely foreign to the competence of the Court as an instance of legal control of the limitations set by the exercise of power.

(c) Judgment on the sufficiency of ordinary measures

This requirement is imposed by the Constitution when it states that the president has the power to declare the state of interior commotion in case of a grave disruption of public order . . . "which cannot be met by the use of the ordinary powers of the police authorities."

In accordance with this phrase, the declaration of a state of internal commotion is the extreme measure in a state's legal and political agenda. It is the last resort to defend the Colombian people and the institutional structure that has been given to them, from the aggression implicit in the grave alteration of public order which in an imminent manner works against institutional stability. By virtue of this principle, the only time it is possible to use the state of internal commotion is when the ordinary legal tools that the state has do not allow it to stop the grave alteration of public order that threatens to dissolve the agreement that makes coexistence possible.

In this context, a disruption in public order is not enough for a declaration of a state of internal commotion. If it was, during long periods in which there was a disturbance in public order we would always be under a constitutional law of exception, that is, under a system of restriction of rights. But that would be opposed to the exceptional, temporary, and restrictive nature of states of institutional abnormality. To that effect, a grave disruption of public order that works in an imminent manner against institutional stability, the security of the state or the peaceful coexistence of citizens is also insufficient. This is because the ordinary constitutional regime cannot ignore the tensions in the life of a community and the frictions that are inevitable in the coexistence of human groups with distinct worldviews. Thus, what ordinary constitutional law regulates is not a nonexistent passive society but an agitated one; a social life that is dynamic. . . . [I]n the structure and functioning of the constitutional state there must be mechanisms to confront the grave disruptions of public order that threaten the democratic state. These include suitable institutional mechanisms such as those inherent to the criminal power of the state or . . . its monopoly on the use of force. . . .

Within this frame of reference, the president is endowed with the power to evaluate the sufficiency or insufficiency of the ordinary attributions of the police to overcome the grave perturbation of public order. . . . [T]he methodology to be used by the Court is an objective judgment of whether or not his evaluation . . . was arbitrary, and whether he made a manifest error of evaluation.

[Finally, the Court applied this framework to the decree at issue. On the factual finding, the Court said:]

Three of the four facts generating the disruption of public order and used by the National Government to declare the state of internal commotion have been verified, since it was demonstrated with documents and figures that they have indeed taken place in the last two years. In relation to them, since there is an objective base, the declaration is legitimate.

This is so because multiple criminal acts have been demonstrated by irregular armed groups, such as attacks against defenseless citizens, violations of their human rights, the violation of the rules of international humanitarian law, and the commission of crimes against humanity; also included are terrorist acts and terrorist attacks against the infrastructure of essential services and, finally, acts to coerce local and regional authorities and their families, who are the legitimate representatives of regional democracy and also administrators of justice.[20]

[As to the value judgment, the Court concluded:]

The application of the objective test considering the value judgment that the president has carried out with respect to the facts showing an alteration of public order, leads the Court to conclude that he has drawn from the factual context implications that are reasonable in the actual context of public order in Colombia.

This is so because the evaluation made by the president of the Republic on the gravity of the facts and their potential to imminently threaten institutional stability, the security of the state, or the coexistence of the citizenry, did not go beyond constitutional limitations—an intensification and expansion of the armed conflict has taken place, as well as violations of exceptional dimensions of human rights and of international humanitarian law. Levels of public disturbance have undergone a qualitative and not only a quantitative change, in the nature of the acts of violence, which have translated into indiscriminate attacks against the civil population, as well as into selective attacks against state officials of all levels and against legitimate leaders of civil society, due to an increase in the capacity of lawless armed groups.

[Finally, the Court referred to the sufficiency of ordinary police measures:]

Among the ordinary attributions held by the president . . . one finds, among others, the granting of exceptions when a police regulation establishes a general prohibition; the issuance of clear, precise, motivated, written, and well-founded orders directed at individuals with the goal of maintaining and reestablishing public order; the employment of force when strictly necessary, if done in a proportional and necessary manner; the utilization of the public service of the police; the carrying out of captures and raids

20. The Court however held that a fourth factual finding in the declaration, that "Colombia has recorded the highest level of criminality on the planet," had not been proven and thus held that it could not be used to uphold the decree.

in accordance with the Constitution and the law; and finally the use of military forces when an alteration of public order cannot be resolved by the police alone.

Within this framework, it is clear that in order to overcome the grave alteration of public order affecting the country and its institutional stability, the ordinary attributions of the police are limited because they are not designed to confront intense situations of institutional crisis such as those invoked in the declaration of a state of internal commotion. . . .

In that sense, the qualitative shift created by organized crime and terrorism and the massive and indiscriminate threat to local and regional democratic authorities requires a reconsideration of state strategies conceived for the maintenance and reestablishment of public order in circumstances of institutional normality. It is not under discussion that acts similar to those being carried out now have been part of the national reality for a long time and, therefore, it could be argued that Colombia is going through a structural abnormality [which] must be dealt with by means of permanent and general state policies and through the use of ordinary police powers from the president. Nonetheless, at the same time it is acknowledged that these acts . . . have acquired an unexpected intensity, that is, they have acquired a new qualitative dimension, in this same sense it must be inferred that the ordinary legal tools that the state possesses to face this unusual and destabilizing qualitative shift must also be endowed with more power. . . .

As we have seen, sufficient elements exist to state the reasonableness of the president's evaluation of the insufficiency of ordinary police power to face the grave disruption of public order affecting the country. . . .

Nonetheless, the declaration of constitutionality . . . in no sense constitutes an endorsement by the Court of the decrees that may be issued under the state of internal commotion. Those decrees will be judged one by one to verify that they respect the Constitution, international human rights treaties, and the statutory law of states of exception.

In particular, the Court notes that the measures adopted under the state of internal commotion must respect . . . Article 213 of the Constitution, which establishes that they must be "strictly essential options to deal with the causes of the disruption and check the spread of its effects. . . ."

[Thus, the Court generally upheld the declaration of a state of internal commotion. However, it struck down Article 3, which stated that "legislative decrees issued under and as a consequence of this declaration will be submitted to the Constitutional Court," as it held that Article implied the Court lacked the power to review the declaration itself. Further, it struck down a statement in the declaration that Colombia had the "highest level of criminality" in the world, as the Court was unable to substantiate it. Justice Jaime Araujo Renteria dissented and would have struck down the entire declaration on the ground that "the state already has ordinary powers contained in many laws" to deal with the facts alleged. Two other justices would have held that some of the facts and measures alleged in the decree were insufficient to justify a state of internal commotion, but would still have partially upheld the declaration.]

2. Review of Decrees Issued during a State of Internal Commotion

If the declaration of a state of internal commotion or other state of exception is struck down by the Court, then, generally speaking, all emergency decrees issued during that state of exception are also void. But even when a declaration of emergency has been upheld, the Court will still review each individual decree to determine whether it is proportional to the emergency and whether it conflicts with rights found in the Constitution, international human rights treaties, or international humanitarian law.

After the declaration of a state of internal commotion in the prior decision had been upheld, President Uribe issued a series of decrees based on the declaration. Legislative Decree 2002 of 2002 was issued by the president, for example, in August 2002. The decree had two chapters.

The first chapter dealt with provisions intended to maintain public order throughout Colombia by limiting otherwise applicable rules concerning warrants in order to carry out an arrest or search. Generally speaking, these provisions established limitations on Article 28 of the Constitution, which establishes in part that "no one may be importuned in his/her person or family, sent to jail or arrested, nor may his/her home be searched except on the basis of a written order from a competent judicial authority, subject to the legal procedures and for reasons previously defined by statute."

Articles 2, 5, 6, and 8, for example, allowed arrest of suspects, interception of communications, and raids and searches of homes and other properties based on "verbal communication of a previously written warrant" in cases where "there is insurmountable urgency and the need to protect a fundamental right in grave and imminent danger." Articles 3 and 7 contemplated arrests and searches of homes without a warrant at all, whenever "there are circumstances that make it impossible to obtain such authorization, as long as there is insurmountable urgency and the need to protect a fundamental right in grave and imminent danger."

The second chapter dealt with the creation of special public order zones, called Rehabilitation and Consolidation zones, in areas with significant guerrilla activity. These zones were seen as a mechanism for the military to fight guerilla and paramilitary activity in especially violent areas; within them, military and administrative authorities would temporarily be given the power to restrict certain fundamental rights.

Thus, Article 12 allowed the president to create Rehabilitation and Consolidation Zones by administrative decree. Article 14 contemplated restrictions on the right to travel and reside in each Rehabilitation and Consolidation Zone through measures such as curfews, military blockades, requirements for special permits in order to move freely through the area, and restrictions on the movement of persons or vehicles at specified hours or locations. Article 17 granted the military commander of the Rehabilitation and Consolidation Zone the power to collect, verify, keep, and classify information regarding persons and things located in those zones. Article 20 allowed for a 24-hour detention of persons found within the zones without their identification document, in order to verify their identity and determine whether they had outstanding warrants against them. Finally, Article 22 placed special restrictions on the movement and residence of foreigners within the zones. Before entering the zones, these foreigners were required to report to the governor or else face the penalty of expulsion from the country, and the governor was given the power to deny or authorize the foreigner's request to move through or reside in the zone.

These measures generated an intense debate because of the restrictions on rights that they contemplated. Several human rights NGOs intervened opposing the legislative decree, while some groups representing victims of illegal armed groups that operated in the areas to be delimited as rehabilitation zones spoke out in favor of the measures. In **Decision C-1024 of 2002 (per Justice Alfredo Beltrán Sierra)**, the Court in a divided judgment upheld some parts of the decree and struck down others.

The Court started its analysis by defining the general framework for limiting rights during the state of internal commotion, reiterating what was stated in Sentence C-802 of 2002. It noted that "legislative decrees dictated as a result of a declaration of a state of internal commotion are necessarily limited not only by the Constitution (Articles 213 and 214), but also by any laws that have not been suspended because of express incompatibility with that state, the statutory law concerning states of exception, and the international treaties and agreements on human rights and international humanitarian law which Colombia has ratified." It then verified that the decree in question was linked to the facts underlying the declaration of the state of internal commotion, and concluded that "the decree . . . considered globally, maintains a connection with the decree through which a state of internal commotion across the entire national territory was declared."

Next, the Court proceeded to examine each individual provision of the decree, beginning with the nationwide provisions restricting the right to a warrant. The Court struck down Articles 3 and 7, which allowed searches or arrests without a warrant whenever there was "insurmountable urgency and the need to protect a fundamental right in grave and imminent danger." It found that the conditions to apply this power were too vague. "[There is] no precise determination regarding which authority is granted the power to make an exception to the inviolability of the private home and to permit it to be inspected or searched, which affects the essential nucleus of the right [to privacy]. Likewise, the norm does not specify . . . any definition of 'insurmountable urgency' or 'the need to protect a fundamental right in grave or imminent danger,' so the citizen is subjected to whatever the authority that wants to do the inspection or search thinks is insurmountable urgency and its free opinion as to whether there is a fundamental right in grave or imminent danger that must be protected. That is, the citizen is left at the mercy of whatever the authority determines . . . , which is contrary to Article 28 of the Constitution."

On essentially the same grounds, the Court struck down the parts of Articles 2, 5, 6, and 8 that provided that a previously-obtained warrant could be communicated verbally in order to carry out an arrest,[21] intercept communications, or search a home or other property whenever there was "insurmountable urgency and the need to protect a fundamental

21. Article 2 also allowed arrests "of those persons about which there are indications regarding their participation or plans to participate in the commission of crimes." The Court upheld this provision, but in the text of the decision read this article narrowly. It noted that arrests should not be carried out on the mere basis of plans

right in grave and imminent danger." The Court found that the decree did not sufficiently explain why these provisions were necessary, and did not explain in clear enough terms the circumstances under which the restrictions would be used, because the standards simply repeated phrasing used in the relevant statutory law governing states of exception, without adding any additional detail.

The Court then considered the Rehabilitation and Consolidation zones. It upheld the power of the president to create these zones. However, it held that this power should be exercised via a legislative decree that would be examined by the Constitutional Court, and not a merely administrative decree that would be examined within the administrative court system, as the object of these measures would be to restrict certain constitutional rights. The Court also upheld most of Article 14, which established restrictions on movement within the zones, as these measures were connected with and proportional to the state of internal commotion, and contemplated by the statutory law regulating states of emergency. It upheld Article 20 allowing 24-hour detention of people found in the zone without their identification card, on the ground that this measure as well was connected with and proportional to the facts that caused the underlying emergency.

However, the Court struck down Article 17, which allowed the military commander of a zone to conduct a census of both people and things located within the rehabilitation zones; the Court made a distinction between a census of the people in the zones and the census of objects found there. "[T]o carry out a population census like the one foreseen in the decree, by virtue of which personal data are recorded by the state, not only about identity but also about each person's residence, their workplace and their individual activities, exceeds the powers granted by the Constitution to the government when declaring a state of exception. . . . It is quite different to collect, verify, preserve and classify data on weapons, explosives, . . . ammunition and telecommunication equipment, or regarding vehicles and other transportation means, be they terrestrial, fluvial, maritime or air, that circulate in specific zones of the country . . . , which could be useful for reestablishing public order and adequate to the end for which the state of internal commotion was declared."

Finally, as to Article 22, which restricted foreigners from entering the Rehabilitation and Consolidation Zones, the Court made a distinction between three types of foreigners: journalists who are protected by the freedom of press and the right to information, members of certain civil assistance organizations protected by international humanitarian law, and other persons. "Article 22 . . . cannot be applied to foreign or national journalists . . . as a prerequisite to perform the duties of their work in any part of the country. The only thing that can be required of them is that they demonstrate their status as journalists, and nothing else. . . . Likewise, foreigners who intend to carry out humanitarian work

to commit crimes unless this were supported by external facts showing at least the "initiation of the execution of the plan." It also read "indications" as clearly requiring "evidence" or "facts," rather than conjecture or suspicion. Finally, the Court noted the absence of any provisions governing the procedure once a person was captured, the duration of the detention, or the rules for bringing the person before a judge. At least in this absence, the Court held that the captured person should have the immediate rights to know why and by whom he was captured, to have the authorities communicate his detention to a person selected by the detainee, and to communicate with a lawyer of his choosing.

or health-related activities, or to provide religious assistance, cannot be limited either in entering, moving through, or remaining in the so-called Rehabilitation or Consolidation Zones, since a contrary rule would violate the norms of international humanitarian law. . . . In regards to all other foreigners . . . , the refusal to grant them the authorization foreseen in the decree must be specifically indicated and justified by circumstances of public order in a concrete case."

The Court therefore struck down or clarified many parts of the law, while upholding many of the core provisions creating and limiting rights in the Rehabilitation and Consolidation Zones. It is worth pointing out that although the Court has sometimes upheld these kinds of zones as temporary measures during states of exception, it has been much less willing to accept them as permanent measures in ordinary laws. In Section B above, for example, the Court struck down the government's attempt to enact similar measures permanently via an ordinary law. The Uribe government would later seek to enact somewhat similar measures in a permanent fashion through constitutional amendment. This attempt was also struck down by the Court on procedural grounds (see Chapter 11, Section A).

As has already been emphasized, states of internal commotion and the measures taken under them are limited in duration. They can only be declared for a term of 90 days, which can be extended twice (i.e., for a total of 270 days). The president may decide on the first extension on his own, with the signature of all of his cabinet ministers. However, a second extension requires the prior approval of the Senate. The 2002 state of internal commotion at issue here was extended once by the president, and Uribe then procured Senate approval for a second extension. However, the Constitutional Court declared its second extension to be unconstitutional on procedural grounds. In **Decision C-327 of 2003 (per Justice Alfredo Beltrán Sierra)**, the Court held that this second extension had not been properly approved by the Senate, because the Senate had approved it less than halfway through the first extension, because the extension had been approved in a rushed and non-deliberative manner, and because the Senate failed to state its reasons for approving the extension in writing. Under the Colombian Constitution, all measures enacted during the state of internal commotion thus automatically ceased at the end of the first extension, 180 days after the state of internal commotion had first been declared.

Since 2002, one other state of internal commotion has been declared, in 2008. This declaration, also under President Uribe, was based on an extended strike by administrative officers of the judicial branch as well as by some judges across the country, which resulted in congestion of the courts, a slowing of judicial processes, and the release of several thousand suspected criminals either because they could not be processed into the judicial system or because the legal time frame for trying them had expired. But in **Decision C-070 of 2009 (per Justices Humberto Antonio Sierra Porto & Clara Elena Reales Gutierrez)**, the Court struck down this declaration. The Court held that many of the basic facts in the decree were adequately supported, but that the declaration did not contain sufficient evidence to justify the requirement that the acts be of such gravity as to affect the institutional order, the security of the state, or the coexistence of the citizenry. Likewise, it held that the declaration did not evaluate the ordinary means potentially within the government's reach to end the crisis.

Note on the State of Economic, Social, and Ecological Emergency: The Constitution includes another significant state of exception known as the state of economic, social, and ecological emergency. This instrument is regulated in Article 215 of the Constitution, which provides that "When events different from those provided for in Articles 212 [state of external war] and 213 [state of internal commotion] occur that disrupt or threaten to disrupt in serious or imminent manner the economic, social, or ecological order of the country or which constitute a grave public calamity, the president, with the signature of all the ministers, may declare a state of emergency for periods up to 30 days in each case which, in all, may not exceed 90 days in a calendar year." The article also states that the president, once he has declared the emergency and justified it in writing, may issues decrees having the force of law so long as they are "slated exclusively to check the crisis and halt the extension of its effects." Unlike decrees issued during a state of internal commotion, decrees issued during a state of economic, social, and ecological emergency are permanent in nature—they become permanent laws of the Republic and do not expire when the declaration of state of emergency expires. The one exception to this permanence is new taxes, which may only be declared provisionally and expire at the end of the next fiscal year unless adopted by Congress.[22]

During the period prior to 1991, the government often used states of exception to write many major pieces of economic and social legislation. In order to prevent this situation from recurring, the Constitutional Court has exercised tight control over these declarations. When the government has faced a genuine crisis based on new events of sufficient gravity, the Court has tended to uphold the emergency. Thus, the Court largely upheld a declaration in response to the deep financial crisis of the late 1990s (see Decision C-122 of 1999), the massive swindling of savings accounts by a Ponzi scheme fed by the laundering of the proceeds of drug trafficking and other illegal activities (see Decision C-135 of 2009), and a response to natural disasters such as those caused by earthquakes (see Decision C-216 of 1999).

However, the Court's long-standing doctrine has emphasized that the government may not use a state of exception to respond to problems that are "chronic" or "structural" in nature. It has held that these problems should instead be dealt with by Congress through ordinary legislative processes. Several recent examples might help illustrate the point. First, about one year after the Constitutional Court issued its structural decision on healthcare, T-760 of 2008 (excerpted in Chapter 6 above), the Uribe administration declared a state of social, economic, and ecological emergency in the healthcare system. The emergency's stated goal was to overcome a crisis in the system and to comply with the Court's decisions in this area. However, in **Decision C-252 of 2010 (per Justice Jorge Ivan Palacio Palacio)**, the Court struck down the declaration because the problems in the system were of a "known, structural, recurring, and foreseeable" nature and thus should be dealt with by Congress rather than through extraordinary lawmaking. But in a highly unusual move, the Court left new taxes that had been created by decree to fund the system intact for an indefinite period, holding that the funding crisis in the system was "grave" and that the Court had the power to avoid negative effects stemming from its decisions.

22. Article 215 also contains a substantive limitation on government power: "The government may not infringe on the social rights of workers through the decrees mentioned in this article."

The president elected in 2010, Juan Manuel Santos, used the device to tackle problems associated with the La Nina weather phenomenon in Colombia, which caused massive amounts of rain and disastrous flooding in parts of the country in 2010 and 2011. In **Decision C-156 of 2011 (per Justice Mauricio Gonzalez Cuervo)**, the Court upheld an initial declaration for 30 days in December 2010, holding that the phenomenon constituted a serious crisis caused by new and non-structural events, thus justifying a state of emergency. The declaration sought mainly to free up funds for relief and reconstruction in affected areas of the country; it also created new taxes to fund the emergency.

However, when the president tried to declare a new emergency for an additional period in January 2011 to deal with the same crisis, the Court unanimously struck down the effort in **Decision C-216 of 2011 (per Justice Juan Carlos Henao Perez)**. The Court noted that the Declaration of a State of Economic, Social, and Ecological Emergency, unlike a State of Internal Commotion, could not be "extended" for additional time, but rather had to be newly declared each time. The Court then struck down the declaration in its entirety, holding that the facts that were stated as justifying the new declaration were identical to those in the previous declaration, and that the government had already, in the prior emergency, established a series of permanent measures to deal with the crisis, which made new measures largely unnecessary.

10

The Congress

Problems of Abdication and Deliberation

During the period prior to the writing of the 1991 Constitution, while the presidency dominated national policymaking, Congress played a relatively minor role in national affairs. It acquiesced in presidential uses of states of exception and frequently delegated broad lawmaking power to the executive. The sources of the dynamic were in part rooted in the two-party, Liberal-Conservative pact of the National Front period, which both made it more difficult to pass major bills through Congress and gave members of Congress incentives to focus on local or pork-barrel projects as opposed to national concerns.[1] The result is that most major acts of policymaking prior to 1991 were done by the president, working around Congress. This affected the model of policymaking, which became more centralized and technocratic rather than deliberative.

The Constituent Assembly sought to reinvigorate Congress so that it could achieve a more significant role in Colombian public life. The Assembly thus altered the electoral rules, especially in the Senate where most members are now elected from a single nationwide constituency, in order to make Congress more representative of the full range of political views in society. It limited states of exception, delegated emergency powers, and other unilateral executive powers, in the hope of forcing Congress to weigh in on most major policymaking decisions. It established a set of restrictions on legislative procedure with the aim of rationalizing congressional deliberations. And it limited the degree of congressional immunity with the goal of suppressing political corruption. A distinction was made between inviolability for opinions and votes, on the one hand, and parliamentary immunity from prosecution of crimes, on the other hand. The latter was abolished.

Some of these goals have been successfully achieved; others have proven more difficult. Congress, for example, has become a far more representative body, and the traditional

1. *See* Ronald P. Archer & Matthew Soberg Shugart, *The Unrealized Potential of Presidential Dominance in Colombia*, *in* Presidentialism and Democracy in Latin America 110 (Scott Mainwaring & Matthew Soberg Shugart eds., 1997).

Colombian Constitutional Law: Leading Cases. Manuel José Cepeda Espinosa and David Landau.

Liberal-Conservative monopoly on political power has been broken. But significant problems remain in terms of levels of legislative corruption, fed by drug trafficking, illegal armed groups, and others issues. Further problems include the quality of congressional deliberation and continued presidential dominance over the policymaking process. This chapter studies some of the Constitutional Court's responses to these dynamics. In one sense, these responses are very particular to the challenges of the Colombian context. In others, they are general problems related to the rationality, incentives, and legitimacy of multi-member legislatures, which are in crisis in many countries around the world.

Section A considers the problem of contamination of political finance by drug cartels in the mid-1990s in light of guarantees of parliamentary inviolability for opinions and votes. In the late 1990s, members of Congress heard impeachment charges against a sitting president, Ernesto Samper, whose campaign had allegedly been financed by drug money. The House of Representatives on a partisan vote declined to impeach the president, and the Criminal Chamber of the Supreme Court opened an investigation of all those members of Congress who had voted against impeachment, probing whether the vote had been based on partisan motives and not the merits. The Constitutional Court held that the Supreme Court lacked the power to conduct the investigation because members of Congress enjoyed inviolability for their votes. After the Court's decision, other cases of illegitimate relationships of members of Congress, mainly with narco-paramilitary groups, were tried by the Supreme Court. The problem in these cases was not the members' votes in Congress, but rather their ties with illegal armed groups. In what is called the "para-politics" scandal several members of Congress were criminally condemned. This is possible because the 1991 Constitution abolished parliamentary immunity and replaced it by a direct investigation and trial ("*fuero*") by the Supreme Court, the only criminal judge of members of Congress. Moreover, members of Congress who violate specific prohibitions enumerated in the Constitution—which range from criminal conduct to absenteeism—may be expelled from Congress and excluded forever from electoral offices by the Council of State, if requested by any citizen. This kind of *actio popularis* to preserve the integrity of parliamentary behavior is called "loss of position" ("*pérdida de investidura*"). It is frequently used, mainly by NGOs. Since 1991 about 60 members of Congress have been stripped of their post by the Council of State.[2]

Sections B and C consider problems of legislative abdication and deliberation. As shown in Section B, the Court has stepped in when Congress has sought to delegate formal lawmaking powers to the president in overly vague ways. In so doing, the Court has sought to prod Congress into exercising its function as the heart of political deliberation, rather than giving the executive a "blank check." Further, as Section C demonstrates, the Court has at times sought to assess the degree of legislative deliberation in light of constitutional mandates, either by controlling legislative procedure or by giving less deference to decisions adopted with less deliberation. This jurisprudence again reflects an attempt by the Court to prod Congress into taking its policymaking responsibilities more seriously, particularly

2. FERNANDO CEPEDA ULLOA, LA PÉRDIDA DE LA INVESTIDURA 1991–2011 (2012).

when they impact sensitive constitutional principles. Of course, there are real questions about whether these forms of control can influence congressional behavior. But the aim of the Court is clear. As stated in **Decision C-816 of 2004 (per Justice Jaime Córdoba Triviño & Rodrigo Uprimny Yepes)**: "Congress is a space of public reason. Or at least, the Constitution postulates that that is what it should be."

A. The Scope of Parliamentary Inviolability

In Colombia, the president is subject to impeachment and criminal trial through a complex process involving multiple actors. All processes require: (1) investigation by a commission of the House of Representatives, (2) accusation by a majority vote of the full House of Representatives, and (3) approval of the accusation by the full Senate.[3] If the accusation involves "crimes committed in the exercise of his/her functions or . . . he/she becomes unworthy to serve . . . ," then the Senate may by a two-thirds vote remove the accused from office and suspend his or her political rights.[4] It must also send the case to the Supreme Court, which has the power to impose criminal punishment.[5]

The president from 1994 until 1998, Ernesto Samper, was accused shortly after winning office of accepting campaign funds from the proceeds of drug trafficking and violating the donation limits fixed by existing law. Investigations were opened by the General Prosecutor's Office after tape recordings surfaced that allegedly discussed these payments. In 1996, Congress opened an impeachment investigation. The Commission of Accusations of the House of Representatives approved the charge, but the process ended at the second stage when the full House decided that there was no cause to impeach the president.

Following that decision, the Criminal Chamber of the Supreme Court opened an investigation against all of the representatives who voted in favor of President Samper during the impeachment process. The main basis for the investigation was that the votes were based on political considerations such as party allegiance, rather than on the evidence presented. Under the Constitution, the Supreme Court has exclusive competence to hear and decide criminal accusations against sitting members of Congress.[6] However, Article 185 provides that "members of Congress enjoy inviolability for their opinions and the votes which they cast in the exercise of their office, without prejudice to the disciplinary rules included in the respective rules of procedure." The decision below, which was based on a *tutela* filed by a member of Congress who was under investigation, required the Court to determine the scope of this inviolability.

3. *See* Articles 174 (Senate); 178 cl. 3 (House).

4. *See* Article 175, cl. 2 ("If the charge refers to crimes committed in the exercise of his/her functions or that he/she becomes unworthy to serve because of a misdemeanor, the Senate may only impose the sanction of discharge from office or the temporary or absolute suspension of political rights. But the accused shall be brought to trial before the Supreme Court of Justice if the evidence should show the individual to be responsible for an infraction deserving of other penalty.").

5. *See* Article 235, cl. 2.

6. *See* Article 186; Article 235, cl. 3.

Decision SU-047 de 1999 (per Justices Carlos Gaviria Díaz and Alejandro Martínez Caballero)

[In a five-to-two decision (two magistrates were recused), the full Constitutional Court ruled in favor of a representative who, along with other members of Congress, was being investigated by the Supreme Court. The Court ruled that the representative enjoyed parliamentary inviolability and thus ordered the investigation against him closed. The Court also ordered the Supreme Court to refrain from "investigating as crimes the facts inviolably linked to the opinions and votes cast by members of Congress in exercise of their duties." The Court thus clarified the scope of parliamentary inviolability. The Constitutional Court began by studying the power of the Criminal Chamber of the Supreme Court to investigate crimes committed by members of Congress:]

The previous Constitution included [a broad conception of] parliamentary immunity, which is the prerogative that members of Congress have not to be judged or investigated while they exercise they functions without the prior approval of their respective chambers. In effect . . . , the prior Constitution stated that no member of Congress could be apprehended or placed before a criminal court without permission of the chamber to which he pertained. This procedure was eliminated by the 1991 Constitution and replaced by a special process for members of Congress, whereby they can only be investigated and judged by the Supreme Court [rather than any lower courts] . . . , but those judicial actions do not require any prior authorization by Congress. In effect, the Constitution states that the crimes committed by members of Congress will be known, "in private session," by the Supreme Court. . . .

On the other hand, basic reasons of common sense and clear constitutional norms indicate that that power of the Criminal Chamber extends beyond crimes committed by members of Congress as private citizens, in order to also cover those punishable acts linked to the exercise of their constitutional duties. For example, a paragraph of Article 235, which states the powers of the Supreme Court in this respect, clarifies that once a person has ceased to exercise the position, the special process will only be maintained for punishable conduct that has a relationship with the functions he carried out. This means that the Constitution distinguishes two situations: while a person is a member of Congress, he will be investigated by the Supreme Court for any crime; however, once he has ceased in his position, he will only be judged by that body for crimes related to his past position. The Constitution therefore implies that members of Congress can commit certain crimes related to their functions, the investigation of which will be carried out by the Supreme Court. . . .

Article 185 of the Constitution establishes that members of Congress enjoy "inviolability for their opinions and the votes which they cast in the exercise of their office . . . ."

All democratic constitutional orders include, with a similar scope, this figure. And it is reasonable for this to be the case, since parliamentary inviolability plays an essential role in the dynamic of democratic legal orders. In effect, the purpose of parliamentary inviolability is to allow representatives to freely deliberate on their votes and opinions, without fear that these could lead to judicial persecution . . . , and thus to guarantee freedom and independence in the formation of the collective will of the parliament or Congress. Thus, only through the concept of inviolability is it possible to comply with the constitutional mandate according to which senators and representatives must act by "in a manner consonant with justice and the common good," (Article 133), and not under fear of possible judicial reprisal.

This inviolability for members of Congress is therefore related to constitutional democracy, since it is the necessary expression of two of its essential principles: separation of powers and popular sovereignty. Also, inviolability assures the independence of Congress, since it avoids interference by other branches when senators and representatives exercise their functions. . . .

[This] prerogative is primarily an institutional guarantee in favor of Congress and democracy, rather than a personal privilege of a senator or representative as such, which explains why it cannot be renounced by its holder and why, in a judicial process, the judge must take it into account *sua sponte*. . . .

Further, the inviolability is perpetual; in other words, the member of Congress will avoid any judicial prosecution for his votes and opinions, even once he has ceased in his functions. And it is natural that this should be the case, since the purpose of the concept is to ensure the freedom of opinion of the member of congress, and it is obvious that this could be limited by fear of future investigations against him, for having voted or given opinions in a certain way.

[Further, the concept] generates a generalized inviolability . . . , since the congressman escapes not only criminal prosecution but also any possible civil demand against him for his votes and opinions taken in exercise of his functions.

Doctrine and jurisprudence, national and comparative, agree also in stating the scope in which the inviolability functions, and it is clear that it is (i) specific or exclusive, but at the same time it is (ii) absolute.

Thus, the inviolability is specific since the actual Constitution, like the previous one, makes clear that this institutional guarantee only covers the votes and opinions taken in exercise of the position . . . [and it] is absolute, since without exception all votes and opinions taken in the process of the formation of the collective will of Congress are excluded from any judicial responsibility.

Finally, from a conceptual point of view, this instrument tries to protect in a general way the liberty and independence of Congress, and thus it is natural that it would protect all of the constitutional functions that senators and representatives develop, as is recognized uniformly in comparative law. . . .

Parliamentary inviolability is thus absolute. However, this does not mean that in a constitutional democracy there is no responsibility for congressmen for their votes and opinions in the exercise of their functions. Thus, most Constitutions, and specifically Article 185 of our Constitution, establishes that members of parliament can be submitted to the disciplinary norms of their chambers, who, with the goal of maintaining order in the debate, can control and internally sanction certain abuses of the freedom of expression.

On the other hand, and even more importantly, the essential control over members of Congress is exercised by the citizens themselves and by public opinion, whose questions can be translated into the imposition of certain forms of political responsibility for senators and representatives. . . .

The prior study shows that while the Criminal Chamber [of the Supreme Court] can judge the crimes committed by members of Congress, it lacks the power to investigate the votes and opinions that the senators and representatives have taken in exercise of their functions, since these are inviolable. According to the evidence incorporated in this petition, the Supreme Court opened an investigation against all of the representatives who voted in favor of the closure of the action against the president, while they declined to open a formal investigation against those who considered that a resolution of accusation should be taken against the president. An obvious conclusion emerges: the primary basis for the investigation carried out by the Supreme Court was the vote issued by the members of Congress, and not other conduct. . . .

Nothing in the text of the Constitution suggests that inviolability does not operate when Congress is exercising judicial functions and investigating a high official, like the president, the justices of the high judicial corporations, or the National Prosecutor.

[One might] think that when members of Congress exercise judicial functions, they lose all of their political discretion, that is, they cease to have any liberty of opinion or to vote, and thus are converted into true judicial functionaries, who have a strict duty to decide impartially, strictly according to the law, and exclusively based on the material incorporated into the [record] compiled by the Congress. [This interpretation of parliamentary inviolability is] unacceptable since, as was stated, it finds no support in the Constitution, and even more importantly, it would lead to an unacceptable erosion of parliamentary inviolability, to the detriment of the independence of Congress and the freedom of democratic debate. . . .

Despite the judicial nature of [the processes in which members of Congress judge high officials], it is clear that the Constitution reserves political discretion to members of Congress when they are investigating and judging high officials, including when common crimes are involved. In effect, the Constitution makes clear that in all activity, including obviously their votes and opinions when they exercise judicial functions, senators and representatives will act according to "justice and the common good," which inevitably has a component of political liberty, given that, in a plural society, not all visions of the common good are identical. For example, a member of Congress can properly believe that strong evidence against a high official exists, but also may believe that his removal would have catastrophic effects for the country, and therefore, consulting the common good, speak and vote in favor of the accused. That conduct is not only unacceptable for an ordinary judge, who is strictly submitted to law, but it could also lead to criminal responsibility, since it could constitute a crime. However, that same behavior in a member of Congress must be immune from any criminal sanction by the broad margin of appreciation [that members of congress enjoy], and by the additional factor that representative bodies need not be composed of experts in law. Parliamentary inviolability therefore continues operating during an impeachment processes taken by Congress. . . .

And there are important reasons of state to justify that model, which is adopted by most republican constitutions: the removal from his charge of a high official, and in particular the head of state, is a fact that has inevitable and profound political consequences. . . . [O]nly when they are protected by inviolability can senators and representatives enjoy sufficient independence to exercise, without fear of repression, this important task of judgment. . . .

[T]he Supreme Court is not competent to investigate, judge, or condemn members of Congress for the opinions that they formulate during the impeachment of the president, or for the votes that they emit in favor or against the closure of that process. . . .

As is obvious, the situation is very different in cases in which some representatives had committed, during the impeachment, other crimes, which are not tightly linked to the manifestation of a vote or an opinion, since those events are not protected by parliamentary inviolability. . . . That would be the case, for example, without making a complete list, of representatives who may have received improper payments or benefits for their actions . . . , since that conduct . . . does not constitute the expression of a vote or opinion. Thus, those facts continue being punishable, and the Supreme Court retains full competence to investigate, judge, and punish them. But it is contrary to the Constitution for the investigation of that high body to be aimed at the exercise of the vote itself . . . , which is what the Criminal Chamber did when it opened investigations exclusively against those who had voted in favor of the closure of the impeachment process against the president. . . .

[In another part of the decision, the Court recognized that the precedent found in two of its prior decisions could be interpreted to mean that there is no parliamentary inviolability in cases where Congress is exercising judicial functions. However, the Court held that the statements to that effect in its prior decisions were merely dicta, rather than the holding, and also stated:]

[This uncertainty] is precisely why the Constitutional Court selected this *tutela*, because it is necessary for the Court to clarify and correct its jurisprudence on this issue, which has unfortunately received interpretations that distort the purpose of parliamentary inviolability and ignore the guarantees that representatives being investigated by the Supreme Court must enjoy. Since the Constitutional Court is the highest interpreter of the Constitution, as our own jurisprudence has stated . . . , we have the duty to clarify the true meaning of parliamentary inviolability, as was done in this decision.

It is rigorously proper for the Constitutional Court to correct and clarify the criteria dealing with parliamentary inviolability in [its prior decisions]. In effect, as has been shown, the doctrine laid down in those decisions . . . would deal a grave blow against parliamentary inviolability, in detriment to the independence of Congress, free democratic debate, and the fundamental right to due process of the officials investigated by the Supreme Court. The arguments that justify the explicit abandonment of those jurisprudential criteria are therefore very powerful, since essential values and principles of the constitutional order are in play. In contrast, the costs generated by a jurisprudential correction, in terms of legal security and equality, are practically nonexistent. . . .

[The Court therefore ordered the Supreme Court to close its investigation. Justice Hernando Herrera Vergara dissented on the ground that parliamentary inviolability did not cover impeachment processes: "[W]hen members of Congress exercise judicial functions . . . they have the same responsibilities and duties that correspond to [judges], and thus, the Criminal Chamber of the Supreme Court enjoyed the constitutional power to investigate and judge possible criminal acts. . . ." Justice Eduardo Cifuentes Muñoz also dissented on various grounds, including the prior precedent on the issue.]

Note on the Criminal Law and Congress in Colombia: The decision reproduced above gave legislators protection for their votes and opinions expressed on the floor of Congress. However, it did not of course protect legislators from accountability for a range of other crimes, including those based on corruption or on links with illegal armed groups such as paramilitaries or guerrillas. In fact, the Criminal Chamber of the Supreme Court has at times been extremely active in investigating members of Congress for these charges. For example, a 2008 report found that in the 2006–2010 term, 34 of the 102 senators, and 25 of 168 members of the House of Representatives, were under investigation by the Criminal Chamber for links to illegal groups.[7] Many of these were either removed from office, resigned, or were put in jail.

B. Legislative Delegation to the Executive

The distribution of legislative and executive powers under the 1991 Constitution is complex. The most common and obvious relationship is that Congress passes laws and the executive branch issues ordinary regulations that are subordinated to those laws and are intended to flesh out their content. This is a dynamic common to most modern presidential systems, in which Congress makes laws and the president issues regulations in reliance on them. During states of exception, however, as the last chapter showed, the president can take on explicitly legislative powers and issue decrees with the force of law. These decree-laws are temporary in the case of states of internal commotion and permanent in the case of states of economic, social, and ecological emergency, until and unless Congress decides to change or derogate them.

Of greatest relevance here, Congress is allowed to delegate to the president, for temporary periods of "up to six months," "precise extraordinary powers to issue decrees with

7. *See* Claudia López & Oscar Sevillano, *Balance político de la parapolítica*, Dec. 2008, at http://www.cronicon.net/paginas/juicioauribe/img/Balance%20de%20la%20Parapol%EDtica.pdf.

the force of law when public necessity or advantage so advises."[8] Thus, under some circumstances Congress may delegate its formal lawmaking powers to the president. The resulting decree-laws issued by the president have the same status as laws passed by Congress.

Constitutional provisions to this effect have existed throughout much of Colombian constitutional history. The Colombian constitutions in force before 1886 authorized Congress to grant delegated legislation to the executive only in cases of internal disturbance and war. However, the Colombian legislative practice during the nineteenth century diverged from these limitations. Congress commonly granted the president legislative power, usually for an unlimited period of time and without setting clear limits, and across a broad range of issues.

The 1886 Constitution regulated this issue in very vague terms, and in practice, Congress continued to delegate legislative powers to the executive on various matters, including in times of peace. The Supreme Court of Justice, during a constitutional review in 1910, adopted a broad interpretation of the relevant article and allowed these delegations to be carried out in peacetime as well as during times of war or internal disturbance. Supported by case law, the granting of delegated legislation in times of peace stopped being only a legislative practice and became a principle enshrined in the constitutional system. Thus, from the onset of the country's republican life and until the adoption of the 1991 Constitution, delegated legislation was regularly granted by Congress and used by the president.

During the decades before the drafting of the Constitution of 1991, as noted in the Introduction and the previous chapter, the president rather than Congress became the main legislator in the system. Many laws were passed by the president during states of exception. Many others, however, were issued by the president in reliance on broad and frequent delegations of legislative power from Congress. This dynamic responded to political conditions created by electoral rules and incentives, in which Congress preferred to focus on local and pork-barrel issues while giving the president the power to legislate on larger national concerns.

In their effort to rebalance the separation of powers during the Constituent Assembly of 1991, the drafters thus focused not only on limiting states of exception (see Chapter 9) but also on placing new limits on the delegation of lawmaking powers from Congress to the president. The relevant article maintains Congress's ability to carry out these delegations, but requires that they be "precise" and temporary, issued for no more than a six-month period.[9] Further, it imposes certain procedural limitations, requiring that the president "request" the delegation from Congress before it can be granted, and requiring their approval by an absolute majority of the members of Congress (rather than a simple

8. Article 150, cl. 10.

9. Article 150, cl. 10 states: "It is the responsibility of Congress to enact laws. Through them, it exercises the following functions: To vest, up to six months, in the President of the Republic, precise extraordinary powers to issue rules with the force of law when public necessity or advantage so advises. Such powers must be requested expressly by the Government and their approval requires the vote of an absolute majority of the members of both Houses. At any time and at its own initiative, Congress may amend decree laws enacted by the Government for the use of its extraordinary powers. These powers may not be conferred for issuing codes, organic or statutory laws, anything referred to in numeral 20 of this Article, or for decreeing taxes."

majority of those present, as for most laws). Finally, the provision prevents Congress from delegating its lawmaking authority on certain issues, including "codes, statutory or organic laws . . . or to decree taxes."

The Constitutional Court has subsequently been active in policing congressional delegations of lawmaking power to the president, particularly on the grounds that they are insufficiently "precise." The following case is an example.

Decision C-097 of 2003 (per Justice Manuel José Cepeda Espinosa)

[In a unanimous decision, the Court struck down paragraph 1 of Article 111 of Law 715 of 2001, where Congress delegated power to the president for six months to "[o]rganize a control and surveillance system to be applied in different types of institutions and regions aimed at addressing special situations. To this end, different kinds of bodies may be created." This provision was included in a much broader law that dealt with the distribution of resources between central and local government entities, and provided rules and institutions governing the provision of healthcare and education services. The Court held that this delegation was insufficiently "precise" to pass constitutional muster. First, the Court highlighted the goals sought by the modifications introduced to the 1991 Constitution regarding delegated lawmaking powers:]

The Constituent Assembly of 1991 wanted to confront the consistent abuse in the recurring and generalized attribution of legislative powers to the government through extraordinary powers. Thus, they sought to strengthen the democratic principle and avoid the excesses of the then-current form of presidentialism. The Court has referred on other occasions to how the institution of extraordinary powers lost its initially exceptional nature for use during disruptions of public order and became an easy expedient for issuing laws outside of public fora and without democratic debate, a historical fact that led the Constitution to modify the regime and reinvigorate the functions of Congress as the natural seat of political deliberation. . . .

The goals that guided the Constituent Assembly in 1991 at the time of modifying the regime of extraordinary powers can be grouped into general and special categories. The first deal with the design of the state, in particular the branches of public power, while the second treat the specific changes in the conditions under which the executive could legislate in an extraordinary way.

The Constituent Assembly in reforming the regime of extraordinary powers sought various objectives, including the following:

1. The strengthening of the Congress and of the separation of powers. . . . [T]he principle of the separation of powers was reinforced by temporal and subject matter limitations for the use of delegated legislation. . . . The idea was to limit the excessive role of presidential power and to foster a greater balance among the branches. . . .
2. The affirmation and furtherance of the democratic principle. It is clear that in a democratic and social state of law founded on the sovereign will of the people,

decisions that greatly impact the community should be adopted by the elected body where pluralistic discussion takes place and not by the executive. Hence, besides strengthening the Congress and the principle of the separation of powers, the Constituent Assembly sought to deepen the democratic nature of the Colombian political system by defining it as a participatory democracy founded on the principles of dignity and solidarity where the general interest shall prevail. In this context, where the participation of all citizens is favored in decision-making processes, the possibility of the executive taking on legislative functions through mechanisms which lack the guarantee of open discussion of the decrees to be adopted, and where minority groups would be excluded and citizens in general would be unable to intervene through their elected representatives, is clearly "extraordinary." This explains why the 1991 Constituent Assembly decided to restrict the granting of legislative powers to the executive and to preserve for the Congress the capacity to modify or repeal the decree-laws issued through delegated legislation.

3. The extension of the principle that Congress should have exclusive powers [over certain issues]. In agreement with the objective of strengthening the Congress, as well as democratic principles and the separation of powers, the 1991 Constituent Assembly adopted the principle that Congress should have exclusive competence over several subject matters.... This guarantees that decisions of special impact on society, such as those regarding people's constitutional rights, are not left in the hands of the executive.

In order to control abuse and excess in the exercise of the extraordinary legislative powers granted by the Congress to the President of the Republic, and to foster the harmonious collaboration between two of the branches of government, the Constituent Assembly added the following new requirements to the granting of delegated legislation:

a. To limit the excesses that occurred in the past, they clearly excluded certain matters such as the adoption of codes, statutory and organic laws . . . and the creation of taxes.
b. They forbade members of Congress from introducing bills authorizing delegated legislation to the executive [since such bills must be requested by the president]. [They did this] in order to prevent the possibility of the Congress deciding on its own initiative to grant temporary legislative powers to the president, which would go against democratic principles and the separation of powers.
c. The need for an absolute [rather than simple] majority of Congress . . . to approve the granting of delegated legislative powers, so as to hinder the temporary transfer of congressional competences to the executive. A simple majority, i.e., a majority obtained from the members of Congress present at the session . . . , is insufficient; instead, more than half of the total number of representatives must vote to grant delegated legislation to the president.

d. The establishment of congressional power to modify, at any time and on its own initiative, any decree-law issued by the government through delegated legislative powers. This was aimed at underlining that the Congress is the holder of legislative functions. Although the Congress is entitled to temporarily transfer to the President of the Republic its legislative powers regarding clearly established matters, when necessity or public interest so demands, it does not relinquish its competence to legislate on those matters, or to modify or repeal the legal provisions issued by the executive through delegated legislation.
e. In this context, it was only natural that emphasis was placed on establishing in a precise manner the limits of delegated legislation by reaffirming that they can be granted only "when necessity or public interest so demands it" and by setting stricter requirements regarding its temporary character, as a maximum six-month term was established while no time limit had existed in the past. . . .

Regarding the demand that these powers be "precise," the jurisprudence has reiterated that the breadth or generality of the grant does not constitute a violation of the Charter. However, the Court has been emphatic in underlining that these powers cannot be vague or indeterminate because that would represent a blank check to the executive and an unacceptable abdication by Congress of the legislative function. . . .

Therefore, . . . this Court [has] developed the constitutional doctrine on the requirements that must be met for a legislative grant to respect the constitutional mandate of precision. . . . The requirements of precision can be summarized in the following congressional duties: (1) to clearly define the subject matter and scope of the executive's authority; (2) to state the objective at which the president's actions should aim while exercising delegated legislation, and (3) to establish the criteria which should guide the executive's decisions regarding public policy . . . within the subject matter for which delegated legislative power was granted. . . .

[Concerning the first requirement, the Court stated that: "[T]he matters that will be regulated by the extraordinary legislator must be described in a clear and precise manner. . . ." Regarding the second requirement, the Court noted that: "[I]t is necessary for the Congress to clarify the purpose and objectives behind the granting of delegated legislative power to the executive so they guide the actions of the extraordinary legislator as to the will of Congress."]

[Last, the Court stated that the third requirement] refers to the specific criteria which allow for the definition of the scope of the authority granted to the executive and whose absence would make it extremely difficult to establish whether the president acted within the scope defined for the granting of delegated legislation. . . .

[I]t is important to note that the requirement of precision and the elements it should encompass aim at defining, clearly and specifically, the scope of the delegated legislative power without necessarily implying that the Congress should itself regulate the matter or must occupy the field of action that the Constitution grants to the executive, since this would change the nature of delegated legislation. If the Congress completely determined the contents of future decree-laws, it would not be granting temporary legislative powers to the executive, but merely carrying out its own duty as the holder of the legislative power. . . .

These requirements help to define governmental authority . . . and [allow for] control over the executive when it acts *ultra vires*. . . . [I]f the scope within which the executive can act is not clearly defined, [this would] hinder the legal control necessary to determine whether the exercise of legislative functions by the executive complies with the goals for which the Congress granted the delegated legislation, whether it is restricted to the subject matter approved, and whether it is adjusted to the criteria established for their implementation.

Within this framework, it is worth laying out the functions played by the requirement for precision within the Colombian context:

1. The law that grants extraordinary lawmaking powers to the president within constitutional parameters can be general but not imprecise. This is because precision in the Act granting delegated legislation is necessary in order to carry out constitutional control over the law itself and the decrees required for its implementation. . . .
2. The mandate of precision prevents the Congress from delegating to another authority the adoption of basic decisions affecting the life of the community in general. In a democratic state the grand democratic political decisions correspond to the organ of popular representation and pluralist deliberation, not to the executive. Grants of a blank check constitute a way to elude this democratic responsibility.
3. Precision guides the executive in the use of delegated legislation. Therefore, the Congress is entitled to delegate powers aimed at the specific design of legislative measures, but it cannot delegate the definition of the fundamental goals of a public policy to which it has been entrusted by the executive. The government can enjoy the power to choose the means for developing the ends of the grant, but cannot completely replace the Congress in the delimitation of the basic aspects of a public policy that by will of the Constitution belong to the legislature.
4. Precision also ensures that no distortion of the goal which has justified the granting of delegated legislation ensues. Its aim is to authorize the executive to legislate, following the parameters established by the Congress, in specific highly technical or complex fields where its expertise is acknowledged.
5. Precision also fosters legislative rationality. Its aim is to prohibit authorizations to the executive without [the Congress] having a clear and specific objective [in mind, thus preventing the] executive from improvising policy design . . . or modifying a policy due to the pressure exerted by interest groups with privileged access to regulatory processes.
6. The requirement of precision aims as well to preserve legal certainty. As we have stated, "the purpose of the requirement of precision in the description of topics or materials . . . is to avoid possible abuses or excesses in its exercises which would create legal uncertainty; because if Congress does not establish limits, then the powers could be used in an arbitrary and overflowing way.

[Once the Court had established the constitutional framework, it examined the extent to which the requirements regarding precision were complied with in this case. The Court concluded that none of the above mentioned requirements had been met, and thus struck down the delegation:]

[T]he contested law does not define in a clear and specific manner the matter for which delegated legislation was granted. The law gives the president authority to "organize a control and surveillance system," but it says nothing on the purpose or beneficiaries of that system. Although later in the law there is an attempt to further define the issue by stating that the system should be "adjustable to different types of institutions and regions," both the system and the institutions and regions where it is to be implemented remain undefined. The text of the law is unclear about the institutions and regions where the system must be implemented. . . . Furthermore, the term "organize a system" is too vague and ambiguous. Nothing is mentioned about the type of system, since there are many different kinds of control and surveillance systems, and no indication is given as to its basic features.

Concerning the goal of the delegated legislation granted to the President of the Republic, the norm specifically establishes that this control and surveillance system aims at managing "special situations." It is evident that this term lacks definition. Establishing what a "special situation" is depends on the criteria used to compare one situation with others so as to be able to conclude that it is special because it has a feature that differentiates it from the rest. Therefore, the quality of being special is established in contrast with the general. The norm under examination does not include any criteria to determine what is special and what is general. So, depending on the criteria used for the comparison, all situations, or none, may be special. . . .

Lastly, the contested norm does not offer any [criteria] to guide the decisions to be made by the executive through delegated legislation. As already mentioned, it does not establish any criteria to differentiate special from other situations. Given the vagueness of the phrase "to manage special situations," the scope of the norm would vary depending on how this phrase were interpreted, which is incompatible with the requirements established in . . . our Constitution. The same problem applies to the "system" to be implemented, since no parameter is indicated to establish that the system to be designed differs from others. To state that the executive will be entitled to "create the necessary bodies" is also vague. The Executive may decide that it is not necessary to create bodies, or it can decide the opposite; in both conflicting cases, its decision would be compatible with the above mentioned phrase, which obviously means that it does not, by any means, define a limit which could guide or restrict the use of the delegated legislation granted.

Notes on the Colombian "Non-delegation" Doctrine: Decision C-097 of 2003 is an example of a broader jurisprudence. The Colombian Constitutional Court has been fairly active in policing the requirements for the legislative grant of lawmaking power, and the Colombian Congress (as in C-097) has at times issued extremely vague delegations of this power.[10] Furthermore, the Court has struck down decree-laws issued by the executive when they have exceeded the limits of the delegation granted by Congress.

At the same time, it is important to understand that the requirements of the doctrine are limited. It is enough for Congress to signal the purpose of the delegation in broad terms, without determining the policy contours of the resulting decree-laws. In **Decision C-211 of 2007 (per Justice Alvaro Tafur Galvis)**, for example, the Court upheld a delegation to the president to "issue norms with force of law that contain the special career system for the defense sector, for the entrance . . . , promotion, training, incentives, performance evaluation and retirement of its public civil non-uniformed employees . . . , its decentralized entities . . . , the military services and the national police, as well as establishing all characteristics and dispositions within the law referring to its personnel regime." The Court noted that the precision requirement did not refer to the "breadth" of the delegation, but solely as to whether it "precisely delimited" the issue on which the president is empowered to legislate.

The context in which the Colombian doctrine has arisen is specific—delegation of formal emergency lawmaking powers to the president. It is not directly comparable to contexts, such as the United States, where the concern of those supporting a revival of a nondelegation doctrine is a broader issue of regulatory power.[11] There is greater similarity to some European countries, where constitutions and courts have policed the parliamentary granting of formal decree-law power to the executive branch.[12] But the underlying animating concerns across cases are similar at an abstract level: the distribution of legislative-executive power. Further, the challenge of articulating and applying a meaningful standard runs across these cases. A court may be more willing to police the boundaries in this area where, as in Colombia, they respond to specific historical concerns about legislative abdication and executive overreach.

C. Legislative Deliberation and Procedure

One of the purposes of the constitutional reforms of 1991 was to reinvigorate Congress so that it could play a greater role in deliberating about the shape of public policy. It also aimed at ensuring procedural regularity as a way to further deliberation and protection of minorities. The Court was expressly empowered to strike down congressional acts adopted with "procedural vices."

As noted in the Introduction, for various reasons Congress has not always met this expectation. For the Court, this raises a basic question: Can Congress be incentivized to act in a more deliberative manner, and how should the Court respond when it does not?

10. For other examples, see David Landau, *Political Institutions and Judicial Role in Comparative Constitutional Law*, 51 Harv. Int'l L.J. 319, 347–54 (2010).

11. *See, e.g.*, Cynthia R. Farina, *Deconstructing Nondelegation*, 33 Harv. J.L. & Pub. Pol'y 87, 95–96 (2010).

12. *See, e.g.*, Donald Kommers & Russell Miller, The Constitutional Jurisprudence of the Federal Republic of Germany 175–76 (3d ed. 2012).

In the case below, the Court reviewed a major tax reform that, among other changes, broadened the base of the VAT tax to include many goods and services that were primary necessities, such as basic food and medicine, previously excluded from the tax. As the Court states, Congress is entitled to significant deference in designing tax policy. However, in light of core constitutional principles, particularly the social state of law and the right to a vital minimum, the Court found the changes broadening the VAT tax to be suspect because they were retrogressive measures that heightened burdens on the poorest members of society, who tended to spend a high percentage of their income on the newly-taxed goods. These principles are covered in more detail in Chapter 6, which discusses social rights.

But the Court also considered it significant that the change was not part of the original proposal but instead was a congressional initiative added to the project very late in the process of legislative approach, and not subject to any congressional debate in committee or the floor. The absence of even "minimal public deliberation," as the Court put it, reduced the margin of appreciation to which Congress would otherwise be entitled in undertaking tax reform. The Constitution expressly requires that the whole tax system be progressive and equitable, but there was no congressional consideration at all about the impact of broadening the VAT tax on the system.

Decision C-776 of 2003 (per Justice Manuel José Cepeda Espinosa)

[In this decision, the Court unanimously[13] struck down a provision of a tax reform that levied a 2-percent value-added tax (VAT) on all goods or services that had previously been exempted or excluded from the tax. The Court first confirmed that among the new goods and services taxed were "primary necessities," defined as "those goods consumed by wide sectors of the population in order to take care of their vital basic necessities." The main legal disposition challenged was Article 116 of the law, which did not list the goods and services to be taxed in a specific way. It only stated that "as of January 1, 2005, the goods and services dealt with in [various] articles will have a two percent (2%) tax." These included (i) entertainment services, (ii) goods and services related to productive activities in the agricultural and farming sector among others, and (iii) primary necessities such as water, rice, corn, meat, chicken, bread, fruit, vegetables, medicines, notebooks and pencils, medical and dental services, education, public transportation, and housing rentals.]

[The Court also confirmed that Article 116 was "a very meaningful expansion of the [VAT] base, carried out in an indiscriminate way on very diverse goods and services." The Court noted that the VAT base had been gradually expanded through the years, and yet, until the enactment of the law at issue, primary necessities—with certain exceptions—had always been excluded or exempt from the VAT. Further, those exclusions and exemptions had been declared constitutional by the Court because

13. Justice Jaime Araújo Rentería dissented from another aspect of the ruling, and issued a concurrence regarding the decision on the VAT tax, arguing that any such indirect tax was per se unconstitutional because it violated the principle of progressiveness.

they fostered "real and effective equality" in a society with high levels of poverty. The Court considered that these conclusions showed that Congress had introduced a major structural change within the tax system. The Court next explained the relevant constitutional principles informing the design of the tax system, in light of broader constitutional principles:]

In accord with what is stated in ... the Constitution, it is a function of the Congress to determine the tax policy of the state ... by law. In a democratic state, it corresponds to the Congress to dictate the economic and social policy of the state, in particular regarding taxes, within the parameters established in the Constitution—the constituted powers have a broad margin of configuration on policy, but must respect the limits created by the constitutional order....

[T]he taxing power of the legislature finds clear limits in the principles that, according to what the Constituent Assembly has stated, inform the taxation system ...; these principles are (i) legality ..., (ii) equity ... and progressiveness, stated in Article 363[14] of the Constitution, and (iii) equality....

[Legality] is derived ... from the maxim according to which there is no taxation without representation, given the democratic character of the Colombian constitutional system; thus, any norm that establishes or modifies a tax obligation must go through all of the steps needed to be adopted as a law of the Republic....[15] The material manifestation of this principle refers to the deliberation regarding taxation on each good and service in the [Congress].

The foregoing is highly relevant for the resolution of this case, since it is necessary to determine if the broadening of the taxable base of the VAT was a legislative decision that was respectful of this principle, especially as to whether it was the subject of a minimum public deliberation by the Congress in terms of its implications for the equity and progressiveness of the tax system....

[T]he principle of equity demands that taxes ... fall on goods and services whose users have the capacity to support the tax ... while exonerating from the duty of taxation those who, because of their economic conditions, would suffer an unsupportable and disproportionate burden....

[T]he principle of progressiveness ... refers to the sharing of the burden of taxation between the different people obligated to pay, according to their respective capacities to contribute, in other words, by applying a criterion of analysis where the proportion of the total burden of each taxpayer is set in relation to his ability to pay.... Along the same lines, a broader dimension of the principle of progressiveness of the system, relevant to this process, invites us to evaluate the destination and effects of public spending financed with the collected resources. In this sense, the impact of public spending is relevant....

14. Article 363 states in part: "The tax system is based on the principles of equity, efficiency, and progressivity."

15. Article 338 states in part: "In time of peace only Congress, departmental assemblies, and district and municipal councils may levy fiscal or fiscal-like dues."

[T]he Court has stated that the constitutional principle of equality should be respected by the legislature at the moment of creating new tax obligations, which implies a duty to take into account the factual differences existing in society so as not to deepen current inequalities. . . .

These special principles that govern the tax system must be interpreted in light of the fundamental principles informing the entire Constitution. Among these, the most relevant is the social state of law. In addition, since . . . one's ability to pay must be appreciated by taking into account the real context, it is necessary to allude to the constitutional right to a vital minimum.

Article 1 of the Constitution establishes the social state of law as a core principle of our political order. The concept of a social state of law was born in Europe in the second half of the 20th century, as a form of state organization designed to "realize social justice and human dignity through the subjection of the public authorities to the principles, rights, and social duties of the constitutional order." In that sense, the central assumption on which one constructs this type of political organization is the intimate and unbreakable interrelationship between the spheres of "state" and "society," which is no longer visualized as composed of free and equal subjects in the abstract . . . but as a conglomerate of persons and groups in conditions of real inequality. The role of the social state of law consists, thus, in "creating the social conditions for the same freedoms for all; that is, of overcoming social inequality;" as this Court has said, "the term "social" means that the actions of the state should be directed at guaranteeing its citizens dignified lives. That is to say . . . , the state is not reduced to demanding non-interference with the freedoms of people, but should also be put in motion to counteract existing social inequalities and to offer everyone the necessary opportunities to develop their abilities and overcome material pressures. . . ." For this purpose, the state has broad powers to intervene in the economy. . . .

[The Court also noted that the social state principle should be read in light of human dignity and equality.]

[Based on the principle of human dignity,] public authorities cannot treat human beings as things or as merchandise, nor be indifferent before situations that endanger the intrinsic value of human life, understood not just as a right of physical survival, but as the right to achieve human capacity and to live a life with meaning, in an environment that is free from the fear of deprivation of those things that are materially necessary and indispensable to live with dignity. . . .

The principle and fundamental right of equality . . . represents a more tangible guarantee of the social state of law for the individual or for groups of people exposed to a deterioration of the conditions of life in a democratic society, where all people deserve the same consideration and respect as human beings. . . .

As a consequence of the foregoing, the measures adopted by the authorities in the framework of a social state of law must consult the factual reality on which they will have an impact, with an eye towards achieving the primordial goal imposed on public institutions under this formula: promoting conditions of dignified life for the entire population. . . .

The fundamental right to the vital minimum has been recognized since 1992 in an extended and reiterated form in the constitutional jurisprudence of the Court. . . . The purpose of the fundamental right to a vital minimum is to demand all positive and negative measures constitutionally ordered with the goal of avoiding a reduction in the worth of human beings because they lack the material conditions that would permit them to enjoy a dignified existence. . . . That right therefore protects the person against all forms of degradation that compromise not only her physical survival but above all her intrinsic value.

The fundamental right to a vital minimum has both positive and negative dimensions. The positive dimension presupposes that the state, and occasionally individuals . . . are required to offer persons found in a situation . . . compromising the material conditions of their existence, the necessary and indispensable benefits so that they may live in a dignified manner and avoid their degradation or annihilation as a human being. In turn, with respect to the negative dimension, the fundamental right to a vital minimum is constituted as a limit or minimum level that cannot be breached by the state, in terms of the availability of the material resources that the person requires to live a dignified life. . . .

[Finally, the Court examined the constitutionality of the provision at issue in light of these principles:]

First, the article violates the limits derived from the protection of the right to a vital minimum in a social state of law.

This decision has already indicated that the exercise of the taxing power of the state cannot be designed or have the clear effect of pushing lower-income people towards poverty . . . nor maintain them below these levels, with due regard for the insufficiency in effective social spending measures that would compensate for the effect on the vital minimum of the neediest people. . . . In effect, the tax laws cannot "place low-income people at grave risk" given their precarious ability to pay that does not correspond to their ability to generate income. This right to a vital minimum is especially relevant on account . . . of the economic context in which the provision in question would be applied. In effect, more than half of Colombians are below the poverty line and close to one quarter are below the line of [absolute poverty or] indigence. In addition, the tendency has been towards an increase in the number of people found in these conditions of manifest weakness. . . .

[Second,] in these conditions, the Court concludes that Article 116 . . . has a particular significance on broad sectors of the population whose income is used practically entirely for the satisfaction of basic needs, given that it will make it more difficult, or in extreme cases impossible, for them to ensure the minimum required to live a dignified life. In this context, it is clear that the broadening of the tax base in the terms contemplated in Article 116 . . . places a significant burden on those people who only have the minimum needed to survive. . . .

Third, there are no elements that indicate the existence of state measures that would compensate for the concrete effect of the obligations contained in the accused norm. . . . Additionally, the Court takes into consideration not only the insufficient nature of the social welfare network but also that the social public spending designed to strengthen that network has been shrinking in recent years, according to official statistics. . . .

Fourth, the broadening of the base of the VAT tax occurred within a system with serious gaps regarding the collection of taxes designed to develop the principle of progressiveness. Article 116 . . . was adopted in a context of high evasion of progressive taxes, like the income tax (with an evasion rate of 33 percent). . . .

[Finally, the Court considered the relevance of the quality of legislative deliberations in Congress:]

Fifth, based on the conception and design of the law at issue, and the manner in which it was incorporated into the taxation system, we conclude that it was the result of an indiscriminate decision to tax a large quantity of goods and services which are completely diverse, and that it was not accompanied by a minimum of public deliberation through which one would realize the principle of no taxation without representation with respect to the implications of broadening the base of the VAT on the equity and progressiveness of the tax system.

On this point, the Court notes that the accused provision was not part of the original project presented by the government. It was incorporated by the House of Representatives and later, since the Senate did not approve it, by the respective conciliation commissions. This indicates that the proposal to broaden the base of the VAT . . . did not respond to a proposal considered in the design of the original governmental project but instead attended to fiscal requirements not originally conceived in that project. . . . This is a fundamental point with respect to the democratic principle because the imposition of taxes must be accompanied by at least a minimum of public deliberation about its scope, implications, and significance for the principles of equity and progressiveness that govern the tax system, especially when these create obligations affecting low-income people. . . .

The Court observes that the project of law [originally] presented by the government . . . extended the base of the VAT, but did not cover all goods of primary necessity and basic services . . . were excluded. [The Court found that the original project in fact emphasized the exclusion of these goods and services for poor families as a way to realize equity and progressiveness within the tax system.]

Three months after the presentation of the project, in front of the full chamber of the House of Representatives . . . , one day before the end of the legislative period and without any discussion . . . , [t]he Minister of Finance stated: "Along with the President, the economic team was considering the convenience of including this levy of 2 percent on goods and services that are currently excluded and exempt . . . ; I know that this is the most complex and difficult decision of this tax reform, but I need to consider it, since we are anticipating a difficult fiscal situation . . . for 2005, and through this measure we can enact a structural solution to the fiscal problems in the country. . . . I want to note to everyone that it is a topic that was discussed at a deep level in meetings and that we measured the benefits and costs and identified that although difficult, this is an important and necessary step in our fiscal reform."

In this way a novel proposal . . . that was not debated was introduced: the universalization of the VAT tax that would . . . cover all goods and services of primary necessity.

The transcribed intervention shows that the decision to tax goods and services of first necessity was not a result of considerations based on a minimum deliberation regarding the legitimacy of the goals sought by the broadening of the base of the VAT tax to all goods and services, which in the original project were excluded precisely in order to justify the reasonableness and equity of the VAT reform according to the explanation of the project presented by the government itself. . . . The proposal of the Minister was based on fiscal requirements that became evident in the moments just before the finalization of the legislative procedure through which the law was passed. . . .

The Court will not discuss the reasons of convenience that were invoked [by the government], since these are beyond its sphere of competence. It will reiterate that the economic stability of the nation, founded on solid institutional structures, has constitutional relevance. However, the fact that Article 116, which universalized the tax base by taxing goods and services of a manifestly varying nature—from weapons of war to milk and even "Bienestarina"[16]—shows that no public deliberation destined to establish the implications . . . for different sectors of society of each one of these taxed goods and services was undertaken. As a result, the Court finds that the decision to tax all goods and services of primary necessity, without discussing considerations regarding the concrete implications of the imposition of the tax on each one of these goods and services in light of the principles governing the tax system, was indiscriminate and lacked the minimum of public deliberation needed to constitutionally allow the extension of the VAT tax base. . . .

[Consequently, the Court struck down the expansion of the VAT tax in the contested provision.]

Note on the Judicial Control of Legislative Procedure in Colombia: The Constitution stipulates detailed procedural requirements for the passage of a law—for example, it requires that the law be approved sequentially by each congressional committee and by each full chamber,[17] it requires that defined periods of time elapse between each stage of the process,[18]

16. Bienestarina is a dietary supplement produced in Colombia and given to low-income children.

17. Article 157 states in part: "No bill shall become law without meeting the following requirements: 1. Being published officially by Congress before being sent to the respective committee. 2. Being approved at the first reading in the appropriate permanent committee of each House. . . . 3. Being approved in each House at the second reading. 4. Securing the approval of the government."

18. Article 160 states in part: "Between the first and second readings, a period of no less than eight days must have elapsed, and between the approval of the bill in either of the Houses and the initiation of the debate in the other, at least 15 days must have elapsed.

and it requires that detailed Committee reports be prepared before a bill can be considered on the floor.[19] It also requires that each bill pertain to only one subject matter.[20]

The Court has actively enforced these procedural requirements (as well as the Organic Law of the Regulation of Congress), both with respect to laws and constitutional amendments. And it has done so with a view toward making congressional procedure more deliberative. There is vast case law on these topics, and we will give only a small sampling here. In **Decision C-754 of 2004 (per Justice Alvaro Tafur Galvis)**, the Court struck down key parts of a pension reform because it held that one of the constitutionally-required debates had merely been formally opened and then closed, with no substantive opportunity for debate, and therefore in effect the required number of debates needed to pass a law under the constitution had not been held. Similarly, in **Decision C-760 of 2001 (per Justices Marco Gerardo Monroy Cabra & Manuel José Cepeda Espinosa),** the Court struck down amendments to the Criminal Code because they had neither been read nor published in the record before the vote, and therefore it appeared that many members of Congress did not know the actual content of the modified text. The Court held that Congress had violated the "principle of publicity": "the supposed minimum of deliberative and decision-making rationality is knowledge of the texts of the projects and the modifications proposed to them."

In comparative law, there appears to be very broad variation in the extent to which courts will police compliance with the rules of legislative procedure and strike down laws that do not follow those requirements. In the United States, for example, the Supreme Court has generally been unwilling to examine even the most basic procedural requirements. Across parts of Europe, however, courts have played a more significant role in policing these processes.[21] The Colombian experience suggests that a court's response to these problems may depend in part on its vision of its own role vis-à-vis the legislature. The Colombian Court's jurisprudence has been an attempt to regulate legislative procedure not for its own sake, but in an attempt to deepen deliberation in light of the problematic history of the separation of powers in Colombia.

19. Article 160 states in part: "In the report to the plenary House for the second reading, the committee chairman shall present all the proposals that were considered by the committee and the reasons why they were rejected. Every draft law or draft legislative act must contain information on how it is to be dealt with by the respective committee competent to discuss it, and must proceed accordingly."

20. Article 158 states in part: "Every legislative bill shall refer to a single issue and any provisions or amendments not germane to it shall be inadmissible."

21. *See* KOMMERS & MILLER, *supra* note 12, at 110–14 (excerpting a decision where the German Constitutional Court closely examined voting rules for a vote in the German Bundestag).

PART FOUR

Constitutional Change

11

Constitutional Amendment and the Substitution of the Constitution Doctrine

The Colombian Constitution is relatively easy to amend. Indeed, 40 distinct packages of constitutional reforms were passed between 1991 and the end of 2015, although several have been partially or completely struck down by the Constitutional Court. These reforms have dealt with a number of different issues and been passed for many different purposes. Some have dealt with relatively technical issues that needed to be updated. Others have been passed in attempts to reverse or modify certain doctrines of the Constitutional Court. Finally, some have treated issues that were politically contentious in 1991 and have remained so, such as the distribution of resources and other powers between the decentralized units of the country and the central government. Some of these contentious provisions have been amended more than once.

As Article 374 states, the Constitution can be amended in three distinct ways: "Congress, a Constituent Assembly, or by the people through a referendum." The most common way of amending the Constitution is via Congress, which can enact amendments through an affirmative vote of both houses in two consecutive congressional sessions, in the first round by simple majority and in the second round by absolute majority. Most of the existing constitutional amendments have been passed through this route. In addition, the Constitution can be amended by referendum, which can be introduced by the government or by a required percentage of voters, passed through Congress, and then set for a public vote. Finally, the Constitution explicitly contemplates the possibility of a Constituent Assembly, although such a mechanism has not been used since the 1991 Constitution itself was written.

The Constitutional Court has exercised control over constitutional amendments in three distinct ways. First, in keeping with its tight control over legislative process noted in the last chapter, the Court has intervened when Congress has not followed all of the required procedural steps in the Constitution. Second, in constitutional amendments

Colombian Constitutional Law: Leading Cases. Manuel José Cepeda Espinosa and David Landau.

involving referendums, the Court has stepped in to ensure that the questions and surrounding material respect the voter's freedom of choice rather than influencing or biasing the voter. This jurisprudence is considered in Sections A and B, respectively.

Finally, and most controversially, the Court has reviewed amendments to ensure that they did not constitute substitutions of the constitution. This doctrine, which is somewhat similarly to the Indian basic structure doctrine, holds that changes to the constitutional text that alter fundamental principles of the existing text are replacements of the constitution rather than amendments to it. Such replacements of the existing constitutional order must be done through a Constituent Assembly, rather than through either a legislative act or a referendum.

The Court has applied this doctrine in several cases, but the best-known examples are those involving amendments to allow a second and then third consecutive presidential term during the mandate of the popular President Alvaro Uribe (2002–2010). The Court, in the decisions excerpted in Section C, held that the amendment to allow a second term was not a substitution of the constitution, but the amendment to allow a third term was. President Uribe complied with this decision and left office at the end of his second term.

The Colombian Constitutional Court is not the only high court in the world to use a doctrine of unconstitutional constitutional amendment. Indeed, recent scholarship suggests that the doctrine has spread considerably over the past several decades to many different regions of the world.[1] Nonetheless, along with the Indian Supreme Court, the Colombian Constitutional Court has perhaps been one of the most active courts in developing the doctrine and applying it to actually strike down significant constitutional reforms.[2]

The Court's rigorous control over the mechanisms of constitutional change, including via the substitution of the constitution doctrine, would appear to be a product of several contextual factors. One of these is the relative flexibility of the mechanisms of constitutional change. Another is the political context, which includes a very strong executive, problems of legislative deliberation, and relatively high levels of popular mistrust of the political process. In this context, the Court has at times stepped in to block constitutional changes that clashed with core constitutional and democratic values.

A. Procedural Review of Constitutional Amendments

Most constitutional amendments have been passed through the method laid out in Article 375 of the Constitution. This provision allows certain groups (including the government, 10 members of Congress, or 5 percent of citizens) to introduce legislative acts reforming

1. *See* Yaniv Roznai, *Unconstitutional Constitutional Amendments—The Migration and Success of a Constitutional Idea*, 61 AM. J. COMP. L. 657 (2013).

2. For a comparison of the Indian basic structure doctrine and the Colombian substitution of the constitution doctrine as responses to their respective political contexts, see Rosalind Dixon & David Landau, *Transnational Constitutionalism and a Limited Doctrine of Unconstitutional Constitutional Amendment*, 13 INT'L J. CONST. L. 606 (2015).

the Constitution. These legislative acts are approved if they are passed by both the House and Senate twice, in two consecutive legislative sessions (each session lasts roughly one semester). In the first round, approval can occur by a simple majority of those present in each chamber, but the second round requires an absolute majority of the members of each body. As the Constitution and the laws regulating Congress require prior approval in each round by the relevant Commission charged with studying constitutional issues, approval of a legislative act requires eight debates and eight votes. The amendment must preserve its basic content during the eight debates. Changes may be introduced during any of the eight debates, but the change must be closely linked to the original subject matter of the respective amendment.

As noted in the prior chapter, the Constitutional Court has exercised a fairly robust review of the procedures through which laws have been passed. As the case below shows, this review includes legislative acts containing constitutional amendments as well as ordinary laws. Indeed, the case excerpted here is emblematic of a broader jurisprudence—several constitutional reforms have been partially or totally struck down by the Court because of procedural problems in their passage.[3]

Decision C-816 of 2004 (per Justices Jaime Córdoba Triviño and Rodrigo Uprimny Yepes)

[In a five-to-four decision, the Court struck down all of Legislative Act 2 of 2003, which would have amended the Constitution to allow the authorities to take a number of restrictive measures to face Colombia's ongoing civil violence. The amendments would have permitted the interception of communications, the search of domiciles, and the detention of persons without a previous judicial warrant. These proposed amendments, called the Anti-Terrorism Statute, were one of the key tools that the government wanted to use to fight guerrillas and organized crime within the context of "democratic security," the security policy of President Alvaro Uribe. In some sense, these measures represented an effort to make permanent some of the tough security measures that President Uribe had attempted to issue during a state of internal commotion in 2002. As was seen in Chapter 9, Section C, many of these measures were struck down by the Court even during a state of exception; those that survived expired when the corresponding state of internal commotion ended.]

[The challengers argued that the constitutional amendments were not approved by using the proper legislative procedures. In particular, they focused on irregularities in the vote in the full House of Representatives to approve a conference report supporting the project in the second round. Under constitutional procedures, this vote required an absolute majority of members of the House. If the vote failed to

3. A more recent example is Decision C-740 of 2013 (per Justice Nilson Pinilla Pinilla), where the Court struck down a set of amendments changing the rules and institutions with respect to criminal cases involving members of the armed forces. The Court held that this legislative act had to be struck down in its entirety because one of the debates in the Committee in the House of Representatives was effectively held simultaneously with a debate on the floor of the House regarding the same bill.

receive an absolute majority, then the project itself would fail and should not advance further. President Uribe had strong support from the leaders of Congress; however these leaders were having a hard time gaining sufficient support for the vote.[4] On November 5, 2003, the House opened a vote on the project. However, when it did not appear that the vote would receive the absolute majority required (the project had received 83 favorable votes, and an absolute majority of the House constituted 84), the President of the Congress first extended the time for voting beyond the normal practice and then adjourned the session without recording the failed vote and consequent failure of the project, citing "disorder" in the Chamber due to protests from opponents of the Act. The next day, a new vote on the conference report took place, and this time it received an absolute majority. The challengers argued that the irregularities in this vote violated core principles of legislative procedure and should result in the entire package of amendments being struck down.]

The parameters applicable to our control of [constitutional amendments] are composed of the norms of the Constitution and the Rules of Parliamentary Procedure (i) whose fulfillment is a basic and necessary presupposition for the adequate democratic formation of the political will of the Chambers; (ii) that are closely related to the materialization of constitutional principles and values, especially the democratic principle; and (iii) which, if ignored, would cause an indirect violation of "the requirements set by the Constitution itself for the approval of those reforms. . . ."

[The Court reviewed the evidence from the November 5 session and surrounding events, including the minutes of the debates and the tape recording of the session, where it was possible, in the midst of the disorganization, to listen to words that were not part of the formally approved minutes. For example, during the November 5 session, the Vice-President of the House could be heard on tape saying: "If it is closed it will fail. If it is closed it will fail. Better to lift the session for order." Based on this evidence, the Court concluded:]

The foregoing elements allow us to infer the existence . . . of a unity of purpose in the Directive Board [composed of the President and Vice-President of the House] and it was the following: to utilize all apparently allowable mechanisms to achieve the approval of the Legislative Act. The Directive Board thus made improper use . . . of the powers conferred by the regulations to maintain order in sessions, in order . . . not to recognize the effects of the vote on the report of the legislative sponsors of the project on the floor of the House on November 5. On November 5, the voting process materially took place, and it was the refusal of the Directive Board to record the result that led it to extend the voting time and to adjourn the session, taking advantage of the disorganization that, to a great extent, its own behavior had generated. And even though the session was then reinstated, the voting process was postponed for the following day. That is, the votes were not counted, nor was the project considered

4. On October 29, 2003, for example, the challengers argued that the President of the House manipulated a vote on the agenda so that a vote would not occur that day, because of uncertainty in the outcome.

defeated as a consequence of the report not receiving approval from the absolute majority required.

In light of this unity of design, and taking into account the expressions quoted from the Vice-President of the House, the apparently not so reasonable decision of the president to adjourn the November 5 session takes on a specific meaning since, if what generated the disorganization was [their own] refusal to close the voting process, why then did the president not proceed to close it, if more than enough time had passed so that all the representatives present in the capitol, even those who had momentarily left the floor, would have been able to vote? And the answer is clear: Because the motivation of the members of the Board was not to bring order to the session, but a different one: to avoid recording the vote that had taken place, because they believed that this would mean the defeat of the project.

Based on this, the Court concludes that the adjournment of the session was not used as a legitimate resource to overcome a disturbance on the floor, but as a mechanism to ignore the legal and practical effects of a voting process that had materially taken place.

It is only logical to suppose that the Directive Board's strategy of not acknowledging the legal and practical effects of the voting process that had taken place aimed at the following purpose: to provide an opportunity so that, off the floor of Congress, a sufficient majority could be obtained to have the project approved. And effectively, such a purpose became concrete in the voting process the following day, when the report on the proposal obtained 104 votes in favor and 32 against, compared to the 83 in favor and the 48 against of the previous day. Also, the Court cannot ignore, given its constitutional relevance, that an essential element of that increase in the majority in favor of the report was the change in votes of at least 14 representatives. . . .

The Court must therefore evaluate the legal significance of this irregularity. Now, since that defect occurred in the vote on a conference report, it is natural that this Court would begin be examining the purpose and value of the vote on a conference report within the legislative process approving legislative acts. . . .

[T]he Court concludes that the conference report is an element of great importance in the formation of democratic will in the chambers. In effect, it is through the conference report that the members of the floor can know the issues raised by the project and can express, through the vote on the report, their agreement or disagreement with it. In that context, the mandatory presentation of a conference report develops the principle of publicity, which is essential in the formation of the democratic will of the chambers. . . . [T]he debates in Congress must be preceded by a public presentation of the reasons that justify the adoption of a law or legislative act. . . .

The legal and practical outcome of the voting process of the November 5 session was thus the failure or archiving of the project. However, the session was adjourned by the Directive Board of the House, without acknowledging the legal and practical effect of that voting process, which is equivalent to suppressing its effects; this is obviously a fault of special gravity, since it ignores a decision of the House and thus distorts the democratic will of Congress. . . .

The suppression of the legal and practical effects of the aforementioned voting process is ... one of those procedural faults that leads to the unconstitutionality of a legislative act, at least for these two reasons: on the one hand, this failure is inexorably bound to the absolute majority required by the Constitution [for approval of constitutional amendments in the second round]. Further, the voting process on the conference report is a critical moment in the process of approval of constitutional reforms.

[Further, the Court held that the procedural error was not corrected by the new vote held on November 6, 2003, in which the conference report was passed.]

It is possible for a fault in voting, despite its seriousness, to be cleansed in the subsequent passage of the bill through the chambers, as has been recognized by the doctrine of this Court and other constitutional tribunals.... This situation is known by some authors as the "test of the prevalence of the vote," according to which a law cannot be annulled if despite errors in voting, it is clear that the project had sufficient support to be approved. An example in comparative law is decision No. 225 of January 23, 1987 of the Constitutional Council of France, which declared that a project should not be struck down, despite the occurrence of a serious fault in voting, because in any case it was clear that it possessed the required majority.[5] In that case, some members of parliament had delegated their vote to others.... The Constitutional Council found that there was a violation of the regulations, but it did not annul the vote because there was no evidence of a distortion of democratic will; even if those irregular votes were ignored, the project had a sufficient majority.

One could thus argue that in this case, despite the suppression of the vote of November 5 ..., we should not strike down the legislative act ..., since ... the conference report received a broad majority the next day.

Despite this, the Court holds that in the process for the accused legislative act, the fault was not cleansed by the vote held on November 6 ... because this new vote, far from correcting the fault, was in reality its materialization. The new vote is in effect a concrete manifestation of the suppression of the juridical and practical consequences of the voting process carried out on November 5, 2003, which should have been respected, with all its effects, by the Board of the House of Representatives and by that Chamber. And this is so because the new vote implied a sort of annulment or repetition of the vote of the previous day, which suppressed the effects of the decision adopted by the House on November 5 that would have caused the project to fail.

[The Court also addressed the question of whether the procedural defect was "remediable." The Constitution provides that the remedy in case a "remediable" procedural defect had occurred during the passage of a law or constitutional amendment would be to send the act back to Congress and allow it to correct the procedural error.[6]

5. *See* CC decision 86-225 DC, Jan. 23, 1987, Rec. 13.

6. Article 241 states in part: "When the Court finds an error in remediable procedures in the drafting of measures subject to its control, it shall order their return to the authority which issued them so that, if possible, that authority should correct the observed flaw. Once the error is corrected, it shall proceed to decide on the validity of the measure."

But the Court considered that in this case it was impossible to send the legislative act back to Congress so it could correct the fault, for several reasons: "(i) because of the nature of the fault, since there was a distortion in the formation of the democratic will of the House . . . ; (ii) [and] because, even if the fault were in principle correctible, in this case it is not possible to correct it, as its correction would take place outside the bounds of the two ordinary consecutive legislative periods that . . . the Constitution requires for the approval of legislative acts. . . ." Finally, the Court concluded by reflecting broadly on the purpose and importance of its jurisprudence controlling the procedure followed by Congress in passing laws and constitutional amendments:]

At a general level, control over procedural errors in the formation of laws and the approval of constitutional reforms is without doubt one of the most important functions of constitutional justice . . . in contemporary democracies. The reason for this importance is clear: popular sovereignty today is expressed, in great measure, by deliberations and decisions submitted to procedural rules, which look to assure the formation of a democratic will in representative assemblies, obviously expressing the majority decision, but in such an manner that those collective decisions, which bind all of society, are a product of a public discussion permitting participation by minorities as well. And in a constitutional democracy like the Colombian one, which is essentially pluralist, the validity of a majoritarian decision does not reside only in its having been adopted by a majority but also in its having been publicly deliberated and discussed, in such a manner that the distinct reasons to justify that decision have been debated, challenged, and made known to citizens, and so that, in addition, minorities have been able to participate in those debates and their rights have been respected. It follows that in this conception, democracy is not the tyranny of the majority, because the rights of minorities must be respected and protected. In addition, in a constitutional democracy, collective decisions must be deliberated in public because that way rational, just, and impartial decisions are reached. . . . The legislative process should not only be a system for aggregating preferences or legitimating private accords or secret negotiations but must constitute a public deliberation, in which the representatives of citizens, without forgetting the interests of the voters who elected them, discuss publicly and offer reasons. . . .

In constitutional democracies in general, and specifically in Colombian constitutionalism, public deliberation and respect for the procedures of the chambers are not empty rituals; respect for those formalities has a profound meaning since they permit the formation of democratic will, in order to make it as public and impartial as possible, and also because they ensure respect for minority rights. The sessions of Congress are not, therefore, a space where decisions and negotiations made outside of the chambers are formalized or ratified. . . . Without denying that there can exist negotiations between political forces outside of parliamentary sessions, in as much as those meetings are inevitable in the modern world, it is clear that constitutional democracies, and specifically the Constitution of 1991, opt for a deliberative and public model of the formation of laws and legislative acts. The meeting of the chambers does not have as its object the mere formality of ratifying a decision that was adopted by political forces outside the parliamentary halls; sessions of Congress must be spaces where distinct positions and perspectives ... are truly discussed and debated in an open forum and before public opinion.... Congress is a space of public reason. Or at least that is what the Constitution postulates it should be.

[The Court therefore struck down the entire package of constitutional amendments. Four justices dissented, under two different theories. Justices Rodrigo Escobar Gil, Marco Gerardo Monroy Cabra, and Álvaro Tafur Galvis dissented because they argued that any procedural error in the November 5 vote was corrected by the vote held the next day. As they argued: "Even if it were admitted, for the sake of discussion, that the President of the House of Representatives had the obligation to continue the voting session that was taking place and which was interrupted by the adjournment of the session, any error that could have occurred would have been corrected in the plenary session of the House of Representatives that took place on November 6, 2003, during which the report ... was voted on for the second time...."]

[Justice Manuel José Cepeda Espinosa wrote a separate dissent, arguing that a procedural error had occurred but that it was remediable, and therefore that the Court had selected the wrong remedy in striking down the law rather than returning it to Congress for correction via a new vote: "what should have occurred in this case was to return the legislative act back to Congress so that, if the latter considered it convenient, it could correct the formal irregularity." He also argued that some parts of the constitutional amendment were unconstitutional as a "substitution of the constitution" (see Section C of this chapter), and that the Court should have analyzed those issues.]

B. Control of Constitutional Reform via Referendum

Article 378 allows the Constitution to be amended by referendum through a multistep process. At the initiative of either the government or a sufficient number of citizens, Congress may approve a law through an absolute majority vote in each chamber to submit a constitutional reform proposal to popular referendum. The popular vote is considered approved if a majority of voters in the election vote in favor of it and a minimum participation requirement is met—at least 25 percent of all registered voters cast votes.[7] The article also contains a special mandate to protect the intent of voters: "The referendum shall be presented in such a manner as to allow the voters to freely choose." The case below focuses on the interpretation of this phrase.

7. Furthermore, Article 377 allows 5 percent of the voters to demand a referendum on any constitutional reform approved by Congress, within six months of that approval, whenever the amendment refers to "the rights recognized in Chapter I of Title II and to their guaranties [Articles 11–41], to the procedures of popular participation, or to Congress."

Decision C-551 of 2003 (per Justice Eduardo Montealegre Lynett)

[Soon after the inauguration of President Uribe in 2002, a proposal to amend the Constitution by referendum became the subject of a heated debate. Three issues were emphasized by the government: (i) a reform of electoral rules and the creation of prohibitions in order to fight corruption, (ii) the need to create a more transparent debate over the budget, and (iii) the overruling of several decisions of the Constitutional Court on diverse topics, from the increase in public-sector salaries (see Chapter 6, Section B) to the admissibility of possessing a personal dose of illegal drugs (see Chapter 3, Section A). President Uribe introduced the referendum proposal into Congress, and during the congressional debates the referendum was substantially modified. The Court studied the constitutionality of the final law approved by Congress, which for the first time since the issuance of the 1991 Constitution called for a referendum to consider a constitutional reform project. The law called for a referendum on several distinct constitutional topics, such as the limitation of labor rights, the modification of the electoral system, the reduction of state expenditures, the changing of rules to approve the budget, and the possibility of punishing the consumption of illegal drugs. The referendum included 18 distinct questions.]

[The Court, in a six-to-two decision, struck down parts of the act through which Congress had called the referendum. The Court began by defining the basic characteristics of the referendum in the Colombian constitutional system.]

The Constitution regulates the constitutional referendum in a careful way, since its objective was not only to establish a mechanism of constitutional reform, but also to ensure that the referendum, in the Colombian constitutional order, would be an instrument in service of citizens, and not a resource in service of the governing class.

Article 378 thus creates precise rules that are designed to avoid these risks: on one hand, they establish that the president cannot directly convoke a constitutional referendum, which must be convoked by a law approved by an absolute majority of the members of both chambers. On the other hand, the Constitution orders that the questions be presented in such a way that the freedom of the voter is protected, and he or she can freely choose whether to vote positively or negatively. Third, the Constitution requires a minimum level of participation for the proposed reforms to be approved. And finally, the Constitution charges the Constitutional Court . . . with controlling the act convoking the referendum.

But the defining characteristic of the constitutional referendum is found in Article 374 of the Constitution. . . . This provision establishes that the referendum is a mechanism of reform of the people, not of the president or the Congress. It clearly states that the Constitution "may be reformed . . . by the people through a referendum." This is a development of participatory democracy as an orienting principle of the entire Constitution. . . .

[T]he Constitution, in establishing the referendum as a mechanism of constitutional reform, did not pretend to consecrate a procedure of pure direct democracy, without judicial controls, and which was totally unlinked from the representative institutions. On the contrary, Article 378 seeks an articulation between representative democracy, the direct participation of the people and the judicial guarantee of the supremacy of the Constitution, and because of this, the constitutional referendum by government initiative can be solicited by the government, be discussed and approved in Congress, which is the organ par excellence of political representation, and also be automatically controlled by this Court for the regularity of the procedure through which the referendum has been called. The Constitution thus aims to "democratize democracy" by setting up a participatory democracy that combines representative institutions with mechanisms of direct democracy. . . .

Article 378 of the Constitution establishes as a prerequisite for the validity of the convoking of a referendum to modify the Constitution that it be "presented in such a manner as to allow the voters to freely choose from the agenda or the various items that which they approve or disapprove." It is clear that there is an express and unavoidable constitutional mandate to guarantee the freedom of voters in referendums, and it obviously corresponds to this Court to verify whether or not the current law complies with this requirement, since it has the power to determine whether the convoking of a referendum is done in conformity with the procedures established by the Constitution. This Court will therefore determine the implications that the constitutional protection of this freedom of the voter has for the control of the referendum law. . . .

Since the freedom of voters must be protected in all elections, but Article 378 orders that it be specially protected in constitutional referendums, it is clear that the Constituent Assembly showed a special preoccupation for that freedom in the case of reform of the Constitution by referendum. . . . [T]he manipulation of the voter is one of the essential means that has been used by authoritarian regimes to legitimate themselves through a plebiscite. . . .

The mandate to protect the freedom of voters in . . . the Constitution is not limited to repeating general guarantees of the right to vote—such as its egalitarian, universal and secret character—but is especially geared towards the way the article is submitted to the people's will. In effect, this norm demands that the topic be written and submitted in such a way that the voter can freely select what he or she supports and what he or she rejects. This implies that the control exercised by this Court . . . inevitably includes the text itself of the Act, as this Court must examine whether the presentation of the article subjected to the approval of the people ensures the liberty of voters.

[The Court began to judge whether the introductory notes that would precede each question violated this guarantee.]

[T]he Court finds that the existence of introductory notes presents important problems. The most obvious, but not the only ones, are those cases in which (i) the questions are written in a way that influences the response of the voter, or (ii) there is no relationship between the content of the [introductory note] and the normative text. . . .

The incorporation in the text of the act of notes or introductory questions that can be considered misleading, that use emotional language, or that are incomplete, threatens the constitutional principle of the right of the voter. . . .

Adding introductory notes to the text of the act calling for a referendum . . . can only be constitutionally justified if the introductory questions aid in the proper exercise of democracy and guarantee the voter's freedom. Consequently, the Court considers that the introductory notes must comply with certain requirements: (i) that they be drafted in simple and understandable language; (ii) that they be value-neutral; (iii) that they be brief . . . ; (iv) that they not be superfluous or innocuous; and (v) that they explain the object of the question. For the Court, compliance with these requirements guarantees that the introductory notes (i) are not used to manipulate the political decision; (ii) do not influence the voter's answer; (iii) do not present partial or misleading information, and therefore do not vitiate political will; (iv) guarantee favorable conditions for the proper exercise of the political right; (v) provide direction and order to the voting process; and (vi) give the decision taken a higher degree of legitimacy.

Beyond the foregoing, the Court finds that the introductory notes incorporated into the text of the law signal some ends or purposes of the reform. This is evident if one examines these introductory notes, which in a recurring manner use expressions such as "with the end of," "in order to," "to carry out," "to reduce," "to suppress." This would seem to indicate a causal relationship between the introductory note and the approval of the text of the article, since the achievement of the ends or purposes stated in the introductory note would depend on the approval of the respective normative text.

This suggests at least two requirements that the introductory notes must satisfy, in order to guarantee the freedom of the voter. The first is the requirement of correspondence, which indicates that . . . there must exist a relationship between the linguistic contents of the introductory note and the normative text. . . . The second one deals with the nature of the causal relationship established between the purpose (introductory note) and the means (proposed reform). For the Court, the guarantee of the freedom of the voter implies that . . . there exists a clear causal relationship, and not merely a hypothetical one, between the purpose (introductory note) and the means (text of article), which implies that once the article is approved the purpose indicated has a greater probability of being achieved.

It is clear, then, that the inclusion of introductory notes that do not satisfy these requirements, by indicating ends that do not correspond to the normative contents they refer to or that are not susceptible to being reached if their approval is given, creates false expectations in the voter and misleads his or her political will, thus totally ignoring the guarantee of the freedom of the voter.

[Based on this analysis, the Court examined all of the introductory notes. For example, the introductory note to the question reversing the Court's personal dose decision stated:]

Against Narcotrafficking And Drug Addiction

Question: To Protect Colombian Society, Particularly its Children And Young People, Against The Use Of Cocaine, Heroin, Marijuana, Bazuco, Ecstasy And All Other Hallucinogens, Do You Approve The Following Article?

With regards to this introductory note the Court finds at least two problems, the first has to do with expressions like "to protect" and "against the use of cocaine . . . ," because it associates a socially desirable situation, like the control of abuse of certain . . . substances, with the approval of the project of the norm. . . .

The second problem is with the . . . causal relationship that can be established between the introductory note and the approval of the article, which includes the criminalization of the possession and consumption of hallucinogenic substances, since there exists many critical analyses of those criminalization strategies, according to which these type of policies, far from protecting, tend to aggravate the situation of consumers by marginalizing them socially.

The employment of emotional language to motivate the voter, and the absence of a clear link between the introductory note and the article to be approved, demonstrates the inclusion of elements that ignore the guarantee of liberty of the voter. . . .

Up until now, the Court has found that various introductory notes threaten the guarantee of freedom of the voter. . . . However, there are more powerful arguments that show that the defects that were already detected in those introductory notes were not casual, but derive from deeper structural problems making these notes unconstitutional in a referendum.

For the Court it is practically impossible to write titles or questions in . . . a neutral, objective, or impartial manner. . . . [A]ny attempt to formulate an introductory note, in these circumstances and with these characteristics, will necessarily imply a prior interpretation of the normative content to which it refers. . . .

The prior consideration is linked to another dilemma regarding those introductory notes, and it is the following: if the title and question do not achieve all of the normative density of the article to be approved, then they violate the double demand for fidelity and clarity; but if they do reproduce that content, then they become useless because they become practically a repetition of the text to be approved. . . .

[Based on these considerations, the Court struck down all of the introductory questions, except for the phrase: "Do you approve the following article?" The Court next considered the question in the referendum that allowed voters to vote yes on all questions simultaneously, or block vote provision:]

The possibility of a block vote in a multi-topic referendum refers to the problem of the thematic unity of the referendum itself and its relationship with the freedom of the voter. . . . [T]he Constitution does not demand that a referendum only treat one constitutional topic, and thus it may include multiple topics; the problem that emerges is with the block vote, in order to protect the liberty of the voter and prevent the referendum from losing its nature and becoming transformed into a form of plebiscitary support for the government. . . .

A block vote on a multi-theme referendum with this degree of heterogeneity violates the liberty of the voter and alters the nature of a constitutional referendum by converting it into an expression of support or disapproval of the proponent of the referendum.

[A] referendum calls upon the people to vote so that they can approve or reject a project of constitutional salience. Consequently, allowing voters to vote on a referendum as a whole is compatible with that legal instrument and with the protection of the voter's freedom only so long as the referendum deals with only one topic, because if various questions deal with the same subject matter, it is reasonable to suppose that they have a similar orientation and aim at common purposes. . . . On the contrary, the situation varies substantially in a multi-theme referendum with a high degree of heterogeneity since, in this event, it is obvious that the purpose of the different themes is not always the same since they are independent and unrelated issues. Why should one authorize citizens to support or reject globally a series of very diverse reforms if, in essence, doing so would permit the referendum to become a manifestation of confidence or mistrust in the proponents of the referendum? Such an election would not constitute a referendum, since a referendum is a decision from the citizens on a legal project and not a manifestation of support or disapproval of a government. . . .

Allowing voters to vote on a multi-themed referendum as a whole, instead of promoting a decision by the citizens on each theme and article, which is the purpose of a referendum, tends to favor the expression of global manifestations of support or rejection for the proponents of the referendum. Voting on a referendum as a whole under these circumstances is unconstitutional. . . .

[The Court thus struck down the introductory questions and the block vote provision. It upheld most of the rest of the referendum questions. However, it did strike down some referendum questions on the ground that there were procedural problems in their passage, and others on the grounds that they were problematic from the standpoint of the freedom of voters. For example, one of the questions involved a number of changes to reduce the size of Congress and modified the system of election law both for Congress and some local political bodies. The question was challenged for hindering the will of the voter, as it included several distinct issues but forced the voter to assess all of them jointly. The Court upheld most of this question, noting that a "complex question in a referendum is constitutionally admissible if Congress aims at the approval of a systematic regulation on a topic." It found this to be the case with the question at issue as all of it aimed at "modifying the structure of Congress and the electoral system with the goal of achieving certain objectives including the rationalization of representation in Congress. . . ." However, it struck down a part of the proposed amendment that would have created "special electoral districts for peace" only for the 2006 election, in representation of illegal armed groups that were willing to demobilize. The Court found that this "paragraph regulates a distinct topic, which does not affect the ordinary dynamic of the new electoral system or the new composition of Congress."]

[Justices Alfredo Beltrán and Clara Inés Vargas dissented, considering that the Legislative Act should have been declared unconstitutional in its totality. They argued that the act being examined, which supposedly called for a referendum, was in reality a plebiscite aimed at expressing support for the president. "The discussion and approval in the Congress of the Republic was carried out as a question of confidence in the person governing and for adherence to a specific policy that, at that time, was presented as a slogan to win a political campaign. . . ."]

Note on Constitutional Referendums in the Colombian System: Only a single article passed the referendum and became part of Article 122 of the Constitution; this article mainly expanded the permanent loss of the ability to participate in politics of individuals who had been convicted of certain kinds of crimes that implied loss of public funds. All other articles in the referendum obtained a majority of the votes cast, but the total number of votes for or against was below the constitutionally required threshold of one-fourth of all registered voters.

In **Decision C-1121 of 2004 (per Justice Clara Ines Vargas Hernández)**, the Court examined the constitutionality of this article against a charge that the list of registered voters had been improperly constructed. The complaint argued that both deceased persons and some new members of the armed forces who could not vote were included on the list, and further that the electoral census excluded persons who had not received the documents necessary to vote. The Court upheld the challenged reform because the census of registered voters had been clearly set out before the vote was held. "Popular sovereignty was respected and participative democracy was guaranteed because both the citizens who went to vote and those who abstained from doing so, acted under the knowledge of clear rules as to the number of votes required to approve the referendum. . . . In other words, an essential principle of participatory democracy was respected, according to which there must be some clear, pre-established and public '*rules of the game*' that guarantee the liberty of those who wish to participate in a democratic event of this nature."

Since 2004, there have been several other attempts to change the Constitution via referendum. In **Decision C-397 of 2010 (per Justice Mauricio González Cuervo)**, for example, the Court struck down a proposed referendum that would have amended the Constitution to allow life prison terms for certain serious crimes, finding errors in its process of passage. And in **Decision C-141 of 2010 (per Justice Humberto Antonio Sierra Porto)**, which is excerpted in Section C below, the Court struck down a proposed referendum on whether to allow presidents to seek three consecutive terms in office.

C. The Substitution of the Constitution Doctrine

The "substitution of the constitution" doctrine is based on the idea that a constitutional reformer has the power to reform the existing constitution, not to replace the existing constitution for a new one. The doctrine allows the Court to exercise a type of quasi-substantive review of constitutional amendments. The doctrine holds that certain constitutional changes are so fundamental that they really create a new constitution rather than amending the old one. These changes can only be done through a Constituent Assembly, an option that is explicitly contemplated in the text of the Constitution,[8] rather than through the usual constitutional amendment processes. Only a popularly elected Constituent Assembly has competence to substitute the 1991 Constitution for an entirely different one, even a text

8. Article 376 states in part: "By means of an Act approved by the members of both Houses, Congress may direct that the voters participating in the popular balloting decide if a Constituent Assembly should be called with the jurisdiction, term, and makeup that the same law shall determine."

with radically opposing institutions (i.e., by replacing a presidential regime with a parliamentary one). The 1886 Constitution was replaced by the 1991 Constitution through the route of a Constituent Assembly.

The jurisprudential foundations of this doctrine were established in Decision C-551 of 2003, the referendum case excerpted above. At the beginning of that decision, the Court examined the scope of its review of constitutional change. In particular, the Court sought to clarify this issue in light of Article 241, which states that the Court can review laws amending the constitution "exclusively for errors of procedure in their makeup."[9] The Court noted that this provision excluded "substantive review" of those changes, which at any rate would be nonsensical because the whole point of a constitutional amendment is to alter the existing content of the text. But it held that it still had the power to determine whether Congress (or other constitutional reformer) had the competence to carry out the amendment at issue:

> In the development of democratic principles and of popular sovereignty, the constituent power lies in the people, who preserve the power to give themselves a Constitution. The original constituent power, then, is not subjected to legal limits and implies, above all, the complete exercise of the political power by the relevant individuals. . . . On the other hand, the power of reform, or derivative constituent power, refers to the capacity certain organs of the state have, on some occasions by consulting the citizens, to modify the existing Constitution, but within the paths determined by the [current] Constitution itself. This implies that it is a power established by the Constitution, and that is exercised under the conditions set out by the same Constitution.
>
> The derivative constituent power, then, lacks the power to destroy the Constitution. The constituent act establishes the legal order and, because of that, any power of reform is limited only to carrying out a revision. The power of reform, which is constituted power, is not, therefore, authorized to annul or substitute the Constitution from which its competence is derived. The constituted power cannot . . . grant itself functions that belong to the constituent power and, therefore, cannot carry out a substitution of the Constitution not only because it would then become an original constituent power, but also because it would undermine the bases of its own competence. . . .
>
> Based on the foregoing, the Court concludes that even though the Constitution of 1991 does not establish any express petrified or unmodifiable clause, this does not mean that the power of reform lacks limits. The power of reform, a constituted power, has material limits, because the power to reform the Constitution does not include the possibility of derogating it, subverting it or substituting it in its integrity. In order to determine whether there has been a defect of competence in an act of constitutional reform . . . , the constitutional justice must consider whether the

9. In addition, Article 379 states in part: "The legislative acts, the convocation to the referendum, the popular consultation, or the act of convocation of the Constituent Assembly may be declared unconstitutional only when the requirements established in this title are violated."

> Constitution was replaced by another one, and to do this it is necessary to analyze the principles and values of the Constitution, as well as those arising from the constitutional block. . . .
>
> For example, a constitutional amendment cannot be used to substitute the democratic and social state of law with a republican structure for a totalitarian state, for a dictatorship, or for a monarchy, as this would imply that the 1991 Constitution had been replaced by a different one, even though the change had formally been carried out through the power of constitutional reform. And therefore, since the Court must analyze whether the power of reform has surpassed limits on its competence, it is necessary for us . . . to examine whether the projects of constitutional reform submitted for approval by the people imply a substitution of the 1991 Constitution.

As can be gleaned from these arguments, the Court has based the substitution of the constitution doctrine on a distinction between "original constituent power," which is the unlimited power of the people to remake their political institutions, and the "derivative constituent power" exercised by constitutional amendment mechanisms, which can amend the existing text but not replace its fundamental principles.[10] Thus, one way to envision the doctrine might be to view it as establishing several distinct tiers for constitutional change.[11] Changes that are mere "amendments" to the constitution can be performed using any of the mechanisms—congressional approval, referendum, or constituent assembly—that are contemplated in the text. But changes that are so radical as to partially or totally replace the existing constitutional order may only be performed by a Constituent Assembly.

1. The First Re-election Decision

Alvaro Uribe Velez was elected President of the Republic for the 2002–2006 term. Halfway through his term, when his levels of popular support were very high, a group of members of Congress presented a constitutional amendment to establish the possibility of presidential re-election for the following term or for a later period. Presidential re-election had been expressly forbidden by the 1991 Constitution in Article 197. At times in the past, re-election had been possible in Colombia, but not for the immediately subsequent term. The legislative initiative amending the Constitution was approved by Congress after a heated debate

10. *See* Joel Colon-Rios, *The Legitimacy of the Juridical: Constituent Power, Democracy, and the Limits of Constitutional Reform*, 48 OSGOODE HALL L.J. 199 (2010); GONZALO RAMIREZ-CLEVES, LÍMITES DE LA REFORMA CONSTITUCIONAL EN COLOMBIA. EL CONCEPTO DE CONSTITUCIÓN COMO FUNDAMENTO DE LA RESTRICCIÓN (2005). For a critique of this conventional position, see Carlos Bernal, *Unconstitutional Constitutional Amendments in the Case Study of Colombia: An Analysis of the Justification and Meaning of the Constitutional Replacement Doctrine*, 11 INT'L J. CONST. L. 339 (2013) (arguing that the doctrine is better founded on limits inherent in the nature of constitutionalism and grounded in the core normative purposes of the existing text).

11. *See* Vicki C. Jackson, *Unconstitutional Constitutional Amendments: A Window into Constitutional Theory and Transnational Constitutionalism*, *in* DEMOKRATIE-PERSPEKTIVEN FESTSCHRIFT FUR BRUN-OTTO BRYDE ZUM 70 GEBURGTSTAG 47 (Herausgegeben von Michael Bauerle et al. eds., 2013).

regarding its convenience and after significant pressure was exerted by the government to achieve the required majority. After analyzing the many actions of unconstitutionality filed by citizens against the amendment, the Constitutional Court declared it constitutional, on the explicit premise that only a single re-election was allowed, thus enabling the incumbent president to run for a new term. President Uribe won the election and took office for the 2006–2010 period.

Decision C-1040 of 2005 (per Justices Manuel José Cepeda Espinosa, Rodrigo Escobar Gil, Marco Gerardo Monroy Cabra, Humberto Antonio Sierra Porto, Alvaro Tafur Galvis, and Clara Inés Vargas Hernández)

[In this decision, the Court examined the constitutionality of Legislative Act 2 of 2004, which amended the Constitution to enable the re-election of the president for one additional term, consecutive or nonconsecutive. In a six-to-three vote on procedural issues,[12] and a seven-to-two vote on flaws regarding whether the amendment constituted a "substitution of the constitution," the Court upheld the key parts of the amendment under discussion.]

[T]he judgment of substitution does not involve a comparison between the amendment and the Constitution to see if the former contradicts the latter, as, by definition, a constitutional amendment does contradict the provision subject to change within the Constitution.

[Instead,] the concept of substitution refers to a transformation of such extent and import, that the Constitution in force before the amendment appears to be so different from the resulting text as to render it incompatible. Case law has referred to total and partial substitutions, holding that the Legislature cannot introduce even partial substitutions when they involve replacing crucial defining axes of the Constitution by others that are completely opposite and wholly different. . . .

In this sense, in the present case the Court will reiterate its jurisprudence in the sense that constitutional amenders are not sovereign and they have limited competence according to the text adopted by the 1991 Constituent Assembly. Article 374 of the Constitution establishes that the Congress may *"amend"* its text, but not abolish,

12. Concerning procedural flaws, the Court examined each of the 10 arguments presented by the claimants in favor of declaring the law unconstitutional. The claims under examination were the following: (i) violation of the requirement of prior notification before a vote; (ii) improper appointment of those members of Congress selected to report on and present the act; (iii) infringement of the right to political representation; (iv) an improper request by the government to call for an urgent discussion of the Statutory Law on Antiterrorism, and then to prioritize the discussion of the draft amendments instead; (v) errors regarding decisions adopted on the recusal of members of Congress; (vi) errors regarding the conformation of the board presiding over the Commission in the Senate where the amendments were approved in the first round of discussions; (vii) infringement of the principle of participation of citizens in the opening debate of the first round of discussions in the Senate; (viii) infringement of principles regarding the timing of amendments, given that language not presented in the first round of discussions was included in the second round; (ix) errors in the way the title of the law was approved; and (x) errors based on the fact that the conciliation report was not discussed in plenary sessions in the Senate or House of Representatives. After examining the evidence presented regarding the procedures to adopt the amendment, the Court rejected all these claims.

undermine or substitute the Constitution. In turn, Article 380[13] establishes the distinction between abolishing the Constitution and amending its text. Amendments to the Constitution may change the content of its provisions, but they cannot substitute it for another contrary or wholly different constitutional text, as was the case when the new 1991 Constitution was enacted. . . . The Constitutional Court must verify that the Legislative Act is in fact an amendment and that it does not abolish or substitute the Constitution. This Court has highlighted that the only holder of unrestricted power to amend the Constitution is the people (Article 3[14] of the Constitution). In 1991, the people bestowed the power, among other things, to amend the Constitution on the Congress of the Republic which, being a body established and regulated by the Constitution itself, can only exercise such power in the terms established by the Constitution and not in an unrestricted manner. Although Congress has the power to amend the Constitution, it is not the holder of sovereignty, which "resides exclusively in the people." Therefore, only the people may create a new Constitution. Additionally, this Court has stated that the people can bestow the power to issue a new constitution on a Constituent Assembly (Article 376[15] of the present Constitution). Therefore, only through such a mechanism may the Constitution be replaced by another wholly different text. . . .

[T]he legal action of substituting the Constitution occurs only when one of its defining elements, instead of being amended, is replaced by an opposing or wholly different one. Substituting implies that the resulting text contradicts the core of the 1991 Constitution and that, therefore, it is no longer recognizable. The Congress of the Republic cannot totally or partially, permanently or provisionally substitute the Constitution, and, naturally, it may not replace the 1991 Constitution by a new and wholly different one. Nor may it introduce the kind of partial amendment that would render unrecognizable those essential and defining elements that give our Constitution its identity. This does not inhibit the Congress from introducing significant amendments to the Constitution to respond to society's evolution and citizens' expectations. . . .

[One deduces] that the judgment of substitution requires the application of a method in three specific stages, which distinguishes it from a judgment of intangibility [of any individual constitutional article] or a judgment of violation of the material content of the Constitution.

The main distinction between a judgment of substitution and the other two types of review is that in the judgment of substitution, the basic proposition is not

13. Article 380 states: "The Constitution, as amended, in force until this time, is hereby repealed. This present Constitution is effective from the day of its promulgation."

14. Article 3 states: "Sovereignty resides exclusively in the people from whom public power emanates. The people exercise it in direct form or through their representatives within the limits established by the Constitution."

15. Article 376 states in part: "By means of an Act approved by the members of both Houses, Congress may direct that the voters participating in the popular balloting decide if a Constituent Assembly should be called with the jurisdiction, term, and makeup that the same law shall determine."

established in any article of the Constitution, and it has to be understood in light of the core elements that define its identity. Besides, a judgment of substitution does not verify whether there is a contradiction between provisions, as is the case when reviewing substance, nor does it refer to whether there has been a violation of some intangible provision or principle. A judgment of substitution of the constitution instead establishes (a) whether the amendment introduces an essential new element in the Constitution; (b) whether it replaces an element originally adopted by the Constituent Assembly, and (c) it compares the new principle with the previous one to confirm, not if they are different, which will always be the case, but if they are different to the point of incompatibility.

Therefore, the argumentative burden in judgments of substitution is much more demanding. The *method* of a judgment of substitution requires that the Court prove that a defining core element of the 1991 Constitution has been replaced by a wholly different one. Consequently, to establish the major premise in a judgment of substitution it is necessary to (i) clearly identify that element; (ii) determine through reference to multiple constitutional provisions its specific character within the 1991 Constitution; and (iii) show why it is an essential and defining principle for the Constitution considered as a whole. Only in this way will it be possible to establish the major premise and avoid legal subjectivity. Subsequently, it is necessary to verify whether (iv) that defining element is irreducible to a specific constitutional article, so as to avoid turning this article into an intangible clause, and whether (v) the analytic statement of this core element would be equivalent to the creation of intangible material limits on the power of amendment . . . , which the Court is not competent to determine. Once the Court has overcome this burden of argumentation, it must move on to determine whether the defining element has been (vi) replaced by another one—and not simply amended, affected, infringed or contradicted, and (vii) whether the new core defining element is opposite or wholly different, to the point of incompatibility, with the defining elements of the identity of the previous Constitution. . . .

[The Court then applied this test to the case at issue, which allowed immediate presidential re-election:]

(i) The Court holds that allowing presidential re-election for a single additional term, subject to a statutory law aimed at ensuring the rights of the opposition and equal opportunities for all candidates during the presidential campaign, is not an amendment that substitutes the 1991 Constitution for another wholly different text. The essential elements that define our democratic and social state of law, founded on human dignity, were not replaced by the amendment. The people will freely decide who to choose as president, institutions with powers of control and review will continue to have full authority, the system of checks and balances will still operate, the independence of constitutional bodies is safeguarded, the executive is not bestowed with new powers, the amendment includes regulations to reduce inequalities in the election process under the administration of institutions which continue to be autonomous, and the acts to be adopted are still subject to judicial review so as to guarantee respect for the social state of law. [Some have argued] that the amendment constitutes a substitution of the Constitution because the president could abuse his power once he can compete in new elections [by] concentrating power in one person, reducing congressional independence and affecting the separation of powers. As pointed out before, such arguments do not aim at proving the lack of feasibility of this institutional design; instead, they evince the fears harbored by some in the sense that [power] would then be exercised in an abusive manner. These are practical considerations on the consequences they fear will ensue from the amendment, but not a result that should necessarily be expected from this new institutional design.

Concerning the form of the state, it is clear that with or without presidential re-election, Colombia is still a social state of law organized as a decentralized republic where regional institutions are autonomous, and founded on democratic, participatory, and pluralistic principles. None of these defining elements is suppressed, subverted, or substituted by the fact that the contested constitutional amendment now allows for the re-election of the president, which was previously forbidden by the 1991 Constitution.

(ii) Based on the arguments presented by the claimant concerning the infringement of political pluralism and equal participation by citizens, and the possibility of an abusive exercise of power and its concentration in the President of the Republic, it would be possible to conclude that when the claimant states that the amendment involves modifying our political system it means that the democratic nature of the Colombian state has been damaged. . . . [I]t cannot be argued that a system which admits presidential re-election will lose its democratic nature by that mere fact, or that our presidential regime will [necessarily] be transformed into an extreme form of presidentialism. Many examples could be drawn from comparative law where such a mechanism exists and does not imply a non-democratic state. On the contrary, in this kind of system the people, through elections, maintain their role as arbitrators in the processes of power.

The foregoing considerations demand a distinct approximation of the charge: The substitution of the Constitution would be produced, not by the consecration in abstract of presidential re-election . . . but by the specific context which it would produce given, in the opinion of the petitioner, the enormous power exercised in Colombia by the president. . . .

Mere reminiscence based on history is not enough. . . . Neither can we base the argument on a legal tradition contrary to immediate presidential re-election, thus attempting to make the norm containing the prohibition intangible. The process of constitutional change is precisely a process of institutional accommodation, and on these matters one cannot say that the book has been closed on institutional design. . . . Presidential re-election was proscribed in the past, in light of very particular circumstances, linked in each case to a determined historical moment in the composition of the Republic, institutional instability, or partisan violence. Before changes in circumstances—and theoretical presuppositions—it is possible that the reformer would newly decide to test the scheme of re-election.

The petitioner, to found his assertion, states that the president is in Colombia head of state, head of government, and supreme administrative authority; directs international relations and is commander-in-chief of the armed forces; [and] that the General Prosecutor, the National Ombudsman, the justices of the disciplinary chamber of the Superior Council of the Judiciary all depend indirectly on him. . . .

Even though the petitioner does not undertake this examination, one might note a general enunciation on the actually existing guarantees in the Constitution [to limit presidential power.] In contrast to other constitutional eras . . . in the Constitution of 1991 . . . , the Constitution consecrates a system of the distribution of public power between distinct branches and autonomous organs with diverse mechanisms of reciprocal control; within the scheme, all actors are submitted to judicial review and there are very developed and independent constitutional and contentious administrative jurisdictions; the possibility of delegated legislation by the executive has an exceptional and clearly circumscribed character; the electoral power is trusted to an organization of constitutional hierarchy and autonomous and independent character before the other powers; there are also autonomous and independent organs managing the central bank and television; the autonomy of territorial entities is consecrated and mayors and governors are popularly elected . . . ; the conditions for calling states of exception are very rigorous and the powers conferred on the president during those states has been reduced; the military forces are clearly subordinated to civil authorities and have a non-deliberative character; the Constitution establishes the administrative career as a general rule, in contrast with a system of free appointment to public posts; there exists a judicial career path and mechanisms to guarantee the independence of the composition of the high courts; the executive power lacks the possibility to interfere in political processes; the rights of the opposition are guaranteed . . . and financing of campaigns is predominantly done by the state; political pluralism is guaranteed and there are distinct instances of popular participation. . . .

Certainly, establishing the possibility of immediate presidential re-election introduces an important modification in some aspects of the design of the distribution of power of the state. It not only permits the influence of the president to project, potentially, for an additional period of four years . . . but also affects certain elements of the constitutional architecture that are in a certain way linked to the duration of the presidential term, such as the participation of the president in the integration of other organs of state like the Board of Directors of the Bank of the Republic, the Disciplinary Chamber of the Superior Council of the Judiciary, and the National General Prosecutor or the Constitutional Court itself. The re-election of the president will project for an additional period his influence in the composition of those organs. However, these modifications to the distribution of power . . . are part of the balancing that is necessary to consider when making constitutional reforms, a balancing that belongs to those who were invested by the Constituent Assembly with the power of reform. . . .

[I]n the opinion of the petitioner, the president as candidate, with the power to intervene in policies relevant to his re-election, would ignore a series of limits imposed by the Constitution. The mere reference to abuse of power makes it evident that the petitioner is not showing a deficiency in the institutional design but expresses a fear that, in practice, the president . . . will decide to ignore the limits and controls established by the constitutional order. This is not a charge of substitution of the Constitution, but an expression of fear that the president-candidate will exceed existing controls. . . . Thus, for example it is said that the president may abuse public spending for electoral means. . . . Along the same lines . . . , some have signaled that he may break the independence of Congress because the members of Congress favored by the political intervention of the president will support all his initiatives and exercise moderated or non-existent political control. These appreciations deal, not with the content of the regulation, but about the manner in which it would be applied by the president during electoral campaigns, or about how political actors would behave. . . . The argument of the petitioner ignores the system of checks and balances written in the Constitution in a general way to proscribe the arbitrariness of power, as well as the specific limitations and controls that the accused legislative act establishes and which must [under the terms of the amendment] be developed by a statutory law. . . .

(iii) It cannot be said that the amendment, which lifted the ban on presidential re-election, has changed the governmental system enshrined in the Constitution. And although it cannot be said a priori that changing the system of government always involves a substitution of the Constitution, the truth is that the amendment established through [the Legislative Act] does not replace our presidential system with a different one because it only modifies one of its elements. According to the accepted doctrine, the defining feature of the system is popular and direct or semi-direct election of the president, who holds the position of both head of state and head of government and who cannot be removed from his position by the legislative body before his term is over, while, in turn, the legislative body cannot be dissolved by the president of the Republic. . . .

In this sense, the possibility of re-election of the president is one of the variable features of a presidential system of government, a conclusion that is based on the theoretical features of the system as well as the observation of its manifestations in states that have adopted it, like the United States, a prototypical example of a presidential system that adopted immediate presidential re-election. . . .

It is interesting to observe that in the Latin American context . . . no consensus has been reached surrounding aspects related to the system of government, electoral systems, the political party regime, or mechanisms of participatory democracy, among others. Not only in Colombia, but across Latin America there has been a permanent process of search and adjustment. . . .

(iv) In conclusion, the reform permitting presidential re-election does not constitute a substitution of the basic structure of the Constitution regarding the form of state, system or government, or political regime. . . .

[The Court also rejected the argument that the amendment infringed the principle of equality.]

The petitioner argues that a suppression of the principle of equality has occurred in the electoral system for the election of the president, because the situation of a president who decides to run for a second term is not comparable to that of any other candidate. . . .

Certainly the possibility of immediate presidential re-election demands that, to preserve equilibrium in electoral debate, one establishes, on the one hand, limits on political activity of those in power, and for another, a group of guarantees for those in the opposition. Both of those are expressly included in the legislative act at issue. . . .

[A]lthough immediate presidential re-election may by itself give some advantage to the incumbent president and to his party over his political opponents, the amendment introduced regulations and guarantees aimed at ensuring adequate balance during the election campaign, as well as equal conditions for all candidates. The result of this provision will depend not only on the specific regulations that will have to be issued through a statutory law, but also on the context of their implementation. In any case, the amendment did include specific mandates to ensure equality during the election campaign. . . .

[However, the Court did hold one provision of the law to constitute a substitution of the constitution. This provision gave the Council of State, the highest administrative court in the country, the power to issue the statutory law governing presidential campaigns if Congress failed to do so within a certain time frame: "If the Congress is unable to issue the statutory law within the deadline established, or if the law is declared void by the Constitutional Court, the Council of State will issue provisional regulations on the matter during a two-month period."]

[T]he provision creates a transitory legislative power subject to no effective control in order to ensure its obedience to the Constitution. The regulation temporarily replaces the Congress and, besides, it eludes the review that the Constitutional Court must carry out for statutory laws referring to the political rights of citizens, campaign finance, the political participation of government officials, and equality during election campaigns, among other issues. The legislative power is granted to a body within the judicial branch which is not directly or indirectly elected by the people, which does not represent society, and which would have to issue regulations with no participation from involved stakeholders, without a previously established legislative procedure, and subject to no congressional control or constitutional review before the 2006 [presidential] elections.

For the Court, this provision in the amendment introduces a wholly different element from those that define the identity of the 1991 Constitution by establishing a legislative power subject to no control, which is not adjusted to democratic principles, and which is granted the authority to define fundamental rights as regards the distribution of public power. This kind of legislative power would be completely different from the legislative power in place now, which is subject to the Constitution, has been elected by the people, and represents our political and social pluralism. Besides, the actual legislative power . . . is subject to a system of checks and balances designed to avoid or invalidate arbitrary restrictions on the fundamental constitutional rights to which all Colombian citizens are entitled. . . .

Therefore, granting such power to the Council of State involves a partial and temporary substitution of the Constitution because for a time the Council of State will be free to arbitrarily adopt mandatory regulations for all citizens and the Constitution will lose its supremacy.

[The majority thus struck down this provision, while upholding the rest of the constitutional amendment. The decision included a number of dissents and concurrences, some of which are excerpted here. **Justice Jaime Araujo Renteria dissented**, arguing that the approval of the amendment had procedural flaws, and it constituted a substitution of the constitution because it changed the form of government:]

The dogmatic and organic design of the Constitution is based on a distribution of political power whose head is the president, for a limited period of time and with no possibility of a new term. In other words, the structure of our governmental system as established by the Constitution was designed by the constitutional assembly under the assumption that the head of the executive branch would be in office for a set term of four years. Consequently, changing the distribution of political power undoubtedly alters the structure of our government system because it was originally conceived for a four-year period and not for an eight-year term.

[**Justice Alfredo Beltran Sierra dissented**, arguing that the amendment should be struck down both because of procedural defects in its approval and because it substituted for the prior constitution by violating basic norms of equality.]

[T]he 1991 Constituent Assembly banned the possibility of any discrimination or privilege that would grant advantages to citizens holding public posts. On the contrary, it established provisions to ensure that candidates running for presidential elections had not held public positions during the year prior to the elections precisely to guarantee equality not only during election campaigns regarding the use of public assets, the access to mass media, or reimbursement [in campaign spending] based on the number of votes obtained, but . . . by clearly forbidding public officials to run for presidential elections. . . .

[The legislative act] authorizes the immediate re-election of the President of the Republic. It is absolutely clear that before the constitutional amendment the president was completely forbidden to run for the presidency while the ban on other high officials . . . in the original text of the Constitution was only a temporary one [which prevented their election as president if they held certain offices within one year of the election]; the new text, however, keeps the ban for the latter, but lifts it for the former. Hence, it must be admitted that the amendment did introduce a significant variation in the Constitution which is not formal in nature, but concerns its substance.

[**Justice Jaime Cordoba Trivino dissented**, holding that the approval of the amendment had several procedural flaws related, among others, to the process of resolving conflicts of interest of several members of Congress and to bypassing debates on the convenience of the amendment:]

As I have mentioned in the different occasions in which I have expressed my dissenting position regarding this amendment, the question that the Court had to resolve in this case was probably one of the most important decisions in its history. On this occasion, the Court had to define, regardless of the consequences and risks implied in the decision, whether Colombia is a democracy exclusively founded on the principle of the majority or a constitutional democracy in which the majority—no matter who leads it—must comply with the limits and restrictions established in the Constitution. After almost fifteen years of contributing to the construction of a constitutional democracy through its decisions, the Court decided that it was not appropriate to continue exerting strict control over the procedures that regulate the shaping of the will expressed in the Constitution. It chose, therefore, to approve procedures which are legitimate only in democracies exclusively founded on the principle of the majority. Accordingly, it disregarded fundamental facts and rendered irrelevant—or turned into mere formalities—procedural requirements that guarantee the principles of transparency, impartiality and ethical conduct during the adoption of laws or constitutional amendments. For a moment, the Court forgot that its own existence is justified precisely by defense of constitutional democracy.

[**Justice Humberto Antonio Sierra Porto concurred** in the decision upholding the amendment; however, he argued that the Court should have declared itself to have lacked jurisdiction to examine claims concerning the substitution of the constitution.]

[T]he category of competence-related flaws is closely linked to the idea of material limits or, in other words, the concept that there is a certain type of procedural flaw that, given its nature, affects the substance itself of acts of Congress. Thus, when the Constitutional Court transferred the concept of competence-based flaws to the review of constitutional amendments . . . , it in fact opened the way to the review of substantive matters in the constitutional amendment process, something which has no support whatsoever in our constitutional text.

2. The Second Re-election Decision

President Uribe won re-election in 2006 and began serving his second term, which lasted until 2010. He remained very popular, and he continued to enjoy the support of most members of Congress. In 2009 and 2010, members of the public affiliated with Uribe's political supporters began gathering the signatures of citizens to call for a referendum again amending the constitution in order to allow Uribe to seek a third term. After a massive campaign to collect citizens' signatures in favor of a referendum to amend the Constitution and allow for a second immediate presidential re-election, the law that convoked the referendum was adopted by Congress. The resulting law was then challenged in front of the

Constitutional Court, which invalidated it both for procedural reasons and as a substitution of the constitution.[16]

Decision C-141 of 2010 (per Justice Humberto Antonio Sierra Porto)

[The Court held that the proposed amendment should be invalided for procedural defects in its passage (by a seven-to-two vote) and because it constituted a substitution of the constitution (by a five-to-four vote).[17] The parts of the opinion explaining the flaws regarding the procedure by which the referendum law was approved are not excerpted here.[18] In its discussion of the substitution of the constitution doctrine, the Court engaged first rejected the argument that the referendum was somehow an exercise of "primary constituent power" that was beyond constitutional control because it was initiated by groups of citizens and not by the government:]

Some argue that there is a difference between the referendum analyzed in Decision C-551 of 2003 [the referendum case in Section B above] and that which is being studied now, and that the difference is that the first was initiated by the government, while this one was popularly initiated, a circumstance that they claim implicates the intervention of the primary constituent power. . . .

[T]he Court holds that the referendum as an instrument of constitutional reform is always a manifestation of derivative constituent power and that not even the intervention of the electorate in order to vote on the proposal after it has been passed by the Congress and revised by the Constitutional Court, has sufficient legal force to transform a referendum into a foundational constituent act of the primary or original power. . . .

[T]he people are also bound to the Constitution of 1991 and therefore cannot modify its defining elements when they exercise their powers of amendment. This point has maximum force when one takes into account that despite deriving from a citizens' initiative, the text submitted to a referendum must be approved by Congress, a process in which it can be exposed to distinct political forces that might end up modifying the initial proposal garnering popular support; thus, the initial manifestation of popular will does not necessarily coincide with the text finally submitted to a vote,

16. For analyses of the political context in which this decision was decided, see Dixon & Landau, *supra* note 2; SAMUEL ISSACHAROFF, FRAGILE DEMOCRACIES: CONTESTED POWER IN THE ERA OF CONSTITUTIONAL COURTS (2015).

17. Justices Mauricio González Cuervo and Jorge Pretelt Chaljub dissented on the procedural defects, and four justices dissented on the substitution of the constitution argument (Humberto Sierra Porto, Mauricio González Cuervo, Jorge Pretelt Chaljub, and Nilson Pinilla Pinilla). Justice Sierra Porto, the author of the decision, thus dissented on the substitution of the constitution argument, which highlights the extent of the internal debate on this issue.

18. The principle procedural flaws were the following: (i) violation of financing limits for initiative campaigns by citizens, (ii) improper changes to the original text during congressional debates, (iii) the fact that Congress was never properly convoked to the extraordinary sessions where the referendum was discussed, and (iv) violation of the Law on Parties by five representatives who illegally voted against the collective position of their own party.

which takes all of the weight out of the argument that the reform stems exclusively from the people acting as a primary constituency and with no limits on their power.

The intervention of Congress and the final participation of the people, which is reduced to approving or disapproving the normative text submitted for a vote, leaves serious doubts about whether the public is acting in this case as an original constituent power; the strict procedural rules to which popular participation is subject cut against the essence of this concept, which has always been characterized as unlimited and not subjugated to procedural regulations.

Based on these considerations, and taking into account the jurisprudence of the Constitutional Court . . . , there exists a common rule according to which all the constituted organs have a limited power of amendment. . . .

[T]he Court has estimated that "the Constitution of 1991 tried to overcome . . . the tension between popular sovereignty and constitutional supremacy by creating an opening for the original constituent power. . ." and in Decision C-1040 of 2005 it indicated that "the people can bestow the power to issue a new Constitution on a Constituent Assembly . . . " and that "only through such a mechanism may the Constitution be replaced by another wholly different text."

Under this theory the people, acting as a constituted power, will decide whether or not to convoke the Assembly and, by defining its competence, can give it powers to carry out a simple reform as a constituted power, or may give it powers that are broad enough to constitute a change from the current Constitution to another, whenever the people . . . so determine. This does not make all limits disappear, because even though [the members of the Assembly] are now not bound by what is stated in the substituted constitution, they must act according to the imperative norms of international law and of international human rights treaties, to give two examples.

Thus, of the distinct mechanisms contemplated in . . . the Constitution, the only one not subject to competence-based limits is a National Constituent Assembly, whenever it has been convoked expressly to establish a new Constitution, and thus, the mechanism of constitutional referendum cannot be used to transform the structural principles originally placed in the constitutional text.

[The Court next summarized its existing case law on the substitution of the constitution doctrine, reiterating the test found in C-1040 of 2005. Having fixed the methodology that it would apply to the question, the Court proceeded to conduct its analysis. The Court first noted that in its decision on the first presidential re-election, the Court had accepted its validity on the condition that the amendment authorized only one re-election.]

According to the Court's previous decision [C-1040 of 2005], "a constitutional amendment that suppresses the ban on presidential re-election, allowing it for one time only, does not constitute, in and of itself, a substitution of the Constitution," and that is the premise on which the Court will base its analysis to determine whether a constitutional referendum designed to amend Article 197 of the Constitution in force, in order to allow a second re-election and thus a third presidential term, substitutes the Constitution. . . .

[Based on a comparative and theoretical review, the Court concluded that] by authorizing re-election for only one time, Colombia appears to be located at the outer limit of permanence of the same person in the post of president because, as we have just seen, the experience of countries with strict presidential systems, doctrine, and institutional history demonstrate that eight years in a presidential mandate constitutes a limit beyond which there are serious risks of perversion of the regime and of the structure defined by the constituent power. . . .

[I]f the president was reelected for a second time, his mandate would be extended for four more years, for a total of 12, a lapse that, in addition to going well beyond the limit that according to Colombian institutional history and practice, is the maximum allowable in a presidential system subject to rules . . . , and would affect the institutional equilibrium based on the coordination of the presidential term with the terms of other high state functionaries. . . .

[The Court proceeded to examine the president's role in composing a number of different institutions, including the National Television Commission, the Board of Directors of the Bank of the Republic, the Inspector General of the Nation, the National Ombudsman, the National General Prosecutor, the Constitutional Court, and the Disciplinary Chamber of the Superior Council of the Judiciary. It found, based on the interaction of these roles with the terms of those officials, that allowing the president to serve two terms gave him significantly more power with respect to some of these institutions, and that allowing him three would give him even more power:]

In effect, the constitutional scheme was based on periods of four years for those responsible for the organisms of control (Inspector General and Ombudsman who can be reelected) and the National General Prosecutor, four-year terms that can be renewed twice for members of the Board of Directors of the Bank of the Republic and individual terms of eight years for the magistrates of the high courts, with a presidential term of four years. Thus, the system of nominations and elections in the distinct branches of public power implied that even when the president could nominate some of these officials, his constitutional period did not coincide with all of them.

[With the reform allowing one presidential re-election] the initial scenario changed because . . . the nominating powers of the president were strengthened, but with a second immediate re-election these would not only increase, since the president would be able to nominate all of the officials mentioned above, but in addition the presidential term would be potentially more extensive than that of the majority of the officials he nominates, in such a way that the majority of them would end their period under the mandate of the president who nominated them . . . and who would in certain cases also propose their replacement. . . .[19]

19. The Court gave examples of this effect in the specific context of the Colombian constitutional order. The Court noted that the president directly names various high officers, such as five members of the Board of Directors of the Bank of the Republic, and sends lists of nominations (*ternas*) for many other key posts to Congress for a final vote, such as in the case of the Inspector General, Ombudsman, General Prosecutor, and three of the nine members of the Constitutional Court. The Court noted that these various posts tended to have

The lengthening of the presidential term to twelve years implies the rupture of the equilibrium between the president invested with relevant powers by the presidential system, with reinforced nomination powers and whose term would coincide with those of the officials in the distinct control organisms and courts which he designated . . . , and the role played by those organisms of control in assuring checks and balances on presidential power. In addition, a president who is part of a political majority with congressional majorities, will control not only the executive and legislature, but also organs of the judicial branch and autonomous and independent organs like the Bank of the Republic and the National Television Commission, precisely by virtue of those previously described nomination powers.

The second immediate re-election will also have direct consequences on the relationship between the executive and legislative branches, because all members of Congress stand for re-election every four years, while the president could remain in power for twelve. It is clear that, given the system of presidential government adopted by the Constitution of 1991, a president with popular support could have a decisive influence on the configuration of legislative power in such a way that the political parties supporting him would have a clear majority in Congress. . . .

Thus, the successive postulation of candidates and the repeated designation of functionaries of other branches or autonomous organs by the same president would cause an evident institutional disequilibrium, distort the structure of the state designed by the constituent power, and given that a good part of the powers attributed to the mentioned authorities is for the purpose of exercising reciprocal control, one must conclude that the recurrent ability of a president reelected for a second time to appoint and nominate these organs would erode the effectiveness . . . of the control over his actions.

Some of the intervenors argue that [the law] proposes a referendum with a singular and particular purpose, in other words that it would allow a constitutional reform designed to permit the actual president to be reelected immediately and for a second time. They also allege that this law violates the equality of electoral campaigns, because the actual president has a privileged position in relation to all the other candidates. . . .

In this case there are various indications that allow us to conclude that [the law] was approved with the specific goal of permitting the actual president to aspire to a third consecutive term, despite the fact that the question that would be submitted to popular vote is written as a general and abstract hypothesis. . . . [The Court canvassed the legislative history and statements by supporters of the referendum inside and outside Congress in drawing this conclusion.]

staggered openings, but showed that over 12 years a president would be able to name all of these various officials at least once, and most more than once. Further, many of these positions such as the Ombudsman, Inspector General, and members of the Bank could be reappointed by the incumbent president after their four-year terms had expired.

[T]he text approved by the Congress demonstrates that ... only one person meets the criteria contemplated in [the law]: the current president. Despite the fact that the formulation is apparently general and could apply to any citizen meeting those conditions, in reality the approved language is designed to favor the actual president in an explicit way....

[T]he possibility of a second re-election affects the equality between candidates for the presidency ... because of the advantage that comes from having served as president for eight years.... The situation of someone who has exercised the presidency for one term and seeks re-election is not equivalent to someone who has been president for two terms and seeks a third ... since the aspirant to a third term has greater negotiating power and higher political recognition, derived from his having remained in power for a greater period of time.

Given this, it is clear that the introduction of a second re-election affects equality in the electoral contest for the presidency, since the progressive increment in presidential periods can allow a leader to perpetuate himself in power and potentially create a vicious cycle permitting the consolidating of only one person in power....

The effect on the equality of opportunities derived from a second re-election not only upsets the possibilities of [other] candidates individually considered, but also interferes with the freedom of voters and thus affects the conditions that make it possible to develop an objective electoral process.

In other words, if elections must be free, any undue influence on the electorate is inadmissible, since the decision whether to support any candidates depends on the existence of objectively free conditions permitting one to adopt that decision based on equal information regarding all of the candidates and their respective proposals. Any advantage that favors one of the options impacts the electoral process and influences the electorate, thus affecting the process through which the electoral body makes it decision....

[Based on this analysis, the Court concluded as follows:]

Because of the primordial role that corresponds to the president and the accumulation of constitutional functions attributed to him in order to carry out his job and to enter into relationships with the other branches of public power and with the autonomous and independent organs that carry out other state functions, it is clear that any alteration in the sphere of power reserved to the president or in his legal status has notable repercussions on the entire state structure and in the aggregation of values and principles that it sustains....

[T]he possibility of exceeding the maximum time allowed for the exercise of the mandate has deep repercussions in the institutional design adopted by the Constituent Assembly and in constitutional rights, values and principles....

Once the second re-election has been allowed, the third period of the president would weaken the rule of alternation in the exercise of public power, preserving for a prolonged period of time the ideological tendencies propounded by the government and the teams in charge of developing policy, and allowing the continued exercise of power by the dominant majority.... [In addition, the president's] possibility of designating, postulating, and influencing the composition of other public organs would destroy the constitutionally-mandated coordination across different periods of time and would result in the growth of presidential power and the loss of effectiveness of controls on presidential action.

In the sphere of rights, principles, and values, in addition to the effect on equality of treatment and opportunities for other [presidential] candidates and on the liberty of the electorate, [the change] would affect minorities not linked to the government and would affect the opposition, whose guarantees have constitutional recognition, because in addition to two periods outside of power, we would need to add a third period in which they would also lack the opportunity to control the state or to contribute to its direction.

Additionally, the growth of presidential power, added to the destruction of controls [on his power] or their merely nominal existence, would have grave repercussions on the structure adopted in the Constitution, because reciprocal controls and in particular those that restrain the president and his government make possible the functioning of the system of checks and balances, without which all equilibrium in high state bodies would be lost. In turn, the loss of equilibrium would make the separation of powers collapse, and this separation exists precisely to assure equilibrium, to impose moderation in the exercise of power, to prevent arbitrariness, and to contain the tendency of the executive to aggrandize his power to the detriment of other powers and public organs.

In the absence of effective controls, of institutional equilibrium, of an operational system of checks and balances and of a real separation of powers, what would exist in truth would be a predominance of the executive that is so marked as to disfigure the typical presidential system and to convert it into the deformed version known as *presidencialismo,* which is characterized precisely by that exaggerated predominance and by the tendency to exceed the maximum time allowed for the exercise of presidential power in order to maintain the *caudillo* and his political project in power.

Based on what we have explained [above], the fundamental objective of the separation of powers in an authentic constitutional state is not merely the effectiveness of the development of state functions, but the guarantee of the rights of citizens, and therefore when the principle of separation of powers has been overcome those rights, and the principles and values that they support, may be diminished.

We have explained ... that the separation of powers creates, in the heart of the state, an institutional pluralism because a diversity of powers and organs with a distinct composition and legal regime are in charge of developing distinct functions[. T]hus the concentration of power in the executive ... would have a negative effect on institutional pluralism and would shackle pluralism in an ideological sense, since the negative effect on the possibilities of minorities and opposition groups for acceding to power would frustrate the opportunities of those who legitimately pertain to tendencies that are contrary to the dominant group and who defend different ideas about governmental direction.

The varied structure of society, whose expression has its basic support in pluralism, would have fewer opportunities to be reflected, with all of its ideological and institutional complexity, in the institutional structure of the state, and as a result the social dynamic, founded on participation, would be openly diminished in its achievements because it could not count on important scenarios to carry out the participatory ideal propounded by the Constituent Assembly.

With opportunities for participation by minorities and opposition groups diminished . . . , the exercise of sovereignty would remain identified with the majority . . . and thus a liberal democracy that promotes pluralism, participation, the inclusion of minority groups and respect for the opposition . . . would lose the essence and value with which it was conceived by the 1991 Constituent Assembly.

All of the variations that have been analyzed would project their influence on the republican form of government . . . , since the hereditary and lifetime character of the monarchy has no correspondence in a republican model that proposes the temporary exercise of power by the president and his guaranteed succession via periodic, disputed, and free elections that are realized when the fixed period has expired or when the maximum number of periods constitutionally allowed has run out.

We must inescapably conclude from all of these considerations . . . that the second re-election and corresponding third term would involve a breakdown of the constitutional order and would substitute various defining axes of the 1991 Constitution. . . .

The breakdown of control, the lack of equilibrium and the consequent effect on the principle of the separation of powers would tend to translate into [presidential] actions free from external evaluation or judgment, disequilibrium, and a concentration of powers in the executive, which are elements totally opposed to those elements originally placed in the Constitution with the aim of avoiding an excess of presidential power and instead in forcing moderation. . . .

If the allowance of a second re-election in the presidential system runs the risk of degenerating into *presidencialismo;* if, in addition, pluralism, participation and the notion of the people created by the constitution would succumb before the permanence of majority government and if, finally, the elements that make up the republican model would be perverted, then the Constitution of 1991 would not be recognizable once a second presidential re-election had been authorized.

As has been explained, separation of powers and a presidential system define the system of government instituted in 1991; participatory and pluralistic democracy . . . is the political regime as established by the Constitution in force; and the republican model is the form of government that was decided upon in 1991. Thus, concentration of power in the executive branch, the *presidencialismo* that would follow . . . , and the disfigurement of the republican conception of government, would replace the political form as adopted in the current Constitution. . . .

We must add that the second re-election would be constructed on two prior presidential periods and that, as currently there is a specific person [Alvaro Uribe] who effectively has occupied the presidency for eight years, . . . the possibility of acceding to a third term would have specific beneficiaries, ... in radical contradiction to the general and abstract character of law.

Further, since the presidential system adopted in the Constitution of 1991 works from the premise of a fixed amount of time allowed for one single person to exercise the presidency, a second re-election would rupture and substitute the Constitution in all cases ..., regardless of whether the third period be ... consecutive or [nonconsecutive].

Based on these considerations, we hold that a second presidential re-election substitutes structural axes of the Political Constitution, and thus [the law at issue] ... violates the Constitution and must be declared unconstitutional.

[**Justice Humberto Sierra Porto** (the author of the decision) also wrote an opinion, where he explained that he agreed with the majority that the proposed referendum must be struck down on procedural grounds.[20] However, he reiterated his opposition to the existence of a substitution of the constitution doctrine:]

As I have stated repeatedly, I think that broadening the reach of the competence of the Constitutional Court [through the substitution doctrine] has the following negative implications: (i) it clashes with the literal text of ... the Constitution and permits material control of constitutional reforms, (ii) it implies a radical and profound change in the concept of the Constitution and moves us towards the concept of a material constitution, and (iii) it is based on an artificial distinction between the distinct ways of reforming the Constitution....

The use of open and indeterminate parameters of control, of a highly charged content, leads to argumentation of a political nature. As is well-known, a large part of the actual doctrine has defended the use of moral argument dealing with convenience and policy in judicial decision-making, particularly by constitutional judges. However, the specific risk of [the substitution of the constitution doctrine] is that these arguments turn into the essential part of the judicial discourse, which places in doubt the legal character of decisions adopted....

In addition, the decision to limit integral reforms that are "important" or "fundamental" to only a single route, that of a national constituent assembly, will cause the freezing of the constitutional text.... That is, the history of the Constitution of 1886 could be repeated, where given its extreme rigidity, due in part to decisions of the Supreme Court of Justice, it had to be entirely replaced through an extra-constitutional proceeding.

In general, all constitutional reform proceedings are an expression of a constituted constituent power, which means that they definitively are decisions made by the holder of sovereignty, by the people, either directly or through popularly-elected bodies. The existence of limits or conditions on the modification of the Constitution only refers to the procedure for making decisions, not their contents.

20. Justice Nilson Pinilla also wrote a concurring opinion in which he agreed with the procedural part of the decision but argued that the "substitution of the Constitution" doctrine should not exist.

Note on the Suppression of Constitutional Re-election in Colombia: President Uribe complied with this decision; the proposed referendum was not held and he did not run for a third term. Juan Manuel Santos, who served in the Uribe government, won election and was sworn in as president in August 7, 2010. Once in office, the new president distanced himself from the old president's policies in important ways, and President Uribe became a leader of the opposition. President Santos also won re-election in 2014, but announced his intent to seek an end to the possibility of presidential re-election in Colombia. In 2015, at Santos's urging and initiative, Congress passed a package of constitutional amendments that included a prohibition on either consecutive or nonconsecutive re-election. Moreover, this prohibition states that it may only be amended by "a referendum of popular initiative or a Constituent Assembly."

3. The Fiscal Sustainability Amendment

Particularly since the beginning of the Uribe administration in 2002, Colombian politics had been marked by a debate about the cost of rights enforcement. Critics of the Court have argued that some of its decisions have been too expensive, or have had excessive effects on public policy or on national budgets. Partially as a response to that concern, the government pushed through a set of constitutional amendments in 2011 aimed at "establishing the principle of fiscal sustainability." The proposal, however, went through significant changes during the approval process, in response to critiques from civil society and some political movements. In relevant part, the final verison of Legislative Act 3 of 2011 amends Article 334 of the Constitution as follows:

> The general direction of the economy will be under the charge of the state. The state will intervene, by mandate of law, in the exploitation of natural resources, in the use of the earth, in the production, distribution, utilization and consumption of goods, and in public and private services, in order to rationalize the economy with the goal of ensuring that the national territory, within a framework of fiscal sustainability, will improve the quality of life of its inhabitants, the equitable distribution of opportunities, and the benefits of development and preservation of the environment. This framework of sustainability must act as an instrument for the progressive realization of the social state of law. In all cases, public social spending will be prioritized. . . .
>
> Fiscal sustainability must orient the branches and organs of the public power, within their competencies, in a framework of harmonious collaboration.
>
> Once a decision has been made by any of the highest judicial bodies, the Inspector General of the Nation or one of the government ministers may solicit the opening of a fiscal impact proceeding, which must be heard. [The courts] will hear the explanations of its proponents on the consequences of the decision on public finances, as well as the concrete plan for its compliance, and they will decide whether to proceed to modulate, modify, or defer its effects with the goal of avoiding serious alterations in fiscal sustainability. In no case will the essential nucleus of fundamental rights be affected.

> In interpreting the current article, under no circumstances may any administrative, legislative, or judicial authority invoke fiscal sustainability in order to weaken fundamental rights, restrict their scope, or deny their effective protection.

A group of citizens challenged this legislative act, arguing that it constituted a substitution of the constitution. They argued that the Act substituted the fundamental principle of a social state of law because it established fiscal sustainability as an overarching principle in the constitutional order and thus forced both judges and other authorities to weigh its importance when trying to enforce fundamental social and other rights. Moreover, they claimed that the provisions substituted the separation of powers because they allowed the executive branch to interfere with the manner in which the judiciary would enforce rights.

The resolution of this case required the Court to apply its substitution of the constitution doctrine in light of fundamental constitutional principles such as the social state of law and the right to a vital minimum, which were developed most clearly in the cases in Chapter 6 on social rights but which run throughout this book. The Court unanimously rejected the demand, suggesting that although the broad interpretation of the amendments argued by the petitioners potentially would constitute a substitution of the constitution, the amendments should properly be interpreted much more restrictively in light of core constitutional principles found elsewhere and developed through the Court's jurisprudence.

Decision C-288 of 2012 (per Justice Luis Ernesto Vargas Silva)

[T]he function of guardianship of the integrity of the Constitution, which Article 241 of the Constitution confers on this Court, includes the power to control constitutional modifications, with the goal of avoiding a situation in which through a supposed reform, which is always limited by and submitted to the conditions existing in the current Constitution, one ends up replacing this constitutional order with another, distinct order. . . .

The establishment of limits on the power of reform is based on . . . questions of political theory, such as the distinction between the constituent power and the constituted powers, also called derivative constituent power. In agreement with this differentiation, when constitutional reforms are advanced by constituted powers, such as Congress, the basis for the validity of those acts is precisely in the Constitution, because this legal document (i) fixes the rules, qualities, and conditions for the composition of Congress; and (ii) assigns a power to the organ of popular representation to carry out the constitutional reform. This clear relationship of subordination . . . implies that the competence to reform the Constitution cannot be extended to the point of subverting the superior order that gives it justification, because a change of this nature would be reserved exclusively to a political power of greater rank than the existing Constitution, namely the constituent power invested in the sovereign people. . . .

With the goal of establishing interpretative tools to understand whether, in a concrete case, one is witnessing the phenomenon of amendment or substitution, the jurisprudence has differentiated between the concepts of intangibility and non-substitutability.

The first phenomenon is present when ... the constituent power decides to exclude certain determined norms or materials from the possibility of being reformed, creating what are commonly called "petrified clauses". . . . In the Colombian case the criterion of intangibility is inapplicable, since the Constituent Assembly did not exclude any provision of the Constitution from the power of reform, and thus any of its contents can be the object of a valid change through the mechanisms of constitutional amendment. . . .

[In contrast,] non-substitutability refers to the existence in any constitutional order of essential and defining axes to that order, which if reformed, would affect the identity of the Constitution, converting it into a distinct text. As was indicated, these structural aspects are not contained in any [single] concrete normative disposition, since the constitution does not contain intangible clauses, but are identified through an analysis of distinct constitutional dispositions that make up those axes. . . .

Further, it is important to understand that the constitutional jurisprudence has not established a complete catalog of those definitive aspects of the Constitution. The identification of those axes must therefore be preceded by an inductive reasoning process, in which ... the Court determines, through a systematic interpretation of the Constitution, the transcendental aspects that make up part of its identity and which, if subverted, would replace the Constitution. . . .

The judgment of substitution obeys strict parameters by necessity, since extensive use lacking sufficient rigor would cause the petrification of the Constitution and would make its mechanisms of reform basically inoperable. The exercise of that competence demands ... careful analysis, guided in all cases by judicial self-restraint, and which permits simultaneous compliance with three objectives: (i) safeguarding the identity of the Constitution from arbitrary exercises of the power of reform that would transform its defining axes; (ii) permitting the Constitution to be adapted to the most transcendental sociopolitical changes through the use of the mechanisms of reform laid out in ... the Constitution, as a condition for the survival of the constitutional order given the dynamic of contemporary societies; and (iii) avoiding ... the confusion of the judgment of substitution with material control of constitutional reforms, a task that is beyond the powers of the Court.

[After explaining the concept of substitution of the constitution, the Court laid out the test from Decision C-1040 of 2005, and proceeded to apply that test to the facts of the case:]

[T]he crux of the accusation in the demand can be synthesized in the following manner: the fiscal sustainability principle subverts the goals of the social state of law by subordinating the protection of constitutional rights to the goals of fiscal discipline. In addition, the instrument that is utilized to guarantee that new purpose will be the "fiscal impact proceeding" before the high courts, a mechanism that serves to place fiscal sustainability above the decisions of those courts, which base their work on the protection of rights. From that perspective, the accused constitutional reform substitutes the principle of separation of powers as well as the social state of law. . . .

As a preliminary matter, the Court points out that its jurisprudence has been . . . invariable in stating that the principle of separation of powers, as well as the social state of law are defining axes of the Constitution without any doubt. . . .

[The Court first dealt with the argument that the provision at issue substituted the principle of a social state of law:]

From the conceptual analysis as well as the historical study of the [amendment], one clearly infers that the operating criterion [of fiscal sustainability] is not a constitutional end in itself, but simply a means for achieving the essential objectives of the social state of law. . . .

There is an express clause, contained in Article 1 of [the amendment,] . . . that affirms this instrumental character of the principle or orienting criterion of fiscal sustainability. In effect, this disposition states expressly that "this framework of sustainability must act as an instrument for the progressive realization of the social state of law." The reasonable interpretation of that disposition obliges us to sustain that the intention of the constitutional reform was to create an instrument, which will work together with the others existing in the Constitution and the law, to achieve the essential ends of the state. . . .

[I]n the original version of the constitutional reform project, the intention of the government was to make fiscal sustainability into a right or duty, with a binding character for state authorities. This original objective was radically modified by the Congress, by (i) reformulating the legal nature of fiscal sustainability, making it an orienting criterion; and (ii) subordinating the application of fiscal sustainability to the satisfaction of the constitutional goals of the social state of law. . . . This point is important, because it forces us to see that fiscal sustainability cannot be considered in any sense to be a new constitutional principle, which has the same nature and hierarchy as the fundamental principles that give identity to the Constitution (Articles 1 through 10). . . .

For the petitioner and others who defend the unconstitutionality of the measure, fiscal sustainability is a constitutional principle that contains a specific mandate, consistent in the maximization of fiscal discipline and deficit reduction. . . . That particular mandate must be optimized and balanced in relation to the other constitutional principles, especially human dignity, pluralist democracy, and the supervision of rights. . . .

The Court finds that this structural argument loses force once we see that fiscal sustainability in reality is not a constitutional principle, but an instrument to achieve the ends of the social state of law. It is invalid to conclude . . . that fiscal sustainability redefines the essential objectives of the state, since an instrument of that character does not impose a particular mandate. It can be understood, in sum, as a rationalizing measure for the activity of public institutions, but in all cases submitted to the achievement of the ends for which it was consecrated in the Constitution. It is incorrect to state that fiscal sustainability must be balanced against fundamental constitutional principles, since a framework or guide for state action lacks sufficient normative hierarchy to overcome those principles, to limit their scope, or to deny their protection through the branches and organs of the state. In other words, we cannot find a normative conflict, and even less a constitutional contradiction, between fiscal sustainability and the fundamental principles of a social state of law, because they are on markedly different hierarchical planes. . . .

[A]mong the additions incorporated in Article 334 of the Constitution by the accused Legislative Act, we find a clause according to which the framework of fiscal sustainability must act as an instrument for the *progressive* realization of the objectives of a social state of law. . . . [T]his disposition integrates the principle of progressiveness of rights into the constitutional reform.

The principle of progressiveness is one of the aspects related to the effectiveness of constitutional rights that the jurisprudence of this Court has most often analyzed, especially in light of international human rights law. . . . The accused legislative act . . . should be understood through the rules that the Court has fixed on this issue, in order to define its content and reach.

The first aspect that must be clarified, especially considering the arguments stated by the petitioner and some of the interveners, consists in affirming that no aspect of the progressiveness principle allows it to be converted into an instrument to deny the effective protection of constitutional rights.

Constitutional jurisprudence states that the progressiveness principle in social rights consists of the obligation of the state to "keep advancing" towards the full enjoyment of these guarantees. This means that states cannot remain immobile before the satisfaction of those rights, but must move towards increases in coverage and in their guarantees, up to the maximum possible, through the establishment of legislative or other measures. Further, the progressiveness principle implies a corresponding prohibition on retrogressive measures: once a determined level of protection has been established, the state cannot reduce that level unless a strict test of proportionality is met under which it is shown that the retrogressive measure is necessary to comply with a critical state interest. . . .

An initial stage of the constitutional jurisprudence established a conceptual division between fundamental rights and so-called positive rights. The first were rights of defense or liberty that were unrelated to the offering of material services and were of immediate effect and application. Examples of these guarantees were the right to due process and to the free development of personality. The second, which required the provision of material services, were above all programmatic mandates for the state, which was called upon to guarantee them progressively in agreement with existing economic resources. . . .

This conception of constitutional rights was soon abandoned by the Court's jurisprudence because of its profound theoretical and dogmatic problems. The theoretical problems are evident upon observing that fundamental rights have various facets, some of them of a service-providing nature. In simple terms, the satisfaction of fundamental rights imposes on the state the duty to provide concrete material conditions, without which their effective enjoyment would be nullified. For example, the minimum efficacy of the right to due process depends on the state providing a system of justice, composed of judges and judicial servants, as well as the necessary infrastructure to carry out their functions. On the other hand, the efficacy of rights that have been conceptually catalogued as social, like the right to join a union, also depend on the state's compliance with negative duties, like non-interference with the formation and activities of unions. . . .

In terms of the inconveniences of a dogmatic nature, constitutional jurisprudence has arrived at a consensus, fed by the norms of international human rights law . . . of the indivisibility and interdependence of [constitutional rights]. It has been concluded that all constitutional rights are fundamental rights, because each of them finds a link with the principle of human dignity. Thus, the thesis of the connectivity between social rights and fundamental rights, as a prerequisite to their justiciability, loses force in preference to this integral vision of the fundamental character of rights. . . .

[T]he properties of interdependence and indivisibility [of rights] have permitted constitutional doctrine to conclude that fundamental rights are those that (i) are functionally related to the realization of human dignity, (ii) can be translated or concretized in subjective rights and (iii) have a dogmatic, jurisprudential, or . . . legal consensus about their fundamental nature. . . .

The prior considerations have direct effects in the interpretation of the orienting criterion of fiscal sustainability, in agreement with its regulation by the Legislative Act under examination. [A] paragraph added by the constitutional amendment . . . orders that the application of fiscal sustainability may not serve as the basis for allowing any state authority to weaken fundamental rights, restrict their scope, or deny their effective protection.

This prohibition, in the Court's view, must be read in harmony with the preceding arguments, especially with the criteria fixed by constitutional jurisprudence for determining the fundamental nature of a particular legal position. . . . That is, when the Legislative Act determines that fiscal sustainability must be compatible with the enforcement and effective enjoyment of constitutional rights, fiscal discipline must give way before the efficacy of those legal norms, in agreement with the Court's doctrine on this point. Thus we must reject as contrary to the Constitution the interpretation under which fiscal sustainability is based on the already-outdated distinction between rights of first and second generation and that, in addition, the criterion of fiscal sustainability has as its object postponing or restricting the achievement of social rights, in opposition to fundamental rights. We have noted that this restriction presents profound dogmatic and theoretical problems, such that constitutional jurisprudence has concluded that the definition of a right as fundamental depends on specific factors related to the link between human dignity and the corresponding provision. . . . This explanation radically departs from conventional distinctions between liberties and service-providing rights, and instead is based on the necessity for constitutional protection in the concrete case, valued in terms of the applicability of the principle of human dignity.

The present analysis shows that the accused Legislative Act contains various provisions clearly designed to show that the fiscal sustainability provision is an instrument that is subordinate to the achievement of the purposes of the social state of law, among which the protection of fundamental rights finds a central place. This purpose is reinforced by the inclusion of specific . . . clauses designed to prevent an erroneous understanding of fiscal sustainability from detracting from those essential objectives.

The first clause of this character is found in Article 1 of the Legislative Act. . . . There it says that social public spending has priority, and thus that fiscal sustainability cannot serve as a basis for postponing its execution. This means that those funds dedicated to the satisfaction of basic unsatisfied needs in health, education, the environment, and drinking water . . . cannot be affected by the application of fiscal sustainability, because that would mean that social spending would cease to be prioritized, thus contradicting the constitutional mandate. . . .

The prohibitive clause of greater effect is contained in the paragraph . . . according to which no state authority can invoke fiscal sustainability in order to weaken fundamental rights, restrict their scope, or deny their effective protection. . . . In other words, whether regarding state intervention in the economy, the transmission of the "fiscal impact proceeding," or the elaboration of the national development plan and the general budget of the nation, the application of fiscal sustainability is submitted, in its instrumental character, to the achievement of the essential ends of a social state of law, including the protection of rights of a fundamental nature. . . .

Thus, the instrumental character of fiscal sustainability implies its permanent subordination to the applicability of fundamental rights. This affirmation inverts the position of the petitioner and some interveners, who argue the existence of an opposing relationship of subordination. We must insist that fiscal sustainability is an orienting criterion for state activity that is clearly aimed, by constitutional mandate, to the satisfaction of the essential principles of the social state of law. Moreover, the Legislative Act does not add fiscal sustainability to [the list of] essential principles of the constitutional state. To the contrary, fiscal sustainability is designed as an instrument for the effective achievement of the objectives fixed by the Constituent Assembly.

[Finally, the Court also rejected the argument that the amendment substituted the constitutional principle of separation of powers, emphasizing particularly that the special judicial proceeding it created did not weaken judicial autonomy in the protection of fundamental rights:]

The Legislative Act creates the "fiscal impact proceeding": a procedure of a constitutional nature designed to permit the ministers of the government or the Inspector General of the Nation to express to the high courts their explanations about the effect of a particular judicial decision on fiscal sustainability. The purpose is to allow the courts to analyze these arguments, in order to determine whether their orders should be modulated, modified, or deferred in order to avoid serious alterations to fiscal sustainability. . . .

[T]he Court finds that the fiscal impact proceeding has a . . . restricted domain, because it does not imply a primary obligation for the high courts in terms of the justification of their decisions. Even though the judicial authorities are called to take into account the orienting criterion of fiscal sustainability, this does not imply that they are obligated to undertake a detailed study about the fiscal implications of their decisions, among other reasons because this would exceed the limits of their constitutional competencies. This type of argument corresponds exclusively to the president, or, in the terms of the constitutional amendment, to the Inspector General or to the ministers when they promote the proceeding in question.

Also, it is notable that the range of action of the proceeding is restricted to different matters than the decision itself. While the original version of the initiative allowed the proceeding to oppose the judicial decision, the definitive text makes exclusive reference to the "effects" of the decision. This is a transcendental modification because it allows us to affirm that the implications of the fiscal impact proceeding cannot affect the res judicata of the judgment. For example, by virtue of the procedure in question, a decision that protects constitutional rights cannot be modified in a way that would change the meaning of the decision to one that denies the protection of those rights. . . .

Based on this understanding, the Court finds that the Legislative Act makes an important distinction between the decision and its effects, a differentiation that has already been noted by the Court with respect to our decisions involving "complex orders." In this respect we have emphasized that it is normal for decisions that protect service-providing aspects of constitutional rights to be submitted to stages or conditions for their compliance, in order to guarantee the material efficacy of these rights. . . .

[T]he text of the reform . . . shows that the possibility of modulating, modifying or deferring the effects of the decision has a discretionary character, because the phrase "they will decide whether to proceed" cannot be understood in any other manner. From this premise one can infer various conclusions: (i) that all that is mandatory is that the proceeding be heard, in the conditions fixed by the Constitution; (ii) that the corresponding high court has the power to evaluate whether it will modify, modulate, or defer the effects of the decision, which signifies the exercise of an autonomous judicial power. . . . This implies, of course, the possibility that the high court will decide to maintain the initial order unaltered; (iii) that the changes made in response to the fiscal impact proceeding are restricted to the effects of the decision, and cannot extend to the decision itself. . . .

These premises, at the same time, make the fiscal impact proceeding compatible with the separation of powers and with judicial autonomy. There is nothing in the constitutional procedure under examination that prevents the high courts from adopting decisions they consider necessary and pertinent in light of the protection of constitutional rights, either in the stage of the decision or in the definition of the particular orders for the effective enjoyment of the vulnerable constitutional rights. Thus, there is no reason to say that the functional powers of the judge have been usurped. . . .

Finally, it is important to emphasize that the fiscal impact proceeding . . . cannot be applied so as to weaken legal rights of a fundamental nature, to restrict their scope, or to deny their effective protection. In the same sense, the fiscal impact proceeding reaffirms the eminently instrumental character of fiscal sustainability and the fact that any action designed to alter the effects of a judicial decision be solely designed to guarantee the compliance of the essential goals of a social state of law. Thus, any order deriving from the proceeding in question must be subordinated to the achievement and effective enjoyment of fundamental rights. . . .

[Based on the interpretation stated in the decision, the Court upheld the constitutional changes at issue.]

Note on Other Cases Involving the "Substitution of the Constitution" Doctrine: The doctrine of substitution of the constitution has also come up in many other cases, some of which are summarized here. The general trend appears to be toward greater deployment of the doctrine through time.

First, in **Decision C-588 of 2009 (per Justice Gabriel Eduardo Mendoza Martelo)**, the Court heard a challenge to Legislative Act 1 of 2008, which it held to be a substitution of the constitution in relevant part. This Act followed a long series of actions in which Congress attempted to create the constitutionally-mandated civil service system for government functionaries, but also sought to shield incumbent officeholders from having to face civil service examinations and procedures in order to maintain their jobs. The Court had struck down such legislative efforts on the ground that they violated meritocratic principles in the Constitution; the Court held that existing posts, and not just future ones, must be opened up to civil service competition. In Legislative Act 1, Congress attempted to amend the Constitution to add a temporary article providing that "For a period of three years . . ., the National Commission of Civil Service will implement the necessary mechanisms to inscribe in the civil service system, in an extraordinary way and without the need for a public competition, those civil servants who were occupying career positions [as of 2004]." Thus, Congress attempted to amend the Constitution in order to protect incumbent civil servants and thus evade the Constitutional Court's rulings.

The Court held that this attempted temporary amendment constituted a substitution of the constitution. It held in particular that the "administrative career path" was a structural constitutional principle linked to meritocracy, equality, and other fundamental principles in the constitutional order. It further stated that the amendment at issue constituted such a significant exception to meritocratic selection that it replaced that principle. The Court also held that the constitutional amendment at issue "was adopted exclusively to be applied to some determined and concrete subjects," and thus lacked the generality and abstractness that should be characteristic of constitutional reform. Finally, the Court noted that the temporary amendment at issue tacitly amended constitutional provisions protecting equality and open access to government posts, without amending the language of those provisions directly. The Court held that such efforts had to be prevented in order to avoid allowing "a fraud upon the Constitution."

In **Decision C-574 of 2011 (per Justice Juan Carlos Henao Perez)**, the Court returned to the "personal dose" issue first treated in Section A of Chapter 3. The Constitutional Court in one of its best-known early decisions held that drug possession of a "personal dose" could not be criminalized by the state. The decision was opposed by certain factions in Colombian politics, who sponsored various efforts to amend the Constitution to overturn the result. In 2009, as part of a broader reform dealing with the healthcare system and other issues, these opponents (led by President Alvaro Uribe) succeeded—Article 1 of Legislative Act No. 2 of 2009 states in part: "The possession and consumption of psychotropic and narcotic drugs is prohibited, except in the case of a medical prescription. For preventative and rehabilitative ends the law will establish administrative measures and treatments of a pedagogical, prophylactic, and therapeutic nature for people who consume these substances. Submission to those measures and treatments requires the informed consent of the addict."

Thus, the constitutional amendment prohibited possession of a personal dose, but provided for administrative measures aimed at education and treatment rather than for criminal penalties. A group of citizens challenged only the following language in the Act: "The possession and consumption of psychotropic and narcotic drugs is prohibited, except in the case of a medical prescription." They argued that this language constituted an invalid "substitution of the constitution," because it violated the fundamental principle of personal autonomy.

The Court held that it was inhibited from reaching the merits of the demand because the language attacked by the petitioners was only a piece of the provision at issue, and its effect could not be understood without also including the other language in the provision. As it stated: "The Court notes that the petitioners limited themselves to making a partial, incomplete and isolated reading of the modification at issue, since they refer only to the prohibition on the carrying and consumption of narcotic and psychotropic drugs, and not to an integral reading of the provision that would make it comprehensible in all of its aspects, [particularly] that the legislature may only adopt administrative measures for preventative and rehabilitative ends, of a prophylactic, pedagogical, and therapeutic nature . . . , and that submission to those measures and treatments will require the informed consent of the addict."

In **Decision C-1056 of 2012 (per Justice Nilson Pinilla Pinilla)**, the Court considered a constitutional amendment passed by Congress that added an exception to the general rule (stated in Article 183 of the Constitution[21]) that members of Congress would lose their seat if they participate in votes and debates despite having a conflict of interest. The amendment at issue stated that these rules would not apply if the vote at issue occurred during consideration of a constitutional amendment. The Court struck down this amendment as a substitution of the constitution. It held that the amendment violated the democratic principle because it "made it possible for the most transcendental collective decisions adopted by the Colombian state to be contaminated by particular interests." The Court also held that the Act also impacted other core constitutional principles, such as the prevalence of the general interest, which required that members of Congress make decisions for the common good and under dictates of morality, as the Court found that the change had "severely limited the capacity of [the sanction of loss of post] to contribute to the purification of Colombian

21. Article 183 states in part: "Members of Congress lose their seat for the following causes: 1. For violating the rules on disqualifications and incompatibilities or the rules on conflict of interest."

politics." Finally, the Court noted that the change had altered the nature of the instruments of constitutional change by "permitting the easy issuance of other legislative actors through which the separation of powers would be harmed and other important instruments of the Constitution could be harmed." Thus, the Court struck down the entire amendment.

Finally, and as detailed in more depth in Section C of Chapter 7, the Court has heard multiple challenges to the legal framework for peace, a set of constitutional amendments that created special "transitional justice" rules for the ending of the Colombian internal armed conflict. In **Decision C-579 of 2013 (per Justice Jorge Ignacio Pretelt Chaljub)**, the Court upheld constitutional amendments that focused the state's prosecutorial resources on "top-level" actors carrying out the gravest crimes under international law and allowed for "conditional renunciation" of criminal prosecution against most other actors. In this decision, the Court held that in carrying out the test of substitution, a Court should consider the fact that the changes—although they threatened some norms found in the Constitution and the constitutional block—also aimed at the very important constitutional principle of peace. Thus, the suggestion was that the test of substitution did not simply assess the degree of change of an isolated principle, but did so in light of an attempt to realize the broader constitutional project, creating something like a balancing dynamic. In **Decision C-577 of 2014 (per Justice Martha Victoria Sáchica)**, the Court likewise upheld parts of the constitutional amendment that would allow many ex-combatants to retain rights of political participation even if convicted for grave crimes such as homicide, kidnapping or war crimes. The Court held that there were few norms of international law on the specific point, and that the overall constitutional framework favored political participation. The Court also upheld the provision stating that ex-combatants convicted of crimes against humanity could not run for office, on the grounds that the reformer of the Constitution had a margin of discretion with respect to the specific prohibitions on political participation, and thus that these did not impact the basic identity of the 1991 Constitution.

These cases can potentially be placed into different, but overlapping, categories. In some, such as the re-election cases, the civil service case, and the conflict of interest case, there seems to be a significant concern with institutional self-dealing. The question in these cases is how far the existing institutional order can be bent in the service of political interests. In some of them, such as the personal dose case, the civil service case, and the fiscal sustainability case, the concern seems to be with challenges to the Court's interpretations of constitutional principles. The task here is to determine how rooted those interpretations are in core constitutional values, and how much of a threat the change poses to those principles. Finally, in a third set of cases, including the peace process cases and the re-election cases, the Court faces changes to truly fundamental pieces of the Constitution, but allegedly in service of other goals of potentially constitutional significance. The challenge here is to determine how to weigh those conflicting goals within the framework of the substitution test.

APPENDIX 1

The Orders of the Constitutional Court

The Colombian Constitutional Court has taken a range of approaches to remedying constitutional violations. Many of the remedies used by the Court have antecedents in the practice of the Colombian Supreme Court before 1991 or in the practices of either European Constitutional Courts or the United States Supreme Court, but the Court's use of them has often been noteworthy both for its creativity and as a response to a particular political context.

The basic constitutional principle allowing the Court to shape remedies for constitutional violations is its constitutional power over the meaning of its own decisions, as stated in **Decision C-113 of 1993 (per Justice Jorge Arango Mejia)**, which was considered in Chapter 2. As the Court is the guardian of "integrity and supremacy" of the Constitution, as stated in Article 241 of the Constitution, it follows according to the jurisprudence of the Court that it has broad powers to shape its orders to make them more effective.[1]

This brief appendix considers some of the types of orders issued by the Court in both abstract review cases and *tutela* cases. The examples are drawn from cases covered in this book. Section A considers the Court's practice of modulating remedies in abstract review cases involving the public action. Here, for example, the Court has issued conditional decisions upholding a statute only on the grounds it be interpreted in a certain way, deferred decisions striking down a law but allowing it to remain in place for some period of time, and integrative decisions adding content to a law in order to make it constitutional. Section B considers the Court's practice of issuing remedies for an individual complaint mechanism—the *tutela*—that normally binds only the parties to the action (*inter partes*). The Court has nonetheless used its power over the effects of its own decisions to issue structural remedies to the state, to give these orders effects among a broader

1. For an early take by one of the justices on these powers, see Alejandro Martinez Caballero, *Tipos de sentencias en el control constitucional de las leyes: La experiencia colombiana*, 2 Revista Estudios Socio-Juridicos 9 (2000).

Colombian Constitutional Law: Leading Cases. Manuel José Cepeda Espinosa and David Landau.

community (*inter pares* or *inter comunis*) and, in the extreme, to issue a state of unconstitutional affairs.

A. Modulated Decisions on Abstract Review

Based both on practices in Europe, where constitutional courts exercising abstract review have used these devices, and precedent under the Colombian Constitution of 1886, the Court from its earliest days has asserted the power to modulate the effects of its decisions issued in abstract review under the public action. These devices have allowed the Court to avoid unnecessary clashes with the political branches, while also increasing the reach of the Court's influence over the political and legal systems.

1. The Conditional Decision

The Court's most common device for modulating abstract review decisions is issuing a conditional decision. The conditional decision upholds a law, but only on condition that it be interpreted in a certain way. The device is appropriate under the Court's jurisprudence whenever one or more interpretations of a norm would be unconstitutional, but other interpretations of the norm would be consistent with the Constitution. The Court has recently noted that it has used this device in "innumerable opportunities . . . giving application to the principle *pro legislatore*. . . ."[2]

There are many examples of conditional decisions in this book, but we will give only two here. The first is the famous case legalizing assisted suicide from 1997, considered in Chapter 3, Section B: **Decision C-239 of 1997 (per Justice Carlos Gaviria Diaz)**. The Court reviewed the constitutionality of a criminal law, Article 326 of the Criminal Code, defining "therapeutic homicide" as "[a] person who kills another one for pity to put an end to extreme suffering resulting from body injuries or severe or incurable illness," and provided for a punishment of "six months to three years imprisonment." The Court did not strike down the provision, but instead held it conditionally constitutional in order to decriminalize some cases of assisted suicide. The order of the Court read as follows:

> First: Article 326 of Decree 100 of 1980 (Criminal Code) is CONSTITUTIONAL, under the understanding that in the case of terminal illnesses in which the free will of the passive subject of the act is manifested, there can be no responsibility for the medical author, since the conduct is justified.
>
> Second: The Congress is exhorted to regulate the topic of dignified death as quickly as possible and in conformity with constitutional principles and elemental considerations of humanity.

The first paragraph of the order thus lays out a conditional decision, under which Article 326 continues in effect but cannot be used to prosecute cases of assisted suicide where the

2. *See* Decision C-171 of 2012 (per Justice Luis Ernesto Vargas Silva).

patient has a terminal illness and freely consents to death. The paragraph may therefore continue to have effect in cases where those conditions are not met, for example where someone kills a severely injured person out of pity but does not have the victim's informed consent. The second paragraph is a request that Congress act as quickly as possible to regulate the problems of assisted suicide and dignified death.

A more complex and detailed use of conditional decisions occurred in the Court's decisions on public sector salaries, covered in Chapter 6, Section B. In **Decision C-1064 of 2001 (per Justices Manuel Jose Cepeda Espinosa & Jaime Cordoba Trivino)**, the Court changed its jurisprudence and held that public sector salaries need not keep pace with inflation in all circumstances. Rather, salary increases could be less than the rate of inflation for wealthier workers under circumstances of economic distress, and particularly where the savings were used on the constitutionally-prioritized purpose of social spending. The Court thus conditionally upheld the budget for 2001, as follows:

> [A]rticle 2 under examination is constitutional under the conditions synthesized here.
>
> 6.2 . . . .
>
> 6.2.1. All public servants have the right to maintain the real purchasing power of their salary.
>
> 6.2.2. The salaries of those public servants must be increased each year in nominal terms.
>
> 6.2.3. The salaries of those public servants that are below the weighted average of the salaries of all employees in the central administration must be increased each year by a percentage that, at least, maintains their real purchasing power.
>
> 6.2.4. The salaries of workers not covered by the prior criterion must be increased in such a way that the annual readjustments of those servants obeys the principle of progressivity in salary scales, thus that the increases of those who earn less are greater in percentage terms. In order to make the progressivity strict, there must not exist a disproportionate difference between one grade or scale and another. Limitations on the right to maintain the purchasing power of the salary of these employees are only constitutionally admissible if they are aimed at achieving a prioritized objective of social public spending and are strictly necessary and proportional to achieve the effective realization of this objective.
>
> 6.2.5. If upon applying the fourth criterion, there is a difference between the nominal annual salary increase and the real annual salary increase, both globally considered, this fiscal savings should be destined for public social spending for the benefit of people specially protected by the Constitution, such as children, mothers who are heads of household, the unemployed, the handicapped, displaced persons or those belonging to other vulnerable groups, or to constitutionally prioritized social programs, such as for

example, those for the feeding and care of the poor, the coverage of pension obligations, or education and training and health.

6.2.6. In order to comply with the Constitution, the authorities will adopt the decisions and issue the necessary acts within their competence, and within the terms of this decision.

The Court finally ordered as follows:

> Article 2 of Law 628 of 2000 is CONSTITUTIONAL under the conditions specified in section 6.2 of this decision.

The Court thus issued a detailed set of conditions upholding a budgetary law that would result in some public employees receiving real decreases in their salaries, but specifying to whom those decreases could apply (employees making above a weighted average), how they should be carried out (in accordance with the principle of progressivity), and what the savings should be spent on (constitutionally-prioritized social spending).

2. The Deferred Decision

The Court has sometimes struck down a law but allowed that law to remain in effect for a temporary period of time. This device is useful in cases where immediately striking down a law would leave a vacuum that would have serious negative effects. Further, it can provide an incentive for the political branches to carry out their constitutional duties within a set period of time, because a failure to do so will mean that they would be responsible for the disappearance of an important regulatory scheme from the legal order. This section examines two cases where a deferred decision was used. The first comes out of the housing decisions from the deep economic crisis of 1999–2000, considered in Chapter 6, Section B. In **Decision C-700 of 1999 (per Justice José Gregorio Hernández Galindo)**, the Court in September 1999 struck down the heart of the existing system, called the UPAC system, on procedural grounds. The Court held that the system should have been issued by a congressional law, rather than by presidential decree. But the Court also deferred the effects of that decision, leaving the existing system in place for a period of time in order to give the political branches time to design a new one. The Court explained the decision to issue a deferred decision as follows:

> The accused norms, making up Decree 663 of 1993, are retired from the legal order because they are unconstitutional, from the date of notification of the present Decision. However, because the flaw found in the them, and which has provoked a decision of unconstitutionality, consists precisely in that the general rules on the financing of housing for the long term must be contained in a law dictated by the Congress and not in a decree issued in the use of extraordinary powers, the Court considers it indispensable to give an opportunity to the legislative branch to exercise its constitutional powers and to establish the necessary directives in order to install a

system that will substitute for the UPAC system, without creating an immediate gap because of a lack of applicable laws.

For the Court it is clear that, with an eye on the adequate transition between the two systems without causing trauma for the economy, the norms retired from the legal order can continue projecting their effects while the Congress, in use of its attributions, dictates the framework law that properly has been placed in its hands. . . .

It is reasonable, then, that the norms excluded from the legal order remain in effect until the end of the current legislative session, that is to say, until June 20, 2000.

The Court finally ordered as in relevant part as follows:

Third. The following articles of Decree 663 of 1993 (Organic Statute of the Financial System), which structured the UPAC system, are declared UNCONSTITUTIONAL in their entirety: 18, 19, 20, 21, 22, 23, 134, 135, 136, 137, 138, 139, and 140.

Fourth. The effects of this decision, in relation to the inapplicability of the norms declared unconstitutional, will be deferred until June 20, 2000, but without prejudice to the ruling that strict, complete, and immediate compliance will be given to the order of this Court in Decision C-383 of 1999,[3] which dealt with the establishment of the factors that bear on the calculation and charging of the units of purchasing power in the UPAC system. . . .

The Court thus deferred the effects of its decision in order to give Congress time to create a new system, but ordered the government to abide by the Court's own prior jurisprudence on the UPAC system in the meantime. As noted in Chapter 6, Section B, the president and Congress passed a new law within the time frame signaled by the Court, and the Court upheld that law while putting important conditions on some articles.[4]

A second example of a deferred decision is **Decision C-577 of 2011 (per Justice Gabriel Eduardo Mendoza Martelo)**, covered in Chapter 4, Section A. In this decision, the Court heard a challenge to a legal framework that allowed same-sex couples to form marital "unions in fact" but did not allow them to be formally married. The Court held that the existing framework led same-sex couples to suffer from a constitutional "deficit of protection" because marital "unions in fact" were not equivalent in all material and symbolic respects to marriages. It recognized however that Congress had some discretion as to how it would remedy the matter, particularly as express constitutional norms referred to

3. This decision on the setting of interest rates within the UPAC system by the Central Bank is covered in Chapter 6, Section B.

4. *See* Decision C-955 of 2000 (per Justice José Gregorio Hernández Galindo).

marriage as being between one man and one woman.[5] The Court refrained from issuing an integrative remedy (see below), which would have immediately added same-sex couples to the coverage of the law, and instead issued the following order:

> First. The expression "a man and a woman," contained in article 113 of the Civil Code, is declared CONSTITUTIONAL under the charges analyzed in this decision. . . .
>
> Fourth. The Congress of the Republic is EXHORTED to legislate before June 20, 2013 in a systematic and organized way on the rights of same-sex couples with the goal of eliminating the deficit of protection that, under the terms of this decision, affects the mentioned couples.
>
> Fifth. If on June 20, 2013 the Congress of the Republic has not issued the corresponding legislation, same-sex couples can go before the competent notary or judge to formalize and solemnize their contractual link.

The Court's order thus gave Congress two years to legislate on the issue, with the aim of allowing the political branches to debate the subject with sufficient time. But the Court's order provided that in the event the two-year period lapsed without Congress issuing legislation, notaries and judges would be tasked with recognizing the rights of same-sex couples immediately, in order to "make effective the fundamental constitutional rights" at issue.

3. The Integrative Decision

When the Court issues an integrative decision, it effectively adds content to an existing law in order to bring the legal order into compliance with the requirements of the Constitution. The Court's jurisprudence has distinguished between two different situations: "absolute [legislative] omissions, that is, those situations where the legislature has not produced any norm in relation to the material being treated, and relative [legislative] omissions, a concept that alludes to cases where legislative development does exist, but it has to be considered imperfect because it excludes in an implicit manner a concrete normative ingredient that in light of the existence of a concrete constitutional duty, should have contemplated the normative development of that material."[6] In other words, absolute legislative omissions occur where Congress completely fails to regulate a topic, and relative legislative omissions occur where Congress has regulated a topic but has excluded some group or topic from its protection, in violation of the Constitution.

With absolute legislative gaps, the Court is limited to exhorting Congress to comply with its duties. But relative legislative gaps can be filled using integrated decisions. The

5. Article 42 of the Constitution reads in relevant part as follows: "The family is the basic nucleus of society. It is formed on the basis of natural or legal ties, by the free decision of a man and woman to contract matrimony or by their responsible decision to comply with it."

6. Decision C-373 of 2011 (per Justice Nilson Pinilla Pinilla); *see also* Decision C-543 of 1996 (per Justice Carlos Gaviria Diaz) (defining these two concepts).

rationale for allowing the Court to fill these gaps is the Court's duty to ensure the "supremacy and integrity" of the Constitution: "[O]n many occasions, a decision of simple constitutionality or unconstitutionality would be insufficient, since it could generate legal gaps that could make the court's decision totally without effect. In those cases, the only alternative in order that the Court may adequately carry out its constitutional function is that, with a basis in the constitutional norms, it proffers a decision that integrates the legal order with the goal of making the decision effective."[7]

Relative legislative gaps are found most commonly with laws that discriminate against a certain group by, for example, leaving them outside the law's protections. Simply striking down the law does not respond to the legal violation in a meaningful way and may do unnecessary violence to the legal order. In those situations, the Court sometimes asserts the power to bring the excluded group into the protections of the law. A prominent example of this use of the integrative decision is **Decision C-075 of 2007 (per Justice Rodrigo Escobar Gil)**, covered in Chapter 4, Section A. The Court heard a challenge to Law 54 of 1990, which considered opposite-sex couples living together for a set period of time and carrying out various other requirements, to be considered a "marital union of fact" and thus to be entitled to various property and status benefits. The law did not create a similar regime for same-sex couples. The Court held that the law was discriminatory and that the appropriate remedy was an integrative decision that would bring same-sex couples into the protections of the law. It thus issued the following order:

> Law 54 of 1990, as modified by Law 979 of 2005, is CONSTITUTIONAL, on the understanding that the regime of protection contained in it be applied as well to homosexual couples.

B. The *Tutela*

The *tutela* was designed as an individual complaint mechanism, allowing individuals who had their constitutional rights violated by state actors or some private actors to get rapid and effective relief.[8] The prototypical order in a tutela case runs only *inter partes*—that is, it affects only the parties to the decision. Yet the Court has again relied on its constitutional power over its own decisions, and its role as the guardian of the "integrity and supremacy" of the Constitution, to issue structural remedies that reach beyond the individual litigants in the case at issue. This section briefly considers three manifestations of this power: first, the Court's willingness to issue structural orders along with individual orders in some *tutela* cases; second, its statement in certain cases that an order should run *inter comunis* or *inter pares* rather than merely *inter partes*, and finally, the Court's use of the "state of unconstitutional affairs" designation in rare cases to assert continuing jurisdiction over massive social problems.

7. Decision C-109 of 1995 (per Justice Alejandro Martinez Caballero).

8. The *tutela* is regulated in Article 86 of the Constitution of Colombia.

1. Structural Orders

In many of the *tutela* cases covered in this book, the Court has issued a combined remedy, issuing both individual remedies to resolve the plaintiff's personalized grievance and structural remedies to reach beyond the case at issue and resolve a social problem. This is by far the most common way in which the Court has broadened the effect of the *tutela* decision in major cases.

An example of this approach is the informal recycling case in Cali, **Decision T-291 of 2009 (per Justice Elena Reales Gutiérrez),** considered in Chapter 6, Section E. The Court held that it would issue "two types of orders in the current decision. First, those orders oriented to resolve the concrete cases of the *tutelas* accumulated in the present decision. Second, complex orders will be adopted, aimed at resolving the problems presented by the recyclers of Navarro and with the situation of the recyclers in the city of Cali in general."

The orders section thus first issued a set of remedies for the 25 individual litigants whose cases had been accumulated, and then added a set of structural orders dealing with the broader problem:

> First. In relation to each one of the individual cases accumulated in the present process:
>
> 1. The decision adopted by Administrative Judge Seventeen of the City of Cali in process T-2094526, which denied the *tutela*, is REVOKED, and in its place the fundamental rights of Cecilio Cesar Izquierdo and his nuclear family are protected. . . .
>
> Second. In relation to each one of the individual cases accumulated in the present process and stated in the prior section, the City of Cali is ORDERED, through its Secretaries of Education, Health, and Social Welfare, to adopt the necessary measures to ensure the effective enjoyment of their fundamental rights to health, education and food within two months . . . , verifying in each concrete case the affiliation or link to the healthcare system, access to education for minor children, and their inclusion in the social programs of the City dealing with food, housing, recreation, labor training and sports. . . .
>
> Third. The company EMSIRVA ESP [which runs waste services in the city] is ORDERED to suspend the Public Convocation 002 of 2009, Contract for the operation and exploitation of the collection services for solid waste, the cleaning of roads and public areas. . . , for three months after the notification of this decision, during such time as the terms of that process can be reformulated as stated in section 9.2.2 of this decision. Once the bidding process has been finalized, EMSIRVA ESP . . . must send to the Constitutional Court by September 1, 2009, a report detailing its conformity with the standards laid out in section 9.2.3 of the current decision.
>
> Fourth. EMSIRVA ESP . . . and the City of Cali and the Autonomous Regional Corporation of the Cauca Valley are ORDERED, within six months of the notification of this decision, to design, adopt, and put in place a policy of effective inclusion for the Cali recyclers in their programs of collection, use, and commercialization of waste in order to strengthen their qualities as businesspeople and the solidarity of their organization.

Fifth. The City of Cali is ORDERED, through its Secretaries of Education, Health, and Social Welfare, to adopt within six months of notification of this decision, the necessary measures to ensure that the recyclers of Navarro included in the 2003 census and identified in 2006 have effective enjoyment of their constitutional rights to health, education, dignified living and food, verifying in each concrete case the affiliation or link to the healthcare system, access to education for minor children, and their inclusion in social programs within the City in the matters of food and housing. . . .

Seventh. The City of Cali is AUTHORIZED to apply the exception of unconstitutionality when necessary to ensure the effective enjoyment of the rights of the recyclers of Navarro and of the street recyclers of the City of Cali, in conformity with the parameters laid out in the present decision. The Mayor of Cali will inform the Court on January 18, 2010 about the use of this mechanism.

Eighth. The City of Cali and the legal representative of EMSIRVA . . . are ORDERED, within two months of the notification of this decision, to form a committee for the inclusion of the recyclers in the formal economy of the city of Cali, in which will participate [various state and civil society groups, including those representing the recyclers]. This committee will participate in the design and implementation of the plan of inclusion for the Cali recyclers into the formal cleaning economy, as well as in the design of the affirmative actions that are necessary to ensure that their participation is effective. The plan of inclusion that the committee designs must be ready and functioning at the latest by November 23, 2009. The mayor of Cali must send to the Court on December 1, 2009 a report with the designed plan and with the affirmative actions that have been adopted and advanced, as well as the indicators of the results that are designed to show the advances of the process of inclusion and the effective enjoyment of rights by the recyclers and their families.

Ninth. The Administrative Planning Department of the City of Cali is ORDERED to complete the census of the Navarro recyclers. . . . Equally, the Department . . . is ordered to design and carry out a census of the street recyclers of the City of Cali, in such a way that the information received permits it to advance in the process of inclusion of the recyclers in the formal cleaning economy.

Tenth. . . . [T]he Autonomous Regional Corporation of the Cauca Valley is ORDERED to create and promote—with the help of the civil society organizations united in this effort—civic and solidarity campaigns aimed at the citizens of Cali, aimed at getting the users of waste services in the city to (a) begin to separate their waste at the source, and (b) to give their recyclable waste to the organized recyclers. . . .

Eleventh. The Ombudsman in the Cauca Valley region is SOLICITED . . . to follow the actions advanced to ensure the inclusion of the recyclers of Navarro and the street recyclers of the City of Cali in the productive activity of collection and use of solid waste, in conformity with the parameters established in this decision, and to send to the Constitutional Court the follow-up reports that it deems pertinent.

> Twelfth. This decision is COMMUNICATED to the organization CIVISOL [a civil society group representing the recyclers], and it is INVITED to continue supporting the organizations of recyclers of the city of Cali and to send periodic reports to the Constitutional Court on advances in the process of inclusion of the recyclers of Navarro and the street recyclers of the city of Cali in the productive activity of collection and use of solid waste in the city of Cali. . . .

The Court thus ordered concrete actions from the city and others to resolve the case for the litigants who had brought individual *tutelas*. At the same time, most of the orders were aimed at resolving broader problems with the informal recyclers in Cali. Among other things, the Court suspended the existing contract that would have pushed the recyclers out and ordered it remade with terms that would include them, ordered the creation of a special committee and a special program to promote the recyclers' inclusion into the local economy, ordered the city and others to link them to defined social programs, ordered the city to take a census of all informal recyclers in the city, authorized the city to disregard existing laws that were contradictory to the fundamental constitutional rights of the recyclers, and invited state and civil society actors to oversee compliance with the Court's diverse orders. In many of these cases, the Court required or invited state and civil society actors to file reports with the Court updating them on compliance.

These sorts of structural orders were also used in a number of other *tutela* cases covered in this book, for example **Decision T-595 of 2002 (per Justice Manuel Jose Cepeda Espinosa)**, covered in Chapter 4, Section C. In that case, which involved access of the handicapped to the mass transportation system of Bogotá, the Court held that the individual did not have an immediate individual right of improved access to the system, but he did have the right to have the system draw up a plan for improved access and execute that plan within two years. Thus, the Court in that case issued a structural remedy without an accompanying individual remedy:

> First. The decision taken by the Fifty-Fourth Municipal Civil Judge of Bogotá, on March 15, 2001, in the process of the *tutela* action by Daniel Arturo Bermudez Urrego against Transmilenio SA [the mass transport company], is REVOKED.
>
> Second. The rights to freedom of movement and equality of Daniel Arturo Bermudez Urrego, in terms of his specially-protected disability, are PROTECTED, and thus the Transmilenio is ORDERED to design a plan within two years of the notification of this decision aimed at guaranteeing the access of the petitioner to the basic public transportation system of Bogotá . . . and once designed the plan must immediately begin being executed in conformity with the timeline indicated in it.
>
> Third. Transmilenio SA is ordered to report every three months to Daniel Arturo Bermudez Urrego is his condition, at the time of presenting the *tutela* action, as a member of the governing board of the Colombian Association for the Development of Persons with a Disability (ASCOPAR), on the progress of the plan so that he, or a representative of the Association, can participate in the phases of design, execution, and evaluation of it. . . .

2. *Inter Comunis* or *Inter Pares* Effects

In very rare cases, the Court will alter the *inter partes* effects normally given to *tutela* decisions in order to give the decision effects over a more widespread community. A good example of this is **Decision SU-214 of 2016 (per Justice Alberto Rojas Rios)** covered in Chapter 4, Section A. In that decision the Court granted a *tutela* on behalf of several couples who were seeking to enter a same-sex marriage, but had been denied by either a notary or a judge. The Court could of course issue individual relief to the petitioner, but such an order would not directly affect all other same-sex couples seeking to marry. The Court therefore decided to issue an *inter pares* remedy that would also incorporate all other couples in the same situation, discussing this issue in the following terms:

> The effects of *tutela* judgments are *inter partes* [among the parties], as a general rule. However, in some cases, given the existence of an objective universe of people found in the same situation as the petitioners, the Court has modulated its decision with the goal of ensuring the exercise of the right to equality.
>
> There exist very special circumstances in which a *tutela* claim is not limited to being a subsidiary judicial action aimed at avoiding the harm or threat of harm to fundamental rights of parties to the process. . . . [T]he *tutela* judge can issue a judgment . . . with *inter comunis* [among the community] or *inter pares* [among equals] effects with the goal of protecting . . . the fundamental rights of those who have not come directly before the Court but require equal protection. This is the case whenever the third parties are found in equal or common conditions to those who made use of the *tutela*, and when the order of the *tutela* judge would have immediate and direct repercussions threatening the fundamental rights of those who are not included.
>
> *Inter comunis* effects refer to situations where the order is extended to a community defined by specific characteristics. . . . In contrast, *inter pares* effects are predicated on third parties who are not linked to the process who are in a similar position to the petitioners. . . .
>
> Based on Decision C-577 of 2011 and the persistent deficit of constitutional protection in the exercise of fundamental rights by same-sex couples, there have been diverse interpretations of the ideal contractual bond to formalize and solemnize the relationships of same-sex couples. This lack of legal definition in the constitution of the family has meant that some same-sex couples have been unable to formalize and solemnize their contractual bond.
>
> In consequence, the Constitutional Court finds that among the various available alternatives to protect the fundamental rights of third parties not linked to the process, that which better protects same-sex couples in order to ensure the effectiveness of inalienable rights and constitutional principles of the human person, is the mechanism of *inter pares* effects, since the case deals with people found in an equal or similar situation, not a defined legal community on which the exercise and enjoyment of individual fundamental rights depends (*inter comunis* effects). . . .

> With the goal of (i) overcoming the deficit of protection recognized in Decision C-577 of 2011 in relation to same-sex couples in Colombia; (ii) guaranteeing the full validity of the Constitution, and more concretely the fundamental right to form a marital bond . . . ; and (iii) protecting the principle of legal security in relation to the civil status of persons, the Court will extend the effects of the present unification decision to all similar cases, in other words, to all same-sex couples that, since June 20, 2013, (i) have gone before judges or notaries in the country and have had their request for marriage denied because of their sexual orientation; (ii) have celebrated a contract to formalize and solemnize their bond, without the title or legal effects of civil marriage; (iii) have celebrated a civil marriage, but the National Marriage Registry refused to inscribe it and (iv) from this point forward, will seek to formalize and solemnize their bond through civil marriage. . . .

This Court this issued the following order in relevant part:

> Eighth. We EXTEND with *inter pares* effects the present unification decision to all same-sex couples who, since June 20 2013, (i) have gone before a judge or notary in the country and been denied in the celebration of a civil marriage, given their sexual orientation; (ii) who have celebrated a contract to formalize and solemnize their bond, without the denomination or legal effects of a civil marriage; (iii) who have celebrated a civil marriage that the National Registrar of Civil Status declined to register and; (iv) who in the future, will formalize and solemnize their link through civil marriage, either before municipal civil judges or public notaries. . . .

3. The State of Unconstitutional Affairs Doctrine

Finally, in a limited class of cases the Court has invoked the doctrine of the state of unconstitutional affairs to justify substantial structural remedies. The doctrine, for example, was used in a 1998 case involving prison overcrowding and other conditions in prisons across the country.[9] But its best-known and most large-scale use was in **Decision T-025 of 2004 (per Justice Manuel Jose Cepeda Espinosa)**, involving internally displaced persons and covered in depth in Chapter 6, Section D. The Court noted that the declaration of a state of unconstitutional affairs was appropriate under the following conditions:

> (1) there is a repeated violation of the fundamental rights of many people—that therefore resort to *tutela* writs claiming protection for their rights and overcrowding judicial courts—and (2) the origin of such infringement is not exclusively ascribable to the authorities accused, but also to structural factors.

9. *See, e.g.*, Decision T-153 of 1998 (per Justice Eduardo Cifuentes Munoz).

> Among the factors evaluated by the Court to define whether a state of unconstitutional affairs exists, the following can be highlighted: (i) a massive and generalized violation of various constitutional rights, affecting a significant number of people; (ii) the prolonged omission of the authorities to comply with their obligations to guarantee those rights; (iii) the adoption of unconstitutional practices, like the incorporation of the *tutela* action as part of the procedure to guarantee the right in question; (iv) the failure to issue legislative, administrative, or budgetary measures necessary to avoid the violation of the rights; (v) the existence of a social problem whose solution requires the intervention of various entities, requires the adoption of a complex and coordinated group of actions and demands a level of resources that requires an important additional budgetary outlay, [and] (v) if all of the people affected by the same problem accede to the *tutela* action to obtain the protection of their rights, greater judicial congestion would be produced.

In the case at issue, the Court held that the huge number of people affected (numbering in the millions), the sustained failure of the state to comply with their constitutional duties or to create a functioning bureaucratic apparatus, the complexity and expense of a comprehensive solution, and the large number of *tutelas* on the topic all supported the declaration of a state of unconstitutional affairs for displaced persons.

The declaration of a state of unconstitutional conditions allowed the Court to issue a large number of structural orders in addition to individual orders for the benefit of the petitioners. There are far too many orders to be reproduced here (23 in all), so in this section we merely translate a few of the key structural orders.

> First. We DECLARE the existence of a state of unconstitutional affairs in the situation of the displaced population given the lack of concordance between the gravity of the violation of rights recognized by the constitution and developed by the law, on the one hand, and the volume of resources effectively destined to assure the effective enjoyment of those rights and the institutional capacity to implement the corresponding constitutional and legal mandates, on the other.
>
> Second. We COMMUNICATE, through the Secretary-General, that state of unconstitutional affairs to the National Council for the Integral Attention to the Population Displaced by Violence [National Council], so that within the orbit of its competence and in compliance with its constitutional and legal duties it can verify the magnitude of the dissonance and design and implement a plan of action to overcome it, giving special priority to humanitarian help within the timeframes indicated below.
>
> a. At the latest by March 31, 2004, the Council . . . must (i) define the actual situation of the displaced population inscribed in the Sole Registration System, determining their number, location, necessities and rights . . . , (ii) fix the scope of the budget effort that is necessary to comply with the public policy designed to protect the fundamental rights of the displaced persons; (iii) define the

percentage of participation in financial resources that will come from the nation, from the territorial entities, and from international cooperation; (iv) indicate the mechanism for achieving those resources; and (v) develop a contingency plan in the event that those resources stemming from territorial entities and international cooperation do not arrive on time and in the quantity indicated, so that those resources that are lacking will be made up through other means of financing.

b. Within a year following the communication of this decision, the Director of the Network of Social Solidarity, the Ministers of Finance and Public Credit, and of the Interior and Justice, as well as the director of the National Planning Department and the other members of the Council . . . , will realize all necessary efforts to ensure that the budgetary effort fixed on them is achieved. If within that year, or before, it becomes evident that it is impossible to assign the established volume of resources, they must (i) redefine the priorities of their policies and (ii) design the necessary modifications to introduce a state policy of attention to the displaced population. In any case, for the adoption of these decisions, they must ensure the effective enjoyment of the minimums necessary to exercise the right to life in dignified conditions, as stated in Section 9 of this decision.

c. To offer to the organizations that represent the displaced population opportunities to participate in an effective manner in the adoption of the decisions that are taken with the goal of overcoming the state of unconstitutional conditions, and to inform them of the advances achieved on a monthly basis. . . .

Fourth. We ORDER the National Council . . . , within three months following the communication of this decision, to adopt a program of action, with a precise timeline, designed to correct the weaknesses in institutional capacity at least in respect to those that were exposed in the reports brought to the present process and summarized in Part 6 and Annex 5 of this decision.

Fifth. We ORDER the National Council, within a maximum span of six months from the communication of this decision, to conclude the actions required to ensure that all displaced persons have effective enjoyment of the minimum of protection of their rights referred to in Part 9 of this decision.

The Court also issued similar orders to other entities within their competencies, including the territorial and local governments and other ministries of the national government. It invited both the Inspector General and national Ombudsman to monitor the decision and to issue reports on compliance.

In the displaced persons case, the Court has continued to exercise jurisdiction over the case and has issued a large number of follow-up orders. The key elements of this model have been well-described by César Rodriguez-Garavito: (1) the Court has maintained jurisdiction over the case, in the displaced persons example for over a decade; (2) the Court requires the state to issue periodic reports, and to appear at periodic public hearings, on compliance and on the effective enjoyment of rights by displaced persons; (3) the Court relies on the aid of civil society (in particularly a Monitoring Commission composed by many of these groups), and on state institutions such as the Ombudsman and Inspector General, to monitor compliance and to develop policy ideas, and (4) the

Court issues new orders through follow-up decisions (called "Autos") as the case develops, and often issues more detailed orders, with tighter time frames, in the event of initial noncompliance.[10]

As an example of the kinds of orders issued in these Autos, one might consider **Auto 092 of 2008 (per Justice Manuel Jose Cepeda Espinosa)**, where the Court dealt with the particular problems faced by displaced women and ordered the state to take special actions of protection on their behalf. A key order in the Auto read as follows:

> Third. To prevent the disproportionate and differential impact of forced displacement on Colombian women, and to protect in an effective manner the fundamental rights of women who are victims of displacement, we ORDER the Director of Social Action to carry out the design and implementation of the thirteen programs outlined in the present decision to fill the critical holes in the public policy of attention to forced displacement:
>
> a. The Program of Prevention of the Disproportionate Gender Impact of Displacement, through the Prevention of Extraordinary Risks of Gender in the Framework of Armed Conflict.
> b. The Program of Prevention of Sexual Violence against the Displaced Woman and of Integral Attention to their Victims.
> c. The Program of Prevention of Intra-Family and Community Violence against Displaced Women and of Integral Attention to its Victims.
> d. The Program of Promotion of the Health of Displaced Women.
> e. The Program of Support for Displaced Women who are Heads of Household, of Facilitation of Access to Labor-Market and Productive Opportunities and of the Prevention of the Domestic and Labor-Exploitation of Displaced Women.
> f. The Program of Educational Support for Displaced Women Older than 15.
> g. The Program of Facilitation of Access to Real Property for Displaced Women.
> h. The Program of Protection for the Rights of Displaced Indigenous Women.
> i. The Program of Protection of the Rights of Displaced Afro-Colombian Women
> j. The Program of Promotion of the Participation of Displaced Women in the Prevention of Violence against Displaced Women who are Leaders or who acquire Public Visibility for their Work on Social, Civic, or Human Rights Promotion.
> k. The Program to Guarantee the Rights of Displaced Women as Victims of Armed Conflict to Justice, Truth, Reparations, and Non-Repetition.
> l. The Program of Psychosocial Aid for Displaced Women.
> m. The Program of Elimination of the Barriers of Access to the System of Protection for Displaced Women.
>
> The Director of Social Action is ORDERED to guarantee that each one of these programs complies in its design and implementation with the minimum conditions and elements of rationality described in detail in Section V.B of this decision. In

10. *See* Cesar Rodriguez-Garavito, *Beyond the Courtroom: The Impact of Judicial Activism on Socioeconomic Rights in Latin America*, 89 Tex. L. Rev. 1669 (2011).

> particular, the Director of Social Action is ORDERED to guarantee the active and effective participation in the design and implementation of these 13 programs to the organizations that represent the rights of displaced women in the country, as explained in detail in Section V.B of this Auto. . . .

Note that as shown above, the Court can, and commonly does, issue structural orders without declaring an unconstitutional state of affairs. In addition, the Court can continue to monitor the progress of those orders even absent such a declaration. In **Decision T-760 of 2008 (per Justice Manuel Jose Cepeda Espinosa)**, examined in Chapter 6, Section C, the Court issued a structural remedy for the right to health, and used a very similar model of retaining jurisdiction, requiring periodic reporting, and issuing follow-up orders, even though it did not declare a state of unconstitutional affairs.

APPENDIX 2

The Constitution of Colombia (1991) (selected provisions)

Preamble

The people of Colombia,[1]

In the exercise of their sovereign power, represented by their delegates to the National Constituent Assembly, invoking the protection of God, and in order to strengthen the unity of the nation and ensure to its members life, peaceful coexistence, work, justice, equality, understanding, freedom, and peace within a legal, democratic, and participatory framework that may guarantee a just political, economic, and social order and committed to promote the integration of the Latin American community, decree, authorize, and promulgate the following:

Political Constitution of Colombia

TITLE I ON FUNDAMENTAL PRINCIPLES

Article 1

Colombia is a social state of law organized in the form of a unitary republic, decentralized, with the autonomy of its territorial units, democratic, participatory and pluralistic, based on respect for human dignity, on the work and solidarity of the individuals who belong to it, and on the predominance of the general interest.

1. These translations are based on: Oxford Constitutions of the World, Constitution of the Republic of Colombia: July 5, 1991 (Max Planck inst., trans., 2012). However, several articles were modified by the authors for the purposes of this volume.

Colombian Constitutional Law: Leading Cases. Manuel José Cepeda Espinosa and David Landau.

Article 2

The essential goals of the state are to serve the community, promote the general prosperity, and guarantee the effectiveness of the principles, rights, and duties stipulated by the Constitution; to facilitate the participation of everyone in the decisions that affect them and in the economic, political, administrative, and cultural life of the nation; to defend national independence, maintain territorial integrity, and ensure peaceful coexistence and the enforcement of a just order. The authorities of the Republic are established in order to protect all individuals residing in Colombia, in their life, honor, property, beliefs, and other rights and freedoms, and in order to ensure the fulfillment of the social duties of the state and individuals.

Article 3

Sovereignty resides exclusively in the people from whom public power emanates. The people exercise it in direct form or through their representatives within the limits established by the Constitution.

Article 4

The Constitution is the norm of norms. In all cases of incompatibility between the Constitution and the statute or other legal regulations, the constitutional provisions shall apply. It is the duty of citizens and of aliens in Colombia to obey the Constitution and the laws, and to respect and obey the authorities.

Article 5

The state recognizes, without any discrimination whatsoever, the primacy of the inalienable rights of the individual and protects the family as the basic institution of society.

Article 6

Individuals alone are responsible before the authorities for violations of the Constitution and the laws. Public servants are responsible for the same violations and for omissions or ultra vires acts committed in the exercise of their functions.

Article 7

The state recognizes and protects the ethnic and cultural diversity of the Colombian nation.

Article 8

It is the obligation of the state and of individuals to protect the cultural and natural assets of the nation.

Article 9

The external relations of the state are based on national sovereignty, on respect for the self-determination of peoples, and on the recognition of the principles of international law approved by Colombia.

In the same manner, the foreign policy of Colombia shall be oriented toward the integration of Latin America and the Caribbean.

Article 10

Spanish is the official language of Colombia. The languages and dialects of ethnic groups are also official in their territories. The education provided in communities with their own linguistic traditions shall be bilingual.

TITLE II ON RIGHTS, GUARANTIES, AND DUTIES

Chapter I On Fundamental Rights

Article 11

The right to life is inviolate. There shall be no death penalty.

Article 12

No one shall be subjected to forced sequestration, torture, cruel, inhuman, or degrading treatment or punishment.

Article 13

All individuals are born free and equal before the law, shall receive equal protection and treatment from the authorities, and shall enjoy the same rights, freedoms, and opportunities without any discrimination on account of gender, race, national or family origin, language, religion, political opinion, or philosophy.

The state shall promote the conditions so that equality may be real and effective and shall adopt measures in favor of groups which are discriminated against or marginalized.

The state shall especially protect those individuals who on account of their economic, physical, or mental condition are in obviously vulnerable circumstances and shall sanction the abuses or ill treatment perpetrated against them.

Article 14

Every individual has the right to have his/her legal identity recognized.

Article 15

Every individual has a right to personal and family privacy and to his/her good reputation, and the state has to respect them and to make others respect them. Similarly, individuals have the right to know, update, and rectify information collected about them in data banks and in the records of public and private entities.

Freedom and the other guaranties approved in the Constitution shall be respected in the collection, procession and circulation of data.

Correspondence and other forms of private communication may not be violated. They may only be intercepted or recorded on the basis of a court order in cases and following the formalities established by statute.

For tax or legal purposes and for cases of inspection, the oversight and intervention of the state may demand the making available of accounting records and other private documents within the limits provided by statute.

Article 16

All persons have the right to free development of personality without limitations other than those imposed for the rights of others and the legal order.

Article 17

Slavery, servitude, and the slave trade in all forms are prohibited.

Article 18

Freedom of conscience is guaranteed. No one shall be importuned on account of his/her convictions or beliefs or compelled to reveal them or obliged to act against his/her conscience.

Article 19

Freedom of religion is guaranteed. Every individual has the right to freely profess his/her religion and to disseminate it individually or collectively. All religious faiths and churches are equally free before the law.

Article 20

Every individual is guaranteed the freedom to express and diffuse his/her thoughts and opinions, to transmit and receive information that is true and impartial, and to establish mass communications media.

The latter are free and have social responsibility. The right to rectification in equitable conditions is guaranteed. There shall be no censorship.

Article 21

The right to dignity is guaranteed. An Act shall provide the manner in which it shall be upheld.

Article 22

Peace is a right and a duty whose compliance is mandatory.

Article 23

Every individual has the right to present respectful petitions to the authorities on account of the general or private interest and to secure prompt resolution of same. The legislative body shall be able to regulate its exercise by private organizations in order to guarantee fundamental rights.

Article 24

Any Colombian citizen, except for the limitations established by statute, has the right to move about freely across the national territory, to enter and exit the country, and to remain and reside in Colombia.

Article 25

Work is a right and a social obligation and enjoys, in all its forms, the special protection of the state.

Every individual is entitled to a job under dignified and equitable conditions.

Article 26

Every individual is free to choose a profession or occupation. An Act may mandate certificates of competence. The competent authorities shall inspect and oversee the exercise of the professions.

Occupations, the arts, and work that do not require academic training are to be freely exercised, except for those which involve social risk.

Legally recognized professions may be organized into professional associations. The internal structure and operation of the latter shall be democratic. An Act may assign public functions to them and establish the appropriate controls.

Article 27

The state guarantees the freedom of teaching at the primary and secondary level, apprenticeship, research, and professorship.

Article 28

Every individual is free. No one may be importuned in his/her person or family, sent to jail or arrested, nor may his/her home be searched except on the basis of a written order from a competent judicial authority, subject to the legal procedures and for reasons previously defined by statute.

A person in preventive detention shall be placed at the disposition of a competent judge within the subsequent 36 hours so that the latter may make an appropriate determination within the limits established by statute.

In no case may there be detention, a prison term, or arrest for debts nor sanctions or security measures that are not prescribed.

Article 29

Due process shall be applied in all cases of legal and administrative measures.

No one may be judged except in accordance with previously written laws which shall provide the basis of each decision before a competent judge or tribunal following all appropriate forms.

In criminal law, permissive or favorable law, even when ex post facto, shall be applied in preference to restrictive or unfavorable alternatives.

Every individual is presumed innocent until he/she is proved to be legally guilty. Whoever is accused is entitled to defense and the assistance of counsel picked by the accused or assigned automatically during the investigation and trial; to an appropriate public trial without unreasonable delay; to present evidence and to refute evidence alleged against the accused; to challenge the condemnatory sentence; and not to be placed in double jeopardy for the same act.

Evidence obtained in violation of due process is null and void by right.

Article 30

Whoever is deprived of his/her freedom and believes to be so illegally is entitled to invoke habeas corpus before any legal authority, at any time, on his/her own or through a third party. Habeas corpus must be complied with within 36 hours.

Article 31

Any judicial sentence may be appealed or adjudicated, but for exceptions provided by statute.

When the accused is the sole appellant, the higher court may not impose a heavier penalty.

Article 34

Punishments of exile, life imprisonment, and confiscation are prohibited.

However, a judicial sentence may nullify ownership of property when same is injurious to the public treasury or seriously harmful to social morality.

Article 37

Any group of individuals may gather and demonstrate publicly and peacefully. An Act alone may establish in specific manner those cases in which the exercise of this right may be limited.

Article 38

The right of free association for the promotion of various activities that individuals pursue in society is guaranteed.

Article 39

Workers and employers have the right to form trade unions or associations without interference by the state. Their legal recognition shall occur by the simple registration of their constituent act.

The internal structure and functioning of the trade unions and social or labor organizations shall be subject to the legal order and to democratic principles.

The cancellation or suspension of legal identity may only occur through legal means.

Jurisdiction and other guaranties necessary for the performance of their administration is recognized to trade union representatives.

Members of the police force do not have the right to form associations.

Article 40

Any citizen has the right to participate in the establishment, exercise, and control of political power.

To make this decree effective the citizen may

1. Vote and be elected.
2. Participate in elections, plebiscites, referendums, popular consultations, and other forms of democratic participation.
3. Constitute parties, political movements, or groups without any limit whatsoever; freely participate in them and diffuse their ideas and programs.
4. Revoke the mandate of those elected in cases where it applies and in the form provided for by the Constitution and statute.
5. Take initiatives in public bodies.
6. Undertake public measures in defense of the Constitution and the law.
7. Agree to undertake public functions and responsibilities, except for those Colombian citizens, native-born or naturalized, who hold dual citizenship. An Act shall spell out this exception and shall determine the cases where they apply.

The authorities shall guarantee the adequate and effective participation of women in the decision-making ranks of the public administration.

Article 41

In all educational institutions, public or private, the study of the Constitution and civics shall be mandatory. In this way, democratic practices for the teaching of principles and values of citizen participation shall be promoted. The state shall publicize the Constitution.

Chapter II On Social, Economic, and Cultural Rights

Article 42

The family is the basic nucleus of society. It is formed on the basis of natural or legal ties, through the free decision of a man and woman to contract matrimony or through the responsible resolve to comply with it.

The state and society guarantee the integral protection of the family. An Act shall determine the inalienable and unseizable family patrimony. The family's honor, dignity, and intimacy are inviolable.

Family relations are based on the equality of rights and duties of the couple and on the reciprocal respect of all its members. Any form of violence in the family is considered destructive of its harmony and unity, and shall be sanctioned according to law.

The children born of a matrimony or outside it, adopted or conceived naturally or with scientific assistance, have equal rights and duties. An Act shall regulate responsibility to the offspring.

The couple has the right to decide freely and responsibly the number of their children and shall support them and educate them while they are minors or non-self-supporting.

The forms of marriage, the age and qualifications to contract it, the duties and rights of the spouses, their separation and the dissolution of the marriage ties are determined by statute.

Religious marriages shall have civil effects within the limits established by statute.

The civil effects of all marriages may be terminated by divorce in accordance with civil law.

Also having civil effects are decrees of annulment of religious marriages issued by the authorities of the respective faiths within the limits established by statute.

An Act shall determine matters relating to the civil status of individuals and consequent rights and duties.

Article 43

Women and men have equal rights and opportunities. Women cannot be subjected to any type of discrimination. During their periods of pregnancy and following delivery, women shall benefit from the special assistance and protection of the state and shall receive from the latter food subsidies if they should thereafter find themselves unemployed or abandoned.

The state shall support the female head of household in a special way.

Article 44

The following are basic rights of children: Life, physical integrity, health and social security, a balanced diet, their name and citizenship, to have a family and not be separated from it, care and love, instruction and culture, recreation, and the free expression of their opinions. They shall be protected against all forms of abandonment, physical or moral violence, sequestration, sale, sexual abuse, work or economic exploitation, and dangerous work. They shall also enjoy other rights upheld in the Constitution, the laws, and international treaties ratified by Colombia.

The family, society, and the state have the obligation to assist and protect children in order to guarantee their harmonious and integral development and the full exercise of their rights. Any individual may request from the competent authority the enforcement of these rights and the sanctioning of those who violate them.

The rights of children take precedence over the rights of others.

Article 45

The adolescent is entitled to protection and integral development.

The state and society guarantee the active participation of adolescents in public and private organs that are responsible for the protection, education, and progress of the youth.

Article 46

The state, society, and the family shall all participate in protecting and assisting individuals in the third age bracket and shall promote their integration into active and community life.

The state shall guarantee to them services of integral social security and food subsidies in cases of indigence.

Article 47

The state shall promote a policy of planning, rehabilitation, and social integration for those who are physically, emotionally, or psychologically handicapped and who shall receive the specialized attention that they need.

Article 48

Social Security is a mandatory public service which shall be delivered under the administration, coordination, and control of the state, subject to the principles of efficiency, universality, and solidarity within the limits established by statute.

All inhabitants are guaranteed the irrevocable right to Social Security.

With the participation of individuals, the state shall gradually extend the coverage of Social Security which shall include the provision of services in the form determined by statute.

Social Security may be provided by public or private entities, in accordance with the relevant statute.

It shall not be possible to assign or use the resources of the Social Security organs for different purposes.

An Act shall define the means whereby the resources earmarked for retirement benefits may retain their constant purchasing power. . . .

[Amendment by Legislative Act No. 1 of 2005 omitted]

Article 49

Public health and environmental protection are public services for which the state is responsible. All individuals are guaranteed access to services that promote, protect and restore health.

It is the responsibility of the state to organize, direct, and regulate the provision of health services to the inhabitants and of environmental protection in accordance with the principles of efficiency, universality, and solidarity; in addition, to establish policies for the provision of health services by private entities and to exercise oversight and control over them; and to establish the competences of the nation, territorial entities, and individuals, and to determine the subsidies to their tasks in the terms and conditions established by statute.

Health services shall be organized in a decentralized manner, according to care levels and with the participation of the community.

An Act shall define the terms under which basic care for all inhabitants shall be free of charge and mandatory.

Every individual has the right to have access to the integral care of his/her health and that of his/her community. . . .

[Amendment by Legislative Act No. 3 of 2009 omitted]

Article 51

All Colombian citizens are entitled to live in dignity. The state shall determine the conditions necessary to give effect to this right and shall promote plans for public housing, appropriate systems of long-term financing, and community plans for the execution of these housing programs.

Article 58

Private property and the other rights acquired in accordance with civil laws are guaranteed and may neither be disregarded nor infringed by subsequent laws. When in the application of a law enacted for reasons of public utility or social interest a conflict between the rights of individuals and the interests recognized by the law arises, the private interest shall yield to the public or social interest.

Property has a social dimension which implies obligations. As such, an ecological dimension is inherent to it.

The state shall protect and promote associative and joint forms of property.

Expropriation may be carried out for reasons of public utility or social interest defined by the legislator, subject to a judicial decision and prior compensation. The compensation shall be determined by taking into account the interests of the community and of the individual concerned. In the cases determined by the legislator, the expropriation may take place by administrative action, subject to subsequent litigation before the administrative law courts, including with regard to the price.

[Amended by Legislative Act No. 1 of 1999]

Article 59

In case of war and exclusively to meet its requirements, the need for expropriation may be decreed by the national government without prior indemnification.

In the said case, real estate alone may be occupied temporarily to meet the requirements of war or to assign facilities to it.

The state shall always be responsible for expropriations effected by the government on its own or through its agents.

Article 67

Education is an individual right and a public service that has a social function. Through education individuals seek access to knowledge, science, technology, and the other benefits and values of knowledge.

Education shall train the Colombian when it comes to respect for human rights, peace, and democracy, and in the practice of work and recreation for cultural, scientific, and technological improvement and for the protection of the environment. The state, society, and the family are responsible for education, which shall be mandatory between the ages of five and 15 years and which shall minimally include one year of preschool instruction and nine years of basic instruction.

Education shall be free of charge in the state institutions, without prejudice to those who can afford to defray the costs.

It is the responsibility of the state to perform the final inspection and supervision of education in order to oversee its quality, for fulfilling its purposes, and for the improved moral, intellectual, and physical training of those being educated; to guarantee an adequate supply of the service, and to guarantee for minors the conditions necessary for their access to and retention in the educational system.

The nation and the territorial entities shall participate in the management, financing, and administration of the state educational services within the limits provided for by the Constitution and statute.

Article 68

Individuals may create educational institutions. An Act shall establish the conditions for their creation and management.

The educational community shall participate in managing educational institutions.

Education shall be in the care of individuals of recognized ethical and pedagogical fitness. An Act guarantees the professionalization and dignity of the teaching profession.

Parents have the right to select the type of education for their minor children. In state institutions, no individual may be obliged to receive religious instruction.

The members of ethnic groups shall have the right to education that respects and develops their cultural identity.

The eradication of illiteracy and the education of individuals with physical or mental limitations or with exceptional capabilities are special obligations of the state.

Article 70

The state has the obligation to promote and foster access to the culture of all Colombians equally by means of permanent education and scientific, technical, artistic, and professional instruction at all stages of the process of creating the national identity.

Culture in its diverse manifestations is the basis of nationality. The state recognizes the equality and dignity of all those who live together in the country. The state shall promote research, science, development, and the diffusion of the nation's cultural values.

Article 73

Journalistic activity is protected to guarantee its freedom and professional independence.

Article 74

Every person has a right to access to public documents except in cases established by statute.

Professional secrets are inviolable.

Chapter III On Collective Rights and the Environment

Article 79

Every individual has the right to enjoy a healthy environment. An Act shall guarantee the community's participation in the decisions that may affect it.

It is the duty of the state to protect the diversity and integrity of the environment, to conserve the areas of special ecological importance, and to foster education for the achievement of these ends.

Article 80

The state shall plan the handling and use of natural resources in order to guarantee their sustainable development, conservation, restoration, or replacement.

Additionally, it shall caution and control the factors of environmental deterioration, impose legal sanctions, and demand the repair of any damage caused.

In the same way, it shall cooperate with other nations in the protection of the ecosystems located in the border areas.

Chapter IV On the Protection and Application of Rights

Article 85

The rights mentioned in Articles 11, 12, 13, 14, 15, 16, 17, 18, 19, 20, 21, 23, 24, 26, 27, 28, 29, 30, 31, 33, 34, 37 and 40 are applicable immediately.

Article 86

Every person has the right to file a *tutela* before a judge, at any time or place, through a preferential and summary proceeding, for himself/herself or by whomever acts in his/her name for the immediate protection of his/her fundamental constitutional rights when that person fears the latter may be violated by the action or omission of any public authority.

The protection will consist of an order issued by a judge enjoining others to act or refrain from acting. The order, which must be complied with immediately, may be challenged before a superior court judge, and in any case the latter may send it to the Constitutional Court for possible revision.

This action will be available only when the affected party does not enjoy another means of judicial defense, except when it is used as a temporary device to avoid irreversible harm. In no case can more than 10 days elapse between filing the *tutela* and its resolution.

The law will establish the cases in which the *tutela* may be filed against private individuals entrusted with providing a public service or whose conduct may affect seriously and directly the collective interest, or in respect of whom the applicant may find himself/herself in a state of subordination or vulnerability.

Article 88

An Act shall regulate popular actions for the protection of collective rights and interests related to the homeland, space, public safety and health, administrative morality, the environment, free economic competition, and other areas of similar nature defined in it.

It shall also regulate the actions stemming from the harm caused to a large number of individuals, without barring appropriate individual action.

In the same way, it shall define cases of responsibility of a civil nature for the damage caused to collective rights and interests.

Article 93

International treaties and agreements ratified by Congress that recognize human rights and that prohibit their limitation in states of emergency have priority domestically.

The rights and duties mentioned in this Charter shall be interpreted in accordance with international treaties on human rights ratified by Colombia.

The Colombian state may recognize the jurisdiction of the International Criminal Court in the terms of the Rome Statute adopted on July 17, 1998 by the United Nations Plenipotentiary's Conference and, consequently, ratify said treaty in accordance with the procedure established by this Constitution.

The admission of a different treatment on substantial matters by the Rome Statute with respect to the guarantees contained in this Constitution shall produce effects only within the scope of application of the latter.

[Paragraphs 3 and 4 inserted by Legislative Act No. 2 of 2001]

Article 94

The enunciation of the rights and guaranties contained in the Constitution and in international agreements in effect should not be understood as a negation of others which, being inherent to the human being, are not expressly mentioned in them.

Chapter V On Duties and Obligations

Article 95

The quality of being Colombian enhances all members of the national community. Everyone has the duty to exalt and dignify it. The exercise of the rights and liberties recognized in this Constitution implies responsibilities.

Every individual is obliged to obey the Constitution and the laws.

The following are duties of the individual and of the citizen:

1. To respect others' rights and not to abuse one's own;
2. To strive in accordance with the principle of social solidarity, responding with humanitarian actions in the face of situations that endanger the life or the health of individuals;
3. To respect and support the democratic authorities legitimately constituted to maintain national independence and integrity;
4. To defend and propagate human rights as the foundation of peaceful coexistence;
5. To participate in the country's political, civic, and community life;
6. To strive toward achieving and maintaining peace;
7. To collaborate toward the good functioning of the administration of justice;
8. To protect the country's cultural and natural resources and to keep watch that a healthy environment is being preserved;
9. To contribute to the financing of the state's expenditures and investments within the principles of justice and equity.

TITLE IV ON DEMOCRATIC PARTICIPATION AND POLITICAL PARTIES

Chapter I On the Forms of Democratic Participation

Article 103

The following are the people's means of participating in the exercise of their sovereignty: The vote, the plebiscite, the referendum, the popular consultation, the open town council meeting, the legislative initiative, and the recall of officials. An Act shall regulate these matters. The state shall contribute to the organization, promotion, and guidance of professional, civic, trade union, community, youth, charitable, or nongovernmental public-purpose associations, without prejudicing their authority so that they may constitute democratic means of representation in the various organs of participation, agreement, control, and oversight of the public actions that they undertake.

Article 104

The President of the Republic, with the approval of the ministers and the prior approval of the Senate of the Republic, may consult the people on matters of great national importance. The people's decision shall be binding. Such consultation may not coincide with another election.

[Amended by Legislative Act No. 1 of 2003]

TITLE V ON THE ORGANIZATION OF THE STATE

Chapter I On the Structure of the State

Article 113

The branches of government are the legislative, the executive, and the judiciary.

In addition to the organs which constitute them, there are others, autonomous and independent, for the execution of other functions of the state. The various organs of the state have separate functions but cooperate harmoniously for the realization of their goals.

Article 114

It is the responsibility of the Congress of the Republic to amend the Constitution, pass laws, and exercise political control over the government and the public administration.

The Congress of the Republic shall be composed of the Senate and the House of Representatives.

Article 115

The President of the Republic is the chief of state, head of government, and supreme administrative authority.

The national government is composed of the President of the Republic, the Cabinet ministers, and the directors of administrative departments. The president and the minister or director of the appropriate department represent the government in any particular issue.

No act of the president, except the appointment and dismissal of ministers and directors of administrative departments and those decreed in his/her capacity as head of state and supreme administrative authority, shall have any value or force whatever as long as it is not countersigned and communicated by the minister of the respective office or by the director of the appropriate administrative department who, by virtue thereof, become responsible for same.

The governorates and mayoralties as well as the superintendencies, public establishments, and industrial or commercial enterprises of the state are part of the executive branch.

Article 116

The Constitutional Court, the Supreme Court of Justice, the Council of State, the Supreme Council of the Judiciary, the Office of the General Prosecutor of the Nation, the tribunals and the judges administer justice. So does the Military Criminal Justice System.

Congress shall exercise specific judicial functions.

Exceptionally, an Act may assign jurisdictional functions in specific subject areas to specified administrative authorities. However, they shall not be allowed to hold summary proceedings or to judge crimes.

Individuals may be entrusted temporarily with the function of administering justice as jurors in criminal proceedings, as mediators or as arbitrators authorized by the parties to issue verdicts in law or in equity in the terms defined by an Act.

[Amended by Legislative Act No. 3 of 2002]

Article 117

The Public Ministry and the Office of the Comptroller General of the Republic are control organs.

Article 118

The Public Ministry shall be made up of the Inspector General of the Nation, the Ombudsman, the delegated inspectors, and the agents of the Public Ministry before the legal authorities, as well as by municipal representatives and other official determined by an Act. It is the responsibility of the Public Ministry to defend and promote human rights, to protect the public interest, and to oversee the official conduct of those who perform public functions.

Article 119

The Office of the Comptroller General of the Republic has the duty to oversee fiscal management and to control administrative performance.

Article 120

The electoral organization consists of the National Election Commission, the Office of the National Registrar of Civil Status, and of the other organs established by statute. It is responsible for the organization of elections, their direction and oversight, as well as matters relating to personal identification.

Article 121

No authority of the state may exercise functions different from those assigned to it by the Constitution and statute.

TITLE VI CONCERNING THE LEGISLATIVE BRANCH

Chapter III On Statutes

Article 150

It is the responsibility of Congress to enact laws. Through them, it exercises the following functions:

1. To interpret, amend, and repeal laws.
2. To draw up codes in all areas of legislation and to amend their provisions.
3. To approve the national development plan and public investments that must be undertaken or continued, with the determination of the resources and appropriations

which are authorized for their execution and the measures necessary to promote their implementation.

4. To define the general division of the territory in accordance with what is prescribed in this text.
5. To confer special powers on the departmental assemblies.
6. To move the present seats of the higher national authorities, under extraordinary circumstances and for important reasons of public convenience.
7. To determine the structure of the national administration and create, eliminate, or merge ministries, administrative departments, superintendencies, public establishments, and other entities at a national level, to specify their objectives and organic structure; to regulate the creation and operation of regional autonomous corporations within a system of autonomy; and, similarly, to create or authorize the creation of industrial and commercial enterprises of the state and mixed economic societies.
8. To issue regulations to which the Government shall be subject in exercising the functions of inspection and oversight assigned to it by the Constitution.
9. To grant authorizations to the Government to enter into contracts, to negotiate loans, and to sell national assets. The Government shall periodically inform Congress on the exercise of these authorizations.
10. To vest, up to six months, in the President of the Republic, precise extraordinary powers to issue rules with the force of law when public necessity or advantage so advises. Such powers must be requested expressly by the Government and their approval requires the vote of an absolute majority of the members of both Houses.

At any time and at its own initiative, Congress may amend decree laws enacted by the Government for the use of its extraordinary powers.

These powers may not be conferred for issuing codes, legal statutes, Institutional Acts, or anything referred to in numeral 20 of this Article, or for decreeing taxes.

11. To establish national revenues and to determine the expenditures of the administration.
12. To establish fiscal contributions and, exceptionally, para-fiscal contributions established by statute.
13. To determine the legal tender, its convertibility and the extent of its discretionary power pertaining thereto, and to regulate the system of weights and measures.
14. To approve or reject contracts or agreements which, for reasons of evident national necessity, the President of the Republic has entered with individuals, companies, or public entities without prior authorization.
15. To decree honors to citizens who have rendered services to the fatherland.
16. To approve or reject treaties which the Government makes with other states or entities of international law. By means of said treaties, the state, on the bases of equity, reciprocity, and national convenience, may partially transfer specified powers to international organizations whose object is to promote or consolidate economic integration with other states.
17. To grant, by a two-thirds majority of the members of both Houses, or for grave reasons of public convenience, amnesties or general commutations for political crimes. In case

those so favored are exempted from civil liability with respect to private individuals, the state must be obligated to make the proper compensations.

18. To enact the regulations regarding the appropriation or adjudication and reclamation of uncultivated land.
19. To enact general rules and specify in them the objectives and criteria to which the Government must be subjected for the following purposes:
    a) To organize public credit;
    b) To regulate foreign trade and specify the international exchange system, in agreement with the functions which the Constitution assigns to the Board of Directors of the Bank of the Republic;
    c) To modify, for purposes of commercial policy, duties, and other provisions concerning the customs system;
    d) To regulate activities concerning finance, the stock market and insurance and any other activity connected with the management, use, and investment of resources received from the public;
    e) To establish the system of wage and benefits concerning civil servants, members of the National Congress, and the Police Force;
    f) To regulate the system of minimum social benefits for official workers.

    These functions pertaining to social security services are not to be delegated to public territorial bodies and may not be claimed by them.
20. To create the administrative and technical services of the Houses.
21. To issue laws concerning economic intervention provided for in Article 334, which must specify their purposes and scopes and the limits to economic freedom.
22. To issue laws concerning the Bank of the Republic and the functions which must be performed by its Board of Directors.
23. To issue laws which shall regulate the exercise of public functions and the provision of public services.
24. To regulate the system of industrial property, patents and trademarks, and the other forms of intellectual property.
25. To unify regulations concerning traffic police throughout the entire territory of the Republic.

It is the responsibility of Congress to enact an organic statute on contracts concluded by the public administration and especially by the national administration.

Article 157

No bill shall become law without meeting the following requirements:

1. Being published officially by Congress before being sent to the respective committee.
2. Being approved at the first reading in the appropriate permanent committee of each House. The rules of procedure of Congress shall determine the cases in which the first reading shall be held in joint session of the permanent committees of both Houses.
3. Being approved in each House at the second reading.
4. Securing the approval of the government.

Article 158

Every legislative bill shall refer to a single issue and any provisions or amendments not germane to it shall be inadmissible. The chairman of the appropriate committee shall reject the initiatives that are not in harmony with this principle, though his/her decisions shall be subject to appeal before the same committee. An Act which is subject to partial modification shall be published as a single text incorporating the approved amendments.

Article 160

Between the first and second readings, a period of no less than eight days must have elapsed, and between the approval of the bill in either of the Houses and the initiation of the debate in the other, at least 15 days must have elapsed.

During the second reading, each House may introduce amendments, additions, and omissions that it deems necessary.

In the report to the plenary House for the second reading, the committee chairman shall present all the proposals that were considered by the committee and the reasons why they were rejected.

Every draft law or draft legislative act must contain information on how it is to be dealt with by the respective committee competent to discuss it, and must proceed accordingly.

No bill shall be put to a vote in a session different from the one which had been previously announced. The announcement that a bill shall be put to a vote shall be made by the president of each House or committee in a session different from the one in which the vote takes place.

[Amended by Legislative Act No. 1 of 2003]

Chapter IV On the Senate

Article 171

The Senate of the Republic shall be composed of one hundred members elected in one nationwide constituency.

There shall be an additional two senators elected in a special national constituency for indigenous communities.

Colombian citizens who happen to be or reside abroad may vote in elections for the Senate of the Republic.

The system of electoral quotient shall apply to the special constituency for the election of senators by indigenous communities.

The representatives of the indigenous communities who aspire to become members of the Senate of the Republic must have exercised a position of traditional authority in their respective community or have been leaders of an indigenous organization, which qualification shall be verified by a certificate from the respective organization, endorsed by the Minister of the Government.

Chapter V On the House of Representatives

Article 176

The House of Representatives shall be elected in territorial and special constituencies and one international constituency.

There shall be two representatives for each territorial constituency and one more for every 365,000 inhabitants or fraction larger than 182,000 over and above the initial 365,000. . . .

For the election of representatives to the House, each department and the Capital District of Bogotá shall constitute a territorial constituency.

Special constituencies will ensure the participation in the House of Representatives of ethnic groups and Colombians residing abroad. Through these constituencies, five representatives will be elected, distributed as follows: two for a constituency of Afro-Colombians, one for the constituency of indigenous communities, and two for the international constituency. This last constituency will only include the votes deposited outside the national territory by citizens residing abroad.

The law may establish a special constituency to ensure the participation in the House of Representatives of ethnic groups and political minorities. Up to four representatives may be elected for this constituency.

For the Colombians residing abroad there shall be an international constituency by which a Representative shall be elected to the House. In this constituency only the votes which have been cast outside the national territory by citizens residing abroad shall be counted.

[Amended by Legislative Acts No. 2 and No. 3 of 2005, and Legislative Act No. 1 of 2013]

TITLE VII ON THE EXECUTIVE BRANCH

Chapter I On the President of the Republic

Article 188

The President of the Republic symbolizes the national unity and, on taking the oath of office to abide by the Constitution and the laws, he/she pledges to guarantee the rights and freedoms of all Colombians.

Article 189

It is the responsibility of the President of the Republic, as the chief of state, head of the government, and supreme administrative authority to do the following:

1. Appoint and dismiss freely Cabinet ministers and directors of administrative departments.
2. Direct international relations; appoint the members of the diplomatic and consular corps; receive the corresponding foreign officials; and make international treaties or agreements with other states and international bodies to be submitted to the approval of Congress.
3. Direct the public force and its disposition in his/her quality of supreme commander of the armed forces of the Republic.
4. Conserve the public order throughout the territory and restore it where it has been disturbed.
5. Direct military operations when he/she deems it appropriate.
6. Provide for the external security of the Republic, defending the independence and honor of the nation and the inviolability of its territory; declare war with the approval

of the Senate or do it without such authorization to repel foreign aggression; and agree to and ratify peace treaties, regarding all of which matters the president shall give an immediate account to Congress.

7. Authorize, during a recess of the Senate and with the prior opinion of the Council of State, the transit of foreign troops across the territory of the Republic.
8. Install and close the sessions of Congress in each legislative term.
9. Approve the statutes.
10. Promulgate the statutes, obey them, and oversee their strict execution.
11. Exercise the power to regulate through the issuing of decrees, resolutions, and orders necessary for the execution of the statutes.
12. Present a report to Congress at the beginning of each legislative term regarding the measures of the administration, regarding the execution of the plans and programs of economic and social development, and regarding the bills which the government proposes to move forward during the new legislative term.
13. Appoint the presidents, directors, or managers of national public institutions and individuals who must occupy national office, positions not to be filled through competitive examinations or which are not covered by other officials or bodies, according to the Constitution or statute.
14. Create, merge, or dissolve, according to an Act, positions required by the central administration, define their special functions, and determine their benefits and emoluments.

The government may not create, at Treasury expense, obligations which exceed the total amount allocated for the respective service in the initial appropriations law.

15. Eliminate or merge national administrative entities or organs in accordance with the applicable statute.
16. Modify the structure of the ministries, administrative departments, and other national administrative entities or organs, according to the principles and general regulations defined by an Act.
17. Assign work according to its nature among ministries, administrative departments, and public institutions.
18. Grant permission to national public employees who may request it to accept, on a temporary basis, responsibilities or benefits from foreign governments.
19. Confer ranks to the members of the public force and submit for the approval of the Senate those that fall under Article 173.
20. Oversee the strict collection and administration of public revenues and credits and decree their investment in accordance with the relevant statutes.
21. Carry out inspection and oversight of education in accordance with the relevant statute.
22. Carry out the inspection and oversight of the provision of public services.
23. Make contracts falling under his/her jurisdiction in accordance with the Constitution and statute.
24. Perform, in accordance with the relevant statute, the inspection, oversight, and control of individuals who undertake financial, stock market, insurance, and any other activities

connected with the management, use, or investment of resources collected from the public. Similarly, those involving cooperative entities and commercial companies.

25. Organize the public credit; determine the national debt and arrange for its servicing; amend the customs duties, tariffs, and other provisions concerning customs; regulate foreign trade; and effect intervention in financial, stock exchange, insurance, and any other activities connected with the management, use, and investment of resources originating from the saving of third parties in accordance with the relevant statute.
26. Effect the inspection and oversight of institutions of public necessity so that their revenues may be protected and be properly applied and so that everything that is essential should be implemented according to the wishes of the founders.
27. Grant temporary patents to inventors of useful improvements in accordance with the applicable statute.
28. Issue naturalization certificates, in accordance with the relevant statute.

Article 190

The President of the Republic shall be elected for a period of four years by one-half plus one of the ballots which, in secret and direct manner, the citizens shall cast on the date and following the procedures determined by an Act. If no candidate should secure the said majority, a runoff election shall be held three weeks later when only those two candidates who received the most votes in the first round of balloting shall participate. The candidate with the larger number of votes shall be declared president. . . .

Article 197

The citizen who under any title has previously exercised the Presidency may not be elected president. This prohibition does not include a vice-president who has exercised it for less than three months, in a continuous or discontinuous form, during the four-year term. The prohibition on re-election can only be reformed or removed by a referendum of popular initiative or a Constituent Assembly.

[Amended by Legislative Act 2 of 2015]

Chapter VI On the States of Exception

Article 212

The President of the Republic, with the signature of all the ministers, may declare a state of foreign war. On the basis of such a declaration, the government shall have the strictly essential options to repeal the aggression, defend the country's sovereignty, meet the requirements of the war, and bring about the restoration to normal conditions.

The declaration of a state of foreign war may be made only when the Senate shall have approved the declaration of war, except when in the judgment of the president, it was necessary to repel the aggression [forthwith].

While the state of war continues, Congress shall use all its constitutional and legal powers and the government shall report to it, giving reasons periodically for the decrees that it has issued and the evolution of events.

The legislative decrees issued by the government suspend laws incompatible with the state of war, are in force during the time which the decrees themselves stipulate, and shall no longer be in effect as soon as normal conditions are declared to have been restored. At any time, Congress may amend or repeal the decrees through a favorable vote of two thirds of the members of each House.

Article 213

In the case of a serious disruption of the public order imminently threatening institutional stability, the security of the state, or the peaceful coexistence of the citizenry, and which cannot be met by the use of the ordinary powers of the police authorities, the President of the Republic, with the approval of all the ministers, may declare a state of internal commotion throughout the Republic or part of it for a period no longer than 90 days, extendable for two similar periods, the second of which mandates the prior and favorable vote of the Senate of the Republic.

By means of such a declaration, the government shall have the strictly essential options to deal with the causes of the disruption and check the spread of its effects.

The legislative decrees that the government may issue can suspend the laws incompatible with the state of commotion and shall no longer be in effect as soon as public order is declared to have been restored. The government may extend its application up to 90 more days.

Within the three days subsequent to the declaration or extension of the state of commotion, Congress shall meet in its own right, with all its constitutional and legal powers. The president shall transmit to it an immediate report concerning the reasons motivating the said declaration.

In no case may civilians be questioned or tried by the penal military system.

Article 214

The states of exception referred to in the previous articles shall be subject to the following provisions:

1. The legislative decrees shall have the signature of the President of the Republic and all his/her ministers and may refer only to matters that have direct and specific connection with the situation which the declaration of the state of exception may have determined.
2. Neither human rights nor fundamental freedoms may be suspended. In all cases, the rules of international humanitarian law shall be observed. A statutory law shall regulate the powers of the government during the states of exception and shall establish the legal controls and guaranties to protect rights, in accordance with international treaties. The measures which are adopted must be proportionate to the gravity of the events.
3. The normal functioning of the branches of government or state organs shall not be interrupted.
4. As soon as the foreign war or the causes that gave rise to the state of internal commotion shall have come to an end, the government shall declare the public order to have been restored and shall lift the state of exception.

5. The president and the ministers shall be responsible when they declare states of exception without the occurrence of a foreign war or internal disturbance, and they shall also be responsible, as shall other officials, for any abuse that they may have committed in the exercise of the powers to which the earlier articles refer.
6. The government shall send to the Constitutional Court on the day following their promulgation the legislative decrees issued under the powers mentioned in the above articles so that the Court may decide definitively on their constitutionality. Should the government not comply with the duty of transmitting the decrees, the Constitutional Court shall automatically and immediately take cognizance of the same.

Article 215

When events different from those provided for in Articles 212 and 213 occur that disrupt or threaten to disrupt in serious or imminent manner the economic, social, or ecological order of the country or which constitute a grave public calamity, the president, with the signature of all the ministers, may declare a state of emergency for periods up to 30 days in each case which, in all, may not exceed 90 days in a calendar year.

By means of such a declaration which shall be justified, the president may, with the signature of all the ministers, issue decrees with the force of law, slated exclusively to check the crisis and halt the extension of its effects.

These decrees may refer to matters that have direct and specific connection with the state of emergency and may, in provisional manner, establish new taxes or amend existing ones. In these last cases, the measures shall stop being in effect at the end of the subsequent fiscal year, except when Congress, during the subsequent year, should give them a permanent character.

In the decree declaring the state of emergency, the government shall stipulate the deadline within which it would use its extraordinary powers in situations referred to in this Article and shall convene Congress if the latter should not be meeting for the 10 days following the expiration of the said deadline.

The Congress shall examine for a period of up to 30 days, extendable by agreement of the two Houses, the report with explanations presented to it by the government on the causes justifying the state of emergency and the measures adopted and shall make an express pronouncement on the convenience and appropriateness of same.

During the year subsequent to the declaration of emergency, Congress may repeal, amend, or add to the decrees to which this Article refers in areas which ordinarily fall under the government's jurisdiction. In connection with those which fall under the jurisdiction of its members, Congress may exercise said powers at all times.

If it is not convened, Congress shall meet in its own right under the conditions and for the purposes provided for in this Article.

The President of the Republic and the ministers shall be responsible when they declare a state of emergency without there being present any of the circumstances provided for in the first clause and shall also be responsible for any abuse committed in the exercise of the powers which the Constitution assigns to the government during an emergency.

The government may not infringe on the social rights of workers through the decrees mentioned in this Article.

PARAGRAPH
The government shall send to the Constitutional Court on the day following their promulgation the legislative decrees issued under the powers mentioned in this Article so that the Court may determine their constitutionality. Should the government fail to fulfill its obligation to transmit them, the Constitutional Court shall automatically and immediately take cognizance of same.

TITLE VIII ON THE JUDICIAL BRANCH

Chapter I General Provisions

Article 230

In their decisions, the judges are bound exclusively by the rule of law.

Fairness, jurisprudence, and the general principles of law and doctrine are auxiliary criteria of judicial proceedings.

Article 233

The judges of the Constitutional Court, the Supreme Court of Justice, and of the Council of state shall be elected for a period of eight years. They cannot be re-elected and shall remain in office while they display good behavior, perform satisfactorily and have not reached the age of mandatory retirement.

Chapter IV On Constitutional Jurisdiction

Article 239

The Constitutional Court shall be composed of an uneven number of members determined by statute. The makeup of the court shall take into account the need to select judges belonging to the various specialized jurisdictions.

The judges of the Constitutional Court shall be elected by the Senate of the Republic for single terms of eight years from lists presented to it by the President of the Republic, the Supreme Court of Justice, and the Council of State.

The judges of the Constitutional Court are not eligible for re-election.

Article 241

The safeguarding of the integrity and supremacy of the Constitution is entrusted to the Constitutional Court in the strict and precise terms of this Article. For such a purpose, it shall fulfill the following functions:

1. Decide on the petitions of unconstitutionality brought by citizens against measures amending the Constitution, no matter what their origin, exclusively for errors of procedure in their makeup.
2. Decide, prior to a popular expression of opinion, on the constitutionality of the call for a referendum or a constituent assembly to amend the Constitution, exclusively for errors of procedure in their makeup.

3. Decide on the constitutionality of referendums about laws and popular consultations and plebiscites of a national scope, in case of these last ones exclusively for errors of procedure in their convocation and implementation.
4. Decide on the petitions of unconstitutionality brought by citizens against statutes, both for their substantive content as for errors of procedure in their makeup.
5. Decide on the petitions of unconstitutionality brought by citizens against decrees with the force of law issued by the government on the basis of Article 150, numeral 10, and Article 341 of the Constitution for their substantive content as for errors of procedure in their makeup.
6. Decide on the exceptions provided for in Article 137 of the Constitution.
7. Decide in definitive manner on the constitutionality of the legislative decrees issued by the government on the basis of Articles 212, 213, and 215 of the Constitution.
8. Decide in definitive manner on the constitutionality of the bills opposed by the government as unconstitutional and of proposed statutory bills, both on account of their substantive content as for errors of procedure in their makeup.
9. Revise, in the form determined by statute, the judicial decisions connected with the protection of constitutional rights.
10. To take a final decision on the execution of international treaties and the statutes approving them. To this end, the government shall submit them to the Court within six days following the adoption of the ratifying statute. Any citizen may intervene to defend or challenge their constitutionality. Should the Court declare them constitutional, the government may proceed to the exchange of notes; in the contrary case they shall not be ratified. When one or several provisions of a multilateral treaty are declared unenforceable by the Constitutional Court, only the President of the Republic may declare consent, formulating the pertinent reservation.
11. Settle conflicts of competence between the distinct jurisdictions.
12. Draft its own rules of procedure.

PARAGRAPH

When the Court finds an error in remediable procedures in the drafting of measures subject to its control, it shall order their return to the authority which issued them so that, if possible, that authority should correct the observed flaw. Once the error is corrected, it shall proceed to decide on the validity of the measure.

[Amended by Legislative Act 2 of 2015]

Article 242

The processes promoted before the Constitutional Court in the matters referred to on this score shall be regulated by an Act in accordance with the following provisions:

1. Any citizen may implement the public actions provided in the preceding Article and intervene as challenger or defender of the provisions submitted to control in processes promoted by others as well as in those cases where no public action has occurred.

2. The Inspector General of the Nation shall intervene in all the processes.
3. Actions to correct errors in form lapse within a year starting from the publication of the said act.
4. Ordinarily, the Court shall have 60 days to decide, and the Inspector General of the Nation 30 days to give his/her opinion.
5. In the processes referred to in numeral 7 of the previous Article, the ordinary deadlines shall be reduced to a third and the missing of the deadline shall constitute cause for a misdemeanor to be sanctioned according to statute.

Chapter V On Special Jurisdictions

Article 246

The authorities of the indigenous peoples may exercise their jurisdictional functions within their territorial jurisdiction in accordance with their own laws and procedures as long as these are not contrary to the Constitution and the laws of the Republic. An Act shall establish the forms of coordination of this special jurisdiction with the national judicial system.

TITLE XI ON THE TERRITORIAL ORGANIZATION

Chapter IV On the Special Regime

Article 330

In accordance with the Constitution and statutes, the indigenous territories shall be governed by the councils formed and regulated according to the uses and customs of their communities and shall exercise the following functions:

1. Oversee the application of the legal regulations concerning the uses of the land and settlement of their territories.
2. Design the policies and plans and programs of economic and social development within their territory, in accordance with the National Development Plan.
3. Promote public investments in their territories and oversee their appropriate implementation.
4. Collect and distribute their funds.
5. Oversee the conservation of natural resources.
6. Coordinate the programs and projects promoted by the different communities in their territory.
7. Cooperate with the maintenance of the public order within their territory in accordance with the instructions and provisions of the national government.
8. Represent the territories before the national government and the other entities in which they are integrated; and
9. Other matters provided for by the Constitution and statute.

PARAGRAPH

The exploitation of the natural resources in the indigenous territories shall be done without impairing the cultural, social, and economic integrity of the indigenous communities. In the decisions adopted with respect to the said exploitation, the government shall encourage the participation of the representatives of the respective communities.

TITLE XII ON THE ECONOMIC AND PUBLIC FINANCE REGIME

Chapter I General Provisions

Article 334

The general direction of the economy will be under the charge of the state. The state will intervene, by mandate of law, in the exploitation of natural resources, in the use of the earth, in the production, distribution, utilization and consumption of goods, and in public and private services, in order to rationalize the economy with the goal of ensuring that the national territory, within a framework of fiscal sustainability, will improve the quality of life of its inhabitants, the equitable distribution of opportunities, and the benefits of development and preservation of the environment. This framework of sustainability must act as an instrument for the progressive realization of the social state of law. In all cases, public social spending will be prioritized. . . .

Fiscal sustainability must orient the branches and organs of the public power, within their competencies, in a framework of harmonious collaboration.

Once a decision has been made by any of the highest judicial bodies, the Inspector General of the Nation or one of the government ministers may solicit the opening of a fiscal impact proceeding, which must be heard. [The courts] will hear the explanations of its proponents on the consequences of the decision on public finances, as well as the concrete plan for its compliance, and they will decide whether to proceed to modulate, modify, or defer its effects with the goal of avoiding serious alterations in fiscal sustainability. In no case will the essential nucleus of fundamental rights be affected.

In interpreting the current article, under no circumstances may any administrative, legislative, or judicial authority invoke fiscal sustainability in order to weaken fundamental rights, restrict their scope, or deny their effective protection.

[Amended by Legislative Act No. 3 of 2011]

Article 338

In time of peace only Congress, departmental assemblies, and district and municipal councils may levy fiscal or fiscal-like dues. Statute, ordinances, and resolutions must determine directly active and passive earnings, the events and bases that are taxable, and the rates of the levies. . . .

Chapter IV On the Distribution of Resources and Jurisdictions

Article 363

The tax system is based on the principles of equity, efficiency, and progressivity. The tax laws shall not be applied retroactively.

Chapter V On the Social Purpose of the State and of the Public Services

Article 365

The public services are inherent in the social purpose of the state. It is the duty of the state to ensure their efficient provision to all the inhabitants of the national territory.

The public services shall be subjected to the juridical regime determined by an Act, may be provided by the state directly or indirectly, by organized communities, or by individuals. In any case, the state shall maintain the regulation, control, and application of the said services. . . .

Article 366

The general well-being and improvement of the population's quality of life are social purposes of the state. A basic objective of their activity shall be to address the unsatisfied public health, educational, environmental, and drinking water needs of those affected.

For such an outcome, in the plans and budgets of the nation and of the territorial entities, public social expenditures shall have priority over any other allocation.

TITLE XIII ON CONSTITUTIONAL REFORM

Article 374

The Political Constitution may be reformed by Congress, a Constituent Assembly, or by the people through a referendum.

Article 375

The government, 10 members of the Congress, 20 percent of councilors or deputies, or citizens totaling at least five percent of the electoral rolls in force may introduce legislative acts.

The bill shall be discussed in two ordinary and consecutive session periods. After having been approved in the first period by a majority of those present, the act shall be published by the Government. In the second period the approval shall require the vote of the majority of the members of each House.

In this second period only initiatives presented in the first period may be discussed.

Article 376

By means of an Act approved by the members of both Houses, Congress may direct that the voters participating in the popular balloting decide if a Constituent Assembly should be called with the jurisdiction, term, and makeup that the same law shall determine.

It is understood that the people shall convoke the Assembly, if they approve it, when they represent at least one third of the electoral rolls.

The Assembly must be elected by the direct vote of the citizens through a balloting that may not overlap another. Beginning with the election, the ordinary powers of Congress shall remain in suspense while the Constitution is being amended during the term stipulated so that the Assembly may fulfill its functions. The Assembly shall adopt its own rules of procedure.

Article 377

The constitutional reforms must be submitted to a referendum approved by Congress when referring to the rights recognized in Chapter I of Title II and to their guaranties, to the procedures of popular participation, or to Congress, if so requested, within the six months subsequent to the promulgation of the legislative act, by five percent of the citizens who make up the electoral rolls.

The reform shall be understood to be defeated by a negative vote of the majority of the voters as long as at least one fourth of those on the electoral rolls participate in the balloting.

Article 378

Upon the initiative of the government or the citizens under the terms of Article 155, Congress, through an Act which requires the approval of the majority of the members of both Houses, may submit to a referendum a bill of constitutional reform which the Congress shall incorporate into the Act. The referendum shall be presented in such a manner as to allow the voters to freely choose from the agenda or the various items that which they approve or disapprove.

The approval of constitutional reforms by means of a referendum mandates the affirmative vote of over half the voters and that the number of these should exceed one fourth of the total number of citizens included in the electoral rolls.

Article 379

The legislative acts, the convocation to the referendum, the popular consultation, or the act of convocation of the Constituent Assembly may be declared unconstitutional only when the requirements established in this title are violated.

Public measures against these acts may be taken only within one year following their promulgation with due regard to the provisions in Article 241, numeral 2.

Article 380

The Constitution, as amended, in force until this time, is hereby repealed.

This present Constitution is effective from the day of its promulgation.

Table of Cases

The full decisions of the Colombian Constitutional Court are all available (in Spanish) from the Court's webpage at the following site: http://www.corteconstitucional.gov.co/.

COLOMBIA

CANADA

FRANCE

GERMANY

SOUTH AFRICA

Index

www.ingramcontent.com/pod-product-compliance
Ingram Content Group UK Ltd.
Pitfield, Milton Keynes, MK11 3LW, UK
UKHW051048150926
475595UK00005B/176